To Mom for Christmas 1977
Love Dianne + Ray.

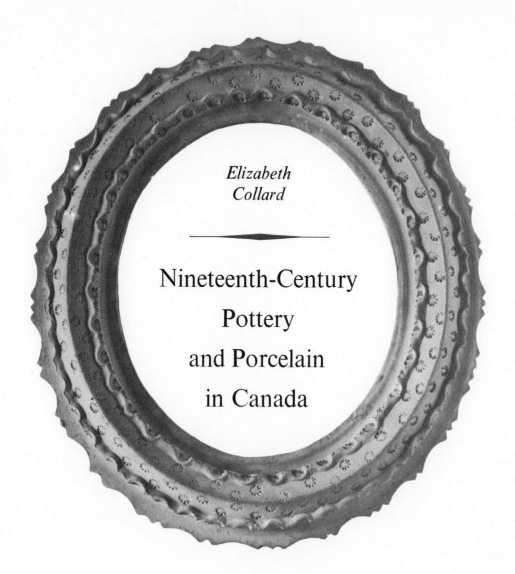

Elizabeth
Collard

Nineteenth-Century
Pottery
and Porcelain
in Canada

With many good with

Elizabeth Collard

Aug 30/80

MONTREAL   McGill University Press   1967

© CANADA 1967
McGILL UNIVERSITY PRESS
Library of Congress Catalog Card No. 67-30576
Printed in Canada
by Gazette Printing Company (Limited)

Reproduced on the title page is an unglazed red earthenware picture frame (*c.* 1867)
made by Anthony Smith, Paris, Ont. Marked on back five
times with Smith's name (incised and impressed). 13 x 11¾ in.

Acknowledgements

In the preparation of this book many persons have helped in a variety of ways; I acknowledge their assistance with gratitude. Mr. John Archer, Director of Libraries, McGill University, and his staff—in particular Mrs. Catharine Cook, Mrs. Elizabeth Lewis, Mrs. Gwen Wright, Mrs. Elizabeth Silvester, and Mrs. Margaret Carroll—aided me at every turn. Mr. Arnold R. Mountford, Director of the City of Stoke-on-Trent Museum and Art Gallery, Staffordshire, gave me repeated help.

I would also thank Dr. W. Kaye Lamb, Dominion Archivist and National Librarian; Miss Edith G. Firth, head of the Canadian History and Manuscript Section of the Toronto Public Library; Mrs. Genevieve Muir of the Paris Public Library; Miss Shirley Elliott of the Nova Scotia Legislative Library; Mrs. M. Robertson, Assistant Archivist, the New Brunswick Museum; Miss Elizabeth Brewster, Reference Librarian, Mount Allison University; Miss N. Gregg, Reference Librarian, the University of New Brunswick; Mr. Janis Bilkins, Reference Librarian, Université de Montréal; Miss Marguerite Mercier, Bibliothèque Saint Sulpice; Mr. David Rome, Director of the Jewish Public Library, Montreal; Miss Margery Trenholme and her staff at the Fraser-Hickson Library; and Mrs. Norah Bryant and her staff at the Westmount Public Library.

For helping me to trace the connection between the successors of the Spodes and the Hudson's Bay Company, I thank Miss Alice M. Johnson, Archivist, Beaver House, London. I am greatly indebted, too, to Mr. Lawrence M. Lande, not only for the richness of the Lawrence M. Lande Collection of Canadiana, which I was permitted to use freely at McGill, but for many personal kindnesses and a continuing interest in this project.

Museums in Great Britain, the United States, and Canada have, on many occasions, given me needed assistance. These include the British Museum, the Ulster Museum in Belfast, the Brooklyn Museum, the Royal Ontario Museum, the Montreal Museum of Fine Arts, and the Château de Ramezay Museum, Montreal. I also acknowledge valuable assistance from the Ontario Archives, the New York Historical Society, and the Vermont Historical Society.

I owe thanks to Mr. R. J. Charleston, Keeper of the Department of Ceramics, and Mr. J. P. Cushion, Research Assistant, the Victoria and Albert Museum; to Miss Nickola Elphinstone, Curator of Applied Arts, the Bristol City Art Gallery; to Mr. J. T. Shaw, Director of the Sunderland Museum and Art Gallery; to Mr. J. D. Boyd, Director of the Dundee Museum and Art Gallery; to Mr. W. A. Billington, Curator of the Wedgwood Museum; and to Mr. Cyril Shingler, Curator of the Dyson Perrins Museum at the Royal Porcelain Works, Worcester.

Mr. Russell Harper, Chief Curator of the McCord Museum, McGill University, has, on several occasions, drawn my attention to material which he has come upon during his own researches, and Mr. George Shepherd, Curator of the Western Development Museum, Saskatoon, has made many enquiries on my behalf. I am indebted, also, to Mr. George MacLaren, Curator of the Nova Scotia Museum; Mr. Barry Lord, formerly Curator of Art, the New Brunswick Museum; Mrs. Connie Ford, of the Lachine Museum; Mrs. J. B. Moore, of the Missisquoi Museum, Stanbridge East, Que.; and Mrs. Jack Wheeler, of the Brant Museum, Brantford, Ont.

Church and burial records have been important to me in the research for this book, and I owe particular thanks to Rev. Robert J. Kirtley of Bethesda Methodist Church, Hanley, Staffordshire; Rev. Carl Gustafson of St. Johns United Church; Rev. Keith Eddy of Beloeil United Church (formerly of St. Johns); and Rev. Peter Davison of St. James Anglican Church, St. Johns. Mrs. D. E. MacNeill, Secretary of the Fernhill Cemetery Company, Saint John. and Mr. John F. Roy, formerly Manager of the Mount Royal Cemetery Company, Montreal, both provided me with information which involved a search through old records.

Some of the British firms who supplied the Canadian market a hundred years ago are still in business. For assistance in tracing early connections with Canada I thank George L. Ashworth & Bros. Ltd., John Aynsley & Sons Ltd., W. T. Copeland & Sons Ltd., Doulton & Co. Ltd., Furnivals (1913) Ltd., J. & G. Meakin Ltd., Mintons Ltd., Ridgway Potteries Ltd., Josiah Wedgwood & Sons Ltd., and the Worcester Royal Porcelain Co. Ltd.

Descendants of Canadian potters and early Canadian china merchants have given me access to family papers. I owe much to Mrs. Effie Farrar Sutherland, only daughter of George H. Farrar, the last of the Farrars to carry on potting in Canada; to Mrs. Lottie Farrar de Bellefeuille, grand-daughter of Eben Farrar (George H. Farrar's younger brother); to Mr. Fenwick D. Foley, great-grandson of Joseph White, the Bristol potter who emigrated to New Brunswick; and to Mr. Lewis Humberstone, great-great-great-grandson of Samuel Humberstone, Loyalist and potter. I have also to thank Mr. W. H. Hayward, grandson of the William H. Hayward who founded a china importing business in Saint John that is now in its second century, and Mr. John Shuter, great-grandson of Joseph Shuter, the most important of all the Montreal china merchants in the early years of the nineteenth century.

Marjorie Lady Pentland most kindly sent me a detailed description of the china painted with Canadian subjects which was presented to her mother, Lady Aberdeen, by the Parliament of Canada. Professor Margaret Griffiths of McGill University, and her sister, Mrs. W. H. Pike, put at my disposal material on their grandfather, John Griffiths, the Minton-trained china painter of London, Ont. Through the kindness of Miss Clare Harrington I am able to illustrate a plate from the service with Bartlett views once owned by her grandfather, Sir

Acknowledgements

William Dawson, and through the kindness of Miss Katherine Torrance Trenholme a plate from the ironstone service made for her great-grandfather, Thomas Torrance of Belmont Hall.

Over nearly twenty years the late Gresham Copeland, grandson of William Taylor Copeland whose earthenware and china were transported to the farthest outposts of Canada, was of assistance to me in ceramic matters. He answered many technical questions in regard to this book, and I have grateful memories of his kindly encouragement.

For further material upon which I have drawn I thank Mrs. Kenneth C. Drury, of Victoria; Dr. D. G. G. Kerr, of the University of Western Ontario, London; Mr. Harold Jarvis, Grimsby; Mr. J. Alex Edmison, Q.C., and Mr. A. J. H. Richardson, of Ottawa; Mr. Donald McLeish, Toronto; Ven. Archdeacon R. Kenneth Naylor, Mr. Eric Reford, and Mr. A. T. Brodeur, of Montreal; and Mr. D. Stuart Trueman, Editor, and Mr. Geoffrey C. Crowe, of the Editorial Department, the Saint John *Telegraph-Journal*. The late Dr. John F. McIntosh, of Westfield Beach, N.B., and Westmount, Que., also supplied me with material relating to New Brunswick.

Mr. Terence Lockett, of Cheshire, England, read the manuscript and, from his own wide knowledge of the field and his experience as a ceramic historian, made valuable suggestions. Though he is not responsible for any errors I may have made, his scholarly criticism was an important help.

I cannot sufficiently thank Mr. Robin Strachan, Director of the McGill University Press, and his staff for their enthusiasm. At every stage of the way they smoothed difficulties, suggested solutions, and gave constructive advice. On Miss Margery Simpson, the Editor of the Press, the heaviest burden fell, but her patience and cheerfulness were unfailing.

My greatest debt is to my husband. It was his suggestion that I expand previously published articles into this book; it was while doing research for him that I made the notes for the articles in the first place. Because of his library of rare Canadiana I have been able to do much of my work in our own home, and because of his unwavering support the task has been greatly lightened. I have drawn so heavily upon his knowledge of the source materials for Canadian history that this is, in very large measure, his book. All the pleasure in the work involved would have vanished had I not been able to share the whole project with him.

ELIZABETH COLLARD
May 1, 1967.

Introduction

This book has been called *Nineteenth-Century Pottery and Porcelain in Canada* because it deals both with wares made in Canada in the nineteenth century and with those imported. The one cannot be properly considered without the other. To consider Canadian-made pottery without relation to the imports from other countries (above all the massive imports from the British Isles) clouds and confuses the picture; for it fails to define just what place the products of the Canadian potteries had among all the ceramic wares used in Canada during the century.

When Canadian pottery is placed against the background of the imports, three things become evident. The first is that the pottery made by Canadians formed only a small part, a very small part, of what Canadians used. The second is that the ascendancy of ceramic imports in the Canadian market severely restricted the scope of Canadian potting. The third is that the unequal struggle of Canadian potters, with their limited skills and resources, explains both why they achieved so little and why that limited achievement was still so remarkable. Whenever they attempted to rise above a small local trade with neighbours to establish a serious industry, they had to wage a struggle against all the traditions and resources of the great ceramic centres of the Old World. It was a battle all the braver because so often doomed to failure. The life of Canadian potteries was all too frequently brief; they appeared, only to fade away. Even the ambitious concentration of industry at St. Johns, in Quebec (though backed, in one case, by capital supplied by St. Johns' 'merchant princes'), in the end faltered and dwindled.

Canada, a land rich in furs and lumber, was less well provided with some of the essential materials needed by any potter who wished to advance beyond the elementary. It is true that common red clay was available in many localities. As James Brown reported in 1851, clay for '*Red Bricks*' and '*Common Pottery*' was 'so widely spread . . . that the localities are too numerous to be mentioned'. But the clays for whiteware and stoneware presented problems. Even well into the twentieth century, as a government report of 1931 showed, it was still cheaper for the Canadian potter to import kaolin or china clay from England than to attempt to make use of the little that was to be found in his own country. For stoneware, most, if not all, nineteenth-century Canadian potters had to look to the United States for their clay. When basic materials were not ready at hand, the Canadian potter started at once with a disadvantage.

By and large it was the imports, not the Canadian wares, that met the needs of Canadians throughout the nineteenth century. There were even large categories of ceramic wares that imports, and imports alone, supplied.

One of these was porcelain. No porcelain whatever was attempted in Canada on a commercial scale during the century. Yet the demand for porcelain was important. Nineteenth-century Canada was a land of contrasts. At the same time that the pioneer settler was contending for survival and was often reduced to a primitive way of life, others, living in the cities, or in the larger country houses, knew affluence and elegance. The households of the higher-ranking members of the official classes—of the church, the government, the army—and of the richer merchants were often luxuriously furnished. Advertisements of the china dealers and inventories for the sale of household goods reveal impressive quantities of fine porcelain. Supplying this sizable and profitable porcelain market was entirely the role of the overseas potter.

Nor can the earthenware used in Canada in the nineteenth century be understood apart from the imports. Except at St. Johns and its vicinity, practically no white-bodied earthenware was produced in Canada during the period. Even at St. Johns only the most utilitarian types of whiteware ('C.C.', white granite, and thick ironstone china) were part of the regular output. The very limited production of whiteware meant, of course, that under-glaze printing formed no successful part of Canadian potting. At the few whiteware factories, little was done in printed decoration beyond an occasional name or identifying device (such as on hotel orders) or some very simple ornamentation; and even this printing was almost invariably on top of the glaze. Canadians had a lively appreciation of the attractions of under-glaze printed wares and bought them in large quantities. But this, too, was a field which Canadian potters, with their limited skills and equipment, could not enter.

Imported wares also supplied a great part of the nineteenth-century Canadian market for even the most elementary types of earthenware: brownware, yellow ware, 'Rockingham', and common stoneware. These wares came into the colonies in quantities that today seem astounding. Dealers offered as many as fifty thousand pieces of imported brownware at a time, or advertised 'Crates of Stone Bottles' and 'red flower pots' as just in from Great Britain in enormous quantities.

It is true that in areas distant from ports of entry the local potter, often a farmer-potter, might for a time have the market for common brown or yellow ware more or less to himself. But the importers were relentless. Advertisements show with what vigour they pressed even the common wares beyond port cities and into country districts.

And yet, in spite of all the difficulties and inequalities of the struggle, Canadian potters succeeded in building up an industry. With persistence they lifted potting from the farm to the factory. They entered Canadian-made stoneware and brownware and even white granite in the great international exhibitions of the day, sending off their wares to Philadelphia, Paris, and Antwerp. They claimed equality for Canadian products, within relatively simple range, boasting that

Introduction

what was made in Elmsdale and Crouchville, in Yamaska, Cap Rouge, and St. Johns was 'warranted equal to English of the same quality'. Some of the Canadian potters joined together as manufacturers, seeking, as an organized group, to control prices and stabilize business. They did all this in the face of the ceaseless flood of imports. But what they contributed was only a comparatively small proportion of the ceramic wares used in nineteenth-century Canada.

Just because imported wares played the major role in meeting Canada's needs, the method of their sale and distribution becomes an essential, at times a dramatic, part of the history of nineteenth-century pottery and porcelain in Canada. The story of these wares only began when they arrived at Canadian ports. Ingenious selling techniques and resourceful means of transportation were needed to carry them to their wide, scattered, and often distant destinations.

With enterprise, overseas potters cultivated the markets of the North American colonies. Pottery owners in Great Britain dispatched members of their families to pick up business in Canada, or themselves crossed by sailing ship to look over the prospects. A few turned out wares with decoration specially designed for Canada. Pictures of Canadian scenery (such as those by Bartlett) or of Canadian sports were printed under the glaze on earthenware. This so-called Historical China, however, although of particular appeal to the modern collector, formed in its own day only a small and incidental part of the vast tide of ceramic imports.

To present the total picture of what Canadians both made and imported in the nineteenth century, a wide variety of contemporary sources has been consulted: inventories (including one listing the entire contents of a Montreal store at the beginning of the period); letters written home by immigrants; diaries, both published and unpublished; lists of wedding presents; descriptions of Canadian life by settlers and travellers; early Board of Trade reports, dealing with the crockery business in Canada. Of all the materials gathered, however, the most important by far have proved to be the advertisements by Canadian china merchants, the advertisements for auction sales, and the occasional advertisements for the products of Canadian potteries.

Nothing gives a more detailed or authentic picture than the contemporary advertisements. Inventories too often mention only 'a sett of dishes' or 'six cups'. Reminiscences have the inevitable errors of memory. But the china merchant's advertisement, even when vaguely phrased, may give a clue to what he actually had for sale at that moment. And some of the merchants were not vague. Upon occasion they mentioned makers' names, or specified patterns and types of ware: the still familiar Willow pattern (and its variants), the 'new English porcelain' (today called 'bone china'), ironstone (introduced by Charles James Mason and ordered for such Canadian 'mansions' as Belmont Hall in Montreal). The auctioneer's announcement tells what he had for the highest bidder. He, too, when settling an estate or selling the contents of a house was sometimes specific about the tablewares and ornaments. Auctioneers considered Wedgwood's black basaltes, Davenport dinner services, and Parian figures by Minton as items with particular sales appeal. They gave them feature billing along with fast driving horses, covered sleighs, and 'superior' milch cows. The local potter's few lines in a newspaper or directory indicate what he was making at that date. Besides brownware, optimistically described as 'not inferior to the English', there was now and then a mention of jugs modelled on 'the latest English Designs', or milk pans coated with a new-type glaze.

As with every study, a little knowledge is often dangerous. One advertisement may be misleading. Twenty suggest a trend. Only a selection of the large number of advertisements indexed have been quoted in this book, but conclusions have been based on the evidence provided by many examples.

Newspapers of every type—east and west, English and French—have been searched for the activities of both potter and china seller. Short-lived country newspapers, like the *Missiskoui Standard*, and all-but-forgotten city papers, such as the *Settler, or British, Irish, and Canadian Gazette*, have contributed their share of facts. The first newspapers established in the widely separated colonies all contained information on the pottery and porcelain used in early days—the *Halifax Gazette* (first newspaper in all of Canada), the *Upper Canada Gazette* (first newspaper of that Loyalist colony), the *Nor'-Wester* (first newspaper in the Red River Settlement), the *Saskatchewan Herald* (first newspaper west of the Red River and east of the Rockies), the *British Columbian* (first newspaper on the Pacific mainland).

One newspaper was of special value in this research. The *Montreal Gazette* (after June 3, 1867, known as *The Gazette*) was the first newspaper in Montreal; it was also the only Montreal newspaper that covered the entire nineteenth century. Since for many years Montreal was the port through which entered, or where was transhipped, nearly all the earthenware and porcelain sold not only in the Montreal area itself but in what is now Ontario, it meant that Montreal had a unique place in the crockery trade of Canada.

Advertisements in newspapers and directories provide not only reliable evidence of the ceramic wares used in nineteenth-century Canada, but a picture of life in the small group of colonies that emerged, during this period, into the structure of a nation. The taste of the times and something of the economic conditions of producer, seller, and purchaser are reflected in the details of shipments from Staffordshire, 'put up with the wants of the colonies in mind', or in announcements of wares locally potted and hopefully priced 'low enough to please'. Ceramic history embraces more than paste and glaze. As a nineteenth-century writer put it, it is, in the full sense, a broad study, 'neither deficient in dignity, nor limited to trifling investigations, nor rewarded with insignificant results'.

Tea cups and stone crocks, pudding bowls and milk pitchers, whether imported or Canadian-made, are true historical documents. Every piece of nineteenth-century pottery or porcelain used in Canada shares the substance of Canada's history.

Contents

Contents

List of Illustrations

Every piece of pottery or porcelain illustrated is from the author's collection, and except where listed as 'attributed' or 'maker unknown', every piece is marked.

List of Illustrations

List of Illustrations

The Tide of Imports: Toils and Hazards

CHAPTER I

Over the Atlantic by Sail

SHUTER & WILKINS . . . expect per first arrivals . . .
1000 Packages of China and Earthenware.
Montreal Gazette, May 10, 1823.

On the bottom of the Atlantic Ocean lie tons of nineteenth-century pottery and porcelain intended for sale in Canada. Crates of creamware delicately painted, black basaltes fashioned into 'table beehives' and teapots with sliding covers, ironstone ware 'new invented' in the days of the Regency, early bone china suitable for the gentleman's table in Halifax or Montreal, all in their day were loaded aboard sailing vessels bound for British North America and committed to the hazards of the sea.

From the ports of London, Plymouth, Bristol, and Liverpool, the ships set out with cargoes eagerly awaited by china merchants in Toronto and Quebec. They sailed from Sunderland and Newcastle and Shields, carrying fifty thousand pieces of brownware at a time; they left Swansea with 'Crockery—Well Assorted' for dealers in Saint John; they put out from Greenock and Glasgow, from Aberdeen and Leith, with Scottish wares that today are often in error assigned to Staffordshire. 'Running swiftly before strong winds' fast-sailing 'regular traders' like the brig *Scotsman*, from Glasgow, or the bark *Coeur-de-Lion*, from Liverpool,[1] carried out to the Atlantic products of the British potteries for the crockery trade of the colonies.

But many of these ships never arrived. The age of sail was full of uncertainties and dangers. In Atlantic storms waves might rise higher than the mast and then strike with such violence that those aboard would expect the vessel to break up at the next blow. Crates and hogsheads from Staffordshire would be beaten loose in the hold, and their contents damaged or destroyed. Some vessels limped into port with crockery that was useless to the merchants who had waited for it. Others disappeared at sea without a trace—and in a Canadian trade report another name would be entered in a column headed simply 'Vessels Lost Or Not Heard Of'.

The toll of the sea was staggering. In a single issue the *Montreal Gazette*, on June 5, 1834, reported nearly twenty vessels gone down since the opening of that year's navigation season. In addition to this list of 'melancholy disasters', the same newspaper carried items from the Halifax *Royal Gazette* and the Miramichi

3

Gleaner, citing further losses known in those ports. Any examination of nineteenth-century Canadian newspapers, with their china merchants' advertisements for goods 'daily expected by the first fair wind' and their lists of 'Vessels Lost Or Not Heard Of', tells a story of thousands of tons of 'Earthenware in New Patterns' and 'English China from the First Manufacturers' that never arrived at all. The wares were advertised and they were expected with each new day, but they went to the bottom of the sea.

A specific illustration of this type of loss and disappointment, always a possibility for the Canadian china merchant in the days of sail, may be found in an advertisement in the *Montreal Gazette* of October 4, 1844. Edward and George Wright, china merchants whose shop was on St. Paul Street opposite the Exchange Coffee House, were the advertisers. On that October day in 1844, when all the crockery sellers of the city were in anticipation of brisk autumn business, and when a number of them were unpacking new fall supplies already come safely to hand,[2] Edward and George Wright announced to the public that they were 'daily' awaiting tablewares 'of the very best manufacture and style'. As soon as these new wares arrived, they would offer them 'at prices not to be surpassed'.

The Wrights' Staffordshire goods had been shipped to them from Liverpool aboard the *Parana* and other vessels, and their advertisement indicated that they expected them at any moment. The *Parana* in particular might be looked for with the first favourable winds from the east, for she was a fine new brig of 200 tons burden, making only her third voyage, and known to be capable of a fast crossing.

But at the very time when the Wrights were advertising the tablewares expected by the *Parana*, and daily awaiting their arrival in Montreal, those same tablewares of 'very best manufacture and style' were already beneath the waves. Gone down with the fast-sailing brig were not only the crates of earthenware intended for the autumn crockery trade of Canada, but the *Parana*'s captain and all but five of those who had sailed aboard her. The tragedy, which to Edward and George Wright meant a serious business setback of a kind only too familiar to Canadian china merchants of the nineteenth century, had taken place before dawn on the morning of September 10—nearly a month before the Wrights, unsuspecting, had placed their advertisement in the *Gazette*. Five days after their advertisement appeared, the news reached Montreal.[3]

Since the *Parana* was believed to have been insured,[4] the Wrights were probably compensated for the wares they did not receive. But loss of stock at a season when the wholesale trade was of prime importance was a serious matter. Country storekeepers from the districts around Montreal and buyers from Upper Canada all laid in winter supplies from autumn shipments to Montreal dealers such as Edward and George Wright, and word only needed to get around that a wholesaler had lost his expected new stock for these trade buyers to take themselves off to his rivals. China-selling in nineteenth-century Canada was a highly competitive business. One of its great hazards was the uncertainty of transportation by sea, and one of the important elements of success was compelling advertising. When a dealer was confronted with the unfortunate news of a ship gone down, he often hurried into print to emphasize that he would still have stock as varied as the next man's, and in ample supply, in spite of disaster.

4

Such was the case with Edward and George Wright in that autumn of 1844. What they had advertised and expected by the *Parana* was gone, but they could make much of what came to them later in the month by other vessels from Liverpool. This was a necessity, because no matter how quickly they wrote off for replacements, nothing that the Wrights ordered from Montreal in October could arrive before the ice was out of the St. Lawrence the next year. In the days of sail not only did it take months for goods ordered from Canada to arrive, but winter brought with it isolation for what are now the provinces of Quebec and Ontario. The supplies that came to the dealers in the autumn were the supplies that had to last for nearly six months. Once the snow fell and the ice formed in the St. Lawrence, there would be no contact with the potteries in Great Britain until the spring break-up.

Even after the middle of the century, when railways first connected central Canada with ports on the Atlantic open to shipping all the year round, the china merchants (whose wares, when packed, were bulky) continued to depend very largely upon the St. Lawrence route. A few enterprising crockery sellers (Edward Wright was one of the first of them)[5] might occasionally get in small shipments through Portland or Boston or New York in the winter months, and bring the goods up to Canada by rail; but even as late as 1876 the *Gazette* could still speak of the china, glass, and earthenware dealers of Montreal as being 'shut out' from the overseas supply centres 'for half the year'. Old ways changed slowly. Sailing ships lasted well into the age of steam, and the St. Lawrence route was not quickly replaced by iron rails. The importance of sufficient autumn stock to see the china merchants of central Canada through an entire winter's business lingered on in the ceramic trade until Queen Victoria's reign was drawing to a close.

The Maritime colonies, with their own Atlantic ports, never experienced the sense of complete isolation that came over the provinces of the St. Lawrence with the first touch of winter frost. Nonetheless, for crockery sellers in Halifax and Saint John, big autumn shipments were also necessary, since they might expect fewer additions to their stock after the New Year, when winter storms made the Atlantic crossing more adventurous than ever for brigs and barks of a few hundred tons. The Maritime china dealers, however, could still look for plentiful supplies in December, at a time when the last sailing vessels out of St. Lawrence ports were racing for the open sea, and when no new arrivals could be expected there until 'the first fair winds' of spring. In an advertisement dated December 9, 1844, the Halifax china merchant, Bernard O'Neil, could announce '300 Crates and Hhds. of China, Glass and Earthenware' as 'just received' from Liverpool, and still look forward to a further assortment 'expected per other . . . vessels to arrive'.[6] In Saint John the crockery seller, Thomas Clerke, could advertise in the *New Brunswick Courier* on December 16, 1848, that he just received 'Dinner, Breakfast and Tea Service, CHINA PLATES by the dozen, assorted sizes, China IMAGES and Common Ware, in great variety'. He, too, could say in mid-December that he was expecting further additions to this stock from Liverpool.

But important as the big autumn shipments certainly were, even for china merchants who could count December as part of this storing-up season, they were scarcely to be compared in significance with those that arrived in the spring.

For all the china sellers of the colonies, spring meant the main upsurge of business. No crockery dealer wished then to be caught without as plentiful an array of Staffordshire's latest patterns or Glasgow's newest shapes as his capital or his credit would permit.

Long before the ships of the spring fleet put out from British ports with their cargoes of earthenware and porcelain, preparations were being made by the Canadian merchants for the new wares. With the end of winter came clearance sales in Canadian crockery shops. There were mark-downs in ironstone jugs, in 'leg pans' and slop jars, 'to make room for . . . Spring Importations'.[7] There were notices to 'Plumbers and Cabinet Makers' that prices had been slashed on earthenware 'Closet Basons' and 'Bidet Pans', to clear off old stock.[8] There were announcements to the general public that 'Reduced Prices' would prevail on 'Rich Dining, Dessert, Breakfast, Tea and Coffee Services',[9] so that space would be free for the new supplies. With the melting of the snow and the running of the sap came anticipation every year in Canada of teapots and dinner plates in 'the most novel and saleable patterns of the day'.[10]

Everything was suddenly stirring again in springtime, after business had died down during the long Canadian winter. Buyers, some from long distances, flocked once more to the china shops, new staff was taken on for the season, and the 'first arrivals', bringing everything from common brown milk pans of Sunderland earthenware to sophisticated tea sets of Worcester porcelain, were looked for with nervous impatience. And then, sweeping across the Atlantic in a mighty fleet, came once more the regular traders to Canadian ports, early to the Maritimes, ice-conscious and cautious into the Gulf. 'Winter suddenly breaks up, the ice disappears, and the majestic *St. Lawrence* opens . . . and all is bustle and hurry.'[11]

At ports like Halifax on the coast, spring meant that everything was all at once shining to greatest advantage. As Captain William Moorsom described the scene in 1830, 'the wharfs are then crowded with vessels of all sizes discharging their cargoes or taking in the returns. Signals are constantly flying at the citadel for vessels coming in; merchants are running about, in anticipation of their freights.'[12]

Back in the newspapers were advertisements for shipments of tablewares 'daily expected'. With vessels crowding into port, bringing news of other ships 'spoken' on the way, the china dealers could announce themselves as not in 'daily' but in 'hourly' expectation of new wares from the British potteries. Captain Salt, whose *Cleopatra* reached Quebec on May 24, 1854, reported having passed 'upwards of 200 inward bound vessels' coming up the river;[13] two days later, as these ships began arriving, one after the other, there were 'anchors going down every minute'.[14]

So eager were the china sellers in eastern and central Canada to lay in new stock at the opening of the season that shipping agents, seeking the business of bringing that stock to them, used as an inducement the fact that their ships would be the first loaded and the first on their way to the colonies at the end of winter. Thus Peter McGill & Co., of Montreal, agents in 1843 for the English sailing ship *Great Britain*, owned by the popular Captain Swinburn, advertised that he would 'as usual' have her off to Canada ahead of all the others in the spring.[15]

6

China merchants, such as Francis Leonard of Montreal (who opened an Earthen, China & Glass Ware store on St. Paul Street in 1823), stressed repeatedly in advertising that they would be able to offer goods from off the first of the spring vessels. Upper Canada dealers like Burns & Bassett, in 1834 proprietors of the Yellow Store in St. Catharines, made a point of telling the public each season that they had crockery selected at the best 'Houses' in Montreal and from the very first spring shipments to be unpacked at those establishments.[16]

It is, then, but the exception that proves the rule when an advertisement offers to the trade earthenware 'imported last fall for Spring Sale'. In this instance Samuel Alcorn, a Quebec merchant, was the seller; his announcement appeared in the *Montreal Gazette* on May 9, 1845.

At a china shop in Quebec's upper town, Alcorn handled fine English tablewares; he also, as on this occasion in 1845, made a practice of consigning cheaper-quality goods to auction sales, or sold off crates of common wares on the wharf by the ship's side.[17] Whether in the 1845 advertisement he was demonstrating foresight in getting ahead of the season, ingenuity in ridding himself of old stock that had not moved during the winter, or an ability to make the best of things when losses at sea had unexpectedly deprived him of spring wares on which he had been counting, is now impossible to say. Few Canadian china merchants would have advertised last fall's goods in their spring trade; most were concerned with publicizing the newness of spring shipments and the early date of their arrival.

The importance attached to these first spring shipments by the nineteenth-century china dealers is sensed in a curt paragraph that appeared in the *Montreal Gazette*. On June 5, 1824, Joseph Shuter and Robert Charles Wilkins, who together carried on one of the largest and most successful china-selling ventures in the colonies, took swift action to stop a rumour harmful to spring trade. The rumour had it that Shuter & Wilkins had lost the greater part of their new supplies with the brig *Cumberland* from Liverpool. Scornfully Shuter & Wilkins denied it: 'S. & W. take this opportunity of informing the Public, that the report of all their goods being lost in the Cumberland, is without foundation, as only a small proportion of the WARE, which they selected in England, consisting principally of such articles as they are not in immediate want of, was shipped on board of her.'

Like others who found themselves without goods on which they had depended and who feared loss of business to rivals thought to be better supplied at this important season, Shuter & Wilkins were at pains to point out that their spring stock would be varied in spite of the toll of the Atlantic. Their advertisement went on to state that they had already that season received 'a complete assortment of Earthen, China and Glassware' by other Liverpool vessels and were in 'daily' expectation of still further supplies. All this they were prepared to sell in Montreal at prices 'lower than ever before offered in this country'.

Shuter & Wilkins had moved quickly, for word that the *Cumberland* had had to be abandoned at sea, when she was about half-way to Quebec, had reached that port only a few days before. As soon as the fate of the *Cumberland* became known, someone in Montreal put about the story that Shuter & Wilkins had suffered heavily by her loss. But so promptly did Shuter & Wilkins act to kill the rumour, that their denial appeared in the same issue of the *Gazette* as the 'Intelligence' from Quebec concerning the doom of this well-known regular trader.[18]

Canadian china dealers depending on importations by sail had more worries than loss of stock at sea. The vessels carrying their orders of tea sets and dinner-ware might arrive in port safely enough, but with cargoes so badly knocked about by the Atlantic that they were fit only for disposal at auctions devoted to 'Goods Damaged on Voyages of Importation', once a frequent sale heading in Canadian newspaper advertising.

Not delicate tablewares alone, but stone jugs and stout baking dishes might be landed in shattered condition after a storm-driven passage. An advertisement in the *Montreal Gazette* on August 31, 1846, indicates what could turn up in an auction sale of damaged goods. In this case the assortment of earthenware had obviously been landed at Quebec from an ocean-going vessel and then brought up to Montreal by barge:

DAMAGED EARTHENWARE

ON THE WHARF, alongside the BARGE
HOPE, opposite Try's Buildings, on TUES-
DAY next, 1st September, will be Sold, for the be-
nefit of the Underwriters, THIRTY CRATES of
EARTHENWARE, consisting of—
Blue Edge Soup and Flat ⎫
    Plates   ⎬ Assorted sizes
Do Bakers ⎭
Painted Cups and Saucers
Do Oval and Round Tea-Pots, Sugars and
    Creams
White Jugs, assorted sizes, Egg-Cups, &c.
White Ewers and Children's Mugs
Black Lustre Tea-Pots, assorted sizes
Stone Jugs (assorted sizes), and Egg-Cups.
      &c. &c. &c.
Damaged on the Voyage . . .

In the days of transportation by sailing ship, the condition in which goods were landed in Canada was of critical importance to a dealer who could scarcely hope for replacements before another season. The fact that china sellers often featured in their advertising the condition of the wares they were offering is significant. An advertisement by John Booth, an early Saint John 'Clock and Watchmaker' who also dealt in goods as varied as cloth and crockery, furnishes an example of this. In the summer of 1800 John Booth received importations by the *America*. These he advertised on July 29 in the *Royal Gazette and New Bruns-wick Advertiser*, and in his announcement he made a point of emphasizing that his 'few crates EARTHENWARE' were all 'in good order'.

Half a century later, Canadian sellers of earthenware and porcelain were still directing attention to the good order of their stock. In an advertisement for an important trade sale of 'China, Glass and Iron Stone', on April 22, 1850, the Montreal auctioneer John Leeming paid for an extra paragraph in the *Gazette* to make clear that what he would be putting up that morning consisted of goods in 'perfect' condition. Many of the sets to be offered had even been packed in special cases 'to prevent risk of breakage'. Those who bid successfully on John Leeming's 'Choice and Expensive Collection' of 'Rich China' would find themselves taking home sets of jugs, vases, pastille burners, ring stands and 'handsome' table services, all of which, they could rest assured, had been transported across the ocean without becoming cracked or chipped.

Some of the British potters made business trips to Canada, gaining, at first hand, knowledge of the conditions under which their products had to travel. One who had impressed upon him the rigours of Atlantic crossing by sail, and the consequent need for careful packing of crockery consigned to Canada, was a young Scot named James Fleming. In later years he would become Sir James Fleming, head of one of Scotland's largest potteries and with Staffordshire interests as well; but at mid-century, when he first set out for Montreal, he came as a salesman representing Robert Cochran, then owner of two important Glasgow potteries, the Verreville and the Britannia.

Fleming's job was to obtain Canadian orders for his employer's wares. In the beginning it looked as if he would never be writing home any orders at all. The 500-ton sailing vessel on which he left for Canada ran into storms so fierce that all able-bodied men aboard had to turn to and help the sailors. Young Fleming, with no previous experience of sails, worked energetically that they might not all go to the bottom.[19]

The man from the Glasgow potteries could have had no more impressive demonstration of the Canadian market's need for tablewares that would stand up to the battering of Atlantic gales. And soon, from the Britannia Works, were coming out to Canada quantities of thick table and bedroom crockery of a kind that was almost indestructible. Much of it not only arrived safely, it has stood up to a century and more of hard use in country districts.

But sometimes sailing vessels survived the worst of Atlantic storms only to be wrecked in the St. Lawrence. Notorious at any season for hidden reefs and dangerous currents, the St. Lawrence route in the springtime was more treacherous than ever because of ice. The *Montreal Gazette* of May 10, 1830, gives an idea of some of the difficulties encountered by an early arrival working her way through ice in the gulf and river. The ship was the *William*, from Liverpool, carrying earthenware as part of her cargo. According to the *Gazette*, her passage after making the Banks had been slow and perilous. She 'was detained North of Bird Islands four or five days by the ice, during one of which she was entirely beset; the ice was one continuous field south of the vessel's station.' Yet in spite of dangers, the *William* landed safely her 'dry goods, iron, earthenware and sugar', and was herself 'only a little chafed' by the heavy ice through which she had navigated.

Not so successful on her way up the St. Lawrence was the *Niagara*, one of the sailing vessels left behind by the steamship *Cleopatra* in the spring of 1854, a year when ice held back sailing ships for a month.[20] In the early hours of a May morning the *Niagara* was wrecked some miles below Quebec. The *Montreal Gazette*, carrying the news on May 27, reported that she was then aground and 'the tide ebbs and flows in her'.

The *Niagara*'s cargo, through which the tide was unhappily ebbing and flowing, included crates of earthenware expected by Montreal china merchants.

James Thomson and William Minchin, for example, who had taken over Robert Anderson's thriving china, glass, and earthenware store near the Customs House, were waiting for spring goods for their first season in business. But the forty-two packages of earthenware which had been shipped to them from Liverpool aboard the *Niagara* never saw the china shop on St. Paul Street. Instead, when a fleet of schooners had brought up all that could be salvaged from the stranded sailing ship, the crates addressed to Thomson & Minchin were piled up in the Thistle Curling Shed, down by the Canal Basin, and there auctioned off as 'Damaged Crockery'.[21]

Another Montreal china seller who lost—although not so heavily—by the *Niagara* was John Sproston. An advertisement in the *Montreal Gazette* on August 17 told his story: 'at the Stores of Mr. JOHN SPROSTON, will be Sold . . . 2 CRATES EARTHENWARE, Damaged on voyage of Importation, *ex Niagara*.'

Not all the crockery came to the colonies in the conventional way by regular merchant ship. Arnold Fleming, son of Sir James Fleming and historian of the Scottish potteries, recorded that once it was a common sight to see Newfoundlanders heaving crates of Scottish earthenware aboard sealing vessels in ports such as Greenock. The crockery had been taken by the Newfoundlanders in payment for their oil.[22] Today in the tenth province it is possible to find nineteenth-century wares typical of the potteries of the Clyde; probably some of them made the trip over the Atlantic in the strong-smelling hold of a sealer.

By the last quarter of the nineteenth century, the age of sailing ships was coming hurriedly to an end; and with the age of sail went many of the delays and risks connected with the early ceramic trade of Canada. Before the old sailing vessels were displaced, however, they managed to compete for some years side by side with the newer steamships. For a while it still seemed open to doubt whether these transatlantic steamships were to have complete advantage over the old-time regular traders they were trying to displace; for in efforts to prove themselves, the early steamships experienced disastrous difficulties of their own. Many of them, too, were wrecked, taking down with them ton after ton of earthenware and porcelain.

But progress would not be denied: the 'A 1 Barques' and the 'First Class Brigs' had finally to give way. Before the century was out, the china merchants of Canada were engaged in a trade in which 'fresh easterly breezes' no longer controlled their hopes or brought their first shipments into port. If a 5,000-ton Allan liner, discharging the latest Doulton art pottery at Quebec, had less of the picturesque about her than the old square-rigged *Leven Lass*, unloading 'Scottish clays' for Robert Anderson in Montreal,[23] the result in the end was far fewer cargoes of crockery lost forever at the bottom of the sea.

Whether by sailing ship or early steamship the voyage over the Atlantic was a hazardous undertaking, and even its successful completion was not always the end of hard travel for crates of earthenware or hogsheads of porcelain. Much of the crockery landed at Canadian ports had to struggle on farther, aboard schooners, bateaux, barges, or paddle-wheelers. Before the age of sail was over, railways, Red River carts, and mule teams were carrying tea sets and dinner services to their journey's end in North America.

10

Halifax was the transhipment point for much that was intended for china sellers in other parts of Nova Scotia and in Prince Edward Island; Saint John was 'the toe of the stocking into which everything ran' for the merchants of New Brunswick.[24] And not only for those in New Brunswick itself. Nova Scotia dealers like John M'Monagle, of Windsor, received their 'China cups & saucers' and their 'Blue and yellow' ware 'VIA NEW-BRUNSWICK'.[25]

For china sellers who had paid transportation costs over the ocean on wares they had waited a year or more to see, there might be further expenses, as well as further delays and dangers, before their goods reached them for unpacking. In 1809, for instance, it cost china merchants ten shillings to have a single crate of earthenware brought up the river from Saint John to Fredericton, a distance of less than a hundred miles.[26]

It was Montreal, however, that became the transhipment point of greatest significance in the ceramic trade of the nineteenth century, and it was the St. Lawrence that carried the greatest inland traffic in crockery as the century wore on. Earthenware, porcelain, and the assorted stonewares that were the connecting link between the two poured into Montreal as into no other port in Canada. Only in part were these wares intended for the buyers of Montreal and the surrounding countryside; in growing quantities they were also for a constantly enlarging market to the west.

Montreal, as the head of ocean navigation on the St. Lawrence, was the port from which were sent on most of the goods intended for sale in what is now the Province of Ontario. Crates of crockery, landed from sailing vessels putting in at Montreal itself or brought up the river from ships unloaded at Quebec, were forwarded to the china sellers of Kingston, Toronto, and Niagara. When the frontiers of settlement moved ever farther on, more and more tablewares 'selected for the western trade' had first to be handled at Montreal. Over the Atlantic by sail was very often but the first stage of the long journey from the potteries of Great Britain to the china shops of Canada. For vast quantities of ware, the second phase involved the risk-taking ascent of the upper St. Lawrence.

CHAPTER II

From Montreal to Upper Canada

Montreal, the great outlet and depot of our whole trade, and the point at which
centre all our shipping relations with Great Britain . . .
Toronto Board of Trade Report, 1841.

When Dr. John Bigsby, an Englishman, first visited Montreal, about 1819, he was
immediately struck by the hustle and stir of the place. In the business section of
the city he noted a sense of purposeful activity that had been absent at Quebec.
To him the Montreal merchants seemed to be engaging in a sort of commercial
'stampado', a term used to describe the gathering together of vast herds of
buffalo, when the very ground for miles around would be made to tremble by
their unceasing and vigorous stamping. The telling effect of the Montreal merchants' stamping was being felt, the doctor noted, 'in the most remote wilder-
nesses', for the merchants were resolutely pushing their wares wherever there was
any chance of a market.[1]

What Dr. Bigsby had to say of Montreal merchants in general was certainly
true of the city's wholesale crockery sellers during the first half of the nineteenth
century. The dealers in china, glass, and earthenware were keenly aware of new
markets opening to the west and quick to exploit every opportunity. Men like
Joseph Shuter, with financial interests ranging from a mortgage on Chrystler's
Farm to huge shipments of 'the choicest tablewares in the country', or Francis
Leonard, opening up his Staffordshire goods in Montreal and advertising them
in Niagara, were businessmen who saw in tea cups and soup plates commercial
success for themselves on the advancing frontiers of Upper Canada.

For much of the century Montreal, through its pushing, watchful china merchants, and because of its geographical location at the head of ocean navigation
on the St. Lawrence (giving it a virtual control of imports into the most populous areas of British North America), held an unchallenged place in the ceramic
trade of Canada. In Montreal's china shops, many of them on St. Paul Street,
were stocked every article of earthenware and porcelain that a constantly
changing fashion dictated and a sophisticated market demanded. In warehouses
near the waterfront stood, ready packed, hundreds of crates of the 'common
goods' considered 'suitable to the Upper Canada and Country Trade'. All summer long, teams of horses and heavy wagons waited about in the streets, their
drivers anxious for the work of conveying crockery or other merchandise to

Lachine, nine miles above Montreal and past the dangerous rapids; at Lachine waited the bateaux and Durham boats and, in later years, the river steamers, their 'conductors' or captains prepared to take charge of starting any amount of earthenware and porcelain on its way to 'western' dealers. By the middle of the century, close to a thousand tons of earthenware alone would be leaving Montreal and going through Lachine in the summer months.[2]

Montreal, to Dr. Bigsby, had appeared a 'stirring and opulent town'. But even before he had commented upon its mercantile activity, another visitor, the Irishman, Isaac Weld, had noted the advantages of Montreal's commercial position, and had foreseen the importance to Montreal's future of expanding western trade. Even in the 1790's, at a time when the population of Upper Canada, founded upon Loyalist emigration from the United States, was not yet of major significance to the trade of Montreal, Isaac Weld had predicted what was to come. He observed that as settlements increased along the Upper St. Lawrence and around the shores of the Great Lakes, so must 'the demand for European manufactures increase among the inhabitants'; and as this demand increased, so must inevitably come significant growth in the commerce of Montreal, 'which of all the sea ports in North America is the most conveniently situated for supplying them with such manufactures'.[3]

Just as Isaac Weld had prophesied and as Dr. Bigsby had observed, Montreal merchants became the suppliers of most of the imported articles needed in Upper Canada at a time when a great tide of immigration was flowing into that province and creating a voracious market. Immigrants themselves, landing in Montreal, noted its highly advantageous position in relation to the new areas where they would make their homes.

One settler, writing of his decision to emigrate from Great Britain and publishing his experiences anonymously in 1834 under the title, *A Cheering Voice From Upper Canada*, invited his readers to 'inspect the map', and thereby observe that Montreal 'is destined, by its locality, to be always an emporium for the supply of the *Upper Province* with merchandise'.[4] Like others before him, the author of *A Cheering Voice* was delighted with the 'bustle and activity' the moment he stepped ashore in Montreal.

By far the greater number of these immigrants flocking through Montreal in the early years of the nineteenth century and bound for new settlements in Upper Canada were from the British Isles. Many of them were able to bring with them across the Atlantic very little other than a desperate hope for a better life in a new land. Such immigrants, travelling steerage, had to equip themselves with utensils for cooking and eating on board ship. That was generally all they brought in the way of tablewares, and even the few simple articles needed for the voyage were often of wood or tin rather than earthenware. 'Wooden noggins and trenchers, and tin porringers are much better than delf-ware which is so liable to be broken in a rolling sea,' wrote Martin Doyle in 1831, in *Hints on Emigration to Upper Canada Especially Addressed to the Lower Classes*.[5] When immigrants, whose status at home had relegated them to the 'Lower Classes', managed to prosper, they purchased in Upper Canada their tea sets and dinner plates, and thereby added to a trade strenuously cultivated by the china merchants of Montreal.

Even the immigrants whose financial circumstances permitted them to come out reasonably well equipped in the way of material possessions were counselled against burdening themselves with anything so fragile and so costly to transport as dishes for the table. All kinds of earthenware and porcelain, they were told, might be obtained easily in British North America, where every quality was available, from the richest to the plainest. Dr. Bigsby himself wrote, for the benefit of those contemplating emigration, that the 'prices of British manufactures are moderate in Canada', and that 'bulky articles', such as 'agriculture implements, furniture, crockery', should not be taken from Great Britain. These things, he stressed, 'can be had cheap and good on the spot'.[6]

In 1850 Rev. William Haw drew upon fifteen years' experience in Canada to give much the same advice as earlier writers. In a list of answers to questions likely to be asked by emigrants, he set down as the first question, 'What shall I take with me?' and answered simply, 'as little as possible.' Household goods of all kinds should be converted into cash before the emigrant quitted his native land, Mr. Haw recommended, for, 'besides a world of inconvenience, they will never pay costs.' Everything, 'and of the best', could be purchased in Canada 'nearly as cheap as in England'.[7]

Many making plans to try life in Upper Canada paid a few pennies for an emigrant's guide, or borrowed such a book from a lending library, and heeded the advice to leave earthenware and porcelain behind them. Others who clung to what they had and attempted to take it with them on the long voyage over the Atlantic often found, before they reached new homes in the backwoods, that they had to say with Catherine Parr Traill: 'Various were the valuable articles of crockery-ware that perished.'[8]

In the first half of the nineteenth century, therefore, Upper Canada, flooded with new settlers who needed to purchase at least some kitchen, dining, or bedroom crockery as soon as they had a place to live, presented the most rapidly expanding market in Canada for the products of the potter. It was a market that the Montreal china sellers were not only able but determined to supply, and although the wholesalers of Quebec might make an effort to share this trade to Upper Canada,[9] the miles told against them. 'The distant and comparatively inconvenient port of Quebec', as a Toronto Board of Trade put in 1841,[10] could never compete successfully with Montreal in the sending of bulky cargoes of earthenware and porcelain to the upper St. Lawrence. And since the Montreal china merchants imported for a large part of the country trade of their own province, as well as for the considerable demands of Montreal itself, theirs was easily the largest share of the ceramic business of British North America. To the mercantile stir of Montreal, so different in the eyes of some visitors from the 'sleepiness' of Quebec,[11] the sellers of tea sets and chamber pots contributed a not insignificant part.

The growing Upper Canada trade was handled from Montreal in several ways. Some merchants from the upper province made regular trips down the St. Lawrence to choose their own goods, including tablewares, from the new shipments arriving in spring and autumn. Wholesalers were on the watch for these out-of-town merchants, and directed advertising to their attention, the more enterprising placing advertisements in the newspapers of Upper Canada itself so as to catch the buyers before they left for Montreal.

15

One of the early York (Toronto) traders to make buying trips to Montreal was the picturesque Quetton St. George, a French *émigré*, who was said to have adopted the name St. George in commemoration of the fact that he first reached safety on British soil on St. George's Day. Almost alone out of a group of French royalists who emigrated to Upper Canada, Laurent Quetton de St. George prospered in the colony. Setting up as an Indian trader and dealer in furs, he opened general stores in several of the settlements, where he sold items as varied as 'segars' and sleigh bells and English porcelain tea cups.

Some of Quetton St. George's goods came to him from New York, as advertisements show. Other advertisements prove, however, that like nearly all Upper Canada merchants, this former officer of the King of France looked to Montreal as a natural supply centre for the wares he handled in pioneer trade in a British colony. The autumn of 1804, for example, saw him in Montreal to lay in new supplies. What he purchased from the Montreal wholesalers on that buying trip was advertised on November 10 in the *Upper Canada Gazette*. The 'general Assortment of Winter Goods' which he announced in York on that day included 'Crockery Ware', as well as 'Hats, Snuff, Hair-powder, Copper Kettles and ready made Carpets', all just in from Montreal.

Another Upper Canada dealer of early days who travelled regularly to Montreal to pick out the blue-printed tablewares that could be had in his general store was John Tannahill of Niagara. The *Gleaner* carried one of his advertisements on June 28, 1823, stating that he was 'just arrived from MONTREAL with a Complete and choice Assortment of GOODS . . . The whole of which were selected by himself and will be sold very Cheap for Cash only'. Dishes for the table (possibly purchased from Francis Leonard, on St. Paul Street, who had advertised earlier that year for Niagara trade)[12] formed part of John Tannahill's 'choice Assortment' personally decided on in Montreal.

But the trip down the St. Lawrence was a long one. Some Upper Canada dealers, in business in a small way, would never have made it at all, while few of those who, like John Tannahill, did follow the practice of buying in person in Montreal would have managed the journey twice in one navigation season; and of necessity much of the travel and nearly all of the transportation of goods was, in early days, restricted to the months when the St. Lawrence could serve as a highway.[13] John Tannahill's advertisements indicate that although he made his own selection in Montreal in the spring of 1823, some one on the spot chose for him the crockery and other merchandise that comprised his autumn stock that same year.[14]

Buying for Upper Canada merchants, catering to their wants when they came to town, or angling for the trade of those who hoped to sell to them became big business in Montreal in the nineteenth century. It was a business carried on not only by the regular dealers, with their china, glass, and earthenware shops; the auctioneers, too, with an eye for a fast turn-over on popularly priced goods, had their important part in the ceramic trade with Upper Canada. In the peak seasons of spring and autumn, the big auction sales of new goods nearly always included some crates of crockery which the catalogues would describe as 'Put up expressly for the Upper Canada Market', or, 'Well suited for Canada West'.

Sometimes an entire trade sale in Montreal would be devoted to crockery intended for the Upper and Lower Canadian markets alike. John Leeming's auction on October 21, 1845, was an example of this practice. According to his advertisement on October 8, in the *Times and Daily Commercial Advertiser* (and on the next day in the *Montreal Gazette*), he was putting up 'TWO HUNDRED CRATES & HOGSHEADS' in what he described as an 'IMPORTANT AND EXTENSIVE SALE OF CROCKERY . . . Packed and assorted expressly for Upper and Lower Canada'. The wares offered were:

> Kaolin or Flown Blue Dinner Sets ⎫
> China Breakfast and Tea Sets   ⎬ Extra quality
> Fireproof Yellow Bakery & Nappies ⎭
> Foot and Chair Pans, Water Closet Pans, &c, &c.
> Crates of COMMON GOODS . . .
> containing every description
> of Earthenware required for the Trade . . .

On occasion the seller at one of these Montreal auctions directed toward the Upper Canada market was the overseas potter himself, and not a local importer. John Leeming handled a large consignment of this kind on June 1, 1846. According to his advance announcement in the *Montreal Gazette* on May 29, he had received from the makers five hundred crates of earthenware to dispose of to the highest bidders. The manufacturers, in making their selections to send out to Canada, had kept the Upper Canada market in mind, and John Leeming's orders were to sell on their behalf 'without reserve'.

At an auction of this kind, open to chance, or at one of the frequent sales of bankrupt stock, there were often bargains to be had. For this reason many Upper Canada dealers found it profitable to put their buying in the hands of a Montreal agent. Such resident agents earned their living by being constantly on watch in the interests of out-of-town dealers. For their services they generally charged a commission of about two and a half per cent. One such agent was James Beatty, a man on the spot, who could snap up an unreserved lot of earthenware slipping through at a manufacturer's sale, benefit by a bankrupt's misfortune, or buy to advantage when the market was glutted.

Some idea of the usefulness of this type of agent can be gleaned from the advertisement that Toronto and Hamilton newspapers carried for James Beatty in the late summer of 1842. Addressing himself 'to the Merchants of Canada West', and looking to the autumn trade, Beatty offered to purchase any type of staple or fancy goods wanted, and he made clear that he was thoroughly familiar with the needs of storekeepers in the upper province.[15]

To make sure of Upper Canada business, some of the bigger merchants opened branches or posted representatives of their own in towns west of Montreal. This practice was noted by the author of *A Cheering Voice From Upper Canada*, when he wrote that 'many of the large houses in *Montreal* have branch establishments, or agents, in most towns of this province.'[16] Joseph Shuter (*Plate* I), the Englishman who became one of Canada's most successful china sellers, and for whom a street was named in Montreal, followed this plan for pushing sales.

It was in 1834 that Joseph Shuter formed the partnership of Shuter & Paterson to open a Toronto china, glass, and earthenware house on King Street, just opposite the Market Place. This was a branch of the business he carried on in Montreal through twenty years and more with Robert Charles Wilkins as a partner. The opening of the Toronto establishment was announced in newspapers in Dundas, London, Niagara, St. Catharines, and St. Thomas; and that autumn the new firm was urging 'Western Merchants' to call at King Street 'before sending their orders to Montreal.'[17] But although Shuter & Paterson made their bid in Toronto for the trade of Upper Canada, they were a Montreal-based firm, and announced themselves as such. The object in opening a Toronto outlet was merely to keep as much as possible of the Upper Canada crockery business in the hands of Joseph Shuter and out of the ledgers of his many Montreal rivals. Branch houses in Upper Canada centres helped to distribute Montreal-imported earthenware and porcelain to the even greater profit of the wholesalers of St. Paul Street.

For those who might not wish to go to the expense of maintaining an Upper Canada outlet or to pay an agent to solicit orders, but who yet wished to sell their wares in the upper province, a Toronto auctioneer of the 1830's had a plan to further his own ends and work to the advantage of Montreal merchants at the same time. A. M. Greig, for many years a partner in the East India house of Lyall, Greig & Co., of London, England, opened the Auction Mart in York in the winter of 1834 (shortly before the name of the city was changed to Toronto). In the spring he decided to seek Montreal business, even as the Montreal merchants and auctioneers sought the trade of Toronto. At the end of May he came down to Montreal, took rooms at Orr's Hotel on Notre Dame Street, and advertised in the *Montreal Gazette* (on June 5) that he was available to discuss the 'peculiar advantages' he could offer Montreal importers. What A. M. Greig had in mind was the organizing of trade auctions in Toronto, and for these sales he wanted consignments of every kind from Montreal. His *Gazette* advertisement, looking for such commissions, reminded the Montreal wholesalers of what they already knew to their gain: 'that in consequence of the great numbers of emigrants daily arriving in the Upper Province, goods of every description are in very great demand.'

In large measure the wares 'suitable for Upper Canada' and sold at auction sales fell into the category of 'common goods', the staple of the colonial trade. Many of the immigrants who arrived in Upper Canada in bands of several hundred at a time found in the cheapest earthenwares the crockery best suited to their needs and means. These made up the bulk of the goods on which the Montreal suppliers reaped their profits, selling literally tons of them to Upper Canada in a season.

There was, however, another side to the ceramic trade emanating from Montreal. As in other parts of the British North American colonies, life in Upper Canada provided for sophisticated taste side by side with pioneer austerity. The settler who, at home, had known nothing better than dirt floors and the simplest of scanty furnishings might well feel that the 'common goods' offered by the Canadian china merchant satisfactorily enhanced his New World prosperity. But along with the hordes of immigrants of this type came others.

A considerable number of those who moved into the Upper Canadian wilderness on the wave of Loyalist emigration were used to luxuries; the French royalists who arrived at the end of the eighteenth century dazzled the backwoods with their jewels;[18] and from the British Isles came those whose names entitled them to a rank which their fortunes had been unable to support. When immigrants such as these were successful in establishing themselves, they provided a ready market for earthenware and porcelain of the 'superior' kind; and before long some of the more enterprising of the working-class immigrants achieved an affluence that permitted them to enjoy luxuries. The buying power of all these groups, combined with that of the official and garrison circles, gave incentive to merchants promoting wares from 'the first manufacturers in England'. An example of what the Montreal china seller was prepared to try out on the Upper Canadian market in the way of 'select' and 'splendid' goods is found in an advertisement which appeared on July 19, 1837. Paradoxically the advertisement was in William Lyon Mackenzie's *Constitution*, an organ devoted to the eradication of rank and privilege. Thomas McAdam, who had begun business two years earlier in Montreal, was the advertiser who offered to 'friends and the Upper Canada public generally . . . a LARGE and SELECT ASSORTMENT OF GOODS . . . STONE, CHINA AND PORCELAIN DINING SERVICES, varying in price from twenty to sixty pounds; together with Dessert, Tea, Breakfast and Toilet Setts, and a great variety of Antique Mantel Ornaments and splendid Flower Vases'.

But even while Montreal wholesalers like Thomas McAdam and a host of others worked up a lucrative trade with the upper province (so that, by mid-century, the Upper Canada trade had become a major part of their crockery business for many merchants), dealers in the upper province itself were slowly making their way to independence. From the first years of the nineteenth century there had been those who, at least occasionally, circumvented the Montreal importers by purchasing direct from the potteries of Great Britain. At the same time as Quetton St. George was making buying trips to Montreal, another early York storekeeper, Henry Drean, was advertising crockery that he had purchased on his own account 'in the cheapest Manufacturing Towns in England'.[19] While Thomas McAdam was tempting the rich of the upper province with £60 'Dining Services' from his rooms in Montreal, William Harris was inviting everyone in Toronto to call at his place on King Street to see china and earthenware just received '*direct from the potteries in Staffordshire*'.[20] And while John Leeming was auctioning off hundreds of crates of flowing blue toilet sets 'well adapted to Canada West', Alexander Christie of Niagara was unpacking supplies of the same type of goods shipped direct to him by 'some of the best makers' in England.[21]

For many years, however, direct importations to Upper Canada china sellers were limited to a relatively small number of dealers. The greater part of the wholesale crockery trade of both provinces remained in the hands of Montreal merchants. Compared with the thousands of crates of earthenware and porcelain they sent west from Lachine each season, the orders sold 'direct from the potteries of Staffordshire' to Upper Canadians like Drean or Harris had little bearing on the ceramic trade of the period. The significance of early advertisements announcing that Upper Canada dealers were receiving crockery direct from the manufacturers lies in their foreshadowing of a future when the upper province would break the stranglehold of the 'mercantile oligarchy' of Montreal, for so Montreal's domination appeared to those restive under her prosperity.

In the story of trade between Montreal and Upper Canada—a story in which the china merchants had an important place—the state of feeling between the two provinces has to be understood. It was not only that dealers in Upper Canada resented the fact that because of geographical location a city in Lower Canada had to be regarded as 'the great outlet and depot' of their trade; there were also causes of dissatisfaction in the prevalent system of credit buying, which each side felt worked to its disadvantage.

Whenever John Leeming held a crockery auction in Montreal to sell goods 'packed with the Upper Canada market in mind', or Edward Wright, the china wholesaler on St. Paul Street, called in trade buyers to inspect new tablewares 'particularly suited to the upper province', he was almost compelled to state in advertisements that 'terms' would be 'very liberal'. The Montreal crockery seller who demanded cash from out-of-town buyers would soon have found himself with an overstocked warehouse full of unsold crates.

Yet, inevitably, when the time for settlement came, there were those who could not meet their obligations, frequently because they, in their turn, had not been paid what was owing them. Others, who had instructed Montreal commission merchants to send orders overseas for shipments of crockery, might be bankrupt by the time their wares arrived the next year from Great Britain. Then would appear advertisements like the one John Dougall placed in the *Montreal Gazette* on October 11, 1842. On that day the young Scotsman (not yet the celebrated founder and editor of the *Witness*) published a list of goods which he would put up for auction at his store on St. Paul Street. Included were '30 hhds and crates first quality assorted Earthenware, imported for a Store in Canada West'. The reason for the sale was to close out the account 'of a Bankrupt Estate'.

In payment for bad debts owed them by Upper Canada merchants, Montreal wholesalers like John Dougall often found themselves the unwilling owners in the upper province of property which they neither wanted when they had it nor were prepared to keep up. In difficult times they were unable to sell it or to lease it, except for trifling sums. As a business transaction, the taking over of property for debt often satisfied no one.

The situation was described by an anonymous writer in the July 1868 issue of *The New Dominion Monthly*. Recalling Canadian business conditions of earlier days, the writer of the article told how once it was a common sight throughout Upper Canada to see 'conspicuous houses built by some merchant who had gone under, which had fallen into a shocking state of dilapidation'. According to this writer, the owners of these eyesores, set in unkempt grounds, were very often unpaid Montreal wholesalers, who had come to feel that taking property for debt in Upper Canada was 'almost worse than getting nothing at all'. Frequently they did not even consider it worth while to pay the taxes on land they had not wanted in the first place.

Since the anonymous writer of the article in *The New Dominion Monthly* was none other than the one-time Montreal wholesaler, John Dougall (by 1868 a dominant figure in Canadian journalism), it is to be presumed he knew the feelings of those in Lower Canada who were saddled with Upper Canadian property in payment for debt. After all, even the astute John Dougall had himself been caught with 'first quality assorted Earthenware' ordered for 'a Store in Canada West', a store gone bankrupt before he could deliver the goods and collect his money.

John Dougall gave the Montreal viewpoint. How Upper Canada felt about it was somewhat different. The attitude towards Montreal in that province was summed up in a letter addressed to a Kingston newspaper and reprinted in the *Canadian Economist* on October 17, 1846. Montreal, to Upper Canadians, was a 'greedy monopolist' battening off the profits of their labour. Proof of this was abundant. It lay in Montreal's 'splendid buildings, public and private' and in her 'unprecedented advance in wealth within the last few years'. 'Whence have all the vast sums expended in public and private improvement been derived ?' asked the Kingston letter-writer. 'Not surely from the profits of petty trade with the inhabitants of the surrounding country, but from the hard-earned resources of the settlements of Western Canada.'

The *Canadian Economist* was a Montreal paper. Its comment on the letter published in Kingston was to wonder how anyone 'with any understanding of these matters' could write such nonsense.

Undoubtedly, over the years, many of those who believed themselves to have been fleeced by Montreal suppliers must have sunk deep into debt weighted down by the wares of the china merchants. In Upper Canadian eyes Montreal took on a sinister aspect. Even those who ordered their stock direct from the makers in England still had to have their goods transhipped at Montreal, paying necessary fees to Montreal-based forwarders. And into the treasury of Lower Canada poured the duties paid on thousands of pounds' worth of goods, purchased, it was true, by Montreal merchants, yet clearly intended by them for the Upper Canadian market. It was, therefore, against a background often coloured by feeling and drawn taut by bitterness that the china wholesalers of Montreal played out their important role in the story of the Canadian crockery trade.

Various solutions to the difficulties were proposed from time to time. A novel plan, its supporters limited to Upper Canada, was the annexation of Montreal to that province. Then what duties had to be paid upon such articles as Worcester porcelain or Glasgow earthenware, supplied by Montreal and sold in Toronto or St. Catharines or London, would enrich the province where the wares were used.

Writing in the *Montreal Gazette* on February 2, 1835, an Upper Canadian businessman declared himself solidly behind annexation. It was, he said, 'the most manly way of obtaining our just rights—*the collection and disbursement of our own revenue*'. This correspondent's viewpoint was shared by many—all in Upper Canada—but probably not even the optimists among them hoped for much success from the proposal. As the author of *A Cheering Voice From Upper Canada* admitted in 1834, the annexation idea was 'not palatable to most of the legislators and big wigs of the *Lower Province*'.[22]

Yet it was only the Act of Union, coming into effect in 1841 and placing the two provinces under one government, that finally put a stop to annexation talk. In the meantime, Montreal wholesalers went on their way, importing on the grand scale and advertising widely their crates of 'assorted Earthenware . . . selected with great care with a view to the UPPER PROVINCE'.[23] They paid their duties and their taxes in one province and they made their money in another.

But whether the tea sets and the dinner plates, the pipkins and the porringers sold in Upper Canada in the first half of the last century came into that province through the agency of a Montreal wholesaler fleecing his Upper Canadian clients, or were shipped by a British potter to the direct order of a York merchant, none of these imported wares reached Upper Canada except by hard travel from Montreal. Hogsheads, crates, and packages of tablewares, which had crossed the ocean aboard some fast-sailing brig running before an Atlantic gale or slipping cautiously through dangerous ice in the Gulf, might yet be lost or damaged before they could be delivered at Kingston or Niagara. To travellers following the St. Lawrence route above Montreal, the sight of wrecked cargo floating downstream or caught on rocks in one of the many rapids was neither unusual nor reassuring.

One writer, Rev. William Bell, on his way to Perth in June of 1817, left a record of the uneasiness which the spectacle of such wreckage might awaken in the mind of a stranger making the ascent of the St. Lawrence for the first time. On June 16, after his bateau had passed the village of Moulin de Roche, above Cornwall, the young Scottish clergyman was told that they were nearing a dangerous rapid: 'Every year both boats and lives are lost in it. Not a week before, a batteau going up with the King's stores, was wrecked, and, indeed the remains of the boat and part of the cargo, which still lay upon a rock, tended not a little to excite alarm.'[24]

Until satisfactory canals were completed, the transportation of goods and people up the river beyond Montreal involved a series of portages and of strenuous poling and dragging of heavy flat-bottomed boats through difficult stretches. That merchandise as fragile as earthenware and porcelain was sometimes smashed *en route* is hardly surprising. Between Montreal and Kingston crates of crockery on their way to Upper Canada were tossed out carelessly onto the river bank, left to the mercy of rains and pillagers, roughly thrown onto farm carts to be jolted over portages, heaved back onto the bateaux, and then subjected to the same process all over again.

From Kingston across Lake Ontario to York, and from York on to the farther west involved more transhipments, and more hazards in handling and travel. There were breakages, and there were delays, and there were additional expenses which had to be added to the original cost. With all these difficulties the china sellers of Upper Canada had to contend. And yet the evidence of their advertisements proves how well stocked these pioneer storekeepers often were in tablewares suitable for Government House or settler's hut.

Long before transportation conditions had begun to improve, fine Queensware could be had in Kingston from John Dowling, advertising in the very first issue of the *Kingston Chronicle*.[25] In the village of Ancaster, John Burwell was handling 'well selected' assortments of the newest earthenware from Montreal and announcing them in the *Upper Canada Gazette*.[26] In William Richardson's store in Chippawa was to be seen a wide variety of table and toilet wares, also from Montreal, and advertised in the *Gleaner*.[27] In Niagara, supplies were large enough for B. Harrison to hold auction sales at his rooms in the Market Place, when tureens, tea cups and saucers, milk jugs, teapots, and all manner of dishes and plates would be offered along with quantities of glassware and Britannia metal goods.[28] All this was in the first quarter of the century.

With so much going to Upper Canada from Montreal, where everything had to be transhipped because of the Lachine Rapids, it was no wonder that farmers, anxious for a little ready money, used to come in from the country with their carts during the season of navigation, hoping for a load of merchandise or travellers' baggage to take out to the bateaux and Durham boats at Lachine. This was the practice when Thomas Storrow Brown, the future rebel, first came to Lower Canada from New Brunswick, in 1818. His reminiscences of Montreal tell of 'the noisy bustle of cart-loading and the long string of carts on the Lachine road'.[29] Four or five shillings was the usual remuneration to a farmer for the nine-mile drive. Frequently farms around the city were neglected, while those who should have been planting the crops were jogging along with crates of fine blue-printed earthenware or hogsheads of early bone china. When the first newspapers of Upper Canada carried advertisements for tablewares just received from Montreal, they were advertising pottery and porcelain that had probably started on the long trip up to new settlements piled high on a farm cart taking its place in the line on the dusty road to Lachine.

From Lachine, in the first years of the nineteenth century, crockery for Upper Canada went up the St. Lawrence to Kingston aboard bateaux (flat-bottomed open boats, narrow at bow and stern). At this period the crew of a bateau might number four to row and a man with a paddle to steer. The man in charge of the craft was styled the 'conductor'. About three tons of merchandise could be taken up on the early bateau, but as river traffic increased larger bateaux were needed and supplied by forwarders, who vied with one another in the number of new bateaux they promised to keep 'constantly plying' each navigation season.

Heavy with freight and passengers, these large, open boats, equipped with oars, sails, and long, iron-shod setting poles, were rowed, sailed, poled, and pulled up the river for nearly two hundred miles. With rapids at the Cascades, the Cedars, and Coteau du Lac, at the Long Sault, Pointe aux Iroquois, Point Cardinal or the Galops, as well as several others of less turbulence to be overcome, the journey up the St. Lawrence for a bateau carrying crockery and other goods for Upper Canada was a battle against obstinate hardships.

What canals there were in the early years were frequently 'repairing' (as contemporary writers put it) and often of little help. Rev. William Bell was one who found this to be the case when he made his first trip in 1817. At one place where a primitive canal usually allowed the boats to avoid a dangerous stretch, the bateau's conductor was told that the lock had been closed for work to be done upon it, 'so that we were forced to ascend the rapid. This we found no easy task.' Rev. William Bell added: 'I had no idea till I came here that the ascent of the St. Lawrence was attended with so much labour and difficulty.'[30]

A year later another newcomer, also making the same journey for the first time, left his account of the hardships of bateau travel. Edward Allen Talbot, noting that in bateaux 'all the merchandise destined for Upper Canada is conveyed', described how the men responsible for the transport of this merchandise would suddenly have to drop their oars and plunge into the icy water to tow the bateau and her cargo 'by main strength up the foaming cataracts'. To him it was a complete mystery how those regularly employed in the forwarding of merchandise by 'this difficult navigation' could ever keep their health: 'They are compelled, almost every hour, when actually melting with heat and fainting through fatigue to jump into the water, frequently up to their arm-pits, and to remain in it towing the boats, until they are completely chilled. Then they have recourse to the aid of ardent spirits, of which on all occasions they freely partake, and, in a few minutes, are once more bathed in perspiration.'

Sometimes the men exchanged their oars for the long setting-poles, 'which they fix in the bed of the river; and, by the pressure of each man upon his own instrument, they propel the boat upwards with astonishing celerity'. For 'hours without intermission' the men would toil in this way to force the loaded bateaux upwards against the current. Talbot noted with astonishment how long they could keep up their fantastic labours.[31]

There were other times when the efforts of the men alone would not be enough to pull a bateau through the resisting waters. At this point a team of oxen or horses would have to be hired from some nearby farmer. With the animals straining on the river bank and the men working from the water, the boat and the valuable cargo would be edged through the dangers of rocks and rapids. At any moment an accident might occur; safety lay only in the skill of the men.

Past the worst of the rapids it was impossible to get a loaded bateau, even by creeping cautiously along close to the shore. At this point the freight would have to be taken off. That weary boatmen, noted for hard drinking and 'horrible oaths', would handle crates of china tea sets with more care than was required for unloading iron bars or bales of dry goods was scarcely to be expected. Crockery took its chance, and crates packed up in Staffordshire thudded down in St. Lawrence mud to stay on the river bank until some farmer's cart came to rattle them over the portage.

Improving service at the portages became a necessity. Horses, wagons, and reliable drivers had to be provided as a regular thing to get the freight over the 'carrying places'. Covered storehouses had to be erected, for merchandise put down and left in the open not only deteriorated, it was often stolen. It is easy to understand why china merchants would have been interested in William Johnson's advertisement in the *Montreal Herald* on August 14, 1819. This announcement dealt specifically with the hazards faced by those taking goods past the Cascades, the Cedars, and Coteau du Lac, three rapids in quick succession, spread over a total distance of about eleven miles, just before the St. Lawrence widens into Lake St. Francis. Pointing out that farmers dragged in from their fields and bribed into service as carters often handled goods 'carelessly', dumping them roughly onto 'the muddy bank of the river' and leaving them there exposed 'to . . . weather and to pillage', Johnson made an offer of 'excellent' horses and carts 'to convey merchandise and passengers' at any time. He guaranteed to move everything safely from the unloading point at the Cascades to Coteau du Lac. He would have extra horses ready to pull up the boats. If required, he would hold goods in a covered storehouse. He even hoped to have covered wagons by 1820.

The rapids at the Cascades, the Cedars, and Coteau du Lac formed only one stretch of difficult navigation on the long journey up the St. Lawrence, across Lake Ontario, and on to new settlements. And Johnson was only one of those ready—for a fee—to expedite the growing traffic up the river. All along the route there sprang up companies who erected storehouses and announced themselves equipped with strong carts and strong horses at portage points. They built new and larger river boats, and, in keen competition, advertised for a share of forwarding profits. In the course of each navigation season these companies handled many tons of pottery and porcelain on its way from Montreal to the dealers of the upper province.

When, for example, Horace Billings of Brockville advertised 110 crates of 'Black Tea Pots' in the spring of 1832,[32] he was advertising goods that had reached him after strenuous river travel under the agency of some forwarding company. Perhaps it was H. & S. Jones, important forwarders with headquarters in Brockville, who brought up the black teapots on one of the bateaux they operated regularly between Montreal and points on the upper St. Lawrence.[33]

When Shriver & Dean opened a general store in 1836 in what had formerly been Chitty's Public House, Upper Bytown, the 'neat' tea sets and the plates— blue, pink, and brown-printed—which formed part of their first stock,[34] must have come to them up the Ottawa. Possibly it was the Ottawa & Rideau Forwarding Company which carried these fashionable tablewares of King William IV's day through or around 'the whirling eddies of contending currents' at Ste. Anne's, Carillon, and Chute à Blondeau.[35]

In Toronto, when Andrew Hamilton advertised china and earthenware 'daily expected' in 1841, he advertised wares at that moment on their way over the Atlantic to Montreal aboard the sailing ship *Souter Johnny*.[36] From Montreal a forwarding company such as that of Ross, Matthie & Co., who promised To- ronto merchants 'increased safety and despatch' in handling their goods, would have to take on the task of seeing the Staffordshire crockery up the St. Lawrence.[37]

In the steadily increasing traffic to Upper Canada the old bateaux kept their place throughout nearly half the nineteenth century. As late as 1835 some fifteen hundred of them were still engaged in carrying crockery and other freight between Montreal and Kingston. Depending upon weather conditions, they could, at this time, worry their way up the river in five to ten days. But the volume of business had early made a place for river craft capable of carrying more crates of china, more bales of dry goods, more passengers per trip. The Durham boat, introduced from the United States, helped to meet this demand from about 1809. Long and shallow, with a rounded bow and a bottom that was not quite flat, the Durham boat, a type of barge, was often several times the size of the largest bateau. Forwarding companies were soon employing Dur- ham boats and bateaux simultaneously,[38] loading them with immigrants and freight, and sending them off up the rivers to fill the demands of new settlements for both men and goods.

With time, and more canals, steamboats began plying over increasingly long stretches of the upper St. Lawrence. Little 'puffers' (small, high-pressure boats) made their appearance pulling behind them 'first-class decked barges', on which crates of earthenware bound for Upper Canada might share space with kegs of nails or cases of pioneers' tools. At first the eerie scream of their whistles terrified both animals and settlers along the shore, but by the mid-1830's puffers, with barges or bateaux tacked on behind, had become an accustomed sight wherever steam navigation was possible on the upper St. Lawrence.

After 1832, when the Rideau Canal was completed, goods might move between Montreal and Kingston by the alternative though longer route up the Ottawa. Some forwarding companies, notably the important Macpherson, Crane & Co., who owned covered barges, bateaux, and a fleet of thirteen steamers, sent their freight up by the Ottawa and Rideau system and brought their boats loaded with produce from Upper Canada down by the St. Lawrence.[39]

All these various developments added to the busy importance of Montreal, able to claim, in 1835, that she was 'the emporium in which has centred the trade of the whole of UPPER CANADA'.[40] Isaac Weld had foreseen it in the 1790's. D'Arcy Boulton, Upper Canada's Solicitor-General, had sensed its beginning when he noted, in 1805, that 'the usual supply' of goods for 'the several very respectable private stores' of York was from Montreal.[41] Dr. Bigsby had felt the pulsating vitality of the city's mercantile stir before 1820.

The Montreal merchants, seizing an advantage handed them by geography and the times, had built up a trade that helped to make the St. Lawrence, the Ottawa, and the Great Lakes alive with flat-bottomed boats, decked barges, schooners and sloops and steamboats which increased in size and importance every year.

Conveying the thousands of crates of earthenware and porcelain that now went from Montreal to the upper country each season had in itself grown into a business that sent many a barge off from Lachine well loaded. To the forwarder, the china merchant was an important customer; to the china merchant, the services of the forwarder were indispensable. Merchant and forwarder, their interests allied but conflicting, kept watchful eyes upon each other.

Sometimes they clashed openly, as in the spring of 1837, when a number of Upper Canada merchants met in Brockville to protest vigorously against the forwarders' proposed 'Tariff of Freight from MONTREAL upwards' for the coming navigation season. One of the major issues at stake that night, when feeling against the forwarders ran high, was the dismaying rise in the charges for taking crockery up the river. Advances so exorbitant as 'almost tantamount to a prohibition of bulky articles' was the accusation hurled against the forwarders by the merchants gathered in Brockville under the chairmanship of Billa Flint (in later years a member of the Canadian Senate). In discussions which lasted long, the proposed cost of transporting crockery provoked angry resistance.[42]

The fuss had begun a few days earlier when five of the major forwarding companies, including the Ottawa & Rideau, Macpherson, Crane & Co., and H. & S. Jones, published a joint advertisement in a number of newspapers giving their new rates for 'the approaching season'.[43] According to the merchants' interpretation of the proposed new rates, based, not as in the past on weight, but, for certain bulky articles, on measurement, the new charge for taking a crate of earthenware from Montreal to Kingston could conceivably represent the staggering advance of 525 per cent over previous rates, and amount to '76 per cent on the Sterling cost of the article'. For taking up one hogshead of earthenware the jump in charges could be as much as '400 per cent over last year's rates and an advance of 84 per cent on the Sterling cost'.[44]

This was the way the china merchants worked it out. The forwarders had a different interpretation. Their case was stated in a letter one of them wrote to the *Montreal Gazette*. It was published on April 15, 1837, and charged the merchants with picking 'extreme' examples so as to paint an 'exaggerated picture' of the probable effects of the new tariff. Defending the introduction of measurement as a basis for setting rates—the basis questioned by the merchants—this forwarder used crockery as an object lesson why measurement and not weight was the only realistic basis for estimating the cost to the forwarder. Crockery was so bulky, he pointed out, that 'on board of one of the boats usually employed, I cannot well stow more than ten hhds'. He ended his letter with a thinly disguised reference to Billa Flint, the chairman of the Brockville meeting, when he regretted that the merchants 'in their abberrations' had not tempered their 'flinty asperity' with more courtesy and understanding.

For their part, the merchants maintained that so far from distorting the picture, they had given what would be the true results of the new rates, results which the forwarders were attempting to disguise. Because of the introduction of the measurement question, an honest appraisal of the situation could not be obtained by any simple comparison of last year's rates with the increases listed in the published tariff for 1837.[45] They cited crockery, a bulky article, as one of the proofs of their contention, and spoke furiously of 'the marks of decided combination, ruinous to the trade of both provinces'. In the end, after their indignant meeting at Brockville, the merchants set up a committee 'to meet this evil threatening the community'. The committee was to get in touch with all dealers in crockery and other goods affected by the new rates. Among firms represented on the committee was Horace Billings & Co., sellers of the 110 crates of black teapots.[46]

Insults and accusations were hotly exchanged by merchants and forwarders that spring of 1837; and earthenware from Staffordshire assumed the guise of heavy ammunition in a verbal battle, its transportation up the St. Lawrence an inciting issue. The emphasis placed on crockery in the wrangle is good evidence of its importance in the trade between Montreal and Upper Canada.

But the end of the Montreal wholesaler's domination of the trade of the upper province was in sight. The commercial 'stampado' of the city on the St. Lawrence began to transfer itself to the newer province. The change was led by Isaac Buchanan, Glasgow shop boy one year, Montreal merchant the next, and pioneer Upper Canada wholesaler within a decade. Direct importers of all kinds of manufactured goods began to set up headquarters in Toronto, London, Hamilton. The number of crockery sellers ordering from the potteries in Great Britain, instead of sending their orders to Montreal to be executed, began to increase rapidly. Upper Canada china merchants, like John Mulholland of London, opened branches of their own in other parts of the province, and had their own agents pushing off 'common wares at low prices'. Alert to new conditions in their overseas market, the potters in Great Britain began sending consignments direct to Upper Canada, with the result that Toronto's Thomas Clarkson was able to come on the scene as a rival to Montreal's John Leeming, with big crockery auctions in Toronto of 'CRATES . . . Packed expressly for this Market, and consigned for Sale on account of the Manufacturers'.[47]

In Montreal, advertisements headed 'Removal of Business to Upper Canada' became a feature of the 1840's and 1850's. One crockery wholesaler, after more than ten years in Montreal, decided in 1854 to transfer to the upper province.[48] When he announced his decision he offered Montrealers some final bargains. To clear out his stock 'as speedily as possible', he was prepared to sacrifice '3 of Ridgway's Complete Pottery Water-Closets, sanctioned by the London Board of Health', and one fine stoneware 'Fountain Basin'. This last was an unusually versatile object, for its seller advertised that it could be put to use by the fortunate purchaser as a 'Baptismal Font', or alternatively employed as a 'Dentist's Basin'.[49]

As for those seeking jobs in crockery establishments, they, too, were looking to the upper province. 'No objection to go to Upper Canada', advertised 'a YOUTH of 19' who wanted 'A SITUATION in a Wholesale or Retail CROCK-ERY STORE' in 1849. His notice, in the *Montreal Gazette* of May 31, gave his qualifications as eight years' experience in the work.

In a report made public in April of 1841 the Toronto Board of Trade had spoken of Montreal as the 'depot' in which was centred all the trade of Upper Canada.[50] At that time the crockery wholesale business of both provinces would still have been very largely directed from St. Paul Street. But in the next few years the picture changed. When the Board came to present its report for 1860, it reviewed crockery-selling in Toronto and came to the conclusion that the old impression 'entertained by some that Montreal is a better market for this class of goods' could 'hardly be so' any longer.[51] Two years later, again in an annual report, the Board was able to note that in Toronto more persons were engaged in selling crockery, 'in proportion to the trade done', than in any other city in Canada. That many dealers, 'buying the bulk of their other goods elsewhere', now came to Toronto 'for their stocks of Crockery' was the best evidence that Toronto, in 1862, had a new place in this trade.[52]

Inevitably the grip of Montreal's wholesalers on the commerce of the upper province relaxed. The city's geographical position would continue to mean that much that was bound for the regions of the upper St. Lawrence and the Great Lakes would have to be transhipped at Montreal from ocean-going vessels, but the days of her resented monopoly were in decline. It was not, perhaps, so much that Montreal was losing ground in the second half of the nineteenth century as that Upper Canada was fulfilling the promise of earlier years. The *Kingston Chronicle* in 1820, seeing the 'mighty host of Emigrants' pouring into the province had cried out:

> They set this way in such o'erwhelming floods,
> Canadians! take your last look at the woods.[53]

The 'mighty host' had cleared much of the woods, and had established flourishing towns and villages. They had created an important market for the Staffordshire tablewares pressed on them by the wholesalers of Montreal. And they had begun to develop their own plans for commercial power. The future Province of Ontario, capable of taking control of her trade, was the assured outcome.

For Montreal's river forwarders, too, the middle years of the century brought changing conditions. The early years had been the hard years, when getting big hogsheads of earthenware and porcelain from Montreal to Upper Canada had involved risks and dangers that called forth the tested skill of the sweating, swearing men of the bateaux. They had been the years when forwarder clashed with merchant, and when the size of crates from Staffordshire had provoked recriminations and insults in the newspapers of the colony. But with the coming of steam on all reaches of the upper St. Lawrence and on the Ottawa, across the Great Lakes, and on the land, many of the old difficulties and hazards of inland transportation vanished. Ahead was a future when steam and iron rails would make it possible for the china sellers of Upper Canada to be ready with 'an assortment of all kinds, and any quantity . . . at any season of the year'.[54]

CHAPTER III

By Red River Cart
and York Boat

Cups and Saucers, Milk Jugs . . . Children's Copper-toed Shoes . . .
Pemmican, Dried Meat and Sinews for Sale . . . E. L. Barber.
Nor'-Wester, Oct. 9, 1862.

Perhaps the most picturesque chapter in the history of Canada's crockery trade belongs to the Northwest. Even though business was at first on a small scale, compared to that in older parts of the country, it was carried on under conditions of frontier enterprise which give it a lively character of its own. In early days the wares sold by pioneer dealers in what are now the prairie provinces reached them only after long months of struggle and risk. Travel time was longer and the hazards even greater than those involved in the transportation of supplies to the china sellers of the east.

Earthenware from Staffordshire bound for the Red River Settlement was exposed to all the uncertainties of navigation to Hudson Bay in vessels often 'too slimly made' to withstand pressure from northern ice, and frequently 'ill-adapted for the critical service required of them'.[1] Again, tablewares awaited by storekeepers of the British settlement had to travel through United States territory, where at times half-starved treaty Indians might be watching for the chance to attack and plunder a freight brigade.[2]

In open boats and slung on the backs of Métis tripmen, wares from Josiah Spode's old factory at Stoke-on-Trent made their way down from Hudson Bay into the interior. Loaded onto creaking Red River carts, products of Longton and Burslem potteries bumped mile after mile over the plains. Urged forward by oaths 'startling to the ear', ironstone china was freighted by mule team to the outposts.

In bleak wooden buildings, standing box-like and lonely against a prairie skyline, earthenware and china were lifted out of packages that had been half a year in transit. In tents and sod huts, white stone cups and saucers were finally unwrapped by the dealers who would sell them. Scalping knives, pemmican, and Indian blankets were the shelf mates of 'Pearl China' tea sets at Fort Garry; furs, trading outfits, and woollen drawers their stock companions at Duck Lake.

As the tide of immigration rolled on to the west, new markets opened up year by year for the products of the potter. That many of the first merchants included crockery as a staple of western trade—in spite of all the difficulties of bringing bulky and breakable goods far inland into pioneer country—is proved by early

31

newspapers, directories, and travel accounts. Troublesome and expensive as crockery might be to transport to the west, it was a commodity that sold well.

The early settlers, travelling to new homes by wagon or oxcart, generally brought little with them in the way of household furnishings. A bride from Ottawa, journeying nine hundred miles across the plains on her honeymoon in 1879, was, perhaps, typical. One who met her on the Carlton Trail on a cold, rainy evening in August described how she and her husband were equipped. They had a small wagon with a tent roof, their home for the journey. A single cart followed behind with all their goods, and one spare animal walked beside the wagon.[3] Edmonton was their goal. The young husband had already secured his grant of land and looked forward to a day when he would be rich and their possessions great, but in the meantime one oxcart transported everything his bride could carry with her to set up housekeeping.

It was to make the necessary travel easier that people like Rev. George Bryce, who knew the country, warned immigrants repeatedly: 'It is not advisable to be encumbered with too much household stuff.'[4] Handbooks such as that issued in 1882 with information on 'What to Bring and How to Come to Battleford' invariably counselled against unnecessary baggage. Not only would it be a burden to transport, it would take up room needed for essential farming equipment, which the settler was told to buy before he struck out for new country. For use on the way tin dishes and not breakable earthenware were recommended,[5] even as they had been advised earlier for emigrants crossing the ocean. These conditions meant that the western housewife was a prospective buyer of tableware as soon as she was well established in her new home. Where there was a demand, the dealers had incentive for finding a way to get in the appropriate supplies.

It was not, however, from the pioneer storekeepers that the earliest settlers bought cups and dishes. The Hudson's Bay Company itself was the first importer of tablewares on a commercial basis in the Canadian west; from the Company's sale shops the first trade in crockery was carried on.

And for the early settlers, dependent for nearly everything they needed upon the Hudson's Bay Company, in the period before the commerce of the west was open to private trade, the best of English earthenware and porcelain was available. Records exist today to name Josiah Spode's successors, William Taylor Copeland and Thomas Garrett, as suppliers of tablewares to Hudson's Bay territory in the 1830's. In the 1840's and 1850's William Taylor Copeland, his partnership with Thomas Garrett dissolved, was still filling orders to go to the remote Northwest of Canada.[6] One such account in the archives of the Hudson's Bay Company states that early in the summer of 1848 Copeland earthenware to the value of £112. 10s. 10d. left England with merchandise bound for York Factory.[7]

Copeland, a Lord Mayor of London, and a Member of Parliament for over a quarter of a century, was one of the most important potters of his day. His business energy brought in orders from all over the world to his factory in Staffordshire. That he included the great Hudson's Bay Company among his customers is further evidence of his success. The Red River settler who took his dinner off a Copeland plate bought at the Fort Garry sale shop may not have been using the same quality of china as royalty, but he was, at least, eating off ware from the same English factory as supplied members of the royal family, dukes of the realm, and foreign potentates.

Undoubtedly some of the Copeland table and bedroom crockery shipped to Canada by the Hudson's Bay Company was sent out to the order of its officers. In the wilderness some Hudson's Bay officials lived elegantly. Heavy silver and crystal so thin 'a person half seas over might easily swallow Glass and all without knowing any thing about the matter' set their tables.[8] But in addition to china and earthenware sent out on the supply ships for those who had given special orders through the Company, there were tablewares sent to the Northwest to stock the Company's sale shops. An inventory of goods on hand at the Fort Garry shop on June 1, 1851, indicates that hundreds of items in tableware were available at a time when stock must have been low, since that year's supply vessel had not yet arrived in Hudson Bay.

Although this particular inventory does not specify the makers of the crockery listed, it shows how ample was the choice. There were china tea bowls and saucers, at two shillings and one penny each; china sugar bowls, at three shillings and sixpence each; 'Octagon Jugs' of various sizes and prices; china butter basins and matching stands (four shillings and sixpence each); dozens of china plates and dozens of earthenware plates in assorted sizes; 'Lucknow' cream jugs, at six shillings each; 'York' teapots, at one shilling each, and brown-glazed 'Rockingham' teapots at slightly more; there were wash basins and ewers, and chamber pots described as 'Pompeian', and there were 'Victoria' jugs and slop basins in blue.[9]

None of this ware had arrived at Fort Garry except by travel involving even more troubles than the route which brought crockery to Upper Canada in the most difficult days. Until the end of the 1850's virtually all the supplies for the Hudson's Bay Company posts in the Northwest came by sailing ship to Hudson Bay. This in itself was often a dangerous voyage. Where ships carrying earthenware and porcelain to Halifax or Montreal might encounter ice hazards on the way, and even, in the case of the St. Lawrence route, be beset by ice for days at a time, sailing vessels bound for York Factory were sometimes for weeks held prisoner by icebergs which threatened to send them to the bottom at the next shattering blow—and sometimes did.

The *Prince Rupert*, loaded with merchandise and supplies, was four weeks coming through Hudson Strait in 1847. James Hargrave, a Chief Factor of the Company was on board. His account of the voyage is preserved in a letter written to a friend in Edinburgh: 'we were in hourly danger', he wrote, 'of being crushed between the mighty masses that were rumbling and crushing around us at every ebb and flow of the tide.'[10] Locked between two tremendous icebergs, the *Prince Rupert* seemed doomed.

In 1847 the passengers and cargo were, in the end, landed safely, but the outcome of a voyage to Hudson Bay was not always so fortunate. The first issue of the *Nor'-Wester*, Fort Garry's first newspaper, which made its appearance on December 28, 1859, carried the grim news that a Company supply vessel must be presumed lost for that year:

there is too much reason to fear that she has been lost on her dangerous voyage to Hudson's Bay. . . . The boats went to York, as usual, for the expected cargo, but came home with the gloomy news of the non-arrival of the vessel. . . . Should the worst apprehensions be realised, this will have been the third chartered vessel which has been wrecked in three years in the ice-bound regions of Hudson's Bay.

When a voyage was successful, and crockery, such as that inventoried at the Fort Garry sale shop in 1851, reached York Factory, it still had adventurous travel ahead of it. It would be landed amid a scene of confusion, excitement, and din. Tripmen, mostly half-breeds and Indians, who brought in the furs and took back supplies to posts in the interior, vied with one another in their haste to collect cargoes and be off. The urgency was great when the supply ship was late in arriving, as the *Prince Rupert* had been in 1847. There was need to be away, lest the early northern winter overtake the freight brigades hurrying along the rivers with the goods from York Factory; and need to get the sailing vessel loaded with furs and on her way home for the same reason.

Scarcely giving over time to sleep, Hudson's Bay men would work frantically to clear the incoming supplies and to check the furs and dispatches that the Company ship would carry back to England. Indians on hand to take part in the excitement of a ship's arrival and passengers just landed or passengers about to sail added to the hubbub. Somehow, in the rushing about, in the general air of frenzy, and in the incessant noise—never letting up day or night in a babel of English, French, and Indian—crockery and other merchandise would be stowed in the right boats; and a brigade would be ready to leave York Factory for the Red River.

To Upper Fort Garry (the future Winnipeg) in the Red River Territory would have gone most of the earthenware and porcelain imported in this way through Hudson Bay. Here, at the point where the Red and Assiniboine meet, was the centre of government for a small, slow-growing colony of free settlers—settlers who were living uneasily under the monopoly of the Hudson's Bay Company, and who were to become the nucleus of the new province of Manitoba in 1870. They, together with Hudson's Bay officials and some former Hudson's Bay men and their families who had elected to remain in the country, created a market for crockery that was the largest the Northwest would offer for many years. This was the market supplied entirely, at the beginning, by the Hudson's Bay Company public sale shop at Fort Garry, and later competed for by private merchants for whom, in the first days of independent trade, the Company also brought in stock through Hudson Bay.

All the goods imported, including fragile porcelain and earthenware, came from York Factory in open boats manned by hardened tripmen, much as the goods for Upper Canada had gone up the St. Lawrence in bateaux and Durham boats. For the transportation of Red River supplies, however, the York boat was used. A Canadian invention, it had been introduced by the Hudson's Bay Company shortly after 1821, and was named for York Factory, where the first such boats had been built. Strong, flat-bottomed, with pointed ends, and sides which sloped inwards, these stout wooden boats, with heavy oars called 'sweeps', were manned by crews of eight or more to row and one to steer. As a rule they travelled from York Factory in brigades of several boats at a time.

Like the river craft of eastern Canada, York boats, laden with their crockery and other cargo, were rowed, sailed, poled, and pulled through a complicated system of inland waters. Dangerous rapids, and channels promising almost certain destruction to anyone unfamiliar with the way, were navigated by men who would even rush through the night when time pressed them on.[11] Standing up among the freight to row, they would send a York boat skimming past dangers narrowly avoided by a quick movement of the bowsman's long pole, or a sudden, powerful stroke of the steersman's sweep. Travelling at the head of the brigade, with responsibility for the whole undertaking, was the 'guide'. James Hargrave's bride, Letitia Mactavish, pictured one of the most famous of them in a letter written home to Scotland soon after she arrived at York Factory in 1840. Alexis L'Esperance she described as wearing a costume composed of a sky-blue capot, a scarlet sash, a sort of high, scarlet 'nightcap' on his head, and moccasins on his feet.[12] To men like Alexis L'Esperance, clad in the traditional dress of the *voyageur*, and familiar with 'every rapid and shoal throughout the long course of his run',[13] many tons of earthenware and porcelain from the potteries of Staffordshire owed their safe arrival in the Canadian Northwest.

The forwarders of Upper Canada, who would have seen similarities between their bateaux and the York boats of the west, and who would have perceived in Alexis L'Esperance, the 'guide', a dominating 'conductor' of bateaux, might, however, have had difficulty in recognizing some of the cargo that was freighted along the rivers of the north. In particular, the familiar crates and hogsheads of crockery, conspicuous by their size and a characteristic feature of the St. Lawrence traffic, took on strange form in northern waters.

When Upper Canada merchant and St. Lawrence forwarder had quarrelled in the spring of 1837 over forwarding costs based on measurement, it was crates of crockery weighing three hundredweight and hogsheads weighing over four that were a cause of angry dispute.[14] On the Hudson Bay to Red River route such large crates and hogsheads could have no place. They were, instead, transformed into what were known in the Northwest as 'inland pieces'. Each piece, or bundle of cargo, was in weight only about one hundred pounds.

There was reason why goods shipped for Hudson's Bay Company transportation had to be sent off from England in cases or packages that were relatively light and more or less uniform in size. The Company's river boats had to travel through hundreds of miles of wilderness, where neither canals nor forwarding companies existed to ease difficulties. Where treacherous rapids made portages necessary, the men of the York boats found no 'excellent Horses . . . with careful drivers to convey merchandize' waiting to help them. William Johnson had provided this service at the Cascades as early as 1819, for those taking goods up the St. Lawrence,[15] but on the route between York Factory and Fort Garry the tripmen, unaided, had to get their own cargoes over frequent and sometimes long portages. Goods put up in pieces weighing no more than one hundred pounds each could be carried easily and reloaded quickly.

An eye-witness account of the way in which the crew of a York boat handled the work at portages was written in the 1870's for readers of a newspaper in the east:

At each of these portages the boats are unloaded and the cargo carried across. Each man takes two of the bundles, fastened together with a strap which is slung across the forehead, the bundles hanging on his back. Thus laden, with their loads of two hundred pounds weight, they cross the portage at almost a running pace. Then the boat is hauled up, and by a long rope at the bow, and rollers under her, is dragged across and launched on the other side. It is not many years since this was the only means of transportation over the water ways of the Northwest.[16]

Five minutes was the time needed for a nine-man crew to reload a York boat with an average cargo of seventy-five pieces. And repacked hastily in this way— perhaps with earthenware from Copelands in Stoke-on-Trent, Twankay tea from a London house, and 'Indian and self-defence knives' from Rodgers of Sheffield —a Northwest boat pushing off from the shore of a lonely river presented an appearance that was 'compact, orderly . . . beyond praise'.[17]

Just as on the journey up the St. Lawrence, so on the four-week trip from Hudson Bay to Red River there were stretches through which the boats, heavy with 'pieces' of crockery and other goods, might have to be dragged. But in the northern transportation system, men, not oxen or horses, normally had to do the pulling from the shore. With a line made fast to the boat, and with harness fitted to their shoulders, the tripmen strained and struggled through thick bush or deep mud on the river bank. In the Northwest this was known as 'tracking';[18] to the men it was often a far more troublesome business than making a portage. Yet all this sweat and toil was inseparable from the problems involved in bringing the products of the potter to the Canadian west.

For long after it was founded, in 1812, Lord Selkirk's Red River Settlement had remained the only area of colonization on the prairies. It was little more than a tiny, isolated band of white settlers cut off from the rest of British North America, surrounded by Indians, and strengthened only by half-breeds divided between two loyalties. Supplying its needs through York Factory was at first no strain upon the Hudson's Bay Company. But as time went on, it became increasingly evident that the requirements of both the Company and the colony would grow too great for this system to continue.

By 1843 James Hargrave was complaining of the work put upon his staff at York Factory by incoming Red River goods. According to him, when the Company's supply ship had sailed into Hudson Bay that summer she had been 'choaked . . . to the Upper hatch with packages for Red River', and he and his men had slaved day and night to the point of exhaustion to check supplies for the inland posts and freight for the Settlement.[19] Four years later the situation had become even worse. Two ships brought in the goods from England in 1847. Before the Red River consignment was away, forty York boats were filled; for the Fort Garry shops alone there were two thousand pieces.[20] Clearly the old system of importations by York Factory would have to give way as the country opened up; already there were signs pointing to the great tide of western expansion.

Slowly but obviously, the tight control of the Hudson's Bay Company over the Canadian west had begun to weaken. By the end of the 1840's, free trade in the Red River Territory was virtually a fact, if not a completely acknowledged one. This meant for independent merchants not only the right to compete with the Hudson's Bay Company in the sale of manufactured goods such as crockery imported from England under the watchful eye of the Company itself, but the right to deal in furs, for so long a jealously guarded monopoly. With trade free and with furs the lure, new merchants went into business around Fort Garry, and, since nearly all dealers dabbling in the fur trade were general storekeepers as well, this increase in the number of merchants came to mean an increase in the flow of crockery entering Red River Territory. Where once the settler had had to choose from whatever the Hudson's Bay sale shop offered, there was now a growing choice for those able to buy or trade.

It was at this point, not long after the 1840's, that the few early independent merchants such as Andrew McDermot, an Irishman who had been at Red River since 1812, and A. G. B. Bannatyne, his son-in-law (ex-Hudson's Bay man who would later hold office under Louis Riel), found themselves being joined by newcomers anxious for a share in a promising future. Men who, in the years to come, would be responsible for bringing quantities of china, glass, and earthenware into the Northwest—before they left general trading for wider business interests— got their start at this period.

From St. Paul, where he had been in the wholesale business, came a man with an impressive name, who was to make for himself an important place in the life of the British settlement. Don Derigo Nojada Gomez da Silva Fonseca, better known as W. G. Fonseca, was the merchant said to have introduced the ladies of Fort Garry to hooped skirts (which at first they regarded as some sort of freak),[21] and who early sold them 'crockery of every kind' at highly remunerative prices. Before his enterprise took him on to become 'the great authority on real estate in Winnipeg',[22] at a time when to be in real estate was to be in a booming market, this native of the Danish West Indies brought huge orders of tableware into the Red River Territory.

A year after W. G. Fonseca had set up at Fort Garry, a Connecticut Yankee, who was also to become one of the capitalists of the region, arrived on the scene. Edmund Lorenzo Barber, grandson of a signer of the American Declaration of Independence, was only twenty-six years of age when he began to lay the foundations of fortune north of the border.[23] In less than twenty years, after he had become one of the largest real estate owners in Winnipeg, the first Manitoba directory would list him simply as 'E. L. Barber, gentleman', but in early days, when cups and saucers were important to his profits, he was E. L. Barber, operator of a 'New Cheap Store' and importer of any article wanted at Red River: 'Scalping Knives . . . Tea Pots, Milk Jugs . . . Powder and Shot, Lead Balls for Buffalo Hunters'.[24]

Without railways and without access to any ocean port except through Hudson Bay (and that by favour of a Company who regarded them as competitors in trade), the early merchants looked for a new supply route. They found that route to the south. Across the border and over several hundred miles of almost trackless plains lay St. Paul, Minnesota. With a population of five hundred in 1850,[25] it was scarcely a metropolis, but, through the Mississippi, it was early connected with railways, which in their turn made contact with Atlantic ports. Goods for the Red River could be brought in through St. Paul, and goods could also be purchased from St. Paul wholesalers.

Crockery was part of the stock Red River dealers used to buy in St. Paul from the importers there, one of whom advertised for orders in this line as soon as Fort Garry had a newspaper. In its first season the *Nor'-Wester* carried advertisements for Pollock, Donaldson & Ogden, St. Paul 'Importers of Crockery and Dealers in China, Glass & Lamp Goods.'[26]

As importers of crockery, Pollock, Donaldson & Ogden would have been handling transatlantic wares, a great part of which would have been of English manufacture; for throughout the nineteenth century the United States was a heavy importer of all grades of English earthenware and porcelain, as advertisements in their own newspapers prove. E. L. Barber, the American established at Fort Garry, is an example of one who regularly bought his stock in St. Paul, and yet who often advertised the crockery he sold under the heading 'English Goods'. His advertisement in the *Nor'-Wester* on January 23, 1865, in which he offered 'English Goods . . . Cheap for Cash, Hides or Wool', cited 'Cups and Saucers, Plates, Sugar Bowls, Milk Pitchers, Salt Cellars, Mustard Pots, Molasses Cups, &c.'

But although much of what the Red River dealers purchased in St. Paul was undoubtedly of British make, it is very probable that they also brought back with them American pottery, in the form of crocks, jars, spittoons, and other plain, utilitarian wares of this kind. 'Ohio Stone Ware' was advertised in the *Nor'-Wester* by Pollock, Donaldson & Ogden on December 12, 1868, in one of the rare advertisements for American-made stoneware to be found in a Canadian newspaper.

While American glass manufacturers actively campaigned for Canadian business in the nineteenth century by advertising extensively in Canadian publications and even, in the case of some of the more important glass factories, by holding trade sales in Canadian centres, advertisements for the work of American potters appear only occasionally until well towards the close of the century. Even these late advertisements are rarely specific, so that sometimes it is impossible to tell whether the word 'American' applies to the glass or earthenware mentioned. In the over-all story of Canada's ceramic imports, American wares were never a significant factor. The advertising of Ohio wares in Red River Territory is accounted for by geographical circumstances.

The first Red River merchants who made the long trip south to St. Paul were remembered there for years. Their 'rude appearance and unsophisticated simplicity' astonished St. Paul storekeepers, who found their new customers prepared to hand over to them 'the entire contents of their purses, while the amount to be retained, as the price of the goods bought, was left to their uncontrolled integrity'.[27]

What crockery was purchased in this trusting way (and such simple trust did not last long) went back to Fort Garry in two-wheeled carts drawn by oxen. The Red River cart, constructed entirely of wood and as characteristic of the plains as the York boat was of the rivers, was the means of bringing countless tons of earthenware and porcelain to western buyers. Oxen, pulling loads of from eight hundred to a thousand pounds of merchandise, could average about fifteen miles a day, which meant that a month or more of steady travelling was needed to cover the distance between St. Paul and the Red River Territory. At night the drivers camped beside their carts, by day they plodded on over roads that were often little better than faint tracks across the plains or rough corduroy crossings through swamps.

In the east the china sellers had waited for the first fair winds to bring new stock into port; in the west they waited for a sound borne on the winds. Long before they could be seen the Red River carts might be heard approaching. The 'simply hellish' screech made by the ungreased wooden axles was said by the Canadian poet (and seller of crockery), Charles Mair, to be 'indescribable; it is like no sound you ever heard in all your life and makes your blood run cold'.[28] The arrival in the Canadian west of many a shipment from Staffordshire was heralded across the prairies by the wail of the Red River cart. This must have been the sound E. L. Barber was waiting for when he advertised in the *Nor'-Wester* on August 24, 1869, that 'A Brigade of nineteen carts will be in very shortly from St. Paul with a large addition to the . . . stock of merchandize.' Crockery was one of the items which he announced would be coming in by the freight brigade.

But even as some of the independent merchants were laboriously jolting in tablewares by oxcart from St. Paul, while others were receiving theirs by the difficult route through Hudson Bay, a new method of transportation opened up. It promised speed and efficiency. At first it gave little of either, but the sense of progress it created was stimulating. The *Nor'-Wester*, then a newspaper of half-a-year's standing, commented upon it optimistically on July 28, 1860:

> We are this year witnessing a complete revolution in the trade of this Settlement. Every week the steamboat arrives at Fort Garry with 20 or 30 tons of merchandize. To a foreigner transportation by means of steam appears natural and common-place enough; but viewed in the light of the past, and taken in connection with the peculiar condition of this country, the change is significant and important. Until recently, the method of importing goods to Red River was slow, unprofitable and vexatious.

What the *Nor'-Wester* saw as a promising substitute for transportation methods that were 'slow, unprofitable and vexatious' was a small steamboat with second-hand engines, the first steamboat on the Red River of the north. This was to eliminate 'the very disagreeable necessity of doing business by York Factory'; this was to promote competitive trade by fast delivery of stock, and breathe 'new life' into the commercial system of the Northwest.[29]

When she first amazed the Indians and settlers of the Red River Territory, the steamboat puffed past under the name of the *Anson Northup*,[30] but, fittingly, her name soon changed to the *Pioneer*. Her career was short. Launched in 1859, she began her first regular season in June of 1860, and two years later was replaced by the larger *International*.

Dealers in crockery were among the first to take advantage of steam on the Red River. In the same issue which hailed the *Anson Northup* as positive evidence of 'hopeful progress', the *Nor'-Wester* carried this advertisement:

> Just received by the Steamer Anson Northup
> a large and varied stock of Dry Goods,
> Groceries and Hardware . . .
> WHITE STONE CUPS AND SAUCERS.
> LARGE AND SMALL WHITE PLATES.
> MILK JUGS, BOWLS, AND PITCHERS.

39

The advertisers were Ross, Buckingham, and Coldwell, operators of a general store. Since William Buckingham and William Coldwell were also the publishers of the *Nor'-Wester*, and James Ross was just on the point of becoming so, it is not surprising to find them turning at once to the new method of transportation which they had praised, and wanting the public to know that they were progressive enough to do so. They should, however, have realized, even at this early date, that the *Anson Northup* was likely to be neither so speedy nor so punctual as they had declared in the editorial columns of the newspaper. After all, a news story in that same July 28 issue had given a hint of navigation conditions on the Red River. The *Anson Northup*, it seemed, had run up a few miles above Georgetown to meet freight caravans from St. Paul, whose non-arrival had been throwing her off schedule, and in the course of this brief excursion she had got herself into shallow water, had had her wheel broken twice, and had very narrowly escaped being completely wrecked on 'fallen timber and still more dangerous snags'.

A stern-wheeler, the *Anson Northup* was owned jointly by the Hudson's Bay Company and J. C. & H. C. Burbank, St. Paul forwarders. While by no means abandoning the York Factory route, the Hudson's Bay Company, like the independent merchants, had been looking for an alternative way to bring in at least part of the growing quantity of supplies needed at the settlement. With the Burbank brothers the Company had worked out a transportation system which was to make use of the *Anson Northup* on the last stage of the long journey from England to Red River Territory. The Hudson's Bay Company in its agreement with the Burbanks had, however, placed no restrictions on the use of the steamboat by private dealers. On the supply vessels coming in to Hudson Bay the Company could, and sometimes did, refuse to carry goods for private merchants when it needed the space for its own shipments, or when a private merchant had clashed with the Company;[31] but the *Anson Northup*, through the Burbanks, St. Paul forwarders and commission merchants in their own right, was freely open to the business of the settlement.

Perhaps nothing illustrates so well the long and involved journey that lay between earthenware and porcelain made in Great Britain and the dealers who sold it in the Northwest of Canada as the new 'fast' route to Fort Garry hailed as progress in 1860. Such progress depended for its fulfilment on an unreliable little steamboat, whose captain considered her 'nothing better than a lumbering old pine basket',[32] and whose hesitant engines had to be stoked with wood which the Indians maintained was stolen from them.

In advertisements running in the *Nor'-Wester* throughout the summer of 1860, the Burbanks gave detailed instructions to merchants who wished to be up-to-date and have their goods hurried to them from England via the Red River and the *Anson Northup*, instead of having them congested in Hudson Bay or dawdling over the plains. A merchant who, for example, wanted a shipment of crockery from an English supplier, and who followed the Burbanks' instructions, would have it delivered to the Burbanks' agent in Liverpool at any time between April 15 and August 1. At Liverpool the agent would see it aboard a vessel of the Montreal Ocean Steamship Company (the early name of the Allan Line, the shipping company cooperating in a through bill-of-lading system worked out in 1859).[33]

Provided all went well on the Atlantic crossing—which obviously could not be taken for granted, since statistics show that the Allan Line suffered the loss of eight ships in its first ten years of operation[34]—the crockery would be landed at Montreal, and there bonded and sealed by customs and taken off to the freight yards of the Grand Trunk Railway. Open boat and portage were all that goods coming in by York factory had ahead of them, but the crockery arriving in Montreal and bound for Red River by the 'fast' route had more varied experience in store.

Since Canada was without connection either by rail or by road with the Red River Settlement, the crockery would have to travel from Montreal to the Canadian Northwest by crossing into the United States at Detroit. From Detroit it would continue by rail as far as La Crosse, Wisconsin, in 1860 'the extreme limit of railway travelling towards the West'.[35] Next would come transhipment to a Mississippi paddle-wheeler, and a 160-mile trip up the river to St. Paul, Minnesota.

At St. Paul the Burbanks themselves would take over. According to their advertisement in the *Nor'-Wester* on June 14, 1860, they owned 'a line of over 100 Transport Waggons', and onto one of these four-wheeled wagons, drawn by horses, the crockery would be loaded for the next stage on its quick trip to the west. For nearly three hundred miles it would then jog across the plains to Georgetown, on the east bank of the Red River. At this tiny post in American territory, the Hudson's Bay Company had erected buildings to house freight, and it was at this point that the *Anson Northup* might be expected to carry on for the final lap of the journey.

Whether the *Anson Northup* left as soon as the freight caravans arrived depended upon a number of things: whether there was freight enough to make a trip profitable, whether she had suffered damage on her last run from Fort Garry, and, most important, whether there was enough water in the Red River for her to go at all. The claims made for her regular service were rarely lived up to, but one thing was assured: when the *Anson Northup* did get off, piled with freight for both the Hudson's Bay Company and private merchants at Red River, the last five hundred miles of the long passage from Liverpool to Fort Garry would not be dull.

Between Georgetown and Fort Garry, the Red River twisted like an eel. There were dangerous rapids. Unexpected obstructions had frequently to be removed before the steamboat could proceed, and stretches that had been navigable on her last trip might, on the next, be so shallow that both passengers and crew would have to get out and pull her along. The crockery that had been tossed on the Atlantic, bumped about in railway shuntings, soaked with torrential rains on the open deck of a Mississippi river boat, and jounced around on the prairie could easily find itself whirling in circles like a cork, as the snub-nosed *Anson Northup* was caught in some unsuccessful navigation manoeuvre. If the crockery had been placed on a freight barge pulled along behind the steamboat, it might suddenly go floating crazily off on its own, when tow ropes were slashed to prevent disaster.

And yet, as they glided along the Red River, skirting the fringes of what was then undisputed Indian territory, crates and boxes of British merchandise managed to maintain, after all their varied travel, an appearance that struck one observer of the 1860's as trim and well-packed, 'doing credit to the London and other firms, the names of which were neatly printed on their coverings'.[36]

Included with the ordinary freight, neat and trim, were equally tidy-looking packages in the form of Hudson's Bay Company pieces, such as the crews of the York boats carried over portages. Even though the reasons for shipping in hundred-pound bundles did not obtain when goods were dispatched to Fort Garry via the Red River, the Company continued for some time to send off all merchandise from England in the distinctive packaging necessary for northern handling. When these pieces first began arriving at the Grand Trunk Railway depot in Montreal, for transhipment to the Red River, the men examined them with astonishment. Very 'peculiar looking' they thought them.[37] Undoubtedly some of these pieces, which appeared most curious to eastern eyes, contained crockery; for the Hudson's Bay sale shop at Fort Garry was, by this time, carrying more of everything in its general stock, under pressure of increasing competition from the independent merchants. At Fort Garry the sale shop was 'an outfitting establishment where one could not only clothe oneself from head to foot, but furnish one's house from attic to cellar'.[38]

Fort Garry was the end of the line for the Burbanks' forwarding system; it was not necessarily the end of the journey for the merchandise brought in by the *Anson Northup*. Had the crockery been ordered by some dealer distant from the Fort, it would then travel on by cart over roads so 'fearful' that, as late as the 1880's, one visitor cautioned that anything transported in a conveyance not well weighted down would be jumped about 'like a pea on a shovel'.[39]

To the original cost of his earthenware or porcelain in England the Red River dealer would have to add ocean, rail, wagon, river, and possibly cart transportation charges; insurance, bonding, sealing, and wharfage fees at Montreal; import duties; and whatever commission the forwarders required for attending to all this. The cheap white ironstone tea set, that retailed for two dollars in eastern Canada at this period,[40] of necessity achieved status by the time it reached the Red River. The merchant who chose his stock in St. Paul, instead of ordering from England, fared no better, since he paid hidden transportation charges in the wholesale price there, and then had to pay more to have his goods taken on to Red River.

But problems other than those of great distance from sources of supply and transportation costs faced the early crockery sellers of the Northwest. They had Indian troubles to worry about. In the late summer of 1862, when the china merchants of Montreal and Toronto were preparing for their autumn shipments, the storekeepers of Red River must have been wondering if there would be any supplies to see them through the winter. With the Sioux restive under bitter grievances against the government of the United States, it looked for a time as if communication with St. Paul might be cut off. Word came to Fort Garry of massacre below the border, and of the impossibility of getting the *International* (the *Anson Northup*'s successor) away from Georgetown, because the water level in the Red River had, as frequently happened, dropped too low.

The Red River merchants were, therefore, on their own. With resolution they continued to go through American territory, bringing in their autumn supplies from St. Paul. On August 18, in the *Nor'-Wester*, both W. G. Fonseca and E. L. Barber advertised crockery just in by cart: 'A VARIED STOCK OF Cups and Saucer, Plates, Teapots . . .'

And in the same issue of the *Nor'-Wester* appeared an advertisement for Harris, Whitford & Bentley, Red River freighters who were prepared to go to St. Paul, purchase any goods wanted in the settlement, and bring them back by flatboat down the Red River. As proof of their ability to carry out what they promised, Harris, Whitford & Bentley pointed to the way in which they had fulfilled earlier commitments that season, 'when there was no sign of that "fast" steamboat'. They stressed, too, their advantages in relation to the Indians: 'the people of the flat-boat have no occasion to fire up with wood belonging to the Indians; and our boat does not disturb their game but [by] puffing and snorting all the way; but she glides silently and swiftly along unnoticed by the Indians.'

Very possibly Harris, Whitford & Bentley were successful in slipping more freight past the Indians, as the autumn of 1862 set in, but what came by cart came neither silently nor swiftly, and not all of it got through. On September 24 the *Nor'-Wester* ran a first-hand account of an Indian attack on a Red River cart brigade. It had taken place below the border two weeks earlier, and the Indians had this time been Chippewas.

It can scarcely have mattered to the Red River merchants whether Chippewas or Sioux did the plundering, the results were the same. Dealers like A. G. B. Bannatyne and William Coldwell, who were both generally well supplied with crockery in their general stores and whose autumn stock had been waiting for some time at Georgetown before the decision to risk it by cart, now lost heavily. Their crates and boxes were 'bounded out of the waggons' and broken open on the prairie. Indians uttering wild whoops smashed up what they did not want. 'Oh! the wanton destruction and waste!' cried the reporter of the scene.

Soon after this raid, winter cut the Red River Settlement off from the world; but when the next spring came, it brought little relief for the anxieties of the merchants. If anything, it added to them. Not only was there increased danger in transporting goods through American territory, but the York Factory route, to which many of the private merchants had turned again, was suddenly closed to them. The news came first in a letter written by Frederick E. Kew, an English commission agent, to one of his clients at Fort Garry. Kew had been planning to send out his orders by the Hudson's Bay Company supply ship, *Prince of Wales*, but this would not now be possible:

> I have just received communication from the Hudson's Bay House to the effect that in consequence of the requirements of the Company for their own supplies they will be unable to furnish freight this year by the Prince of Wales for the private traders of the Settlement . . . I am compelled to adopt the alternative of forwarding your order by the route advertised by Messrs. Burbank of St. Paul.[41]

Kew, who regularly shipped crockery to his customers, and who later dispatched great quantities of it for the trading and retail establishments that he himself founded in the Northwest,[42] went on to admit fears for the safety of the merchandise now on its way to Red River. He concluded his letter by repeating that he would write again to the Burbanks to urge 'every precaution' in getting these spring supplies through the dangerous country lying between St. Paul and Fort Garry.

His urging was unnecessary. The Burbanks, 'being disappointed in frontier protection' on the part of their government, were not taking anything farther north than Fort Abercrombie (250 miles by cart from Fort Garry, and about 50 miles up the Red River from Georgetown). In the *Nor'-Wester* of June 2, 1863, they stated flatly that they were not going to 'jeopardize' the *International* while 'Indian depredations' continued. As far as the Burbanks were concerned, Red River clients would have to deal with their own transportation problems from Fort Abercrombie on.

Theoretically, of course, it was true that Red River freighters would travel with greater safety between Fort Abercrombie and Fort Garry than Americans. The Indians had no quarrel with the Hudson's Bay Company nor with the people of the Red River Settlement. This was a point emphasized by the leaders of the Sioux when they paid a visit to Fort Garry in the spring of 1863. They could easily, the Indians insisted, tell the difference between an American wagon and a Red River cart. They could distinguish at a glance the bright British complexion from the sallow tint of the American skin. With quick ears they could catch accents which marked travellers on the plains as from the Red River.[43]

Yet friendly feelings had not saved the cart train journeying from Georgetown to Fort Garry the previous autumn, although the Indians had spared lives on that occasion. The excuse had been then that the Chippewas, kept waiting by American agents negotiating for their lands, had been reduced to starvation. But the truth was that danger lurked at all times in travelling through territory where Indian unrest had already resulted in massacre.

As if these worries were not enough, other troubles followed for the Red River merchants that summer. As it turned out, there was not nearly as much freight as usual for which transportation had to be arranged from Fort Abercrombie on. The Allan steamship, *Anglo-Saxon*, carrying the greater part of that year's English supplies for the Red River, was wrecked in fog off Cape Race. A second vessel (and it may have been on this one that Frederick Kew's orders were shipped) fared no better—all her cargo, too, went to the bottom.[44]

The stock that was in the wholesale establishments at St. Paul became a necessity for many of the merchants. Red River cart brigades were willing to go after it. Travelling by routes that changed according to what could be learned of Indian movements, Red River freighters kept supply lines open. And in carts over which sentinels maintained watch through each night's camp in the anxious journeying over the plains, packages of crockery made up a substantial part of the cargo. For some merchants at least there was new earthenware as usual during that troubled summer of 1863. On August 19 Fonseca & Logan advertised in the *Nor'-Wester* that they had new merchandise to open up; when it was unpacked there would be 'crockery of every kind'. And again, on October 28, E. L. Barber announced that he was ready with autumn stock just in the day before from St. Paul. In part it consisted of 'a large lot of Crockery, including Coffee Cups, Pitchers, Plates.' Dishes for the table had slipped past dangers undreamed of in Staffordshire.

When the first steamboat had made her exciting appearance on the Red River, the editors of the *Nor'-Wester* had urged all merchants to hand over freighting business to her. The Burbanks had paid for advertising space to make known that they felt 'justly entitled to the whole patronage of the Settlement'.[45] They had even sounded almost querulous because some Fort Garry dealers persisted in bringing in their goods all the way across the plains by cart, or employed men with flatboats to help them over part of the way. But the Red River cart, slow and lumbering and a terror to the eardrums, had proved its dependability when Indians and drought had effectively knocked the fast steamboat out of action.

Not until the 1870's was the Red River cart finally to be displaced in the transportation system between southern supply centres and Fort Garry (Winnipeg). By this time Confederation with the Dominion of Canada had taken place, and improved steamboat service and railways had entered the picture. For the Red River Territory, now part of the new Province of Manitoba, the old methods of bringing in merchandise, with their dangers and their difficulties, were almost over. The tide of immigration was moving west again, and henceforth what had been the Red River Territory was regarded as the old settled part of the prairies.

When the 1870's opened, the crockery trade in Winnipeg belonged, as it had from the first days of Red River commerce, to the general merchant:

LOOK HERE!
GEORGE BLACK is still to be found at
his old stand . . .
where he still continues to conduct business
as a
GENERAL MERCHANT & TRADER
Dealer in all sorts of Fancy and Staple
DRY GOODS . . . BOOTS & SHOES . . . PROVISIONS
CROCKERY . . . HARDWARE . . . TINWARE, &c. &c.[46]

But by the 1880's Winnipeg, like the cities of the east at an earlier date, had its China Halls and Staffordshire Houses, boasting stocks that included everything 'pertaining to the keramic art' wanted 'between here and the Mountains'.[47]

Now it was from Winnipeg that carts set out with miscellaneous assortments of crockery, dry goods, hardware, and groceries for the newer settlements. Winnipeg, in its turn, had become a supply centre, and the whole pattern of freighting in goods by cart, flatboat, and steam was to be repeated in areas that would, in the twentieth century, become the Provinces of Saskatchewan and Alberta. And here, in these newer areas of colonization, before pioneer conditions were banished, the sellers of crockery would again have their day of troubles brought on by half-breed and Indian warfare.

That tablewares were, from the beginning, an essential part of the merchandise handled by pioneer dealers setting up in the farther west is shown by contemporary accounts. In the first issue of the *Saskatchewan Herald*, first newspaper west of Winnipeg and east of the Rockies, there was one local advertisement, and it particularized crockery as part of a stock which might be traded for 'furs or pemican'. Patrick Gammie Laurie, a Scots Canadian, hauled his printing press six hundred miles across the prairies by oxcart as far as Battleford. There, on August 25, 1878, the first copies of his newspaper, set in six point solid to crowd in the most type in the least space, advised readers that Mahoney & Macdonald, storekeepers, would supply them with wares for the table or boots for the feet.

Alexander Macdonald, pioneer merchant of Battleford, had freighted in his crockery and his boots the same way that P. G. Laurie had brought in his printing press—over a trail unimproved by a single bridge and with only the most primitive of ferries. A young man from Montreal, who travelled the same route at this time, described it in the spring of 1878, in a letter written to a friend back home: 'The journey over the prairie is, I need scarcely say, rough, and you would be required to put up with some hardship. This must be undertaken if you wish to get here.'[48]

It was by a rough route that the tablewares first sold by private dealers in the Northwest Territories arrived at their destination. Under conditions of hardship Thomas O. Davis, for example, took in a general assortment of goods from Winnipeg to Prince Albert in 1880. When he had disposed of his share of the load at a profit, the future 'Whirlwind Orator' of the Canadian Senate[49] turned to the business of bringing in merchandise for other people. Probably much of the crockery sold in Prince Albert in those early days owed its safe arrival to a large white ox, the lead animal in the future senator's brigade of nine carts. A better judge than a man of the safest spot to cross a 'sleugh' or the firmest ground in an ocean of mud, the ox was credited with knowing the freighting business to the satisfaction of all.[50]

When Thomas O. Davis had prospered, and was selling crockery 'at Rock Bottom Prices' in his own 'Horse Shoe Store', erected in Prince Albert at a spot where the old Carlton–à la Corne Trail passed, he may have had his printed earthenware and white granite brought in to him at least part of the way by steamboat on the Saskatchewan. But steam, in the late 1870's and 1880's, did not always guarantee fast delivery, or even delivery at all, in the Northwest. As one traveller from Montreal noted, rapids on the Saskatchewan River were frequent, and almost more formidable than those at Lachine. Awesome manoeuvres, which he could only describe as a sort of 'steamboat pole-vaulting' were required for Saskatchewan navigation; and when all these exertions had been gone through, it was as likely as not that the water was too low, a little farther on, for the freight to be delivered by steamboat after all.[51] York boats or carts would then have to be called back into service.

Many dealers in the Territories, like the Fort Garry merchants of an earlier day, continued to depend on cart brigades until railways brought easier transportation to at least some areas. On trails criss-crossing the country, earthenware and porcelain were freighted over the last stages of the long journey from overseas potter to frontier storekeeper.

This crockery, taken on by cart from Winnipeg, or from the station or landing where the train or steamboat had put it off, was mainly of sturdy English make. At the site of Fort Carlton, the old Hudson's Bay post on the Saskatchewan, destroyed in the Northwest Rebellion of 1885, Dr. Ralph Russell collected fragments of earthenware in the 1940's. These, together with other shards from

Fort Qu'Appelle, gave evidence of the ironstone and printed ware that were the staples of the colonial market from the beginning of the nineteenth century to its end.

One fragment only of those discovered by Dr. Russell bore a maker's mark, COPELAND.[52] The connections that the firm of Copeland & Garrett formed with the Hudson's Bay Company in the 1830's, and which W. T. Copeland maintained, undoubtedly took the Stoke earthenware throughout the Northwest. At least some of what had been brought into the Saskatchewan area with difficulty must have perished in the spring days of 1885. In the rebellion in which Indians joined with Louis Riel and his half-breeds, Hudson's Bay stores were looted, private merchants' supplies plundered, and settlers' houses fired.

American Indian troubles had harassed the transportation of supplies to the Red River dealers in the 1860's. In 1869-70 and again in 1885 the Métis agitation in Canadian territory disrupted business for some and caused apprehension throughout the country. In Saskatchewan many merchants lost seriously in 1885, not because their supply lines were cut off—the rebellion lasted for too brief a period and came too early in the season for that—but because what they had brought in the year before, with toil and expense, was stripped from them.

While the fighting was actually in progress, from March to May, 1885, the sellers of crockery in the area had more than mercantile pursuits to occupy them. George Kerr is an example. With his brother he ran a general store at Duck Lake, and there, at one time or another, he sold everything from white stone cups to Indian blankets. The rebels looted the Kerrs' store, and George Kerr 'shouldered a rifle and helped smash Riel'.[53] Charles Mair, seller of crockery, hardware, and groceries, who had moved from Portage-la-Prairie to Prince Albert when Saskatchewan began to open up, fought in the rebellion with the Governor General's Body Guard. Merchants of Battleford had their work cut out to help North West Mounted Police keep control of the fort and hold off Indians until troops arrived. When the rebellion was over, and they surveyed their plundered and wrecked places of business, ruin stared many a Saskatchewan storekeeper in the face.

But though apprehensive in 1869-70 at Red River, and though suffering severely in Saskatchewan in 1885, western Canadians were, at least, spared the insistent Indian 'depredations' which plagued frontier life south of the border. Indians had not really been involved when Louis Riel set up his provisional government in 1870 (with A. G. B. Bannatyne, one of the principal merchants of the Red River, as postmaster-general). In 1885, although Big Bear and Poundmaker were forces to be feared, the rebellion which had broken out in March was decisively crushed in May.

The reverses which this brief rebellion brought with it for the settlers took time to repair, but soon the merchants and freighters were making efforts to resume normal trade. Back on the trails came the carts, loaded with both farming equipment and household necessities to replace those lost by fire and plunder. With the tools and the groceries came fresh supplies of English tea sets and soup plates. Dealers like Thomas O. Davis, of the Horse Shoe Store in Prince Albert, were quick to get back on their feet. Only a little more than two years after the rebellion of 1885, Davis had a stock worth between $10,000 and $15,000,[54] all of which—dishes for dining, ploughs for the field, patent medicines for what ailed—had come to him from Winnipeg.

While carts were transporting goods from Winnipeg to the areas around Prince Albert, Duck Lake, and Battleford, and while the Hudson's Bay steamboat was toiling up the North Saskatchewan to Edmonton with merchandise for the Company's sale shop, supplies for traders in the south were arriving through the United States. In wagons drawn by mules or oxen thousands of tons of assorted goods came from Fort Benton, Montana, some 150 miles below the border. What St. Paul had been to Fort Garry, Fort Benton became to places like Fort Walsh in the Cypress Hills of Saskatchewan.

Fort Benton, at the head of navigation on the Missouri River, exported more than goods: it exported mercantile establishments. As early as the 1860's the important American firms of T. C. Power & Co. and I. G. Baker & Co. were both in business in Montana. Both brought up the Missouri everything needed for the Indian and settlers' trade in the American west; both owned steamboats and freight wagons; both were anxious to supply, or freight in, goods to British territory; for both had their eyes on the profits to be gained there. By the 1870's both had opened Canadian branches.

Calgary's first independent store belonged to I. G. Baker & Co.[55] When Fort Walsh, headquarters in 1877 of the North West Mounted Police, had two trading establishments, one bore the name I. G. Baker and one T. C. Power. Battleford, Fort McLeod, and Lethbridge were other Canadian settlements where these enterprising Americans set up for trade.

Both I. G. Baker and T. C. Power stores distributed crockery in nineteenth-century Canada. 'Wholesale and Retail Dry Goods, Groceries, Crockery, &c.' was the way Baker & Co. advertised in Calgary in the 1880's.[56] The tough ironstone tablewares typical of a Baker or Power store travelled from Montana under conditions as rugged as their composition, their guardians on the trip north bullwhackers, who relied on their language almost as much as their whips to force the goods along the way. 'With the help of their tongues, they will throw an oath as long and startling to the ear of an outsider as the crack of the whip to the oxen.' So wrote a traveller, in a letter reproduced in 1880 in the brief-lived magazine, *The Canadian North West*.[57]

Conveyed in freight caravans of 'about eighteen wagons, usually three wagons hitched together, drawn by 20 head of oxen',[58] cups and plates for the table crawled along, ten or fifteen miles a day, towards Canadian settlements. Memories of tableware that arrived in this way still survive from the time of Fort Walsh, where everything had to be freighted in from Fort Benton. One who was born at Fort Walsh, when his father was with the North West Mounted Police, recalls that 'the tableware my family used, and was brought from Fort Walsh . . . was a heavy crockery ware of a dull white'.[59] This was ironstone china that had been dragged to the Canadian outpost under the crack of the notorious bullwhacker's lash and the explosion of his profanity.

Charles Mair had looked on the Red River carts for the first time and had burst out: 'strange rigs and strange drivers'.[60] To the potters of Hanley, or Longton, or Stoke-on-Trent, whose products were to be found in a North West Mounted Police barracks or in a settler's hut, the bull trains, freighting earthenware through Saskatchewan, would have appeared just as startling. The York boat, with the tripmen standing to wield the twenty-foot sweeps, or the *Anson Northup*, her pilot perched high, a target for Indian marksmen, would have been to them an outlandish sight. Yet every one of these methods of transportation was an essential part of a crockery trade that brought tablewares from the smoke-blackened potteries of the Old Land to the settlements and outposts of the new Northwest.

CHAPTER IV

Around the Horn and On By Mule

NO MONOPOLY—NO COMBINATION . . . Mining Utensils, Hardware,
Crockery . . . bought at my store will be delivered free of charge
to all portions of Williams Creek. S. ELSASSER.
British Columbian, Nov. 29, 1865.

In no part of Canada did the business of crockery-selling get started so late or make such rapid progress as west of the Rocky Mountains. When the second half of the nineteenth century opened, although there was an important Hudson's Bay post at Victoria, there were scarcely thirty settlers, as distinct from Hudson's Bay employees, on the whole of Vancouver Island. Colonization of the mainland had not even begun. As in earlier days at Red River, any crockery sold came from the Company sale shop.

But when gold suddenly brought thousands scrambling to the west coast, at the end of the 1850's, the country began to develop so rapidly that within only a half-dozen years scores of private merchants in Victoria and New Westminster were selling the ironstone and the printed earthenware popular in all the colonial markets. In addition to mentioning crockery in long lists of goods handled in the new business establishments leaping into existence, some dealers were even beginning to take special newspaper advertisements to feature shipments of it. An example is found in an early issue of the *British Columbian*, first newspaper published on the mainland:

ALFRED FELLOWS
HAS JUST RECEIVED,
per "RETRIEVER," a large
and extensive assortment of
CROCKERY AND GLASSWARE
OF EVERY DESCRIPTION
which will be sold
Cheap for Cash.
Victoria, V.I., Oct. 24, 1861.

By 1864 there was on Vancouver Island at least one pioneer storekeeper who billed himself as dealing in china, glass, and earthenware exclusively.[1] Before the

51

period was much further advanced, ceramic importations on the Pacific coast had progressed to 'Fancy VASES and CHINA ORNAMENTS', as well as to 'articles of vertu' enthusiastically described as 'nice, neat and natty'.[2] Even the vulgarities of spitting were soon taken care of in a superior way by the china sellers of Victoria. They offered fine Chinese spittoons as early as the 1860's.[3]

To obtain these wares was not easy for the first crockery dealers in what is now the Province of British Columbia. Their problems of supply, though of the same kind as those of the china merchants of both eastern Canada and the Northwest, were magnified. The ocean voyages necessary to bring them new stock from the British potters were twice as long, and they involved some of the worst navigation hazards known to sailors. Transportation routes over which crockery had to be forwarded to storekeepers in the interior of the mainland colony demanded even greater toil and worse hardship than cart travel over the prairies. Many a teapot or stoneware cup sold in a shanty in mining country had to make the last stage of the journey packed on the back of a mule; no cart or wagon could possibly have gone over the trail.

In the first days of the colonies on the Pacific coast, goods from England came by sailing ship by way of Cape Horn. This was the route that had been followed for years in bringing the annual supplies for Hudson's Bay posts west of the Rocky Mountains. Long before the colonies of Vancouver Island or British Columbia existed, and when the whole territory was still a fur-trading preserve, the Company's vessels fought their way round Cape Horn and into the Pacific, bearing in their holds shipments from Copeland & Garrett, potters 'to the Royal Family' and suppliers of tableware and other goods to the Honourable Company.

One invoice, dating back to the time of King William IV and preserved today in Hudson's Bay archives in London, records that in May of 1836 Copeland & Garrett wares to a total of £145. 7s. 6d. were forwarded to the Hudson's Bay Company for delivery in North America. According to this statement, some of these wares were for shipment aboard the *Eagle*, an imposing brig of nearly two hundred tons employed, in those years, as a Pacific supply vessel.[4]

Tablewares which came round the Horn at this time were for the use of Hudson's Bay people only. There were as yet no free settlers to whom they might be sold. But in later years, when Victoria was both a Hudson's Bay post and the capital of a tiny colony, the annual Company ship from England sailed into port with merchandise that settlers and Company servants alike hurried into the sale shop to buy.

Mrs. Arthur Fellows, daughter of Sir Rowland Hill of penny-postage fame, and sister-in-law of the Alfred Fellows who was himself selling 'crockery of every description' in Victoria, in 1861, recollected that the Hudson's Bay ship used to come laden 'with everything that heart in reasonable mood could desire'. Her arrival was 'the one great event of the year'.[5] After the cargo had been unloaded there would be new patterns and shapes in English tea sets and dinnerware at the 'Universal Provider', as Mrs. Fellows called the Hudson's Bay sale shop in Victoria, just as there had been at Fort Garry, when the boats arrived from York Factory.

It is probable that the same Staffordshire factory that had supplied earthenware and porcelain to the Hudson's Bay post at Victoria in its earlier days continued to send in its wares as the colony developed. William Taylor Copeland and Thomas Garrett had dissolved partnership in 1847, but the pottery that had once belonged to Josiah Spode continued under Copeland's ownership, and Copeland retained the Hudson's Bay Company as a customer for many years.[6] Some of the wares purchased from him for North America went to York Factory, but others must have been loaded onto sailing vessels preparing to make the long and dangerous voyage around Cape Horn.

'Everything came out from England in those days.'[7] So the wife of the first Surveyor-General of British Columbia remembered the early years of the colony. In Victoria the fortunate lived 'in comfort', thanks to the cargoes unloaded from the sailing ships. Tablewares and bedroom crockery came from the first manufacturers of Staffordshire, carpets from Kidderminster, wallpapers from Lancashire, and books of steel engravings and new novels from the best London publishers.

But the long wait for these wares was not without uncertainty. Crockery and all the other merchandise brought by the Hudson's Bay Company ships, and by others carrying goods for independent merchants, could arrive only after one of the longest and most dangerous of sea voyages. Few storms were comparable to the hurricanes that swept round Cape Horn—that 'notorious Cape', as the *Emigrant Soldiers' Gazette* called it in 1859.[8] On a voyage of five or six months (or even longer) one month or more might be spent by the sailing vessel in battling her way through the gales that almost invariably raged in far southern latitudes. 'We were off the Horn for six weeks,' a pioneer housewife of Yale recorded. During those long days and nights the ship tossed with such violence that none expected she would last out the passage. In the end the captain had to order cargo jettisoned to lighten her.[9]

Tossing cargo into the waves in order to save a ship was a not unusual step in navigating Cape Horn, and crates of Willow plates or flowing blue hand basins must sometimes have gone overboard instead of into the shops of the merchants waiting in Victoria or New Westminster. There were many times, too, when even the most desperate efforts were not enough to keep a vessel afloat; then both passengers and cargo would disappear, their only trace a bit of wreckage drifting on the sea.

Not until the twentieth century, when the Panama Canal was opened, was it possible to sail from England directly to Vancouver Island without facing dangers dreaded by sailors. After 1855 the voyage could be shortened, and Cape Horn avoided, by taking advantage of a railway across Panama; but, in the early years of the British colonies on the Pacific, passengers rather than merchandise went by this more expensive route, which involved transhipment. Even as late as the end of the 1880's, when the Canadian Pacific Railway had linked Canada's Atlantic coast with the Pacific, crockery from England might still be shipped by sail around the Horn to British Columbia.[10]

In addition to supplies brought in sailing vessels from Great Britain, merchants of the Pacific colonies frequently purchased stock in San Francisco, or received goods transhipped at that point, even as the merchants of Red River traded through St. Paul. These wares came up the coast by sea. In the relationship between Victoria and San Francisco, however, there were certain significant factors which did not enter into the situation on the prairies. Not only was Victoria itself a port; until the union of the colonies of Vancouver Island and British Columbia in 1866, it was a free port. This meant that dealers in crockery doing business in Victoria paid no duties on their wares, while their competitors south of the border had these extra charges to add to the original cost of all they imported direct.[11]

Being a free port gave Victoria an advantageous position, particularly in the importation of certain goods such as crockery, in the manufacture of which the United States could not compete successfully with England.[12] As a letter in the *Times* commented: 'British goods paying no duty pour from Victoria in Vancouver Island into California, whose citizens are thus enabled to clothe themselves in purple and fine linen without paying tribute to the Washington treasury.'[13]

Matthew Macfie, publishing his account of Vancouver Island in 1865, and taking note of what the *Times* had said, urged the dealers of Victoria and the manufacturers of England to exploit this 'merchant's paradise' to the full. Earthenware was one of the examples he gave of duty-free British products purchased in Victoria the previous year by 'foreign' buyers.[14]

Victoria, the new town growing up hurriedly around a Hudson's Bay fort, became the main supply centre for British earthenware and porcelain, if not for the wide 'foreign' market envisaged by Macfie, at least for the dealers in the neighbouring colony on the mainland. But as this mainland colony itself grew, ambitious merchants there began to do their own ordering from abroad, and came to resent Victoria's domination of their trade. In particular, those from 'Stump-ville' (as the people of Victoria were apt to refer to the 'little bantling town' of New Westminster) became impatient with Victoria's commercial superiority.[15]

One of the first sellers of crockery in British Columbia was also one of the first to challenge the Victoria wholesalers. William James Armstrong, a Canadian of Irish ancestry who later became a member of the provincial cabinet of British Columbia, built one of the first houses in New Westminster and opened a general store near the Liverpool Wharf. By 1861 he was selling 'anything and everything' and this meant 'Crockery and Glassware of every description' ranged alongside codfish, hatchets, farming implements, and cross-cut saws.[16] On February 7, 1863, in an advertisement in the *British Columbian*, Armstrong made a fighting bid for the wholesale trade of the up-river dealers ('third-rate traders' Macfie called them) who had been giving their patronage to Victoria:

OPPOSITION
to all who send to VICTORIA for their
GOODS
Buy of me by
WHOLESALE
as you do when you send to VICTORIA
pay me the cash
as you do when you buy in VICTORIA
Just Received

— AND —

FOR SALE . . .
Crockery, Glassware, Hardware
Paints, Oils and a thousand-
and-one other articles
W. J. ARMSTRONG

Whether the storekeepers in the interior took note of W. J. Armstrong's 'op-position', or continued to send their orders for crockery 'and a thousand-and-one other articles' to Victoria suppliers, such as Alfred Fellows, the durable earthen-ware suitable for the needs of their customers had a hard trip ahead of it. British Columbia, like other North American colonies, suffered from what was generally called 'the young-country road grievance'. In her case, however, geography had conspired to make the interior of the country accessible only with difficulties that could scarcely be credited in the east. When the hordes of gold-seekers descended upon the Pacific coast, they found that they had to push through territory where only the faintest of trails led through dense forests and over high mountains, and where the very idea of road-building strained the imagination. Relentlessly they pressed on, but the physically weak fell by the way and their pack animals died by the hundreds. Nevertheless, transportation routes of a kind were forced into being, and over these trails by mule-pack went the goods needed in the mining country.

Surprisingly early in the gold-rush days, crockery took its place in the shacks and shanties where supplies were sold at inflated prices. Often the early sellers of tablewares in the interior were themselves men who had arrived at Victoria or New Westminster with the throngs of prospectors, but who had come not as miners but as merchants sensing opportunity. One of these was Robert McLeese, an Irishman from the glens of Antrim.

McLeese reached New Westminster with the frenzied mobs of 1858 gold-hunters. He had prospected in California earlier, and perhaps because of that experience he chose to remain in New Westminster to open a general store, in-stead of going straight on to the gold country. But as soon as the interior began to open up, in the wake of mining, McLeese sold out and turned towards Cari-boo. For him, in 1863, the way would have been in part by uncertain river steam-boat and in part by the fantastic new wagon road which, by the end of that year, had been hacked out of mountain sides and compelled through canyons as far as Soda Creek.

At Soda Creek McLeese stayed, to deal in crockery, mining implements, cigars, liquors, and furs, 'raw and manufactured';[17] to become postmaster and hotel keeper; and, finally, to represent Cariboo in the Legislative Assembly of British Columbia. In later years it was said of him that he had been 'most suc-cessful in his commercial ventures'.[18] At Soda Creek, where he found a per-manent place in the life of a young colony, those commercial ventures began with the selling of such goods as crockery, wanted in even the most rugged of new country.

All the tablewares that Robert McLeese sold at Soda Creek in these beginning years—tablewares that had first crossed the Atlantic and sailed through the

Pacific—came to him in great freight wagons, travelling two, three, and four to-gether, and pulled by a dozen mules or sixteen or eighteen oxen. They followed a route thrust into the wilds, and along which passed heavily armed escorts bringing out gold, camels strangely transplanted from another continent, mules struggling under packs too heavy for them, and six-horse coaches racing at seemingly careless speed down slopes where a brake giving way, a wheel coming off, or an animal shying could mean only destruction.

Another of the early sellers of tablewares whose goods came to him through the cruel tests of the Cariboo road was S. Elsasser, one of the pioneer Jewish dealers of the Pacific colony. Like McLeese, he dealt in anything wanted, and found that there was a call for crockery. He had arrived in British territory with excited gold-hunters, and had stayed behind in Victoria to open a store. Later he had been led by ambition to try his luck in the mining country.

Continuing past Soda Creek, where Robert McLeese was already doing well, Elsasser settled in at Cameronton. Here fortunes had been made in a day, and here Elsasser set out his jugs and plates, his pans for washing gold, and his flour for slap-jacks. With enterprise he offered a free delivery service to any of the mining camps on Williams Creek, and he advertised tablewares in wholesale as well as retail quantities.[19]

At least some of the crockery Elsasser offered for sale at Williams Creek prob-ably came to him not by freight wagon but by mule-pack over the last stage of the journey. The Cariboo wagon road had reached only as far as Cottonwood when work stopped in 1864, and was not forced on until the next year.[20] Early in the spring of 1865, before frost was out of the ground or the appalling task of road-building likely to have been completed over the forty-five miles between Cottonwood and Williams Creek, Elsasser was advertising crockery for sale.[21]

In those days, when life in the interior of British Columbia was raw, pioneer storekeepers such as Robert McLeese and S. Elsasser not only saw profits in tablewares from potters thousands of miles away, they chose to feature crockery high on the list of articles wanted in even the most remote areas of a new land. And British tablewares, exported to all parts of the world, travelled no more daring route than over the Cariboo Trail of British Columbia.

But the freight roads, which Governor Douglas had been determined the colony must have, could not be built everywhere at once. Many parts of the country were to remain inaccessible for years, except by difficult trails or water-ways, and yet crockery still made its way into isolated places. At Hudson's Bay trading posts, such as Kamloops, the famous horse brigades were needed for yet a little longer to bring in supplies over the last laps of the journey. There is evi-dence that these supplies included crockery.

To see a horse brigade arriving at Kamloops in the old days had been 'a thrill-ing sight'. So it was spoken of by the American writer, Hubert Howe Bancroft: 'Through the deep ravines, round precipitous mountainsides, and over hills and plains they had come; sleek, fat animals, usually perfect in form and color, bear-ing the burdens which had been carefully brought so far, from beyond continents and seas.'[22]

Crockery from beyond the seas came with the horse brigades to Kamloops. Its presence there at a time when no wagon road led in to the fort, and when a few Hudson's Bay servants and a handful of half-breeds and Indians were the only inhabitants, is unexpectedly proved by Dr. Walter Cheadle. An episode confided to his private diary, and omitted from the version of that celebrated journal published jointly with Lord Milton in 1865, records the evidence of smashable tablewares in Kamloops on a September morning in 1863.

A few days earlier Lord Milton and Dr. Cheadle had staggered down the trail to the fort. They had completed the adventurous journey across the Rockies that was to make them famous, a saga of hardship and danger that had come very close to being the end of them. At the Hudson's Bay post at Kamloops they had been welcomed, taken in, and fed and clothed from the sale shop.

But so near had Lord Milton and Dr. Cheadle been to starvation that even after several days of hearty eating they were still eager for a summons to the next meal. It was, therefore, with annoyance that the visitors found their enjoyment of breakfast being disturbed on the morning of September 2. It began with words between two of the Hudson's Bay men. A clerk of the Company referred to the Chief Trader at Kamloops, who was absent at the time, in terms far from complimentary. A relative of the Chief Trader took exception to them. They exchanged cups of hot tea—in the face. After that they progressed to what Dr. Cheadle called 'a regular scuffle', which ended with 'plates being smashed . . . & an awful mess'.[23] In his journal Dr. Cheadle wrote that it had all been 'a most disgraceful scene', but he slipped quietly back to the table and went on eating, as soon as the crockery, which had travelled almost half way round the world to be broken in a breakfast brawl at a fur-trading post, had been swept out of sight.

Bancroft's reference to 'sleek, fat animals' packing in goods to Kamloops would not have been entirely borne out by Dr. Cheadle. He examined horses at the post in 1863 and noted that some were 'shockingly injured by bad packing & brutality; ribs broken, &c.'[24] Another diarist, travelling to the mining country that same year, saw dead pack horses 'lying in every direction . . . the wretched animals so overcome with fatigue and deficient feed that they died in the mire.'[25]

Many of the pack animals needed for the transportation of crockery and other merchandise to the interior of British Columbia would have been better off if they had died quickly. Most visitors to the country who later wrote of their experiences commented upon the hard lot of these tormented beasts of burden, whether employed by inexperienced individuals or in long pack trains. 'Broken-down mules and Indian ponies . . . packed in so ill a manner that one could well imagine how little skin would remain on the backs of the wretched quadrupeds when their journey was completed' were pitied by R. Byron Johnson in the 1860's.[26] Some twenty years later J. A. Lees and W. J. Clutterbuck, 'rambling' in British Columbia, were moved by the same compassion. 'It is most distressing to see the backs of almost all the pack animals in the country; hardly any of them are free from huge raws, and the poor things must suffer terribly. A sore once started has scarcely any chance of recovering, for men cannot or will not give the necessary time and trouble to attend to it and so arrange the packs as not to bear upon it.'[27]

Just as the making of cheap ceramic ornaments in the nineteenth century was often the work of pinched, undernourished little children, or the carrying-out of certain ceramic processes the work of men whose lungs rotted with industrial disease,[28] so the transporting of 'crockery of every description' to the far frontiers of North America must often have been the killing work of animals whose backs were rubbed bloody with the weight of the Staffordshire products they bore. Crockery and all other manufactured goods sold by pioneer dealers or made available to settlers near Hudson's Bay posts in early British Columbia went on their way by pack animals whacked and goaded beyond endurance, by bull teams straining agonizingly up mountain roads that had cost countless animal and even human lives to construct, by open boats loaded dangerously to the water-line, and by explosive river steamers whose captains charged as much as twenty dollars a ton for freight,[29] and depended upon a supply of tarred blankets and few old boards to plug up leaks.[30]

But gradually, as the century advanced, improvements in transportation facilities came to British Columbia. The completion of the Canadian Pacific Railway in 1885, and the opening of branch and other lines, meant that in at least some parts of the province crates of earthenware reached the dealers of the interior with comparative ease. In Kamloops, for instance, where once the only tableware obtainable had been from the same Hudson's Bay sale shop where Lord Milton and Dr. Cheadle had been thankful to purchase clothes to replace their rags in 1863, a number of dealers were doing business in crockery by the 1880's. One of these was R. E. Smith, on Victoria Street, whose customers were smaller dealers 'along the line of Railway'.[31] It was the railway, too, that now brought R. E. Smith the wares he was able to sell to these other storekeepers at prices 'as low as in the eastern and western cities'. Yet it was not many years since crockery had made its way to Kamloops only by painful travel over a trail that even Dr. Cheadle, who had struggled overland across the Rockies, found unusually 'rugged'.

Most of the crockery sold in British Columbia had been, from the first, imported direct from England. This was the case with the 'well assorted' invoice of thirty crates of earthenware that Dickson, Campbell & Co., of Victoria, received in 1864.[32] After Confederation, however, commission agents and crockery sellers in other parts of Canada gave increasing attention to the province on the Pacific. Harris H. Fudger, of Toronto, was one of these. Early showing the flair for mail-order merchandising that brought him to the presidency of the Robert Simpson Company before the end of the century, Harris Fudger went after business in British Columbia even before the Canadian Pacific Railway had eliminated the barrier of the Rockies. In an advertisement in *The British Columbia Directory for the Years 1882-83* Fudger and his partner, Henry Smith, offered any earthenware or china needed on the west coast. In this they were acting as agents, who would have the orders filled in England and shipped direct.

Another Ontario house determined to sell the best English tableware to dealers on the Pacific was W. J. Reid & Co., of London, proprietors of Crystal Hall, where 'the largest, most complete, and finest stock of crockery in the Dominion' was to be seen;[33] or so the firm claimed. Five travellers were put on the road in the 1880's to bring in orders 'from Halifax to British Columbia', and dealers using Reid & Co. as their importers could choose from Coalport, Copeland, Derby, Minton, Worcester, Wedgwood, or a range of continental porcelains.

Customers were strongly urged to try Reid & Co.'s 'Boadley ware' from Stafford-shire. Glittering with high-quality gold, dinner sets in this line were held by Reid's to be rightly 'fit for the royal table';[34] but, given an order, they would ship them for use in Lillooet or Wild Horse Creek or Conklin's Gulch.

If British Columbia buyers, now regarded as within range of the wholesalers of central Canada, did not wish to supply themselves through Smith & Fudger, or Reid & Co., or John L. Cassidy of Montreal (who opened a Victoria office), there were prairie importers anxious for their crockery trade. Once the Canadian Pacific Railway was through to the west coast, a pair of travellers from Winnipeg's Crystal Hall was 'constantly on the road between Rat Portage and British Col-umbia'.[35] Porter & Ronald, two Toronto men, were the owners of the Winnipeg emporium. Their firm was young, but they had already been infected with western push, and their salesmen went confidently beyond the Rockies with samples of 'the rarest novelties and oddities, the quaintest designs and the most curious specimens . . . ever contributed to the keramics of the world'.[36]

For Oriental wares the dealers on the Pacific coast had their own sources of supply. Because of geographical position they had long had contact with the Orient, either by direct trade or through dealers in San Francisco. At a period when Chinese porcelain would have been virtually unknown on the prairies it was available in Victoria. In 1863, for instance, merchandise to a total value of $45,434 was imported direct from China.[37] At trade sales, J. P. Davies & Co., the Victoria auctioneers, frequently had Chinese wares to offer, as in the spring of 1869, when vases from China were put up with a consignment of English wall-papers and steel engravings.[38]

But the bulk of the ceramic goods sold on the Pacific were from the British potteries, just as they were in other North American colonies. They were wares like the Copeland & Garrett products that the Hudson's Bay Company was bringing round the Horn in the 1830's, or the Parian china stocked by Henry Gribble at his Victoria Bazaar in the 1880's,[39] or the Minton tiles set round fire-places in British Columbia houses.[40] In supplying these goods Hudson's Bay sale shop competed with private merchant, and Canadian agent with English commission house.

In proportion to the population, probably more English earthenware and porcelain came in with immigrants to British Columbia than to most other parts of the country. Those making the long journey all the way by sailing ship thought only in terms of loading their household goods on board at an English port and then taking them off when the end of the journey was reached at Vancouver Island. Yet even Pacific colonists were often proved unwise in the belief that it was possible to transport these goods easily to a new country. A British Columbia pioneer, Mrs. Robert Burns McMicking (born Margaret Leighton, a distant cousin of Lord Leighton, P.R.A.) told of 'family gods' having to be heaved over-board at the Horn during a wild storm in the 1850's.[41] A few years later R. Byron Johnson stood and watched recently arrived immigrants disposing of all kinds of goods at street-corner auctions in Victoria.[42] At these forced sales household possessions, brought all the way from England, changed hands for pathetically small sums.

To bring household goods from England to Vancouver Island in a sailing ship often seemed relatively simple to the emigrant, and so it might be, if Victoria was to be the end of the journey. But there was disillusionment for those who reached Vancouver Island and then wanted to pursue fortune into the interior of the mainland, where transportation might be by pack animal or on foot. Then it often became necessary to sell what had been brought so far but was now an intolerable burden. The storekeeper might take a pack train into the far regions of British Columbia, but the immigrant in pursuit of gold was lucky if he could afford one nondescript animal to carry his supplies. Many transported what they needed on their own backs.

On one occasion Byron Johnson looked on while an immigrant hawked a prize possession, specially purchased at home as 'just the thing for that country, you know'. In this case it was a fine iron wash-stand, 'with fittings complete',[43] which would have included basin, ewer, soap dish, tooth-brush holder, probably a sponge dish. What in England had seemed suitable for the colonies presented a problem when the immigrant reached the Pacific. Since he was headed for the mining country, the possessor of the wash-stand was confronted with the unpleasant fact that he would have to carry it, and all its fine fittings, on his back for three or four hundred miles, 'if he wished to avail himself of the prodigious facilities for open air ablutions *en route* which it offered'.[44]

Byron Johnson's observations on bringing out household goods to British Columbia echoed the opinions of those who had counselled emigrants to other parts of British North America to leave such possessions at home: 'the money spent on them in the first instance would have been better carried in the pockets of the luckless wights'.[45] Many had to part with the wash basins and the soup plates, transported round the Horn at expense, to buy again, when they had struggled into the interior of British Columbia, from dealers who matched enterprise with business shrewdness in providing crockery in the most remote settlements of a formidable country.

How Pottery and Porcelain Were Sold

CHAPTER V

Anybody's Business

Wallis, James, blacksmith and dealer in crockery.
Listing under Yorkville, C. W., in
Mitchell's Canada Gazetteer for . . . 1864-65.

Crockery-selling in Canada was anybody's business. Wherever a general store opened in a backwoods settlement or a shack was run up for trade on the prairie, the products of overseas potters were to be found. Ships' captains, fur traders, auctioneers, commission agents, pedlars, country storekeepers, pottery representatives, and specialist china merchants, all had a part in distributing tablewares in a pioneer country. Even harness makers, butchers, or blacksmiths might deal in crockery as a sideline. In the older cities of the east it was sold in impressive establishments by men who personally visited the British potteries to make their selections. In the Northwest it was sold in tents by freighters speculating with goods from Winnipeg and using profits to bring in more the next time.

The men who dealt in this china and earthenware for gain were as varied as their stock. W. H. Hayward, grandson of a soldier who fought in the American Revolution wearing the King's uniform, imported earthenware into Saint John. In Red River Territory, Edmund Lorenzo Barber, grandson of a signer of the Declaration of Independence, brought in the same goods through Minnesota. Joseph Wedgwood, bearing one of the most famous names in potting, sold Queensware in Montreal. In Toronto, James Jackson, captain of a fire brigade, offered plates made to his order. Charles Mair, the poet, advertised toilet sets in Prince Albert. His business rival in crockery was Thomas Osborne Davis, 'lineal descendant of . . . ancient Irish kings', who traded tablewares for pemmican.

Most of the early crockery sold was handled by general dealers. To be 'well assorted' was once the goal of every Canadian merchant, and it remained the aim of country storekeepers and traders on the frontier. The crockery business belonged originally to men like William Macnider, of Quebec, whose boast, in 1789, was not that he was a specialist dealer of any kind, but, on the contrary, that few men in trade were 'so well assorted' as he. His advertisement in the *Quebec Herald and Universal Miscellany* of January 19, in which he made this claim, specified a great quantity of Queensware, both 'gilt and green edged', in a diversified stock.

Gradually, however, in the nineteenth century, there emerged a type of Cana-

63

dian dealer described as a china merchant. His shop was known as a china, glass, and earthenware house, even though it included many varied items besides crockery and glassware. Joseph Shuter, one of the most important of all the early china sellers of Canada, was listed in Montreal's first directory as a china merchant.[1] His advertisements regularly referred to his 'China, Glass & Earthenware Store', yet at that same china store Joseph Shuter and his partner sold tarred cordage, gunpowder, and cheese.[2] When William Turner, who dealt in Wedgwood and Worcester, first opened his Montreal business in 1832, he proclaimed it under the heading 'NEW WHOLESALE AND RETAIL CHINA AND EARTHENWARE STORE', but his announcement ended with 'BOOTS and SHOES'.[3] Nonetheless it was a long step towards specialist china-selling when merchants came to be known for their crockery, no matter what additional stock they carried.

Before the middle of the nineteenth century was reached, some Canadian dealers selling crockery in large amounts, if not necessarily exclusively, began to emphasize the predominantly British character of their wares by giving their shops names such as 'Staffordshire House' or 'Yorkshire House'. This was following an English practice: directories indicate that by the beginning of the century London had well over 150 china sellers who called their premises Staffordshire warehouses, and who were, presumably, doing a big trade in Staffordshire products.

One of the early dealers to adopt this fashion in Canada was Charles H. Jones, of York (Toronto). He opened a 'Staffordshire Ware-House' in the Market Square in 1830, with a 'superb' stock from the Potteries.[4] In the Maritime colonies Samuel Cooper, of Saint John, a merchant who made buying trips to England, was calling his Dock Street store the 'Staffordshire & Yorkshire Warehouse' by 1838.[5] Another Saint John dealer, A. B. Buxton, was different: he named his shop the 'Liverpool House', and what he sold there in the way of crockery is revealed in an advertisement in the *New Brunswick Courier*:

LIVERPOOL HOUSE
Water-street

A. B. BUXTON . . . has just received by ship WARD . . . from Liverpool, decidedly the most superior assortment of CHINA and EARTHENWARE, ever offered for inspection (at one time) in St. John, consisting of *Dinner, Tea, Breakfast and Toilet sets, Pitchers, Ornaments,* &c. &c. selected from the first Manufactories of Stafford and Yorkshire . . . January 27, 1838.

None of these merchants dealt in crockery alone, nor did very many of those who followed in the 1840's and 1850's with a rush of Staffordshire Houses, China Halls, Porcelain Houses, and crockery 'signs' (such as Thomas Clerke's 'Sign of the Jug' in King's Square, Saint John).[6] One of the country's biggest china sellers, Francis Clementson (who took over Samuel Cooper's premises after his death) for years carried a line of Havana cigars in his china shop.[7] Towards the end of the century in Windsor, Nova Scotia, C. P. Shaw stocked such incongruous items in his China Hall as wheelbarrows and children's sleds.[8] In Winnipeg 'Bird Cages and Perambulators' were promoted in the advertising for Hodges' Staffordshire House & China Hall on Main Street.[9]

Even when groceries, clothing, boots, shoes, and general hardware had been eliminated from the 'china shop', crockery-selling on an 'exclusive' basis in Canada almost always meant that glassware, papier-mâché, some woodenware, silver-plated or Britannia metal goods, wax flowers, and lamps and their fittings went along with the earthenware and porcelain. This was the case with William H. Hayward, the Saint John dealer who set up in early Victorian days, and who had a better right than most to the title of china merchant; for the crockery firm he founded was to survive fires, depressions, and changing conditions. When it completed its first century and entered upon its second, in 1955, it was still in the hands of his descendants.[10] What he, as a china merchant, sold in a shop 'exclusively' for crockery is indicated by an entry in a city directory: 'HAYWARD WILLIAM H, dealer in CROCKERY, CHINA, GLASSWARE and Silver Plated Ware, Lamps, Chimneys, Burners, Fancy Goods, Looking Glasses, Vases, &c.[11] Advertisements, such as that in the *Daily Sun* on December 23, 1878, show that Hayward's china shop also stocked toys—'WAX DOLLS . . . WOODEN TOYS . . . EARTHEN TOYS'.

In 1860, the annual report of the Toronto Board of Trade, commenting on crockery-selling, contained a significant statement: 'Formerly this business was not carried on exclusively, but formed an adjunct to other trades. Now, however, it has a distinct character.'[12] The 'distinct character' that crockery-selling in Canada assumed in the second half of the nineteenth century resulted in city shops like the new china, glass, and earthenware depot erected by William Hayward, after he had been wiped out in the terrible Saint John fire of 1877; like Glover Harrison's China Hall in Toronto, famous for forty years as a place where Canadians learned about new ceramic fashions; like Reid's four-storey Crystal Hall in London, up to Victorian modernity with electric bells, speaking tubes, and sixty employees; like Hodges' Staffordshire House & China Hall in Winnipeg, one of the chief 'crockery establishments' in the west.

And as early Victorian days gave way to the middle and last phases of the Queen's long reign, the China Halls and Staffordshire Houses, never at any time as exclusively ceramic as their names implied, began to handle goods that were no longer almost entirely from British potters. The name, in 1870, might still be Staffordshire House, but the tablewares and ornaments could be representative of 'well known and famous manufacturers in every part of the world'.

Throughout the century, nearly every Canadian dealer of any kind aspired to sell to other dealers, and thus be in the wholesale business. The crockery merchants were no exception. Many in port cities, such as Saint John and Montreal, offered special inducements to those who would buy from them in bulk lots as the goods were being unloaded from the sailing vessels. 'Just landing, per ship *Commodore*, and *Sarah Louise* from England . . . 47 assorted Crates of Earthenware, well adapted for the country trade . . . will be sold low while landing'— so ran Henry Robertson's advertisement in the *New Brunswick Courier* on July 17, 1852.

In Montreal, auction sales by the ship's side were a regular occurrence in the crockery trade over many years. Sometimes they were held on behalf of English potters or exporters, who sent out consignments to be sold for their own account; sometimes they were organized by local commission agents who wanted to make a quick profit and who, in certain cases, had no regular store in which to place the goods; sometimes they were arranged by china merchants who sold fine-quality tablewares in fashionable shops in the city, and who disposed of 'common wares' in a fast turn-over down by the river.

Even before Montreal had wharves, sales of earthenware took place on the bank of the St. Lawrence, with the crates from Staffordshire or Newcastle often standing in mud, or with thousands of pieces of brownware from Sunderland—milk pans, stew pots, covered crocks, and foot baths—put down 'loose' for the inspection of a shrewd-eyed band of colonial storekeepers. Advertisements for these auctions used to read: '*on the Beach opposite Clamp's Coffee House . . .* 6000 Pieces Brown Earthenware';[13] or: 'THIS DAY . . . *On the Beach at Pointe Calliere, will be Sold, peremptorily without reserve . . .* 118 Crates well assorted Earthen Ware'.[14] Frequently in damp weather there was more mud than 'Beach' on the river bank that served as a crockery auction room in Montreal; 'the clayey and generally filthy bank', John M'Gregor called it in the 1830's.[15]

Everything considered, selling by auction was one of the most important aspects of the nineteenth-century crockery business in Canada. There were auction sales on the beaches and on the wharves. There were huge sales in auctioneers' rooms. There were auctions held in the offices of commission merchants, where the buying was all done from samples, the earthenware and porcelain being still afloat or in the customs warehouse. There were auction sales held in stores.

While many crockery auctions were obviously arranged for the trade, at others the dinner services and the bedroom wares would be put up 'in lots to suit private families'.[16] Often the advertising for a crockery auction was directed to the 'housekeeper', to whom choosing a new tea set at an auction was almost as accepted a practice as stepping in to the nearest China Hall or Staffordshire House. 'The . . . attendance of Ladies (both on view and sale days) is particularly requested.' This advertisement by Lawrence Devany, in the *Montreal Gazette* on May 15, 1866, was typical of many. Devany's aim was to interest the house-keepers of Montreal in a consignment of Parian porcelain, ironstone tableware, papier-mâché, and cutlery.

Just as the earlier sellers of crockery in shops had invariably been general merchants—their tablewares displayed with groceries, dry goods, and hardware —so the earlier sellers of crockery at auction included it in mixed sales, such as that arranged by Deblois & Mitchell, the well-known Halifax auctioneers, for noon on June 16, 1826. In the *Novascotian* they indicated what was in store for those who attended at Creighton's Wharf the next day: '2 handsome desert setts China' would be sharing the bidding with fifteen barrels of nuts, ten bags of almonds, and two bales of sponges.

Throughout the century, general auction sales of both new and second-hand goods usually included a few lots of crockery, from the common brown earthenware for kitchen use to the finest of porcelain. Before long, however, there was a place for the special crockery auction. Adam L. Macnider, of Montreal, held a particularly good sale of this type in the autumn of 1832. His advertisement for it appeared in the *Gazette* on September 20, and was headed 'ELEGANT CHINA AND EARTHENWARE'. How elegant were the wares offered at this china auction in a colonial city may be judged by the fact that the porcelain was Derby, Rockingham, and Worcester, and the earthenware 'from the much admired WEDGWOOD and LIVERPOOL Manufactories'.

Sometimes fashionable tablewares of 'recherche styles and patterns' found themselves being auctioned off in Canada in unusual surroundings. The famous Tattersall's Yard in Great St. James Street, Montreal, was known for horse sales, where old nags often went for as low as two dollars to the tobacco-spitting 'Jehues and habitants' who met there regularly in excited hubbub.[17] It is remembered as the gathering place of 'the horsey men', and of the card-playing, bowling-alley set, all of whom had frequent recourse to the numerous nearby taverns as an auction progressed. Few today familiar with the stories about Tattersall's would connect it with china. But there was another side to Tattersall's. On occasion the horse-yard would be cleaned up, and John Jones, the auctioneer, would mount his 'throne' (a sort of cross between a sentry box and a pulpit) to sell not horses but fine tablewares to discriminating buyers. The *Gazette* of September 5, 1846, carried an advertisement for one of these strangely circumstanced china sales:

TATTERSALLS,

THIS DAY . . .

THE Subscriber will sell, by Auction, in TATTERSALLS' YARD, Great St. James-street, without reserve . . . A very large and varied assortment of China Tea and Breakfast Services, Stone China Dinner, Dessert, Tea and Toilet Services, &c., &c.

  Hotel-keepers, Private Families, and Dealers, will find this an opportunity of purchasing which seldom offers itself; all of which are of the most recherche styles and patterns. On view the morning of sale . . .

JOHN JONES,

Auctioneer.

A really good crockery auction might develop when a china merchant gave up business, went bankrupt, or died. Then everything in the store would be auctioned off, sometimes including crates 'in the original package', just as they had come from England. At these sales housewives jostled dealers and hotel-keepers in the scramble after a crockery bargain.[18]

Some merchants made regular use of the store auction as a selling technique. In the west this was common practice. Quantities of stout white ironstone and heavy pearl china must have been knocked down at Red River sales advertised with characteristic western flourish. John Higgins, a Fort Garry dealer who had begun in a small way peddling goods from a wagon in the 1850's, and who would be able to retire to the position of successful 'patriarch' before the end of the 1870's,[19] arranged an auction at his store in 1869. His advertisement for it, in the *Nor'-Wester* of February 5, mentioned that crockery 'of all description' would be included. The announcement started off:

Hold Up! Stop! !

DON'T YOU SEE THIS?

GREAT NOTICE OF AN

Auction Sale

A great Auction Sale will take place at John Higgins store, on the first day of March.

  The people of this settlement are invited to attend, as the Sale will consist of the best stock of Goods, Groceries &c., ever brought in . . .

67

According to the *Nor'-Wester,* no old stock was to be pawned off in the sale. It was to be just:

> ... step in, pick for what you please. Cash down, and go away as contented, as if nothing had struck you ...

The advertisement ended:

> ... Don't forget my sign is over the door, and inside you will find my Stock consisting of Clothing of all cuts and styles. The best assorted patterns of Ladies Bonnets ... Crockery of all description. Hardware ... Jewelry &c.
> Remember on the 1st day of March, this Great Sale will take place. Fetch all your friends along and you will find John Higgins at his old stand waiting for your bid ...

Whatever articles made up John Higgins' crockery of all description, those wares must have been well talked up when they went on the auction block in 1869.

Another kind of auction, peculiar to the times, was responsible for distributing china and earthenware in Canada in the nineteenth century. The wares sold were not, strictly speaking, new; they had all been used once. Yet they were scarcely second-hand in the accepted sense of the term. A sale of this kind was advertised in the *Montreal Daily Argus* on May 8, 1857. It was to be held three days later at Compain's Restaurant, not far from Tattersall's Horse Market. To be auctioned off were all the articles of crockery, glassware, and cutlery that had been used 'at the Grand Trunk Celebration Banquet', presumably the 'splendid affair' held some six months earlier to mark the arrival of the first train from Toronto:

> 600 dozen Knives and Forks
> 600   do   Tea and Table Spoons
> 600   do   Table, Desert and Soup Plates
> 2000 Dishes and Jugs
> Tumblers, Wine Glasses, Decanters to match.
> — ALSO —
> A large assortment of Cake Ornaments &c.
> As the above were only used once, and are in perfect order, parties attending the Sale are sure to get great bargains, as the whole will be sold without reserve ...

Selling off what had been used at some special event like this was a curious practice of Victorian Canada. It reached its climax when the Prince of Wales (later King Edward VII) visited the North American colonies in 1860. Royalty had hardly left a city before everything purchased for the visit was up for public sale. Even the 'mammoth ballroom' erected in Montreal was taken apart and sold in pieces. 'Obtain a souvenir', the advertisements shouted—and thousands did. This is one reason why so many plates, glasses, and spoons (many bearing the Prince of Wales' Feathers as decoration) are today in the hands of families who cling to the tradition that His Royal Highness personally used them during his visit.

In Halifax a 'grand ball' was given for the Prince on the night of July 31. The next morning the Prince left Halifax for Saint John, and five days after that everything that had been used at the ball—the tables and all that had furnished them, the ornaments, the carpets, and the muslin curtains—was sold by William M. Allan. The auction took place 'in the Ball Room, in the Province Building', which less than a week before had been the scene of quadrilles, galops, waltzes, and polkas danced by Queen Victoria's heir.[20]

The Saint John merchant, Francis Clementson, rented to the provincial authorities all the china used in the residence occupied by the Prince in that city (the 'Duke of Kent's Lodge', owned by the widow of the Hon. Ward Chipman).[21] He also supplied, on a rental basis, what was needed for a banquet given in connection with the visit. As soon as the banquet was over, Clementson's china and glass were rushed aboard the *Forest Queen*. While the Prince steamed up the River Saint John to Fredericton, the tablewares were put to use a second time. After the New Brunswick visit was over Francis Clementson got back his dishes, glasses, and china ornaments, and then quickly disposed of them to eager buyers. Not all the pieces came up for resale, however: a few had disappeared, apparently filched by ladies granted permission to view the apartments furnished for royalty.[22]

In Montreal several different auction firms shared the business connected with the Prince's visit. While one was selling the gold fringe that had decorated a platform, another was stressing the souvenir value of bedroom crockery and china plates. C. F. Hill & Co. had the sale of much of the porcelain and earthenware, for they were commissioned to auction the contents of Rosemount, the residence of Sir John Rose, newly furnished for the use of the Prince of Wales. 'The articles have obtained historic value', C. F. Hill told the public. 'Those desirous of obtaining a souvenir of H.R.H. the Prince of Wales should embrace this opportunity . . . which will not be met with in a life-time.' Wash-stand sets were among the items listed in his advertisement as having obtained 'historic value'.[23]

A month later C. F. Hill & Co. had a new selection of royal visit souvenirs under the hammer, this time 'Plate and Plated Ware, CROOKERY [*sic*] AND CHINA, BED AND TABLE LINEN, &c., used by H.R.H. the Prince of Wales and Suite throughout Canada'. In the *Gazette*, on October 23, Hill stated that everything had been 'made expressly for His Royal Highness', and that many items were 'richly' decorated 'with the Prince of Wales Feather and Crown'.

It was the same story in Ottawa. There H. McLean, auctioneer, sold the contents of forty rooms fitted up in the Victoria House for the use of the Prince and his suite. 'Ornaments, Rich China and Glassware' went to the highest bidder wanting 'a souvenir of H.R.H.'[24]

New and all-but-new crockery was sold by auction in Canada in astonishing quantities. So, too, were tablewares and bedroom wares that were, in fact, second-hand. These came on the market when the contents of private dwellings were put up for sale. In a new country the number of such auctions was greater in proportion to the population than it would be in an old, settled land such as England. In Canada there was a constant moving on to new opportunities farther west, and there was also the come and go of government officials and garrison officers. Even those whose business took them to Great Britain or the Continent for a matter of months, or a year or two, frequently sold off their household goods before they left, and furnished anew when they returned. Simon Mc-

Tavish, head of the North West Company, and probably the richest man in Montreal in the days of the fur lords, gave orders for such a sale before he left for England in 1791. On that occasion he put his 'entire elegant and genteel Household furniture, Plate, Linen, China and other effects' into the hands of an auctioneer.[25] It was another lot of household goods, including 'setts of the most fashionable china', that was sold at his house on St. Jean Baptiste Street after his death in 1804.[26]

Emigrants were counselled to watch for house sales when they got to Canada and to take advantage of the opportunities offered. Rev. William Haw, writing in 1850, after fifteen years' experience in Canada, told intending emigrants that at auction sales in Toronto good-quality household goods of every kind could be purchased cheap, sometimes cheaper than at home in England.[27]

Some of the best of the second-hand china and earthenware came from government officials, or garrison or naval officers. Those dispatched to serve in the colonies sometimes brought fine tablewares with them; if they came unequipped, they generally chose what they needed from the better goods available in the colonial shops. When it was time for them to move on again, they put these household furnishings up for sale. When Sir Peregrine Maitland, Lieutenant-Governor of Nova Scotia, returned to England in the 1830's he handed over to the Halifax auctioneers, Deblois & Mitchell, his china, his pictures, his grand piano, and his four-post beds with curtains. They sold them at the King's Wharf on November 8, 1834.[28] Lord Metcalfe, dying of cancer and recalled, at his own request, as Governor-General of Canada, sailed from Montreal in November of 1845. His porcelain dinner services were left behind to be sold at auction the next spring.[29]

One garrison officer, Sir R. I. Routh, put on the second-hand market one of the biggest china services recorded in nineteenth-century advertising in Canada. The Montreal newspaper, *La Minerve*, described it on October 20, 1842, as 'un service de Porcelaine contenant plus de 800 morceaux, et qui a coûté plus de £200'.

Newspapers of the day show that other officers left behind them tablewares of Wedgwood and Worcester, of Dresden and Sèvres. They sent to the auction rooms china teapots that were silver-mounted, china jars filled with preserves, supper sets in mahogany trays and 'Chamber Crockery, very elegant'. Thousands of pieces of earthenware, stone china, and porcelain came on the market because garrison officers had been transferred.

Why they nearly always left behind what some had even gone to the trouble of bringing across the Atlantic was explained by Sir James E. Alexander, who served in Canada in the 1840's. Writing of his experiences as a garrison officer, he pointed out that moving goods like crockery, even from one military post to another in Canada, was impracticable, 'the risk of breakages being so great'. In addition, there was the heavy 'expense of transport'. In his case, when he was suddenly transferred from London, Canada West, to Kingston, there 'was no time to advertise a sale; the only thing to be done was to send for an auctioneer, to divide all my moveables into lots, carry them out into the garden, and send round the . . . Bellman . . . to announce a sale on the following day.[30]

All this second-hand earthenware and porcelain was added to the quantities dispersed at sales when Canadians themselves died, moved, or 'declined house-keeping', as the phrase of the time went. The delft that belonged to the Hon. Joseph LeMoyne de Longueuil (an officer under Montcalm), was advertised for sale at auction in the *Montreal Gazette* on April 29, 1799. Andrew McGill's creamware dinner service in parsley leaf design was disposed of the same way six years later.[31] In the 1860's, when Jesse Joseph, the Jewish financier, died, someone went to the auction sale of his goods and came home with a 'rich White and Gold China Tea Set'.[32]

Others flocked off to auctions where tablewares made for hotels or steamboats were sold. Sometimes fires or a going out of business had occasioned these sales, but at other times tablewares were sold off when a refurnishing program was put into effect. According to newspaper advertisements, crockery made for such famous Montreal hotels as the Albion, the Masonic Hall, Donegana's, and the St. Lawrence Hall was sold by auction. In the *Montreal Gazette* of April 15, 1867, for example, Lawrence Devany announced the sale of 'the complete and costly Furnishings' of 'THE DONEGANA HOTEL', including the entire contents of 'DINING ROOMS . . . CUISINES and PANTRIES'. In other parts of the colonies similar hotel auctions took place during the nineteenth century.[33]

With regard to tableware from Donegana's, it should be noted, however, that ironstone plates bearing a sepia-printed view of the hotel, which are today in such museums as the Château de Ramezay, Montreal, and the McCord Museum, McGill University, would not have come from Devany's 1867 sale. The view of the hotel on these pieces shows that they belonged to the first Donegana's Hotel, destroyed by fire in 1849. This first Donegana's was said by Lt.-Col. B. W. A. Sleigh, a visitor of the 1840's who later wrote of his experiences in *Pine Forests and Hacmatack Clearings*, to be 'a magnificent establishment' where everything was 'in the first style'. The Staffordshire firm that supplied 'first style' tableware decorated with the hotel's picture was William Ridgway, Son & Co., whose mark appears on surviving pieces.[34]

The frequency of auction sales in Montreal caught the attention of an English visitor, John Palmer, in 1817.[35] By 1876 a Canadian writer, A. Baumgarten, was worrying that auctions of one kind or another were giving unfair competition to merchants 'of first class standing'.[36] In the history of Canada's crockery trade the auctioneer looms almost as large as the china merchant. Both handled imported wares in huge quantities, both dealt in first-quality goods as well as in the 'seconds' that formed a considerable part of the crockery exports from England to British North America, and both faced many of the same difficulties of business. The chief of these was getting paid for what they had sold.

A ruinous credit system meant that few were able to sell for long on a strictly cash basis. As Henry Taylor wrote in 1850, 'in Canada the scarcity of money is almost always a general complaint'.[37] There were, of course, some who did their best to operate on a cash system. There was an early woman dealer, Mrs. J. Wilson, who opened the China Shop in Quebec in 1819, and proposed carrying tablewares 'of the best English manufacture . . . cheap for cash'.[38] And there was the Staffordshire China and Glass House in Halifax, which advertised in 1845 that business was 'conducted on the cash principle'.[39] Most crockery dealers and most auctioneers, however, had to be willing to take 'approved notes'; though probably all the storekeepers followed the practice announced in 1833 by Burns & Bassett, of St. Catharines. In an advertisement dated July 25, and published in the *British American Journal*, Burns & Bassett stated that their prices for crockery and other goods would be reduced 'without the smallest hesitation', if cash was put down in front of them.

Credit-buying and the barter system continued throughout the century. Table-wares made in potteries on the other side of the Atlantic were exchanged in Canada for 'peltries' and 'country produce', for pemmican and hand-knit socks, for 'good merchantable promises', pot ashes, dried sinews, cords of wood, and 'Old Pot Metal'. In advertisements listing crockery for sale, it was usual to see a statement similar to that which Lovitt & Burrell, of Milton, Nova Scotia, added to an advertisement for 'Crockery, Earthen, China and Glass Ware' in 1854. In the *Yarmouth Herald* on October 26, Lovitt & Burrell cited their latest shipments, and then added:

IN EXCHANGE FOR GOODS

We take Lumber, Shingles, Timber, Cord Wood, Laths, Butter, Cheese, Eggs, Fish, Mitts, Socks, Homespun Cloth, &c.

But it was this type of barter that Henry Taylor blamed for the scarcity of money, and the scarcity of money continued the need for credit. When a crockery seller went under, as a high percentage of them did, the cause was frequently that he could not get in what was owing him, which meant that he, in his turn, could not pay his suppliers. 'Merchants must take a firm stand to abolish the pernicious credit system', A. Baumgarten declared urgently. 'We feel its bad effects every day.'[40]

Yet even when a merchant attempted to run a store on the 'Ready Pay system', which would, in theory, eliminate the carrying of charge accounts, he felt almost compelled to allow barter. Robert Meighen, who opened a store at McDonald's Corners, near Perth, Canada West, advertised in the 1860's that he had 'determined upon doing business on the Ready Pay system'. This would 'reduce . . . prices to the lowest point'. But Meighen, selling dry goods, groceries, and crockery, for 'Ready Pay' also announced that 'ALL kinds of Produce' would be taken in exchange for these goods.[41]

To bring in business the crockery sellers—general merchants, specialist dealers, and auctioneers—relied heavily on advertising. They distributed hand-bills and catalogues, very few of which have survived; and they also made constant use of newspapers and other publications. It is their advertisements in these publications, and particularly in newspapers, that make up today the most important general record of the types of earthenware and porcelain used by Canadians in the nineteenth century.

In a single issue of the *Quebec Observer*, an Upper Town china merchant, Thomas Bickell, had eleven different advertisements. Nine were for crockery, one for Kelly's Pure Cod Liver Oil, and one for 'Japaned' ware. Long ahead of twentieth-century advertising experts, Bickell realized that no one advertisement could be of equal interest to everybody, but in his nine ceramic announcements on September 4, 1854, he reached out to every possible market. Separate advertisements appealed to those who wanted porcelain ('French China . . . richly gilt'); earthenware ('from Staffordshire'); ornamental wares ('3 CASES of French Flowers in China Vases'); cheap durable goods ('White Granite Ware'); 'Garden Pots', or 'Preserve Pots, Pickling Jars, &c.' There was even an advertisement directed to invalids who might be interested in bed pans 'on an improved principle'.

Another china dealer who relied strongly on advertising was Robert Anderson of Montreal, a very canny Scot, who felt it good business to pay for advertisements in more than half a dozen newspapers at the same time, French as well as English. As a general rule Anderson did not follow the plan of small, separate advertisements, directed to different sections of the buying public. His method was to compel attention by the sheer bulk and variety of his stock, and at other times to use half-price sales as bait. There was telling impact in the heading that Anderson put on his advertisement in the *Montreal Gazette* on August 12, 1846:

A MILLION PIECES OF
GLASS, CHINA AND EARTHENWARE
FOR SALE . . .

A vast assortment, from dinner services to toy tea sets, from mortars and pestles to scent jars, and from foot baths to table candlesticks, was listed in this announcement, which appeared in French two days later in *La Revue Canadienne:* '1,000,000 D'ARTICLES EN Verrerie, Porcelaine et Fayence . . .'

Nineteenth century china sellers believed in repetition: 'CHINA! CHINA!! CHINA!!!' screamed the heading for A. Harley's 'elegant China TEA SETTS' in the *Yarmouth Herald* on August 10, 1838. John Monro, who owned the Tea, China and Glassware House in St. Catharines, used repetition within the advertisement. In the *Weekly News* of September 4, 1873, he headed his announcement 'GOLD BAND!' and then went on to list:

China Fruit Stands
China Fruit Sets
China Sauce Plates
China Water Jugs

and so on, for nineteen more articles, repeating the word 'China' every time. Few who looked at that newspaper in 1873 could have been left unaware that somebody was selling gold-banded 'China', even if the advertisement were not followed to the end to learn that this was all French porcelain.

Many aimed at catching attention by the heading itself. 'WAR IN CHINA' was the startling sweep line on one of A. T. Wiley's first advertisements for China Hall in Montreal.[42] 'PHEIHO,' sighed the heading for a mark-down sale at Cleverdon's Staffordshire House in Halifax.[43] 'The Wants of the People Regarded', declaimed W. Burrell, in an advertising caption in the *Yarmouth Herald*.[44] (Lustre ware and fancy jugs went into his list of the people's wants.)

Nearly every crockery seller put advertising emphasis on the possibility of a bargain. 'On the utmost discounted terms' and 'cheaper than the cheapest' was the way tablewares were publicized from Prince Edward Island to Upper Canada as early as the 1820's.[45] One of the most ingenious ceramic advertisements of the century, however, was that placed in Montreal's *Daily Witness* by A. T. Wiley, at the time of the Dominion Exhibition in 1880:

BEWARE OF PICKPOCKETS
at the coming Exhibition, and hold fast to your
money to buy
FANCY GOODS
— IN —
Crockery, Glass and China
At   WILEY'S CHINA HALL
425 Notre Dame street.[46]

But not all the pottery and porcelain was sold by auctioneers or dealers in the regular way. Some of the old wares held in esteem today as family possessions may have been acquired because an ancestor had the instincts of a gambler. China lotteries were once common in Canada, and lucky ticket-holders might find that such famous names as Wedgwood or Worcester were theirs because they had risked something on the drawing of a number.

Dealers frequently resorted to lotteries as a way of drumming up business in slack periods. 'On account of the dullness of trade and the scarcity of money' was the reason given for the holding of one lottery in the 1850's.[47] It was undoubtedly to work up business in the dull winter season, when the city was cut off from the outside world, that William Turner, the Montreal china merchant, decided on a lottery in January of 1833.

Of all the advertisements to be found for china lotteries in Canadian newspapers, Turner's detailed announcement in the *Montreal Gazette* is one of the most important. It appeared on January 10, 1833, and cited famous makers and gave values for the prizes offered. 'ALL PRIZES—NO BLANKS', was the way it began: 'A LOTTERY OF SUPERB CHINA TEA AND DESSERT SERV-ICES, JUGS, &c. just imported from ENGLAND, selected from the best . . . Manufactories'.

First prize, valued at £20, was to be 'A China Dessert Service, most superbly Painted in Enamel, each piece having a Boquet [*sic*] differing from every other piece—the whole most tastefully and profusely decorated with rich Burnished Gold, consisting of twenty-seven pieces,—supposed to be the richest China ever offered for sale in Montreal'.

Worcester porcelain, valued at £9, came fourth on the list of seventy-five prizes: 'an elegant Worster [*sic*] Service of China for Tea and Coffee, Tastefully decorated with Burnished Gold and chastely Enamelled on a Fawn Coloured Ground, the newest shape and device—forty pieces'.

Wedgwood was farther down, prize number nine, with a value of thirty-five shillings: 'A Wedgwood's Green Embossed Dessert Service—twenty-seven pieces'.

The list was alluring: white and gold porcelain, Broseley pattern blue and white, sets of jugs, and china punch bowls. The seventy-five prizes totalled over £80 worth of first-quality tablewares. A ticket cost four dollars,[48] so that the holder stood the chance of getting a dessert or tea service for a fraction of its cost, or, on the other hand, of paying only about twice too much for a trio of jugs.

In spite of the fact that it took a disappointingly long time to get the tickets sold—in the end the goods were put on view in a pastry shop, where the drawing was at last held[49]—William Turner must have found that a china lottery was good business. The next winter, with a partner, he was back before the public with another lottery. An advertisement for this one appeared on March 13, 1834, in the short-lived and almost forgotten Montreal newspaper, the *Settler, or British, Irish, and Canadian Gazette*:

GRAND LOTTERY OF SUPERB
CHINA

CONSISTING of 1 superbly decorated burnished Gold China Desert Service; 2 Semi-China Desert Services; 4 superbly decorated burnished Gold China Tea and Coffee Services; 1 elegantly moulded double Dinner Service, best Earthenware, 300 pieces; 1 double Dinner Service best Earthenware 270 pieces . . . total, 100 prizes . . .

Sometimes china formed only a part of the lottery prize list. Almost any article imaginable could share it. Advertisements give evidence of such diverse rewards as pairs of porcelain vases 'beautifully painted', cuckoo clocks, 'a learned Parrot', a stuffed rat, and 'Ringlets and Wig for the use of the Stage'.[50] In the west, when the troubled days of the first Riel Rebellion had slowed trade in Winnipeg, Bannatyne & Begg (A. G. B. Bannatyne and Alexander Begg) turned to a 'Monster Lottery' to get business going. They were dealers in crockery, dry goods, groceries, and hardware—a general store—and they threw in a bit of everything in the prize list of 'A LOTTERY on a larger scale than any which has yet taken place in this Settlement'. The *New Nation*, the newspaper whose stormy existence paralleled the days of Riel's provisional government, carried their advertisement on April 29, 1870, citing a rifle as one of the top prizes in this very mixed bag.

Probably few who bought tickets on William Turner's Worcester tea set, 'chastely enamelled', or hoped, the next year, for the 300-piece dinner service, were actually connoisseurs of fine china. Rather, they were likely to have been those who the next day would have been willing to have a fling on a learned parrot, or, had they lived in the west at a later date, would have hoped for the top prize of a sportsman's rifle. But selling china by lottery allowed the dealer, whether china merchant or general trader, to tap a new market. It was a market in which the china seller would have found it harder to make sales by regular business methods than by the lure of 'ALL PRIZES . . . NO BLANKS . . . an excellent opportunity of obtaining a splendid Prize at very small cost'.[51]

As crockery-selling in Canada was anybody's business, people got started in it in strange ways. A ship's captain might try his luck with a few clay pipes and some salt-glazed tablewares when he reached Halifax.[52] 'A PERSON going through the COUNTRY WEST OF TORONTO' might advertise that he would 'undertake the sale of STAPLE ARTICLES, such as OILS, CROCKERY, &c. on COMMISSION'.[53] Some set up as specialist china merchants—and many ended in failure. But for a few the china business brought its final rewards. They survived the hazards of this highly competitive, often tough, rough trade to achieve solid security. They were the successful few, like S. L. Willett, who retired from china-selling in Montreal in 1866, and could offer for sale a 'fine business . . . established, safe and profitable'.[54]

CHAPTER VI

A Wedgwood in Montreal
and Other Unexpected Links

JOSEPH WEDGWOOD, manufacturer, POTTERIES, STAFFORDSHIRE,
ENGLAND; or No. 51 St. Paul Street, Montreal . . .
Montreal Herald, Nov. 2, 1816.

Until well past the middle years of the nineteenth century, St. Paul Street, down near the waterfront in Montreal, could claim to be the very heart of Canada's crockery trade. Most of the city's important china sellers carried on their business in the vicinity of the Old Market, later known as Customs House Square and now as Place Royale. To these merchants came supplies of earthenware and porcelain not only for Montreal itself and the surrounding districts, but, in increasing quantities, for the rapidly expanding trade of Upper Canada. For a considerable time the china sellers of St. Paul Street were to be in virtual control of the market of the most populous area of British North America.

Thomas Storrow Brown, the rebel grandson of a Loyalist, left a vivid impression of what business on St. Paul Street was like when he first arrived in Montreal in the spring of 1818. 'All doors and no windows' described many of the one- and two-storey shops, whose goods were often set outside for better display. Merchants stationed clerks in the street, to accost passers-by and inveigle them into the stores. Country buyers were frequently dragged in forcibly, their protests merely adding to the general air of brisk business. As Thomas Storrow Brown remembered it, 'the excitement on market days between these vociferous sellers and wary buyers, pulled into one shop after another, made St. Paul Street lively.'[1]

On this lively street in Montreal, at the period just described, a member of one of the most famous potting families of England was selling china and earthenware. A few doors from the Old Market, in the best business section of St. Paul Street, was Wedgwood's China Store. Its proprietor was Joseph Wedgwood, cousin of Josiah Wedgwood II, who was by this time head of the Wedgwood Works at Etruria.

According to the ceramic historian, Llewellynn Jewitt, the father of the Joseph Wedgwood who emigrated to Canada (Joseph Wedgwood, Senior) and the great Josiah Wedgwood (father of Josiah Wedgwood II) were second cousins.[2] They were further related by marriage, for Joseph Wedgwood, Senior, married a niece of Josiah Wedgwood (the daughter of his elder sister, Ann).[3] Through both his father and his mother, therefore, the Joseph Wedgwood whose china shop was

77

on St. Paul Street in Montreal was closely connected with the successful potters of Etruria.

His father, Joseph, Senior, had himself been a potter. In the 1780's and early 1790's he was at the Churchyard Works, in Burslem. Evidence indicates that Joseph Wedgwood, Senior, leased this pottery from his cousin, who owned it, and there made wares for him, wares which Josiah Wedgwood's biographer, Miss Meteyard, says 'were chiefly consumed for the export trade'.[4] In 1793, however, Joseph Wedgwood failed. He died soon after his son emigrated, leaving him a legacy of debts amounting to over £1,000.

In Montreal Joseph Wedgwood the younger made a bold start. He took premises in the best district and arranged to advertise his new establishment extensively. Probably he himself, as was the custom of the day, took round to the newspaper offices the copy for his advertising, written in his own hand. Dated June 22, 1816, the announcement of the opening of Joseph Wedgwood's china shop in Montreal ran over a period of months in several newspapers:

> *China, Glass & Earthenware House,*
> *No. 51 St. Paul Street.*
> JOSEPH WEDGWOOD, of the Staffordshire
> Potteries in England, begs leave to inform the public that he has opened the said Store, wherein he will dispose of all kinds of articles in the above line on the most reasonable terms.
> *June 22, 1816.*[5]

Memories of the opening of the Wedgwood china store in Montreal lasted for many years. Joseph Charles, writing to the *Daily Witness* in the 1890's, recalled his mother's saying 'there was a rush at the store when it first opened', and that the stock carried was 'superior'. His father had been among the early customers. He had purchased 'a beautiful set of the finest kind'. Joseph Charles described this set as having been decorated with classical figures. Unfortunately, this decoration was not approved when the new tableware was unpacked at home, because the classical figures were insufficiently clothed. The tableware went back to Joseph Wedgwood, who exchanged it 'for a set with ornaments of grape vines and fruit'.

There is no evidence that Josiah Wedgwood II actually set up his colonial cousin in business, but there is clear evidence, in letters preserved today in the Wedgwood Archives in England, that he was interested in his success, and was supplying him with Wedgwood products to sell. Josiah Wedgwood's interest in the china shop near the Old Market in Montreal would have been twofold: in the first place it represented a new outlet for Wedgwood wares, and the Wedgwood firm had had a keen eye for Canadian business since the eighteenth century. A second, and probably equally compelling reason why Josiah Wedgwood must have hoped for signs that Joseph was making good in Montreal was a debt owed the pottery by the elder Joseph Wedgwood at the time of his death. That Josiah Wedgwood expected his cousin in Canada to pay off his father's debt is evident from letters to Joseph, Junior. These letters, from Josiah Wedgwood in England to Joseph Wedgwood in Canada, ask for settlement of the father's liabilities, and give £1091 as the sum still to be paid.[6]

A Wedgwood in Montreal and Other Unexpected Links

Joseph Wedgwood, Junior, by virtue of his connection with the Wedgwood potters of Etruria, was able to style himself a 'manufacturer' in Canada.[7] In advertisements he made much of the fact that the wares he offered for sale were 'direct from the manufactory in Staffordshire'. The *Montreal Herald* carried an advertisement of this kind on June 21, 1817, and, incidentally, spelled the name 'Wedgewood', an error commonly made by Canadian compositors throughout the century:

> THE Subscriber has just imported per the late arrivals from Liverpool, an extensive, and valuable assortment of CHINA, GLASS, AND EARTHENWARE, all of which are of the most recent patterns, direct from the manufactory in Staffordshire, and will be disposed of on the most reasonable terms.
>
> Joseph Wedgewood.

A postscript to this advertisement added that orders for wares 'from the manufactory in England' would be taken in Montreal by Joseph Wedgwood, who would ask only a 'reasonable' commission for having them attended to.

One of these orders has survived. In a letter written from Montreal on November 18, 1817, and addressed to Josiah Wedgwood in Staffordshire, his cousin Joseph says: 'I have just rec'd a small order from a Gent'n here for some Dairy Tiles &c. and if you think proper to execute it I shall feel obliged.' Then follow details of 'An order to be sent out in the first Spring Vessel'. Included with a quantity of tiles, at that time fashionable for use in dairies, and which were to be in 'any cheap showy pattern', were the following articles in cream-coloured earthenware intended, like the tiles, for dairy use:

12 Oval milkpans with lips border'd to match
 2 Milksieves C C about 6 qts
 6 Cream Vases — 4 qts — do —
 2 Skimmers C C
 4 Milk bowls with covers, — do —[8]

Joseph Wedgwood was a typical Canadian china merchant of the early days. He called his store a 'China, Glass & Earthenware House', advertising that he would take orders for 'articles in the above line from the manufactory in England'; and yet a very large part of his business must have been concerned with goods not even remotely connected with crockery of Wedgwood or any other make. In one advertisement he is expecting, 'by the first fair wind', not only '100 crates assorted Earthen Ware' and '16 casks elegant burnished Gold China', but also fish sauce, capers, Hessian boots, 'real Staffordshire ale in bottles', pickles, coals, and flannel shirts.[9] Again, he is advertising 'Newly Discovered Garden Seeds', at five dollars a packet, or advising 'Medical Practitioners' that he has 'Genuine Drugs' for sale.[10] On another occasion, although starting off his advertisement with 'A large and elegant assortment of China, Glass and Earthenware', he goes on to list carpenter's tools, clocks in 'handsome Mahogany cases', gigs, 'Prime Cheshire Cheese, in hampers' and 'Bristol Pickled Tripe, in kegs'.[11]

In other ways, too, Joseph Wedgwood ran a typical Canadian china business: he found it necessary to deal in 'Country Produce',[12] and he had difficulty collecting what was owing him. Financial troubles set in early, as is seen in the letter addressed to his cousin, Josiah Wedgwood, in 1817:

> Mr Wedgwood
>> Sir
>>
>> It gives me great uneasiness to have to address you on the present subject, which is to request of you a still farther indulgence in the payment of my former account,—this request I should not make if it was in my power to collect in my just demands, But such is the scarcity of Money here, that out of from £3 à 4000 which was due in the Month of October, I could only get in about £1500, to send home, in Bills & produce together,—I have . . . remitted the Money to pay you the last a/c, & if you would indulge me with a still farther credit on the former a/c, the obligation will ever be remember'd.[13]

Of Joseph Wedgwood's father, the elder Joseph, Miss Meteyard wrote: 'For some cause or another he was not a prosperous man'.[14] The same, in the end, had to be said of his son, at least in so far as his attempt at china-selling in the colonies was concerned. In less than three years Joseph Wedgwood, Junior, was back in England, bankrupt. In Montreal the store on St. Paul Street was put up for rent,[15] and on May 1, 1819, the firm of McLean & Wilson advertised in the *Canadian Courant* that they had been empowered to collect 'all debts of whatever nature, due in Upper or Lower Canada' that were still owing to 'Mr. Jos. Wedgewood late of this city, Mercht.'

Josiah Wedgwood, far away in Staffordshire, was not, however, done with his cousin's unsuccessful Montreal shop. He had not been fully paid for the stock which he had sent out to Canada for it, and he now found himself having to answer enquiries from Montreal concerning his cousin's affairs. On June 25, 1819, Josiah Wedgwood replied to the important Montreal merchants, Irvine, Leslie & Co.: 'I wrote to you on 22nd instant that Mr. Joseph Wedgwood was returned to England'.[16] It took time not only to collect as much as possible of what was owing to Joseph Wedgwood but to 'put into a train for settlement' what he himself owed in Canada.[17]

Obviously the Wedgwood china shop on St. Paul Street had not been very profitable for anyone. Yet it played a part in putting Wedgwood wares on the Canadian market, and because of the importance of the name of Wedgwood, this brief venture into china-selling, unsuccessful though it was, must be regarded as one of the most interesting examples of hitherto almost unsuspected direct family connections between British potters and those distributing their products in Canada.

Another of these significant relationships between overseas potter and Canadian china merchant was on a very different basis. Joseph Wedgwood was the poor relation. Francis Clementson, who opened a china, glass, and earthenware house in Saint John, New Brunswick, at mid-century, was the eldest son of Joseph Clementson, prosperous master potter of Hanley. From the first, Francis Clementson had behind him in Canada the strong financial backing of his father's firm. This is indicated by the credit rating accorded him in *Mercantile Agency Reference Books*. The most important of the crockery merchants in the largest cities of central Canada found it difficult to push their credit rating past 'Good', but Francis Clementson's rating was regularly higher, even when his total capital was estimated at an equal or lesser amount than that of others in the same line of business.[18] In 1872 he was given the unusual rating of 'Un-

limited Credit'. The explanation was not that he was doing a bigger china business than anyone else in the whole of Canada, although his business was certainly
large; he was solidly backed by the unquestioned financial resources of his
father's firm in Staffordshire. For Francis Clementson there was no need to write
humbly home to England, praying that a small order would be filled and time
extended on an overdue account.

Joseph Wedgwood stayed in Canada less than three years and then had to
return home in a state of bankruptcy, leaving behind him creditors who wrote
off to his cousin in an effort to trace him. Francis Clementson, on the other hand,
remained in New Brunswick for more than a quarter of a century; and when
he went back to England to live, it was to return as the eldest son, and to settle
into his father's house in Staffordshire. Behind him in Canada he left a crockery
business that flourished under his name for another twenty years or more.
Francis Clementson's had just as obviously been a colonial success story as
Joseph Wedgwood's had been a failure. Today Clementson's portrait, fittingly
reproduced on porcelain, is preserved in the New Brunswick Museum. It shows
a china merchant who was portly and balding and the very essence of Victorian
confidence.

The connection between the British North American colonies and the Clementsons of Staffordshire antedated Francis Clementson's coming to Saint John.
It went back to the early days of his father's career as a master potter. Apprenticed to J. & W. Ridgway in the 1820's, Joseph Clementson (1794-1871) later
formed a partnership with Jonah Read for the manufacture of earthenware. That
was in or about 1832, the year Joseph Clementson crossed to North America
by sailing ship and visited the colonies looking for business.[19]

Like the Ridgways, under whom he had served his apprenticeship, and like
many another Staffordshire potter of his day, Joseph Clementson was a staunch
Methodist. In Canada on this first business trip he had an eye out for the Methodist cause as well as for the sale of his earthenware. During week days he
worked hard to secure orders for the pottery, and on Sundays he 'worked for
the Lord', preaching to Methodist congregations who turned out to hear a man
from the Potteries, where John Wesley had had such marked effect. Joseph
Clementson was, however, shocked, when he reached Upper Canada and found
that there many New Connexion Methodists (the branch of Methodism to which
he adhered) were 'destitute of the ordinances of religion'. It was in large part
due to Joseph Clementson's influence, after he returned to England, that increased missionary support was forthcoming for the work in Canada.[20]

If Canadian Methodists benefited from Joseph Clementson's interest in their
spiritual needs, the potteries which Clementson soon acquired in his own name
in Staffordshire were not without benefit in their turn from the Canadian and
Methodist ties so early formed by their owner. When Llewellynn Jewitt came
to write the history of the ceramic art of Great Britain, he noted of the Clementson potteries that the Canadian market took up an important part of their output.[21] Joseph Clementson had effectively laid the foundations for this Canadian
trade, and his Methodist associations brought in orders of a special kind as well.
Evidence of this has been handed down in Clementson tablewares printed with
a religious device and identified as having been made for the Methodist New

Connexion Church, Toronto. Later wares from the Clementsons' Phoenix Works (one of Joseph Clementson's two potteries) were printed with the same religious symbols and the name THE METHODIST CHURCH OF CANADA (*Plate* 2A). These last belong to a period after 1874, when 'Methodist Church of Canada' became the official title of the united Wesleyan and New Connexion Methodists.[22] By this time Joseph Clementson was dead, but his sons were still profiting from his interest in Canada.

The eldest of these four sons, Francis, was the one who chose to come to Canada himself and set up in business under his own name as a 'Manufacturer and Importer of Glass, China, and Earthenware'.[23] The manufacturing was done in Staffordshire, at the family potteries, the selling in Saint John by Francis. When he first came to Canada, at the end of the 1840's, Francis Clementson was a young man still in his twenties.[24] To assist him he had one of his father's trusted employees from Staffordshire, Thomas Stubbs,[25] whose son, Joseph Balfour Stubbs, was brought into the Saint John business in 1855, and was manager for many years.[26]

More fortunate by far than the unhappy Joseph Wedgwood, who was compelled to address his Staffordshire cousin with 'uneasiness', hoping for a few supplies to be sent out to him, Francis Clementson began his career in Canada with the experienced help of one of his father's men. Aided by his counsel, he sold to advantage the wares shipped to him in abundance. By 1853 Francis Clementson was able to move into premises well known for crockery. That year he rented Samuel Cooper's old Staffordshire & Yorkshire Warehouse on Dock Street, announcing the move in the *New Brunswick Courier*, in an advertisement dated August 20:

CHINA,

GLASS, AND EARTHENWARE

The Subscriber having imported a large Stock of the above Goods from the Manufactory in England with which he is connected, and having reopened the Store of the late Mr. S. Cooper, respectfully calls attention to the choice selection of BREAKFAST, Dinner, Dessert & Tea SETS, CHINA ORNAMENTS . . . FIGURES, STATUETTES, VASES, &c. . . .

FRANCIS CLEMENTSON,
DOCK-STREET.

Like other Canadian china merchants, including Joseph Wedgwood at an earlier period, Francis Clementson handled wares that had nothing to do with china. He re-opened Samuel Cooper's old store not with ornaments and tea sets alone, but with English ale and boxes of window glass.[27] The cigars he imported to sell with china were known as 'Clementson Queens'.[28]

His business soon went beyond New Brunswick. In the summer of 1855 he was seeking Nova Scotian orders in an advertisement in the *Yarmouth Herald* on August 16:

FRAS. CLEMENTSON,
Manufacturer and Importer of Glass,
China and Earthenware,

NO. 11 DOCK STREET,
ST. JOHN, N.B.

A Wedgwood in Montreal and Other Unexpected Links

NOW opening a beautiful selection of the above Goods, of the newest patterns and designs, (imported from our own Manufactory, Staffordshire, England,) in China, Ironstone, &c. . . .

   The Wholesale Department will be found to contain a full and varied assortment from which any description of Goods can be selected or had in the original Package.

The advertisements show that Francis Clementson became an importer on an unusually large scale. Common wares, such as stone crocks and milk pans, came to him from England by the thousand.[29] In tablewares he handled goods ranging in price from two dollars for a cheap tea set to nearly two hundred dollars for something stylish.[30] It is not to be supposed that everything he sold in crockery was necessarily of Clementson make. He was, after all, renting out Minton porcelain at the time of the Prince of Wales' visit in 1860,[31] but it was to his distinct advantage to stress his own pottery connections, and this he did repeatedly: 'THE SUBSCRIBER invites the attention of the Public to his extensive Assortment of CHINA, EARTHENWARE and GLASS, (imported from our own Manufactory . . . Ironstone, Whitestone and Earthenware . . . '[32]

The New Brunswick Museum, in Saint John, contains a number of plates and other articles whose donors stated that they had originally been purchased from the long-remembered Clementson china house on Dock Street. One cup and saucer, of printed earthenware, is of particular interest. The body is warped and discoloured, and the glaze marred by gritty blemishes. But these defects only serve to link the history of china-selling in the Maritimes with a Saint John tragedy. This cup and saucer were salvaged by Robert Gale, a Saint John merchant, from the smouldering ruins of Francis Clementson's china, glass, and earthenware store.[33] When the Great Fire of June 20, 1877, plunged down Dock Street, in the course of levelling almost half the city of Saint John, the building that housed the Clementson crockery business was one of twenty-six to be burned out on that street alone.[34]

By the time of the fire the business on Dock Street had become Francis Clementson & Co., and was officially 'a branch of Clementson Bros. of England'.[35] Francis Clementson was dead, but his business continued. He had died in England at what had been his father's house, Prospect House, Hanley. At the time he was only fifty-seven years of age. The funeral service took place in the eighteenth-century Bethesda Methodist Chapel, where his father had worshipped (and where Methodist services are still held today). In a churchyard that is now no longer used, Francis Clementson was interred in the family vault, and his name inscribed on the north side of the obelisk-type memorial erected to Joseph Clementson and his sons. The wording on this north side of the stone reads:

In Remembrance of Joseph Clementson
of Prospect House, Hanley,
who died August 22nd 1871
Aged 77
also of Francis, Eldest son
of Joseph and Martha Clementson
who died at Prospect House
August 12th 1875
Aged 57 years.[36]

83

In Saint John the news was received in black-bordered formal announcements, such as the Victorians sent out to friends whenever there was a death in the family:

IN REMEMBRANCE OF
FRANCIS CLEMENTSON
of Hanley,
(Late of St. John, New Brunswick,)
Who died at Prospect House, Hanley, on the
12th of August, 1875
Aged 57 years;
And was Enterred in the Family Vault at Bethesda Chapel,
August 17th, 1875.[37]

Francis Clementson's widow, Calista Ann, returned to live in New Brunswick. She died there in 1885, and is buried in Fernhill Cemetery, Saint John.[38]

The Clementson china shop in Saint John remained in business until almost the end of the century. In 1891 it was 'the oldest house in its line . . . in the city'. Its record was said to have been one of 'continued and honorable success'. Francis Clementson, the son of a British potter, had established an outlet for his father's and brothers' wares that became known 'over the Dominion'.[39]

Outside the Maritimes there were other dealers who imported Clementson products direct—there was at one time a Clementson pattern room in Montreal,[40] and the Quebec crockery sellers, McCaghey, Dolbec & Co., had their own name added to Clementson wares—but probably none was so effective a Canadian distributor of the 'Ironstone, Whitestone and Earthenware' that poured from the Bell and Phoenix Works in Hanley as the china business that bore the family name. Today both the Bell and the Phoenix potteries in Staffordshire, like the china shop in New Brunswick, have disappeared.

In the 1850's, while Francis Clementson was selling his wares in the Maritime colonies, a member of another English potting family set about gathering in the growing wholesale trade of Upper Canada. This time it was a new crockery warehouse in Toronto and a pottery near Liverpool that were linked in an expanding business. An announcement in the *Globe* on July 3, 1856, told the story:

CROCKERY AND GLASS-WARE
GOODWIN & CO.

From Seacombe Pottery, Liverpool, England, Manufacturers and Importers of Earthenware, Glass, and China, having taken that large Store in Wellington St., opposite the Commercial Bank, for a Wholesale Warehouse are now receiving their goods, which they are prepared to sell lower than any other person in the trade.

The attention of all Dealers is specially directed to the fact of G. & Co.'s being their own manufacturers, and they are thus enabled to offer their goods at such prices as have never been known in Upper Canada.

Toronto, June 30, 1856.

Directories state that it was George Goodwin who was in charge of Goodwin & Co. of Toronto. He was not, actually, a newcomer to Canadian mercantile affairs. Even before the new Toronto warehouse was opened, 'Goodwin Brothers' had been importing 'a well selected Stock' of tablewares to Quebec, where they had established themselves at the beginning of the 1850's. Their advertisements indicated that in Quebec they were operating 'in connection with an extensive manufactory in England',[41] and the *Supplement to the Canada Directory*, published in 1853, identified that manufactory as the 'Seacombe Pottery, Liverpool'. In opening a branch in Upper Canada (while still maintaining their Quebec outlet), Goodwin Brothers were following the trend of the day. The upper province promised a rapidly growing market. Many merchants in Lower Canada were not only anxious to have a share in it, but believed it wise to be on the spot to seize every advantage.

The expansion of Canadian business came at a time when the Seacombe Pottery was on the crest of success. J. Goodwin had founded a pottery in Staffordshire, in the 1840's, but at the beginning of the 1850's he had made the decision to remove to Seacombe, on the opposite side of the Mersey from Liverpool. Joseph Mayer, the Liverpool ceramic historian, summed up the advantages of such as move as 'a great saving in carriage, as the raw materials . . . can be laid down on the quay close to the works; and again, when packed and ready for the market, vessels can load in the Great Float at Birkenhead, and at once proceed to sea without re-shipment, as is the case with the Staffordshire ware on its arrival at Runcorn.'[42] Clearly Goodwin anticipated a growing export trade, and the Canadian advertisements bear this out.

The export side of Goodwin's business was stressed by Mayer, who pointed out that he shipped goods to 'the east and west coast of South America, Turkey, California, and India',[43] but Mayer made no mention of Canada. Yet it was in Canada that at one time a Goodwin was resident in order to direct the operations of not one but two distributing centres.

Although writing in some detail of Goodwin's activities, Mayer gave him no first name or even a distinguishing initial. Subsequent ceramic historians who have mentioned Goodwin have based their material very largely on Mayer, with the result that he has passed into encylcopedias and histories simply as 'Goodwin'. In Canada, however, Goodwin products which have survived give his mark as:

J. GOODWIN
Seacombe Pottery
LIVERPOOL

The most frequently found examples of his work are printed earthenwares. One pattern that must have had a large sale in Canada, to judge by the amount that has been handed down, featured galloping horses, apparently in a South American setting. It was usually printed in brown, and the backstamp gives the pattern name as 'Lasso' (*Plate* 2B).

In its day the Seacombe Pottery was considered a model, so that manufacturers came from France and Germany to inspect it, admiring its lay-out and its new machinery for speeding up production. For a time everything seems to have prospered, but by the 1870's the factory was closed.[44] George Goodwin had given up the Toronto warehouse some years before that date.[45] In Quebec, however, the Goodwin name outlasted the pottery itself. The members of the family who had originally come out to Canada returned to England, but the business continued as a china-importing house. The Goodwin connection with the crockery trade of the colonies is another of the little-known and surprisingly close ties between the nineteenth-century potters who produced the wares and those who marketed them in British North America.

One of the most successful of the Canadian china sellers, though having no such family connections with overseas potters, was himself a direct link with a vividly picturesque figure in Scottish ceramic history. Robert Anderson of Montreal ultimately became a millionaire. The man who trained him for the work of china-selling, starting him on the way to fabulous riches, was none other than John Geddes, the potter of Finnieston.

The historian of the Scottish potteries, Arnold Fleming, has described Geddes as tall and handsome but with an unfortunate nose that was the delight of the caricaturist. He liked to be addressed as 'Colonel', and when he rode at the head of the Anderston Volunteers, whom he raised in 1803, and who were dubbed 'the Anderston Sweeps' (because of their black uniform) he was a never-to-be-forgotten figure.[46] Mounted on a coal-black charger and wearing a large cocked hat with flowing plumes, he was a glorious spectacle. Blind Alick, a Glasgow character, who was himself immortalized in pottery, described him as vividly as anyone blessed with sight:

> Like the fiery God of War
> Colonel Geddes does advance
> On a black Arab that belonged
> To the murdered King of France.[47]

This imposing man was well-educated, quick-tempered, and generous at heart. In his business outlook he was far in advance of his time. After he acquired the Verreville Pottery, at Finnieston, then outside Glasgow—a pottery that would later belong to Robert Cochran, who sent agents to Canada—Geddes set up a technical school for his workers. Visitors from England were deeply impressed by the rapid progress made at Verreville under Geddes' direction. And not only did he make progress in the manufacture of earthenware and porcelain, he also built up a distributing system that pushed sales ahead. His wares were sold in quantity on both sides of the Atlantic.[48]

It was under this remarkable man that Robert Anderson, the young son of Archibald Anderson, the Laird of Bloward Hill, began his training in the china business. Undoubtedly Anderson early noted the extent of the orders that came to Verreville from North America, but he could hardly have foreseen in those years that he himself would one day be on the way to millions by the sale of British tablewares in the colony of Canada. In time Robert Anderson rose to be head of sales for the Verreville Pottery in the Glasgow area; later, when Geddes opened a warehouse in Belfast, he took charge of it. But changes came in the firm. Geddes sold out his interests, and Anderson began to be uneasy about his future. He decided to strike out on his own. For a brief period he tried crockery-selling in Galway (surely not too hopeful a field for a man with large ambitions). Then he emigrated.[49]

A Wedgwood in Montreal and Other Unexpected Links

When he arrived in Montreal in 1840, Robert Anderson was thirty-nine, with his fortune still to make. The only business he knew was china-selling, but in that his training had come from a man who knew both how to make and how to sell earthenware and porcelain. It must have been with considerable confidence, if not with an equal amount of capital, that he opened a china, glass, and earthenware store near the Old Market, not far from the address that had once been Joseph Wedgwood's.

The outcome of Anderson's story was to be very different from that of Joseph Wedgwood, and successful beyond anything that Francis Clementson achieved in the way of personal fortune. With Scottish shrewdness, however, he began with sturdy, sensible wares for which there was always a demand. An advertisement in the *Montreal Transcript* (October 24, 1844) gives a glimpse of his stock:

EARTHENWARE
200 Crates and Hhds, consisting of
Black Teapots, White Chambers,
Dipt Bowls, Pitchers, Blue Edge
Plates, Twifflers, Muffins,
Yellow Bakers, White Soup
Twifflers, Irish size Coffee
Cups and Saucers, Painted Lon-
don Teas, &c. &c. . . .
For sale at low prices by
ROBERT ANDERSON

From the very first Anderson believed in advertising, in French as well as English, and in newspapers outside Montreal as well as in every one published in the city. Low prices and bargain sales kept stock moving. He never forsook the inexpensive utilitarian wares — the dipt bowls, sponged cups and saucers, goods 'Suitable for the Country Trade'—but he was very soon catering also to buyers who wanted 'Rich Gilt Tea and Coffee Setts' and 'Vases en Porcelaine pour Corniches'. He imported every article made by the potter: tableware in every form and quality, toilet ware, stone spirit bottles, ornamental figures, sick feeders, toy tea sets, foot baths, carpet bowls (the 'marbles' of a *Gazette* advertisement of 1845),[50] closet basins and cream crocks and clay pipes by the thousand. He advertised 'A MILLION PIECES . . . FOR SALE AT LOW PRICES'[51] and kept on hand six hundred crates and hogsheads ready to be shipped wholesale at a moment's notice.[52]

As might be expected, Robert Anderson, although he brought with him no family connections with a Scottish china firm, had close ties with the pottery where he had been trained under John Geddes. In 1847 Verreville came into the ownership of Robert Cochran. Cochran was alert to the value of the Canadian market, and it is virtually certain that much of the earthenware and porcelain that came to Anderson in these years from Glasgow was of Verreville production. During every shipping season the lists of importations published in Montreal newspapers were dotted with Glasgow arrivals for Robert Anderson: there were ten crates by the *Lady Charlotte Guest* in 1841,[53] a hundred crates by the *Erro-*

manga in 1845,[54] eighty-nine crates by the *Caledonia* in 1850.[55] By the brig *Favourite*, owned by the Allans, there were hundreds of boxes of 'Scottish clays'.[56] In less than a decade Robert Anderson's money would be backing the Allans to found a line of steamships,[57] but in the 1840's and 1850's he was building his fortune on the products of the potter. Like every other china merchant of the day, he handled Staffordshire wares; but, in greater quantities than most, he imported from Glasgow.

From the time that he opened his shop on St. Paul Street at the beginning of the 1840's, Robert Anderson never looked back. Tea sets and soup twifflers and tobacco pipes gave him the start that enabled him to retire in 1854.[58] That year he sold his china business on St. Paul Street to James Thomson and William Minchin, and turned from tea cups to bank stocks. John Geddes had trained him for success. From him Anderson had learned to know his wares and how to sell them. For fourteen years in Montreal he had sold crockery to such advantage that never again would he have to deal in any merchandise. In the future he was to be occupied only with the world of investment and finance. Ahead, for this ambitious Scot, who 'carefully nursed' his profits from china-selling,[59] who never married, and who always lived unostentatiously, lay directorships in insurance, shipping, and paper companies, and the vice-presidency of a bank.

When Robert Anderson died in Montreal, on March 24, 1896, at the age of nearly ninety-five, he left behind him a fortune estimated by the *Gazette* at something between one and a half and two million dollars,[60] and that with the buying power of the Victorian dollar. His long obituary notice, the day after his death, put particular emphasis upon his start in the crockery business and the extraordinary success that made him one of the richest men in the Dominion.

Anderson's name was linked with that of his old master, John Geddes, in that final appearance in the *Gazette* of one who had often advertised tablewares in its columns. On the day of the funeral, the board of directors of the Merchants Bank of Canada summed up the qualities which the members felt characterized their late vice-president: constant attention to business concerns, vigilant watchfulness at every turn, judgment that was sound, and the ability to stand fast when times were bad. They were the very qualities that had raised John Geddes himself from the status of employee at Verreville to that of forward-looking pottery owner; they were the qualities that had made his pupil a millionaire in the New World.

Many in nineteenth-century Canada earned a living by selling crockery. A small band of china merchants, however, came to this country with direct personal links with British potteries. Some of them, like Joseph Wedgwood and Francis Clementson, bore famous names; some, like Robert Anderson, owed an unmatched knowledge of selling crockery to men who made it. To the trade of the colonies they brought traditions that must always set them apart in interest.

CHAPTER VII

Canadian China Dealers' Marks
on Imported Wares

RENDRE LE PEUPLE MEILLEUR.
French-Canadian slogan and dealer's mark on English
wares made for McCaghey, Dolbec & Co., Quebec.

In the nineteenth century, some Canadian china merchants ordered their own names printed on the back of the wares they sold. These articles, marked with their names, and often with the names of the Canadian cities where they carried on business, were imported from overseas suppliers. The marking was done at the factory where the wares were made.

Today pieces that can be identified with a particular china seller have taken on added interest. As a record of the dealer's enterprise, they are tangible evidence of the types of ware and patterns that once stocked his shop. A Canadian dealer's mark may now recall that a blue-printed plate was once displayed in a china, glass, and earthenware store near the Old Market in Montreal, in the days of King William IV. An earthenware coffee pot becomes more meaningful when it is associated with a china shop that brought the carriages of the fashionable to Palace Street, in Quebec, when Queen Victoria was young. A painted sugar bowl moves into historical perspective when it is taken back in time to a King Street crockery house in Toronto, whose proprietor made sales to Princess Louise.

Pieces of old china bearing the names of the dealers who imported them are valuable guides in dating shapes and styles popular with Canadians of the past. With such pieces there is no need to speculate on the circumstances that brought them to Canada, perhaps at a date long after they were produced. Here are wares 'imported expressly for the trade of this country', and sold in Canada when they were new.

Earthenware or porcelain marked with a nineteenth-century dealer's mark and belonging to the first half or three-quarters of the century is, however, relatively scarce. Only a few of the many who hopefully established china warehouses in the colonies had bedroom crockery and tablewares identified with their names; of these dealers, some had their names added only to pieces in certain patterns. On the other hand, this is a field where new information frequently turns up, and where there is always a possibility of discovery.

One of the earliest and one of the most interesting of the Canadian dealers whose marks have been found on imported tablewares was Joseph Shuter (1782-1864)[1], an Englishman who came to Montreal at the end of the eighteenth century. He was only a boy in his teens when he arrived in Canada with his elder brother, John. When he died, at the age of eighty-two, he left a fortune behind him and property holdings throughout the province. The foundations of his highly successful business career were built on china.

As a china merchant Joseph Shuter was unique. Not only did he become one of the biggest dealers in the country, importing on a tremendous scale for both Upper and Lower Canada; the china, glass, and earthenware business he founded, though no longer bearing his name, is still in existence today. Montrealers have known it for a century as 'Cassidy's', but Cassidy's as a china business can be traced back directly, through the various firms which preceded it, to Joseph Shuter, the merchant whose name lived on for years in Shuter Street.[2]

On tablewares Joseph Shuter's name is recorded with that of his business partners. Robert Charles Wilkins was his first partner, and the mark Shuter used when in partnership with him appears on the bottom of pieces of tea and dinner ware as:

SHUTER & WILKINS
MONTREAL

Pieces that may in date be ascribed to about 1830 have been noted with this printed mark. It cannot be later than 1836.

Joseph Shuter's first experience with china-selling must have been in the 1790's. At that time, when he was little more than a boy, he probably worked for his brother at the latter's 'commission and vendue store'. Porcelain and earthenware were among the goods John Shuter sold from an address almost opposite the building Cassidy's owns today on St. Paul Street. A *Gazette* advertisement of November 14, 1796, gives both John Shuter's address and some idea of a part of his varied stock. 'John Shuter . . . has for sale at his Store No 114 St. Pauls street opposite the Hospital church a large and general assortment of China, Glass and Earthen Ware which he will sell on the lowest terms for cash.'

John Shuter was able to retire in 1815,[3] going to England to live two years later.[4] On his own, Joseph progressed eventually to business interests on a far wider scale than John had known. Joseph's business was, however, seriously interrupted by the War of 1812. At that time he joined the militia, actively recruiting volunteers, and taking part himself in the defeat of the Americans at Châteauguay in 1813. The next year he was with the British forces defeated in their turn at Plattsburg. But when peace was concluded at the end of 1814, Joseph Shuter once more gave wholehearted attention to mercantile affairs. It is following the war years that he emerges as a china merchant.

John Shuter had dealt in china as part of a general business, but Joseph Shuter, while dealing in a stock almost as varied as John's, came to be known for his china. In Montreal's first directory, published in 1819, Joseph Shuter and Robert Charles Wilkins are listed as 'china merchants'.[5] Theirs was one of only two such listings, although a number of merchants were selling china in Montreal at that time, as John Shuter had done in his day.

The partnership between Joseph Shuter and Robert Charles Wilkins, entered into in the early years of the century, lasted until May 1, 1836. It was then dissolved 'by mutual consent'.[6] To wind up the affairs of Shuter & Wilkins a public auction was held of all their stock-in-trade. The sale took place on May 9, 1836; and it was a big one, for the firm had imported heavily throughout the years. It had not been unusual, for instance, to find Shuter & Wilkins advertising importations of 1,000, 1,200, 1,500 packages of china, glass, and earthenware at a time.[7] When the final selling-off came there were 1,000 lots of crockery alone to be put up, including 'splendid China Dinner and Dessert Setts, also China Tea Setts, China Ornaments, &c. &c.'[8]

Though a certain amount of the multitude of wares imported by Shuter & Wilkins must have survived, only rarely is a piece found today with the firm's name, and such pieces as have turned up belong to the closing years of the partnership. This would seem to indicate that Shuter & Wilkins ordered their mark printed on only some of the 'beautiful China Desert Setts, and China Glazed Blue Printed Dinner . . . Services' that were 'selected in England by one of the firm'.[9] It may indicate, too, that the practice was not adopted at all until the 1830's.

But even before the stock of the old firm of Shuter & Wilkins had been disposed of, Joseph Shuter had entered into a new alliance to sell china. The successors to Shuter & Wilkins were Shuter & Glennon. In an announcement dated May 7, 1836, Joseph Shuter informed the public that he had taken 'Mr. JOHN GLENNON, of this city, Merchant, a Partner', and their business would be 'carried on in the name of SHUTER & GLENNON, at the same Old Stand'.[10]

The mark that appeared on wares sold during the partnership of Shuter & Glennon is in date 1836-42. It was printed within a wreath on the bottom of the pieces:

SHUTER & GLENNON

MONTREAL

Joseph Shuter was the senior partner, as he had been in the partnership of Shuter & Wilkins. An error, however, was made by at least one of the firm's suppliers in Staffordshire. The mark has also been noted as GLENNON & SHUTER (on an earthenware vegetable dish printed in pink with a European scene).

By 1842 Joseph Shuter was a very rich man, with a large estate on Sherbrooke Street. His business interests now extended into many fields. Although he would retain some financial interest in china-selling for a few years yet, his active days as a merchant were over. On May 17, 1842, the *Montreal Gazette* carried the notice of the 'dissolution' of partnership between Joseph Shuter and John Glennon.

For over a quarter of a century, Joseph Shuter's name had been connected with the china and earthenware trade in Montreal. With first one partner and then another he had been responsible for importing thousands upon thousands of crates and hogsheads from Staffordshire. Much of what he brought into the colony was 'Common Crockery . . . for the country', but much that he also sold from St. Paul Street was 'of the most elegant China, richly gilded'.[11] His own tablewares belonged in the latter category. Davenport porcelain at its most opulent was what Joseph Shuter, the china merchant, chose for himself in his later years. A dozen pieces of a dessert service that he ordered painted with the family crest on the border of each piece are today in the possession of his great-grandson in Montreal.[12] With moulded rims heavily outlined in gold and enamelled in dark green, the pieces are each one handsomely decorated with a different bouquet in the centre, the flowers being those favoured by the Staffordshire ceramic artists of the day: iris, rose, tulip, passion flower, poppy, primula, convolvulus. Joseph Shuter's porcelain of Davenport make was certainly 'elegant China'.

When Joseph Shuter gave up china-selling, his firm was continued by his partner, John Glennon. Glennon in his turn took a partner named Bramley. The same issue of the *Gazette* that made public the end of Shuter & Glennon carried the announcement of their successors, Glennon & Bramley:

THE undersigned have formed a connection under the firm of GLENNON & BRAMLEY and have now, and daily expect a further supply of CHINA, GLASS and EARTHEN-WARE, in the premises heretofore occupied by SHUTER & GLENNON.

J. GLENNON
C. C. BRAMLEY.

John Glennon and C. C. Bramley were in business together from 1842 until 1847, or the early part of 1848. They remained at the 'Old Stand' on St. Paul Street during these years, and they continued the practice of having the firm's name printed on wares they sold. A sugar bowl, in flowing blue, has their mark, again printed within a wreath:

GLENNON & BRAMLEY
MONTREAL

In the early years, wares with a Canadian china dealer's mark did not usually carry the maker's identification as well, but at least one of the Staffordshire suppliers of Glennon & Bramley is known. In an old ledger, preserved today in the City Museum and Art Gallery of Stoke-on-Trent, Staffordshire, is an entry for April 12, 1847. On that day was dispatched pottery to the value of £8. 1s. 10d. to 'Messrs. Glennon & Bramley, Montreal, Canada'. The potter whose long-closed accounts contain this record of Canadian trade was John Wood, of Brownhills, a distant cousin of the more famous Enoch Wood.[13]

Before he joined Joseph Shuter in 1836, John Glennon had been in the china business on his own account. An advertisement in the *Montreal Gazette* on October 8, 1829, announced the opening of his shop:

CHINA, GLASS & EARTHENWARE

—No. 65, *St. Paul Street*.—The Subscriber has opened, opposite Messrs. JONES & SMITH, where he will always keep on hand a general assortment of articles in the above line, (Wholesale and Retail,) which will be disposed of on as reasonable terms as any other house in the trade.

J. GLENNON.
Montreal, October 8, 1829.

Glennon had continued on his own account until he joined Shuter. Later, after his partnership with C. C. Bramley was dissolved, he again carried on alone

92

for a period of about two years.[14] In 1850 he re-organized the old china business that had once been Joseph Shuter's firm as John Glennon & Co. From 1848 to 1850, and again from 1850 to 1857, when he was operating under his own name, Glennon sold wares carrying the dealer's mark printed within a wreath, but with the wording changed from 'Glennon & Bramley' to:

GLENNON
MONTREAL

(or)

GLENNON & CO.
MONTREAL

The next phase of this historic china-selling story began on May 11, 1857. On that day, according to an almost forgotten Montreal newspaper, the *Argus*, the old china, glass, and earthenware house opened its doors to the public under yet another management. Renaud, Prieur & Co. were the new owners, and the *Argus* carried their invitation to prospective customers on May 12:

CROCKERY
Messrs. RENAUD, PRIEUR & CO.,
(SUCCESSORS TO MESSRS. GLENNON & Co.)

... invite their friends, and among others the Country Merchants, to favor them by visiting their establishment, where they will find articles combining elegance and good taste ... at very low prices. They flatter themselves that all who are good enough to take the trouble of inspecting their assortment which is one of the largest and most varied in North America will be satisfied by the cheapness and novelty of all they see ...

Renaud, Prieur & Co. do not seem to have had a dealer's mark, possibly because the firm stayed in business less than three years. The partners did, however, leave a record of their activities printed on earthenware. In the museum at the Château de Ramezay in Montreal may be seen a small plate, of the kind that china sellers used to distribute as an advertisement. It is a child's plate, printed with a picture and the letters of the alphabet; around the face of the plate, along with the decoration, are the words: 'RENAUD PRIEUR, & Co Importateurs PORCELAINE VERRERIE FAIENCE et autre OBJETS en MÉTAL RUE ST. PAUL MONTREAL'.

This same type of advertising plate is in the collection of the New Brunswick Museum. There it carries the name and address of Francis Clementson, the crockery dealer of Saint John. Similar plates, supplied for advertising purposes by overseas potters to Canadian china sellers, were probably handed out by merchants in other parts of the country.

Directories indicate that two members of the Renaud family, Charles and the better-known Louis, were connected with François Xavier Prieur in the china business taken over from John Glennon.[15] At the beginning of the 1860's Prieur dropped out of the firm, and Hon. Louis Renaud, who had made a fortune in flour and grain, became the senior partner in the firm of 'L. Renaud & Cassidy, (successors to Renaud, Prieur & Co.,) importers of china, glass and earthen-

93

ware'.[16] Again the partnership was brief. In 1865 the Irish Canadian, John L. Cassidy, became the head of 'John L. Cassidy & Co. (late L. Renaud & Cassidy)'.[17] He was now in charge of the china business originally established by Joseph Shuter.

Before the end of the 1860's, Cassidy had decided upon an important move. Across the street was a new commercial building, one of the finest in Victorian Montreal. It was owned by the Sisters of the Hôtel Dieu, and had been put up by them on the site of their original seventeenth-century hospital. Cassidy decided to rent space from the Sisters in the 'Nuns Building'. Back in 1824 Joseph Shuter and Robert Charles Wilkins had advertised that they were selling china 'opposite the Hospital in Saint Paul Street';[18] John L. Cassidy moved the business to the site of the hospital itself. His firm, eventually formed into a joint stock company and incorporated by letters patent in 1896,[19] has remained there ever since.

In 1963 Cassidy's Ltd. (the twentieth-century style of the firm) became the owners of the 'new' building of which the company had been tenants for nearly a hundred years.[20] It was a purchase not only of a building associated with John L. Cassidy himself, but of land granted by Maisonneuve, the founder of Montreal, to Jeanne Mance, and held by the Sisters of the Hôtel Dieu for three hundred years.

To walk past Cassidy's today is to walk back in time in the history of china-selling in Canada. Joseph Shuter and Robert Charles Wilkins, John Glennon and C. C. Bramley, Hon. Louis Renaud and François Xavier Prieur, and, finally, John L. Cassidy are shades of the past that come to life very easily in the area of St. Paul Street that once knew their daily comings and goings in the china business. Theirs is a crockery history that must have few parallels on the North American continent. And it is all the more remarkable for being a history that may be traced nearly all the way in dealers' names on earthenware or porcelain. The missing link lies in the 1860's. Though Renaud, Prieur & Co. may not have had a dealer's mark, they did have their name printed on advertising plates. But no printed mark of any kind has been recorded for L. Renaud & Cassidy. With John L. Cassidy & Co. the printed name on tablewares returned. The mark CASSIDY & CO. on the back of a Worcester porcelain plate made shortly before 1891 takes the history of Joseph Shuter's firm to the last years of the century.

While no other china, glass, and earthenware house in Montreal, and probably no other in Canada, had a history to equal that of the firm organized by Joseph Shuter, and carried into the present century under the name of Cassidy, other nineteenth-century dealers had their printed marks. A mark that belongs to the 1873-93 period is:

DOUGLAS & McNIECE
MONTREAL

This mark, on white ironstone made by T. Furnival & Sons perpetuates an error. The name of the senior partner in this case was John Douglass, and he cannot have been entirely satisfied to have found it misspelled on his orders from Staffordshire. Both John Douglass and James McNiece had had experience in the crockery business before they joined in partnership, their separate firms dating to the 1860's.

A late mark frequently seen, although the company was in existence for only five years, is that of:

BOXER BROS.
AND CO.
MONTREAL

In date, the Boxer Brothers' mark is 1885-90, unless 'Staffordshire Hall' is added to it, in which case it dates from 1886. The mark itself may appear within a garter, within a circle surmounted by a crown, or within some other ornamental device. Sometimes the advertising slogan 'The Latest for Boxer Bros.' accompanies the mark.

In 1885 R. J. Boxer, S. S. Boxer, and T. W. Boxer took over John Watson's long-established crockery business on Grey Nun Street (near the old St. Ann's Market, now known as Place d'Youville). The following year they opened Staffordshire Hall on St. Catherine Street. The Grey Nun Street building was retained as a wholesale warehouse. Four years later, in 1890, the business was given up, but not before a considerable amount of earthenware and porcelain of good quality, marked with the Boxer Brothers' name, had been distributed throughout the province.

One English firm that supplied the Boxers with marked wares was W. Brownfield & Sons, Staffordshire potters capable of such ceramic feats as porcelain vases twelve feet high and majolica fountains as tall as a man.[21] The Boxers also bought from Scottish makers, as is shown by an advertisement in the *Daily Witness* on September 12, 1885:

New Goods just to hand from England and Scotland. Please call and examine our stock and you will find quality of the best and prices very low. We are showing some very handsome patterns in TOILET, DINNER and CHINA TEA SETS.

BOXER BROS. & Co.
Successors to John Watson & Co. . . .

In the Quebec City area, several nineteenth-century china merchants had their own marks. One of the earliest of these was Samuel Alcorn, of Palace Street in the Upper Town. His mark sometimes appears on printed earthenware as:

S. ALCORN
IMPORTER
QUEBEC

In date this mark belongs to the 1830's and 1840's.

Samuel Alcorn was a dealer who conducted business in two ways: on Palace Street, he had a china shop where he sold the latest in ceramic ornaments and the most fashionable patterns in tableware;[22] on the wharf, he held trade sales of common crockery as it was unloaded from the sailing vessels.[23] At the auctions by the ship's side, trade and country buyers bought 'in the package' (crate or hogshead), hoping for bargains while the goods were 'landing'. The wares found

95

today with Alcorn's mark were probably sold originally from Palace Street, where his best-quality wares were displayed to a discriminating clientele.

One of the most elaborate of all the Canadian china dealers' marks belongs to another Quebec firm, McCaghey, Dolbec & Co. John McCaghey and Edouard Dolbec were in business together from the end of 1868 or early part of 1869 until about 1874.[24] The mark they had printed on ironstone wares from Staffordshire incorporated a French-Canadian nationalist slogan, RENDRE LE PEUPLE MEILLEUR, with the Canadian beaver and maple leaves (*Plate* 3A). With this combination of motto and symbols, McCaghey, Dolbec & Co. were appealing to French-Canadian sentiment. This same arrangement of the beaver and maple leaves joined with 'Rendre le Peuple Meilleur' had been adopted by French-Canadian nationalists some years before. It appeared, for example, on the masthead of the Montreal newspaper *La Revue Canadienne*, in the 1840's.[25] St. Jean Baptiste societies made use of it in their celebrations.[26] It was a motto and device well known to a buying public, and McCaghey, Dolbec & Co. turned it to their advantage by having their own names and the words IMPORTERS and QUEBEC added to it. One English firm that supplied them with tablewares bearing this mark with French-Canadian appeal was Clementson Brothers, of Hanley (the sons of Joseph Clementson, who had taken over their father's potteries in 1867).

Before he joined forces with Edouard Dolbec, John McCaghey had operated a crockery and lamp store in the Upper Town of Quebec, but a fire, thought to have been set by burglars, gutted his premises in the early morning hours of April 13, 1867.[27] Insured for only about one-third of his stock, John McCaghey was hard hit. When he re-opened, it was with Edouard Dolbec as a partner. Together they bought out Henry Goodwin's crockery business in the Lower Town. For about five years McCaghey, Dolbec & Co. continued in partnership. At the end of that period the company, with its ornate dealer's mark, dropped out of the directories. A new china merchant, soon to be one of the best known in the province, hung out his sign on the store in the Lower Town.

Francis Thomas spent his first year or two as a 'commission merchant and crockery importer' in the store that had formerly known McCaghey, Dolbec & Co. After that he moved to larger quarters. His dealer's mark, F. T. THOMAS and QUEBEC, cannot be earlier than 1874.[28] Under the style of F. T. Thomas, the firm continued until almost the end of the century (it was being operated as 'the Estate of F. T. Thomas' in 1897).[29] In the twentieth century it became The Thomas Company, Limited.[30] During his career as a china merchant, Francis Thomas handled not only imported wares but also locally made crocks and pots; and at times he described himself as a 'manufacturer' of these goods (indicating a financial interest in a local concern). Almost from the beginning he was a success. In January, 1881, when he had been in business for only six years, the *Mercantile Agency Reference Book* gave him a credit rating of 'Good' and estimated his capital at $10,000-$20,000. This early rating placed him on a par with many much longer-established china merchants throughout the Dominion. In volume of business his firm was to rise quickly.

Francis Thomas imported on a large scale, but he confined his own printed mark to a limited range of patterns. Chief among the wares that bore his name were products of a Scottish pottery, printed with views of Quebec and its vicinity.[31] As these wares were imported in fairly large quantities and are late in date (the Quebec views were still being made for the Thomas Company in the twentieth century), a number of specimens have survived. This fact, added to the special interest now felt by collectors in Canadian views, even those on earthenware relatively modern in date of production, have made the Thomas mark better known today than that of any other Quebec china merchant of the nineteenth century.

As was the case with Montreal and Quebec dealers, Toronto china sellers had their own printed marks. One of these recalls both the days of Victorian crockery and the time of volunteer fire brigades. James Jackson was a King Street merchant known alike for his china and his fire-fighting. 'The Jackson Hose' was his volunteer company,[32] Jackson's Crockery Store his business. The period of his activity as a merchant began in the early 1850's. By 1868 he was gone from the directories. His mark, printed within a wreath of berries was:

J. JACKSON
IMPORTER
TORONTO

This mark has been found in two forms. One is evidence of somebody's inability to spell. On the bottom of a sugar bowl, with a transfer printed pattern in blue, the word IMPORTER appears incorrectly as IMPORTOR (*Plate* 3B). Jackson must have complained. A small plate has this same printed mark, with a correction. The second 'o' in the misspelled IMPORTOR has been obviously and awkwardly converted into an 'E' in the original stamp.

In the Toronto Board of Trade's annual report for 1860, James Jackson was listed among the 'principal dealers' of the city in the crockery line. He was a merchant who dealt direct with Staffordshire, generally ignoring the trade sales of Montreal. An advertisement in *Brown's Toronto General Directory, 1856* gives an idea of his way of business:

J. JACKSON,
No 3, KING STREET WEST,
TORONTO . . .
IMPORTER OF
EVERY DESCRIPTION OF
CHINA, GLASS, & EARTHENWARE,
WHICH HE IS PREPARED TO FURNISH . . .
At such prices as cannot fail to give satisfaction.
ASSORTED CRATES KEPT CONSTANTLY ON HAND.
Every description of Ware imported to order direct from the Manufacturers.

One of the best known today of the nineteenth-century Toronto china merchants was another King Street dealer, Glover Harrison, from the west of Ireland. The Queen's daughter made purchases from him, and his China Hall through forty years commanded 'the best patronage of the city and surrounding country'.[33]

97

Marks containing Harrison's name, or the name of China Hall on King Street, span the years from the mid-1860's until the close of the century. The actual number on King Street, which generally appears in the mark, is a clue to dating. For about fourteen years, from the autumn of 1866 until the end of the 1870's, Glover Harrison was at 71-73 King Street East. At the beginning of the 1880's his number was 49 King Street East.[34] This was the address of China Hall until 1899, although Glover Harrison had died some years before. By the end of the 1880's, the business was being managed for the 'Estate of Glover Harrison'. When the estate was settled, Joseph Irving became the new proprietor, and in 1900 he moved China Hall to Yonge Street.[35]

In the 1860's and 1870's, Glover Harrison advertised that the 'Big Jug' was the registered sign of China Hall.[36] This sign appears in a mark printed in blue on white ironstone imported by him. The jug is to the left in the mark; on the right is his name and address.

Another mark, belonging to the later years, when China Hall was at 49 King Street East, occurs on porcelain made in France. This mark is printed in red within a shield:

CHINA HALL
49 King St. East
TORONTO

In view of the reputation that China Hall in Toronto acquired in its own day, it is surprising to learn, from *Mercantile Agency Reference Books*, that Glover Harrison never commanded the capital that backed some of the other well-known china merchants of the period;[37] yet his China Hall, widely advertised and widely known, must be ranked as one of the most important Canadian china houses of the last century. From Glover Harrison, Canadians learned about new wares and new fashions. Belleek, the Irish porcelain, was sponsored by him when it was new on the market. Behind his much-admired show windows Copeland, Derby, Royal Worcester, and Wedgwood tablewares shared space with the finest Parian ornaments of the day.[38] To select these wares, and others from continental potters, Glover Harrison made personal buying trips abroad. His enterprise in this regard was highly commended by contemporaries, who credited him with 'educating' the taste of Toronto.[39]

At the Industrial Exhibition of 1879, Glover Harrison's spectacular ceramic display caught the eye of Princess Louise. The *Mail* reported (on September 12) that the royal visitor 'minutely inspected' his exhibit, and ordered from him a set of ironstone jugs of antique form. This Irish china merchant was perhaps one of very few persons ever to set Queen Victoria's daughter right on her facts. When the Princess, generally exceedingly well informed on most subjects, asked Glover Harrison if seaweed was not considered the most satisfactory packing for china, he gave her a firm denial. Straw, he told her, was always used by the best English houses.

A growing interest in dealers' marks on earthenware and porcelain will bring others to light. Joseph Shuter's Montreal marks are known, but did he have a different mark for the wares sold in Upper Canada in the 1830's, when Shuter &

Paterson was his Toronto outlet ? Is there a mark to be discovered for L. Renaud & Cassidy to complete the story of that historic firm ? How many of the Maritime china sellers of colonial days had their own names added to imported wares ? Shortly after Confederation the Halifax firm of J. R. Jennett & Co. sold tablewares 'manufactured expressly' for them by E. F. Bodley & Co. in Staffordshire, a fact indicated by a printed mark; but is the pre-Confederation record of this firm, when it was Jennett & Taylor, also to be traced on cups from Staffordshire ? How many Victorian china merchants advertised themselves on free samples ?

The field of dealers' marks is one of the most rewarding for research in the history of nineteenth-century pottery and porcelain in Canada. Such marks serve three important historical purposes: they throw light on the dealings of the china merchants; they are an unusually reliable guide to wares actually used in Canada —on dining table, drawing room whatnot, or bedroom wash-stand; and, since these marks can generally be dated with precision, they are accurate evidence of the periods when such wares were new furnishings for Canadian homes.

The Earthenwares

The Earthworms

CHAPTER VIII

The Wedgwood Tradition in Canada

GEORGE BROWNE ... HAS FOR SALE ... Wedgwood's finest cream-coloured
Earthen Ware, in crates each containing a complete dinner-service.
Quebec Mercury, Jan. 7, 1811.

Canadian china merchants of the first half of the nineteenth century were more concerned with the elegance and newness of their wares than with the names of the potters who produced them. That their customers, too, attached more importance to 'the best patterns, newest shapes' than they did to knowing what firm had made them may be deduced from the fact that merchants rarely felt it necessary to include this information in advertising.

In the second half of the century, although identification of earthenware and porcelain by factory became more frequent, especially in the last years, the newspapers continue to show that with the Canadian china buyer of Victorian days novelty and fashion still had greater promotional value than a potter's name. In a typical advertisement of 1865, John Patton, of Montreal, offered china that was 'new and peculiar'.[1] He was using 'peculiar' as the Victorians commonly used it, in the Biblical sense, meaning distinctive or unusual; and it took him a quarter of a column to list his first-class wares of this type. He went into details about the latest styles in 'Lava' and 'Terra Cotta'; he specified new models in Parian ornaments; and he cited a wide choice in English and French table sets. But John Patton did not identify one maker of his fashionable wares.

In 1881 Edward Hagar, another Montreal china merchant, announced in the *Daily Witness* that he had received a handsome assortment of goods by the steamship *Peruvian*. He tempted the public with 'New Colors! New Shapes! New Designs!'[2] Yet he said not a word about who had turned out such saleable articles. It was obvious that when Hagar had come to draft an advertisement for the new shipment he had ranked novelty a better drawing card than a name.

Patton's and Hagar's announcements were characteristic of the vast majority. In the advertising of the day, makers of stoves were more often identified than makers of tea sets. Furniture makers, particularly Canadian and American, were frequently indicated. Shoe blacking, spermaceti candles, and castor oil were promoted by maker's name. But the best of English china and the finest of earthenware were generally advertised in Canadian newspapers under a cloak of anonymity and disguised by novelty.

103

Even when an agent was appointed to represent a particular potter, he might advertise for orders without a hint of whose wares he was pushing. Thomas Heaven did this in 1828, as the *Montreal Gazette* of June 16 shows:

> THE Subscriber having been appointed AGENT in CANADA, for an extensive CROCK-ERY MANUFACTORY in ENGLAND begs to announce, that he has just opened a crate of *patterns,* to which he invites the attention of dealers, as he is now ready to take orders for any quantity.
>
> THOMAS HEAVEN.

Thomas Heaven's mode of advertising was in no way unusual. He was a merchant active in Lower Canada over many years, who understood the business of selling and carried it on with profit.

There were, of course, exceptions to what was almost a rule. And the most consistent exception was the name of Wedgwood. Even in the earliest years, when identification of tablewares with their actual makers was very rare in Canadian advertising, Wedgwood products were repeatedly mentioned in the newspapers. A Halifax paper, for example, referred to 'Wedgwood's Ware' in an advertisement at the end of the eighteenth century.[3] Quebec advertising specified 'Wedgewood' in 1802.[4] The next year 'A table service of Wedgwood' was featured in the *Montreal Gazette.*[5] In Saint John, in 1811, an advertisement offered Wedgwood in New Brunswick.[6] A garrison officer leaving Canada in 1817, and another in 1850, instructed auctioneers to advertise their Wedgwood.[7]

It would, in fact, be literally true to say that nineteenth-century crockery advertising began and ended with Wedgwood, for Henry Morgan & Co. brought 1899 to a close with an advertisement inviting Montrealers to view 'choice sets' of Wedgwood in their 'Ladies' Parlor'.[8] Misspelled Wedgwood might be more often than not through the hundred years; what is significant is the astonishing frequency of the name in print.

The fact that auctioneers and merchants particularized Wedgwood in this remarkable way does not mean that the Wedgwood factory was the biggest exporter to Canada. Some Staffordshire and Glasgow firms specializing in the cheap, durable ironstones, for which there was an obvious need in a pioneer country, probably sent more crockery to Canada than the factory at Etruria ever did. During many years Wedgwood produced no porcelain,[9] and this at a time when Canadian advertising stressed 'superior china, richly gilt' as the height of sophisticated taste. The frequent mention of Wedgwood wares cannot be accounted for by the size of the factory's exports, large as they must have been; rather it is an indication that the name meant something to Canadians. Montreal's oldest newspaper offering 'a handsome set of Wedgwood ware' together with a 'calash' and a 'horse chair', at an 1808 auction sale,[10] is in itself a tribute to a potter who strove for 'something new . . . to give a little spirit to the business'.[11]

One of the new wares with which the first Josiah Wedgwood (1730-95) gave 'spirit' not only to his own business, but to the whole history of English potting, was an earthenware that formed a staple of Canadian trade from the latter part of the eighteenth century. The perfected earthenware body that was known as cream-coloured ware, the 'C C' and 'Queen's Ware' of Canadian advertising, was Josiah Wedgwood's most important contribution to English commerce (*Plate* 4A). When Queen Charlotte, wife of King George III, became a user of it, Wedgwood began calling his cream-coloured product 'Queen's ware', and this name was taken up by other potters. In the Canadian advertising of the day, Queensware, spelled in a variety of ways, became synonymous with 'cream-coloured earthenware', regardless of the maker.

Wedgwood did not invent English cream-coloured earthenware: what he did was to take an existing body and to make of it something lighter in colour, more refined and elegant, more perfectly potted, more evenly glazed, more fashionably decorated than had been known before. Where he led others hurried after. Soon English cream-coloured tablewares were competing successfully for markets once almost exclusively the property of oriental and continental potters.

Wedgwood's creamware made its appearance about 1763; by 1799 this thoroughly English contribution to ceramic history had gained such ground that a French scholar, Faujas de St. Fond, professor of geology at the Museum of Natural History in Paris, made the observation: 'in travelling from Paris to Petersburg, from Amsterdam to the furthest part of Sweden, and from Dunkirk to the extremity of the South of France, one is served at every inn with English ware.'[12]

The 'English ware' of which Faujas de St. Fond spoke was not all from the Wedgwood factory (by this time under the management of Josiah Wedgwood's heirs), but it was the same cream-coloured earthenware that owed its popularity to the first Josiah Wedgwood's efforts. It had all but driven imported French earthenware from the English market, and had pursued it into its own territory. It had cut tellingly into the sales of continental porcelain. It had threatened continental faience (earthenware) of every kind. In self-defence, the potters of Europe began to make the English-type cream-coloured body for themselves.

At home the perfected creamware, lead-glazed, dealt a death blow to the older, tin-glazed earthenware potted at a number of places and known as delft. It put an end to the production of the salt-glazed stone ware, 'rejected from genteel tables'[13] in favour of the new product. The mottled or 'tortoise-shell' ware, introduced by Thomas Whieldon about 1750 and made by others, including Wedgwood himself, eventually gave way to the sweeping fashion for tablewares that were light cream in colour, and sophisticated and practical at the same time.

All these older products had once been important in the small Canadian market of the eighteenth century, and although both delft and white stone (as the salt-glazed ware was often called) held out perhaps longer in the colonies than at home,[14] the story in North America was the same as in Great Britain: the creamware that owed its position to Josiah Wedgwood became, in the end, the common ware of the British settlements overseas.

Advertisements in the first Canadian newspapers give evidence of the gradual taking over of the market by creamware. Delft and white stone predominated in the first years; tortoise-shell had its place; the old redware teapots, made but not admired by Josiah Wedgwood,[15] were an important selling item, but, bit by bit, the creamwares came crowding in. The *Quebec Gazette* of June 22, 1769, illustrates this in a significant advertisement, one that foreshadows the importance of cream-coloured earthenware and at the same time indicates that the Canadian market, only a few years after the conquest, was supplied with the popular English wares of the day:

Just imported, and to be Sold by Wholesale and Retail
by GEORGE KING, *in Palace-Street,*

. . . Stone Tea Toys, fine Cream colour'd and Tortoise Shell Ditto . . . enamel'd Stone Tea-Pots, painted and enamel'd Cream colour'd Ditto, fine red China Ditto, large and small Stone Dishes, Ditto flat and Soup Plates, Breakfast Ditto, painted and white Stone Bowls, Ditto Wash-hand Basons, Ditto Decanters, Ditto small Bowls and Saucers, Butter-Tubs and Stands . . .

In Fredericton, in the spring of 1790, delft, salt-glazed ware, and Queensware were all offered by the same dealer.[16] But the time was fast coming to an end when the older bodies, less practical in use and more capricious in the kiln, could make any pretence of holding their own with what a contemporary writer described as 'a firm and durable body . . . manufactured with ease and expedition'.[17] With the new century creamware won the day completely. Virtually unchallenged by any other earthenware for the table, it dominated the Canadian market until it was its turn to share popularity with the newer printed earthenware and ironstone china.

The decoration of the early creamware exported to Canada was often of the simplest: 'a blue line varnished',[18] a green-painted line, or a brown edge. When dealers like Martin Chinic, of Quebec, advertised 'a few crates of blue and green edge table services of Wedgewood',[19] it was cream-coloured or 'Queen's ware' that was being offered.

Martin Chinic, in 1802, specified Wedgwood; a surprising number of other merchants did the same. Much Wedgwood, however, must have been sold in Canada in the usual way, without identification and in odd company. There is no way now of telling whose Queensware was being auctioned by James Dunlop in Montreal in 1804. His advertisement in the *Gazette* merely stated that he would sell '2 hhds. Queens-Ware Soup Plates, 63 doz. each' on October 23. Unidentified, this creamware was to take its place on the auction block with baskets of English cheese, cases of Havana sugar, and puncheons of Jamaica rum.[20]

When the 60th Regiment of Foot was withdrawn from the garrison in Montreal, in 1797, the tablewares used in the mess were disposed of at public sale. The *Gazette* advertised the auction on June 26, but described the crockery only as 'Queen's Ware Dishes, Flat and Soup Plates'. They may have been Wedgwood dishes; they may have been from one of a number of other makers of cream-coloured earthenware at this period.

While the kind of 'Queen's Ware' the 60th Regiment dined off in Canada remains a matter for speculation, what set the tables for the officers of the Royal Fusiliers is known: it was Wedgwood. In August of 1791 the 7th Regiment of Foot (Royal Fusiliers) marched ashore at Quebec. The commander was H. R. H. Prince Edward, later Duke of Kent and the father of Queen Victoria. Soon after the Prince's regiment had settled into its quarters, the crates of earthenware, ordered from the Wedgwood showrooms in London, were unpacked and their contents examined with interest. Everything had come through the Atlantic crossing intact. Yet very soon there was a strange complaint: the blue edge on the new cream-coloured dishes was showing wear in an unaccountable manner.

In Staffordshire, at the factory carried on by Josiah Wedgwood's descendants, a letter regarding this Canadian order was preserved. Captain John Ashton Shuttleworth, of the Royal Fusiliers, wrote it from Quebec, on September 14, 1791: 'We arrived here about three weeks ago; and I have since examined the earthenware . . . it all came perfectly safe and very much approved off [sic]; what it is owing to I do not know; but the Blue edge does not stand heat so well as what I should have expected.'[21]

No detail was too small to escape the attention of Prince Edward, who was noted for his minute inspection of every aspect of garrison life. When Captain Shuttleworth wrote to the Wedgwood firm that the tablewares for the officers' mess had been 'very much approved off', it may be taken to mean that Prince Edward himself had been satisfied with the 'Queen's ware' (given this name because of his mother's patronage). Not even the defective blue caused any serious difficulty; the Wedgwood firm was to expect further commissions, and Captain Shuttleworth cautioned the London office to keep 'patterns of all that have been sent out, in order that we may replace any deficiencies that may happen in the future'.[22]

The Wedgwood Archives are by no means complete. Eliza Meteyard, writing in the 1870's, told how ledgers and huge bundles of papers were sold for scrap after the death of the second Josiah Wedgwood in 1843, and also of how some of this material was rescued five years later, when Joseph Mayer, collector and ceramic historian, came upon old Wedgwood documents being used to wrap butter and groceries in Birmingham.[23] But what has survived, and been carefully gathered together in Staffordshire, constitutes one of the largest collections of documents in Great Britain devoted to the history of a single pottery. Enough Canadian material is included to give an indication of the extent of Wedgwood's trade with this country from an early period. Ample proof is offered of the popularity in the colonies of Wedgwood's creamware, graceful in shape and 'chaste in decoration'.

From Wedgwood papers it is learned that in Canada the fashion for the firm's cream-coloured earthenware was set in high places. In England it had been royalty and 'persons of rank and affluence' who had first taken up the Wedgwood product, and their example had brought orders streaming into the factory. In Canada an Attorney-General and a Lieutenant-Governor were soon dining off Wedgwood. The owner of Monklands (to be a vice-regal residence when Montreal became the capital of Canada) ordered Wedgwood's cream-coloured ware in 1787. James Monk, not at that time knighted, was Attorney-General of Quebec when Josiah Wedgwood shipped his new tableswares to him, a fact noted on the order preserved with the Wedgwood papers.

When Robert Shore Milnes arrived in Quebec as Lieutenant-Governor of Lower Canada, he brought with him a set of brown-edged Wedgwood creamware. That was in 1797, and in 1800 he needed an additional dinner service to match. Two documents exist concerning the Lieutenant-Governor's order for this dinner ware: a copy of the order itself, dated July 28, 1800, and a letter dated September 24, 1800.[24] The tableware had been expected in Quebec with the autumn convoy, but it missed the September sailing, probably to the Lieutenant-Governor's displeasure. By being held over until the shipping season of 1801, however, the Wedgwood creamware was new for the dinner in celebration of the baronetcy conferred upon Richard Shore Milnes that year.

Another Canadian order, of which the details are known, is of interest as an illustration of the custom of having the owner's initials painted upon tableware of the period. In 1815 J. Besserer of Quebec not only wanted Wedgwood creamware, he wanted Wedgwood creamware with his own initials, J B, done in a 'Cypher' and surrounded by a 'ring'. In an old ledger containing orders for November of 1815 is a sketch of how Besserer's initials were to be painted upon each of the many pieces to go out to Quebec: 'sallad' dishes, oblong dishes of various sizes, soup plates and flat plates, soup tureens, compotiers, a large centrepiece for dessert, and 'Scollop Shells'. The pattern chosen by Besserer for the decoration of his monogrammed tableware was a border design in brown, known as 'strawberry leaf with drop' in the Wedgwood pattern books of the early days.[25]

Important as was the cream-coloured earthenware in the Canadian market, it represented only a part of Wedgwood exports. Another of Josiah Wedgwood's improvements concerned a body frequently advertised by the china sellers of British North America in the eighteenth and throughout the nineteenth century. Again, like the cream-coloured earthenware, it was a body to which Wedgwood gave a name of his own, and again, it was a ware that has continued in production down to the present day.

Josiah Wedgwood's 'artificial basaltes' (called 'a fine grained black stoneware' in modern advertisements,[26] and 'a black porcelain biscuit' by Wedgwood himself)[27] was long known to the potters of Staffordshire as 'black Egyptian' ware. Iron and manganese accounted for its colour, and materials needed to make it were readily available. William Pitt, in a history of Staffordshire published in 1817, described how some of the necessary ingredients for 'that kind of ware called Egyptian black' could be obtained from the sediment at the bottom of streams draining from the coal mines in the district. When the sediment had been dug out and thoroughly dried, it sold to potters for a guinea a cart-load.[28]

William Evans, who was accused of revealing secrets of the potting industry in a book published in Staffordshire in the 1840's, gave the components of '*Egyptian, best black, or vitrified basalts*' as blue clay, china clay, calcined ochre, manganese, and black marl combined in stated proportions.[29] There was little secret about this, for the black body was common knowledge to the potters of Staffordshire. Yet of the many who made it, few ever produced black ware to equal Wedgwood's. In his hands Egyptian black became 'black basaltes', finer, darker, and smoother to the touch than the traditional product.

He had begun experimenting with it towards the end of the 1760's. By 1773 he was claiming for his artificial body 'nearly the same properties as the *basaltes*', declaring that it would resist 'the attacks of acids', and be 'a touchstone to copper, silver and gold, and equal in hardness to agate or porphyry'.[30]

Wedgwood used his polished black body for much ornamental work. In

Canada, however, it was his practical wares that were advertised most frequently, and in these colonial advertisements the old name of Egyptian black often persisted, even though Wedgwood products were probably meant in many cases where makers were not identified.

'Egyptian black tea pots, sugar boxes and milk pots' were advertised in Halifax in 1786.[31] Earlier (1780) the black body, which at this period owed most of its fashionable popularity to Wedgwood's promotion, had been offered to Novascotians as the 'new fashion Egyptian Ware'.[32] It requires imagination to think of it, stark and handsome, displayed amid the incongruity of the other goods that shared those early Maritime advertisements—nails, running rigging, cables, cod lines, and pocket microscopes.

In Montreal two ceramic bodies that owed much to Wedgwood, even if his firm was not the maker of what was being advertised (and it is impossible to know), were announced on November 4, 1799, in the *Gazette*. Black Egyptian was named and Queensware was implied in a sale at which Joseph Provan proposed putting up earthenware in company with 1,283 raccoon skins, 116 'muskratts', and assorted deer, elk, wolf, bear, mink, and otter pelts: '. . . will be positively sold without reserve . . . One hundred crates and seven hhds. of Earthen Ware, consisting of . . . flat and soup plates, plain, green and blue edged; plain, laurel and painted cups and saucers; bowls, jugs, chamber pots, twig baskets and stands, oval Egyptian black tea pots.'

In another Montreal advertisement, appearing in a supplement to the *Gazette* on December 2, 1805, the attribution to the Wedgwood factory of the 'black' and 'cane' teapots mentioned is a possibility, since Wedgwood made both black and cane-coloured bodies, and since N. Graham, the china seller in this case, stated earlier in the advertisement that he had 'elegant wedgwood'. He also listed 'pearl' wares, and this may, perhaps, refer to the white earthenware (as distinct from cream-coloured) to which Josiah Wedgwood gave this particular name. He himself did not develop his white, or 'pearl' wares to any extent, but at the period of Graham's advertisement his successors were attempting to put the pearl body into competition with the bone porcelain of other makers. White bone china was the rage of the day, and the Wedgwood factory lagged behind in getting into its production.

One Wedgwood item in black basaltes that had wide popularity in Canada and was advertised in many parts of the country was the ink pot. 'Wedgwood black inks' was the usual way of describing them. James Brown, publisher of the *Montreal Gazette* from 1815 to 1825, who was also a stationer, used to advertise them regularly in his bilingual newspaper. They were 'Wedgewood Black Inks' in the English columns, and 'Cornets Noirs de Wedgewood' in French.[33] In Quebec another stationer, George Cowan, was selling them in 1838,[34] and in Saint John a dealer in Ward Street, George Thomas, had a half dozen for sale in 1845.[35] Both Cowan and Thomas, like James Brown, identified their wares specifically as Wedgwood, and offered them as an alternative to pewter ink pots.

There were other Wedgwood bodies of importance, in particular the close-grained stoneware known as 'jasper', which, like black basaltes, is still being made. With jasper it was once more a case of Wedgwood's name for his own products being taken up by competitors. For this reason it cannot be said with certainty, although it is possible, that it was Wedgwood that Glover Harrison was selling at Toronto's China Hall when he advertised 'Jasper Cheese Covers and Game Pies'.[36] Probably every type of ware produced at the Wedgwood factory came to Canada at one time or another—'Wedgewood in every possible design'[37] ran a Montreal advertisement of the 1870's—but the cream-coloured wares and the black wares are the types in which the Canadian trade can be shown to have been the greatest in the first half of the century.

After 1850 the crockery trade in Canada began to expand rapidly. A growing population created a bigger market, and it was a market that more manufacturers wanted to supply. As the years went on, competition from foreign wares became keener, yet there is nothing to suggest that Wedgwood products lost their grip on Canadian business. It is true that potters like Copeland and Minton stand out as stronger figures in the history of Victorian ceramics, and that the Wedgwood factory did not lead in the nineteenth century, as it had done when Josiah Wedgwood himself was in command. But although Canadians bought heavily from all the great makers of the day, the reputation that the founder of the firm had first won for his wares when Canada was an unimpressive little group of colonies, in part new to British rule, continued to mean that the name of Wedgwood had power.

Some idea of what the Canadian china merchant of Victorian days might order from the factory may be gained from the Wedgwood Archives. The shipments that went out to Simon Levy, a Quebec dealer, in 1850 and 1851 serve as an illustration. Simon Levy had fashionable goods. He ordered jugs in shapes that were shown at the Great Exhibition of 1851, in London;[38] he had honey pots in black basaltes, and butter tubs and stands in 'buff' coloured ware; he had a selection of 'toy' items, and more than one supply of 'Tom Thumb' teapots, sugars, and creams; he had candlesticks, vases with covers, and cups, saucers, and plates; and he kept a stock of mortars and pestles in the famous stoneware body that Josiah Wedgwood had introduced for such ware, and which he himself had called a 'compact, hard porcelain' that made marble appear soft by comparison.[39]

In Victorian advertisements it gradually became more common for makers of earthenware and porcelain to be identified, yet not many advertisements were headed by a potter's name, as was this one appearing in a Montreal newspaper in 1885:

WEDGWOOD

Just received in the above well-known ware a large assortment of CHRISTMAS GIFTS, including Jugs, Caraffes, Vases, Ash Trays, Cups and Saucers, Five o'clock Tea Sets, Sugars and Creams, &c. . . .

ADAM DARLING,
203 St. James Street.[40]

In the earlier years it had been the practical items, the cream-coloured earthenware for the dinner table and the black-ware teapots, that had been mentioned most often in Canadian newspapers; now it was Wedgwood novelties that were advertising features. A Montreal china seller with a flair for the spectacular in advertising copy publicized his supply of them in the *Daily Witness* on September 21, 1885:

SO THEY ALL SAY
—THAT THE—
NEWEST GOODS
AND LATEST NOVELTIES
ARE TO BE HAD AT
WILEY'S CHINA HALL
These are a few of them:
WEDGEWOOD BISCUIT JARS
WEDGEWOOD ICE TUBS
WEDGEWOOD CHEESE STANDS . . .

But the Victorians, enamoured of novelty and enthusiastic over every new form of ceramic production, from their own version of 'majolica' to wares called 'malachite' and 'lava' and 'ancient Flemish',[41] were still open to the appeal of the utilitarian bearing the name of Wedgwood. It was an appeal that George Browne, a Quebec dealer, had recognized in 1811, when he had advertised 'Wedgwood's finest cream coloured Earthen Ware, in crates';[42] it was an appeal that Edward Hagar exploited in Montreal in 1882, when he put an advertisement in the *Daily Witness* for brown-glazed teapots:

WEDGEWOOD Rockingham
We have just opened an assortment of
WEDGEWOOD ROCKINGHAM
Teapots, Sugars, Creams, Bowls, &c.
This Ware is far superior to any other made.
For a cup of good tea get a Wedgewood Brown Tea pot.[43]

According to Llewellynn Jewitt, the Wedgwood Rockingham was just what Edward Hagar claimed—superior.[44] The cups were pleasingly white-lined, and the brown glaze known as 'Rockingham' was of the richest colour. Sometimes there was even etched or engraved decoration.

In this advertisement for useful Wedgwood wares Edward Hagar of Montreal struck a note that would have appealed to Josiah Wedgwood himself, for of him it would have been true to say that his triumphs in ornamental potting—his busts in black basaltes, his heads of the illustrious in jasper, his cabinet cups in the Etruscan style— were no more important than a teapot whose lid fitted to perfection, whose spout poured well, and whose glaze stood up to the 'vicissitudes of heat'.

Canadians paid their own tribute to the potter who first made English wares a force to be reckoned with in the world market; they paid it in the way most satisfactory to a maker of goods for sale: by buying his tablewares from the earliest days of the colonies; by advertising them consistently in their newspapers as the 'much admired' Wedgwood ware;[45] by remaining loyal to the factory's products, despite competitive distractions, till the century's end, even long after Josiah Wedgwood himself had become part of the Staffordshire clay.

111

CHAPTER IX

Printed Wares:
From Willow to Flowing Blue

SHUTER & WILKINS BEG leave to inform their Friends . . . that
they expect . . . Blue Printed Dinner and Desert Services.
Canadian Courant, Aug. 16, 1823.

Of all the tablewares imported into Canada in the nineteenth century those with decoration printed under the glaze enjoyed the greatest popularity over the longest period. The protected decoration itself was durable; the wares were relatively cheap; and with this new process, whereby a printed picture could be transferred to a piece of pottery, the whole world of the engraver's art was brought to the dinner table. Beside the printed wares in their infinite variety of patterns, the glaze softening the decoration and giving it depth and tone, the hand-painted creamwares began to have the look of something out of date. 'Best blue printed' was taking the place of 'finest cream-coloured earthenware' on the tables of those who kept up with the times, even while living in the colonies.

Zabdiel Thayer's advertisement of June 17, 1815, published in the *Canadian Courant*, shows how the old and new fashions were offered side by side in the early years of the century; just as the cream-coloured wares, while they were the new style, had once been sold in Canada with the delft and salt-glazed tablewares of an earlier period. With six hundred crates of 'well assorted Earthen Ware' on their way up to Montreal from Quebec, where they had been landed from an Atlantic sailing ship, Thayer announced himself as expecting 'Table and Desert Services' in both 'Blue Printed' and 'C.C.', the latter with painted decoration in brown, blue, or green.

C.C. (cream-coloured earthenware) did not disappear from the Canadian crockery stores, in spite of the pressure of competition from newer wares. It continued to be advertised throughout the century. But the C.C. of the later years was a cream-coloured earthenware that had bowed to the demands of mass production. As the nineteenth century wore on, it became an altered and generally coarsened product, turned out largely for the cheapest market. Where once Canadian advertising specifying C.C. ware had indicated a fine earthenware ornamented with delicate hand-painting (such as was offered by Zabdiel Thayer in 1815), it later came to mean a thick body, often crudely daubed with gaudy colours. A line from a Montreal crockery advertisement of the 1860's, '50 Crates

SECONDS and C.C. WARE',[1] illustrates pointedly what happened to the earthenware called cream-coloured.

Before the 1820's the under-glaze printed wares had effectively snatched the lead from the older painted wares and had, in their turn, become the best-selling item in the Canadian crockery trade. They owed their success to an eighteenth-century invention that waited until the nineteenth century for full development.

For the beginning of the story of under-glaze printing on British earthenware it is necessary to go back to Staffordshire's Josiah Spode (1733-97). He did not himself invent the technique, nor was he even the first to try it out in Staffordshire, but his was the grasp of its possibilities. At his factory, carried on by his son after his death, under-glaze printing was brought to perfection (*Plate* 4B). Where the Spodes, father and son, charted the way into realms of picture-printed earthenware, a legion of potters thronged after. Much of the prosperity of nineteenth-century Staffordshire was based on what Josiah Spode did at the end of the 1770's.

At that time he began to ponder the future of under-glaze printing. It had been used earlier outside Staffordshire for the decoration of porcelain. The earthenware makers, however, although one or two had made tentative experiments, had not developed it. Josiah Wedgwood, for instance, the most important of them all, was ornamenting his creamware with hand-painting, or else sending it all the way to Liverpool, there to be printed over the glaze by the firm of Sadler & Green. Not only was this a trouble and expense, but such printed decoration, put on top of the glaze, was subject to wear. Spode wanted something more practical, and he wanted to be able to carry it out at home. Accordingly he laid his plans.

His first move was to bring into his employ a printer and an engraver from Caughley, in Shropshire, where under-glaze blue printing had been used on porcelain. With these experienced men to help him, Spode next took the bold step of introducing under-glaze printing on earthenware at his own factory in Stoke-on-Trent. Trial, error, and years of experimentation lay ahead; but from that day in the early 1780's, Spode wares pointed the way to the industrial achievements of which under-glaze printing was capable. For technical reasons this printing was at first almost invariably in blue, hence the name 'blue printing' for the process, used even after other colours had been mastered.

What the elder Spode began, his son, the second Josiah Spode (1754-1827), continued, with all Staffordshire ready to share in the rewards. Hurriedly nearly every potter of the early nineteenth century seized on this way to decorate table-wares quickly and attractively. 'Blue Printed' reached out to every market, and nowhere was its acceptance greater than in North America.

The method by which a picture was transferred from a piece of metal to a piece of pottery was a complicated process, testing the skill of a number of different workers. There are many descriptions of the operation, but one, written at a period when printed wares were flooding into the crockery stores of colonial Canada, is in itself of particular historical interest. Since the first half of the nineteenth century, certain improvements have taken place, but basically transfer

114

printing on pottery is today the same as it was when William Evans set down the steps to be followed in 1846, in his now rare *Art and History of the Potting Business Compiled . . . for the Especial Use of Working Potters.*[2] '*Blue printing,*' he wrote at that time, 'is the name for the manipulations of taking impressions (in colours . . .) from copper-plates engraved in a style peculiar to the artists of the pottery districts; and of sizes varied to the different vessels.'

When the artist, working in the style 'peculiar . . . to the pottery districts' had engraved his design or pattern onto a copperplate, the next step was to rub colour into the lines of the engraving, the copperplate being kept heated during this stage to facilitate the working of the colour: the 'colour is well mixed . . . into a fluid, called technically an *oil* . . . The printer places his plate on the stove, rubs in the colour, with a broad pallet knife scrapes off the excess, and then with his boss [a pad for cleaning the copperplate] cleans the plain sides, and places it on the bed of the press.'

With the copperplate engraved and loaded with colour, the preparation of the tissue paper, which would receive the impression from the copperplate, was then attended to by the printer: 'he . . . brushes the sheet of paper over with a solution of soft soap and water, puts it on the plate, rolls it between the rollers [of a press] and . . . carefully takes it off, and examines that the impression is a good one, and that the colour properly adheres'.

Several sections of a design intended to fit the different parts of a vessel, as, for instance, the sides and lid of a teapot, might be engraved onto one copperplate. These different sections would, therefore, all appear on the one tissue-paper impression. Separating them, so that they might be applied in the proper places, was the work of a cutter, 'a little girl, training up for the next manipulation'.

This little girl would collect all the tissue-paper impressions from the printer: she 'takes the impression, cuts away all the white paper, then separates the impression into its parts, which she places in the order most readily facilitating their application to the ware'.

At this stage a woman operator, a 'transferer', took over. Hers was an exacting task, requiring what Evans called 'tact and judgment'. Using the tissue-paper impressions, which the cutter had separated and made ready for her, the transferrer 'places on a biscuit [unglazed] vessel the several parts in their proper arrangement; and then, with a rubber of flannel, six to sixteen inches long, and firmly rolled and tied together . . . she rubs the paper upon the article, with much force, often resting one end in the right arm-pit, until it [the paper] cannot again be taken off'.

The paper, with its coloured impression rubbed hard against the biscuit, or unglazed vessel, was, in this way, 'stuck' to the piece of pottery: the 'dry and absorbent porosity of the ware aids the adhesion of the colour in the oil, and when the task is completed, each vessel is taken off the board on which it was placed by the transferer, immersed in water, and . . . with soft water and a sponge the paper is washed off, and leaves in the ware only the . . . colour, and a little of the oily medium'.

In this way, the design which had been engraved onto a copperplate, and

115

transferred from the plate to tissue paper, was finally transferred again to the piece of pottery. After the tissue paper had been washed away, leaving its coloured design behind, ware decorated by this method was 'kept in a heated room to evaporate much of the water imbibed in washing off the paper, which is requisite to prepare it for the fluid glaze; and also, is heated to red heat to *harden on* the colour, and volatilize the oily particles, else the glaze would not adhere'.

Every stage of the process was important: the right temperature for the copperplate, the care with which the paper was laid upon the plate, and the way in which it was taken from it, when excess moisture had been pressed and dried out. The difference between cheap, hurried work and the type of blue printing that came from a factory like Spode's was often to be seen in the way the pieces of the printed pattern had been fitted to the pottery. An awkward or careless transferrer left the evidence of her ineptitude in permanent form. A master who provided only inferior materials and expected too much work from an underpaid, tired-out woman had a poorly decorated product to sell.

In Canada there was a market for both the 'superior blue printed' and the 'common printed'. Firms like Shuter & Wilkins, of Montreal, handled wares from the 'first houses in England' for their city trade; a village storekeeper, selling a crate of cheap dishes along with farming implements and ox and steer bows would not be particular. It was the genius of the Staffordshire potter that he always produced what his market wanted, and what Canadians wanted in the nineteenth century was printed earthenware of every quality.

Because blue looked better against a white background, the cream colour of earthenware used for tablewares was changed to white by those who turned to under-glaze printing to decorate their products. Newspaper advertisements and the details of auction sales of household effects, always a sure guide to what Canadians were buying at any period, show that soon almost everyone was using these new tablewares printed in 'pure blue and white'.[3] In Charlottetown, for example, Samuel Nelms was advertising 'Best blue' in 1827. He had to offer: 'Breakfast sets, Soup Tureens and Ladles, Sauce do. complete, Ewers and Basons, Bowls, Mugs, Pitchers, &c. &c.'[4]

Shuter & Wilkins, in Montreal, angling for the trade of both Upper and Lower Canada, announced that their blue-printed was selected for them in England 'by a house which has shipped Goods . . . to this country for upwards of twenty-five years', and was, therefore, well able to judge the patterns 'fit for this Market'.[5]

Blue printing was not confined to earthenware; it could be, and was, used on the new bone china, and on the stone china which was the connecting link between earthenware and porcelain. But in this early part of the century a 'blue dinner set' meant blue-printed earthenware, and many who could afford porcelain tea cups chose to take their dinner and dessert from the popular earthenware. In times past, these same persons would have dined from painted creamware.

One of those who followed fashion in this way was Hon. Henry Byng, captain in the Royal Navy. When he was stationed at Isle aux Noix near St. Johns, Lower Canada, in the late 1820's, Captain Byng furnished his living quarters handsomely. He had Chinese ornaments for his mantel, mahogany tables and chairs of latest style, over a thousand books on graceful bookshelves, porcelain cups and saucers for his tea—and dinner and dessert services in blue-printed earthenware.[6]

A garrison officer who also had a porcelain tea set but blue earthenware dinner and dessert dishes was Rev. Brooke Bridges Stevens. To this day in Canada this indefatigable military chaplain of the 1820's and 1830's is remembered as the founder of churches in Queenston, Chambly, and Lachine. In 1832, two years before he died of tuberculosis and was buried under the chancel of St. Stephen's in Lachine, Rev. Brooke Bridges Stevens sold all his household belongings at auction. The sale revealed that his 'splendid' porcelain came in teaware; his dinner and dessert services were blue earthenware.[7]

Samuel Gerrard, president from 1820 to 1826 of the Bank of Montreal (then known as the Montreal Bank), was a man of varying fortune but fashionable tastes. He, too, dined off blue-printed.[8]

Still another whose table appointments are known was John Try, one of the important cabinet-makers of early nineteenth-century Montreal. Formerly on his own, John Try had later gone into partnership as Foster & Try, with premises on St. Paul Street. To Foster & Try had come the urgent, pre-dawn message on an August morning in 1819 to hurry to Lachine with a hearse. Like everyone else in Montreal, John Try must have been stunned to learn that the Governor-General, the Duke of Richmond, whom the city had only recently turned out to cheer on his way to Upper Canada, had been brought back dead from the bite of a rabid fox.

By the time dawn broke the most massive coffin Montrealers had ever seen was being rushed to completion in Foster & Try's workroom. It was of mahogany, and had to enclose not only the shell in which the Governor-General's body had been brought down from Upper Canada, but also the 600-pound lead box in which the shell was placed in Montreal. People talked for years about the huge mahogany coffin fashioned hurriedly that day at Foster & Try's, and of how the soldiers staggered and swayed under its weight as, watched by silent, weeping crowds, they carried it onto the steamboat *Malsham* for the last journey back to Quebec.[9] Whoever bought John Try's blue-printed earthenware, when it was auctioned five years later,[10] may well have remembered the part Foster & Try had been called on to play in a tragedy that was whispered about for years, because of the madness of hydrophobia.

From naval officer to garrison chaplain, from coffin-maker to bank president, Canadians were ready to buy the blue-printed wares Staffordshire wanted to supply. But ceramic taste was a restless, changing thing in the nineteenth century. No sooner had blue-printed earthenware come within the reach of all, than fashion was off again on something new. Simeon Shaw, in his history of the Potteries published in 1829, revealed what caused the first slipping from favour of the 'best blue': it was simply that everybody had it, and therefore it was 'common'.[11]

The potters of England had an answer for this new problem. They already knew how to print in under-glaze black (as well as blue), they learned how to produce wares in brown, pink, lavender, green, orange, grey, and a new light blue—never to be mistaken for the older, sparkling blue, that gave life to the engraving, or the deep, sapphire blue, that had attracted by the very strength of its colour.

The paler shades had an appeal of their own, and the details of the engraving often tended to be clearer. They gained favour in England before the end of the 1820's; by the early 1830's they were selling well in British North America, not only in the larger centres, but in country districts, like the Eastern Townships of Lower Canada. In an early issue of the *Missiskoui Post*, published at Stanbridge in 1835, A. L. Taylor advertised that he had 'Pink, Brown and Blue Tea-Sets' (*Plate* 6A). He would exchange them for all kinds of country produce 'at a fair price' and 'No Mistake'.[12]

Up in Bytown, the future Ottawa and capital of Canada, the *Bytown Gazette* was carrying an advertisement for Shriver & Dean, in November, 1836. Shriver & Dean had taken Chitty's Public House in Upper Bytown, and were running it as a general store, stocked with furs, groceries, and a few 'neat DINNER AND TEA SETTS'. The colours of their 'neat' earthenware included 'Blue, Pink and Brown', which meant blue, pink, and brown printed wares.[13]

By the 1840's printed wares were off again on a new whim of ceramic fashion, and once more Canadian china merchants were quick to import the latest. Up to this point it had been the object of the best under-glaze printers to make their pictures on pottery sharp and clear; now suddenly the whole aim was to blur the outline of the engraving. Colours that had moved or 'flowed' in the glost oven started a fad in printed wares that lingered till the end of the century.

It has been suggested that the first flown decoration was an accident, resulting from materials left by chance in the sagger, or container in which the pottery was fired.[14] This may or may not be true, but there was no chance or accident about the printed wares advertised in Canadian newspapers as 'the new . . . FLOWING STONE WARE'.[15] They had all been fired in an atmosphere into which volatile chlorides had been purposely introduced. The result was that the colour of the printing spread or flowed into the glaze, creating the much-admired blurred or misty look.

A deep blue was the colour most in demand, but others were given the same treatment. Next to blue in popularity came flowing mulberry, a shade variously described as purplish-brown (puce) or purplish-grey. Printed wares with the flown or flowing effect (both terms were used) were also produced in black, yellow, brown, and green.

The first flown ware was put on the market in England before Queen Victoria came to the throne, but essentially this was a fashion of Victorian days. The 1840's and 1850's represented the peak period of its popularity in Canada, and ironstone, or 'stone ware', was the favourite medium for its display.

A Saint John advertisement of 1847 illustrates the range of flowing colours offered to Canadian buyers by that date. Francis Clerke was the advertiser; his announcement appeared in the *New Brunswick Courier* on November 27: 'Just received per ships Themis, and Lisbon, from Liverpool—36 CRATES EARTHENWARE, comprising a general assortment of flowing blue Dinner, Breakfast, and Tea Wares; brown, green and olive do. Toilet Wares . . .'

118

Printed Wares: From Willow to Flowing Blue

Flowing colours were advertised by Alexander Christie in the *Niagara Chronicle* on July 17, 1851:

. . . just received direct from
THE STAFFORDSHIRE POTTERIES
SEVENTY FOUR CRATES OF CROCKERY
CONSISTING OF . . .
FLOWING DEMASINE
FLOWING MULBERRY
FLOWING BLUE
IN BREAKFAST, DINNER, TEA AND TOILET SERVICES.

The Ware is of the very best quality and from some of the best makers, and it will be sold very low.

In Toronto, when Patton & Co. first opened their Staffordshire Warehouse on King Street, towards the end of 1846, they featured 'Flowing Blue Stoneware' in advertisements in both the *Globe* and the *Examiner*.[16] In Montreal at this same time John Leeming, organizer of huge trade auctions, was promoting 'Flown Blue Dinner Sets' as particularly suitable for the Canadian market.[17]

When Canadian dealers were selling printed wares, whether the earlier 'blue-printed' or the later flowing colours, they tended to follow their practice in selling other kinds of earthenware or porcelain: they sold them by type and not by maker. Their advertisements were alert in stressing the latest fashions, but the names of the overseas potters who had produced them were rarely mentioned.

An exception to this general rule was an advertisement of 1817, apparently referring to blue-printed ware. On May 10 that year, in the *Montreal Herald*, the auction firm of Cuvillier & Co. announced a sale of household goods belonging to a garrison officer. In their advance publicity, the auctioneers picked out certain items for special mention, with the result that 'a complete Dinner Set' of what was identified as 'blue Wedgwood's Ware' found itself sharing advertising interest with 'a superior Milk Cow'.

Early in the nineteenth century the Wedgwood factory, conscious of the growing market for the under-glaze blue wares such as Josiah Spode had set on the path of fame, began to produce top-quality blue printing of its own. This underglaze blue work was done at the Wedgwood factory itself, in contrast to the first over-glaze printed decoration on the creamware, which had been carried out at Liverpool, to Josiah Wedgwood's order. The Wedgwood blue-printed patterns, like those of other makers, were set against a white background.

When the printed ware in flowing colours came into fashion many of the 'first' potters of the day exported it to Canada—Copeland & Garrett (successors to the Spodes), Davenport, the Ridgways, Podmore, Walker & Co. Yet contemporary Canadian advertising stressed their products and not their names. One supplier of the Maritime market is known, not from advertisements of bygone days, but from the curious fact of his wares' remaining unused for nearly half a century. In the 1940's an unopened barrel of crockery was discovered in an outbuilding on a property at Westfield Beach, New Brunswick. It had obviously been purchased at some time in the previous century from a Saint John dealer. When unpacked, it was found to contain a complete dinner service of ironstone

china in new condition, decorated in an under-glaze blue just slightly flown.[18]
The set bore the mark of John Meir & Son, a Staffordshire firm in business
between 1837 and 1897. In date the ironstone discovered in New Brunswick was
mid-Victorian.

Under-glaze printing of every type had tremendous selling power in Canada.
Fashions changed throughout the century, but the printed wares, whether in
sharp, clear monochromes, in purposely blurred tones, or in the multi-colour
printing introduced by the 1840's, accounted for the greater part of the crockery
trade of the colonies. With the introduction of under-glaze printing on earthenware, the variety of patterns became almost limitless, and the protective glaze
meant that these patterns were permanent, a decided improvement over decoration put on top of the glaze.

In the earlier years subjects inspired by the Chinese predominated. Then came
a vogue for landscapes, real or fanciful. Floral designs had an appeal that never
faded, although their best days were in the first half of the century, when bold
representations of English garden flowers were strewn over the printed surface
with a confident hand. In the 1840's there was a taste for religious themes, and
towards the end of the century a tendency to follow Japanese arrangements which
were asymmetrical and often fan-shaped.

Borders became important with printed decoration, and as much attention
was given to them as to the main theme. It seemed a matter of no consequence
that there was sometimes complete incongruity between the printed border and
the printed pattern. A Spode series of views in Asia Minor had, for example, a
border composed of subjects taken from big-game hunting in India. On the other
hand, there was often an inspired matching of border to central theme, as on a
blue-printed series by Charles James Mason, depicting ancient ruins, and framed
by a border of fragmented stone columns.

For immigrants, printed pictures on tablewares must often have served as
poignant reminders of places for which they were homesick and which most of
them would never see again. On a piece of earthenware, the County Antrim man
might gaze once more on the wild splendour of Carrick-a-Rede, the Londoner
walk in Regent Street, the Scot return to the banks of the Clyde. Staffordshire
made all this possible. In time, scenes of the new land itself appeared on dishes
for the table, but these, though highly valued today, were only incidental and
never dominant features of the nineteenth-century crockery trade of Canada.

With the introduction of under-glaze printing on tablewares, came a growing
practice of identifying the pattern on the back of at least some of the pieces in
a dinner or tea service, or in a toilet set. It was not a universal custom by any
means but many makers of printed wares did add a backstamp, often itself of
ornate design, that gave the pattern name and sometimes included the maker's
name or initials.

Many pattern names were obvious; many were surprising. Some potters, for
example, chose the title of the pattern not from the design itself but from the
border. This accounts for the name 'Olive' given by Mellor, Venables & Co. to
a European river scene, and for the name 'Wild Rose' chosen by the Middles-
brough Pottery in Yorkshire for an English landscape. A pattern entitled 'California', registered just before mid-century by a Staffordshire firm, bore no re-

semblance whatever to the scenery of the United States. T. J. & J. Mayer's 'Oregon' was equally remote from reality.

Makers of printed wares in the flowing colours frequently turned to the Orient for their patterns and pattern names, but sometimes they attached an eastern name to a view that had looked to the architecture of the Rhine for inspiration. Upon occasion the discrepancy between name and pattern in printed wares was an error in the use of the backstamp itself; the wrong stamp got onto the wrong pattern. Thomas Mayer's 'Canova', popular in North America about 1830, made use of classical urns set against appropriate background. But pieces of the Canova pattern have been found with the backstamp of Mayer's 'Olympic Games' (an entirely different series of views).

Pirating of designs was not uncommon. There were, however, other circumstances that might account for the appearance of the same printed pattern at different factories. Copperplates might be sold, or made available by one potter to another. Many factories purchased patterns from ceramic engravers working on their own, and these engravers often sold variations of a pattern to different firms. Thus J. Goodwin's 'Lasso', distributed in Canada in the 1850's,[19] became 'Peruvian Horses' when Anthony Shaw, of Burslem, was the maker.

With all the naming of patterns, and the great importance the nineteenth-century china merchants continually put upon 'new patterns' in their advertising, it is surprising that this same advertising in Canadian newspapers rarely, with one great exception, attempted to sell printed wares by pattern name. There were scattered references to patterns, such as Richard Calvert, Junior's announcement in the *New Brunswick Courier* of July 20, 1833, that he had chamber sets in Chintz design, and Joseph & John Tooker's advertisement in the *Yarmouth Herald*, on January 2, 1841, that they had plates in 'cattle scenery, lakes and Mayfield patterns'. But no real general effort was made to capitalize upon the popular appeal of pattern names. The one important exception was the Willow pattern.

Of the countless patterns printed on tablewares and exported to Canada in the nineteenth century, none exceeded the Willow in selling power. It was one of the first under-glaze printed patterns on the market; it was still being promoted a hundred years later. Everybody knew, and still knows the Willow pattern. Charles Dickens spoke of it as 'the ugly old willow', and, in 1852, wrongly predicted its disappearance from the ceramic scene.[20] Henry Wadsworth Longfellow thought of it nostalgically as:

The willow pattern that we knew
In childhood, with its bridge of blue[21]

The Canadian china merchant, selling printed Willow by the crate, decade after decade throughout the century, advertised it by name and put it in a class of its own; to him printed was 'printed' but Willow was 'Willow'.

Contrary to the general belief, the Willow pattern was not a true Chinese pattern, nor was there any authentic 'old Chinese legend' to go with it. Willow was Chinese in inspiration, but English in execution, and the legend came after the pattern, made to fit a particular version of it. The birthplace of Blue Willow, in the form in which it soared to a spectacular popularity that has never completely waned, was not the Orient. The Orient supplied the different parts of the pattern, but it was in England that these different parts, borrowed from the Chinese, were assembled in the eighteenth century to create something new.

The first Willow pattern made its appearance at the Caughley porcelain factory in Shropshire. Thomas Turner was the owner of the factory, Thomas Minton the young engraver who worked on the plates for the new pattern, little dreaming that he was cutting into copper the first likeness of what would prove to be the most popular design in ceramic history. For Minton, the engraving of the Willow pattern was a step towards a future which saw him become one of the best-known ceramic engravers of his day, and, in time, the owner of a pottery himself.

Shortly after the appearance of the Caughley Willow pattern, Thomas Minton set up as an engraver in London. Josiah Spode was quick to give him commissions. Soon Minton moved to Staffordshire to be nearer Spode. For the Spode factory, where under-glaze blue printing was being developed to its utmost capacity, Minton engraved more than one Willow pattern. Possibly he engraved the version that is best known today. From the Spode factory at an early date came the familiar Willow pattern with the fence in the foreground, the bridge with three figures on it, the willow tree by it, the pagoda to the right, with the apple tree behind it, the small boat, the island, and the two birds high against the sky.

This is the Willow pattern that lent itself to the 'old Chinese legend' of two lovers fleeing before a father's wrath and pursued by the rich mandarin who had been promised the young bride, of temporary escape by means of the boat to the island, of vengeance and tragedy, and of two souls changed into two immortal doves by the gods who pitied them. Just how the 'legend' originated has been lost in time, but its value in selling the Willow pattern has been undoubted.

There was no 'real Willow pattern'. There were many versions of the same theme, having certain features in common, but often arranging them differently, and adding or omitting certain details. The Spode factory alone produced more than a dozen Willow or Willow-type designs. By far the most popular, however, was the one with three figures on the bridge and the drooping willow tree in the foreground. Almost every potter in Great Britain took it up, and to assign an unmarked piece to any particular factory, or to put credence in tricks of identification is always to tread on uncertain ground. European potters copied the English Willow pattern and made it their own. In time the Orient borrowed back again what had been inspired by its ceramists in the first place, producing for export the pseudo-Chinese design that the Occident inexplicably wanted.

During part of the nineteenth century, the Willow pattern was 'commonly known in the trade as "Broseley pattern" '[22] (Broseley being the market town near Caughley, where the Willow pattern was first produced). 'Broseley' was advertised in Montreal in the 1830's.[23] 'Willow and Rock' was the name of another Willow design, and in the 1840's this, too, appeared in Canadian advertising.[24]

In days when extensive promotion of printed wares all but ignored the existence of pattern names, Willow stood out everywhere: 'fine Willow dishes' were for sale in Halifax (announced in the *Novascotian*);[25] 'Willow Ware' headed the list of items in a big crockery auction in Montreal (publicized in the *Gazette*);[26] 'BLUE AND BROWN PRINTED WILLOW . . . from several of the first Potteries in Staffordshire' was a mid-century special in Niagara (advertised in the *Chronicle*).[27]

Printed Wares: From Willow to Flowing Blue

That printed Willow was put into a category of its own by the Canadian china merchant is illustrated by John Patton's advertisement in the *Commercial Advertiser* of Montreal (October 4, 1862):

CROCKERY
BY WHOLESALE

THE Subscribers have now on hand a full assortment of Goods suitable for the Country Trade.

Painted, Sponged and Printed Teas, C.C., Blue Edge, Willow and Printed Plates . . .

If, in the end, it became 'Willow and common wares', that in itself was evidence that the Willow pattern could not be dislodged from the market; on the contrary, it had been swept into the great flood of production for the masses.

At the beginning of the nineteenth century British potters were still experimenting with under-glaze printing; at the end of the century the technique had been so perfected that a North American writer enthusiastically declared: 'Printing has come to such perfection that one can find abundance of really wonderful art in decoration at very low prices. And it must be a difficult taste to satisfy which cannot find among the cheap earthenwares of our day an abundance of color and decoration such as will meet the most fastidious demand.'[28]

But with all the new patterns which had come upon the market, Canadians retained a taste for designs and colours belonging to the days when under-glaze printing was struggling with technical problems, and bursting upon the ceramic world with startling achievements. In 1904 the Willow pattern was a century and a quarter old, and flowing blue an accomplishment of sixty years and more ago, yet the new Robert Simpson catalogue that spring still featured both in one advertisement: 'We furnish the old original Dark Flow-blue Willow design . . . The Ware is splendid quality English . . . printed under the glaze, and warranted to wear.'[29]

CHAPTER X

Stone, Ironstone, and Granite

For Sale, by G. HENDERSON, *No. 7, Sault-au-Matelot Street*
. . . the new Invented *Iron Stone ware.*
Quebec Mercury, June 6, 1820.

The most important nineteenth-century development in the earthenware body itself, as apart from its decoration, was the ware generally known as 'ironstone'. Intermediate between earthenware and porcelain, but technically an earthenware, ironstone was in every respect suited to the needs of a pioneer country such as Canada. It was strong and hard-wearing, and, in its later stages, very cheap. When decorated, it often relied on the highly popular transfer print. Sometimes this print might be in flowing colours; sometimes bright enamels and gilding were added by hand over a printed outline. The effect could be attractively vivid and lively; yet the ware was tough enough to stand up to hard travel and long use. Ironstone was one of the great wares of the colonial trade.

There are two distinct phases in the history of ironstone as the Canadian market knew it. At the beginning it was an earthenware influenced by the porcelain of the Orient. Later it became an earthenware ranged in competition with the flood of cheap china from the Continent. The first years found it a relatively expensive, showy earthenware, fine enough for the tables of rich merchants in eastern Canada. The second half of the century saw ironstone, plain and cheap, bumping its way to the farthest frontier.

The story of the earlier and finer type of dense earthenware, which in time came to be commonly known as ironstone, goes back to two men potting in Staffordshire at the beginning of the nineteenth century. One was the second Josiah Spode (1754-1827). The other was Charles James Mason (1791-1856), who was to become Spode's nephew, by marriage to his niece. It was Spode who first made a commercial success of a fine-grained, high-fired earthenware approximating porcelain. It was Mason who invented the name 'ironstone', the name handed down to the twentieth century as a general term for a tough earthenware.

Spode used a different name for a ware very like that which Mason shortly after christened ironstone. He called his body 'Stone China', and he put it on the market in 1805. This was eight years before Mason made a lasting impact upon the ceramic world with 'Ironstone China'.

Possibly Spode, with his stone china, owed something to John and William

Turner, Staffordshire potters who had made a somewhat similar body for which they had been granted a patent in 1800. Simeon Shaw, writing in 1829, stated that Spode had purchased the Turners' patent, and that Spode's stone china was, therefore, based on the Turner product.[1] William Evans, on the other hand, declared in 1846 that it was Mason's ironstone ware that 'imitated' what the Turners had made.[2]

The truth was that little was done in Staffordshire that was not immediately known to everyone else. Spode and Mason both produced a strong earthenware that set a pattern for a horde of copyists, who borrowed not only their new earthenware bodies, but their names for them as well. In Canada 'stone china' and 'ironstone' were soon in every crockery merchant's advertising vocabulary, though often the wares announced under these titles must have borne only slight resemblance to the stone china of Josiah Spode or the ironstone china of Charles James Mason.

The earlier of these two wares, Spode's stone china, had been in part developed in the natural course of business. Like other English potters of his day, Spode received orders from those who owned Chinese porcelain services, and wanted replacements made at home for breakages. It was necessary for Spode to provide as close a copy as possible of the oriental body. This he did with great success, but not with a porcelain. Spode matched the china of the Orient with an English earthenware. His early stone china was a startlingly good imitation of the Chinese porcelain, when the English glaze was faintly stained to tone with the blue-grey hue of the foreign ware.

Although he later produced a stone china that was whiter in appearance, much of Spode's earthenware of this type was given the distinctive tone of oriental porcelain, and on these wares he used patterns adapted from oriental prototypes. The mark devised for this stone china was also reminiscent of the East: a pseudo-Chinese fretted square with the name SPODE and STONE CHINA added.

That the Canadian dealers soon accorded stone china a place of its own, setting it apart from the blue-printed earthenware of ordinary body, and from china proper, is shown by advertisements in the first quarter of the nineteenth century. An illustration is the Shuter & Wilkins announcement in the *Montreal Gazette* on June 11, 1825:

SHUTER & WILKIN [*sic*]

RESPECTFULLY inform the Public, that they have received their usual assortment of CHINA, GLASS & EARTHENWARE, selected from the first establishments, in England, amongst which are:—

> Stone China, Dinner and Desert Services,
>
> Blue printed table and desert Sets . . .
>
> China Tea-sets, of elegant patterns.

By the 1820's stone china was also turning up frequently in house auctions; this is **evidence** that it had been established in the Canadian market for some time. Hon. Charles William Grant (who would inherit the historic title of Baron de Longueuil) was one who owned a 'Stone China Sett'. His 'China' was sold at his house in Montreal, in 1829.[3]

In stone china, no matter who made it, the Canadian dealers and auctioneers had an assured selling line, and they imported huge quantities of it. George Rhynas, a Montreal merchant, announced he had in stock '8 casks (200 setts) Stone Breakfast and Tea Services' in 1839.[4] This would have represented many hundreds of pieces, for most services in stone china were large: 266 pieces in one 'sett' is mentioned in a Yarmouth advertisement of this period,[5] and 'upwards of 280 pieces' is given as the size of a 'very Superior Stone China Service' in a Montreal sale.[6]

At the same time as the merchants were advertising these vast amounts of the earthenware known as 'stone china'—Spode's name—they were also announcing 'ironstone china', Charles James Mason's invention. Throughout the century the two names continued in use, both signifying a dense, hard-fired earthenware, although the terms had long ceased to refer to wares made only by Spode or Mason.

Mason, a flamboyant, brilliant young master potter, patented his product in 1813. It was very like the Spode body in many ways, but for it Mason claimed the merit of a new invention. His ware, he declared in his application for a patent, contained slag of ironstone, something hitherto unknown in pottery manufacture. To his new ware, like Spode's an earthenware, he gave the fine-sounding, imaginative name of 'Ironstone China'. It was as much the name as the ware itself that made 'Mason's Patent Ironstone China' a fantastic success. Whether or not it actually did contain any prepared ironstones in its composition matters little today. Mason's lasting contribution to ceramic history lies primarily in the invention of a name which has passed into general use.

Enormous quantities of ironstone came to Canada. In the early part of the century much that was advertised here was probably of Mason's own make. An announcement in the *Quebec Mercury* on June 6, 1820, is almost certainly a reference to Mason's ware:

For Sale by G. HENDERSON,

No. 7, Sault-au-Matelot Street, near the Bank:

NAILS and Spikes, Hoop Iron, Window-glass, Putty . . . a few hogsheads blue Printed ware, china, and the new Invented *Iron Stone Ware* . . .

Mason's ironstone was, like Spode's stone china, faintly coloured to resemble oriental porcelain, and on it he, too, used patterns owing their inspiration to the East. Like the Spode ware, the ironstone of Charles James Mason could be strikingly attractive. It was bought by Canadians who wanted something both good and practical. With Mason's ironstone they had an approximation of porcelain with a ware that was well-nigh indestructible. An example of one who had Mason's ironstone on his table when it was still a new product is Thomas Torrance, a prominent Montreal merchant.

The Torrance china was used in a setting of colonial grandeur, for Thomas Torrance, a Scotsman who had emigrated to Canada in 1804, was the original owner of Belmont Hall. In its day Belmont, at what is now the northwest corner of Sherbrooke Street and St. Lawrence Boulevard, was considered a 'palatial mansion'.[7] Torrance built it shortly before 1820: Thomas Storrow Brown, arriving in Montreal in 1818, noted that Belmont Hall was then under construction,[8] and Rev. Robert Campbell, writing at a later date, stated that Torrance 'built and occupied the fine house' in 1819.[9]

When it was first built, Belmont was far out of the city, so far, in fact, that the notion of a merchant's residing at such a distance from his place of business caused people to dub it 'Torrance's Folly'. Nonetheless, they drove out in their carriages to marvel at its handsome appearance. Commanding a magnificent view over Montreal, the gardens of Belmont sloped down to cover the site of the old Sherbrooke Street Methodist Church (later Holy Trinity Greek Orthodox Church). The famous apple orchards reached out to the Royal Victoria College of today. In the building itself a special feature was a spiral staircase of great elegance. With seven daughters, all of them said to be handsome girls, and all of whom secured husbands, Thomas Torrance gave numerous balls and entertainments at Belmont. These were attended by the first families of the city and by all the young garrison officers, with their eyes on the beautiful daughters.

Family tradition has it that Thomas Torrance ordered the double dinner service of Mason's ironstone china as part of the new furnishings of Belmont, and that it was used at many dinner parties attended by garrison officers. Although Torrance chose a well-known Mason's pattern, his was a special order. On each piece of the Torrance ironstone a section of the border design was removed, and in its place appeared Thomas Torrance's initials, T T, done in gold and surrounded by a wreath (*Plate* 7A). Today some seventy-five pieces of this service survive.

After Torrance's death in 1826,[10] his widow gave up Belmont Hall (which then passed into the hands of the Molson family). Torrance's executors disposed of some of the furnishings,[11] but the ironstone china, with Thomas Torrance's initials painted in gold, remained with his descendants until early in the twentieth century. At that time it was unexpectedly willed out of the family and disposed of by its new owner to an American. But the china that had been purchased for Belmont Hall did not stay long in the United States nor out of Torrance possession. Hon. Norman William Trenholme, husband of Thomas Torrance's granddaughter, Grace Shaw, traced it across the border, re-purchased it for his wife, and brought it back to Canada. Upon Mrs. Trenholme's death, it became the property of her daughter (Torrance's great-grand-daughter), Katherine Torrance Trenholme of Montreal.

Even more colourful in design than the Torrance ironstone was the Mason's dinner service originally the property of an early member of the Knowlton family, for whom the town of Knowlton, in the Eastern Townships of Quebec, was named.[12] Bold and striking in appearance, this ironstone ware was ornamented with an unusually handsome floral pattern in enamel colours. Like the Torrance china, the Knowlton service was marked with Mason's name and PATENT IRONSTONE CHINA. In 1951 the surviving pieces from this service went to an unknown buyer at a country auction, following the death of a collateral descendant of the original purchaser.[13]

The amount of Mason's ironstone still to be found in old settled parts of Canada, such as the Eastern Townships, is testimony to the trade Mason built up with the colonies. His was ware greatly admired in its day, as is shown by its purchase for a 'palatial mansion' like Belmont Hall. Around much of this ware, however, has grown up a strange legend. It used to be cited of the Knowlton china and only recently it appeared in a newspaper account of another historic service in Ontario. The fanciful story is to the effect that this ironstone of the Mason or Spode stone china type was 'sent to China to be decorated'. Surprising credence is given to this claim in North America, where it is frequently offered as one of the unusual facts of ceramic history. And yet these English wares need no tales of impossible journeys to the Orient and back again to give them interest. Spode's achievement in making a Staffordshire earthenware look like Chinese porcelain and Mason's triumph with a name are greater wonders than the fiction of decoration painted in Canton.

But the lives of Spode and Mason had very different endings. For Josiah Spode there were great financial rewards from potting. Spode's commercial drive and his competence carried him from one ceramic success to another. Stone china was only one among them. He died a rich man. For Charles James Mason, who invented the name of ironstone in a flash of genius, and whose wares must have come to Canada literally by the ton, there was failure. Clever and resourceful but mercurial, Mason tumbled into bankruptcy in 1848. In a small way he managed to make a brave showing again at the time of the Great Exhibition in 1851, but for him time was fast running out. He died in 1856, without having recovered his sure footing. Yet to the end of his days, even after adversity had overtaken him, and when the rich furnishings of his house had been sold and others owned his famous patterns and his moulds, Charles James Mason would describe himself with justifiable pride as 'the Patentee of the Patent Ironstone China'.[14]

Mason's bankruptcy did not deprive Canadians of the ironstone china they had long admired. Francis Morley, who himself cultivated the Canadian market, bought the right to use the Mason name, together with copperplates and moulds. From him they eventually passed to George L. Ashworth & Bros. (the firm that owns them today, although the Ashworths are no longer connected with it). It was an Ashworth service that Sir William Dawson, the principal of McGill University, chose in 1870. The service itself was new that year, but the pattern was an old Mason design in rich Imari colours, and on the back of each piece, together with the Ashworth mark, was Mason's famous name of 'Ironstone China'.[15]

The wares of Spode and Mason type represented one aspect of the huge trade in strong, hard-fired earthenware. These were wares of superior quality, often with colourful decoration and even rich gilding. They were eminently practical, but not necessarily cheap. The second phase of the trade in stone china and iron-stone was mainly concerned with wares of a different order. The Victorian wares had the same durability as the earlier products of the nineteenth century, and they were descendants of them, but they were, generally speaking, heavier, clumsier, thicker, and cheaper — wares well suited to the rough usage of pioneer life on the new frontiers of British North America. The old names introduced by Spode and Mason were retained in various forms, but the 'Patent Stone China', 'Pearl Stone China', or 'White Stone'[16] of the later nineteenth century bore as little resemblance to the stone china of Josiah Spode as the Victorian wares named 'Royal Ironstone', 'Imperial Ironstone' or 'Genuine Ironstone' did to the dashing products of Charles James Mason.

Some of these new cheaper earthenwares still harked back to the Chinese wares that had inspired Spode and Mason. Edward and George Wright, Montreal china merchants, were, for instance, advertising a 'stone ware' in 1843 that they claimed was 'a perfect fac-simile of the famous antique Nankin China'.[17] A large proportion of the popular flowing blue wares were of stone china bodies decorated with patterns borrowed from the East.

After about 1850, however, a new factor entered the picture. From the middle of the century on, the French potters became a force to be reckoned with by the British in the Canadian market. They offered little competition in earthenware, but they began exporting quantities of cheap porcelain. Some of those who would ordinarily have bought British earthenware were tempted by the cold, hard glitter of continental china. They began to wonder if it were not more genteel to dine off French porcelain than British earthenware.

But the British potter of Victorian days was nothing if not resourceful and adaptable. If the market wanted cheap white porcelain, then an imitation of that porcelain could be made cheaper still in earthenware. Stone china and ironstone had originally imitated Chinese porcelain; they could now be made to simulate French. The blue-grey tint that had characterized much of the stone china of Josiah Spode and the ironstone of Charles James Mason began to give way to a whiter look. With either the body or the glaze tinged the grey-white of hard French china, the tough British earthenwares surged back on the market to hold their own successfully in Canadian sales.

Nor did British potters stop with a new look. They retaliated with new names playing upon the idea of porcelain. 'Opaque Porcelain' and 'Demi-Porcelain' were adopted by some for wares that were the same as the stone chinas and ironstones of others. A number of British potters went a step further and gave 'Opaque Porcelain' a French air by calling it 'Porcelaine Opaque'. One English manufacturer, Sampson Bridgwood, made a dense earthenware body known as white granite and stamped it 'Limoges' (sometimes adding 'P. G.' to stand for 'Parisian Granite'). This 'Limoges', however, originated in Staffordshire. 'Parisian Porcelain' and 'Paris White' were other markings found at this period on heavy English earthenwares. 'Paris White' sometimes appeared on the back of pieces printed with a French-Canadian nationalist slogan made for sale in the Province of Quebec. These pieces had acquired their Paris white glaze and their nationalist slogan not in France but at Edward Walley's pottery in Staffordshire.

One of the finer types of hard earthenware flirting with porcelain, which came on the market at mid-century and which is known to have had a good sale in North America, bore the curious name of 'Chemical Porcelain'. George Grainger, of Worcester, was its maker. He put it on display at the Great Exhibition in 1851,[18] and declared that it had the 'advantage of being so completely vitrified that the inside, in case of being chipped or broken remains of its original whiteness'.[19] This met the challenge of certain French porcelain manufacturers. In the 1850's these French potters were making a determined effort to publicize a thick ware of their own as being more economical simply because chips mattered less.

This French propaganda found Canadian expression in advertisements such as that of Patton & Co., in the Toronto *Globe* on September 5, 1856:

> Thick French China Plates, Dishes, Bakers, Cups and Saucers.
> This ware being much more durable than English stoneware, and never turning black if chipped will be found much more economical than the former for hotels, steamboats, &c. It may be seen in use at Russell's and the American Hotel.

But Russell's and the American Hotel in Toronto notwithstanding, it was usually a British earthenware and not a French china that was to be found in Canadian hotels and on steamboats of the nineteenth century. Donegana's Hotel in Montreal ordered 'Patent Iron-Stone' from the English potter, William Ridgway; ships of the Beaver Line sailed the Atlantic fitted out with Bodley's 'Genuine Ironstone' from Staffordshire; the Montreal Ocean Steamship Company (forerunner of the Allan Line) bought Ashworth's 'Royal Stone China' for its first ships; and the Canadian Navigation Company's paddle-wheelers plied the Upper St. Lawrence with an 'Opaque Porcelain' in the dining saloons.[20]

In addition to bearing a variety of names suggesting the porcelain or china they were not, many thousands of pieces of earthenware intended for sale in Canada were stamped 'Granite' or 'White Granite'. This was merely another name for a body similar to the Victorian stone china or ironstone. Sometimes both 'Granite' and 'Stone China' or 'Ironstone' appeared on the same piece. Wedgwood & Co. (successors to Podmore, Walker & Co., and not to be confused with the firm founded by Josiah Wedgwood) produced earthenware looking very like a thick French porcelain, which they identified on the back as both GRANITE and STONE CHINA.[21]

Further proof of the way in which these names for the dense earthenwares might be interchanged in their own day comes from James Torrington Spencer Lidstone. In his tour of the Staffordshire potteries in the 1860's, Lidstone visited the factory of T. & R. Boote in Burslem. There he inspected their 'Granite or Opaque Porcelain, Otherwise Iron-Stone China'.[22]

In quantities which stagger the imagination these long-lasting wares poured into Victorian Canada. The Britannia Pottery in Glasgow was only one of the potteries supplying North America, and this pottery alone was capable of turning out a thousand dozen white ironstone plates and as many cups and saucers in a day.[23] To push these wares in the colonies, the Britannia Pottery at one time kept an agent in Toronto.[24]

Few advertisements identified actual makers of stone, ironstone, or granite. The common practice was to publicize them by type: 'a general assortment of China, Stone China, Imitation Stone China' (Montreal, 1833);[25] 'Desert, Tea Breakfast and Toilet SETS in flowered blue ironstone' (Halifax, 1846);[26] 'Direct from THE STAFFORDSHIRE POTTERIES . . . PEARL WHITE GRANITE' (Niagara, 1851);[27] 'Among the Crockery . . . Pearl China Tea setts' (Fort Garry, 1869).[28]

Occasionally, however, there were departures from the accepted way. Francis Clementson of Saint John used to advertise 'Ironstone &c.' whose make was implied in the phrase 'imported from our own Manufactory, Staffordshire, England'.[29] Since Francis Clementson was the son of Joseph Clementson, whose two potteries in Hanley made ironstone for the Canadian market, his own name was an advertisement for his father's wares.

The products of Thomas L. and Richard Boote, whose establishment was visited by Lidstone, the poet, were sometimes referred to specifically in Canadian newspapers. John Leeming, the Montreal auctioneer, made clear it was their wares he would dispose of at a trade sale in 1861:

"BOOTE'S"

WHITE GRANITE

EARTHENWARE

&c. &c. &c.

By the "LADY EYRE," from Liverpool,

now at Quebec, we have a consignment of

55 crates of the above Cel-

ebrated Ware,

TO BE SOLD BY AUCTION . . .[30]

Another advertisement of particular interest, for the reason that it identifies suppliers of the Canadian market, appeared in the Montreal newspaper *La Minerve*, on May 7, 1873. This announced sixty crates of white granite from the Hanley pottery of J. & G. Meakin, which had come to Canada aboard one of the beautiful sailing ships of the Beaver Line. In the advertisement the Meakin name was spelled phonetically:

60 HARASSES

DE

Granit Blanc

Actuellement débarquées en bon ordre

Ex LAKE SUPERIOR, de LIVERPOOL

Nous vendrons par encan, dans nos salles de ventes . . .

60 Harasses de Granit Blanc

FABRIQUE de "MEEKAN,"

assorties et convenables pour le commerce

de la ville ou de la campagne . . .

BARRET & RAE,

Encanteurs.

In the closing words of Barret & Rae's advertisement in *La Minerve* lay the secret of the overwhelming success of the stone chinas, the ironstones and the white granites. They were 'convenables' (suitable) for the country trade; and by the middle of the century this country trade included a frontier trade leaping ahead with every tree felled in the backwoods or every sod broken on the prairie. The stout earthenwares which had succeeded to the heritage of Spode's stone china and Mason's ironstone were equal, as were no other imported wares, to the struggle into new settlements in the east, the jolting of Red River carts over the prairie, or the strains of mule travel in the farther west. In price the cheapest of them were suited to the immigrant's means—a cup for a few cents, a white ironstone tea set for less than two dollars. When Catherine Parr Traill described the furnishings of a log cabin in Upper Canada, the wretched home of an Irish immigrant family, the few pieces of crockery she noted were probably of this type of cheap earthenware: 'Few and simple were the articles of household use. Two or three shelves of unplaned boards held a few crockery cups and cracked saucers, some tin plates and mugs, and a battered tin teapot, minus a handle.[31]

In her own *Canadian Settler's Guide* Mrs. Traill had warned of the unsuitability of attempting to introduce 'gay, showy, or rich and costly articles' of any kind into 'so rough and homely a dwelling' as a log hut.[32] Even if they survived the hardships of travel into the bush, they would look strangely out of place and be less than useful in such surroundings. There was nothing 'showy' about stone, ironstone, or granite ware, when it was left plain white and potted half an inch thick. Nor would it break easily, leaving the housewife who lived far from sources of supply without needed dishes. Many who could afford something fragile found by experience that the heaviest of durable earthenware was more practical for the first years in new country. Anne Langton, living, as was Mrs. Traill, in the Peterborough area, once wrote of the difficulties of obtaining replacements for broken dishes: 'Peterboro cannot at present supply the articles . . . chiefly wanted here, viz., crockery. Things will break here as elsewhere, and we want replenishing sadly. You have no idea of the extra value which glass, china, etc., acquire by removal to the wilderness.'[33]

It was best to be equipped with crockery that would last, saving finer wares for the day when the log hut in the woods became the house in the growing settlement, or the sod shack on the prairie was vacated for the frame dwelling which at first would seem strangely bright.

It is obvious why advertisements in the east stressed ironstone for the country trade, and why the first newspapers of the west carried repeated announcements of the arrival of white stone and pearl china. It was 'white stone cups and saucers' that the *Anson Northup*, first steamboat on the Red River, brought to Fort Garry dealers on one of her earliest adventurous trips.[34]

In frontier outposts this heavy white crockery was the usual tableware of pioneer days, not only with the settlers, but with the North West Mounted Police, who made the country safe for settlers. One whose father was at Fort Macleod with the force, immediately following the Northwest Rebellion, was able to recall the heavy white tablewares with the crest of the North West Mounted Police.[35] Another, who joined the famous frontier police in the 1890's, remembers that in barracks 'we had the common white cups and saucers and plates, I think the material is called stoneware'.[36]

The collections of the Western Development Museum, at its headquarters in Saskatoon, contain tablewares typical of those used by pioneers of the west. 'Opaque China' (in a moulded design named 'Canada', registered in the 1870's by Clementson Brothers) and 'Royal Ironstone China' are characteristic markings on these pieces. Some have printed decoration; many, like the Clementsons' 'Canada', are all white.

In every part of the country, from the east to the newer west, Canadian merchants learned to stock the strong earthenwares as a staple. It was a lesson, however, that some had to learn by mistakes they could ill afford. There were those with slender capital, hoping to make good 'keeping store', who misjudged the crockery market painfully when they were new to the ways of the colonies. This was the case with William and Sarah Thompson who came from Walker, just outside Newcastle, in the north of England. In 1857, with their two young sons, the Thompsons arrived in Upper Canada. Sarah wrote home in November that after looking around carefully William had 'fixed upon Lindsay, a small new & rising town . . . in which to take a store'. There he would 'keep groceries, crockery, glass and hosiery in a small way—a general store'.[37]

The Thompsons moved into 'a tiny house' (so cold the ink froze as Sarah forced herself to write cheerful letters to England). Hopefully they arranged their first stock in the 'small store', which Sarah was confident 'we shall manage . . . without any hiring, as I can often be in it'. All this stock had been anxiously chosen with much thought, but the Thompsons had been too new to the country to select wisely. A year and a half later most of the crockery that they had believed to be highly saleable was still on the shelves. Sarah wrote home about it on May 6, 1859: 'if we could only get rid of our quantities of good china, we should do very well—as it is, we may be thankful things are not worse with us, but it is annoying to have so much of our small capital locked up in this way.'[38]

Had the Thompsons known more about Canadian ways they would not have tied up their 'small capital' in 'good china' to sell in Lindsay in the 1850's. They would, instead, have invested it in the durable earthenware marketed under a dozen different names but which most people called ironstone, and which outsold every other ceramic body in nineteenth-century Canada.

It outsold every other ceramic body because it met every requirement of the country or frontier trade, while at the same time commanding a continuing sale in the cities. Every Victorian home had a use for ironstone. Those with limited means could be accommodated with plain, cheap wares; those with more to spend could find something splendidly practical. Accounts of a lawless night in Montreal, when the Earl of Elgin was Governor-General, provide evidence that stoneware had its place in the fashionable suburban or town house, just as it did in the backwoods shanty.

In 1849 Hon. Louis Hippolyte Lafontaine, of the Baldwin-Lafontaine administration, moved into an imposing residence in the St. Antoine Suburbs of Montreal, then the capital of Canada.[39] The house was new furnished for him from cellar to attic. But scarcely had he begun to enjoy his comfortable new surroundings when political troubles erupted into a violent storm. The Tories became outraged at the controversial Rebellion Losses Bill, which Lafontaine had introduced. They declared vehemently that it made no adequate distinction between the rebels and the loyalists of 1837; in ensuing riots the Parliament Building was burned down on the night of April 25, 1849. The next night, looking for fresh ways to vent their displeasure, the Tories took themselves to the St. Antoine Suburbs. There they fired the stables of Lafontaine's new house. The house itself was saved, but when the Tories had gone home to bed Hon. Louis Hippolyte Lafontaine was missing, among other things, two complete sets of bedroom crockery, of a kind later described as 'stoneware'. Every piece was either carried away by the protesting Tories or else completely demolished by them. Foot baths, ewers, basins, soap trays, pots de chambre, all were missing from

134

their accustomed places. When an inventory was published of what the government leader had lost, his blue stoneware was valued at five pounds, his plain white set at half that amount.[40]

In time, however, the fastidious began to look down on ironstone and all the related wares. By 1882 Adam Darling, the Montreal china merchant, was speaking of 'White Granite and the commoner goods'.[41] American writers on ceramics and taste, such as Charles Wyllys Elliott and William C. Prime, whose works were circulated in Canadian libraries, compared using thick white granite cups to drinking out of horse troughs,[42] or expressed the hope that public taste everywhere might be elevated by 'expelling' white stonewares 'from all tables'.[43] Yet those same durable wares, stronger and tougher than ordinary earthenware, had an essential part to play in the crockery trade of a new land. Another writer declared that 'a certain rough efficiency' was the chief requisite for success in nineteenth-century Canada,[44] and this was exactly the quality possessed to an extraordinary degree by the Victorian stone, ironstone, and granite wares.

CHAPTER XI

For the Kitchen and the Country: Brownware to 'Portneuf'

. . . a grand assortment of Common Glass and Earthenware for the country trade.
Montreal Gazette, June 14, 1830.

The crockery seller in nineteenth-century Canada stocked a multitude of earthen-wares. Creamware, printed ware, ironstone china, each in its turn was brought forward by fashion and retained by utility. But there were other wares besides these of cream or white body intended primarily for the dining-room table or the bedroom wash-stand. There were, for instance, the humble but eminently useful wares, made of clays that burned grey, buff, tan, pink, or dark red. These wares, some fired as ordinary coarse earthenware, some given the prolonged and high firing required for stoneware, met the crockery needs of the very poor, or found their places in the kitchens of the better-off.

In both earthenware and stoneware, these were wares meant for the storage cellar, the laundry, the pantry, the milkhouse, and the conservatory. They had certain uses in hotels and taverns and in the shops of grocers and wine merchants. Some were coloured a dark brown, some mottled and streaked; some of the earthenware, lead-glazed, was lined with white; the stoneware was frequently salt-glazed. In lots of 5,000, 10,000, 25,000, even 50,000 pieces at a time, these common wares were shipped to Canada. Sunderland and Newcastle were im-portant sources of supply for the earthenware; either earthenware or stoneware, sometimes both, arrived also in vast quantities from Derbyshire, Staffordshire, Bristol, and Glasgow.

In Canadian advertising such goods came under the heading of 'Brownware', 'Stoneware' or 'Common Staple Goods', and what type of article this implied

137

may be learned from advertisements such as that which appeared in the *Quebec Gazette* on April 29, 1823:

Sales by Auction
Brown Ware, without reserve
on Messrs. Heath & Meir's Wharf,
to-morrow morning . . .
The following Brown Ware, now landing
ex Swan, Lee, Master, from Newcastle, viz.:
4829 Pieces, consisting of Brown
Dishes, Milch Bowls, Beef Pots,
Hand Basins, Broth Pots,
Stew Pots, Jars, Pipkins, Jugs,
Chamber Pots, Porringers and
Butter Pots . . .
Sale to commence at nine o'clock
by Jonathan Wurtele
A. & B.

The heavy, coarse earthenware that Jonathan Wurtele auctioned off in Quebec would have been of an ordinary red or buff body covered with a lead glaze. Common brick clay was frequently used for such ware and the glaze itself was often coloured with manganese to darken it. Some of the brownware advertised in Canada as 'superior' may have had decoration in coloured slip (clay watered to the consistency of cream). Much of the brownware in the form of bowls, tureens, porringers and the like was given a white or light-coloured lining. Llewellynn Jewitt pointed out in the 1870's that this lined ware, 'i.e. brown ware, white inside', became known in the trade as 'Sunderland Ware', no matter where it was made.[1]

Probably it was Sunderland Ware that was advertised in Saint John as 'BROWN WARE . . . white glazed' in 1836[2] and as 'BROWN AND WHITE EARTHENWARE' in Montreal in 1841.[3] The Saint John advertisement was for milk pans—1,645 of them all imported at one time. The Montreal advertisement put 11,000 pieces of this white-lined brownware on the market, offering it for sale off a brig from Newcastle.

When the heading on an advertisement was 'Stoneware', implying a hard body fired to the point of vitrification, the articles listed were often the same as many of those produced in the softer 'brown' earthenware. Francis Clementson's advertisement in the *New Brunswick Courier* of November 3, 1855, is an illustration:

STONE BUTTER CROCKS
AND
MILK PANS
WHOLESALE AND RETAIL
LANDING ex Ship "Indian Queen":
4000 Butter Crocks;
3000 Jars,—1, 2, 3, and 4 gallons;
500 dozen Milk Pans.

138

Most of the common stoneware of this type was salt-glazed. Shortly before 1840, however, British potters perfected a liquid glaze for stoneware that was more satisfactory in use.[4] When colonial importers referred to 'Improved Stone-Ware' shortly after this date, they were probably offering this type of ware. A typical advertisement was that of Cuvillier & Sons, in the *Montreal Gazette* on August 2, 1844: '23 crates Improved Stone-Ware, consisting of 1 to 3 gallon Jars, Pickle-Pots, Pitchers, Ginger Beer and Cider Bottles, Cake and Milk Pans, Tobacco Pots, &c.'

From the pages of the newspapers emerges evidence of a tide of imports in both earthenware and stoneware that must have added up to an astounding total over the years. Advertisements picked at random from the papers of port cities tell the story: from the Montreal *Canadian Courant* of October 2, 1821, comes the notice of a sale of '22,000 Pieces assorted Brown Ware from New-castle'; from the *Quebec Gazette* of July 28, 1823, the announcement of an auction of '13,000 pieces Loose Earthenware, principally Brown Dishes' from Sunderland; from the Halifax *Novascotian* of May 13, 1829, the news of a sale on the Market Wharf to dispose of 'THE cargo of the Brig SPET . . . from New-castle' and offering '8000 pieces brown Ware, loose'; from the *Quebec Gazette* of May 4, 1838, word of '6750 PIECES BROWN STONEWARE,—comprising a complete assortment'; from another Quebec paper, the *Literary Transcript & General Intelligencer*, of June 10, 1839, notice of the arrival of '47,348 PIECES Loose Earthenware . . . consisting of Brown Dishes, Milk Pans, Basins, Jars, Chambers, &c.'; from the *Montreal Gazette* of September 1, 1852, an advertisement publicizing an auction of 'Forty to Fifty Thousand pieces of BROWN EARTHENWARE in Lots to suit the Trade.'

This brown earthenware and common stoneware from Great Britain began arriving very early and was distributed everywhere. Quebec had shipments, some from Glasgow, in the 1760's, shortly after the conquest.[5] Saint John and Fredericton merchants were receiving their supplies from Liverpool at the beginning of the nineteenth century.[6] In the 1820's country storekeepers in the Eastern Townships of Lower Canada were getting brownware from Montreal and offering it in exchange for farm produce.[7] Bytown (Ottawa) dealers in the 1830's were also trading in brownware imported from Glasgow and obtained through Montreal.[8] Glasgow was again the source of supply for Yarmouth merchants advertising 'brown, yellow and black Crocks and Pans' in 1856.[9]

It was in the face of such a massive volume of imports as this avalanche of brownware and stoneware from Great Britain that Canadian potters offered their own output of similar wares. No understanding of Canadian potting as an industry can be complete without full knowledge of the extent of the importations in common earthenware and stoneware, and no appreciation of the Canadian potters' difficulties possible without recognition of the formidable competition offered by rivals working on the other side of the Atlantic. In the second half of the century, colonial potters made important strides towards the establishment of the industry in Canada, greatly increasing and improving the quality of their own products; but this did not stop the importations. They pressed steadily in. In 1853, for instance, the year in which potters from St. Johns exhibited their brown earthenware at an industrial fair in Montreal, hoping for new orders,[10] the importations of that same ware were enormous. In one week two huge shipments arrived from Shields alone. On June 21 the *Montreal Gazette* announced that 'a quantity of Loose Brown Earthenware' would be sold the next morning, 'alongside the KEEPSAKE, from Shields'. The articles offered would include: 'Milk Dishes, Starch or Broth Pots, Beef Pans, Plain Trays, Cream Pots, Stew Pots Covered, Jars, Bottles, &c. &c.'

Two days later, the same newspaper carried an advertisement for another 'Brown Earthenware' auction, this time 'alongside the Brig "ROCKCLIFFE"', also from Shields. For the wholesalers on this occasion there were '12,000 Pieces BROWN EARTHENWARE': dishes, jars, cake pans, cream pots.

In an attempt to meet competition, local brownware makers sometimes employed an agent to represent them in port cities, such as Quebec or Montreal. In this way they tried to force their own products before the attention of the wholesalers who bought so readily at the shipside auctions. The Yamaska Pottery and Brick Works had an agent in Quebec in 1853:

YAMASKA POTTERY AND BRICK
WORKS,

HAVING been appointed AGENTS for the above Works, the undersigned are prepared to receive orders for a superior manufacture of BRICKS, Roof and Drain Tiles, Jars, Crocks, Milk Pans, Garden and Chimney Pots, and a general assortment of BROWNWARE.

A. JOSEPH & CO.

Quebec, 11th May, 1853.[11]

This same pottery in Yamaska (near Sorel) claimed that its brownware was 'equal to English manufacture',[12] but the orders taken for it by Abraham Joseph were secured only in the face of determined competition. Quebec, at this period, had potters of its own turning out the ordinary red-bodied earthenware adapted to such uses as garden pots and milk pans. The Bell brothers, William and David, were working on the outskirts of Quebec, making many of the same articles advertised by the Yamaska Pottery, but both the Bell Pottery and the Yamaska Pottery, when they offered common brownware in the middle years of the century, offered it in competition with shipment after shipment from Great Britain.

Even in the later Victorian days, when Canadian potters had advanced a long way from primitive beginnings and were ready with every article of common earthenware and stoneware, the crockery sellers were still advertising importations in this line. Glover Harrison, the Toronto dealer, whose China Hall on King Street was filled with fine porcelain, used also to carry plainly practical articles. In the 1870's these included stoneware chicken troughs and water filters, advertised as 'just arrived' with the importations from overseas.[13] Toronto stoneware makers had been offering these same articles for years,[14] but at China Hall the practical, even as the luxurious, came from potteries three thousand miles away.

Though it was from British potters overseas that Canadian potters had almost overwhelming competition throughout the century, those working in border areas faced a certain amount of competition from American makers of brownware and stoneware. There was never any substantial importation of American ceramic products of any kind into Canada in the nineteenth century—the main stream of the Canadian crockery trade was fed from across the Atlantic—but there was always a going-back-and-forth over the border, with the consequent bringing in of American goods, legally or illegally. American storekeepers, such as William Farrar of St. Albans, Vermont, used to advertise for business in the *Missiskoui Standard*, published in the Eastern Townships of Lower Canada.[15] Other Vermont merchants advertised at an early date in the *British Colonist and St. Francis Gazette*, also published in this border region.[16] Vermont-made earthenware very possibly formed part of the stock of these dealers, particularly of William Farrar's stock, for he had relatives potting in the state. Later in the century, Vermont potters who transferred activities to the Eastern Townships, while still maintaining business interests at home, were the contact through which some importations of Vermont stone and earthenware entered Canada. It is not surprising, therefore, that nineteenth-century crocks and jugs of Vermont manufacture are found in the Eastern Townships. In Ontario, New York stoneware turns up, and Ohio stoneware was, as has already been seen, imported into Red River Territory through St. Paul, Minnesota.[17] In the Maritime colonies, New England pottery undoubtedly came in, though advertisements show that here, as in other parts of British North America, the dealers waited for the ships from old England to bring them even the common wares advertised as 'wanted for the country trade'.

In the earlier part of the century, the term 'brownware' took care of nearly all the common earthenware, dark-bodied and utilitarian in every sense. After about 1840, however, the crockery sellers of the colonies began advertising 'yellow' and 'Rockingham' wares in addition to brownware. The yellow wares were made of clays that burned to a light buff shade intensified by a transparent glaze; Rockingham wares were covered with a rich, manganese-brown glaze. Both were generally potted from clays more refined than those used for ordinary brownware.

The yellow ware, in Canadian advertisements, was also referred to as 'yellow ironstone'[18] or as 'cane'. As cane, this Victorian yellow ware is not to be confused with the caneware introduced by Josiah Wedgwood in the eighteenth century, and continued in production by the Wedgwood factory. Wedgwood's dry, or unglazed body called 'cane' was a stoneware that represented a very much refined version of the body produced by the brownware potters. Wedgwood, and those who copied him, used it for decorative articles and for delicate teaware (generally glazing the inside of any hollow piece intended for use). By contrast, what the later nineteenth-century crockery sellers frequently meant by caneware was a glazed body employed for articles more at home in the kitchen than the drawing room. John Patton's advertisement in the *Gazette* of Montreal on October 7, 1867, gives a good illustration of the type of caneware imported in large quantities in the second half of the century: 'CROCKERY WHOLESALE. —The Subscribers have now on hand a large stock of Crockery suitable for Country Stores, comprising ... CANE BAKERS, BOWLS and JUGS, ROCKINGHAM TEAPOTS.'

The Rockingham teapots, mentioned by Patton, like the caneware, had little to do with earlier products of the same name. They were not from the Rockingham Works in Yorkshire, which were, in any case, long out of existence by this time. They did, however, hark back, in the colour implied by their name, to a type of ware associated with the factory. That ware, as introduced early in the nineteenth century, was described by Llewellynn Jewitt as a 'fine hard and compact white earthenware' covered by a 'reddish brown, or chocolate, colour'.[19] At the Yorkshire factory itself, where this ware was first made, it was known as 'brown china'; later, when everyone else was attempting a version of it, the name 'Rockingham ware' became attached to it, regardless of maker. According to Jewitt, 'every manufacturer in the kingdom' tried to make an earthenware covered with a Rockingham-type brown glaze. And not only in Great Britain: in North America what passed for Rockingham became the pride of local potters.

But few who copied the Yorkshire product achieved anything like it in quality. Over the years the name 'Rockingham' came to mean the dark brown glaze only. The body it covered was not often of the 'fine, hard and compact white earthenware' described by Jewitt. He had declared the original 'brown china' to be 'one of the smoothest and most beautiful wares that has ever been produced'. Only a small percentage of the Rockingham sold in Canada would have even approached this standard.

Tea and coffee pots were the main items imported in this ware. A Montreal advertisement of 1846 indicates that the demand for them was such that a wholesaler would bring in '20 crates ROCKINGHAM TEAPOTS' at a time'.[20] Robert Anderson, the crockery-selling Scotsman who imported what would sell easily, kept Rockingham tea and coffee pots constantly on hand. His advertisement in the *Montreal Gazette* on August 12, 1846, headed dramatically 'A MILLION PIECES OF GLASS, CHINA, AND EARTHENWARE FOR SALE', listed 'Rockingham Tea and Coffee Pots' among items picked out as specially wanted by the public. In Halifax, in 1860, they were selected by R. Hannah to feature from his first shipment of a New Year. The advertisement appeared in the *Novascotian* on January 9: 'Plates, Jugs, Bowls, and Toilet Sets of all sorts and sizes; Tea Pots, Black and Rockingham, Brown Ware and Toys.'

Comparatively little of what was imported in cane and Rockingham would have been marked, but one firm known to have supplied Canada over many years with cane milk pans, 'fireproof' yellow baking dishes, Rockingham teapots, and blue-printed earthenware was that of the Sharpe Brothers of Burton-upon-Trent. An advertisement mentioning their earthenware by name appeared in the *Montreal Gazette* on October 2, 1847:

BY JOHN M. TOBIN
EXTENSIVE SALE OF EARTHEN-
WARE, GLASSWARE, &c.
ON THURSDAY next . . .
at the stores of the subscriber—
156 crates of superior assorted Earthenware, the
manufacture of Sharpe, Brothers
& Co.

Thomas Sharpe had founded the firm in 1821. When he died, in 1838, the business was carried on by his brothers. Much of the Sharpe ware was marked, first with the name or initials of Thomas Sharpe alone, and, after 1838, with the name of Sharpe Brothers & Co. In the 1890's the firm added 'Ltd.' to the mark. Marked examples of useful kitchen wares manufactured by the Sharpes are often found in Canada, but on some of the very hard cane or yellow wares the mark is so faintly impressed that it often goes unnoticed.

Wedgwood's superior-quality earthenware with a Rockingham glaze was generally marked.[21] So, too, were the equally fine wares of this type that came from the Spode, and later, the Copeland factory. But thousands of tea and coffee pots, jugs and other articles calling themselves Rockingham, and even greater numbers of yellow ware bowls and baking dishes came anonymously to Canada. Today it would be impossible to know who made them, or even to distinguish some of them from similar wares made in North America.

Yellow and Rockingham wares, like brownware and ordinary stoneware, fell within the range of Canadian potting. And here again the local product was often hard pressed by the imported ware. In the 1870's the Farrars of St. Johns (the Canadian branch of the Vermont potting family) sought business as 'MANU-FACTURERS OF Stone, Yellow & Rockingham Ware',[22] but at the same time as the Farrars' advertisements appealed to buyers of these wares, Montreal importers, less than thirty miles from St. Johns, were not only bringing in shipments of yellow and Rockingham wares from overseas, they were careful to advise the public that what they were offering was the imported article. Firms like Devany & Co. of Montreal knew well the promotional value in stressing that their Rockingham teapots were English make. This was how they described two crates of them advertised in the *Gazette* on December 6, 1876.

As they had done with brownware and stoneware, Canadian potters claimed hopefully that what they made in yellow and Rockingham ware was 'in no way inferior to the imported'.[23] In some cases this may have been true, but many small potters, working under the handicap of very limited resources, must have produced wares that fell far short of the standards of industrial potting set by manufacturers like Sharpe Brothers of Burton-upon-Trent. As for Rockingham, which had begun as a finely potted ware, it came, in terms of Canadian production, to mean almost anything covered with a dark brown glaze. 'Brownware' vanished from the acknowledged output of Canadian potteries and 'Rockingham' took its place.

The brownwares and common stonewares and some of the yellow and Rockingham wares belong in feeling, if not necessarily in fact, to what is generally thought of as country pottery. Another type of earthenware which came to Canada in the nineteenth century, and which combined something of the simpler spirit with industrial potting, was known in its day as 'dipped' or 'dipt' ware. Robert Anderson's advertisement in the *Montreal Gazette* of October 7, 1844, is typical of many announcing the arrival of dipped wares throughout the colonies:

CROCKERY AT LOW PRICES

LANDING, ex "Lord Lambton," and for sale, a large assortment,—consisting of assorted Crates . . . Painted Teas, White Chambers, Dipt Bowls . . .

According to William Evans, who was writing at just this period, dipped ware was of three main types: marbled ware, banded ware, and Mocha ware.[24] The last type today attracts much interest. Obviously it came to Canada in considerable quantity, for a certain amount of it has survived, particularly in country districts, in spite of the fact that it was cheap ware put to hard use.

Mocha ware is unmistakable. Whether it is of a cream or white earthenware or of a hard cane body, its distinctive feature is the 'seaweed' or fern-like decoration thought to resemble the markings of the quartz called Mocha stone. This decoration, different in every piece, appears on a wide band of coloured slip, and may be in brown, black, blue, green, or pink. The pink decoration seems to have been introduced towards the end of the century; the other colours were all in use earlier.

First made late in the eighteenth century, Mocha reached the height of its popularity in the nineteenth. The Canadian advertisements show that all kinds of dipped wares, and these undoubtedly included some Mocha, were in particular demand from the 1840's through the 1860's. This does not mean that no Mocha ware was imported into Canada after 1870. Mocha outlasted the century. Canadians were probably importing it long after the Victorian era had come to an end.

Little Mocha ware was marked, and dating is difficult. Some of the lightweight, cream-coloured ware belongs to the earlier days, but the cane body must have been typical of most that was sold in Canada (*Plate* 9). Many potters in Staffordshire and in Newcastle and Gasgow, all areas exporting heavily to British North America, made Mocha ware.

Just how the dendritic or tree-like effect of the decoration was obtained is a matter of debate. The fact that the ware has also been called 'tobacco spit ware' indicates what some potters, at least, used in the mixture required to produce the 'Mocha tea' or colouring agent. The necessary quality of the 'tea' was that, aided by gravity, it would creep or 'ramify' into the characteristic forms. Evans declared that on the band to be decorated 'a drop is let fall, of a saturated infusion of tobacco in stale urine and turpentine, and it ramifies into the resemblance of trees, shrubs, &c.'[25] Others cited a brew containing tobacco and hops. Sometimes the spot of colour was allowed to flow naturally into its patterns by inclining the object being decorated; sometimes it was scattered on its way by the use of a blow-pipe. When the Mocha decoration takes thistle-like form it is frequently attributed to Glasgow potters, who very possibly were the suppliers of at least some of the 'Fancy Dipt' bowls and jugs that Robert Anderson, the Glasgow-trained crockery seller, used to import for Canadian buyers.

Another class of ware whose place was in the kitchen or on the tables of the unsophisticated, was earthenware with sponged decoration. With sponged wares belong many of the imported bowls and other articles long called 'Portneuf' (the name of a town near Quebec City). Once thought to have been made in Canada, before it was realized how little whiteware was ever potted in this country, these so-called Portneuf wares were later assigned to Staffordshire; it is Scotland, however, that should be credited with many of them.

The sponged ware advertised in Victorian Canada as crockery excellent for country trade was of a cheap white or cream-coloured earthenware. Its name implied the nature of its decoration. This, according to Arnold Fleming, the Scottish potter and historian, was put on the biscuit (or unglazed) ware by means of 'designs cut out of the roots of sponges' and used 'in conjunction with "underglaze colours" '. The pattern was thus stamped on, a rapid and cheap method of colour decoration.[26] At other times a bright effect, although not a formal pattern, was obtained by merely dabbing at the ware with a sponge impregnated with colour. Sometimes the sponge technique was combined with enamelling, occasionally with transfer printing.

Most sponged ware had what Llewellynn Jewitt called 'a bright fancy character', which he observed was much admired in the 'out-markets' of the world.[27] Canada was one of the 'out-markets' where earthenware of this 'bright fancy character' had lasting sales appeal, as the advertisements show. It was equally popular in the United States, where much of it has now come to be called 'spatterware'. In Great Britain, where it was made, it was and is called sponged ware,[28] and as sponged ware it was sold in its day in Canada.

It first came on the Canadian market about mid-century. Alexander Christie, whose store was on Queen Street in Niagara, advertised it in the summer of 1851: 'The Subscriber has just received direct from THE STAFFORDSHIRE POTTERIES . . . SPONGED, PAINTED, DIPT, AND WHITE WARE.'[29]

The same month as this advertisement appeared in Niagara, Robert Anderson, always to the fore with whatever was new, quick-selling, and cheap, publicized sponged ware in Montreal. With 250 crates of earthenware at 'very low prices', he had ample supplies of sponged 'Cups and Saucers, Plates all sizes, Pitchers, Chambers, Bowls, Platters'.[30]

In a later advertisement, this one by James Patton & Co., of Montreal, sponged earthenware was again included with the cheaply painted wares and dipped wares—all 'country goods':

CROCKERY
BY WHOLESALE
THE subscribers have now on hand a full assortment of Goods suitable for the Country trade.
Painted, Sponged and Printed Teas . . .
Dipped and Sponged Jugs, Bowls . . .
for sale by the crate or dozen.[31]

Scottish pottery made extensive use of sponged decoration; some believe it originated with them. Staffordshire potters, led by William Adams of Greenfield (1798-1865), began producing it in quantity just before mid-century, or only shortly before it became a feature of Canadian advertising.

With sponged earthenware, which today is regarded as having the ingenuous appeal of country charm, must be classed at least some of the 'Portneuf' wares. Over the years this term (a misnomer in the first place) has come to be used very loosely to include a variety of types of decoration, but what are generally regarded as characteristic 'Portneuf' wares are those on which the design, in under-glaze colours, has been stamped or stencilled, the colour applied in some cases by sponge stencil. The typical 'Portneuf' decoration is not transfer-printed.[32]

That many of these wares have a Scottish ancestry is apparent from material presented some years ago in the English magazine, *Apollo*. In December, 1957, Commander H. J. S. Banks, writing on Scottish ceramics, illustrated a mug

145

typical of many nineteenth-century wares from the Bo'ness area. Of ordinary white earthenware, its coloured decoration was, he pointed out, 'applied by sponge stencils'. To many Canadians the decoration of this Bo'ness mug would be startlingly familiar: it is 'Portneuf' in its best form. A bowl with similar decoration is in the McCord Museum of McGill University. Acquired a number of years ago, the bowl was at that time labelled 'Portneuf'.

Again, several border designs are known to be common to both 'Portneuf' and to nineteenth-century wares found today in Scotland. The narrow branching border on the mug illustrated by Commander Banks is one. Not only border designs but the main decoration is sometimes the same on wares found today in both Scotland and Canada. The bowl decorated with a robin, illustrated in *Plate* 10A is an example. This particular bowl was purchased in Scotland in 1966; similar bowls have come from farm houses in the Province of Quebec. Significant points of resemblance have also been noted between 'Portneuf' and some of the characteristic motifs used as decoration on Scottish 'taws' (balls of earthenware for carpet bowling).

Floral decoration abounds on what is called 'Portneuf'. There are bluebells, convolvuluses, fuchsias, marguerites, peonies, thistles, and nameless blossoms of no botanical standing. Rosettes (often scattered profusely), medallions, and stylized motifs appear in many forms. Crossed flags belonging to no country decorate some bowls; sailing ships, fans, ferns, and butterflies have a place. Animal and bird subjects are generally thought to be among the most interesting. These include deer, cows, goats, rabbits, partridges, turkeys, robins, peacocks, and birds unknown to ornithologists. The border designs are varied. The peacock bowls, for example, occur with at least two different borders: one a narrow floral border in pink, another a stylized border in brown (*Plate* 10B).

One bowl with typical animal decoration serves to set the date of many. This piece, the decoration repeated around it in characteristic 'Portneuf' manner, is ornamented with an elephant—an elephant who is named beneath his coloured picture. 'Jumbo' was a resident of the London Zoo for nearly twenty years. When the Zoo decided, in 1882, to accept P. T. Barnum's offer of $10,000 for him, Jumbo sprang into the news. The public outcry over parting with him was deafening. It reached Parliament. An injunction was taken to stop the sale, but the case went against those who wanted to keep Jumbo in England.

At this time Jumbo's name was everywhere. There were Jumbo polkas, Jumbo cigars, Jumbo books, Jumbo handkerchiefs. It was inevitable that he appear on pottery, and he did, in various forms. Before the furore had entirely died down, Jumbo was in the news again: this time in Canada, and this time was the last. Jumbo, the mammoth elephant billed by Barnum as the largest pachyderm ever seen, was killed near St. Thomas, Ontario, in the early autumn of 1885. The exploited animal had been allowed to wander onto the railway track, and his massive skull was fractured by a head-on collision with a train.

Only a few of the wares which have survived to be called 'Portneuf' in the Province of Quebec can be dated as early as the introduction of sponged earthenware to the Canadian market. Most, with their cheerful colours—pinks, blues, greens, lavenders, rusty reds, yellows, browns, and a bright navy blue—date from about the time of Jumbo's fame. Tea bowls and saucers and other items similarly

146

decorated with pink rosettes may predate Jumbo by some years; but it should be remembered, in regard to tea bowls, that the old-fashioned cup without a handle was in use much longer than is generally realized. Tea bowls, or cups without handles, were being imported into Montreal from Glasgow as late as the 1870's.[33] Many of the wares collectors buy as 'Portneuf' cannot be dated even as early as Jumbo.

Very little of this cheap white or cream-coloured earthenware was marked, but one of the suppliers of some of the earliest of the sponged wares to come to Canada was an English potter of the 1850's. Edward Walley, of Staffordshire, had close connections with the Canadian market.[34] Today his name is found occasionally on tablewares with a sponged design in pink and blue. When this sponged Walley ware turns up in Canada it is tagged 'Portneuf'. A plate in a pattern some call 'Maple Leaf' has a two-line impressed maker's mark that is indistinct but which is relatively late in general appearance.[35] Some bowls with 'Portneuf-type' floral decoration have a mark of the Britannia Pottery in Glasgow. A few pieces turn up not with a maker's mark but with the mark of a Glasgow crockery merchant.

It will never be possible to know who made all the decorated bowls and tablewares 'suitable for the country trade' that have been called 'Portneuf'. They very obviously come from a number of sources. But there is little doubt that much of the most interesting and attractive 'Portneuf' originated with those Scottish and Staffordshire potters whose earthenware of 'a bright fancy character' held the Canadian market for over half a century.

CHAPTER XII

Earthenware for Decoration:
On Mantel, Table, and Wall

TERRACOTTA AND MAJOLICA . . . perfection of design and color
. . . applied upon principles laid down in the English schools of art.
F. & J. Morgan, in *Cherrier's Quebec Directory for . . . 1880.*

Even in the early days, there was a market in Canada for earthenware that was more ornamental than useful. At the same time as they were buying crocks by the thousand and soup plates by the crate, Canadians were purchasing, albeit in smaller quantities, 'Chimney Ornaments', 'Fancy Figures', and 'Images'. They put Queen Victoria on the mantelpiece and made a place on the whatnot for Sir Rowland Hill, the father of penny postage. They hung up plaques with John Wesley's picture on them, and delighted in 'Lustre Ware' for decoration.

There is evidence that a merchant of Quebec imported earthenware figures of William Wilberforce, the great emancipator, whose efforts helped to make slavery illegal in British territories years before it became an issue in a civil war in the United States. 'Fancy Jugs' in coloured stoneware, intended for show rather than use, and parlour knick-knacks in terracotta are proved by advertisements to have been as popular in Canada as in Great Britain, where they were made.

Mrs. Traill advised emigrants that 'rich' furniture was out of place in a log cabin, and counselled against the expense of taking unnecessary equipment into remote places, yet she recommended ornaments to relieve the bleakness of a home in the forest. A glazed print or two and a set of corner shelves for 'little ornamental matters' were, in her opinion, desirable, if not really essential.[1]

In mid-nineteenth century, the period at which Mrs. Traill was writing, 'little ornamental matters' very often took the form of small figures to stand on a corner shelf, busts of 'celebrated personages', or the chimney ornaments whose name indicated their place on the mantelpiece. These were all advertised in both earthenware and porcelain (in the Canadian advertising it was customary to specify china, or porcelain, where that was meant, otherwise to imply earthenware).

Most of the ornaments sold in Canada came from Staffordshire, a few from the Scottish potteries. Those with lustre (metallic colour) decoration were sometimes imported from Sunderland, although Staffordshire, too, made earthenware figures and other articles decorated in this way. When John McDonald, china merchant of Halifax, advertised in 1843 that he had 'received . . . from Liverpool

149

. . . Lustre Ware Ornaments',[2] he was probably offering Staffordshire goods regularly shipped from that port.

Nearly all specialist china sellers in Canada handled ornaments along with their tablewares and kitchen crocks. Robert Anderson, for instance, the Montreal dealer who stocked the useful and the quick-selling to do business on a tremendous scale, announced 'Fancy Figures' with 'Yellow Ironstone Pie Dishes', and 'Images' with preserve pots and milk pans.[3] When he publicized them in French they became 'figures d'ornements' and he put them in the same advertisement as 'Vases à bidet' and 'Pots de Nuit'.[4] All were in earthenware and all were imported by Anderson with shipments from Glasgow and Liverpool.

'Chimney Ornaments', frequently sold in pairs or sets, must have come to Canada in considerable quantities, to judge by the evidence of the crockery advertisements in newspapers. Francis Rasco, the future owner of the famous Rasco's Hotel in Montreal, where Charles Dickens would be a guest, was selling them in his shop in 1817;[5] Robert Anderson had them 'at low prices' in 1848.[6] Evidence of their popularity comes, too, from the auction sales. When garrison officers were transferred, their auctions frequently included chimney ornaments in earthenware. A lieutenant of the Royal Engineers left chimney ornaments to be sold in Kingston in 1831.[7] A grocer's household auction in the St. Lawrence Suburbs of Montreal, held on an April morning in 1857, gave to the highest bidder a blue and white stone china dinner set, a selection of chimney ornaments, and an English thrush in a cage.[8]

Although many earthenware ornaments were well modelled and well potted, they were, in the main, intended for the cottage rather than the mansion. They could sell as low as a few pennies in some general store or cost shillings in a china shop. Many were brightly decorated; a cobalt blue, a vivid orange, and a strong pink were favourite colours. Often gold was used sparingly to add to their impressiveness, or to spell out the title on a figure.

Few who made these images and fancy figures marked their work. Some of the earthenware ornaments are known to have been produced by such important makers as Enoch Wood (1759-1840) and Felix Pratt (1780-1859); but the vast majority came from small pot-works, their inspiration drawn from history, literature, and current events.

Members of the royal family gave the potters subjects for many of their most popular figures. Queen Victoria, Prince Albert, and the young Prince of Wales issued forth in clay in a variety of poses. When the royal children grew to marrying age, they and their marriage partners were saleable as ornaments at home and abroad. Statesmen had decorative value; so, too, did authors and actors. Prizefighters and murderers sold well. Animals, especially dogs in pairs for the mantelpiece, were turned out by the thousand, along with rustic cottages and coy country lovers. Religious figures, of both Protestant and Roman Catholic interest, were produced in quantity, and earthenware plaques to hang on the wall set forth religious texts in stylish form.

Few Canadian advertisements for earthenware figures or ornaments of any type specify titles. One that did, however, appeared in the *Quebec Mercury* on December 28, 1839. On that day Samuel Alcorn invited colonial connoisseurs to come to his Palace Street shop to view earthenware figures of very superior quality: 'WESLEY—WILBERFORCE—HANNAH MORE—ADAM CLARKE—ROWLAND HILL, and QUEEN VICTORIA! ! !'

Today the minor poetess Hannah More and the Methodist divine Adam Clarke are almost forgotten, but in 1839 they had sufficient popular appeal in Canada to be offered as 'splendid' figures suitable for New Year's gifts.

In Great Britain, figures and chimney and other inexpensive ornaments had enormous popularity. That they were also an important part of the Canadian crockery trade has not been so well known, yet the newspaper advertisements make clear that china merchants like Robert Anderson in Montreal, Samuel Alcorn in Quebec, and John McDonald in Halifax were importing large stocks of this British earthenware made for decoration. In both price range and forthright sturdiness these decorative pieces were compatible with the blue-printed dishes and ironstone cups that were the characteristic tablewares of a new country.

Another earthenware article made for show and greatly admired in nineteenth-century Canada was the 'fancy jug'. It was possible to put these jugs to use, but the ornate decoration, often moulded in relief, was scarcely functional. The fact that many such jugs have survived suggests that they were often kept for display in Canada.

Repeatedly advertised in the middle years of the century were fancy jugs in what was called 'drab stoneware'. The colour was an olive grey, or putty shade. 'Drab Stone Jugs, uncovered and covered with Britannia Metal' was the way Thomas M'Adam announced them in the *Morning Courier* of Montreal, in 1835.[9] He listed them with 'Mantel Ornaments' and separated them from the 'cheapest articles of manufacture' with which country merchants could be supplied.

G. M. Fairchild, writing of the old things to be found in the vicinity of Quebec at the end of the nineteenth century, told of coming upon one of these drab stone jugs discarded on the beach at Cap Rouge. It was a marked specimen, bearing the name of Jones & Walley of Staffordshire, and a registration date for its relief decoration of July 1, 1842. When its broken handle had been restored 'by the deft hand of Côté' (Jean-Baptiste Côté, the Quebec sculptor), George Fairchild had a piece such as might once have been seen by customers visiting Samuel Alcorn's china shop in the Quebec of an earlier day.[10]

Fairchild's stone jug, salvaged at Cap Rouge, had what he called a 'gipsy' pattern. Others, sometimes in drab colour, sometimes in grey-white or a distinctive light blue, and potted by many different makers, had hunting patterns or classical scenes. At mid-century Charles Meigh of Hanley produced a whole series of jugs in the Gothic taste, with figures appearing in ecclesiastical niches. Cork & Edge of Burslem followed with others. A fine example of the early Victorian Gothic jug, with the Apostles in their niches, was in the collection that Percy Inglis, of Mahone Bay, patiently put together over many years. The Inglis collection illustrated the wares once typical of Nova Scotia homes.

In white stoneware T. & R. Boote, whose products were considered 'celebrated' by Canadians,[11] made fancy jugs with Biblical figures in relief. They also put on the market large jugs with scenes from the poems of Robert Burns. A number of potters issued Burns jugs in tan stoneware, and many of these must have had a sale in the British North American colonies, where fancy jugs were held in high esteem for their decorative value, and where thousands boasted of Scottish blood.

Many fancy jugs of the middle and later years of the nineteenth century depended upon plant forms for their relief decoration. Others, in white or cream-coloured earthenware embellished with enamel colours, were modelled as portraits of some of the 'celebrated personages' who also appeared as 'fancy figures'. Robert Burns himself, the Duke of Wellington, John Wesley, and Princess Louise, at the time of her marriage to the Marquis of Lorne, were all to be seen standing as ornaments or decorating the sides of jugs that were rarely used.

As the nineteenth century moved into its second half, new types of earthenware ornaments began to crowd the Staffordshire figures and the older-style fancy jugs on the dealers' shelves. With restless achievement, British potters gave the public new fashion after new fashion. For many of these they looked to history for a name, while producing wares characteristic of their own times and conditions. Two of the most popular of these Victorian ornamental earthenwares with historical associations were advertised together in the *Gazette* of Montreal on September 21, 1876. The occasion was a store auction at one of W. H. Barber's two china shops. 'Just opened' and offered as particularly tempting was 'a fine lot . . . of Majolica and Terra Cotta Ware'.

The Minton firm in Staffordshire was probably responsible for resurrecting the name of majolica, originally a tin-glazed and painted earthenware whose great day had been the sixteenth century in Italy. In time for the exhibition 'of the works of industry of all nations', held in London in 1851 (the Great Exhibition), the firm produced a display of vases and flower pots 'in imitation of Majolica Ware'.[12] The relationship of the Minton majolica to the majolica (or maiolica) of the Italian Renaissance was not readily apparent, but the name was taken up enthusiastically by both potters and public.

Soon potters throughout Great Britain, and even on the Continent and in America, were manufacturing highly ornamental earthenware with rich coloured glazes and calling it majolica. Their work caused little confusion with either the antique or the imitations and outright forgeries of the antique made in Italy itself. The Victorian potter started with a name from history, but he made of majolica an earthenware that could have belonged to no other time but his own. Even when painted (as the early tin-glazed ware had been) Victorian majolica retained its nineteenth-century approach. In the hands of the British potters it became a confident modernity, a 'massive ware, of bold design, and bolder ornaments, and positive colours'.[13]

Massive, bold, and positive described much that was admired as majolica in Canada. The name came to be used as a very general term for any earthenware with coloured glazes, but such ware was usually of ornamental character with conspicuous relief decoration. Of a cane or buff body, its colours derived from glazes used in a variety of ways, this was the ware of innumerable fern jardinières, of umbrella stands, and of the more refined of spittoons which once adorned the lobbies of Canadian hotels like the Rossin House in Toronto, the St. Lawrence Hall in Montreal, and the Victoria Hotel in Saint John.

Majolica was used for figures, for wall plaques, and for fanciful candlesticks and commanding vases. Its rich blues, turquoises, yellows, and greens were seen to advantage, in Victorian eyes, in the huge ornamental cheese covers such as Glover Harrison was selling as majolica at China Hall, in Toronto, in 1879. In the same *Mail* advertisement, on November 28, he was also offering the fashionable majolica boxes (usually with crossed fish on the covers) known as 'sardine boxes'.

The line between ornamental and useful was loosely drawn with majolica wares. Much majolica was actually produced in useful forms and yet kept by the Victorian housewife solely for display. 'Unique' cheese stands and porridge sets (a bowl and small pitcher) were advertised in majolica by Montreal china merchants,[14] but how often these came to the table with cheese or oatmeal may be questioned. In the country, many a Methodist minister on his circuit rounds baptized the baby from a majolica berry bowl—the best bowl in the house, and never used for berries.

Majolica belonged in the categories of both 'utility' and 'vertu', as a Winnipeg china seller described it in the 1880's,[15] but it was as an article of 'vertu', or ornament, that most Canadians knew it. A. T. Wiley, offering it in Montreal, classed it under 'New Novelties' and 'Bric-a-Brac', and this is how a high proportion of it was sold.[16]

Differing from majolica, in that its body was usually red in tone and it was generally left uncoloured and unglazed, was Victorian terracotta, a name borrowed from the Italian and meaning simply baked clay. Historically terracotta was associated with Italian work at the time of the Renaissance, and it was, therefore, another case of the nineteenth-century potter looking to the past for inspiration and taking an old name for a new product.

English potters had, of course, produced biscuit redwares since the seventeenth century, but these earlier English wares had generally been hard-fired to render them serviceable as stonewares. When the Victorians adopted unglazed redware as a new ceramic style, they thought of it as a ware produced from 'brick clay', fired below stoneware temperature, and particularly suitable for decoration in high relief. In body colour it could range from a dark red to near white.[17]

Canadians took terracotta seriously. In Montreal crowds used to turn out for great auction sales where 'elegant and costly . . . fancy goods' included 'Splendid Terra Cotta' in designs based upon the antique. In the Montreal *Gazette* of December 20, 1852, Young & Benning, holding such a sale in their rooms on St. François Xavier Street, urged 'all lovers of the ingenious and beautiful' to attend. Not only would the auction offer a wide selection of artistic 'holiday gifts', it would provide a rare opportunity for Montrealers to view articles said to be duplicates of those exhibited the previous year at the Great Exhibition in London.

The successors of Young & Benning (the firm of Benning & Barsalou) held another sale of this kind in 1866. The advertisement in the *Gazette* on July 13 read:

SALE OF TERRA COTTA WARE

The Subscribers have received instructions to Sell at their Stores . . . the contents of THIRTY PACKAGES TERRA COTTA WARE consisting of—VASES, WATER FOUNTAINS, STATUARY, ORNAMENTAL FLOWER POTS, FERN STANDS, &c. &c.,

Modelled from Copies of Designs both Ancient and Modern, and being principally of an embossed character . . .

Although most terracotta was untouched by any addition of colour, some was given this type of decoration. 'COLOURED TERRA COTTA' was the heading on an advertisement in Montreal's *Daily Witness* in 1881. On Christmas Eve a group of auction-goers gathered in the Ottawa Hotel on St. James Street to bid for these novelties.

Terracotta for the china shop (as distinct from terracotta in the form of architectural and large-scale garden ornaments) was made by many of the same potters who made majolica. Mintons was a leading firm. Copelands, successors to the Spodes, produced figures and busts in terracotta that were considered handsome. They advertised their 'Ceramic Statuary', of which they produced a number of different types, in a Canadian publication of the 1870's.[18] Doultons also made impressive terracotta wares. All three firms were heavy exporters to Canada in the nineteenth century.

In the 1860's a lesser-known pottery, that of F. H. Brewer & Co., of Longton, was visited by the self-styled Canadian poet, James Torrington Spencer Lidstone. At Brewer's Stafford Street Works fancy rustic wares, 'that . . . even in Terra Cotta seem'd to grow', were seen by Lidstone, who made note of a number of terracotta items familiar in Canadian advertisements of the period: hanging flower baskets, cigar ash trays, garden seats imitating rustic stumps, and 'Stands for Ferns and every kind of Flower'.[19]

Several firms came into being to work in terracotta exclusively. One of these was the Watcombe Terra Cotta Clay Co., in Devonshire, who put on the first important showing of their wares at the South Kensington International Exhibition in 1871. Watcombe terracotta was of a fairly hard body, and the Company made what the Canadian advertisers called 'Coloured Terra Cotta'. Small figures, busts, vases, jugs, and tobacco jars were among the items produced.

Like majolica, terracotta came in useful as well as ornamental forms. 'TERRA COTTA Tea Sets . . . something new' were announced in Montreal in 1862 by Savage & Lyman, prominent silversmiths who also handled decorative ceramic wares.[20] Some years later terracotta 'Ice Cream Sets' were an innovation at Edward Hagar's china shop on St. Paul Street.[21] But again like majolica, terracotta was regarded as a ware more suitable for display than for table use.

Terracotta ornaments—as highly recommended for Christmas presents by a New Brunswick china seller in 1858[22]—ranked for many years with the most popular earthenwares bought for decoration. 'Handsome ware and very durable' Canadians considered it,[23] but when they brought home teapots (glazed inside) and jugs in terracotta they were more apt to put them beside the figures and the vases in cabinets than on tables set for tea.

New earthenwares for decoration became a Victorian craze. Majolica, terracotta, and related wares called by other historic names—Palissy, Della Robbia, and Henri Deux—emanated from British potteries and were snatched at by the art-conscious in Canada. For those of small means or less elevated taste, who still wanted earthenware ornaments in their homes, there were the perennial Staffordshire figures and commemorative pieces (which had never ceased to keep up with current events) as well as cheap copies of the newer art pottery. Captain Webb, first to swim the English Channel and drowned, in 1883, while attempting to conquer Niagara, appeared in earthenware in the traditional Staffordshire manner. In 1891, when Princess May of Teck (the Queen Mary of the twentieth century) became engaged to the Duke of Clarence (elder brother of the future King George V) the young couple were in chimney ornaments almost at once. Queen Victoria's Golden Jubilee in 1887 and the Diamond Jubilee ten years later released a torrent of figures, jugs, mugs, plaques, all to be had in earthenware.

In the last quarter of the century, Canadian china marchants, not only in the old cities of the east but in Winnipeg and the farther west, did business in untold numbers of the cheaper ornaments, and ventured on supplies of the new wares of the aesthetic movement. From 'all the leading European makers . . . ORNAMENTAL POTTERY. CABINET BRIC-A-BRAC' was the boast in Montreal;[24] 'the rarest novelties and oddities, the quaintest designs, and the most curious specimens' was the 'puffery' in Winnipeg.[25]

Towards the end of the century, however, Canadians were visiting shops other than those of the china merchants for their ornamental earthenware. Fine art dealers began to handle much of what is thought of as the art pottery of the period. Buying from them, some Canadians formed important collections of 'modern' wares. The day of the studio potter was slowly dawning, and even in Canada there was an early interest in the new direction earthenware was taking.

One firm whose products were imported by both art dealers and china merchants was that of Doultons of Lambeth. The new Doulton pottery, Canadians learned from Montreal's *Daily Witness* (November 1, 1885), was 'very elegant'. That they accepted this judgment is evident from the status accorded Doulton ware in the late nineteenth century as the appropriate gift for the fashionable bride. A wedding of 1893 furnishes an interesting example. On October 18 that year, Montague Allan, son of the founder of the Allan Line (and later Sir Montague Allan), married the daughter of Hector MacKenzie, one of the largest shareholders of the Bank of Montreal. Next day the *Herald* called the wedding 'one of the greatest social events that have stirred Montreal's best society', and then proceeded to publish a detailed list of the presents. The list revealed that some of the most prominent citizens had chosen Doulton ornaments for Miss MacKenzie. Each of these pieces would have been unique, a work created by an artist in Henry Doulton's Lambeth studio.

The story of Doulton art wares of the later nineteenth century actually goes back to the 1860's. At that time, because of a friendship existing between Henry Doulton (1820-97), then head of the firm, and John Sparkes, headmaster of the Lambeth School of Art, students from the art school were admitted to the pottery. Ornamental salt-glazed stoneware, for which Doultons had been noted in earlier years, was revived, and turned over to the students for its decoration. At the South Kensington Exhibition of 1871 the public was shown what a co-operative effort on the part of an art school and a pottery could produce. On the whole it liked what it saw. By the time of the American Centennial Exhibition held in Philadelphia in 1876, Doultons, having brought into their employ their own staff of artists, were well on their way to the reputation accorded them in the 1880's by Marc Louis Solon—that of being the creators of a new style of stoneware 'known and admired by the amateurs of Ceramic art all the world over'.[26]

An American critic, commenting on the British display at Philadelphia, found 'the peculiar stone-ware' of the Doulton factory to be of extraordinary merit.

'The wonderful variety of the different shapes into which this Doulton-ware is manufactured,' wrote J. S. Ingram, 'is rendered still more so by the fact that no one form is ever repeated. It is the pride of the makers that they have never willingly duplicated a single article.'[27]

Ingram then went on to explain the relationship between decorator, modeller, and potter under the Doulton system:

> The Doulton-ware is made out of a very common stout clay, capable of resisting an excessively high temperature. The modeler draws his shapes upon paper, and these are handed over to the decorators, who consider in their own minds what form of decoration will best conform with them. Having determined upon this, the potter is next consulted, and he throws upon the wheel the desired shape. Then the decorator seizes it while still wet, and proceeds to ornament it.[28]

One of the early and best-known of the Doulton stoneware decorators was a woman, Hannah B. Barlow. Her love of animals contributed to her reputation as a ceramic artist. She became famous and made Doulton stoneware famous for the drawings of animals which she incised in the unfired clay. Into the lines of a drawing, pigment would be rubbed. In the fired result the drawing then stood out against the salt-glazed ware with the effect of an etching. Ingram did not name Hannah Barlow, but it was her work he described at Philadelphia when he spoke of Doulton pots with 'animals in every variety of posture . . . deer lying down among high ferns, lambs suckling their mothers, cats watching with eager eyes the heedless hops of unwary sparrows'.[29]

Other artist members of the Barlow family were also employed at Doultons, notably Florence E. Barlow, a younger sister of Hannah. The work of both sisters was known in Canada. Edward Black Greenshields of Montreal, for instance, one of the important art collectors of his day, was a connoisseur of pottery, as well as of the Dutch paintings with which he filled his house on Peel Street. A stoneware vase decorated by Florence Barlow and bought, when it was new in the 1870's, for the Greenshields collection, is illustrated in *Plate* 11.

A Doulton artist whose work had surprising diversity was George Tinworth, a wheelwright who yearned for an art education and who found the opportunity for it in evening study at the Lambeth School of Art. In 1866 Tinworth, urged by John Sparkes, made the decision to give up his occupation of wheelwright. At that time he entered the employ of Henry Doulton, as a modeller, and he remained at Doulton's Lambeth pottery until his death in 1913. Early encouraged by his mother in his ambition (even as he was discouraged by his father) Tinworth was strongly influenced by his mother's love of the Bible. In the Bible he found all the romance and sense of history he craved. His work, consequently, was often 'Scriptural' as Ingram described it at Philadelphia. The American writer was impressed by Tinworth's 'great power as a modeler', and noted in particular the religious character of his 'most wonderful' productions.[30] But while Tinworth became best known for his great terracotta panels on Biblical themes (such as his altar screen for York Minster) he also executed models in stoneware, sometimes in a light, even whimsical vein. Perhaps his most attractive work of this type depicted animals playing human roles. These may be found with such titles as 'The Cockneys at Brighton' (a group of mice) and 'Going to the Derby' (frogs). In stoneware he also executed a set of figures illustrating Aesop's Fables.

Doulton artists usually signed their pieces. Names, initials or monograms, and often dates are, therefore, to be found on the bottom of ornamental stoneware of this period having the name of Doulton as the maker. These wares are always in the distinctive muted colours to which stoneware was necessarily confined because of the very high temperature at which it was fired, but the styles of decoration vary according to the individual artist responsible for the work. Even the colours themselves have individual qualities, the result of a particular firing. As Ingram explained it, the salt-glazing could cause blues to change 'to the most exquisite greens and browns', or produce 'cloudings' that could only be compared to the shading in the folds of velvet dresses, or, again, eat away the actual colour, leaving the natural buff of the clay to glow dimly like an antique gold.[31]

When the stonewares proved a success, Doultons tried the studio method with other forms of pottery. Designs were conceived and painted on a new 'faience', or earthenware body, by another group of artists. Nor was Doultons by any means the only firm to swing ceramic productions into the stream of the aesthetic movement. Copelands, Wedgwoods, and all the leading potteries were part of it; new bodies, new shapes, new approaches to decoration were the evidence. Art potteries were founded, and even the newest of these were soon known in Canada. William Scott & Son, Montreal fine art dealers who exerted a strong influence on Canadian taste in late Victorian and Edwardian days, sponsored the work of some of them. For example, Scott's Christmas advertisement in the *Daily Witness* on December 20, 1883, read:

BEFORE BUYING ORNAMENTS
INSPECT THE FAMOUS
BARUM WARE
At SCOTT'S

Barum ware came from an art pottery in Barnstaple, Devonshire, started only a few years earlier by Charles Brannam. When it was still relatively new, and before it had received the attention of royal patronage, Scott's of Montreal, as their advertisements show, were offering to Canadians this richly glazed or slip-decorated art ware.

Among the most famous potters of the late Victorian art movement whose work Scott promoted in Canada was William De Morgan (1839-1917): 'Artist: Potter: Inventor: Novelist'.[32] In his own time it was as a novelist that he achieved greatest fame, yet his heart was in his pottery. Today William De Morgan's novels are little read, but the pottery, with its glowing lustre or equally stirring 'Persian' colours has come to be considered one of the most important artistic creations of its period.

On De Morgan vases painted with strange beast-forms sweeping round them in spreading triumph, and on huge circular dishes magnificently echoing an ancient past, William Scott & Son put their paper label. Some of these pieces, a few with the Scott label still in place, have found their way into Canadian museums.

Very possibly it was from Scott's that E. B. Greenshields and R. B. Angus, another important Montreal collector of the time, acquired at least some of the De Morgan pottery that was in their collections. In the Angus collection, seem-

157

ingly representative of every phase of De Morgan's work, was a memorable vase painted in blues and greens, and in shape identical to the one that De Morgan chose to hold in his hands for the portrait painted by his wife. The Greenshields collection included examples of the tiles that were among De Morgan's most famous productions, as well as vases and dishes. Formerly in the Greenshields collection were the copper and ruby lustre pieces illustrated in *Plate* 12A.

In admiring De Morgan pottery—little of which was actually made or painted by De Morgan himself, but all of which was done to his design—the Montreal collectors shared the taste of the Tsar of Russia and of that Victorian giant, Lord Leighton, P.R.A. And yet the De Morgan pottery never paid. The venture, which began in the 1870's and which managed to survive until shortly after the turn of the century, would have staggered into complete financial failure at many points along the way, had it not been for De Morgan's wife, the artist Evelyn Pickering. As her sister has recorded, she was a woman who was willing to stake everything she owned to enable her husband 'to make one more splendid pot'.[33]

The De Morgan work was carried on in London, or in the vicinity of London. Pieces that were made by the De Morgan pottery, and not purchased in the white from Staffordshire, sometimes had the name impressed on the bottom. On wares only decorated at De Morgan's workshop, a mark was painted. This mark often included the initials of the artist who had carried out De Morgan's design. After 1888, when William De Morgan entered into partnership, first with the architect Halsey Ricardo, and, after 1898, with Frank Iles and Charles and Fred Passenger, the mark might be W. DE MORGAN & CO.

In these closing years of the nineteenth century, Canadians were chooseing their earthenwares for decoration from a far wider field than had been open to them earlier. Wares other than British were everywhere. Specialist dealers like Scott's sold 'modern' art wares from the Orient, and from Europe. China merchants like Edward Hagar & Co. of Montreal imported 'Danish Majolica',[34] and Henry Morgan & Co. advertised 'Pottery, a fine assortment' from Vallauris, in France.[35] Establishments like Moore's China Hall in Winnipeg had earthenware and porcelain both 'curious' and 'useful' from 'potters and artists' in England, on the Continent and in America.[36]

Nor was it necessary for Canadians to confine their earthenware ornaments to cabinet or table. They were offered every facility for laying their floors, panelling their walls and outlining their fireplaces with decorative earthenware slabs and tiles. In the main it was with English tiles that they did their interior decorating.

Like so much that pleased the nineteenth century in ornamental earthenware, tiles were of ancient origin. In England they had been known since the days of the Roman occupation. They were used for pavements in the interiors of churches in the Middle Ages. In the seventeenth and eighteenth centuries they were important in the earthenware called 'delft'. Their great revival in the nineteenth century dated from about 1830. By mid-century many of the best firms were making tiles in quantity for a public bent on tearing up floors and ripping out fireplace surrounds in order to walk on new earthenware and gaze at tilework patterns on the wall. These Victorian tiles—produced by makers like Bootes, Copelands, Doultons, and Mintons—were sometimes painted, sometimes printed, and sometimes manufactured in the majolica style, with embossed designs covered with thick glazes. Often the pattern was 'inlaid', an effect achieved by pouring stiff slips of coloured clays into an intaglio design impressed into the face of the tile. When the coloured clays had hardened sufficiently, the surface of the tile was scraped level with special tools, and the 'inlaid' pattern revealed in sharp outline.

A potter who early foresaw the future that tiles were to have in the nineteenth century was Herbert Minton (1793-1858), son of Thomas Minton, founder of the Minton Works. He turned his attention to tiles some years before Queen Victoria came to the throne, carrying out experiment after experiment. The traditional story is that when his scrap heap of failures had reached enormous proportions and the bills had mounted equally, his business partner remonstrated with him. But Herbert Minton was determined to make tiles. 'I will make these tiles, Man, if they cost me a guinea each', was the answer he gave.[37] His determination paid in the end. No firm was better known than Mintons for tiles, in a day when this form of earthenware reached the height of its popularity. After Herbert Minton died, his pottery passed into the hands of two nephews, Colin Minton Campbell and Michael Daintry Hollins. Ten years later the tile business was separated from the other branches of manufacture. It became the concern of Michael Hollins alone, and was continued under the style of Minton Hollins & Co.

Both before and after the tile part of the business came under separate management, there was a market for Minton tiles in Canada. As early as 1849 an advertisement for these tiles appeared in the *Montreal Gazette*. On May 29, Edmonstone, Allan & Co., general merchants, announced that they had just received 'a set of PATTERNS of MINTON'S PATENT TESSELATED TILES', and they informed colonial readers that in Great Britain 'These Tiles are now extensively used'.

A few years later, at the provincial exhibition held in Montreal in 1857, Minton tiles were put on display. Thomas D'Arcy McGee's newspaper, the *New Era*, commented on them, saying that they were exhibited 'by the agent of Messrs. Minton & Co., an English firm', and were 'in several patterns', producing 'a very handsome effect'.[38]

In all parts of Canada many persons came to think that Minton tiles produced 'a very handsome effect'. From east to west they were installed in new houses put up in the opulent taste of the times. In Victoria, John Weiler's house (now demolished) had Minton tiles in a number of rooms, including a handsome set illustrating scenes from Shakespeare.[39] Since Weiler was both a china, glass, and earthenware dealer and a furniture maker, it is probable that he imported the tiles himself, for setting Minton tiles into furniture was another fashion of the period.[40]

In Cote St. Antoine (now Westmount, Quebec), when Robert Harvie, partner of Hugh Brodie, the flour manufacturer, decided on the fittings for a new house in 1870, he chose, for a drawing-room fireplace, Minton tiles with English pastoral scenes in a style reminiscent of Birket Foster. They were set into a frame of rich mahogany and brass, and combined with majolica slabs. There they stayed for close to a hundred years. When the Harvie house was demolished in the

1960's the fireplace and mantel—mahogany, brass, and tile—were carefully removed, so that they might begin a second century of use in a new setting.[41]

A building that did not have Minton tiles on either floors or walls was the parliament building erected after Ottawa was made the capital of the united Province of Canada. The Prince of Wales laid the corner-stone in 1860, and when the building was completed many persons considered it perfect in every detail. But Lidstone, the poet, thought Minton tiles would have improved it:

> O, they contractors, Ottawa, should full well be shent,
> Those edifices the glory of the Western Continent,
> Disgraced, alas! with floors paved with Yankee cement.
> Had I been there when that same contract was being given out,
> I would have put the Vandal horde unto an utter rout,
> And with Mintonian products have paved the halls thro'out . . .[42]

A Shropshire firm specializing in tile-making, and who, like Mintons, maintained agents in Canada, was Maw & Co., of Broseley. Patterned tiles in a combination of terracotta colour, yellow, and black were characteristic of this firm (*Plate* 12B), who also, however, could produce pictorial and majolica tiles which won high awards at international exhibitions. In Quebec city, in the 1870's and 1880's, Maw's agents were Felix and James Morgan, who advertised the tiles they handled as the best produced in England for 'perfection of design and color'. The Morgans not only promised to decorate houses with tiles worked into designs approved by the best English art schools, they guaranteed that any tiles installed by them would stay in place, since they had twenty-five years' experience with the effects of the Canadian climate.[43]

Unlike much nineteenth-century decorative earthenware, tiles were both functional and ornamental. Sir Charles Eastlake, the arbiter of Victorian taste, approved of them, praising Maw tiles in particular, and declaring that this branch of 'art-manufacture' had become 'a means of decoration' capable of combining beauty, durability, and cheapness to an extraordinary degree.[44] Earthenware tiles set into the wall of an entrance hall were specially recommended by Sir Charles, for a reason that reflects the conditions of his time. He recommended them not only because of their decorative effect, but because, if carried from the floor to a height of about three or four feet, they would effectively protect the walls from the shower of street dirt that was inevitable when the Victorian lady came in the front door.[45] In other words, it was in the entrance hall that the Victorian lady usually shook off the dirt from her long skirts (which had been sweeping the streets) before proceeding farther into the house.

In nineteenth-century Canada, where streets were muddier and roads dirtier than anywhere else in the world, if contemporary accounts can be believed, ornamental earthenware tiles must have been highly valued as a protection from the ladies in long dresses.

The Porcelains

CHAPTER XIII

British Porcelain
in the Canadian Market

IMPORTED *In the Brig* SUSANNAH . . . *and for* SALE *by* DANIEL KING
. . . A few Table and Tea sets of Liverpool China.
Royal Gazette, Nov. 11, 1800.

Porcelain was never as important in the Canadian market as earthenware. This is not surprising. The general needs of a pioneer country were better served by common brownware and tough ironstone than by 'RICH AND VALUABLE . . . China Dinner Setts' selling, in 1824 in Montreal, at thirty guineas apiece.[1] The significant fact is not that porcelain came to nineteenth-century Canada in very much smaller quantities than did earthenware, but that, from early years, there was a strong and decided demand for it.

Before the nineteenth century was even ushered in, the dealers of Halifax were opening up hogsheads of Liverpool china, and those in Saint John were advertising Worcester. Montreal merchants, supplying the first settlers in the wilderness of Upper Canada with earthenware that was durable and cheap, were, at the same time, ready with costly porcelain, fit to catch the eye of a lavishly spending Nor'Wester.

Canada of the nineteenth century was a land of contrasts, and this was from the first strikingly reflected in the ceramic trade. On the one hand the crockery sellers catered to the pioneers, for whom there was hardship and plain living as they cut farmland out of forest; on the other they courted the business of fur lords 'rich beyond the dreams of avarice', and of an official and ruling class that brought cultivation to a colonial society. Merchants themselves often became men of great affluence, who wanted in their own homes the best of everything, including tableware. 'The better class of people, most of whom are in the mercantile line, live in good style', so wrote John Howison in the 1820's, after he had visited Kingston.[2] Earlier, the first Anglican bishop of Quebec, Rt. Rev. Jacob Mountain, dining in Montreal with one of the chief merchants of that city, had noted in his diary that the house of John Forsyth, his host, was 'elegant', and that people of his class in Canada 'are fond of good living and take care to want no luxury'.[3]

For the pioneer there were fantastically large importations of common earthenware, and for the town dweller, of a certain financial status, porcelain if he wanted it. After mid-century, when cheap china from the potteries of both Great

163

Britain and the Continent came to Canada in increasing quantities, old distinctions relaxed, but still earthenware dominated the Canadian market.[4]

An advertisement for an auction of unusual interest gives a picture of the furnishings, both table and otherwise, to be found in a rich man's house at the beginning of the century. It appeared in the *Montreal Gazette* on May 27, 1805, and shows that 'fashionable china' was part of the luxurious living noted by Bishop Mountain. Up for sale were the contents of No. 2 St. Jean Baptiste Street (a house, 'built in the English taste',[5] that still stands). This was Simon Mc-Tavish's house, for McTavish, head of the North West Company, had never been able to move into the extravagant mansion which he had planned outside the city on the slope of Mount Royal. He had died in 1804, while his country house was still under construction. It was never to be finished. In the spring of 1805 his widow, having decided to go to England, sold the furnishings of the house in the city. They were described in the *Gazette* advertisement:

BY AUCTION

Will be Sold . . . at the house of Mrs. M'TAVISH, going to England, all her most valuable furniture—consisting of FEATHER BEDS, Mattresses, mahogany bed steads, chests of drawers, desks, a new piano forte, large dining tables, chairs, &c. setts of the most fashionable china, knives and forks in cases, a quantity of silver mugs, spoons, forks, servers, &c. &c. sophas, sconces, looking glasses, carpets, old Madeira, Claret, Port, Burgundy, and other wines of the first quality, in bottles; an elegant new Phaeton, carioles, gig and chair, several covered carioles, an excellent horse for a chair, &c. double and single stoves, with a great number of other articles.

ALEXANDER HENRY.

Simon McTavish, lord of the fur trade, was a very rich man; some said the richest in Montreal. Not many were able to maintain his standard of living, but many, like Simon McTavish, used 'fashionable china' on their tables in early Canada. Most of this porcelain was English, as was the earthenware imported in far larger quantities, although at the end of the eighteenth and the beginning of the nineteenth century there was still some importing of 'India china' (*Plate* 13A). This was Chinese porcelain brought to England by the East India Company, and from England later shipped to Canada.

'India china' was what Canadians called it in its day. In Victorian times an error in understanding what type of work had actually been done at Lowestoft, on the east coast of England (where a porcelain factory was in operation from 1757 until 1802), caused these oriental wares to be widely known as 'Lowestoft'. It was all a mistake. Porcelain of the 'India china' type was never made, nor even extensively decorated at Lowestoft in England. To call it 'Lowestoft' was an unfortunate blunder that was to prove surprisingly difficult to set right. Today, however, it is generally realized that this was Chinese ware made for export. 'India china' was its contemporary name in Canada; 'Lowestoft' it could never have been; 'Chinese export' describes it. The term 'Oriental Lowestoft' which, in spite of everything, still persists in North America, is both a misnomer and a contradiction.

In England the porcelain of the Orient held a large place in the ceramic trade of the eighteenth century; to a certain extent it was still imported in the early nineteenth. Those who dealt in it were known as 'china-men'. Miles Mason,

164

father of Charles James Mason, inventor of ironstone, was a seller of oriental porcelain, a 'china-man'. The decline of this porcelain in England set in just as Canada began to emerge as a market for ceramic wares imported from England. The decline was hastened by high import duties imposed by the British government on 'India china'. The British potters themselves had worked for the imposition of these duties, for, as the eighteenth century moved on towards its close, the makers of both earthenware and porcelain gained the confidence that was to mark their rise to world importance.

In Canada the 'India china', or Chinese export porcelain, never had quite the place it attained in the United States. Americans began to trade freely with the Orient immediately following the Revolutionary War, and in the United States sending an order to China for a dinner or tea set to be painted with the owner's initials or some special device became a mark of gentility. In Canada some people of wealth certainly had such tablewares; but others who, had they been living south of the new border, would probably have been dining off Chinese porcelain, used instead British wares. British potters maintained a commanding position in the British colonies, and Wedgwood's creamware, for example, decorated to special Canadian order, undoubtedly took the place of Chinese porcelain to a considerable extent.

One who did use Chinese export porcelain in the great house he built for himself in Montreal was William McGillivray, nephew of Simon McTavish, and, after McTavish's death, chief director of the North West Company. In 1805, the year following his uncle's death, McGillivray moved into his new St. Antoine House. According to his biographer, Marjorie Wilkins Campbell, he furnished St. Antoine House with fine paintings, fine furniture, and Chinese export porcelain ornamented with 'its owner's recently acquired Scottish coat-of-arms'.[6]

That William McGillivray and other prominent Nor'Westers had Chinese porcelain does not necessarily mean they purchased it through a Canadian china seller. They may well have ordered it through a dealer in England, or, as seems probable, through the North West Company itself or its connections. At one time the North West Company had limited permission from the East India Company to trade with the Orient on its own.

There were, however, frequent advertisements in Canadian newspapers at this period for Chinese or 'India' tablewares. In Saint John the *Royal Gazette* of March 14, 1786, announced 'fashionable sets of tea and other China, of curious patterns and real India'. This oriental porcelain was to be offered to the New Brunswick colonists at an open-air auction in two days' time, 'or the first fair day after', together with 'a genteel assortment of silver', gilt swords, and plated shoe buckles.

In Montreal a prominent importer, Thomas Schieffelin, had '300 sets India Cups and Saucers' in 1798.[7] In 1815 Forsyth, Richardson & Co. (partners in the North West Company and agents for the East India Company) were selling 'Table sets of India China' and 'Cups and Saucers do.'[8] But the direction which the ceramic trade was taking had been indicated in a *Royal Gazette* advertisement on March 9, 1790. On that day a Fredericton merchant, A. Allen, advertised both 'East-India and English China'. It was English china that was to supplant Chinese not only in Canada but in many other markets.

In a few years 'India china' would fade out of the advertisements, pushed aside by 'rich' porcelain 'from the first manufacturers in Staffordshire' and ousted in the colonial trade by wares 'guaranteed to be of English make'. Tableware such as William Mackie advertised in Montreal in 1824 as 'Burnished Gold China Tea Setts . . . of the newest fashion'[9] were the accomplishment of English potters, not Chinese. And Shuter & Wilkins' 'China Tea-sets, of elegant patterns', imported into Montreal the next year from 'the first establishments in England',[10] came from potters who had successfully invaded the world of the oriental masters and who had, by this time, made a contribution of their own to ceramic history. That contribution was 'bone china'.

What came to Canada as 'India china' was what is termed a 'hard-paste' or 'true porcelain'. This was the porcelain of the Orient. What most English potters made was something different, and what they finally evolved, after the experimental period of the eighteenth century, led to a revolutionary advance in industrial potting. It is known today as 'bone china', but Canadians who bought it when it was new on the market never heard that name. It was just English china then, something whiter, newer, and more desirable than the old wares which belonged to a receding past.

English bone china, known the world over, became the standard English porcelain body early in the nineteenth century. It was a hybrid product, combining something of the 'hard-paste' porcelain of the Orient and the Continent with certain elements of 'soft-paste' or 'artificial porcelain' made in eighteenth-century England. The first Josiah Spode is credited with experiments in it in the 1790's. He was not the first to use calcined bones in his porcelain formula: bone ash as an ingredient of porcelain had been known in England since the middle of the eighteenth century. But at the Spode factory in Staffordshire, in the last years of Josiah Spode's lifetime, an adjusted and dependable formula was worked out for a porcelain with bone as an essential ingredient. It could be counted on to come from the kilns white and strong and evenly translucent, capable of standing up to wear and of showing off to advantage many styles of decoration. With kiln losses, and hence costs, reduced, porcelain was to become available to larger markets.

Josiah Spode (1733-97) and his son, the second Josiah Spode (1754-1827), had not invented something new, but they had realized, as had no one else, the full competitive possibilities of a bone porcelain. At the Spode factory this body was standardized. In time it was to displace entirely the older types of English porcelain, and to be copied not only at home but abroad. With bone china, England made a permanent contribution to porcelain technology.

Canadians had begun to use English porcelain before bone china became the standard. In the first newspapers of both the Maritime colonies and Lower Canada there is a sprinkling of advertisements for porcelain imported from England and not specifically identified as 'India china'. In most cases these advertisements certainly refer to English-made wares—wares produced in the period when English porcelain makers were still hovering on the threshold of the commercial triumphs that were shortly to be theirs. For proof that such porcelain was exported to Canada, it is not, however, necessary to rely on advertisements whose intent seems clear but whose wording is indefinite. A few important advertisements actually mention by name the type of English porcelain offered in these early days.

One such announcement appeared in the *Royal Gazette and Nova Scotia Advertiser* on June 7, 1791. James Wainwright, in a store at the 'upper-end of Copland's Wharf' in Halifax, was selling goods imported from England in the *Aurora*, and he identified his tablewares: they were 'Liverpool china' and 'Staffordshire ware'. The earthenware, then, came from Staffordshire, the porcelain from Liverpool, where several factories were still in operation at that date.

Again, in the *Royal Gazette and New Brunswick Advertiser* of January 22, 1793, Ludlow & Fraser, of Saint John, listed their importations 'from the principal MANUFACTORIES and WAREHOUSES, in Britain'. Purchased 'by MR. FRASER' in person at these establishments, and available in exchange for furs, if cash was not easy, were 'Worcester china cups and saucers, Ditto tea pots'.

This Worcester teaware, imported into New Brunswick when the Loyalist colony was still new, could have been from one of two porcelain factories: it could have been from the old Worcester factory associated with the name of Dr. Wall, which, about this time, came under the direction of Joseph Flight and Martin Barr; or it could have been from the factory of Robert Chamberlain, a china painter who had left employment with the older factory in the 1780's to found a decorating establishment of his own, and who had recently started to manufacture a greyish porcelain.

Very little of the English porcelain sold in Canada in the earliest days was even identified as to type, or area of origin. This makes all the more interesting newspaper announcements like those of James Wainwright, offering Liverpool porcelain in Halifax, or Ludlow & Fraser, willing to exchange Worcester teapots for furs in Saint John.[11]

It was always customary for the china merchants to distinguish between earthenware and porcelain (generally referred to as 'china') in their advertising, and frequently to emphasize that what they were selling was English-made. About new styles, patterns, and shapes they became enthusiastic in print, calling them 'modern', 'elegant', 'beautiful', 'saleable', 'neat', 'rare', 'novel', even 'fabulous' and 'meritorious'. They promised repeatedly that their porcelain was 'splendid', and they spent much advertising money in describing colours and styles of decoration. 'Burnished gold' was considered a detail no customer would wish to miss. 'White and gold' china was nearly always worth mentioning. If porcelain was 'pencilled' (a type of painted decoration) or 'enamelled' (painted over the glaze) the fact was frequently included in the advertising. When 'hand painted' centres occurred on dessert dishes the public was informed. 'Embossed' china, and china ornamented with 'sprigs' in blue were matters for special advertising. Porcelain decoration with lustre sent the china merchants rushing to the newspapers. But as for who was responsible for making what was advertised so profusely, this would seem to have been a matter of such secondary sales importance that it is necessary to turn hundreds of pages of old newspaper files to gather together a handful of names.

The china sellers' advertisements do, however, present a picture of refinement for the tables of pre-Confederation Canada, for those in circumstances that enabled them to buy the porcelain imported by the dealers. In Quebec, for instance, in 1777 there was 'dragon and enamell'd China';[12] in Halifax in 1788 'Blue and white China . . . coffee cups';[13] in Montreal in 1817 'Tea China, Gold burnished';[14] in Charlottetown in 1826 'elegant china, white and gold';[15] in Saint John in 1839 'Hhds. English PORCELAIN';[16] in Toronto in 1841 china 'from some of the first Manufactories in England'.[17] Even in Fort Garry, where strong white ironstone was better suited to the rigours of the transportation route than porcelain, there were 'China Cups and Saucers . . . designed for CHRISTMAS AND NEW YEAR'S GIFTS' in 1860. This last advertisement, in the *Nor'-Wester* on December 17, was headed in large letters: 'GREAT EXCITEMENT'.

Sometimes, but only sometimes before about 1860, these porcelain advertisements identified the make of tablewares offered. So it was that Adam L. Macnider, arranging a trade sale in the 1830's, advertised in the *Montreal Gazette* that his '22 packages of China Tea, Coffee, Breakfast, Dessert, and Supper Setts' represented wares from 'the ROCKINGHAM, WORCESTER, and DERBY Manufactories'.[18] And William Turner, another Montreal merchant of the period, dangled 'Worster [*sic*] . . . tastefully decorated' before prize seekers in a china lottery.[19]

Rockingham and Derby, in Macnider's advertisement, could refer only to specific potteries. At the Rockingham Works, in Swinton, Yorkshire, on property owned by Earl Fitzwilliam and backed by his money, Thomas, John Wager, and George Frederic Brameld were at this time manufacturing the fine-quality porcelain admired in all the fashionable circles of the day. Montrealers who read in their *Gazette* that Rockingham wares would be sold at the Old Distillery Stores could not have known that financial disaster was looming ahead of the Bramelds; as potters they had less than a decade left to them. The colonial buyers would, however, have been well aware that Macnider was offering them tablewares which were, in the words of his advertisement, 'elegant china' (*Plate* 14B).

The Derby advertised for that same trade sale came from a china manufactory actually owned by Robert Bloor; but, as he was at that time 'mentally incapacitated from taking any part in the business'[20] (in other words, hopelessly insane), the Derby ware offered in Montreal was porcelain produced under the direction of James Thomason. For over fifteen difficult years Thomason kept the Derby Works going. After he retired, in the mid-1840's, it faltered to a close.

By 1832 the Worcester porcelain on sale in Montreal had three possible makers. The old firm of Flight & Barr continued, with younger members of the Barr family in the business, so that now it was known as Flight, Barr & Barr. Chamberlains was not only still going, it was soon to absorb the older firm from which Robert Chamberlain had broken away. And by this time, too, a third Worcester porcelain factory was at work. Thomas Grainger, a nephew of Humphrey Chamberlain (son of Robert), had had his training at Chamberlains, and had then started up on his own. This was early in the century; by the time of Macnider's trade sale in Montreal, the Grainger factory was producing porcelain considered very fine by the artistic world of the day.

The advertisements show that Worcester was a name much valued by Canadians. Taking the nineteenth century as a whole, porcelain announced as being of Worcester make was advertised with unusual frequency, even if the early advertisements did not state from which Worcester factory the wares came. After 1862 the Canadian china merchants very often did name Royal Worcester as the product offered. The firms of Flight, Barr & Barr and Chamberlains had been amalgamated in 1840. In 1862 the company, which had experienced difficulties and changes of partnership since 1840, was reorganized as a joint stock company, and renamed the Worcester Royal Porcelain Company Limited (the name it bears today). The Grainger factory remained as a separate concern until 1889, when the business was taken over by Royal Worcester, although production continued under the Grainger name for another few years.

Very shortly after the Royal Worcester firm came into being, the Canadian china merchants began to publicize it by name. For Christmas of 1863, for example, John Patton & Co., of Montreal, advertised tablewares 'suitable for the season' particularizing dinner and dessert services from the 'celebrated Royal Porcelain Works in Worcester'.[21] In 1865 John Leeming devoted an entire advertisement to the 'VERY HANDSOME' china 'Manufactured by THE ROYAL PORCELAIN WORKS, WORCESTER, ENGLAND', which he was selling at a 'positively Unreserved' auction in Montreal. Included were twenty-six dinner services, all 'genuine' Royal Worcester, in 'choice patterns and styles', featuring gold decoration and blue, pink, and green borders.[22] The *Montreal Gazette* commented in the editorial columns that ladies would do well to attend this Worcester auction.

Further evidence of the sale of Worcester porcelain in nineteenth-century Canada comes from the ledgers preserved at the Works in England. An entry under the date of March 16, 1857 (when the company was operated by W. H. Kerr and R. W. Binns), gives an indication of what patterns in Worcester porcelain were to be seen in the best china shops of mid-century Canada; it also shows that Worcester was executing special orders for Canadian customers.

The shipment, of which the details have been preserved, filled two hogsheads and was invoiced at £129. 5s. 3d. It was for Alexander Levy, whose large shop stood at the corner of Notre Dame and St. Gabriel Streets in Montreal. There Levy presumably unpacked the teapots, covered dishes, tureens and 'twiflers' (9½ inch plates) sent to him by that year's spring fleet. 'White and gold' decoration and 'blossoms' in colours, as well as 'Colored Vine', and 'Gold Vermacelli' were included among his patterns. In 'Egg Shell' (very thin) porcelain, he had articles painted with cupids and 'leaves and turquoise spots'. Two of the patterns sent to Montreal have been identified from examples bearing the same pattern numbers in the Dyson Perrins Museum at the Worcester Works. One of these (Pattern 5738) had a 'celeste' blue band with 'ivory and gold french edge'. The other (Pattern 5739) combined a wide maroon border with rich gilding and a gold medallion in the centre of each piece.

Crests in gold were specially painted on some of the pieces shipped to Canada for Alexander Levy's customers. Others had crests printed on them. One crest is described in the ledger as 'Lion & Motto in Ribbon'. This was painted at a cost to Levy of one shilling and fourpence. Packed in with the order, according to a notation on the old records, were Worcester's new price lists for 1857.[23]

It was during this same period—when Kerr & Binns were operating the firm that represented the amalgamation of Chamberlains and Flight, Barr & Barr—

that Worcester was called on to fill a special order for Canada in connection with the visit of the Prince of Wales in 1860. At that time were produced the plates and dishes ornamented with green maple leaves and the Prince of Wales' Feathers (*Plate* 15) which are to be seen in a number of Canadian museums. These pieces are not always recognized as Worcester porcelain, for the order was given through the London firm of Sharpus & Co., and the name of this firm appears on the back of many of the pieces. The presence of the Sharpus name, and a failure to observe that the impressed mark of Worcester is also there, sometimes results in the erroneous conclusion that Sharpus was the potter. Sharpus & Co. were merely the London suppliers; Kerr & Binns of Worcester, the makers.

The distribution of these Worcester plates throughout what are now the provinces of Quebec and Ontario (the united Province of Canada at the time of the royal visit) suggests that they were among the table furnishings ordered in connection with entertainments given for the Prince. Many of the tablewares ordered in this way were later disposed of to a public anxious for souvenirs.[24] One of these Worcester plates, now in the City of Lachine's museum (Manoir Lachine), is believed to have been used at the luncheon given by Sir George Simpson, Governor-in-Chief of the Hudson's Bay Company, for the Prince of Wales. According to museum records, this plate was said to have been presented by Sir George as a memento of the occasion to one of the guests. The luncheon took place on August 20, 1860, at Sir George Simpson's country estate on Dorval Island (three miles above Lachine). The Prince was transported to the island in a large barge escorted by a flotilla of canoes manned by one hundred Indians, costumed '*en sauvage*'.[25] The tradition subscribed to by many that each Worcester piece printed with the Prince of Wales' Feathers was 'used by the Prince himself' obviously rests upon an impossibility, but probably many did acquire such Worcester pieces in one way or another as souvenirs of the Prince of Wales' visit to Canada.

But while Canadians were consistent buyers of Worcester, the bulk of the porcelain they used in the nineteenth century would have come from Staffordshire. 'CHINA, GLASS & EARTHENWARE *direct* from Staffordshire' was what William Johnson & Son of Niagara advertised in 1845,[26] and scores of other dealers said the same thing. 'Staffordshire' was the drawing card, the individual potter who had made the wares did not seem to matter.

With the mid-Victorian period, however, came a change. While cheap porcelain continued to be widely publicized without identification, 'selling rapidly' at a few dollars for several dozen pieces,[27] better-quality china was now more frequently offered by name. The two Staffordshire names that stood out most prominently in the Canadian porcelain market of the second half of the century were those of Copeland and Minton. China from these two firms must have been known in Canada for years, yet it waited until Victorian days for full acknowledgement in print.

The Copelands were the successors of the Spodes, and were, therefore, inheritors of traditions upon which much of the prosperity of Staffordshire has been based. That they sought to keep alive the Spode reputation is shown by their own advertising in North America: 'W. T. Copeland and Sons beg to state that the Original Moulds, Pattern Books, and Copper Plates are still employed by them in the reproduction of the highly esteemed SPODE WARE, in the unequalled Bodies of that Eminent Potter.'[28]

William Copeland, who died in 1826, had been connected with the first Josiah Spode in the London, or selling, end of the business, and had been a partner of the second Josiah Spode. His son, William Taylor Copeland (1797-1868), bought the Spode Works, in 1833, from the executors of the third Josiah Spode. He brought in Thomas Garrett as a partner, but in 1847 their partnership was dissolved, and for twenty years William Taylor Copeland carried on alone. In 1867 the firm became W. T. Copeland & Sons.

In the early years of the nineteenth century Canadians knew William Taylor Copeland's name in more than one connection. The *Montreal Gazette* reported it when he was sworn in as an alderman of the City of London in the 1820's.[29] In the 1830's, when he was Lord Mayor of London, his name, at least, would have been familiar to prominent colonial merchants in England to select their goods. He himself secured orders from the Hudson's Bay Company; and through the Company, Copeland & Garrett and later Copeland wares were distributed throughout the Northwest, beginning in the 1830's.[30] The bulk of the shipments to Hudson's Bay Company posts would have been of earthenware, but porcelain must have been included from time to time. An inventory of the Fort Garry sale shop in 1851 showed both porcelain and earthenware in stock.[31]

An article in the *Art Union* magazine at the end of the Copeland & Garrett period, describing the factory's products and going into details about porcelain, stressed the big colonial trade carried on by the Spodes' successors.[32] Canadian publications ran Copeland advertisements for 'Vases, Ornamental Works and Services' in porcelain, as well as earthenware and stoneware.[33] In the newspapers, the Canadian dealers of the second half of the century picked Copeland's name to list with 'the first . . . manufacturers in Europe' in announcements that offered 'Fancy China'.[34]

Frequently the name of Minton appeared together with that of Copeland in the advertisements for porcelain.[35] Thomas Minton (1766-1836), the engraver of the Willow pattern at Caughley, had founded the firm at the end of the eighteenth century. Herbert Minton (1793-1858), his son, under whom the porcelain side of the business was greatly developed, had brought French artists to Staffordshire, and much of the Minton porcelain of the Victorian period was under French influence in matters of decoration. Under Herbert Minton's nephew, Colin Minton Campbell, who succeeded his uncle as head of the Minton Works, such French techniques as 'pâte-sur-pâte' were introduced. Translated this meant simply paste on paste, or clay on clay. It was a delicate process whereby reliefs were slowly built up on porcelain. This was the type of porcelain which would be sold by dealers like Scott's of Montreal, specializing in costly wares, and which was acquired by nineteenth-century Canadian collectors who valued De Morgan pottery and Doulton stoneware. In 1883, two years before the death of Colin Minton Campbell, the firm became Mintons Limited. Today it makes porcelain only, and Canada remains an important customer.

Minton porcelain, like Worcester, was considered sufficiently grand for use when Queen Victoria's heir came to British North America. In Saint John, where the committee in charge of arrangements decided to rent and not to buy what was needed, Francis Clementson, the china merchant of Dock Street, was commissioned to furnish all the glass and porcelain needed. His choice fell on Minton. Supplying himself with suitably handsome goods, Clementson rented out Minton porcelain for the table, and Minton ornaments to decorate the rooms of the house taken over for the use of the Prince of Wales. One who was familiar with the arrangements in Saint John recalled in later years that the ornaments included Minton 'hand-painted' china vases, a particularly large and impressive pair being placed in the drawing room.[36]

The high opinion in which Minton porcelain was held by Canadians of Victorian days was implied in an advertisement in Montreal's *Daily Witness* in 1879. Five days before Christmas that year Scott's announced a special sale. Those who hurried down to Notre Dame Street would find sets of Minton china selling at no more than 'ordinary ware'.

Although the service was not made for the Canadian market—and was not even made to be put on general sale—it is, somehow, fitting that one of the most celebrated exploits of Canadian travel was recorded on Minton porcelain. Lord Milton and Dr. Walter Butler Cheadle were Canada's first transcontinental tourists. In 1863 they made their epic journey overland across the Rocky Mountains. It was a fantastic journey, and it nearly cost them their lives; its successful accomplishment made them famous. They published their account of it in 1865 under the title *The North-West Passage By Land*, an account illustrated by skteches done on the spot. The published version, which had run through nine editions by 1891, is known to every Canadian interested in pioneer travel. Virtually unknown, however, is the fact that the illustrations which have become so familiar to many were reproduced on porcelain. They were painted to Lord Milton's order on a dessert service of Minton manufacture shortly after the travellers returned to England. The work was done by a Minton artist or artists never identified, although the views themselves were named on the back of each piece. Today some thirty pieces from this porcelain record of Canadian travel are to be seen at the Minton Works Museum, in Stoke-on-Trent. They were acquired for the museum in the 1940's, after the death of Lord Milton's grandson.[37]

Some Staffordshire firms of the nineteenth century did put Canadian views on porcelain made for general sale. John Aynsley's pottery, founded shortly before 1860, was one of these.[38] On the testimony of the poet, James Torrington Spencer Lidstone, this Longton pottery must have begun exporting to the colonies soon after the business was established, for Lidstone, who had earlier been in Upper Canada, wrote in 1866 of having seen Aynsley china 'o'er th' reddening western seas'.[39] At the beginning of the 1880's the firm produced a series of porcelain dessert services with landscape centres and mazarine blue borders embellished with gold. (A registry mark sometimes appears on these pieces to date them before 1883.) The views on each service concentrated on a particular theme, such as English lake scenery or English castles. On at least one service the views were Canadian, depicting the Muskoka district of Ontario (*Plate* 19A). Each view was identified on the back of the piece.

Services such as the Aynsley Muskoka service, where every piece was decorated with a Canadian subject, obviously differ in purpose from those where one or two Canadian views were included casually. About 1850 Coalport, for example, produced a handsome dessert service bordered in vibrant turquoise, in which William Henry Bartlett's view of the Chaudière Bridge (copied from the engraving in *Canadian Scenery*) decorated a plate.[40] Other views painted on this service, however, had nothing to do with Canada, and it would be wrong to assume that the service was necessarily made for the Canadian market. Only rarely does a nineteenth-century porcelain service turn up with a Canadian theme in decoration carried throughout.

But though Coalport cannot be said to have been catering to the Canadian market with this particular dessert service of 1850, the Shropshire firm,[41] founded in the eighteenth century, was one well known to Canadians. In the nineteenth century, Coalport wares were imported in quantity by dealers like Reid & Co., of Crystal Hall, in London,[42] and advertised, generally under the old name of Coalbrookdale, by china merchants like Patton & Co., of Montreal. For Christmas, 1870, John Patton published a list of suggested holiday gifts in the *Gazette* of December 21, and included porcelain 'From Coalbrookdale Works'.

In the later years of the century, Derby was back again in the Canadian advertisements, as the Royal Crown Derby Porcelain Company, founded in 1876. After having made no porcelain since the brief attempt in the years between 1812 and 1822, the Wedgwood factory put a bone china on the market in 1878. Doulton began making porcelain at its Staffordshire plant in 1884. Wedgwood and Doulton wares were exported to Canada; and, until the factory closed in the mid-1880's, Davenport china was also sold extensively. Sometimes the advertisements of Victorian days were for the wares of porcelain makers now all but forgotten. The products of Charles Ford serve as an illustration. Ford was a Staffordshire potter who had formerly been in partnership as Thomas & Charles Ford; during the last quarter of the century he worked alone, making a good-quality bone china that was highly regarded in Canada. Adam Darling, the Montreal importer, ranked Ford's wares with those of Copeland and Minton.[43] Dessert services, with landscapes painted by hand, were typical of the Ford wares fashionable in the 1880's.

But important as were all these porcelain makers—from Worcester, from Staffordshire, from Shropshire—and frequently as they may have been mentioned by Canadian advertisers who had formerly been reticent about putting a factory name to a cup or a dish, the attention they received in the newspapers was all but eclipsed by a publicity campaign in the 1870's and 1880's for an Irish china. Belleek, the ivory-coloured, eggshell-thin porcelain made in County Fermanagh, swept into the Canadian market on a wave of unprecedented enthusiasm. Dealers who had rarely been known to utter a pottery name in years of advertising suddenly put 'BELLEEK!' headings on their copy. 'COME AND SEE IT', cried Glover Harrison in Toronto.[44] Exclaimed Edward Hagar in Montreal: 'This ware is the perfection of Art.' [45]

Founded in 1857, the Belleek china factory was born in the mind of an Irishman named Robert Williams Armstrong (1824-84), an architect by profession. A tour of Ireland with W. H. Kerr, of Worcester, when the latter was seeking materials for the making of porcelain, had given Armstrong the idea of establishing a pottery himself, where Irish felspar (found near Belleek) could be used to produce an Irish china. Lacking capital to set up alone, Armstrong enlisted the financial help of David McBirney, of Dublin, and together the two embarked on a project that was to make the name of a village in the north of Ireland known throughout the world.

The porcelain they produced was not a bone china, like the standard English body, but a variety of Parian porcelain, used at that time for ceramic statuary.[46] Felspar was an important ingredient of Parian, and tests had shown that the Irish felspar was of particularly fine quality. This was employed at Belleek to make both tablewares and ornaments characterized by thin potting, marine forms, and glazes that were reminiscent of the sheen of mother of pearl.

In North America this Irish china made its appearance about 1870 (*Plate* 19B). Jennie J. Young, writing in 1879, spoke of it as having found 'considerable favor' in both the United States and Canada, and said that it had come to their markets 'within the last ten years'.[47] Montrealers had it for 1870 Christmas giving, recommended by John Patton.[48] In Toronto it was Glover Harrison, himself an Irishman, who first promoted it strongly. To his customers, in 1871, it was the 'New Irish China', a ware he identified with 'First-class quality' and 'superior taste'.[49] Eight years later, in 1879, he was still promoting it, in several newspapers, as among 'the most beautiful . . . Ornamental Goods ever offered to the public'.[50]

Edward Hagar, the Montreal dealer, held the opinion in print that this Irish ware was 'very handsome', and for last-minute Christmas buying in 1881 he offered (in the *Witness* of December 16):

IRISH BELLEEK CHINA

Dejeuner Sets, Shells, Tea Sets

Baskets, Milk Tumblers, Wall Brackets

Centre Pieces, Biscuit Boxes, Honey Pots, &c.

But not everyone agreed with the dealers—or with Queen Victoria, who ordered Belleek for herself and members of the royal family.[51] Sir Charles Eastlake, the watchdog of British taste, suspecting vulgarity at every turn, spoke of 'what is called "Irish porcelain" ' as 'a detestable ware of recent invention, which glistens like wet barley-sugar'.[52] Sir Charles found Minton more acceptable.[53] In Canada, however, the china merchants carried on with 'IRISH BELLEEK CHINA! Very Elegant . . .'[54]

A porcelain made in Ireland had been R. W. Armstrong's dream. This he had brought to reality by establishing a pottery on an island in the River Erne, a pottery that has lasted for over a hundred years. His grandson, Brigadier James Price, stated in 1958 that some of the characteristic glazes—to which Sir Charles Eastlake objected but which others praised for their 'silvery, lustrous appearance'[55]—were of his own devising, written down in a cookery book and kept as a family secret.[56] In addition to working with technical problems, Armstrong was the factory's art director and designer. Yet he did not die a rich man. As his grandson has pointed out, he was never 'concerned about profits: what he really wanted to do was to make good china at home in Ireland . . . when he died he left nothing except the fame of Belleek.'

174

That fame was sufficient to send the Canadian china merchants into unusual particulars when they drew up their hand-written advertising copy. Some of them even visited the factory in Ireland, and must have known Armstrong. C. C. Taylor, of Toronto, not a dealer but a buyer for dealers, left a record of a visit to Belleek when he was shown 'beautiful wares', including 'hand-painted dishes priced from twenty to fifty guineas each; the painting being done by first-class artists'.[57] Glover Harrison was another who 'periodically' inspected 'the sources of production',[58] and the Belleek that he advertised in 1871 was announced in Toronto's *Evening Leader* on October 7 as 'selected with care . . . personally'.

Other British porcelains, not publicized in campaigns such as that put on for Belleek or particularized, like Minton, as being above 'ordinary ware', were nonetheless sold in Canada in large quantities. Significant as were the advertisements for Rockingham, Worcester, and Derby, or porcelain 'from the Celebrated Houses of Minton & Co. and Copeland', those that told the full story of the trade in porcelain mentioned no names. China from dozens of British factories was to be met with in nineteenth-century Canada as anonymous ware, just in from Liverpool, or London, or Glasgow. The dimensions of the trade were given by 'beautiful China . . . Setts' picked out at an English manufactory for Shuter & Wilkins in Montreal;[59] by 'Lustre China . . . in hampers', shipped from Liverpool to Saint John;[60] by 'China Toys and figures . . . chastely gilt', made in the Potteries and sold in Halifax.[61]

If china was never needed in the same quantities as earthenware, there was always a steady demand for it. This demand was met from early days by the new British porcelains that forced 'East India' wares from the market, and then held their own against an onslaught from powerful continental rivals.

CHAPTER XIV

Parian Ware

... a beautiful collection of genuine parian ware ... consigned from
England for peremptory sale ... at Mr. Shaw's stores ...
Montreal Gazette, Dec. 22, 1865.

Of all the ornamental wares produced in porcelain and sent for sale in Canada the most popular by far were those in Parian, the china that looked like marble. No well-furnished Victorian drawing-room was without Parian in some form. John J. Arnton, the Montreal auctioneer, recognized this when he advertised a house sale comprising 'the general goods of a comfortable Private Residence', and featured, with the 'Hair-seat Sofa', the 'What-not' and the 'Crimson Damask curtains', a 'Parian Vase and Ornaments'.[1] This was in 1864. Two years later he was again talking about a 'comfortably furnished residence', and again naming 'Parian Ornaments' as part of the accepted furnishings.[2]

The Canadian market was amply supplied with all the most fashionable Parian articles. Models of statuettes and busts admired at the Great Exhibition in London were later for sale in Toronto. In Montreal, statuary in Parian after such eminent artists as John Gibson, R.A., W. C. Marshall, R.A., and Sir Richard Westmacott, R.A. was shown at a provincial exhibition, and then offered to the highest bidder at auction. From one end of the country to the other, Canadians would have agreed with John Arnton that 'really splendid objects of Art' were to be had in the porcelain called Parian.[3] Nor were these art objects confined to the purely decorative. Parian came in useful as well as ornamental form. Candlesticks were made in it, so were jugs and honey pots. Trinket boxes in Parian were on every dressing table, and watch stands and spill vases, 'richly flowered and graped',[4] had their place on the mantel. Some of the Parian was cheap, all of it was greatly admired.

Parian belonged to the Victorians. Its first appearance seems to have been in the 1840's, although undoubtedly there were experiments at an earlier date leading up to it. Once again it was at Josiah Spode's factory in Staffordshire that initial steps were taken. Others, notably Bootes and Mintons, claimed that they had produced Parian as early as Copeland & Garrett (the firm operating the Spode Works from 1833 until 1847), but William Taylor Copeland and Thomas Garrett are generally credited with having first put Parian on a commercial basis. Their successors, W. T. Copeland & Sons, claimed the invention

for them in such Canadian advertisements as that in Polk's *Ontario Gazetteer*
... *1884-5*: 'INVENTORS AND ORIGINAL MANUFACTURERS OF THE
CELEBRATED . . . PARIAN STATUARY'. Copeland & Garrett themselves
did not, however, call it Parian; to them it was 'statuary porcelain'.

This statuary porcelain, later known as Parian, was china of a particular kind,
eminently suited to the reproduction of marble statuary. Even if it had points of
resemblance to other porcelains, both earlier and contemporary, it attained a
distinction quite its own. Its formula included ingredients of hard, or 'true'
porcelain, such as was made on the Continent, but not in the same proportions
used by the Continental potters, and it was fired at a lower temperature. Parian
differed from the celebrated Derby biscuit of the eighteenth century, yet it was
not just an unglazed (or biscuit) porcelain of the newer bone variety. Though
spoken of as unglazed, Parian was frequently given a very fine coating of glaze
by the 'smear' technique. This left it with a dull sheen, instead of an obviously
shiny surface, giving rise to the belief that it was in fact unglazed. Parian was
called a white porcelain, but its surface could be tinted, a later and not always
successful innovation.

Probably every important maker of Parian used a formula that differed slightly
from his neighbour's, but in every case a high proportion of felspar was essential
to its composition, the quality of the felspar affecting the tone of the porcelain
body. The cheaper Parian was often dry-looking, almost rough to the touch,
but the better products rivalled marble in appearance. John Gibson, the English
sculptor who had been a favourite pupil of the great Canova, declared that
Parian was 'decidedly the next best material to marble', and he was anxious to
have his own work reproduced in it.[5]

The exact date at which Copeland & Garrett introduced their statuary porcelain is difficult to determine. The year 1842 is often given, although this is open
to question. It is, however, clear that by the end of 1844 statuary porcelain was
in production, since the January, 1845, issue of the *Art Union* magazine made
reference to it. By the time of the Manchester Exhibition of British Industrial
Art, opened later that same year, Copeland & Garrett were in a position to make
a strong showing of their new porcelain body. The statuettes in it which they displayed at Manchester brought the influential *Art Union* to their side. 'It is impossible,' said the magazine, 'to devise more apt or desirable ornaments for the
drawing room'.[6] This sentiment was shared by Victorians for the rest of the
century.

Though Copeland & Garrett, and, after 1847, Copelands called their body
'statuary porcelain', Mintons, who disputed with Copeland & Garrett the invention of the new ware, called theirs 'Parian', after the marble from the Greek
Island of Paros. At Wedgwoods the name of an Italian marble, 'Carrara', was
adopted. It was the Minton name of 'Parian' that finally came into general use,
although Copelands were still referring to their ware as 'statuary porcelain' at
the time of the Great Exhibition in 1851.

The official catalogue of the Great Exhibition contained an explanation of
how the various figures and groups were made in this porcelain body of several

178

names but one overwhelming popularity. After being cast in plaster moulds, the different parts of a figure or group would later be assembled by the figure-maker. Sometimes as many as fifty separate parts would be involved, and then the joining of the 'seams' would become an intricate process. Allowance had to be made for shrinkage in firing, which was considerable. The firing itself was of the utmost importance: overfiring would result in a shapeless mass; underfiring would give an imperfect surface to the ware. What the catalogue called 'a series of difficulties' presented themselves to every maker of Parian porcelain.[7] These difficulties scores of potters overcame successfully.

Parian, like anything new in the Potteries, was taken up by nearly everyone who could manage to procure the equipment and materials to make it. Soon all over Great Britain 'the delicate new material called Parian' (as Charles Dickens termed it),[8] was being used for porcelain ornaments. The important makers commissioned well-known artists to provide models, or they paid for the right to reproduce sculpture that had received awards or public recognition.

It was this reproduction of sculpture—art for the masses—that won the approval of the *Art Union* and of those concerned with elevating Victorian taste. Said the *Art Union*, in November of 1846: 'We attach very great importance to this material, as offering a valuable medium for the multiplication of works of a high order of art, at a price that will render them generally available.' Very few might be able even to see an original Canova; almost everyone could own a copy in Parian. It was cheaper than bronze and better than plaster.

Canadians, who lived far from the cultural centres of the older world, suddenly found themselves able to view exhibitions where the works of acknowledged masters were set before their eyes in dazzling displays of porcelain. Such a show greeted visitors to the provincial fair held in Montreal in 1865. At the stand of Watson & Co., the china dealers, was an assortment of what the *Gazette*, on September 28, called 'beautiful specimens of Parian ware statuettes after Westmacott, Canova, Marshall, Gibson, Thorwaldsen, Bell, and other eminent sculptors.' Combined with a collection of Parian vases, 'exquisite in their floral ornamentation', these copies of sculpture were later sold off at a public auction. They ran to over 150 lots.[9]

In Toronto, in 1853, Patton & Co. were selling Parian busts and figures that included at least one model much admired at the Great Exhibition in London two years earlier: the bust of the Duke of Wellington after Count d'Orsay (a dandified French nobleman of military aspirations and artistic talent), which had been exhibited by Copelands in 1851.[10] The *Examiner* advertisement offered d'Orsay's Wellington in Toronto with another hero of the Napoleonic Wars, Lord Nelson (after Flaxman).[11]

Parian specified as from 'the Celebrated Houses of Minton & Co. and Copeland' was advertised by Patton & Co. in *Brown's Toronto General Directory, 1856*. That same year, in the *Globe*, Patton & Co. published one of the most interesting Parian advertisements to be found in any Canadian newspaper. Though it named no makers of what was offered, it gave a list of Parian models after some of the most prominent sculptors of the day, and most of these models are known

179

to have been produced by either Copelands or Mintons. The list, as it appeared on September 5, 1856, read:

PARIAN STATUETTES

DANNECKER'S Ariadne (two sizes)
Carrier's Prometheus, Psyche and Pandora
Canova's Dancing Girl
Cumberworth's Paul and Virginia
Bell's Una and the Lion
Bell's Shakespeare
Theed's Ruth and Rebeckah
Marshall's Sabrina
Power's [*sic*] Greek Slave
The Angel of the Annunciation
The Madonna
Bust of Michael Angelo (large size)
Theed's Bust of Napoleon
Durham's Bust of Jenny Lind
Busts of Shakespeare and Milton
Bust of Washington
And a number of smaller figures, just received.

PATTON & CO.
49, King Street East

In that list of top-quality ceramic sculpture one of the most popular items was the Greek Slave. The work of an American, Hiram Powers, the original marble had taken the artistic world by storm at the Great Exhibition. Daily crowds had gathered to gaze at the exquisite nude figure of a young woman, her hands pitifully chained. Displayed on a revolving dais, against a velvet backdrop, the Greek Slave in marble took on an ethereal beauty. Critics were astonished to find so excellent a work 'from the hand of a sculptor whose country has hitherto made comparatively little progress in this, the highest department of Art'.[12] Hastily they praised his effort.

Potters were quick to note the excitement created by the Greek Slave, and chief among the potters alert to public enthusiasm was William Taylor Copeland. He secured rights of reproduction, bringing out his porcelain version of the Powers masterpiece in 1852. Unmarked examples should not, however, be attributed automatically to Copeland, for many other potters, over many years, also issued models of this famous sculpture, and it should, perhaps, be noted that one writer of the day thought he saw a copy of the Greek Slave in Parian on the Minton stand at the Great Exhibition itself.[13] He may have been mistaken, although the possibility exists, for the Greek Slave (executed in 1843) had actually been shown in London, in a publisher's rooms, in 1845. It had then attracted the attention of 'the nobility and gentry', had caused a *Times* reporter to marvel at the 'beautifully rounded' limbs, and had received notice as 'the first specimen of progress' in sculpture ever produced by an American.[14] But it was not until it was viewed by the masses at the Great Exhibition that the Greek Slave soared to the peak of its popularity in England.

In Canada the interest in Parian reproductions of the Greek Slave was undoubtedly stimulated by the fact that many had seen it even before it drew the staring crowds in the Crystal Palace overseas. One of the six replicas in marble had been brought to Montreal in 1850, and put on display in a hall over the Mechanics Institute, on Great St. James Street, with one shilling and threepence charged for admission. Beside the Canadian appreciation, London's 1851 reaction to the Greek Slave seemed almost mild. In Montreal many went day after day 'to enjoy the contemplation of its rich and varied beauties'. The *Gazette* reporter was one. On July 30 he wrote: 'For ourselves, we can say, that from each visit, we have derived increased pleasure and increased good. We sincerely hope, therefore, that none who would add to their knowledge of the truly beautiful, or purify and elevate their moral sentiments, will allow the present opportunity to pass by unimproved. Once gone, it may perhaps be gone forever.'

The next day he was back again, 'gazing with rapture on the most beautiful Work of Art ever exhibited in this city'. With such publicity was a ready-made market created in Canada for copies of the Greek Slave in statuary porcelain. Hiram Powers' 'beautiful Work of Art' need not 'be gone forever', as the *Gazette* writer had feared. It could be purchased in the china shops, and all its 'varied beauties' contemplated anew in the drawing room.

So popular was the Greek Slave in Parian ware that even the second-hand market in Canada was offering it by 1855. An advertisement for an auction sale of household goods in the Montreal *Pilot*, on June 27, itemized a Parian statuette of the Greek Slave in 'perfect' condition.

For the china buyers of Toronto, one item in particular in Patton's 1856 list must have had special interest, and that was 'Durham's Bust of Jenny Lind' (*Plate* 20A). Like the bust of the Duke of Wellington, it was one that had formed part of the Copeland exhibit at the Crystal Palace in 1851, the very year in which the people of Toronto (to the envy of Montrealers) had had a chance to hear 'the Swedish Nightingale' for themselves. In Toronto she had been a sensation. So great was the crush to get tickets for her concert that the doors of Nordheimer's music store on King Street had to be barricaded, and the crowd admitted in batches. Even then, coats were torn from the backs of men scrambling to secure the ten-shilling seats.

The bust of Jenny Lind by Copeland has today added interest because of the marks generally impressed on the back. Like much of the Parian from the better makers, the bust of Jenny Lind after Durham was marked by the firm that made it. The name COPELAND is nearly always found upon it, together with the name of the subject ('Mlle Jenny Lind') and the name of the sculptor who executed the original bust ('Joseph Durham Sc. Oct. 1847'). On this bust, however, another mark is frequently found: 'Reduced by B. Cheverton'.

Reducing a large marble sculpture to a small porcelain copy was a process requiring much skill. Unless the proportions were kept exact, the lines of the original would be distorted and art defeated. Here a machine invented in England in the 1840's by Benjamin Cheverton proved an important aid to the potters of Parian. For a fee, Cheverton, by means of his machine, would produce an exact scale model of a piece of sculpture in any required size. From this model the potter could make his mould. As the popularity of Parian gathered momentum, Cheverton and his reducing machine became of increasing value, and ceramic statuary in which he had a part, such as the bust of Jenny Lind after Durham, frequently bore his name as well as that of the maker. Those who

181

purchased Jenny Lind from Patton & Co., in Toronto, were not only purchasing a bust of the singer whom they had tumultuously welcomed, they were purchasing a piece of ceramic sculpture that had been reproduced by the aid of one of the most ingenious machines utilized by the potter.

With earthenware ornaments it had been unusual to list titles, but with the advent of Parian the china sellers and auctioneers became more conscious of the value of letting the public know what models were in stock. The names of those who made the Parian did not seem to matter very much; what they made in it did. It was all part of an increasing Victorian awareness of art, with sculpture considered art's most important expression, and Parian china the popular form of sculpture available to all. Through the pages of Canadian newspapers, then, run the titles of Parian busts and statuettes which were once the latest in fashionable taste: Prince and Princess of Wales, Havelock, Milton, Clytie, and Amazon.[15] The firms of Copeland, Minton, and Wedgwood are known producers of some of these titles. All three firms were large exporters to Canada, and in their Parian ware sometimes included titles inspired by this interest in the North American colonies. Minton, for example, put out a model entitled 'Canadian Trapper' that is sometimes found today in drawing rooms where Victoriana has remained undisturbed.

Newspaper advertisements for household auctions contribute to the list of Parian models known to have been admired in Canada and also reveal that, when these wares were new, Canadians formed collections of them. One such collection came on the market in 1876, when a Mr. A. R. Brown, of Montreal, decided to 'decline housekeeping'. The *Star* of April 4 carried the advertisement for his sale on Lorne Avenue, and reported that it would include 'a choice collection of Parian Busts . . . Napoleon, Prince Albert, Prince of Wales, Peabody [the American philanthropist], Handel, Shakespeare, Dickens and others'.

A booklet published in 1865 gives another glimpse of the Parian statuary sold in Canada. *Montreal Business Sketches* contained a description of a china seller's shop window on St. James Street. Amid a glittering array of the best imported articles in glass and porcelain was a display of Parian statuettes, 'representing such historic personages as King Robert Bruce, Sir William Wallace, Michael Angelo, Raphael, and other equally illustrious and known to fame'.

One English firm responsible for Parian busts of fine quality maintained an agent in Montreal. John Ridgway, Bates & Co. appointed an Irishman, Andrew Hayes, to take orders for them throughout British North America. Hayes placed his business card in the *Canada Directory for 1857-58*, and advertised earlier in the *Montreal Gazette* (May 16, 1856):

POTTERS TO THE QUEEN.
JOHN RIDGWAY, BATES & CO.,
CAULDON PLACE,
Staffordshire Potteries.
Office and Pattern Room, 7 St. Sacrament Street,
Opposite the Merchants' Exchange.
ANDREW HAYES,
Agent for Canada and the B.N.A. Provinces.

John Ridgway (1785-1860) was the potter, a son and grandson of master potters of Staffordshire; Bates was a financier.[16] During the mid-1850's John Ridgway, Bates & Co. produced Parian of a superior quality, for which Hayes secured orders in British North America. He would appear to have been unusually successful with a bust of the hero of the Crimean War and Indian Mutiny, Sir Colin Campbell (later Lord Clyde). Today in Canada this piece with the impressed mark of J. RIDGWAY, BATES & CO., may be found in sizes from five inches to well over one foot in height (*Plate* 20B). The sculptor whose work was reproduced in this Parian body was Joseph Durham, and sometimes Durham's name is included with the maker's mark.

Although others also produced the popular military hero in Parian, it was possibly the J. Ridgway, Bates & Co. bust that William Edmonstone, one of the principal merchants of Montreal, had in his drawing room. When he disposed of the contents of his house on Sherbrooke Street, in 1866, the sale was handled by John Arnton, who advertised that a Parian bust of Sir Colin Campbell would be included.[17]

Some Montrealers may have remembered when Colin Campbell, as a young officer, fought in the War of 1812. In the 1860's they heard for themselves the famous pipes that had heralded his relief of Lucknow. Marching to the aid of that besieged garrison in 1858 had been the Ross-shire Buffs, part of the force commanded by Sir Colin Campbell in India. It had been the distant sound of their pipes playing 'The Campbells Are Coming' that had first told the all-but-hopeless within Lucknow that help was on the way at last. At first the sound had been but a faint note on the wind, scarcely to be believed, but then it had grown strong and clear, firing the courage of the exhausted to hold out a little longer. In the 1860's the Ross-shire Buffs, their duty in India completed, were with the garrison in Montreal. On a chill November Sunday, when the St. Andrew's Society went in parade to St. Andrew's Church on Beaver Hall Hill, the same Lucknow pipes of the Ross-shire Buffs led them along their way.

But Canadians had celebrities of their own who began to make their appearance in Parian. Sir John A. Macdonald, father of Confederation and the first prime minister of Canada, was one. His fellow Scot and political foe, Hon. Alexander Mackenzie, was another. The Parian busts of the two political leaders were obviously issued at the same time, for they show both men as they were in the 1870's (*Plate* 20C) when they faced each other across the floor of the House of Commons in Ottawa. When Macdonald's government fell in 1873, Mackenzie, as prime minister, then formed the first Liberal administration that the new Dominion had known. His party was sustained in the general election of 1874, but in 1878, after one of the bitterest political campaigns ever fought in Canada, the Conservatives were back. It was not for nothing that their campaign song had been 'Johnny Comes Marching Home Again'. After 1878 Alexander Mackenzie dropped quickly from prominence, being succeeded as leader of his own party by Edward Blake in less than two years. He would not have been portrayed in Parian after 1878. The date, therefore, of this pair of busts, produced in medium-quality Parian, lies within the 1870's. Presumably they were made to sell cheaply, and were in demand at election time.

Each bust is marked with the name of the subject: MACDONALD or MACKENZIE.

Neither was given a maker's name, although both have the initials 'R C' impressed with a number, the numbers being consecutive (264 for Mackenzie and 265 for Macdonald). Various names, including that of Robert Cooke, a Staffordshire maker of Parian in the 1870's, have been suggested to fit these initials, but until a fully marked specimen has been found, attribution must remain speculative. 'R C' whoever he may have been, was a potter who supplied both the home and colonial markets liberally over a period of time. In addition to the busts of the first two Canadian prime ministers, 'R C' produced classical busts and large figure groups, as well as statuettes of young women in contemporary Victorian costume, and busts of famous authors and poets.

Another Canadian, this time an international figure in the sporting world, appeared in Parian. Edward Hanlan ('Our Ned' to the newspapers) was a Toronto oarsman who won the championship of the world in 1880, rowing his greatest race along the Thames in England to defeat a lanky 'giant' of an Australian. Born in Canada West, in 1855, Hanlan had first made an international name for himself during the American centennial year of 1876. As a virtual unknown, he had entered a race arranged in connection with the Centennial Exhibition in Philadelphia. To the amazement of everyone, except his enthusiastic Toronto backers, he had won. Two years later, in a race at Lachine against the famous American sculler, Charles E. Courtney, the Canadian had emerged a champion to be reckoned with. On that occasion Adam Darling, the Montreal china merchant, had been one of the chief organizers of the race, and had presented Hanlan with the prize money. It was said that when the news of Hanlan's victory at Lachine came through to Toronto the enthusiasm was so great that 'staid old men were seen to cut capers' in King Street.[18]

Nothing, however, compared to the fever pitch of wild excitement into which the whole of Canada had worked itself in November of 1880. Edward Hanlan of Ontario and Edward Trickett of New South Wales were to meet in England for the championship of the world on the morning of November 15. In England the day dawned foggy and drearily wet. Whether the race could be held was a question. It was to be rowed from the Star and Garter Pier, just above Putney Bridge, to Mortlake, but the atmosphere was so murky that crowds gathered along the river bank appeared like phantoms in the mist. Then, suddenly, the clouds lifted, a clear stretch of water was revealed, and the waiting throngs saw the contestants take their places in their sculls, Hanlan's being a Toronto-built one of white cedar. In a moment they were away, Trickett moving ahead, but with Hanlan quickly drawing even. For well over a mile it was the close contest that had been anticipated, but then, as Hammersmith Bridge was reached, Hanlan shot into a commanding lead. English crowds, 'gifted with lungs of brass', yelled him on. Hanlan needed no urging; the race was his. 'He won as he pleased.' Said the London papers: 'It was a triumph of skill over strength.' 'The Little Sculler Walks Away from the Cornstalk. THE GIANT NOWHERE', ran the headline in the *Montreal Star*.[19]

While the Governor-General, the Marquis of Lorne, was awaiting a special cable to give him the results of the race, and all Canada was standing by, it was, naturally, in Toronto that the excitement mounted to the highest pitch. Long before seven o'clock in the morning, the hour at which it was anticipated word would arrive from overseas, crowds were milling around newspaper and tele-graph offices. When the machines finally began to tap out the cables from London, the first word of victory turned the city into one surging, madly cheering mob. King Street was completely blocked, business offices closed, flags ran up on many buildings, bells began to ring, and betting money changed hands in unheard-of amounts.

In Parian china Edward Hanlan of Toronto, champion oarsman of the world, was 'the handsome, grave-looking gentleman' that the *New York World* had called him[20] (*Plate* 21A). Issued in large size (over eleven inches in height), the bust showed Hanlan in rowing costume, and identified him on the back. Fine-quality Parian was used, but the potter who capitalized on the Canadian's fame does not seem to have added his own name to his work.

Although Parian began as a porcelain for the reproduction of sculpture, it was soon turned into other types of ornamental ware, and even into articles intended for use. In the same 1856 issue of the *Globe* in which they published their hand-some list of Parian statuettes, Patton & Co. of Toronto announced other Parian articles:

PARIAN VASES

THE Portland or Barbarini Vase
The Warwick Vase (small size)
A pair of Vases after Cellini
The Vintage Garden Vase
Lily of the Valley, Primrose, and Cowslip Vases,
Hyacinthe Vases
Hanging Baskets for Creeping Plants, in Terra Cotta and
Parian just received . . .
Parian Jugs and Butter Coolers in great variety,
Parian Cups and Saucers and Plates
Parian Loaf Plates, with wheat border
Parian Match Boxes, Pin Boxes, &c.
Parian Candlesticks, &c.
PATTON & CO.

Copeland and Minton probably were the makers of at least some of these pieces, but a number of the patterns indicated in the *Globe*—lily of the valley and cowslip vases, for example—were produced by other makers as well.

Articles such as jugs (*Plate* 21B) and cups (more ornamental than really useful) would have been glazed on the inside; but dessert services, which were occa-sionally advertised in Canada,[21] had only the smear glaze commonly found on most Parian wares.

Another advertisement which gave an excellent idea of the variety of hollow wares to be had in Parian appeared in the *Montreal Gazette* on May 15, 1866. Lawrence Devany, holding an auction to dispose of consignments from over-seas, was the advertiser who sought the patronage of both trade and private buyers: 'A MAGNIFICENT ASSORTMENT of the celebrated EGG-SHELL PARIAN, comprising Sets of Jugs, with grey-hound handles; Shell Ice Jugs, Jewel Boxes, Cupid Watch Stands; Greek, Etruscan and Ricmond [*sic*] Vases; Dolphin Trinket Stands, Lisbon Ewers, Ice Butter Coolers, Vases, Ornaments.'

Druggists used to sell Parian with perfume. At Davidson's Central Drug Hall, in Montreal, 'PERFUMES in Parian-ware Jugs' were advertised in 1864 as 'USEFUL AND ELEGANT CHRISTMAS & NEW YEAR'S GIFTS'.[22] Into

185

Parian containers, often of classic form, went such Victorian favourites in scent as New Mown Hay, Moss Rose, Peruvian Balm, Jockey Club, and Jenny Lind.

Whether found in china shops, 'drug halls' or what were called 'fancy goods stores', Parian was a Victorian porcelain that commanded a wide sale in Canada. Henry Gribble, 'Importer and dealer . . . in FANCY GOODS', stocked it at his Victoria Bazaar in British Columbia.[23] Francis Clementson, operating one of the finest china shops in the colonies, advertised it in New Brunswick.[24] It was offered at auction with Jacques & Hay furniture made in Toronto,[25] and at trade sales that put 'Best Parian Vases' on the same bill as 'fine skates'.[26]

But Canadians had yet another way of obtaining Parian porcelain. Many took the opportunity of buying a chance on a Parian prize at one of the great art lotteries, which were a distinctive feature of Victorian life in Great Britain. The art union movement, art on a gamble, began in the 1830's; for half a century and more the unions were an influence in the distribution of various forms of art, including paintings, engravings, sculpture, and ceramic wares. According to Canadian advertisements for these British lotteries, the principle on which the art unions operated was that of 'mutual combination', their object 'to promote the knowledge and love of Fine Arts and their general advancement in the British Empire'.[27]

They were, in brief, lotteries in which all the prizes were works of art. Since extending appreciation of the arts, even to distant colonies, was one of the main purposes of the art unions, most of them advertised in Canada. Canadians were told that this type of lottery offered 'peculiar advantages to persons of taste', and they were promised that 'works of art of the highest class' would be theirs 'at the lowest price',[28] if the ticket number turned out to be lucky.

By paying a subscription to a local representative of an art union, a resident of Halifax or Montreal or Toronto would be in the running for one of the many prizes to be drawn on the appointed day in England, Ireland, or Scotland. Tickets, or 'subscriptions', cost anything from one shilling to one guinea. Generally a free engraving or some other inducement, said to be 'fully equal' to the price of the ticket, was presented to each subscriber. The Art Union of London also gave a long-membership reward. In 1848 this union advertised in Nova Scotia that everyone who paid one guinea for ten successive years would receive not only the annual premiums, and, perhaps, valuable prizes, but a silver medal as well.[29]

The Art Union of London, 'well known and popular' in Canada,[30] was the most influential of them all. It was actually credited with having played a decisive role in the development of Parian porcelain itself. According to S. C. Hall, editor of the *Art Journal* (formerly the *Art Union* magazine), Copeland & Garrett's new statuary porcelain had made a disappointingly slow start, as far as sales went: 'at the outset, the experiment was not only discouraging, but would have been ruinous to a producer of limited means.'[31] After a meeting was arranged by the magazine, at which representatives of the Art Union of London were present to examine samples of this new ware, the whole picture changed. A commission from the Art Union of London followed, and Copeland & Garrett's statuary porcelain was launched on the swelling tide of art lottery prizes. Its future was assured.

Parian Ware

When Parian was included as an art union prize it was usually one of the lesser awards, statuettes or busts being given to several dozen ticket holders at that particular drawing. One art union, however, specialized in ceramic prizes. This was the Ceramic and Crystal Palace Art Union, which distributed great numbers of Parian statuettes and busts. A Canadian who subscribed to the Ceramic and Crystal Palace Art Union in the 1860's and whose Parian trophies have survived, was Andrew Angus, of Montreal. Two of the Parian busts he received have passed into the possession of his grandson, Dr. Donald M. Angus. One, entitled 'The May Queen', is after Joseph Durham, and was 'Published April 1, 1863'. The other, made by the Copeland firm, reproduces a work by Raffaelle Monti, an Italian sculptor.

Parian marked as a premium or a prize by an art union had the name of the union and the pertinent information impressed upon it. Many of the important makers, such as Copelands, Mintons, Wedgwoods, and the porcelain factories at Coalport and Worcester, frequently put their own names upon Parian, whether made for lotteries or for regular sale. On the other hand, much Parian went unmarked, or was marked only with the initials of the maker. T. & R. Boote, for instance, who disputed with Copeland & Garrett and Mintons the invention of Parian, often marked their ware with their initials only, T. & R. B. The most prolific of all Parian makers, the Staffordshire firm of James Robinson and Edward James Leadbeater, apparently used no mark at all for many years and, when they did begin to mark their wares, identified them only with initials. Llewellynn Jewitt, writing in the early 1880's (and stating that Robinson & Leadbeater exported to Canada), declared that at that time no mark was in use.[32] Although subsequently some, at least, of their wares bore the initials R & L,[33] it seems strange that this firm, which devoted the entire output of two factories to Parian, did not identify its products more fully. Long after Parian had been abandoned by most other potters for newer ceramic fashions, Robinson & Leadbeater continued to make it. Well past the turn of the century they were still producing busts and figures in this porcelain which was characteristically Victorian.

Although used for other articles, Parian was in origin related to statuary. The Victorian interest in sculpture, added to the Victorian belief that popularizing art was a matter 'of high national importance', made a particular place for statuary porcelain. In 1851 Cassell's *Illustrated Exhibitor* had looked on the Parian ware displayed at the Crystal Palace in London and had admired it extravagantly. Said the *Exhibitor*: '. . . we long to see the day when the creations of the sculptor's genius, destined as they are to pioneer the way along which mankind advance in their siege upon ignorance and superstition, shall no longer remain as isolated specimens of human power in the halls of the wealthy, but be spread by the potter's agency through the humblest cottages of the land.'[34]

The day for which Cassell's *Exhibitor* longed had dawned with the invention of Parian, not only for those dwelling in the humblest cottages of Great Britain, but for those in the colonies beyond the seas. Parian made it possible for Canadians to share in the admiration accorded 'the sculptor's genius'. For the Canadian china merchants, Parian also meant a thriving business in groups, statuettes and busts—'classical, portrait and imaginative'.

187

CHAPTER XV

Porcelains Other Than British

JUST received a very small supply of FRENCH CHINA in Vases,
Ornaments and Tea Setts . . . For Sale by THOMAS BICKELL.
Quebec Observer, Sept. 4, 1854.

It was the French potters who gave the British the keenest competition in the
Canadian market, and it was in porcelain that they made their effect felt. Their
strength became apparent towards the middle of the nineteenth century. Even
earlier, however, when the great bulk of tablewares sold in the British colonies
of North America was of British make, French china had been brought to
Canada in the hope of profit. In the pages of the *Montreal Gazette* for September
3, 1827, is the record of a selling venture that anticipated the important trade
which would be done in French porcelain at a later date.

J. B. Martinucio, who had recently arrived in Montreal and taken rooms at
Rasco's Hotel, informed 'the Gentry and Public' that he had with him 'an
assortment of FRENCH GOODS, such as have never been imported before in
this country'. With musical clocks, musical snuff boxes, silk braces, flowers 'for
chapeau' and cases of 'sparkling champaigne', he had for sale 'a rich assortment
of PORCELAIN DE CÈVE, consisting of Vases, with fine Paintings, Tea-Setts,
rich Porcelain Trays, with small setts, Drawing Room Chimney Ornaments, and
a variety of other articles of this celebrated Factory.'

Two years later, in 1829, Scott, Montgomerie & Co., Montreal merchants,
advertised an auction sale at their stores which would include 'Ornaments from
the celebrated Severe [*sic*] Manufactory'.[1] These were to be put up with a quantity of other goods, such as 'China Tea, Dinner and Coffee setts' (probably
English), Britannia metal, and Sheffield wares.

In the Maritime colonies, Ratchford & Lugrin, of Saint John, tested the New
Brunswick market with a consignment from Paris in 1833. Furniture described
as 'elegant' and porcelain that was 'handsome' made up part of it.[2] Another
Saint John merchant, A. B. Buxton, brought in two cases of French china in
1839, and advertised them with his regular stock of English earthenware and
porcelain.[3]

But mention of French china in Canadian advertising was not common until
the 1850's. Previously it was generally limited to special importations or to
ornamental wares which fell into the luxury class. In this the Canadian market

differed from that of the United States. There advertisements for French table-wares direct from Paris were frequent in the earlier part of the century.[4] In Canada it was not until the flood of cheap continental china at mid-century that French wares were a constantly recurring item in crockery advertising.

Where formerly French china had been a novelty, mentioned only occasionally in the newspapers, it now became usual to see advertisements listing French with English tablewares. Patton & Co., of Toronto, had an announcement of this kind in the *Globe* on September 5, 1856:

DINNER SERVICES
Plain French China Dinner Services, very low . . .
English Ironstone and Earthenware Dinner Services in a
great variety of forms and   patterns.

DESSERT SERVICES
French China Dessert Sets at unusually low prices.
English Stoneware Dessert Sets, Gilt and Plain.

BREAKFAST SETS
Breakfast and Tea Sets of French and English China.
English Stonware Breakfast Sets of new pattern.

TOILET SETS
French China Gilt and Enamelled Toilet Sets
English Stoneware Toilet Sets, Gilt, Coloured and Plain.
Slop-Jars, Foot Baths . . . Basins to match.

Expensive French tablewares and rich ornamental wares were imported as well as the 'French China . . . at unusually low prices', but it was the flood of cheap china that cut most seriously into British sales. Patton's advertisement shows how this French ware challenged not only English porcelain but earthenware. With its prices reduced to competitive levels, porcelain of French make seemed to many more stylish than good-quality earthenware costing as much. And for those disposed to weigh durability against prevailing fashion, and who might feel that hard-wearing 'English stoneware' was more practical than brittle con-tinental porcelain, the French potters were ready with an answer. The rest of Patton's advertisement gave it when it listed 'Thick French China Plates, Dishes, Bakers, Cups and Saucers', and went on to declare that this heavy-weight foreign porcelain was even 'more durable than English stoneware'.

Elsewhere that same year, Patton & Co. advertised 'the *thick French China* now coming into general use'.[5] They held up as a mark of its superiority the fact that it never turned 'black if chipped', and was, therefore, 'more economical' than English stoneware.[6] But the English earthenware makers were equal to the threat from France. They fought back with porcelain-sounding names applied to dense earthenwares covered with thick, stiff glazes, stained to imitate the look of continental china.[7] In their turn they publicized new semi-porcelains so highly vitrified that they, too, retained their original whiteness if chipped or flaked. For earthenware, they claimed the advantages of standing up better to heat, and of holding heat longer—important considerations in the case of dinner or tea ware. In the end, the dense earthenwares retained their full place in the Canadian market; for nothing ever really met the ordinary needs of a new country so well as the stout ironstones and stonewares from Great Britain.

In the porcelain market itself the story was different. For the rest of the century, the British porcelain makers exporting to Canada had to maintain active competition with French potters. The evidence of the advertisements shows that the British wares never lost supremacy in Canadian sales; the bone china of England was advertised in greater quantity than the hard porcelain of France, and names like Copeland, Minton, and Worcester remained at the top where quality was concerned. But their rivals were both aggressive and effective. French porcelain never supplanted English wares in Canada, but it created for itself an important place in an expanding market.

For a time fashion swung appreciably to French china. In the lower-priced wares in particular Canada now began to look to England for earthenware, to France for porcelain, and to the United States for glass. John R. Monro's advertisement in the St. Catharines *Weekly Times* of October 2, 1873, is an illustration:

OUR CHINA
Is all new, and direct from the FRENCH
POTTERIES
———
OUR CROCKERY
Is largely assorted and direct from
the ENGLISH POTTERIES
———
OUR GLASSWARE
Is direct from Pittsburg and Boston,
and contains all the new and best
patterns.

Canadian china merchants, seemingly hesitant about identifying English potters in their advertising, appeared even more reluctant to name French makers. A brief 'French China' generally sufficed. Occasionally porcelain from what had once been the Royal Manufactory at Sèvres was announced. This had been the case when J. B. Martinucio brought his 'rich assortment of PORCE-LAIN DE CÈVE' to Montreal in 1827. In Victorian times Henry J. Shaw, a Montreal auctioneer, was another who particularized Sèvres in his advertisements. Over a period of years Shaw handled consignments sent to Canada by a Paris exporting house. These he disposed of at annual or semi-annual sales, and from time to time named Sèvres in the announcements, as in the *Gazette* on October 21, 1876, when he advertised 'an almost matchless selection of Porce-lain from . . . Sèvres'.

Perhaps the name Limoges was more frequently mentioned in Canadian china advertising than that of any other French ware. During the Christmas season of 1863 John Patton, of Montreal, included 'Limoges' dinner and dessert sets in the same advertisement as tablewares from the 'celebrated Royal Porce-lain Works in Worcester'.[8] Edward Hagar, another Montreal dealer, announced 'LIMOGES CHINA! The Newest Designs' for the Christmas trade of 1880.[9]

In the nineteenth century the products of a large number of hard-paste porce-lain factories were covered by the term 'Limoges China'. The first porcelain had

191

been made at Limoges in the eighteenth century, but it was only after 1820 that hard-paste porcelain factories and decorating establishments began to spring up in numbers in this area of France, where certain raw material for potting was readily at hand. In Victorian times several of the Limoges factories built up a strong trade with Canada. One in particular, Haviland & Co., a French china factory founded by an American, supplied some of the most important Canadian dealers.

David Haviland had been an importer of English china to the United States. In the 1840's he decided to become a maker as well as a seller of china, and for the location of his manufacturing he chose Limoges in France. With selling outlets in New York, and with a sound knowledge of what would be admired in the United States, the American, David Haviland, was a success as a French potter. His fellow Americans were soon convinced that his porcelain 'invariably' reflected 'refined taste'.[10] Many Canadians agreed.

To own a set of 'Haviland Limoges' became the goal of housewives in Victorian Canada. Glover Harrison of Toronto found the demand sufficient to arrange with the manufactory to have the name of his China Hall added to wares shipped to him. Adam Darling in Montreal, a dealer in a large way, bracketed Haviland with such great names in potting as Copeland, Minton, and Wedgwood.[11] It was Adam Darling who brought to Canada a replica of the most famous porcelain service Havilands ever made. For weeks it was on display in his shop on St. James Street, attracting hundreds of visitors and winning praise in the *Herald* as 'the most unique exhibition of a work of Art which has ever been gathered in Montreal'.[12]

The story of this service goes back to 1879. In the spring of that year the wife of the President of the United States, Mrs. Rutherford B. Hayes, gave an order to Havilands for new White House china. But it was not to be just another service of porcelain suitable for state occasions. What she wanted was something 'strictly native American', as the *Montreal Herald* put it. It was finally decided that each piece for the White House would be painted with an American scene or subject. Since Havilands had no artists sufficiently familiar with the United States to produce the required designs, the services of Theodore R. Davis, Civil War veteran and well-known illustrator of the American scene, were engaged. Davis did not do any of the actual painting on the china, but he submitted designs to be followed by the china painters in Limoges.

The results were considered spectacular. Plates with snowshoes raised in gold upon them were executed for ice cream (the association of snowshoes and ices being considered appropriate). Shell-shaped dishes were painted with marine subjects. Platters were realistic representations of birch bark. Wild turkeys, moose, and buffaloes ranged over china surfaces, and maple-sugar making, unknown to Europe, was glorified on French porcelain. The name of Theodore Davis, together with a coloured representation of the Great Seal of the United States, appeared on the back of each piece.

Copies of the White House china were made for sale by Havilands. It was one of these copies that Adam Darling imported to Canada in 1881. His, however, was a special 'Canadian edition'. The *Herald* explained it: 'the enterprise of Mr. Darling, in importing so rich a triumph in the art, deserves all praise, and he has made it especially a Canadian edition as every piece is marked with the Arms of the Dominion in colours; in short, nothing has been omitted to make it perfect.'

The praise Adam Darling 'deserved' for bringing this special Haviland tableware to Montreal was probably translated into increased sales for the 'Haviland Limoges' in his regular stock. Such an exhibition must have had great promotional value. The *Herald* alone devoted over half a column to it, and throughout the summer of 1881 Adam Darling never allowed the public to forget that 'the famous White House Dinner Service' was on view at his establishment.[13]

David Haviland died in 1879, but for some years his sons, Charles and Théodore, carried on the business. When they dissolved partnership in 1892, it was to start separate concerns of their own, so that Haviland products continued to come to Canada. One of the last crockery advertisements of the century, which appeared in the Montreal *Gazette* in December of 1899, was for dinner sets by such 'well known names as Minton, Doulton, Wedgewood [*sic*], Haviland, etc.'[14]

While a set of 'Haviland Limoges' was the object of many Canadian buyers, there were countless others who were content with cheaper French china which bore no maker's mark. One type of floral decoration which had great popularity, and which occurred on much unmarked French china of the Victorian period, as well as on Haviland products, made use of the moss rose as the central theme (*Plate* 22A). It is not surprising that the moss rose was frequently incorporated in china decoration on both tea and dinner ware, since it was one of the favourite flowers of the day. As many as two dozen varieties of the moss rose were cultivated in Victorian times, and it appeared on wallpapers, on textiles, in paintings, on Valentines and Christmas cards. Its distinguishing feature was the almost exaggerated 'mossiness' covering the buds. In china decoration this was sometimes depicted in brown or buff tones, as well as in green. The French potters used variations on the theme of the moss rose for years, particularly for the North American market. English makers of earthenware in competition with French china were not long in copying the moss rose onto their wares, and white granite and ironstone are often found painted with this Victorian flower. It was the moss rose decoration and not the maker of the ware itself that was the selling point, as Edward Hagar's Montreal advertisement of 1885 shows:

LOW PRICES

FOR THIS WEEK WE ARE OFFERING

China Tea Sets, 44 pieces, Moss Rose

and Gilt at $5 . . .[15]

Towards the end of the century porcelain tablewares from Germany added another element of competition in the Canadian market. 'Dresden' of ornamental type, had been popular in the North American colonies before Confederation—'DRESDEN CHINA FIGURES, VASES, &c.' were suggested as presents by John Patton, advertising in the *Montreal Gazette* on Christmas Eve, 1863—but ordinary German wares for the table did not become a typical feature of Canadian advertising until about the last quarter of the century, and their great day was after 1900.

As with English and French porcelain, however, German tableware was sometimes brought to Canada by persons who arrived equipped with household possessions. Such porcelain frequently made a later appearance on the second-hand market. In a particularly luxurious auction sale of 1819 'a very handsome Dinner Service of Dresden China' was specified. This had certainly been purchased abroad and brought to Montreal by the seller, Major Henderson of the Royal Engineers.

Garrison officers often lived elegantly in Canada, but few can have outdone Major Henderson. The details of his auction, as set forth in the *Herald* on February 20 (shortly before he returned to England) reveal that his 'very handsome' Dresden china had been used on a clawfoot mahogany dining table large enough to seat twenty persons. The table, and all his furniture, was advertised as having been made 'by the best workmen in England'. His silver, in the King's pattern, was 'superb', and had cost originally £1,800. His cut glass was 'rich', his carpets, paintings, prints, sofas, chairs, and pianoforte the most fashionable that could be found. His library was 'valuable', with every book bound in 'Russia Leather'—and all new. His cellar comprised more than one hundred dozen 'Superior Wines', including port of 1812 vintage, and excellent champagne. It is no wonder that the auctioneers advised Montrealers wanting good things to hurry to Major Henderson's house in the 'Quebec Suburbs'.[16] Presumably somebody who attended that auction came away the owner of a porcelain dinner set of unusually fine quality, and possibly this service was a product of Meissen. The English commonly spoke of Meissen wares as 'Dresden'.

Both French and German potters deluged the Canadian market with porcelain ornaments. Two hundred and fifty dozen 'China Ornaments' of continental origin were announced for a Montreal trade sale in 1880.[17] At an earlier sale Montreal importers offered 'magnificent' fancy goods which included ornamental china from Germany, Austria, and France. These wares were 'rich and costly',[18] but many continental ornaments were sold in Canada for very little: twenty cents each and upwards at Henry Morgan's Colonial House in the 1890's.[19]

Immensely popular, especially in the closing years of the century, were the continental bisque figures, once to be seen standing on most parlour organs. Some, like many from Galluba & Hofmann (porcelain manufacturers in Thuringia, in the latter part of the century), were left in the white (*Plate* 22B). The vast majority, however, were coloured over the unglazed body. While some might sell for a few cents, others were retailed for dollars.[20] Classical figures were among the ornaments from Galluba & Hofmann (whose hard-paste wares were marked with their monogram or name), but sentimental, even saccharine figures or groups had wider appeal in their day. In a *Witness* advertisement on December 18, 1880, Wiley's China Hall in Montreal attracted attention with the heading 'SANTA CLAUS SUGGESTS', and among the wares which had this hallmark of holiday approval were bisque figures. In this case details were given as to models available. Paul and Virginia (the tragic lovers in a Rousseauistic novel by Bernardin de St. Pierre), Masqueraders, Skaters, Fruit Vendors, and a Flower Girl were specified. The Ontario importers, W. J. Reid & Co., of London, regularly carried both Dresden and French 'Bisco', and declared that every figure in stock was 'a complete work of art'.[21]

Another ornament usually from continental potters, although made by some

British firms, was the lithophane (porcelain moulded in *intaglio* in such a way as to produce a 'picture' by transmitted light). 'Transparent Porcelain Pictures!' John Armour called them in a Montreal Gazette advertisement, dated June 16, 1853. Armour was a bookseller, not a china merchant, but vast quantities of ceramic ornaments were sold in shops other than those devoted to china. Women teaching 'Berlin wool work' in their 'fancy goods' stores often added to slender incomes by dealing in cheap china; booksellers such as Armour handled china goods for the writing table, as well as a wide variety of other decorative items from the potter. In announcing his shipment of 'Transparent Pictures', Armour suggested them as suitable for 'Hall Lights, Lamps, &c., &c.' His collection was priced at from one to seven shillings each.

Depending for their effect on a light arranged behind them, most lithophanes were made as panels, some of which ambitiously reproduced old master paintings. They may, however, be found in other articles, such as small night lights. They were even formed in the bottom of beakers or tumblers (presumably the user was expected to upend his drink against a bright light, otherwise the presence of the lithophane might escape him). Made at a score of factories, some of the best lithophanes came from the Königliche Porzellanmanufaktur in Berlin. These Berlin panels generally have the initials K.P.M. impressed, but the intials do not always stand for this royal manufactory; other continental firms also used them.

In addition to all these continental ornaments offered to 'Admirers of the Ingenious and Beautiful' (as one Montreal auctioneer put it),[22] and all of which were ranged in competition with the Parian and other ceramic ornaments from British potters, there was another type of china ornament which invaded the Canadian market from the continent in late Victorian times. This was the small, glazed, and very cheap porcelain figure or group (sometimes perched on a box lid). Such ornaments differed from the cheap bisque or unglazed wares not only in the appearance of the porcelain itself, but in approach. The bisque figure, cheap or otherwise, was often sentimental and nearly always 'pretty'. These little glazed figures and groups, on the other hand, were crude, occasionally rude little ornaments which appealed greatly to the Victorians, whose sense of humour could be bawdy. Even when the subject touches the heart, as is the case with a little street sweeper or a ragged news-boy, a sense of bravado seems to supplant pathos. Perhaps the most engaging of them have to do with animals acting like humans. Such wares were probably made at a number of continental factories. Later they were copied in Japan.

Some modern collectors of these wares call them 'fairings', since, like cheap Staffordshire ornaments, they were sold at country fairs in England. In their own day they would have been classed merely as cheap novelties, 'the sixpenny line'. In Canada they must have formed part of the stock of many a 'bazaar' or 'fancy goods' store, such as Henry Gribble's Victoria Bazaar in British Columbia, where French and German wares were advertised along with English china,[23] or at the 'Ark' in Montreal, where 'FANCY CUPS AND SAUCERS . . . little Statues and Ornaments' were available at low cost.[24] Older people, recalling the turn of the century, remember them as being hawked in country districts by itinerant pedlars, who would have stocked up with them, at a few cents a dozen, from an importer.

Typical of the titles which appear in English on the front of these ornaments, made mostly in Germany, are 'Modesty' (a bedroom scene), and 'The delights of Matrimony' (the baby walker). Victorian 'scraps' (sold in sheets for albums) and music covers provided some of the themes. Although ceramically they have little interest, these ornaments, which appear to have come to Canada in vast quantities, serve to illustrate in yet another way the competition eventually offered the British potter.

Compared to the outpourings of the British and European potteries, what was manufactured in the United States was, relatively speaking, negligible, as far as Canada was concerned. Huge importations from abroad flowed steadily into the country, but there is little evidence that American porcelain makers attempted to enter into very hopeful competition with them. For porcelain, the United States itself was primarily dependent in the nineteenth century upon foreign wares. Yet there was one early New York china manufacturer who made a determined effort to secure Canadian business. He was British-born Charles Cartlidge, whose name generally appeared as 'Cartledge' in Canadian advertising.[25] To promote his wares in Canada, the Staffordshire-trained Cartlidge appointed as agent the same Andrew Hayes, of Montreal, who represented John Ridgway, Bates & Co., Potters to the Queen.[26]

Cartlidge had himself been an agent in the United States for one of the Ridgway firms. He may possibly have had an acquaintance with the Canadian market at that time, particularly since his employer, William Ridgway, visited Canada.[27] About 1848 he decided to go into business on his own account as a manufacturer of porcelain door furniture and other articles, and took as partner Herbert Q. Ferguson, a former Ridgway representative in New Orleans.[28] Together they set up Charles Cartlidge & Co., in Greenpoint, Long Island. Before the firm failed (about 1856) not only porcelain door furniture but Parian busts and china buttons had been accomplished. The Canadian advertisements, such as that in the *Montreal Gazette* on April 14, 1851, suggest that Cartlidge did not come to potting in New York without previous practical knowledge gained at home in Staffordshire:

Charles Cartledge & Co.

Sole Manufacturers of American Porcelain

Door Furniture, &c. &c.

GREEN POINT, KING'S CO., N.Y.

C. C. & CO. having been brought up to the business, have given their attention to the production of an article which will withstand the rigours of the severe Winters of the North, which their Manufacture is warranted to do.

It took the first premiums at the Fair of the American Institute, New York, and the Franklin Institute, Philadelphia, and is at once the most beautiful and cheap article that has been introduced.

Specimens may be seen at the Office of their sole Agent for Montreal and the British Colonies,

ANDREW HAYES,
No. 124, St. Paul St.

Since Hayes represented the New York pottery for several years, he probably also attempted to put on the Canadian market the Parian china and the other ornaments which came from this factory during its years of struggle to compete with imported goods. That Cartlidge tried for Canadian sales is undoubtedly explained, at least in part, by his own British background.

Towards the close of the Victorian era Canada shared with the western world a revival of interest in oriental wares. At the end of the eighteenth century, Chinese porcelain had come to Canada as 'India china', imported into England through the East India Company, and from England sent to British North America. In the second half of the nineteenth century, it was arriving 'direct from China' to be offered in trade sales from Halifax to Victoria. Thomas J. Potter, the Montreal auctioneer, held such a sale just before Christmas, 1880. His advertisements in several newspapers featured Chinese vases, 'quaint' tea cups, rice bowls, and platters—'A Rare and Beautiful Collection direct from China'.[29]

On the west coast, direct trade with the Orient belonged to the earliest days of the colony of British Columbia, and auctioneers like J. P. Davies & Co., of Victoria, frequently had consignments of Chinese porcelain. This was the case in the spring of 1869, when Davies offered 'Chinese Spittoons and Vases'.[30] At an earlier period dealers on the east coast were handling Chinese porcelain 'imported direct from Canton'. Sometimes this porcelain came in with shipments of tea. It is possible that the 'Elegant China' advertised by Street & Ranney, of Saint John, with '6000 PACKAGES OF TEA' received *by the Clifton, from Canton*' was also oriental.[31]

Japanese wares as well as Chinese were sold in Canada in Victorian times. In 1883 Matthew Hicks & Co., of Montreal, advertised 'a rare and choice collection of JAPANESE ART GOODS', picking out for special mention 'Kioto, Awata, Kutani, Kaga, Owari, Himeja, Saitogo and Kinran Porcelains'.[32] Hicks had conducted a similar auction the year before, when a wide variety of Japanese porcelains had been offered, including those of Hizen. On this occasion, however, Hicks had been selling the Japanese porcelains on behalf of the customs authorities. A whole shipment had been seized, after government appraisers had compared their estimates with the declared values and had found a discrepancy of about two hundred per cent.[33]

Cheap Japanese porcelain gained ground in the popular market during the mid-Victorian period, claiming, with French and German wares, a share in a crockery trade once almost exclusively supplied from the British potteries. By the 1880's it was possible to buy a 'Five o'Clock Tea Set' of Japanese porcelain for 'only one Dollar' in Montreal.[34] At higher cost the same type of set was available in 'FRENCH WHITE CHINA . . . from Limoges', or in Belleek china from Ireland.[35]

It was all part of the growth of the Canadian market, growth accounted for by an enlarging population, improved transportation, and an awakened interest in ceramic wares from the ends of the earth. In 1800 Daniel King, a Saint John merchant, had been well supplied when his porcelain comprised 'a few Table and Tea sets of Liverpool China';[36] by the end of the century the picture had changed. Canadian buyers expected to see a complete assortment of British porcelain in any well-run china shop, but they also expected to have their eyes bewildered by 'a magnificently arranged and judiciously selected stock . . . from all quarters of the globe'.[37]

Printed Earthenware with
Canadian Views and Emblems

CHAPTER XVI

Enoch Wood:
His Canadian Views and Montreal Agent

Such as have not done business with Messrs. ENOCH WOOD & SONS, and
who may be desirous of opening an account, may have Prices Current.
Montreal Gazette, Oct. 29, 1829.

Some nineteenth-century earthenware made in Great Britain was decorated with transfer prints depicting Canadian scenes. This is the so-called Historical China —a term borrowed from American usage. It is easy to understand why it is of special interest. Not only has it the appeal of its period, and the interest of under-glaze printing, a technique on which much of the prosperity of the British potting industry was founded, but it has also the particular attraction of an easily recognizable Canadian connection.

Yet the term 'Historical China', when applied to Canadian views, is in a sense misleading and to a certain extent distorts the position of this printed earthenware in the history of pottery and porcelain in Canada; for only some of these 'historical' wares were ever intended primarily for the Canadian market, and those that were formed only a very minor part of the whole trade in printed crockery. Never in their own day were they a dominating influence. Relatively few Canadians seem to have given them preference over other patterns in their choice of tableware, and only very occasionally did a china merchant consider Canadian views of sufficient sales value to feature them in advertising. There is, too, every indication that some of the views most sought after today as Canadian were originally sold in greater quantities in the United States, being intended in the first instance for that larger and more lucrative market. Productions of Enoch Wood's pottery illustrate this.

Enoch Wood (1759-1840), the 'Father of the Potteries', as Simeon Shaw called him in the 1820's, was a son of the famous modeller and block-cutter, Aaron Wood. After serving his apprenticeship to Humphrey Palmer, of Hanley, he began to make earthenware in partnership with his cousin, Ralph Wood. Later, from 1790 until 1818, he was in partnership with James Caldwell, and from 1818 until his death, in 1840, with three of his sons, the firm then being known as Enoch Wood & Sons. Under this style the business continued for six years after his death. In 1846 it was closed.

Shaw, writing in 1829, described Enoch Wood's establishment in Burslem as 'very extensive', covering the site of five old factories.[1] Some years later John

201

Ward, who published in 1843 material that had in part been prepared earlier by Shaw, declared that the firm of Enoch Wood & Sons had become the largest exporter of Staffordshire earthenware to the United States.[2] This tremendous business had been built up because the Woods catered shrewdly to American taste. They produced wares in the brilliant dark blue greatly admired in the United States, and they gave careful thought to subjects that would appeal particularly to Americans.

Though producing the wares some years after the events depicted on them, the Woods capitalized, for example, on the War of 1812. With a choice of subjects before them, the Woods selected such events as were favourable to the Americans. Today tableware decorated with these scenes is sometimes included in Canadian collections of 'Historical China'. In its own day it would have been received with little enthusiasm in the Canadian market. It was made for American sale. The teaware commemorating Commodore Thomas Macdonough's victory on Lake Champlain is an example.

This naval engagement between British and American forces took place in September of 1814. The result was a reverse for the British, which Canadian colonists, smarting under a severe blow to national pride, took very badly. They reviewed the leadership of the Commander-in-Chief of the British forces, Sir George Prevost, and blamed him for an alleged failure to direct operations effectively in the Lake Champlain area. A number of Montrealers, including the china merchant, Joseph Shuter, had served under Prevost; they were savage in their criticism of his handling of affairs. From Montreal a scathing denunciation of Prevost was written by Hon. John Richardson in the 'Letters of Veritas'. These appeared in the columns of the *Montreal Herald* in 1815, one letter being devoted to the humiliating defeat on Lake Champlain. When the Woods produced their ceramic picture of the battle, they showed the sound judgement that had brought in a host of American orders, but they were obviously not trying to cultivate Canadian sales with this ware. Even years later Canadians held the War of 1812 in bitter memory.

In yet another series of North American views, Canadian subjects made their appearance on Wood earthenware, and here, again, it is possible to show that these were wares produced with an eye not on the Canadian but on the United States market. Of some sixty North American landscape views turned out by Enoch Wood and his sons, two or three only were Canadian, and these few were of places that were favourites with Americans—as indefatigable travellers in the nineteenth century as in the twentieth.

There was, first of all, a handsome view of Quebec, a picturesque city popular even with the earliest of American tourists. The Woods used this Quebec view, printed in dark blue, on various items of tableware, including a square vegetable dish. The cover of this dish they decorated not with further Canadian scenes (as would be expected were it for the Canadian market), but with American subjects: West Point Military Academy, Lake George, and the Hudson River.

Another Canadian view made use of by the Woods on tableware was titled on the back of each piece FALL OF MONTMORENCI NEAR QUEBEC (*Plate* 23). In the early nineteenth century, Montmorency Falls, below Quebec, was an important tourist attraction. Everyone who visited Quebec drove out to see the falls, considerably greater then than now. One American who made the trip was Dr. Benjamin Silliman, professor of chemistry at Yale, who travelled to Quebec in the autumn of 1819, and wrote an account of his journey. Like everyone else he made the excursion to Montmorency. On him the falls left an impression of grandeur: 'the thundering noise, and mighty rush of waters, and the never-ceasing wind and rain produced by the fall, powerfully arrest the attention: the spectator stands in profound awe.'[3]

For both the Quebec view and the Falls of Montmorency, the Woods used the same shell border that appeared on such American scenes of theirs as the Capitol at Washington and the Highlands, Hudson River. The sources of these two Canadian views appear to be unknown. Ellouise Baker Larsen, in *American Historical Views on Staffordshire China*, stated that the view 'most nearly resembling the one used by Wood' for Montmorency was W. H. Bartlett's view, published in *Canadian Scenery* in the 1840's.[4] The Bartlett view, however, could not have been the source drawn upon for the Wood decoration, even though Bartlett did provide material for a number of Canadian views produced by other potters.

Apart from the fact that the Wood view of Montmorency would have to date from the beginning of the 1840's, if Bartlett is to be regarded as possible source material (and some of the Wood plates decorated with this view may, perhaps, be earlier), and disregarding entirely the fact that the style of the engraving reproduced on Wood earthenware is obviously of an earlier period than that of Bartlett, there remains one conclusive reason why Bartlett is ruled out as a source for the Wood decoration. The engraving, as it appears on Wood earthenware, has a distinguishing feature not present in Bartlett's view of the same scene. It is not to be found in the Bartlett view for the very good reason that it had disappeared before Bartlett ever saw the falls. It is significantly present in the view used by Enoch Wood & Sons.

This important feature of the picture on Wood tableware is the small building standing on a platform and projecting into the air over the water. On the earthenware it is clearly visible on the left-hand side of the waterfall, slightly below the top.

A number of contemporary accounts described this structure perched perilously over the rushing waters of Montmorency. Mrs. John Graves Simcoe, wife of the first Lieutenant-Governor of Upper Canada, spoke of it in 1792, noting in her diary that Sir Frederick Haldimand had built it as a 'summer house'.[5] Baroness Riedesel, whose husband fought on the British side in the American Revolution, stated that it had been put up at her suggestion in 1782. In later years she recalled how she had gone with Sir Frederick Haldimand, Governor-in-Chief of the colony, to see Montmorency. 'I happened to say to the general,' she wrote, 'that it must be delightful to have a little dwelling opposite to it. Three weeks later (in the summer of 1782) we accompanied him thither a second time . . . the General begged my hand to show me into a small house, which was, as it were suspended on the cataract . . . The foundations of the house consisted of eight strong beams laid athwart beneath which the cataract hurried down with tremendous velocity.'[6]

Isaac Weld, the Irish visitor, found the little summer house still hanging over the rushing torrent in the 1790's, but he wondered about its safety: 'It is said that the beams whereon this little edifice is erected are in a state of decay . . . That the beams cannot last forever is certain.'[7] As the years went on, the state of the rotting beams became a preoccupation with visitors to Montmorency. Long before Bartlett ever saw the falls, 'the decays of time' (as one American tourist put it)[8] had taken the beams and the summer house. Eventually another wooden structure was erected near the same spot, but not until many years after Bartlett's visit, and not until Enoch Wood & Sons had gone out of business. Anthony Trollope, the novelist, described this later structure in the 1860's. It was, he said, 'horrid'.[9]

Making use of earlier topographical material was common practice on the part of the English potters looking for subjects for ceramic decoration. Enoch Wood & Sons were doing nothing unusual when they turned to an earlier period for their view of Montmorency. They did the same thing when they came to chose some of their American views.

In addition to the views of Quebec and Montmorency, Enoch Wood & Sons also made tableware, printed in the same dark blue and with the same shell border, depicting a third Canadian tourist attraction familiar to Americans. For this one, the source of the view is known. It was taken from an engraving of Table Rock, Niagara, published shortly before 1820, in a book of travels by Paul Svinin, a Russian diplomatic officer resident in the United States from 1800 to 1813. Translated from the Russian, the title of the book (published in St. Petersburg), was *A Picturesque Voyage in North America*. Between the published engraving of Table Rock, done from a water colour by Svinin himself, and the ceramic engraving as issued on Wood earthenware, there are very few differences. The pottery engraver in this case made an almost literal translation.

Strangely enough, this well-known Canadian subject has long been classed as American by ceramic writers, even though Table Rock was indisputably on the Canadian side of the border. From it visitors from all over the world were accustomed to view the stupendous wonder of the Canadian or Horseshoe Falls. Yet as far back as the 1890's, an American collector and writer, Alice Morse Earle, made the error of classifying Table Rock as American. In her *China Collecting in America*, she stated that Quebec and Montmorency were 'the only views of Canadian scenery' known to her on old Staffordshire—and then on the very next page she listed 'Table Rock, Niagara' with American titles.[10] Later writers, including Ellouise Baker Larsen, have followed Alice Morse Earle in this error.[11] In one way they have all been correct: Enoch Wood certainly intended all three of his Canadian views for his important United States market. This does not alter the fact, however, that Table Rock, even as Quebec and Montmorency Falls, was in Canada, and any view so titled belongs in the Canadian division.

The error in assigning Table Rock to American territory is perhaps explained by the fact that it disappeared over a hundred years ago, and its location can be ascertained only from historical accounts. But these accounts abound, and they are very clear. One of the most succinct is to be found in *Travels in South and North America*, published in the 1850's by a Scottish visitor, Alexander Marjoribanks. 'The best view of the Falls,' he wrote, 'is from Table Rock, on the Canadian side.'[12]

According to a nineteenth-century guidebook, Table Rock was 'a magnificent crag' which at one time jutted out beside the Canadian falls, providing a natural platform from which to admire them.[13] But in the summer of 1850 the main part of Table Rock suddenly cracked and hurtled down. The *Montreal Gazette* reported on July 6 that the first portion to break off was from a hundred and fifty to two hundred feet long and from thirty to ninety feet broad. It fell with one 'tremendous crash'.

Even the marks on these Canadian subjects chosen by Enoch Wood & Sons show how definitely they had the American market in mind when they made them. They used on them marks commonly applied to the wares produced for export to the United States, and which would have been quite unsuitable for a specific Canadian trade. In addition to an impressed eagle and shield and E. WOOD & SONS (or E. W. & S.) pieces such as the Montmorency plates had also a printed mark in which an eagle and shield were combined with the motto of the United States: E. PLURIBUS UNUM. To understand now repugnant such American symbolism would have been in Canada at the time when this earthenware was produced, it must be borne in mind that this was the day of the harassed and defended border.

Even before the War of 1812 Canadians had had to fight against invading armies from the south. At the time of the Revolutionary War, the Americans had seized and occupied Montreal and had attacked Quebec. When war was declared in 1812, those of American birth living in Montreal were speedily told to take the oath of allegiance to the British Crown, or get out. Over the peace concluded at the end of 1814 hung for years the brooding threat of another war with the United States. Ugly incidents often troubled the border, notably in the 1830's. Again in the 1840's, war seemed near over boundary disputes. Even as late as 1861 the Trent affair brought massive reinforcements of British troops to strengthen the garrisons in the face of imminent hostilities. In the days when Enoch Wood & Sons were adding American symbols to their identifying marks, few in Canada had a good word to say for 'Brother Jonathan', as the American was called then. The American motto, 'e pluribus unum' (one out of many), prominently displayed on the back of the Enoch Wood wares intended for the United States trade had a sinister meaning for Canadians, understandably suspicious of American expansionist ambitions.

This is not to say that there would have been no sale at all in Canada for Enoch Wood's Canadian views when they were new, but the evidence is beyond doubt that it was for United States sale that they were primarily intended. The fact remains, too, that these Wood views of Quebec, Montmorency, and Table Rock are today found in far greater quantity in the United States than in Canada itself. Only rarely do they turn up in Canada with proof that they have been long in the country—and even then there remains the possibility that a nineteenth-century traveller to the United States made the purchase there. The Wood views of Canada added to Canadian collections in recent years have nearly all come from American sources, whether through a Canadian antique dealer supplied from the United States, or purchased direct by the collector himself, or by the return to the market of a collection previously put together from these sources.

In spite of the fact that Enoch Wood's views, classed today by Canadians as their own 'Historical China', were actually produced in the first instance for American buyers (regardless of any minor sales effected in Canada), there is clear proof that Enoch Wood and his sons did have an interest in the smaller Canadian market. That proof is to be found in the pages of the *Montreal Gazette*. On October 29, 1829, William Peddie, a St. Paul Street importer, took space in the newspaper to make an announcement:

A CARD.—WILLIAM PEDDIE & Co. beg to inform the Correspondents of Messrs. ENOCH WOOD & SONS, of STAFFORDSHIRE, and the Importers of CROCKERY generally, that they have within these few days received a sett of Samples, which may be seen at any time, by those intending to order any of their manufacture.

   Such as have not done business with Messrs. ENOCH WOOD & SONS, and who may be desirous of opening an account, may have Prices Current, with terms of payment stated, on application by letter or otherwise.

Montreal, Oct. 12, 1829.

There is no way of knowing now just what the 'sett of Samples' sent to William Peddie in Montreal included, but it should be borne in mind that, important as their big United States trade was, earthenware printed with North American subjects was only a part of the Woods' total output. They produced tablewares printed with views in Great Britain, Europe, Asia, and Africa. They made wares decorated with lustre and with enamel colours. Enoch Wood was celebrated as a figure maker, and he and his sons eventually attempted porcelain.[14] To the United States itself, the Woods shipped wares whose decoration had nothing to do with North America. Canadian crockery dealers did well with patterns which they could guarantee as the latest thing in London. They were, after all, catering in part to colonial officials, to garrison officers, and to immigrants. All wanted to keep in touch with the world they had left behind them. If the 'sett of Samples' on view in Montreal included North American views of any kind, William Peddie did not consider the fact of sufficient sales importance to make a point of it in his advertising.

The man seeking business for Enoch Wood & Sons in Montreal was a Scotsman from Perth. He was a general merchant who imported crockery with hardware and other goods, and who carried on a big wholesale trade with Upper Canada. Few merchants in the colony were more respected than William Peddie, a bachelor sharing living quarters with his clergyman, Rev. Henry Esson, of St. Gabriel Street Presbyterian Church. With Scottish vigour he had built up an important business on St. Paul Street. It was typical of William Peddie that he had secured the agency of a firm so well known in the potting world as Enoch Wood & Sons, and typical of Enoch Wood that his company was allied with a merchant of William Peddie's acumen.

The trade that Enoch Wood & Sons did with the United States was gigantic; they sometimes shipped thousands of pieces in a single order to one dealer. Peddie's *Gazette* announcement, however, shows that they were also anxious to pick up Canadian business. The reference to 'the Correspondents of Messrs. ENOCH WOOD & SONS' implies that they had been supplying Canadian dealers for some time.

Unfortunately there were only a few years left for the alert Scotsman, to act as Enoch Wood's Canadian agent. When the terrible cholera epidemic descended upon Montreal in 1832, William Peddie escaped, but only to fall a victim to its return two years later. He died on July 27, 1834, at the age of only forty-five.[15]

It is very possible that the wares of Enoch Wood & Sons continued to come to Montreal through William Peddie's firm, for his younger brother, Walter, who had earlier been in business on his own account, acceded to William's dying request, and joined the two businesses under the old name of William Peddie & Co. For a number of years all went well, and then, at about the same time as the affairs of Enoch Wood's sons began to slip into difficulties in Staffordshire, catastrophe overtook William Peddie & Co. in Montreal. Upper Canada merchants who owed the Montreal firm substantial accounts went bankrupt. William Peddie & Co. were ruined.

In Staffordshire the blocks and moulds that had belonged to Enoch Wood, 'Father of the Potteries', were sold. In Montreal the name of William Peddie & Co. disappeared from the business scene. In time the potter's name came before the public again, but in advertisements for others, who now owned the right to 'th' blocks and moulds o' that illustrious race'.[16] The Peddie name, too, eventually reappeared—in that refuge of embarrassed gentility, a young ladies' seminary, conducted in Montreal by William Peddie's niece.

CHAPTER XVII

Bartlett for the Table

Dinner Sets . . . with Patterns of . . . British North
American Views, which can be got to order.
Novascotian, Dec. 11, 1843.

Of all the nineteenth-century engravings of Canadian views by far the best known today are those after drawings by William Henry Bartlett, the English topographical artist. In their own times these steel engravings were fully as popular as they are now. Then Canadians not only bought them to look at, they dined off them as well. Enterprising British potters, capitalizing on Bartlett's fame, produced tablewares decorated with a number of his Canadian scenes. Some of these were made for sale in the United States, but some were intended primarily for the Canadian market. It is possible that sample patterns of Bartlett for the table were ready for the colonies as early as 1843. By the 1850's several Staffordshire potters had made use of Bartlett's views of Canada, and at least one firm was still producing them in the last quarter of the century.

William Henry Bartlett (1809-54) earned a living by travelling through many lands making sketches as he went. A publisher would then arrange to have a selection of the sketches engraved on steel, and would provide descriptive material to go with them. After issuing the pictures and descriptions by instalments —'in parts'—the publisher would later offer them in bound volumes.

Bartlett's sketching tours took him through the British Isles, the Low Countries, Germany, Switzerland, the Near East, the United States, and Canada. His Canadian sketches, accompanied by descriptions compiled by the American writer, Nathaniel P. Willis, were published by Virtue & Co. of London, under the title *Canadian Scenery*. An advertisement in Fredericton's *Royal Gazette* on October 21, 1840, announced them in the colonies:

NEW ILLUSTRATED PUBLICATIONS
*Published under the Patronage of Her Most
Gracious Majesty the Queen.*
Canadian Scenery Illustrated,
FROM original Drawings by W. H. Bartlett, whose labors have already illustrated Scotland, Switzerland, Syria. Asia Minor, Palestine, &c. &c. . . .
A part will be published regularly every month; each part will contain four exquisite Engravings from original Drawings, and eight or twelve pages of Historical and descriptive text;—price 3s. 9d. each part . . .

The advertiser was W. Dunbar, who had been appointed agent in New Brunswick and Nova Scotia for the publisher, and who announced himself as 'now prepared to take Subscribers names and deliver the first numbers . . . received per Edwin and Thetis, from London'. In Upper and Lower Canada others solicited orders. Well over one hundred of Bartlett's Canadian views were published in these monthly parts and sold to subscribers throughout the colonies. In or about 1842 the publishers issued the engravings in two handsomely bound volumes.

Such a skilful topographical artist as William Henry Bartlett met the need and taste of his time in two ways: he supplied the views of many lands in the period before photography; and his romantic spirit appealed to the Victorian wish to see things not quite as they were but rearranged, softened, heightened by a romantic feeling. It was a period when the lore of distant lands was influencing architecture, household furnishings, dress, literature, painting, and sculpture. Bartlett's way of looking at things not only made faraway places seem more than ever alluring; he also gave people a renewed vision of their own countries. He brought out the romantic quality of Scottish loch and Irish seacoast; and, in North America, he gave to the hard facts of ports and backwoods the wished-for gleam and glamour.

It is not surprising that prints made from the sketches of so popular an artist as Bartlett should have been used to decorate the wares of the Staffordshire potters. Pottery with Bartlett views certainly had a sale in Canada. But there is danger that the modern collector's natural interest in everything depicting old Canadian scenes may distort the true historical perspective.

Earthenware decorated with Bartlett-inspired scenes was incidental rather than characteristic in nineteenth-century Canada. It never amounted to more than a tiny proportion of the crockery sold and used in British North America. The vast majority of wares on Canadian tables were without any distinctive Canadian appeal: they were the same wares (with the same patterns) being sold at home in Great Britain. Many Canadians still felt themselves primarily British in background and outlook and would certainly have preferred tablewares decorated with flowers and views that recalled their homeland, or which appealed to the general taste of the period for far and romantic lands in Europe or the East.

But while the place of the Bartlett-decorated earthenware used in Victorian Canada should not be exaggerated, there is no doubt that it did make an appeal of its own to the awakening pride of some Canadians in the new land that had become their adopted home, and which would be their children's native soil. The spirit of 'British Americanism' was stirring, as the first movement towards a larger Canadian consciousness. To this spirit there was a positive appeal in tableware decorated not with old remembered scenes, or castles on the Rhine, or glimpses of the sultry Bosphorus, but with the rising Canadian towns, the engineering triumphs of Canadian bridges and canals, or the Indian encampments on the river banks.

There was something quite natural, for example, in the fact that William Dawson, when he left Nova Scotia to become principal of McGill University in 1855, brought with him a set of Staffordshire tableware printed with views taken from Bartlett's *Canadian Scenery*.[1] The spirit of British Americanism was strong in Dawson. Born in Pictou, Nova Scotia, he visited only in later years his mother's old Scottish home in Lonerig. 'Standing on a rising ground,' he wrote, 'where a turn of the road gives a last view of the old homestead and the ridge on which it is built, I have attempted to realize the feelings which must have wrung hundreds of Scottish hearts transplanted from homes in the motherland to take root in the New World of the West.'[2] Perhaps in nothing could the spirit of the native colonist be better revealed than in this admission that he could only attempt to imagine how a British emigrant might feel on leaving the Old World. It was fitting that at Principal Dawson's table in his residence at McGill in the 1850's his guests were served from dishes decorated with Bartlett's Canadian views.

The first of the Staffordshire potters to make use of *Canadian Scenery* may have been the firm of Ridgway, Morley, Wear & Co. (William Ridgway, his son-in-law, Francis Morley, and William Wear). Since this partnership lasted for only a brief period, ending about 1842, any use made of *Canadian Scenery* was almost certainly from the parts. One of the firm's patterns was entitled 'Agricultural Vase', the name being printed on the back of the pieces, sometimes with the initials R. M. W. & CO. added. The pattern name was taken from a large vase ornamented with farm subjects which was a prominent feature of the design. But seen around and beyond the conspicuous vase in the foreground was, on each piece, a scenic view. It has been suggested that for one or two of the views in this series the source was Bartlett's *Canadian Scenery*.[3] There is nothing to indicate, however, that Ridgway, Morley, Wear & Co. intended this series for special Canadian sale. If the pottery engraver who supplied their copperplates did derive inspiration from *Canadian Scenery*, that inspiration obviously took second place to other elements of the design, as far as the producers were concerned. No extensive or important use of Canadian views was made by Ridgway, Morley, Wear & Co. That was left for Francis Morley, when potting under his own name.

Just when tablewares decorated with Bartlett's Canadian scenes were first offered by Canadian china merchants has never been established, but possibly an advertisement that appeared in a Halifax newspaper in 1843 holds the answer. John McDonald took space in the *Novascotian* in the autumn of that year to describe his 'Fall supply of CHINA AND EARTHEN-WARE' received from Liverpool 'by the Helena and Father Mathew'. In an announcement dated November 6 he offered, among other things, 'a few choice Dinner Sets of FANCY and Wilton [Willow] Patterns, together with Patterns of do. with British North American Views, which can be got to order'.

'Wilton' was clearly a typographical error for 'Willow', as another advertisement by McDonald, a few months earlier, shows.[4] On that earlier occasion, however, he had no samples of 'British North American Views' to offer. The phrase 'fancy and willow' was one commonly used in Canadian advertising of the day to indicate transfer-printed earthenware in both 'fancy' patterns and the familiar Willow. Often the word 'fancy', when used by the china merchants in this way, implied new patterns. The dinner sets which could be 'got to order' in November of 1843 were, then, of earthenware with printed decoration showing 'British North American Views'.

211

The appearance of an advertisement for printed earthenware with British North American views at the very time when Bartlett's *Canadian Scenery* had become available, suggests that what John McDonald was offering in Halifax was Bartlett for the table. If this was the case, then the firm most likely to have been ready with samples at this date was Podmore, Walker & Co., of Tunstall, Staffordshire. Not only did Podmore, Walker & Co. have a flourishing business, doing a big trade with Canada; they alone of all the potters who decorated their wares with Canadian subjects emphasized the British American location of the views. They actually chose the pattern name 'British America' for their series of pictures on earthenware, and printed it on the back of each piece (together with their own initials, P. W. & CO., and the title of the particular Bartlett engraving used).

The firm of Podmore, Walker & Co., in business under that name from the early part of the 1830's until about the beginning of the 1860's, was made up of Thomas Podmore and Thomas Walker, with Enoch Wedgwood as the '& Co.' (Enoch Wedgwood later began potting on his own account, as Wedgwood & Co.).[5] In 1843, the year in which John McDonald's advertisement appeared, Podmore, Walker & Co. were operating two manufactories, both in Tunstall.[6] As well as ordinary earthenware they made what they called 'Pearl Stone China' and 'Opaque China', and some of their Canadian views appeared on these hard bodies. Large shipments of their earthenware—printed, blue-sprigged, and brightly painted—were exported to Canada. It must have been because of the importance of the already established Canadian trade that the partners decided to risk the heavy expense of bringing out the series of views entitled British America. Unlike most of the potters who produced Canadian views on earthenware in the first half of the century, Podmore, Walker & Co. would seem to have intended their ware primarily for Canadian sale. The name they chose for the series and the amount of this earthenware found in Canada today bear this out.

In many ways the Podmore, Walker & Co. earthenware with Canadian decoration is the most attractive of all the nineteenth-century tableware of this kind. Not only was it produced for the Canadian market itself—a fact that adds historical significance to it—it has to a marked degree the compelling vigour and zest of the early Victorian period. There is about Podmore, Walker & Co.'s work a confidence typical of the time. The shapes of the dishes have solid force, the potting is good, the printing well done, the border, with its fern-like effect, is eminently suitable as a frame for Canadian scenes, the colours are sharp and effective. The most popular shades were a spirited light blue, a sepia, a reddish-brown, and black. Less frequently green was used. Many pieces were marked. In dinner or tea services a number of different views would appear; in toilet sets the same view was sometimes carried on all the pieces.

When a pottery engraver or artist came to adapt published engravings to ceramic use, certain problems faced him. The different shapes and sizes of the articles to be decorated meant that only portions of some engravings could be employed, and frequently these had to be changed in certain ways to meet the requirements of pottery. Yet even when this has been acknowledged, it is often puzzling to account for the choice of the engraving selected or the changes made in it. Sometimes the best of the published views seem to have been ignored. Again, with a whole series of engravings from which to choose, the ceramic artist will have interpolated a view from some other source.

When Podmore, Walker & Co. put out their 'British America' tableware, with decoration based on *Canadian Scenery*, they included views of Quebec (*Plate* 24) and Montreal. In both cases their artist took liberties with the published views; yet in both cases he produced ceramic interpretations capable of striking effect, particularly when seen on the broad surfaces of large platters. Another handsome ceramic picture was achieved for use on a platter by working from Bartlett's 'View of the City of Halifax . . . From Dartmouth'. Bartlett's view of Kingston furnished decoration for a smaller platter, as did his view of Port Hope. Sometimes segments of these larger views were taken for the decoration of such articles as pudding plates or stands for footed dishes.

For ornamenting tea bowls and saucers, Podmore, Walker & Co. chose Bartlett's view of Navy Island, in the Niagara River. At the end of the 1830's, about the time Bartlett visited it, Navy Island was much talked about in Canada. What had happened there would still have been vividly remembered when the Podmore, Walker & Co. teaware came on the market. It was on Navy Island that the rebel, William Lyon Mackenzie, had made his last stand. After the fiasco of events in December of 1837, Mackenzie escaped across the border, where he found willing listeners to anti-British talk. When he and some of his supporters established their headquarters on Navy Island, they were able to obtain supplies from the United States. The seizing of their supply ship, the *Caroline*, by a body of volunteers under Capt. Andrew Drew, led to repercussions that at one time strained the uneasy peace between the British and Americans. The Americans were indignant at British 'interference' with the *Caroline*; the British awaited with grim determination the outcome of the trial, in the United States, of one of the Canadians who had taken part in the successful cutting off of supplies to Canadian rebels. Alexander McLeod was tried for murder in Utica, New York, for his part in the destruction of the *Caroline*, but fortunately diplomatic considerations were not without influence, and he was acquitted. Some of those who later stirred their tea in bowls marked on the bottom 'Navy Island' must also have stirred memories of the exciting days of '38.

In all, Podmore, Walker & Co. adapted more than a dozen Bartlett views of British North America to table and toilet ware. In addition to those already mentioned, the views used from *Canadian Scenery* included Saint John and Portland, Lily Lake (near Saint John), the Governor's House at Fredericton, the Village of Cedars (some miles above Montreal), the Chaudière Bridge (*Plate* 25), a Toronto view, a view from the citadel at Kingston, and an Indian scene on the St. Lawrence River. These appeared on a wide variety of articles—on huge soup tureens and on small cup plates, on ewers nearly a foot in height, and on ladles with delicately slender handles. It was possible to wash from a basin depicting Quebec, or to take gravy from a tureen showing the Chaudière Bridge. Sugar came from the 'Village of Cedars' and fruit from a bowl marked 'Lily Lake'.

In catering to Canadian taste with these British American views Podmore, Walker & Co. soon had an important rival. That rival was Francis Morley & Co.

Of all the potters who seized upon Bartlett's *Canadian Scenery* for ceramic decoration, Francis Morley was, perhaps, in himself the most interesting to Canadians. Not only was he son-in-law to William Ridgway, one of the Staffordshire potters who visited Canada in person to appraise the market; it was Morley who had had the enterprise to acquire the famous moulds and copperplates of Charles James Mason, when Mason sank in a sea of financial troubles. Mason's wares had been known throughout the colonies, and had been used in fine houses such as Belmont Hall, in Montreal. When the much admired shapes and patterns appeared again under Morley's name, they sold readily. As for Morley's views taken from *Canadian Scenery*, they were to remain longer on the market than any others. Morley's successors were producing them in the 1880's.

Francis Morley and his father-in-law had been partners in the firm of Ridgway, Morley, Wear & Co. When this partnership was dissolved, William Ridgway and Francis Morley remained at the Broad Street Works in Shelton (now Hanley), and for about two years potted together as Ridgway & Morley. (During this period they continued to produce the printed series known as Agricultural Vase, marking the pieces made at this time with the initials R. & M.) In the second half of the 1840's Francis Morley potted on his own account; about 1850 he began working under the business style of Francis Morley & Co. The maker's mark most frequently seen on earthenware printed with Canadian views after Bartlett and made at the Broad Street Works in Shelton is that of F. M. & CO. Pieces so marked belong to the period from about 1850 to 1858. In the latter year Taylor Ashworth joined the firm, and the name changed to Morley & Ashworth. In 1862 Francis Morley retired; the firm then became George L. Ashworth & Brothers. As George L. Ashworth & Brothers Limited it continues to the present day, although the Ashworth interest was bought out in the early part of the 1880's by John Hackett Goddard. Goddard acquired the pottery as part of the patrimony of his eldest son, John Shaw Goddard, whose descendants continue the business.[7]

Francis Morley, like Podmore, Walker & Co., made extensive use of Bartlett's views of Canada, but unlike Podmore, Walker & Co. he did not stress the British location of those views. His series of pictures on dinner and tea ware was produced under the vague title of 'Lake'. This name was printed on the back of the pieces in an ornamental device incorporating the central span of the Chaudière Bridge. (The bridge itself decorated the soup plates.) No attempt of any kind was made to identify the views used. Possibly this was because Francis Morley intended his wares from the first for sale in the United States as well as in the British colonies. Evidence of this comes from the large amount of Morley's Lake series, found in the United States, and also from pieces bearing the additional printed marks of American china importers, such as Tyndale & Mitchell, Philadelphia china merchants in the 1850's.

Francis Morley would have been made aware of the Canadian market by his father-in-law, William Ridgway, who had evaluated that market for himself. But from William Ridgway he would also have heard much of the lucrative market in the United States, where Ridgway at one time had his own agents.[8] Probably both Podmore, Walker & Co., and Francis Morley & Co. found that Americans and British Americans alike were willing to buy Canadian views for their dinner tables. Podmore, Walker & Co., however, made a definite bid for

British sentiment with their name, 'British America'. Francis Morley & Co. offered some of the same ceramic pictures, but under the innocuous name of 'Lake'.

Though there are over a hundred views in Bartlett's *Canadian Scenery*, Francis Morley still chose to give the public a number of the same views produced by Podmore, Walker & Co. The reason for this duplication is now lost in the past, but a possible explanation lies in the fact that many potteries did not have engravers on the staff, but bought designs from ceramic engravers working on their own. From such a source the same view (with slight changes) might go to several potters. Possibly the engraver or engravers responsible for adapting Bartlett's Canadian views to pottery decoration worked not from the bound volumes, where all the views were to be seen, but from a selection of the parts, which would limit the choice. Again, the success which one potter had with a pattern often inspired a competitor to try another version of it. At other times an understanding between two potters might result in pattern material passing from one to the other. And there were, too, the occasions when sales of moulds and copperplates put one man's former property into the hands of old rivals.

Whatever the explanation, Francis Morley & Co. came on the market with their own version of the Chaudière Bridge (*Plates* 26 & 27) and their Indian encampment on the St. Lawrence,[9] with their view of Kingston and their Village of Cedars. The views, as they appeared on the tablewares of Podmore, Walker & Co. and of Francis Morley & Co., differed in certain respects, but all had a common source—Bartlett's *Canadian Scenery*. On the Morley wares the views appeared within a border of garlands of flowers. They were printed in a blue sometimes decidedly darker than the blue of Podmore, Walker & Co. They appeared, too, in a somewhat harsh pink, a brown, and a pleasing, soft grey.

In addition to these views, which were also to be found on the products of Podmore, Walker & Co., the Morley adaptations of Bartlett included views of Georgeville and Lake Memphremagog (in the Eastern Townships of Quebec), Hallowell (Bay of Quinté), the Rideau Canal at Bytown (Ottawa), and a church at 'Point-Levi' (a Protestant Church at Lévis, opposite Quebec) (*Plates* 28 & 29).

Into this series of views, all taken from *Canadian Scenery*, Francis Morley & Co. injected a typical European lake scene of the period, complete with castle. This view generally appears on large platters; the pieces decorated with it carry the same 'Lake' mark as the rest of the series.

Inserting a view into a series with which it was totally unconnected was nothing new for Staffordshire. An example of this practice is to be found in an earlier series of views of Caramania (in Asia Minor) put out by the Spode factory. The engraver employed by the second Josiah Spode had a whole book of views, published in 1803, from which to work. His choice was ample. Yet into Spode's Caramanian series he thrust a view alien to it. Morley's European lake scene, like Spode's pseudo-Caramanian view, 'belongs' only by right of the Staffordshire potter's whims and incongruities.

An early purchaser of one of Morley's 'Lake' dinner services was William Dawson, whose leadership was to raise McGill University from an unknown and almost moribund institution to a university of the world. When he bought his earthenware dinner service, however, he was a young man not many years married, and as yet unfaced by the challenge of McGill. The move from Nova Scotia to Montreal came shortly after, in 1855. With the Dawsons' other household belongings, the grey-printed dinner ware, with its Canadian views, was shipped to Montreal aboard the *Lady Head*. In Montreal it went into use at the principal's residence at McGill (now the East Wing of the Arts Building).

About 1870 the future Sir William and Lady Dawson decided that something more colourful than the tableware bought nearly twenty years ago was needed for their dining room. They sent the 'Lake' plates and dishes to the kitchen, and gave an order for a service by Morley's successors, the Ashworths. What they chose at this time was a reproduction of a Mason's pattern—one of the patterns which Francis Morley had had the perspicacity to buy up when Mason had to sell.[10]

Much of the ware decorated with views from Bartlett and produced by Francis Morley & Co. is marked only with the pattern name 'Lake'. But not all of the wares so marked belong to the years when Francis Morley was connected with the Broad Street factory. Some of them are much later. A coarser style of engraving, and dishes in shapes that post-date the 1850's indicate a continuing demand for this 'Lake' tableware. A certain amount of the later ware is clearly marked ASHWORTH, and many pieces with this mark can be dated in the 1880's. What is harder to ascertain is exactly when production stopped. Today at George L. Ashworth & Brothers Limited, in Hanley, old copperplates with the pattern name LAKE cut into them are preserved. Although probably none of them has been in use for half a century or more,[11] they remain as evidence of the popularity of an English artist named William Henry Bartlett, and of Staffordshire potters quick to recognize his value in transatlantic markets.

Another of these potters who capitalized on Bartlett was Thomas Godwin, potting in Burslem from the 1830's until towards the end of the 1850's. Godwin directed his sales of Bartlett for the table to the American rather than the Canadian market, but he made use of at least two views from *Canadian Scenery*. They were 'Village of Cedars, River St. Lawrence' (also used by both Podmore, Walker & Co., and Francis Morley & Co.) and 'Outlet of Lake Memphremagog' (used by Morley). These views he included in a series with the general name of 'American Views'. His inspiration for other views in this series came from Bartlett's *American Scenery*, published just slightly earlier than *Canadian Scenery*. The American views used by Godwin included the Capitol at Washington, Bunker Hill, and Yale College. Why he pushed into this series of American views two relatively unimportant Canadian scenes is another of the inconsistencies of Staffordshire. He obviously intended his 'American Views' for sale in the United States.

The Godwin views were given a floral border and printed in brown, light blue, or pink. The body was an 'Opaque China'. The mark included Godwin's name, the general title (American Views), and the title of the Bartlett engraving used. Towards the end of the century some of the Godwin views were reissued by Edge, Malkin & Co., also of Burslem.

William Henry Bartlett, whose drawings furnished Staffordshire potters with new material on which to base decoration, led a restless life, moving from country to country. In the end his way of life killed him. On his way home from

216

the East, and with his last book still in the press, Bartlett, one of the best-known topographical artists of the day, took ill with a fever and died. In September, 1854, he was buried at sea, somewhere between Malta and Marseilles.

Today Bartlett's work survives to give one of the most vivid insights into the spirit of the nineteenth century. His way of looking at scenery—his effective method of combining the literal with the romantic—made a profound appeal to the Victorian mood. Evidences of his popularity linger not only in the volumes of his views of many lands, but on the crockery that brought his engaging vision of British North America to the comfortable Victorian intimacy of the dining table and the wash-stand.

CHAPTER XVIII

Other Canadian Views and Emblems

A traditional knowledge of the beaver is the birthright of every Canadian.
Horace T. Martin, *Castorologia*, 1892.

In addition to the Canadian views used by Enoch Wood and his sons and the engravings after Bartlett issued by several potters, a number of other Canadian views and emblems (such as the beaver and maple leaves) appeared on both English and Scottish wares. The earliest had to do with General Wolfe, but it is to the eighteenth and not the nineteenth century that the best of these representations of Wolfe belong.

As would be expected, the death of the hero of Louisbourg and Quebec appealed to British potters. The porcelain makers were probably the first with commemorative printed ware. Worcester, for example, produced a black-printed bust portrait of Wolfe on cylindrical mugs. Bernard Rackham, revising the catalogue of the Schreiber Collection in the Victoria and Albert Museum, stated that this particular portrait was taken, with modifications, from an engraving by Richard Houston, after a sketch by Captain Hervey Smyth, Wolfe's aide-de-camp at Quebec.[1] From the Liverpool ceramic printers, Sadler & Green, came another bust portrait of Wolfe. This one, also printed in black over the glaze, and signed 'J. Sadler Liverpool', may possibly have been based on one of the three portraits of Wolfe attributed to Gainsborough. As it appeared on a mug from the Longton Hall factory in Staffordshire, it showed Wolfe flanked by military trophies, including flags inscribed 'Louisbourg' and 'Quebec'.[2]

The earthenware potters of the later eighteenth century found in Benjamin West's painting, 'The Death of Wolfe', their subject for over-glaze printing, in either black or purple on creamware. West, born in the American colonies, was one of the founders of the Royal Academy, and it was at the Academy, in 1771, that his historically inaccurate but immediately successful painting was exhibited. It was inaccurate because West, possibly for a price, included persons not even at Quebec at the hour of the battle.[3] The original painting, however, found a buyer at once in Lord Grosvenor,[4] and commissions followed for copies.

A few years later, when William Woollett's engraving of the painting was published, West's 'The Death of Wolfe' became known to almost everyone. The success of the engraving was phenomenal. It made a fortune for Woollett, and a

219

greater fortune for John Boydell, the publisher, who secured full ownership of the plate after Wollett's death in 1785. Thousands upon thousands of copies were sold; it is probably true to say that no other military print in the history of art had greater popularity.[5]

It was an adaptation from the central portion of West's painting, and probably from Wollett's engraving of it, that appeared on Wedgwood jugs, printed in either black or purple over the glaze. According to Joseph and Frank Kidson, creamware made at Leeds was similarly decorated, the printing for both Wedgwood and Leeds being carried out at Liverpool.[6] Some unmarked jugs with this same decoration have, in the past, been attributed to a Staffordshire potter named Thomas Wolfe, who claimed to be a distant relation of the military hero.[7] Although all these jugs would have been produced primarily for the home market, it is not without interest that in the early years of this century such pieces were occasionally found in the Maritimes. Percy Inglis, of Mahone Bay, Nova Scotia, acquired one of them.

Artistically inferior, and with even less basis in historical fact than the West representation of the death of Wolfe, was a blue-printed version on earthenware of the nineteenth century. Jones & Son of Staffordshire produced dinner services in the 1820's decorated with scenes from British history. The series was given the name 'British History' as a general title, and the different events portrayed were identified in an ornate printed mark that also included the name of the makers.

One of the events in the series was the 'Death of General Wolfe' (pictured on large platters). This death scene bears no relation to Benjamin West's painting, which had inspired the earlier potters. Its source was either some other painting or engraving—and there were many others—or the uninformed imagination of a pottery artist. On this nineteenth-century earthenware the scene is very differently arranged from that in West's painting, and in addition there is a startling interpolation. Immediately behind the dying Wolfe appear a horse and rider. Even West had not attempted to introduce British cavalry on the Plains of Abraham. Cavalry had no part in the British capture of Quebec. The desperate climb of Wolfe's men up the face of a cliff did not include the impossible task of dragging horses up with them. Between Benjamin West's famous painting, 'The Death of Wolfe', and Jones & Son's 'Death of General Wolfe' printed on earthenware there are no real points of resemblance. A subject in common is their only relationship.

A date in the 1820's is generally ascribed to this British History series because one of the events included is the coronation of King George IV. The Prince Regent came to the throne as King George IV in 1820, but it was not until July 19, 1821, that his coronation took place. He died in 1830. After that date the coronation of this little-loved and disreputable monarch would hardly have been considered a memorable event in British history.

Interesting as the naive version of the death of Wolfe produced by Jones & Son may be, there appears to be nothing to connect the British History series specifically with the Canadian market. It was produced by obscure potters in business only briefly. Whether or not they ever had an export trade would be difficult to trace now. It seems improbable.

Two unknown Staffordshire potters of the first half of the nineteenth century were responsible for views of the heights of Quebec, scene of Wolfe's victory, but both of these ceramic views were intended for sale in the United States. They were produced in the dark blue popular in that market. One was issued by a potter who turned out articles of tableware decorated with pictures of cities or towns, all the pieces having the same floral border, and each city being identified on the back of the piece. Proof that this was a series of views made with the United States market chiefly in mind comes from the fact that of more than a dozen different towns or cities portrayed, only two, Quebec in British North America and Buenos Aires in South America, were outside the United States. A number of pieces in this ceramic series have also been found bearing the additional printed marks of china merchants in such places as Louisville, Kentucky, New Orleans, Louisiana, and Wheeling, Virginia. Plates printed with the view of Quebec have been reported with the name of a Cincinnati, Ohio, china seller on the back.[8] The series appears to date from the 1830's.

For the Quebec view in this series (*Plate* 30A) the pottery engraver may have drawn, either directly or indirectly from 'A General View of Quebec, from Point Levy', published in London in 1761. This engraving was the first in a series of twelve views of the small North American city, so recently the scene of one of the decisive battles of history. The drawings, from which the engravings were done, were 'taken on the Spot' by Richard Short, a naval officer present at the capture of Quebec. Certain features of the ceramic view are similar to those in the left foreground of the published engraving—the stone house, half hidden by a bushy tree is one of these. Any view of Quebec from Lévis would, however, have features in common with Short's view, so that identifications of this type are often inconclusive. Similarities may be merely inherent in the scene itself.

The second view of Quebec by an unknown English potter is little more than a vignette, showing buildings perched upon a height, with water below. It appears on tableware designed with a prominent eagle and scroll border, indicating for what market it was intended. The earthenware is not marked, either with the name of the maker or of the city depicted. In date it is probably about the same period, or a little earlier, than Quebec in the city series.

A pair of earthenware views printed in a lighter blue and belonging to this same period are believed to commemorate yet another stirring event in British North American history. An English potter, who again did not mark his ware, produced dinner and dessert services decorated with a series of views pertaining to the sea. On large platters in this series the decoration depicts a naval engagement, and on plates and shell-shaped dishes is a sailing vessel, probably intended to represent a ship of war. The background—it is more than a border—for the views in this series is a strikingly effective arrangement of sea shells and plant forms.

In 1909 the English ceramic writer, Arthur Hayden, illustrated one of the platters printed with this naval engagement in his *Chats on English Earthenware*. At that time he attributed the ware itself to the pottery operated in Staffordshire from the end of the eighteenth century to the beginning of the 1840's by members of the Rogers family, and he stated that the naval engagement shown was 'the . . . Fight between the *Chesapeake* and *Shannon*'.[9]

This naval engagement of the War of 1812 took place just outside Boston harbour, on the afternoon of June 1, 1813. Only the two ships, evenly matched, were involved. The result of their meeting was one of the briefest engagements of the war: fifteen minutes was the time required for the British ship to overcome her American opponent.[10] Dramatically the *Shannon* carried off the *Chesapeake*, literally under the eyes of Boston. She was taken to Halifax, where the American captain, James Lawrence, who had been killed in the fight, was buried with fitting ceremonial in the churchyard of old St. Paul's.[11]

While Arthur Hayden's identification of the naval engagement seems to have been accepted without much question, the attribution of the earthenware itself to the Rogers factory has long awaited the finding of a marked specimen for actual proof. On the basis of the ware alone it would be virtually impossible to assign it to any particular factory. Several other views in this series have not been identified, but it is thought by some that the single sailing vessel, pictured on plates and dishes, is the victorious *Shannon*. With reference to this particular identification, however, it should be noted that there is only faint resemblance between the ship on earthenware and the woodcut entitled 'The Shannon Frigate' (published by Simms & M'Intyre of Belfast) which has been cited as the source of the earthenware view.[12]

On the whole, English potters concerned themselves more frequently with American victories in the War of 1812 than with British successes. This was not from any lack of patriotism, but from a desire to sell earthenware to American buyers. To cultivate the American market, the potters were fully prepared to immortalize the enemy, and a whole series of American heroes and American victories appeared on earthenware made after the war for export. Almost none of this would have been sold in Canada.

An appropriate theme for both the Canadian and American markets was Niagara Falls. In addition to Enoch Wood, a number of potters pictured Niagara on earthenware, and several of the views included the Canadian Falls. Like Enoch Wood, however, the other potters who chose Niagara as a subject for earthenware decoration generally included it with ceramic views intended primarily for sale in the United States. Andrew Stevenson was one who produced a view of Niagara that Dr. E. A. Barber, writing in 1899, identified as 'Niagara (Falls on Canadian side)'.[13] The view, with floral border, is printed in dark blue. Stevenson, who worked in Staffordshire from the early years of the nineteenth century until about 1830, catered to the American trade with well over a dozen American views printed on tableware. It is more than probable that he considered Niagara, whether Canadian or American Falls, as decoration made to sell in the United States.

About mid-century another Staffordshire potter produced a view to which he gave a Canadian name. J. Heath (possibly Joseph Heath) was responsible for a fanciful scene entitled on the back of the pieces 'Ontario Lake Scenery'. Presumably he had Lake Ontario in mind when he fixed on the name, for the province was, at that time, known officially as Canada West (and unofficially still called Upper Canada). In Heath's completely imaginary version of a Canadian scene, printed generally in light blue, a large, castle-like building stands on one side of the water, and on the other are what some have seen as Indian tepees. Mountains and a waterfall are in the background, figures in the foreground.

This scene on Heath's earthenware is not unlike the curiously un-Canadian view awkwardly introduced by Francis Morley into a series otherwise based on Bartlett's *Canadian Scenery*. It is conceivable that the same pottery engraver furnished both Morley and Heath with their pseudo-North American pictures. No stretch of the imagination could credit either view to Canada. In Heath's case, he was equally incongruous when he gave the Californian name 'Monterey' to another European-type scene featuring a Gothic castle. The composition of 'Ontario Lake Scenery' and 'Monterey' is almost indistinguishable. These are not American views but artistic fantasies.

Soon after mid-century, beavers and maple leaves began to make their appearance on British earthenware made for sale in Canada. With some potters these symbols took the place of Canadian views, by others they were employed as fitting borders to frame such views. An early and interesting use of the beaver and maple leaves on earthenware was made by Edward Walley, a Staffordshire potter active in the 1850's (*Plate* 30B). Walley evidently received from a French-Canadian source an order to work the beaver and maple leaves into a design combining a Latin motto, 'Labor Omnia Vincit', and a nationalist slogan, 'Nos Institutions, Notre Langue et Nos Lois'. The date at which he received this order would not have been earlier than 1856. His grey-printed ware carrying these mottoes and symbols came on the market in an ironstone body whose moulded design was registered with the Patent Office in London on November 29, 1856. The pieces were produced in what Walley called his 'Niagara Shape', and this information is usually impressed, along with his own name and the registry mark, on the back of the pieces.

Walley's printed design, produced in Staffordshire to French-Canadian specifications, was a 'special order' only in a certain sense. It was not an order for one service only. A fairly large number of these services must have been sold in what is now the Province of Quebec, for over the years they have been found in both institutions and private homes. They were made with several different border designs, and in dinner, dessert, tea, and toilet ware. On some services there is a narrow, grey-printed floral border. On others the edges of the pieces have a gold line, sometimes with an inner line in blue. On some services there is no border or edging, only the moulded design registered by Walley. Again, on still others, a blue band, with a second narrow band in red, has been used.

The inspiration for these services obviously came from the St. Jean Baptiste Society. The slogan 'Nos Institutions, Notre Langue et Nos Lois' was the Society's own. It had appeared on May 7, 1832 on the front page of *Le Canadien*, the revived nationalist newspaper; from that time on, it had been a rallying cry for nationalist sentiment in Lower Canada. In 1844 the newly formed Quebec branch of the St. Jean Baptiste Society adopted 'Nos Institutions, Notre Langue et Nos Lois' as its motto; almost at once other branches took it up. On every occasion for St. Jean Baptiste demonstrations the motto was heard on the lips of speech makers and was seen waving on banners. As P. G. Roy pointed out, in *Petites Choses de Notre Histoire*, 'la plupart de nos sociétés nationales ont adopté la même devise et, aux jours des démonstrations populaires, les orateurs puisent leur inspiration presque uniquement dans cette devise . . . '

The Latin motto, 'Labor Omnia Vincit', was the official motto of the Department of Public Instruction of Lower Canada. It appeared, combined with the beaver and maple leaves and certain religious symbols, on the department's printed forms, book labels, and other identifying material at the period when Walley was making his earthenware. This may explain why tradition, over the years, has associated the purchase of Walley earthenware both with members of the St. Jean Baptiste Society and with educational institutions. It is certainly very possible that a number of the services were bought for use in colleges and seminaries, for the ware was a tough ironstone. It would have been eminently suitable, both in body and decoration, for use in institutions. It is clear, however, that whatever may have been owned by schools or colleges, a number of services were in private hands.

Orders for all these services were undoubtedly placed through a Canadian china merchant. E. Z. Massicotte, the archivist and historian, believed that merchant to have been Henry Howison.[14] In the 1850's Howison had a china, glass, and earthenware store in the Upper Town of Quebec. At a later date the family moved to Montreal. In this regard it should, perhaps, be noted that in the 1870's a Henry Howison was in the china-importing business in Montreal: Sentenne, Howison & Massue, at the corner of St. Paul and St. Gabriel Streets.[15]

A second Staffordshire firm to turn the beaver and maple leaves into earthenware decoration was that of Thomas Furnival & Sons, who, like Edward Walley, worked in Cobridge. In this case the beaver formed the central part of the design; the maple leaves made up the border. Printed usually in brown, sometimes in light green, and occasionally in autumn colours, the pattern was named 'Maple' by the makers (*Plate* 31A). This pattern name was often printed on or impressed in the wares. The printed mark of T. FURNIVAL & SONS (in use from the 1870's until about 1890) was also on many pieces.

Furnivals was an old firm, said by Llewellynn Jewitt in the 1880's to 'rank high' with Canadian buyers.[16] This would be at the very time when the Maple pattern was introduced, as the shapes of the hollow pieces indicate. It was not, as is often believed, a pattern brought out to celebrate Confederation in 1867, but one that made its appearance at the time of the 'New Square Shape' popular in the late years of the century.[17]

Introduced in the 1880's, the Maple pattern was not limited to that decade; it continued in production at least to the end of the century, as pieces bearing later variations of the Furnival mark testify. Until recently copperplates from which it was printed were still in existence, although no use had been made of them since the present Furnival firm assumed direction of the pottery in 1913. In 1963, or early in 1964, the Maple copperplates, all badly worn, were disposed of with a quantity of old copper.[18]

All these makers of earthenware whose decoration was Canadian in theme were from Staffordshire. But Staffordshire potters were never able to keep the Canadian market exclusively to themselves. They had, at all times, formidable rivals in the potters of Scotland. From the end of the eighteenth century Scottish wares were in active competition with the products of Staffordshire. Scottish potters not only gave Canadian buyers the stout brownwares and the sturdy white granites that North America wanted; they supplied them with tablewares decorated with Canadian pictures. Two series of Canadian scenes on earthenware belonging to the later years of the nineteenth century are of Scottish origin: the black or brown-printed 'Canadian Sports' (*Plate* 31B), and the brown or pink-printed views of Quebec and its environs (*Plate* 31C).

John Marshall & Co. of Bo'ness (Borrowstounness in Linlithgow) were the makers of 'Canadian Sports', the earlier of the two series. These pictures illustrate such typical sports as lacrosse, which reached its heyday in the second half of the nineteenth century; snowshoeing, enjoyed by all the young people and encouraged by well-organized snowshoe clubs; skating, which tempted even those who could only wobble over the ice; tobogganing, a sport which often caused spectators to shudder, as they watched its devotees flying down icy slopes; and rowing, a competitive sport in which a Canadian eventually became champion of the world.[19]

Marshall's quaint pictures of these Canadian sports were usually in a heavy black; less often the printing was done in a dark brown. Sometimes colour was crudely added over the transfer prints—a raspberry pink, a bright blue, yellow, and green. A gold easily worn off was occasionally used on rims of jugs and on handles. Both tea and dinner services were made in 'Canadian Sports'. Toiletware and such items as children's mugs and large milk pitchers were also decorated with these lively scenes. The printed border was floral; on some small plates and other ornamental items, however, the views were sometimes used with a moulded border.

Although the series was not always marked, it may be found with the pattern name (Canadian Sports) printed on the bottom of the pieces, together with the initials of the makers (J. M. & CO.). Occasionally BO'NESS is impressed in the paste, in addition to the printed marks. The earthenware body itself is generally of very ordinary quality and the transfer printing sometimes carelessly done. It would appear that 'seconds' were marketed, for it is possible to find plates so badly potted that they will not lie flat upon the table but may be spun like tops.

The Scottish pottery that made these Canadian scenes for the overseas market was founded in the eighteenth century. In the middle of the nineteenth century John Marshall became the owner. He bought it shortly after 1854. At first he operated it under his own name alone, and then, in the later 1860's, '& Co.' became part of the business style of the firm. Pieces marked J. M. & CO., therefore, date only from this period. Marshall himself died in 1870, but the pottery continued under the old name of J. Marshall & Co. until near the end of the century.[20] Possibly the Canadian Sports series was introduced before Marshall died, although the evidence of many of the female costumes depicted suggests a date after 1870 as more probable. In any event, the series was still being produced long after Marshall's death. Ornamental jugs in shapes belonging to the 1880's are known with this decoration.

Even if John Marshall was not himself responsible for the Canadian views on Bo'ness earthenware, it was he who had built up an overseas trade of sufficient importance to make it practical for the firm of J. Marshall & Co. to bring out a special Canadian series. The solid basis of the pottery's Canadian business had been established with earlier printed patterns as remote from the Canadian theme as the popular brown-printed 'Bosphorus'. Marked J. MARSHALL and BO'NESS, the 'Bosphorus' is a pattern that must have been sold in quantity in Canada, for it still turns up today in old houses.[21] The sales success of such earlier patterns as this made it a sound investment for J. Marshall & Co. to go to the expense of catering to the Canadian market with Canadian subjects.

Another Scottish pottery, the Britannia (carried on by the successors of the Robert Cochran who once sent agents to Montreal and Toronto),[22] was the maker of a series of views of Quebec. In date these pieces cannot be earlier than 1875; they remained in production into the twentieth century. If these Quebec pictures do not have the interest of the earlier views after Bartlett, nor the magic of the Enoch Wood name attached to Montmorency Falls, they have the late Victorian mood that has an attraction all its own.

As with the earlier productions of Podmore, Walker & Co. and Francis Morley & Co., a number of different topographical views were used in a dinner or tea service. All the views were named—not on the back, as was the earlier custom, but on the face of the pieces, the titles appearing in both English and French. The scenes depicted included a view of the Quebec harbour, Quebec from Lévis, Cape Diamond, the Dufferin Terrace and Citadel, a view looking north from the Citadel, the St. Louis Gate and also the St. John Gate, the Breakneck Steps on the way from the Lower to the Upper Town, the Basilica and Seminary, the monument erected to mark the spot where Wolfe died on the Plains of Abraham, the monument erected to both Wolfe and Montcalm in the Governor's Garden, Montmorency Falls (which had attracted Enoch Wood many years before), the Falls at Lorette (near Quebec), the Chaudière Falls, and the Natural Steps on the Montmorency River. The views were printed on an ivory or cream-coloured earthenware of good quality, and given a border of beavers and maple leaves combined with the rose, the shamrock, and the thistle.

Generally (although not always) the earthenware with these Quebec views was marked with the name of the Quebec dealer who had ordered them from Scotland. Francis T. Thomas set up in the crockery business about 1874. He died shortly before the end of the century, but his firm continued into the twentieth.[23] Since most of this earthenware bore only the name of the importer—F. T. THOMAS/QUEBEC—the question of identifying the maker became one of speculation. While it was early recognized that Thomas was not himself the potter, but only the dealer who had ordered these wares, a tradition grew up that they were, nonetheless, a Canadian product, and that this printed earthenware had, in fact, been made at the pottery of the Bell brothers (William and David) near Quebec. It was a theory that seems to have been founded on the shifting sand of oral testimony. Marius Barbeau referred to it in June, 1941, when he wrote, in the American magazine, *Antiques*, that 'some old people' of the Quebec area claimed that Thomas procured this tableware 'from the Bells'. The next year, in *Maîtres Artisans de Chez-Nous*, published in Montreal, he identified Sir Charles Fitzpatrick, of Quebec, as one who had made this statement. Since the 1940's this theory has been resurrected from time to time, although no one advancing it has ever produced a shred of evidence that the Bells made whiteware for the table, let alone whiteware decorated with under-glaze transfer printing. Dr. Barbeau, himself, in *Maîtres Artisans*, noted that the claim for the Bells was open to doubt.[24]

226

The theory that any Canadian pottery of the nineteenth century could have been responsible for this accomplished under-glaze transfer work on excellent-quality tableware is not only inconsistent with the state of Canadian potting during the period, it is at variance with contemporary accounts of the Bells' productions. To credit the Bells, therefore, with the making of fine ware for the table—finer-quality ware than was produced by the St. Johns Stone Chinaware Company, the only really successful producer of whiteware in Canada—is to be optimistic; but to credit them in addition with skilled under-glaze transfer work is to credit them with being able to produce what no pottery in Canada was then attempting on a commercial scale.

The pottery operated by members of the Bell family over a long period was on the outskirts of Quebec, on 'the Little River road' (Little River St. Charles). Directories show that the factory was at this address, while in the city itself a sales depot was maintained.[25] The pottery was founded in the 1840's, and from mid-century on there is contemporary evidence to show what the Bells made: bricks in quantity, common brownware, yellow ware and Rockingham ware, smoking pipes and drain pipes. In 1850, for example, the *Montreal Gazette* (on October 24) reported that the Bells had won a prize at that year's provincial exhibition. The prize was for 'pottery', a term used at that time to denote common brownware. Three years later, in the same newspaper (December 19), the Bells were mentioned once more as exhibitors of 'pottery ware', this time at the world's fair in New York. In a progress report of the Geological Survey of Canada, published in 1854, the Bells were named as manufacturers of 'vessels for the use of the dairy and the garden'. This was in addition to their extensive brick-making.[26]

There are many references to the Bells as makers of tobacco pipes and of drain pipes. The *Gazette*, on August 10, 1877, carried an advertisement for 'Tobacco Pipes—Bell's Make'; and the official catalogue of the Canadian Section at the American Centennial Exhibition, held in Philadelphia the year before, gave the Bells' entries as 'Drain Pipes and Tobacco Pipes'. These are the products that the Bells can be shown to have made. No contemporary evidence of this kind links them with printed tableware. In the 1880's, when the tableware with Quebec views came on the market, the Bells were listed in the Quebec directories simply as 'drain pipe manufacturers' ('tuyaux d'égouts').[27] Possibly the Bells themselves owned, used, and discarded tableware printed with views of Quebec; they did not make it.

In point of fact, the views of Quebec sold by Francis Thomas may occasionally be found with the printed or impressed marks of the pottery responsible for them. In the McCord Museum of McGill University is one of the 'pulls' or proofs from the copperplates for these views. It is from a set of proofs sent out from the Britannia Pottery in Glasgow to the Thomas china shop in Quebec, and it shows both the familiar printed mark, F. T. THOMAS/QUEBEC, and the names COCHRAN and ST. ROLLOX (St. Rollox being the north-east district of Glasgow where Cochran's Britannia Pottery was situated). Since these views were in production over many years, marked pieces are a guide to the changing business styles of the Britannia Pottery which supplied them. In addition to pieces bearing Cochran's name alone, there are also wares marked with the name of Francis Thomas which have the additional identification of COCHRAN & FLEMING, or FLEMING/GLASGOW, or B. P. & CO.

The earliest date at which any of these views could have been produced is the late 1870's, since Thomas was not in business until about 1874, and could not have given an order to the Britannia Pottery before that date. The evidence actually points to the 1880's, rather than the late 1870's, for the introduction of this series. The shapes of some of the earlier pieces of hollow ware (like those of Thomas Furnival & Sons' Maple pattern) are of the 'Square Shape' advertised as new in Canada in 1885. Also, one of the views depicted shows the extended terrace which came to be known as Dufferin Terrace, and which incorporated the old Durham Terrace. The corner-stone of the extended terrace was not laid until October of 1878.[28] Even if an order had been given at once, earthenware printed with a view of Dufferin Terrace could not have been produced and shipped to Canada before about 1880 at the earliest. That this ware was, however, sold by Francis Thomas in the 1880's is proved not alone by the shapes of certain pieces, but by old invoices for 'Quebec Views' dated in the 1880's, and by family records which name such wares as wedding presents of the same period.

In the 1880's Alexander Cochran was the proprietor of the Britannia Pottery. He had inherited it from his father at the end of the 1860's, and it is his ownership that is indicated in the mark COCHRAN. The managing partner in the business was James Fleming, who had earlier represented Cochran's father in Canada. According to Arnold Fleming, the son of James Fleming, the firm became known as Cochran & Fleming in 1896. Earthenware decorated with Quebec views and marked COCHRAN & FLEMING would, therefore, date from 1896. A few years later Alexander Cochran died, and the Flemings, father and son, worked the Britannia Pottery together until 1911, when the elder Fleming retired. Between 1911 and 1920 Arnold Fleming carried on the business alone. In 1920 it was sold to the Britannia Pottery Company Limited.[29] Quebec views marked FLEMING or B. P. & CO. belong to the twentieth century.

On the twentieth-century pieces the printing is often in a darker tone than on those of the nineteenth century, and the earthenware itself is generally thinner and whiter. Pieces made in either century may carry the familiar F. T. THOMAS/ QUEBEC mark. Francis Thomas died before the end of the nineteenth century, but the Britannia Pottery continued, for some years, to use the old backstamp on wares supplied to the firm carrying on under his name.

In producing printed patterns specifically for the Canadian market, Bo'ness and Glasgow earthenware makers, like John Marshall and Alexander Cochran, were merely providing further evidence of the long-established connections between the potters of Scotland and the china sellers of British North America. As far back as the second half of the eighteenth century sailing vessels were calling regularly at colonial ports with Scottish earthenware. An announcement in the *Montreal Gazette* on August 27, 1798, listed 'Queens Ware' as part of the cargo of the *Lucy* from Greenock. Earlier that same year another vessel from a Scottish port brought 'Earthen Ware in Hogsheads' to Halifax.[30] The trade which the Scottish potters were building up at this period with merchants in Boston and Philadelphia and other parts of the United States has long been recognized; the Canadian trade is also significant. There is proof in the first newspapers of Canada that such a trade was systematically pursued. Delft, stoneware, Queensware, brownware, and clay pipes came in sizable quantities from Scotland, even in these early years; and while it would be impossible to say with certainty that all the earthenware arriving in ships from Scottish ports came from Scottish potteries, it would be equally far from the truth to neglect the probability that much of it did.

By the nineteenth century, when transfer printing on earthenware was to be developed to the full — at Scottish as well as at English potteries — Canada had become a very important market for Scottish wares. It was in the nineteenth century that thousands of Scottish immigrants poured into the colonies. In every aspect of mercantile life industrious Scotsmen became influential. As china, glass, and earthenware importers, some of them had marked success, the outstanding example being Robert Anderson of Montreal. Trained in Scotland by old John Geddes, potter and china merchant both, Robert Anderson went on to become a millionaire in North America, laying the foundations of his fortune with cups and plates. He and other Scottish dealers in the colonies gave many an order to a pottery back home. When the potters of Scotland looked for expanding markets for their increased production, they found encouragement in British North America, and not only from Scotsmen in the crockery business, but from thousands of Scottish-Canadian buyers who welcomed something from the Old Land. In the colonies Scottish wares were highly regarded. Joseph Burrell's advertisement in the *Yarmouth Herald* of January 31, 1856, speaks of crockery from Glasgow as 'very desirable'.

Side by side, English and Scottish wares competed for Canadian business. Advertisements that name the two together emphasize this. In 1844 Blackader, Wilkes & Co. of Montreal announced 'CROCKERY AND CHINA—From Staffordshire and Clyde Potteries'.[31] In 1853 Edward Wright, one of the best-known china merchants in the country, advised the public of Lower Canada that his orders for new stock had been placed in both 'the English and Scotch markets'.[32] In the spring of 1873 John Leeming, opening a new season with a big trade sale, advertised in the *Gazette* that of seventy crates of crockery to be put up, thirty-nine would be from the Staffordshire potteries, thirty-one from Scotland.[33]

Scottish potters sent agents to Canada to snatch orders from their Staffordshire rivals, and placed their own advertisements in colonial publications.[34] How well they succeeded in capturing business is shown in the way Canadian china dealers featured 'SCOTCH CROCKERY' in headlines,[35] and went out of their way to stress that 'New Goods just to hand' included the latest patterns 'from Scotland'.[36] It was only the natural outcome of a long and carefully cultivated trade relationship that earthenware with Canadian views should be made in Scotland as it was in Staffordshire.

CHAPTER XIX

Nautical Crockery

Under Contract with the Lords of the Admiralty . . . Acadia . . . Britannia
. . . Caledonia . . . Columbia . . . S. Cunard & Co., Halifax.
Montreal Gazette, Oct. 2, 1841.

The lore of early shipping in Canada has left its record on tablewares of the period. These wares, which meant new business for British potters, belong to two main classes. There were, first, the tablewares whose printed decoration recalled ships famous in Great Britain and Canada alike. In addition to these, there were the heavy ironstone wares made especially for use on vessels of Canadian lines, such as the Montreal Ocean Steamship Company, and the Beaver Line. In all these tablewares the enterprise of the potter is linked with the stirring record of struggle and achievement in the history of transportation. They belong to the days when steam across the Atlantic was new, and when auxiliary power for any steamship meant 'a suit of sails'.

Among the most interesting of the wares inspired by nautical events is a series to which the name 'Boston Mails' was given by the Staffordshire brothers who made it (*Plate* 32A). They clearly intended this printed earthenware for sale in the United States, but by right of historical association it belongs even more to Canada. It was a Canadian's achievement it celebrated, for the views in this series depict Samuel Cunard's four wooden side-wheelers, with which he established the first regular transatlantic mail service by steam.

In its day nothing so caught the imagination of people on both sides of the Atlantic as this spanning of the ocean by a little fleet of steamships endeavouring to keep to defined schedules. Others had dreamed of such a service, but it remained for Samuel Cunard of Halifax, son of Abraham Cunard, Loyalist, to bring it about.

Cunard got his chance at the end of the 1830's. At that time the British government, hoping to speed communications between Great Britain and the colonies, called for tenders for certain steam services. Three bidders were ready to take on the formidable task of establishing the transatlantic service. Samuel Cunard was the successful bidder, and to him went a seven years' contract with the Admiralty. He was to carry the mails by steam across the Atlantic, from Liverpool to Halifax. In addition, he had to provide a coastal steamer to run between Pictou and Quebec in the summer season, and he proposed, also, to link Boston with the Liverpool-Halifax route.

231

When Cunard secured the Admiralty's contract, there was resentful criticism from his English competitors. What had this man from Nova Scotia to offer except promises ? Cunard, however, had supporters as well as critics in Great Britain, and with the aid of British backers he formed the British & North American Royal Mail Steam Packet Company. It was this company that began service with four ships—*Britannia, Acadia, Caledonia,* and *Columbia.* Insignificant by modern standards, they were considered 'mammoth' in their day. A *Montreal Gazette* advertisement of October 2, 1841, described them as '1250 Tons and 440 Horse Power' each. They were built on the Clyde, supplied with engines by Robert Napier, equipped also with the needful sails, and fitted to carry troops if required. Both Nova Scotians and Bostonians took immense pride in them: Nova Scotians because these steamships were the tremendous achievement of a native son, Bostonians because with the opening of Cunard's Liverpool-Halifax-Boston service the port of Boston had no longer to take second place to New York.

The *Britannia* inaugurated the service. She sailed from Liverpool on July 4, 1840, with Samuel Cunard himself on board. Exactly twelve days and ten hours later she arrived at Halifax, and the greatest excitement immediately spread throughout the North American colonies. On July 19, fourteen days and eight hours from the time of leaving Liverpool, the *Britannia* was at Boston. There enthusiasm ran wild. New York was put in the shadow, Boston was ahead with this new fast transatlantic communication. Free wharfage was granted Cunard for his steamships, and it is said that he received nearly two thousand invitations to dinner in Boston during the first twenty-four hours after the *Britannia's* arrival.[1]

It would have been surprising had the alert British potters not seen in Cunard's achievement a subject for ceramic celebration. Several seized the opportunity, naming patterns after the famous ships. One firm, however, made use of all four Cunard steamships as earthenware decoration. James and Thomas Edwards, of the Kiln Croft Works, Burslem, registered their designs on September 2, 1841, according to the printed mark sometimes found on the wares. From the beginning, the unwieldy name of Cunard's company, the British & North American Royal Mail Steam Packet Company, had been shortened in popular parlance to Royal Mails or Boston Mails (according to whether a British North American or a citizen of the United States was speaking). By printing BOSTON MAILS on the back of their earthenware, the Edwards brothers made clear what market was uppermost in their minds. Yet their tablewares are, historically speaking, more closely connected with Canada than with the United States. Possibly some of them were sold in Canada when they were new, even though the larger sale was most certainly in the market for which they were obviously designed.

The Edwards tableware features the four Cunard steamships in medallions in the border. Sometimes all four ships appear on one piece, sometimes only two or three of the ships are used. They are always identified in the medallions, although no real attempt was made to produce exact portraits of the quartette. Occasionally the border is omitted, the main decoration then being carried to the edge of the piece. For this main decoration the Edwards brothers turned to the interior arrangements of the 'noble steamers'. A series of views showing the saloons, ladies' cabins, and gentlemen's cabins is used on articles which include small cup plates, ladles, teapots, large platters, and outsize milk pitchers. The transfer printing is frequently in a light blue, but black, lavender, and brown-printed views are also found. Most of the pieces carry on the back the printed mark of a steamship, over which appears the name of the series, BOSTON MAILS. Some pieces also have J. & T. EDWARDS, and the data concerning the 1841 registration.

James and Thomas Edwards dissolved partnership about 1842[2] (not long after they registered their designs for the Boston Mails tableware). At this time James Edwards acquired the Dale Hall Pottery, which had formerly belonged to the Rogers family, and here he carried on business for many years. He retired in 1861, leaving his son in charge. Whether James Edwards continued to produce the Boston Mails series after he and his brother had dissolved their partnership has not been determined, but there remains the possibility that some of the wares unmarked as to maker, and giving evidence of copperplates well worn, may have been the work of James Edwards alone.

Of James Edwards it was said that he was 'an entirely self-made man, and was one of those bright examples of indomitable perseverance, unflinching rectitude, steadiness of purpose and genuine benevolence which crop up every now and then among . . . successful manufacturers'.[3] As a self-made man of indomitable perseverance and steadiness of purpose James Edwards, the Staffordshire potter, had much in common with Samuel Cunard, the Halifax ship owner, whose impressive achievement of 1840 furnished striking material for pictures on earthenware.

If Edwards did continue the Boston Mails series when potting on his own account, it would probably have been for only a few years, since the *Britannia*, *Acadia*, *Caledonia*, and *Columbia* were all taken out of the transatlantic service within a decade. They were replaced by still bigger and faster steamships.

The *Columbia* was the first to go. On July 2, 1843, she was wrecked on 'the Devil's Limb', a rocky ledge off Seal Island, some miles from the Nova Scotia coast. The mails were rescued and no lives were lost, though over 150 passengers and crew were aboard; but the *Columbia* herself was finished. Her end was mourned by the whole colony of Nova Scotia. Before her fate was confirmed, there had been mounting anxiety in Halifax over her non-arrival. Strangers stopped one another in the street to ask if anything was known of the *Columbia*, and when finally a passing American brig spotted her, and brought her third mate on to Halifax to get help, the news of the disaster spread like wildfire. Said the *Novascotian*, sadly, on July 10: 'There can be little doubt that the tidings of the loss of this noble Steamer (for such news travels fast) ere this has reached the remotest corner of Nova Scotia, and perhaps few events, not involving the loss of life, could more universally have awakened feelings of public regret.'

In 1849 both the *Britannia* and the *Acadia* were sold to the North German Confederation for reconstruction as frigates. The *Caledonia* went the next year to the Spanish government, and was wrecked within twelve months.

While the Edwards brothers seem to have been the only potters to grasp the possibilities of using all four of these historic steamships on tableware, others recognized the imaginative appeal of Samuel Cunard's achievement and pictured individual ships on their products. Charles James Mason was one of these. He used a print of the *Britannia* on his famous patent ironstone china. Set within a frame of appropriate symbols and identified by name, the first of this fleet to cross the Atlantic made a handsome appearance under Mason's sure touch. It was unusual for him to turn to contemporary events: a pseudo-oriental style was more characteristic of the decoration on his famous ironstone. The fact that he did produce this view of the *Britannia* is evidence of the stir that Samuel Cunard created with four paddle-wheelers.

It is not surprising that Mason's choice fell upon the *Britannia*. She was more frequently in the news than any of her sister ships. Not only did she inaugurate the transatlantic service, she was much talked about on at least two other occasions. In 1842 Charles Dickens booked passage on her for his first trip to North America. Illustrated papers of the day hurried once again to give the public pictures of the *Britannia*, including views of the cabin the famous author would occupy. But the famous author was not too well pleased with his trial of the most modern means of transportation. On the way to Halifax he noted with alarm that sparks flew from the smoke-stack of the *Britannia*, and that the wind carried these sparks back over the steamship. He expected her to catch on fire. When the time came for Charles Dickens to return to England, he decided that sails were safer than steam.

In another two years the *Britannia* was again in the news. In February, 1844, during a winter of unprecedented cold, she became ice-bound in Boston harbour. The hour of her sailing drew near, and seven miles of heavy ice stood between her and open water. It seemed that hope of maintaining the mail schedule was doomed.

To keep the mail contract, Cunard had to meet regular schedules. When the *Columbia* had been wrecked, another Cunard steamer had salvaged the mail and rushed it on its way. The ice in Boston harbour, however, presented an entirely new type of problem. But the worry was not Samuel Cunard's alone. The reputation of Boston as a port was at stake. Quickly the merchants of the city organized. A plan was devised and money hastily subscribed. Through the seven miles of heavy ice a great canal was cut, and through this canal, only two days behind schedule, steamed the *Britannia* out to sea. Crowds of cheering Bostonians saw her off, and along the ice on each side of her veered and tacked small sailing craft, racing on blades of iron that served as giant skates. The Admiralty offered to repay the merchants of Boston for expenses entailed in freeing the *Britannia*, but it is said that Boston would not be paid. Let New Yorkers speak of a harbour that did not freeze over, Boston had kept faith with Samuel Cunard.

The *Acadia* also appealed to the Staffordshire potters. She was the fastest of these first Cunarders, cutting thirty hours off the *Britannia's* time on her first run.[4] A British potter who did not put his name on what he made used the *Acadia* on tableware printed in mulberry and sometimes edged in gold (*Plate* 32B). This heavy earthenware, showing a side-wheeler equipped with sails, has the name ACADIA printed on the back. In date it appears to be mid-to-late 1840's. All the usual articles of dinnerware were made in this pattern, which has been found in the possession of old families in both the Maritime Provinces and in Quebec. The *Acadia*, reconstructed as a frigate after her sale in 1849, came again on the market in 1852, when the North German fleet was broken up. She finished her days as a troop ship at the time of the Indian Mutiny. It was, however, as a steamship celebrated for swift crossings of the Atlantic, that she appeared on earthenware used in Canada.

In 1857 another event in shipping history was recorded on pottery. This had no Canadian origin, as did Cunard's steamship service, but Canadians took the liveliest interest in it, and waited impatiently for their chance to view the nautical wonder in their own waters. It is very probable that they were early given the opportunity of buying souvenirs of the event in earthenware, for the potters who capitalized on it had a big trade with Canada. The *Great Eastern*, the world's largest steamship, was completed in 1857. Her ceramic picture was widely distributed, not only at the time of her completion, but in the next few years, when she was vainly trying to live up to the glorious future predicted for her.

This time it was the potters of Sunderland who were conspicuous in turning a famous ship to ceramic advantage. Several of the Sunderland potters produced earthenware, both useful and ornamental, decorated with a black transfer print of the *Great Eastern*. Sometimes the print had colour added, and generally lustre was used on the rims of plates or wall plaques. Most of this Sunderland earthenware was unmarked, but two of the potteries responsible for items depicting the *Great Eastern* were the Wear Pottery of Samuel Moore & Co., and Scott's Pottery. These were both in Southwick, then just outside Sunderland. Since Canadian advertisements make very clear that Sunderland shipped earthenware to Canada in a steady trade—common brownware, printed earthenware, and lustre-trimmed ornamental ware—it is reasonable to suppose that items showing the *Great Eastern* must have been exported, too. Anything depicting her would have had a popular sale in Canada.

In modern times it is hard to realize what a sensation the *Great Eastern* caused, but in the nineteenth century, even when she had proved a gigantic failure, the *Great Eastern* had the power to conjure up alluring visions of scientific progress. Canadian newspapers devoted columns to her. One Montreal paper, the *Pilot*, stole a march on rivals by obtaining an exclusive eye-witness account of the *Great Eastern* from the point of view of a Canadian. A Montrealer who was visiting England in the summer of 1857 made a special trip to the shipyard on the Thames where she was being built, and sent back his reaction for the benefit of *Pilot* readers. He wrote that he was 'stunned' by her 'towering grandeur'.[5]

Far off in the Red River Settlement, the *Nor'-Wester*, three years later, carried lengthy details of the *Great Eastern*'s construction. She was of unbelievable size (and not until the twentieth century would her 22,500 tons be surpassed). Built of iron, she was fitted with a screw propeller and equipped also with paddle-wheels and sails. Enviously the first newspaper of the Canadian west noted that those in the east had had a chance to see for themselves 'the noblest triumph of engineering skill . . . the pride of her country, the wonder of the world'.[6] This was in 1860, when the *Great Eastern* had sailed to New York, stopping at Halifax on the way home. Thousands of British Americans had then viewed her in awe, either in Halifax or in New York (for many from Upper and Lower Canada had crowded excursion trains to the United States).

The next year the *Great Eastern* came to Quebec, and the promoters of excursions had another field day. By every available means people flocked to Quebec. It was fifty cents for adults and half price for school children to go aboard the leviathan of the Atlantic.[7] Again the colonial newspapers were full of astonishment at the great ship. They were more critical when she proved almost unmanageable during a storm on the way home. The *Pilot* was prophetic on this occasion. On October 7, 1861, the Montreal newspaper said: 'The ill-luck of the Great Eastern, born within her, has closely followed on her track, and now it is likely to gain the mastery.'

There was, however, one more close connection between Canada and the giant steamship built before her time. In 1866 she laid the first effective Atlantic cable, a feat which brought her again into prominence, and no doubt stimulated a new sale of her portrait on earthenware.

All these wares, decorated with printed pictures of famous ships in which North Americans had a special interest, bring back to life spectacular events of the energetic Victorian years. Nautical history is also vividly recalled in tablewares made to the special order of early shipping companies. Cunard's British & North American Royal Mail Steam Packet Company once equipped its ships with ironstone from the Burslem pottery of E. F. Bodley & Co. An example of this earthenware is today in the possession of Mr. Eric Reford, himself president of an old shipping company (the Robert Reford Co. Ltd.). Mr. Reford's cup and saucer are printed in brown with the name BRITISH & NORTH AMERICAN ROYAL MAIL COMPY, and the crest of the company, a lion (rampant, regardant, and crowned) holding a globe. A gothic design covers the rest of the surface.

Some thirty or forty years ago wares similar to Mr. Reford's cup and saucer were brought up from the bottom of Boston harbour during dredging operations. They were found near the place where the early Cunard steamships used to dock.[8] In date, wares marked with both Bodley's name and the original name of the Cunard Company cannot be earlier than the 1860's nor later than the 1870's. The Bodley firm which made them was established in 1862, and in the 1870's the old Royal Mails title gave way to that of the Cunard Steamship Co. Ltd.[9]

Edward F. Bodley, who secured the order for supplying crockery to Cunarders of mid-Victorian days, industriously sought business of this kind, a fact noted by James Torrington Spencer Lidstone, when he spoke extravagantly of Bodley wares 'Hail'd on ev'ry land of the Globe and all its seas'.[10] It was Bodley's 'Genuine Ironstone China' that was used on vessels of the Canada Shipping Company, popularly known as the Beaver Line. Both the official and popular names appear on the face of wares made for this company, which was founded in Montreal in the year of Confederation. Also printed on them in black, and then touched with colour, is the company's flag, on which a beaver is prominently displayed (*Plate* 33A).

Tablewares made for Cunard ships speak of the dynamic success of a Nova Scotian; those with the symbols of the Beaver Line tell of disasters and disappointments. Beaver ships never seemed to pay. As a nineteenth-century writer put it, this 'necessary element of success' was wanting.[11] Both sailing vessels and steamships flying the Beaver flag were beautiful and swift, but one after another they came to grief. In the 1890's the Canada Shipping Company, 'an out-and-out Canadian enterprise', had to go into liquidation.[12]

236

Another North American company whose ships were fitted out with Bodley wares was the Newfoundland Coastal Steamship Co. Ltd. Printed with the name and crest of the company in green, this ironstone has the same nautical 'rope' border used on the Beaver Line crockery. It was supplied to the Newfoundland ships through a firm of Glasgow china sellers, whose name appears on the back of the wares, often obscuring the impressed Bodley mark.

The Bodley mark itself gives the period at which the wares were produced. In the 1860's and 1870's the mark was E. F. BODLEY & CO., or the initials E. F. B. or E. F. B. & CO. About 1880 Edward F. Bodley took his son into partnership, and the mark thereafter reflected the change. Up until 1881 the works were in Burslem. Just before his death that year E. F. Bodley purchased a pottery in Longport. The business, carried on by his son until the end of the 1890's (under the old style of E. F. BODLEY & SON), was removed to Longport before the end of 1881.[13] The actual date (month and year) of production is often impressed in the wares turned out at Longport.

But the Bodley firm did not have a complete monopoly of Canadian shipping business. Francis Morley's successors, George L. Ashworth & Brothers, supplied tablewares to another line closely identified with nineteenth-century Canada. In the Montreal board room of the Shipping Federation of Canada is a soup plate marked on the back ASHWORTH BROS. and ROYAL STONE CHINA. On the face of the plate, printed in brown and framed by rose, thistle, shamrock, and beaver, is the name of the MONTREAL OCEAN STEAMSHIP COMPANY.

The Montreal Ocean Steamship Company, although founded by Scotsmen, was in some ways more distinctively Canadian than the Cunard Company, founded by a Nova Scotian. Its origins go back to the close of the Napoleonic Wars, when a Scots merchant mariner named Alexander Allan sailed a small brig to Quebec. In time his sons, Hugh and Andrew, emigrated to Canada. In 1854 they brought a dream to reality when they announced the opening of a new steamship line to run between Great Britain and Canada.[14] The Allan brothers, who, with members of their family, later came to own all the shares of the company, could not have founded it without financial backing from others. Merchants in both Upper and Lower Canada helped to establish the Montreal Ocean Steamship Company, and among those whose capital was essential was Robert Anderson, the Glasgow-trained china merchant.

For some years the company operated under the name adopted in 1854, but gradually advertisements began to appear headed simply 'Allan Line'.[15] It was ALLAN LINE that was printed on the back of Willow pattern ironstone used on the company's ships in the closing years of the century (*Plate* 33B). The maker of this tableware was no longer Ashworth Brothers, however; Edward Bodley's son had brought the Allan Line onto his order books with the many others.

Any tableware bearing the Allan name has the power to bring back a tale of typical Scots resolution in the face of reverses. In its early years the Montreal Ocean Steamship Company lost ship after ship, sometimes with tragic loss of life. Yet the Allans always found ways to keep the company going. They had obtained contracts for carrying the mails, and their orders to the ships' captains were to meet their schedules. Probably a relentless pressing on for the sake of getting the mails through on time accounted for some of the losses, but sheer bad luck and the hazards of the difficult St. Lawrence route were responsible for others.

Inland shipping companies also purchased wares made by British potters. For example, the Canadian Navigation Company, which operated under that name on the upper St. Lawrence and on Lake Ontario, from the beginning of the 1860's until 1875, equipped its ships with an opaque porcelain made by an un-identified potter.[16] The title of the shipping company, worked round a small blue-printed picture of a river steamboat, appears on the face of this heavy crockery. Since the printing is over the glaze in this case, it is possible that the decoration was done in Canada by a firm such as that of Hurd, Leigh & Co., of Toronto. English wares made to the order of Canadian shipping companies usually carried the names of those companies in under-glaze printing. As china merchants, Hurd, Leigh & Co. imported wares in the white, and as Canada's first china decorators,[17] they supplied them with crests and monograms to order. Of necessity, however, their work was on top of the glaze.

It was probably ware ornamented in this way that was in the dining saloon of the Canadian Navigation Company's ill-fated *Grecian*, and the small blue-printed picture of the river steamboat gives an idea of how she must have looked, before she went banging down the narrow channel at the Cascades on a May day in 1869. Refusing to answer her helm as the gateway to the dangerous passage was reached, the *Grecian* came down broadside, reeling from rock to rock, each crash more resounding than the last.

The wrecking of the *Grecian* was summed up by the Montreal *Gazette* as one of those dangers 'against which human skill is unable at times to guard'.[18] No printed decoration on any nineteenth-century earthenware recalls more strikingly the courageous facing of dangers impossible to guard against, and the meeting of challenges inherent in progress, than that on nautical crockery.

CHAPTER XX

Davenport and Canada

On Sunday morning at 5 o'clock the new steamboat British America,
left this for Quebec which she reached at 9 P. M.
New Montreal Gazette, Aug. 12, 1830.

The first Cunarders, used for ceramic decoration by the Edwards brothers, and the *Great Eastern*, adapted to the same purpose by the potters of Sunderland, were all ocean-going ships whose pictures were printed on tablewares sold to the general public. Another ship also made her appearance on earthenware of this type, but in this case she was not an Atlantic vessel, joining continents with steam, but a river boat, the *British America*, built in Canada itself and celebrated on inland waters for the speed and power of her engines (*Plate* 34A). The finely potted and well-printed earthenware on which she was depicted was the product of the Davenports, a family whose wares were admired in Canada through nearly the whole of the nineteenth century.

The pattern featuring the *British America* was actually called 'Montreal' by the Davenport firm, but it was the St. Lawrence steamboat that dominated the view; the city appeared as her background. That this ceramic portrait of a Canadian ship, with Montreal as the backdrop, is today one of the most sought after of all the Canadian views on tableware is not surprising. Not only is the earthenware the product of a pottery capable of great technical excellence, the scene itself is easily one of the most evocative of the 'historical' subjects. Davenport's printed plates revive memories of days when paddle-wheelers crowded with passengers and towing great sailing ships were a vital part of St. Lawrence commerce. 'The ease of travelling by steamboat is so very great,' wrote a satisfied visitor to Canada.[1] It was paddle-wheelers like the *British America* that provided this ease.

When she was new, in the 1830's, the *British America* was considered 'superb': so Catherine Parr Traill, the future botanist of the backwoods, described her.[2] Mrs. Traill, a British bride, arrived at Quebec in 1832. With her husband she had crossed the Atlantic on the brig *Laurel*. At Quebec the *Laurel* was taken in tow by the *British America*. On a serene August evening, just after sunset, the 'superb steam-vessel of three decks' and the brig started off up the river together. Mrs. Traill, watching the *British America* from the deck of the *Laurel*, found her 'a brave sight . . . to look upon; ploughing the bright waters which foamed and

239

sung beneath her paddles', while the Atlantic ship, 'with her white sails, followed like a butterfly in her wake'.[3]

Far away in Staffordshire a pottery artist, working up a view of Montreal for Davenport's extensive North American trade, put the 'superb' *British America* in the foreground. Lest anyone be in doubt as to which of a number of steamboats plying the St. Lawrence was intended, he named her clearly in the picture done for earthenware. It is the fact that the ceramic artist identified the *British America*, and made her the most prominent part of his picture, that strongly suggests he had access to material other than the published engraving usually cited as the source of the Davenport view.

The source generally suggested is an engraving published in 1830, with the title 'View of Montreal From St. Helen's Island' (*Plate* 34B). The artist was Robert A. Sproule, miniature painter, drawing master, and decorator of window blinds.[4] It is one of the most familiar of all the nineteenth-century views of Montreal. In 1950 the American ceramic writer, Ellouise Baker Larsen, named it as the source material for the Davenport decoration.[5]

The Sproule view was one of a series of six views of Montreal advertised in the *Montreal Gazette* on November 12, 1829:

VIEWS OF MONTREAL

ROBERT A. SPROULE *proposes publishing* a set of SIX VIEWS, *comprising some* of the principal Streets, Public Buildings and Squares in MONTREAL with a general VIEW of the CITY—to be executed in a style fit for colouring, and superior to anything of the kind yet got up . . .

On the day before Christmas the artist announced in the same newspaper that 'two of the ORIGINAL DRAWINGS are now finished'. In 1830 all six were published by Adolphus Bourne, of Montreal, with William S. Leney, 'An Engraver of first rate talent',[6] responsible for the plates.

The view of Montreal taken from St. Helen's Island, although published in 1830, did not show the Montreal skyline as it actually appeared at that time. Sproule anticipated the future, for he gave Notre Dame Church its well-known twin towers, 'La Persévérance' and 'La Tempérance'. These towers were not completed until 1841 and 1843. Moreover, Sproule must have worked from plans not even in existence when he first advertised his views of Montreal in 1829. The towers, as they appear in the engraving after Sproule, and as they are known today, were not designed by James O'Donnell, architect of Notre Dame. The original plans by O'Donnell called for towers with gables. But O'Donnell died suddenly in January of 1830, leaving Notre Dame unfinished. He was succeeded as architect by John Ostell, and the pinnacled towers of Notre Dame, rising against the Montreal skyline in Sproule's view and on Davenport tableware, were this Englishman's contribution to one of the most tremendous efforts at Gothic revival in North America. Another of Sproule's six views of Montreal showed Notre Dame as it really was in 1830—without the towers.

It is certainly possible that the Davenport artist did work from the engraving after Sproule, as Mrs. Larsen suggested. But he must have had additional information at his command. This information caused him to identify the steamboat as the *British America* and to shift the centre of attention to her. Neither in

Sproule's original water-colour drawing (now owned by the McCord Museum, McGill University), nor in the engraving done from the drawing, is the steamboat identified, nor is she the dominating feature of the scene. In the Davenport view the steamboat is not only named as the *British America*, she is named three times. The Davenport artist lettered the words BRITISH AMERICA on his steamboat, then he spelled out her name on a pennant, and, going still further, he added a flag with a large B A prominently displayed.

In the published engraving after Sproule, the unnamed steamboat is almost incidental to the view of Montreal in the distance. She is no more prominent than any of the three other craft on the river. In the Davenport version the city recedes in importance; the focus of attention is a steamboat, no longer anonymous but brought into prominence and emphatically singled out as the *British America*. Even her course is altered on earthenware. In Sproule's drawing a nameless boat was headed downstream towards Quebec. In the Davenport picture the *British America* steams in the opposite direction. On tableware she forever battles the difficult St. Mary's Current. This in itself is of interest, for conquering the St. Mary's Current was one of the accomplishments of steam on the St. Lawrence.

The St. Mary's Current, flowing between St. Helen's Island and Montreal, was long an obstacle to navigation. Sailing vessels used to be crowded together in a veritable fleet, waiting for winds strong enough to take them up it to Montreal. Often, in the end, they had to be dragged up by oxen pulling from the shore. The *Accommodation*, the earliest steamboat on the St. Lawrence, was unable to get up the St. Mary's Current; and not until 1824 did a steamboat—the *Hercules* —ascend these rapids.[7]

It was always the custom for an artist adapting a published engraving to pottery decoration to make slight changes, and even occasionally to make a major change. Between Davenport's Montreal and Sproule's 'View ... From St. Helen's Island' there are a number of differences. The design of the steamboat itself does not correspond exactly, and on earthenware she flies two British flags instead of one. The city in the distance corresponds reasonably well, but the whole view has been moved slightly upstream, and the river, as pictured on tableware, has become alive with activity. Sproule put only four craft on the river: the unidentified steamboat, a large raft with two sails, a row boat with sail, and a small sailboat. In contrast, the St. Lawrence on earthenware is crowded. The *British America* is the dominant presence, but there are also some ten or twelve small craft, and, to the far right, a second steamboat. Although the large raft with its two sails has disappeared, there has been added a picturesque birchbark canoe, manned by what were undoubtedly intended as Indians.

Another difference immediately apparent between Sproule's interpretation and that of the Davenport artist is the omission of the sentry and sentry box. St. Helen's Island was garrisoned in the nineteenth century, and Sproule acknowledged this fact with a sentry and sentry box in the foreground. They are not present in the earthenware picture.

Montreal taken from St. Helen's Island was not in any way an uncommon view. Many artists approached it from this aspect, and others besides Sproule included both a steamboat on the river and the pinnacled towers of Notre Dame

241

rising against the skyline ahead of their time. Sproule's view, however, was probably the one to provide the pottery artist with necessary material. That the pottery artist was commissioned to produce a view of Montreal itself seems clear, since the Davenport pattern was entitled 'Montreal'. But it is equally clear that the pottery artist departed from Sproule—if Sproule was his inspiration—in bringing the steamboat into greater prominence. In making her a particular steamboat he revealed knowledge that did not come to him from Sproule; from Sproule alone he would not even have learned the name of the steamboat he so conspicuously identified.

Built in 1829, and 'new' in the 1830 season, the *British America* belonged to John Torrance & Co. of Montreal, who also had other steamboats in service on the St. Lawrence in competition with those of rival lines. The Torrance steamboats came to include the *St. George*, built in 1830, and the *Canada*, built in 1831. Both were constructed in the same Montreal shipyard as the *British America*, and were similar to her in size and power.[8]

For years the *British America* was a familiar sight in St. Lawrence shipping, as she hurried back and forth between Quebec and Montreal. Perhaps her busiest time came in the rebellion summer, 1838. As unrest festered, she was constantly employed in bringing in troops and military equipment. On June 20, for example, she towed up the river the transport ship *Venitia*, with a detachment of the 7th Hussars aboard. Once she had the *Venitia* up the St. Mary's Current, she turned back and struggled up again with a supply ship.[9] On July 5, troops of the 1st Dragoon Guards arrived aboard her.[10]

But the most stirring occasion in which the *British America* had a part that anxious summer came earlier. At a little after seven o'clock on the evening of May 17 the *British America* steamed into Montreal with five companies of the 71st Highlanders. The Highlanders had been rushed up the river the moment they arrived at Quebec. In a city with as many Scots as Montreal, the arrival of a Highland regiment was an event of importance. On this occasion a Scottish regiment already known in Canada was returning—and returning at a time when it was felt to be sorely needed. Word of the 71st Highlanders' expected arrival at Quebec had reached Montreal before them, and all day on May 17 the *British America* was looked for 'with the greatest anxiety'. At last crowds waiting on the wharf and along the shore caught sight of her. As she stemmed the St. Mary's Current the band of the 71st filed on deck. Soon a medley of gay airs floated across the water, and then, as the *British America* slowly came opposite the wharf, the band suddenly struck up *Auld Lang Syne*. From on shore the cheers rang so loudly that the whole city was aroused. From every direction 'hundreds were seen running at full speed to the wharf'. The cheering increased by the minute. When the piper of the 71st began *The Campbells Are Coming*, the skirl of pipes was drowned out by the delighted din.[11]

Even when her fame among the ships of the St. Lawrence had been eclipsed by new names and her active days had come to an end, the reputation of the *British America* was a compelling memory. The engines that had caused the waters to 'foam and sing' beneath her paddles were offered for sale in a *Montreal Gazette* advertisement on Christmas Day, 1850. Said the auctioneers: 'the speed and power of the "British America", so well known, is a guarantee against disappointment, when these engines are again put to use. They are at SOREL, and can be examined . . . '

At Sorel, which the old *British America* had passed innumerable times on her goings up and down the St. Lawrence, her engines awaited buyers of the second-hand. It was all very different from the early days, when, bordered by flowers, the celebrated *British America* was new decoration for platters and salad bowls, plates and footed dishes.

The earliest date at which any of this earthenware could have come on the market was about 1831. The *British America* was built only in 1829, and it would have taken time for Davenport to bring out the new pattern featuring the steamboat. In actual fact, the tableware with this decoration was in production over some years, and it may be found with different border designs. On many pieces the transfer print shows that it has been taken from a copperplate worn by use.

The colours used by Davenport for the printing of this pattern were the shades that became popular after the 1820's: lavender, pink, sepia, and a light blue. The mark on the earthenware was the regular Davenport mark of the name impressed over an anchor. In addition a printed mark gave the name MONTREAL.

The city of Montreal was as well known to Americans of the early nineteenth century as Quebec. Most of those travelling to Quebec and Montmorency Falls from the United States had to journey first to Montreal, and from there go on by stage coach or by water. Many must have made the trip up and back by the 'superb' *British America*. That the Davenport firm originally intended the pattern called 'Montreal' for sale in the United States as well as Canada is proved by the amount of this earthenware found, over the years, in the United States. More of this Davenport pattern actually turns up in the United States than in Canada. The indefatigable gatherer of Canadiana, David Ross McCord, whose collection founded the McCord Museum at McGill University, obtained his example of Davenport's 'Montreal' in New York. A note on the back of the plate that belonged to him reads: 'Bought in N. Y., April 1915'. The price he paid at that time was ten dollars. This was a sizable sum for a 'Montreal' plate in 1915, and probably indicates that David Ross McCord did not find these pieces abounding at home in Canada.

In both countries Davenport ware of every kind was well known for almost a hundred years. The firm was founded in Staffordshire at the end of the eighteenth century by John Davenport; it lasted until the 1880's. Every type of ware was made: creamware, printed ware, stone china, black basaltes, 'yellow ironstone', porcelain. Royalty patronized Davenport, and special orders went off to Peru. At the same time the home and colonial markets were supplied in their every rank. As James Torrington Spencer Lidstone, the poet 'late of Toronto, Upper Canada', noted, Davenport made wares for 'all Society's less'ning grades'.[12] There were showrooms and warehouses in London and Liverpool and on the Continent. Even in Canada, where it was not the usual custom for the makers of earthenware or porcelain to be mentioned in advertising, the name of Davenport got into print. An advertisement in the *Novascotian* on December 6, 1827, supplies an example. In announcing a sale of household furnishings, the Halifax auctioneers Deblois & Mitchell publicized the fact that they would be offering 'a dinner set, DAVENPORT WARE, 274 pieces'. They would also be selling 'tea china' at the same auction, but this did not merit identification. It was described only with the usual vagueness: 'white and guilt [*sic*] . . . 68 pieces'.

In Montreal big trade sales of Davenport wares used to take place on the wharf by the ship's side. A sale of this kind was advertised in the *Gazette* on June 14, 1851:

Morning Sale
OF
EARTHENWARE

THE Subscribers have been instructed by Messrs. TYRE, COLQUHOUN & CO. to offer for Sale, on TUESDAY MORNING next, the 17th instant, alongside the Brig "BRITON'S PRIDE,"—
50 crates assorted Earthenware,
From the well-known House of WILLIAM DAVENPORT & CO., of Liverpool.
Catalogues are now ready for delivery.
Sale to commence at ELEVEN o'clock punctually.

YOUNG & BENNING.

Again that autumn, when supplies were coming in for the winter, Young & Benning announced an auction 'from the Ship's side on the arrival in port of the "CITY OF MANCHESTER" ', then on her way up the St. Lawrence from Quebec.[13] At this sale '64 Crates and Hhds. assorted EARTHENWARE', said to be 'well adapted' to Canadian trade, were to be put out on the wharf for buyers. All the earthenware was from 'the well known Firm of WILLIAM DAVENPORT & CO.'

John Davenport had retired from the business about 1830, leaving the management of his potteries to his sons. When Henry, the second son, was killed in an accident in 1835, William, the youngest, took charge; the firm then traded as William Davenport & Co. Through the years a huge business was built up; glass was made as well as earthenware and porcelain; and at one time more than 1,500 workers were said to be employed in Davenport factories.[14] Sales were enormous, particularly in North America, where Davenport became a household word. John M. Clarke's description of the furnishings of the old Mauger house on lonely Bonaventure Island in the Gaspé illustrates how widespread was the use of Davenport. When he visited the house shortly after the turn of the century, Clarke came upon 'a cupboard full of English Davenport and willowware'.[15]

But in spite of what appeared to be unusual success, difficulties set in for the Davenport firm. Some said it was because the Davenports had become too prosperous and had lost touch with the realities of commerce. Others said that Henry Davenport, William's son who succeeded him in the business, had inherited none of the commercial drive or the potting skill of his grandfather.[16] Whatever the reason, one by one the Davenport factories were sold off and showrooms closed. In the end the name of Davenport dropped from the ranks of English potters.

The view entitled 'Montreal' and featuring the steamboat *British America* was not the only North American subject produced by this firm with a tremendous North American trade. Earthenware depicting Franklin's experiments with electricity was made for the United States, as were creamware plates with portraits of some American heroes of the War of 1812. But on the whole, the Davenports had no need to try to build up sales with special patterns for either the United

States or Canada. Even firms like Enoch Wood & Sons, who did produce a very large number of North American views, still relied for a great part of their overseas business on other patterns as popular abroad as at home. The Davenport patterns marketed in England were the patterns that accounted for the volume of Davenport sales in Canada. The merchant in Montreal or Halifax who could offer what was selling well in England offered what the fashionable wanted in the colonies.[17] Earthenware printed with the view of Montreal and the *British America* was but a minor incident in Davenport's North America trade; it has the power, however, to revive memories of an age when steam was bringing something of the exciting marvels of the Industrial Revolution to Canada. With steam on inland waters there was 'ease' in colonial travel, and a new freedom from the long tyranny of wind and current.

Canadians Compete

CHAPTER XXI

The Range of Canadian Potting

... it is hardly to be expected that infant industries, comparatively speaking,
such as our potteries are, can jump at once to perfection.
W. W. Johnson, *Sketches of the Late Depression*, 1882.

Only when set against the imports is the limited range of nineteenth-century Canadian potting seen in perspective; and only when judged in relation to the overwhelming flood of these imports is its true achievement realized.

Potting in nineteenth-century Canada was typified by the brownware bowl and the stoneware crock. The red flower pot and the yellow milk pan were part of the Canadian output. So, too, in a smaller way were the 'ornamental items' in a red or buff earthenware body: the brown-glazed dog figure, the terracotta picture frame, the 'artistic ware' that included in its scope a type of Victorian majolica. But whiteware was not achieved commercially until nearly the last quarter of the century, and then the successful production of thick stone china and utilitarian white granite was almost entirely restricted to one area. No porcelain at all was produced by Canadian potters in any serious way during the century. They did not even attempt the finer qualities of white earthenware. As William Wickliffe Johnson wrote in 1882: 'All the finer qualities of crockery and glassware are still imported . . . as also are all china goods, none of the latter ware being made in Canada'.[1]

It was not that Canadian potters were unambitious: Simon Thomas Humberstone dreamed of making Parian porcelain in Newton Brook,[2] George Whitefield Farrar would not rest until stone china had been tried at St. Johns,[3] William Livesley hoped to turn a defunct glass works in St. Cunegonde into a manufactory for 'fine ware, such as porcelain'.[4] But the Canadian potter was beset by difficulties, and the range of his work was dictated by them. He operated nearly always with inadequate capital;[5] he had to import certain raw materials, sometimes from across the Atlantic;[6] and whenever his ambition soared he was met at once by the relentless competition from overseas potters with larger resources and long experience. Even protective tariffs, which came into force early to defend the types of ware that could be made in Canada, were not enough to give him an equal chance with his rivals.[7] He worked in their shadow, his best advertisement the cry that his products were 'warranted equal to English make'. Yet surprisingly Canadian potters entered world exhibitions, hoping for triumphs, applied for patents for new earthenware bodies, persuaded themselves that new ventures would succeed where old ones had failed, and, in time, achieved a consciousness of common interests that banded them together in an industrial association.

Potting did not come late to Canada. Wherever the settler went, the potter was to be found. The earliest French settlers, cut off from civilization, had of necessity to fashion crude pots from local clay. When the first British settlers came they, too, had the potter with them. At the dawn of the nineteenth century there must have been many potters working in the British North American colonies. John Lambert, travelling in Upper and Lower Canada between 1806 and 1808, noted that 'saddlers, blacksmiths, carpenters, mill-wrights, potters' were all to be found, and that more trades and professions were represented than was generally realized.[8] There were potters in Saint John or its vicinity at the end of the eighteenth century and the beginning of the nineteenth. Samuel Bullen, a potter, was a freeman of Saint John in 1797.[9] Another Maritime potter, John Thomas, was advertising wares made near Portland (now part of Saint John) in 1815.[10] By 1813 a former resident of Upper Canada had been able to record that 'Hats, shoes, boots, tin and crockery ware' were there manufactured 'in great plenty'.[11] But while at no time in the century was there any dearth of local potters operating in a small way, potting as an industry grew slowly.

It is significant that those giving advice to emigrants scarcely ever mentioned that Canada offered opportunities to the potter. Dr. William Dunlop ('Tiger' Dunlop), writing under the pseudonym of 'A Backwoodsman' in 1832, stressed that blacksmiths, tailors, shoemakers, and tanners had a very promising future in Canada; he also named carpenters, millwrights, masons, and bricklayers as among those likely to do well. But he said nothing at all to encourage potters to emigrate.[12] It was the same when James B. Brown, after eight years' residence in Upper Canada, came to set down his advice to emigrants. In *Views of Canada and the Colonists*, first published in the 1840's, Brown went into details concerning opportunities for the emigrant. He discussed the prospects for carpenters, bricklayers, stone-masons, plasterers, painters, blacksmiths, carriage makers, wheelwrights, tinsmiths, bakers, shoemakers, tailors, printers, farm labourers, and even seamen. He made no mention whatever of potters.[13]

One of the very few persons to specify in an emigrant's guide that there was any demand for potters was Alexander Begg, writing in 1871. Begg, however, was not encouraging potters to emigrate to a land where there was a thriving industry with jobs for all who could handle clay. He was, on the contrary, encouraging emigration to the new Province of Manitoba, a part of Canada where, according to his information, there was not a single pottery to be found. He felt, however, that it was reasonable to suppose there would be a need for 'one or two potteries'.[14] In so far, therefore, as an emigrant potter might have the courage to become a true pioneer of the Northwest, the opening would be considered 'good'. That same year of 1871 Begg himself joined with seven others in forming the Manitoba Brick and Pottery Company.[15]

As an industry, potting in Canada lagged behind in offering opportunities to the emigrant. In 1863 the compilers of *Eighty Years Progress of British North America* had been able to find only one pottery of any size in the whole colony of Nova Scotia. They estimated its value at $500.[16] But though potting grew slowly on this industrial level, the combined output from all the little local potters, many of whom were never mentioned in directories or newspapers and who have left scant documentary evidence behind them, must have added up to a considerable total. In numbers of small communities throughout the colonies, particularly in the little French-Canadian communities with their self-sufficient economy, the local potter at one time found enough work to keep going in a limited way. It was the improvement in transportation, allowing the imported wares to move freely into the interior of the country, that very often struck the local potter his most serious blow. This was clearly illustrated in Upper Canada. In the first quarter of the century the potters there, making at that time only coarse brownware, had less effective competition from imported wares than was the case in the later years. As Peter Russell wrote from York in 1825: 'The only sort of Pottery made in Canada is brown ware, which is often of a very good quality; enough is made for the use of the upper province. Very little of the English brown ware comes far beyond Montreal.[17]

Although perhaps more imported brownware was even then reaching Upper Canada than Peter Russell realized, it was certainly true that in the early years of the century very much smaller quantities of the imported brownware than of the finer white tableware made the expensive and difficult ascent of the upper St. Lawrence. The common brownware was heavier and bulkier to transport, and it was a product that was in part at least supplied by the local potters. Whiteware was another matter. Commenting on the necessity for importing all the colony's requirements in this line, Peter Russell wrote prophetically to his brother: 'You and I will not live to see the day when America will rival England in white ware, painted and blue ware, and china'.

But with the coming of steam on inland waters and on the land and the improvement in roads, many of the difficulties of transportation were eased; the heavy brownwares and stonewares from the British potteries accordingly increased their threat to local potters everywhere in the colonies, even those working far from ports of entry. When the Port Dundas Pottery Company of Glasgow advertised its Rockingham ware and its stoneware in *The Canada Directory for 1857-58* it was sure of orders from the upper as well as the lower province. One of the few patents to be granted to a potter in pre-Confederation Canada was to a Toronto potter whose discovery concerned a superior body for common earthenware, and whose petition for a patent cited the need to match 'Home Manufacture' against the rapidly expanding volume of importations in this line.

John Brown (1814-66) was an English-trained potter and modeller who endeavoured to extend the range of Canadian potting by making use of local clays in ways 'not known . . . by others before'.[18] He came to Canada in 1849, accompanied by his wife and by young sons who, before many years, would be potting with him. The family settled first near Bowmanville in Upper Canada.[19] Here John Brown began potting at once. He worked to good effect. Barely twelve months after he arrived in the country he was awarded a prize for his wares at the provincial exhibition, held that year at Niagara.[20] The next year, 1851, he introduced what was claimed to be the first machine for making earthenware drain tiles ever seen in Upper Canada.[21] This machine he imported from Albany, New York, putting it into operation in company with another Bowmanville potter, James Bailey. It is said that the partners were given a hundred pounds as a reward for furthering the tile-making industry in Canada.[22] They themselves won a prize for 'Draining Tile' at the provincial exhibition in Toronto in 1852.[23]

But John Brown's original inventions in potting concerned the earthenware body itself. For the discoveries that he made in the use of local clays he was granted a patent in 1859. By this time the family had moved to the Toronto area, and John Brown applied for his patent in association with John Worthington, the Toronto builder, who may have had a financial interest in his pottery.

The patent was granted on February 9, 1859, upon the recommendation of John A. Macdonald, at that time Attorney-General for Upper Canada. It was stated officially that the patent was for 'the invention of a new species of clay adapted to the manufacture of Drainage or Sewerage Tiles or Pipes and stone crockery ware or common yellow earthenware'.[24] 'I have examined the . . . papers, they seem to me to be correct,' John A. Macdonald had noted on them.[25]

The 'new species of clay' which John Brown and John Worthington wished to make use of under a patent depended upon a seam of clay found in Halton County, a section being visible 'on Lot *No. 22* in the *3rd* Concession of the Township of Esquesing, where the line of the Grand Trunk Railroad cuts through the Hill.' In its natural state this clay was 'mixed with a species of shale or stoney marle' and generally occurred 'underlaying the Lime stone'. The specifications for the patent maintained that when the clay was properly 'wintered' (pulverized by exposure to frost), or crushed by machinery, or 'washed and cleaned by the ordinary washing process', and then either used alone, or mixed with stated proportions ('from ten to fifty percent') of 'common red clay' or 'a similar proportion of pulverized Freestone from the Quarries in the neighbourhood', it produced a superior earthenware body. This body was suited to the manufacture of 'Drainage or sewerage Tile or Pipes . . . or for manufacturing stone crockery-ware, or common yellow Earthenware'. Further, if the prepared clay was mixed with 'from five to fifteen percent of Borax' a glaze of 'the best description' resulted 'for the several articles . . . enumerated'.[26]

To strengthen the claim for a patent, John Brown and John Worthington declared that any earthenware made from their clay and glazed with their glaze produced 'a decided improvement on the same article . . . Imported from England'. The English ware coming into the colonies was, they said, porous; and they submitted a specimen of the imported earthenware to prove it. In their own product, however, the glaze 'vitrifies and incorporates itself through the entire body of the Tile Pipe or Crock and by so doing makes the articles impervious'. This, too, they endeavoured to prove by submitting a sample of their manufacture. They advised those examining their application for a patent to test each sample 'by the simple method of Touching it with the Tongue'. The tongue test would show instantly the superiority of the Canadian earthenware since it would indicate that it was non-porous.[27]

The inevitable growth of Upper Canada and the consequent increase in importations were used by John Brown and John Worthington to support their petition for a patent. They pointed out that 'a variety of almost indispensable articles' of superior quality could be made from their formula, and that, unless 'checked by Home Manufacture' of this type, the imported wares would rapidly gather momentum.[28] They swore that no one else had put on the market an earthenware body similar to theirs, and they humbly prayed that Letters Patent be allowed them.[29]

The clay from Esquesing Township was used not only for tiles and drain pipes but, as the specifications for the patent had indicated, for articles which came under the heading of common 'crockeryware'. It was even turned into ornamental items. The proof that it was used for ornaments is to be found in a large dog figure (*Plate* 35A) which carries the name of the Brown pottery and PATENTED 1859. Made as a huge penny bank, the dog is a commanding piece, much superior to the usual figures produced at Canadian potteries. It is modelled with competence and Victorian vigour. John Brown by his own statement was both a modeller[30] and potter, and this dog is the product of modelling skills brought with him from England. Its earthenware body is Canadian, fashioned of clay from Esquesing Township and patented with the approval of John A. Macdonald.

Two of John Brown's sons, Joseph and William O., went into the potting business with him. According to directory listings and prize lists and other documentary evidence (such as the signatures on the Ontario Earthenware Manufacturers Association agreement) the brothers potted with their father, together, and separately. With potting families, however, it is not always easy to determine the exact business relationships. The business style of the firm sometimes masks the fact that all members of the family were part of the same concern. Prior to John Brown's death in 1866, it is probable that both Joseph and W. O. Brown were part of a potting business more or less dominated by their father, in spite of variations in the business style of the firm.[31] In 1866 Joseph Brown assumed control of the concern, which was then in Carlton West, a few miles outside Toronto. William O. Brown eventually gave up potting. In the early years of the twentieth century he was the proprietor of Brown's Hotel at Toronto Junction. Joseph Brown turned to brick-making exclusively in the 1880's, his business being carried on by his own sons after his retirement in 1900.[32]

John Brown endeavoured to extend the range of Canadian potting by improved methods and new inventions making use of Canadian materials. Another Englishman made his contribution to the industry in a different way. Joseph White (1799-1870) brought with him to the colonies a determination to transplant to the shore of Courtenay Bay in New Brunswick the typical products of a successful pottery in Bristol. Stoneware glazing as the Bristol potters carried it out was part of his plan. Conditions in the New World cramped and confined his efforts, but his was a conspicuous attempt to enlarge the scope of potting in a colony by introducing English standards. From Crouchville he advertised the same wares (at least in name) that he had made at home in England. *Hutchinson's New Brunswick Directory for 1867-68* tells what he was trying to do:

JOSEPH WHITE & SONS,
Manufacturers of Earthen & Stoneware,
ROCKINGHAM AND BLACK TEAPOTS,
Common and Fancy STONE PITCHERS of the latest English Designs,
STONEWARE SPIRIT JUGS, MILK PANS, & PRESERVE JARS,
COMMON AND ORNAMENTAL FLOWER POTS, VASES, &c.,
COURTNEY [sic] BAY POTTERY,
ST. JOHN, N.B.

J. WHITE & SONS (of the Potteries, Bristol, England) have lately commenced manufacturing a superior description of Stoneware, coated with a glaze, impervious to acids, to which they respectfully invite the attention of Wine and Spirit Merchants, Chemists and Importers.

It was at the beginning of the 1860's that Joseph White and his family arrived in Saint John from Bristol.[33] Trained as a potter in England, where the Whites had been working with clay for generations, Joseph White acquired a small pottery already in operation at nearby Crouchville on Courtenay Bay (now known as East Saint John). It is said that he very soon put into effect 'new ideas pertaining to pottery manufacture in conformity with the English practice of the day'.[34] His advertisement in Hutchinson's directory would bear this out, for in that advertisement he specified products for which the Whites as potters were known in Bristol.

According to W. J. Pountney, the Bristol ceramic historian, Joseph White, son of Joseph White, potter, was apprenticed to John Decimus Pountney (W. J. Pountney's father, and a master potter) in 1814, 'to be educated as a turner'. In 1828 this younger Joseph White started a potting business of his own in Bristol, with his brother James as partner. Their ancestors had made clay pipes, but the brothers Joseph and James White became noted for wares of a different kind. Their particular products came to include Rockingham and black teapots, fancy stoneware jugs, and utilitarian articles (spirit kegs and the like) glazed not with salt but with a much more practical leadless liquid glaze 'impervious to acids'.[35] The wares that Joseph later advertised in the colonies were, therefore, the very wares he had earlier made in England. And in England these wares had brought him a modest prosperity. By 1855 Joseph and James White had been able to retire from the Bristol pottery, leaving it to sons to continue. James was eventually to go blind; Joseph was to have a new career across the Atlantic.

That Joseph White became a Canadian potter, after he had retired from his Bristol business, was probably due to the example of his second son, William Daniel. One of the many in England whose imagination was fired in the 1850's by the discovery of gold in the far west of North America, William Daniel White left Bristol for the Pacific in 1858. His departure set other members of the family thinking about the opportunities in the colonies. Soon a younger brother, Frederick J. White, was also on his way to the New World. It was Frederick who first arrived in Saint John (after a short time in Nova Scotia); in Saint John he learned of a small pottery for sale at nearby Crouchville.

To Frederick, taken with the New World in his turn, the Crouchville pottery seemed to offer a splendid opportunity for development by skilled and experienced potters. He returned to England to persuade his father to emigrate. The business in Bristol was being managed capably by Joseph's eldest son, another Joseph. There seemed, therefore, nothing to hold him back and even much to urge him on. With his wife, two daughters (of whom Mrs. James Foley was one), and his sons, James A. and Frederick J. White (*Plate* 37A), Joseph White, the Bristol potter, embarked for New Brunswick. At Crouchville he attempted to introduce the products that had brought success in England, as his advertisement in the New Brunswick directory shows.

In this 1867 advertisement, Joseph White's reference to his stoneware glaze is of particular interest, for it is undoubtedly a reference both to a technique that had greatly improved stoneware manufacture in Great Britain and to a particular specialty of the Whites as potters in Bristol. W. J. Pountney credits William Powell of Bristol with the invention, about 1835, of a liquid glaze for ordinary stoneware. Since the old method of salt glazing produced an article not always satisfactory when certain liquids, such as spirits, came in contact with it, the invention of a stoneware glaze guaranteed impervious to the action of acids was of decided importance. In addition, kitchen and dairy wares, such as stone pie dishes and milk pans, looked more attractive with the new glaze. All over Great Britain potters began to experiment to find the secret of the Bristol glaze. In Bristol itself the firm of Joseph and James White made a specialty of manufacturing a stoneware glaze, theirs being of such quality that potters in other parts of the country purchased it from them.[36] When Joseph White established the colonial pottery he was justified in making an advertising feature of 'a superior description of Stoneware, coated with a glaze, impervious to acids'. Such ware was undoubtedly one of the improvements that he introduced at Crouchville 'in conformity with the English practice of the day'.

In Bristol, the White pottery, founded in 1828 by Joseph and James White, lasted until the 1890's; in Crouchville the Whites—Joseph and then his sons, Frederick J. and James A. White—potted from the 1860's until the end of the 1880's. For a brief while William Daniel (who had failed to find a fortune in gold) was also connected with the Crouchville venture, but his potting experience in Canada was but an interlude; he is said to have been by profession a dentist. It was Frederick J. and James A. White who carried on after their father's death in 1870, and it was James who was eventually left alone in Crouchville. Frederick was called back to England to assist his brother Joseph's widow and young sons with the Bristol business. Later he went to the United States.[37]

Introducing 'the lastest English designs' and improved techniques cannot have been easy in a colonial setting, in spite of the bright future that Frederick had believed possible in Crouchville. The *Mercantile Agency Reference Books* indicate that the Whites found business no more rewarding financially, even at the best of times, than did the average Canadian potter.[38] And yet the White products at one time commanded a good sale beyond the boundaries of the Maritimes. A White Pottery account book, now in the New Brunswick Museum, reveals that one of the customers was John L. Cassidy, the important Montreal china merchant. There were a number of potteries nearer at hand from which John

L. Cassidy could have bought his crocks and jars, if he wanted a Canadian product, and he did buy from some of them, including the Farrar pottery in St. Johns; nonetheless, he gave orders totalling large sums to the firm of F. J. & J. A. White in New Brunswick. He was billed by the Whites for $549.27 on April 3, 1878. Only a month before he had paid another bill of $554.22.

But the same storm clouds gathered over the White pottery in Crouchville as darkened the horizon of many another Canadian pottery. Fire devasted the plant in 1885;[39] bankruptcy closed it not many years after.[40]

John Brown in Upper Canada had sounded the warning that 'Home Manufacture' would have to compete with an ever-increasing flow of imports in common earthenware; articles of 'superior quality' were his answer. Joseph White's plan for success was to make the same articles in New Brunswick as could be imported from England. But no potter working in the colonies who entertained any hope of building up large-scale business could escape the competition offered by imported wares. That the range of Canadian potting did not go far beyond the humble brown dish and the stoneware crock in no way set the colonial potter free from the need to match his output against that of English manufacturers. A striking example of the way in which the imported wares rolled over and about the colonial work is found in the *New Brunswick Courier* of May 12, 1849. On that day appeared an advertisement for locally made earthenware:

PROVINCIAL POTTERY
NEAR THE VALLEY CHURCH
Portland, St. John.
MR. THOMPSON having imported from
England, superior Ore for glazing with, is
now prepared to supply Country Merchants and
the trade generally with the undermentioned
Wares at twenty per cent less than the same
quality can be imported from Great Britain, viz:

MILK PANS,	BUTTER CROCKS,
PUDDING PANS,	PRESERVE JARS,

BOTTLES, ½ and 1 gallon,
GARDEN POTS, &c. &c.
Warranted equal in quality to English of the same description.
Orders left at the Store of JOHN GILLIS, Esq., will be attended to.

But in another column of the same newspaper appeared a different advertisement. This one, inserted by Richard Calvert, a merchant on Dock Street in Saint John, drew the attention of the crock-, pan-, and jar-buying public to importations:

Earthenware, Milk Pans, Cream
Crocks, Stone Jugs, &c. &c.
The Subscriber has received per ships
Infanta and Thomas, from Liverpool:—
100 PACKAGES of the above articles,
selected at the Potteries expressly
for this Market, which he is now opening.

Not only did Richard Calvert have on hand ample imported stocks of the same type of ware as the Provincial Pottery was trying to make, he was actually expecting further large supplies at any moment. His advertisement went on:

Hourly expected per ship "Majestic"
5000 Pieces Milk Pans and Cream Crocks, Gallon
and half gallon JARS, &c.

No doubt the Provincial Pottery would have been thankful for orders for a few hundred pans and crocks; Richard Calvert was bringing them in by the thousand. And he was only one of a number of Saint John importers, all of whom would be supplied with wares from across the Atlantic, and all of whom would be prepared to sell at highly competitive prices. The local potters in Canada had need of protective tariffs and price reductions and the fiction of superior quality to get their products moving on a market glutted with earthenware and stoneware from Great Britain. Even after any costs of transatlantic transportation were added, these imported wares, landed in their thousands at Halifax, Saint John, Quebec, and Montreal, could be offered for trifling sums, so that underselling them was not easy. The potter least affected was the one in an isolated community who was content if a small output gave him a simple living. With every year his isolation was eroded, and what was good enough for him in the way of a living might not be enough for his sons. Potting as an industry had to face up to competition.

It was not easy. The imported article was extolled as being the more desirable: 'warranted to be of English make' was the way a Montreal dealer publicized soda water and ginger beer bottles in 1847;[41] and '*very superior*' was how a Saint John merchant advertised 'pop bottles' imported that same year from Joseph Bourne's pottery in Derbyshire.[42]

The Canadian potter's defence was not often to claim superiority to English wares (as John Brown had done when applying for a patent), but to assert equality. This was the theme of an advertisement by the Yamaska Pottery & Brick Works in *McLaughlin's Quebec Directory* for 1855:

YAMASKA
POTTERY & BRICK WORKS
ST. MICHEL D'YAMASKA, C.E.

———

THE ATTENTION OF
MERCHANTS & TRADERS
Is invited to the above Manufactory

———

BUTTER CROCKS, BREAD PANS, LI-
QUORS JARS, half Gallon, Gallon and two
Gallons each. MILK DISHES of all sizes: PRE-
SERVE JARS; GARDEN POTS; FANCY
VASES; and every article of Brownware, war-
ranted, equal to English manufacture.

Other potters made the hopeful boast that in Rockingham and yellow ware they could meet English standards. L. P. Gauvreau & Frère, whose pottery was at Cap Rouge, nine miles from Quebec, and who sometimes advertised under the name of the Cap Rouge Pottery,[43] provide an example of this attempt to meet the competition that so often was overpowering in the end. Their advertisement appeared in the *Quebec Daily News* on May 27, 1864:

L. P. Gauvreau & Frere,
MANUFACTURERS OF

Yellow and Rockingham Ware, HAVE the honor to inform the public that they have established a depot of their Ware in ST. PAUL STREET, No. 30, next door to the Hon. L. Renaud's Store. As they are manufacturing this Ware themselves which is in no way inferior to the imported one, and that they are in a position to give it at a lower price than the Importers they hope for a liberal support from the public.

The stoneware potters of Brantford, Morton & Co., claiming in 1851 that theirs was 'the *only* stoneware factory' in Canada West, did not reach as high in their aspirations as equality with the stoneware makers of Derbyshire, Gloucestershire, or Staffordshire. They advertised only that their work was 'warranted equal to any in North America'.[44] To be simply Canadian seemed not enough. The potting reputation had insufficient sales appeal.

Nonetheless, potting in the British North American colonies moved steadily if slowly away from the farmer-potter and into the realm of an industry. Enterprise such as that displayed by John Brown in seeking to patent a new earthenware body, or by Joseph White in attempting to reproduce Bristol products in Crouchville, eventually carried this infant industry to the point where Canadian potters not only challenged the imported wares on home ground, but met them in world exhibitions.

The nineteenth century was an age of technological advance achieved with a rapidity and variety never known before. This was particularly true of the second half of the century, when the Victorians were keyed to a sense of wonder and excitement at the changes taking place about them and the new products being offered. In such an age it was only natural that the exhibition should become the means on the part of industry of marking progress and displaying new wares. The first of the international fairs, the Great Exhibition of the Industry of All Nations, was promoted by Prince Albert and held in London in 1851. Canadian potters were not ready for it. *The Official Descriptive and Illustrated Catalogue of the Great Exhibition* lists specimens of minerals, woods, and agricultural products, furs, snowshoes, birchbark canoes, and furniture from the North American colonies, but no pottery. At the New York world's fair, held two years later, Yamaska and Quebec pottery (the latter the work of W. & D. Bell) made a 'very good' display, and was said to be 'a branch of Canadian industry that ought to be supported',[45] but it was not until the American Centennial Exhibition of 1876, held in Philadelphia, that Canadian potters made any important showing of their wares internationally. At Philadelphia more than half a dozen of them contributed to a Canadian exhibit of manufactured goods of various kinds, comprising 'all the articles necessary for the use, if not for the ornament and luxury of life'.[46]

The report of the Canadian Commission at Philadelphia pointed out that there were 'a number of branches of human art' in which a country as young as Canada could not hope to compete, and that this was 'especially the case with painting, sculpture and ornamental industries'. These 'ornamental industries' included the manufacture of 'the finer descriptions of china, glassware and pottery'.[47] Yet in submitting practical, useful wares in ordinary, plain bodies, the Canadian potters who competed at Philadelphia were following their historic role. All the nineteenth-century Canadian potter was actually capable of doing was attempting to match home manufacture against importations of this kind. The range of his potting on a commercial basis aimed only at the earthenware and stoneware bodies suitable for such wares. When his work included whiteware it was heavy stone china and durable white grainite, not the 'finer descriptions' of white earthenware. Any ornaments the Canadian potter made—figures, picture frames, urns, and vases—were fashioned from the bodies devised for his practical pottery. They were only a by-product.

But Canadian potting, making almost its first appearance at an exhibition outside the country, and confined as it was to the practical, won an international award at Philadelphia. The St. Johns Stone Chinaware Company, the only whiteware manufactory in the country, then in operation scarcely three years, brought home a medal from Philadelphia for its white granite ware.[48] When ranged in competition with the products of Great Britain and the United States, the table and toilet whiteware from St. Johns had won 'the good opinion of many . . . able to judge'.[49]

In the ordinary dark-bodied earthenware and stoneware there were a number of optimistic Canadian exhibitors at Philadelphia. The Farrars from St. Johns (who would be burned out later that year) sent specimens of pottery and samples of the clay from which their wares were produced. The Cap Rouge Pottery Co. (not Gauvreau & Frère, but a later firm, backed by John Ross & Co., the Quebec wholesale grocers) made a display of common earthenware, as did Smith & Kaye, the Nova Scotia potters who were also brickmakers.[50] Ontario, with the greatest number of potters working on the industrial level, had the greatest number of exhibitors at Philadelphia. They were five in all: Charles Pratt of London, J. H. Ahrens of Paris, William Wells of Beamsville, and Robert Romaine and Robert Westcott of Peterborough.

The report dealing with the Ontario entries listed Charles Pratt's exhibit as composed of a nest of flower pots, a preserve jar, a spittoon, and a sample of the clay from which these wares had been made. J. H. Ahrens also sent a sample of the clay used for his spittoon and nest of flower pots and saucers. William Wells submitted a flower pot and saucer and a sample of the clay employed in making it. The Peterborough potters sent flowers pots and an 'Assortment of Earthenware'.[51]

The Ontario government issued a report of its own on the 1876 world's fair. An enthusiastic paragraph was devoted to the bricks sent to Philadelphia,[52] but the work of the five potters merited no special attention. The range of their wares was certainly limited, but it was limited by conditions that had hampered the Canadian potter from the earliest days. That Canadian potters exhibited as much as they did at Philadelphia was an achievement; that there was even one whiteware factory anywhere in the country capable of bringing home an award for its granite ware was almost incredible. Even at that moment the St. Johns Stone Chinaware Company, which had accomplished this feat, was tottering on a crumbling foundation. It would have to be propped up the next year by the financial support forthcoming when it passed into the private ownership of Edward and Duncan Macdonald, bankers.

At least two of the potting firms who had competed at Philadelphia went on to take part in the Universal Exhibition held in Paris in 1878. When the S.S. *Newfield* steamed away from Montreal at the end of the shipping season in 1877 she carried Canadian exhibits to be viewed in Paris the next spring.[53] Both J. H. Ahrens and the firm of G. H. & L. E. Farrar, who had taken part in the Centennial Exhibition at Philadelphia, submitted samples of their wares for display in Paris. In addition, Henry Schuler (like Ahrens, from Paris, Ontario) sent a selection of his stoneware for competition abroad. In the official catalogue of the Canadian section at this European world's fair the German-born Ahrens was given the most space. He was described as a 'Manufacturer of Flint, Enamelled and Common Earthenware'. His 'Common Earthenware' exhibits included 'Samples of Cream Pots, Milk Crocks, Milk Pans, Butter Pots, Jugs, Molasses Jugs, Fruit Jars, Preserve Jars, Fancy Flower Pots, Water Pitchers, Flower Pots.' In 'Rockingham or Flint Enamelled Ware' he showed 'Water Pitchers, Tea Pots, Spittoons, Hanging Flower Pots, Vases, &c.'[54]

At the time of the Paris exhibition Ahrens had been potting in Canada for almost twenty years. He had learned the business in Germany and had continued it after he emigrated to Upper Canada in the 1850's. A hard worker, he had prospered in the New World, but at the end of the 1860's he had suffered a serious financial reverse. It was not the usual fire that wiped out Jacob Ahrens' pottery in 1869; it was the breaking away of the dam at Paris. He had, however, recovered his losses, and must have been confident when he exhibited his flint enamelled and common earthenware in France. Unfortunately, there was still trouble ahead for Jacob Ahrens. In the summer of 1883 a flash flood on the Nith washed away his pottery a second time (*Plate* 37B).[55]

Henry Schuler also potted on the banks of the Nith, not far from Jacob Ahrens. He, too, brought something of the German tradition to Canada. Born in the United States of a German father and a German-American mother, he spent his childhood in New Hamburg, Upper Canada. In the 1860's he became another of the effective band of German-Canadian potters who helped to build up the industry in Ontario. At first he made only common earthenware; then, in 1873, he branched out into stoneware.[56] It was stoneware he showed in France. The Canadian catalogue described his display as composed of 'Butter Pots, Preserve Jars, Cream Pots, Jugs, Tomato Jars, Churns, Common Pitchers, Spittoons, Molasses Jugs, Flower Pots, &c.'[57]

The Farrars exhibited an 'Assortment of Stone Ware' and 'Fancy Flower Pots'. In the catalogue their display was listed under the name of the 'St. John [*sic*] Pottery Works',[58] although they were, from now on, to be identified with Iberville, across the Richelieu River. For George H. and Lucius E. Farrar, getting together a suitable exhibit to send abroad at the end of 1877 may have presented certain problems. In the autumn of 1876 their business had been brought to a standstill, when fire gutted the Works in St. Johns.

It was hardly to be expected that Canadian earthenware and stoneware would attract much attention, when viewed against the background of industrial potting of which Europe was capable, but even within their own Canadian section the Quebec and Ontario potters found interest diverted from them. The 'novelty feature' of the Canadian display in Paris, in the eyes of the French visitors, was the rocking chair. The *Canadian Illustrated News* reported on June 15, 1878, that rocking chairs seemed to be unknown to the general public of France, and that those sent to the exhibition by Canadian furniture manufacturers had created a sensation. People had little time to look at any other Canadian manufactured goods, they were too busy trying out the rocking chairs: 'all day they are occupied by people delighted with the new sensation. There is not one left unsold'.

But while many a visitor, hurrying by to rock again, may have given the Canadian pottery and stoneware only a cursory glance, the judges were more impressed. Henry Schuler won an honourable mention for his stoneware.[59] The Farrars received a certificate stating that their contribution had formed part of 'a joint exhibit representing the Dominion of Canada' which had been awarded a diploma. Signed by Thomas C. Keefer, the Canadian Executive Commissioner, the certificate was ornamented with a picture of the walnut and pine trophy, eighty-five feet high, which was a picturesque part of the Canadian display.[60] Decorated as it was with birchbark canoes, moose heads, and a huge buffalo head, the trophy, together with the rocking chairs, was probably remembered longer by the Europeans than the flint enamelled jugs of Jacob Ahrens, the spittoons of Henry Schuler, or the fancy flower pots of the Farrar brothers.

Canadian potters, however, had reached a stage where they were prepared to show what they could do in international competitions, even those held on another continent. Though they must certainly have hoped to sell what they sent abroad, their real object in taking part in such exhibitions was to impress Canadians themselves by this progress. It was the Canadian market and no other that would keep the Canadian potters in business. By having their wares accepted for international display, Canadian potters sought a status at home that would help in some measure to offset the long-established conviction that the imported article, even in common goods, was of necessity a superior product.

At two other nineteenth-century exhibitions abroad Canadian potters displayed their wares. On May 2, 1885, the King of the Belgians opened an International Exhibition in Antwerp. One Quebec pottery and three from Ontario were represented. As at Philadelphia, the St. Johns Stone Chinaware Company was the only exhibitor of whiteware from Canada. The catalogue of the Canadian section listed the St. Johns contribution as table and toilet 'chinaware' (stone china), both 'plain and decorated', and white granite ware for 'domestic purposes'. Once again this Canadian factory, whose skilled workers included potters brought over from Staffordshire, held its own in international competition. At Antwerp tablewares from St. Johns again won acclaim.[61]

The exhibitors of Ontario stone and earthenware at Antwerp were Gray & Betts of Tilsonburg, W. E. Welding of Brantford, and Hart Brothers & Lazier of Belleville. William Gray and S. H. Betts, who had been only a short time in business together as 'Manufacturers of Stone, Rockingham and Bristol ware', showed bowls, spittoons, teapots, pie plates, and soap drainers in Rockingham. In salt-glazed stoneware their assortment included 'Dutch pots', fruit jars, butter pots, and oil and water kegs. In 'Bristol ware', or stoneware coated with a liquid glaze (such as Joseph White had attempted to make earlier in New Brunswick), they had sent over ink and beer bottles, jars for pickles, and mustard jugs.[62] W. E. Welding, who had once been a travelling salesman for Morton & Co.'s stoneware, and who was now conducting a business of his own on a larger scale than most potters in Canada, included 'fancy dogs' in his Antwerp display. He also showed the usual churns, pickle jars, stew pots, spittoons, pie plates, teapots, and milk pans.[63] The exhibits from Hart Brothers & Lazier (a Belleville firm made up of George I. Lazier, of Picton, and Charles A. and Elwin E. Hart) were described in the catalogue as an assortment of 'butter pots, preserve jars, flower pots, &c.'[64] At home at this period Hart Brothers & Lazier advertised stoneware of every description, and kept circulars on hand to send out to prospective customers. An advertisement for their wares in Polk's *Ontario Gazetteer* for 1884-85 shows covered stone pots with ornate floral decoration. Two years later a similar advertisement makes clear that all this stoneware was made 'from the best Imported Clay'.

A year after the Antwerp International Exhibition, a huge Colonial and Indian Exhibition was organized in London. Canada was naturally one of the main contributors to this event. The same four potteries that had sent wares to Antwerp represented Canada among the colonies.

In the catalogues of these great fairs held outside the country is an important record of what nineteenth-century Canadian potters could do—their achievements and their limitations. There were many potters, however, who, for a variety of reasons, took no part in international events but who frequently displayed their products in provincial or Dominion exhibitions. Provincial exhibitions had begun in the colonies in the early years of Queen Victoria's reign, Dominion exhibitions came at the end of the 1870's. Again the picture of ceramic products is primarily one of 'articles necessary for the use, if not for the ornament and luxury of life'. Common brownware bowls, stone churns, Rockingham teapots, yellow jugs, and red flower pots made up the bulk of the potters' goods. Whiteware in the form of stout granite and stone china represented the peak of refinement in Canadian potting as seen at home or abroad.

Some potters demonstrated what they could do by making special show pieces for these Canadian fairs. W. E. Welding, who took part in provincial as well as international events, was one who sometimes exhibited a tour de force of practical type. At the exhibition in Toronto in 1879, he had on display 'a meat-packing jar' specially made for the occasion. It was no ordinary meat-packing jar, however; its capacity was all of two hundred pounds.[65] In reporting that year's fair the *Evening Telegram*, on September 3, published a description of W. E. Welding's exhibit. The account was headed 'ELEGANT NOVELTIES', and the elegant part of the Welding display was evidently made up of brown-glazed hanging baskets for plants, the baskets being ornamented with raised 'wreaths of flowers' in pale yellow.

According to the *Telegram*, the potter from Brantford had a grievance: 'He complains that at all the fairs and exhibitions he attends he cannot get other makers in his line to compete with him, and that consequentls [consequently] he has always carried off the prize.' W. E. Welding, with his 'fancy dogs' (shown at Antwerp) and his 'elegant' plant holders (shown in Toronto) did not, it would seem, find competition unduly keen when he strayed with common earthenware into the realm of the ornamental.

Provincial exhibition accounts provide some of the few contemporary descriptions of the wares of certain potters who, though in business for many years, did not often, if ever mark their wares, or spend much money on advertising. The Dions of Ancienne Lorette furnish an interesting example. Although these French-Canadian potters never took part in the big exhibitions outside Canada, they were contributors to the industry over a long period. Contemporary comment on their work is, however, scarce. The body of information concerning them has been almost wholly built up on the never entirely satisfactory authority of oral testimony, and on the evidence of unmarked wares found in the Quebec area (where other potters were also at work throughout the period).

To establish the type of ware made by the Dions in the twentieth century should present no real problems. The days of their later productions are still within living memory. But determining what they made in the nineteenth century means entering upon more speculative ground, for here recollections must often become only memories of memories. Such recollections as have come down from the earlier days have not always been historically convincing. References to Dion work in nineteenth-century provincial exhibition accounts, brief as they may be, give some of the few contemporary glimpses of this French-Canadian contribution to potting. From them it may be ascertained that Antoine Dion, in 1873, could show a creditable variety of articles in earthenware,[66] and from these same accounts come two different opinions of what that Dion earthenware was like. Each was given by a person who actually examined Dion wares for himself.

In 1877 the *Gazette* reporter, viewing the provincial exhibition at Quebec, paused at the earthenware display. He found that 'Dion of Lorette' was the only exhibitor of 'Quebec-made pottery' (earthenware). In his published opinion the Dion wares were 'principally coarse stuff'. He specified items shown: teapots, spittoons, and pitchers.[67]

Four years later another reporter, this time from the *Daily Witness*, examined what Antoine Dion had sent to the provincial exhibition in Montreal. The Dion wares shown in 1881 struck him as being of 'excellent finish', even though they were of ordinary 'brown earthenware'.[68] The prize for the 'Best collection of Pottery ware' went that year to Antoine Dion.[69]

Both opinions of Dion products were undoubtedly justified. All brownware is in essence 'coarse stuff'. And it was of 'coarse stuff' that Canada's ceramic output in the nineteenth century was almost entirely made up. But there were at all times those who were capable of giving 'excellent finish' to their work in a pedestrian body. If the more accomplished pieces attributed to the Dions are rightfully theirs, they show that in Victorian days these potters of old Lorette drew upon English and American methods to produce French-Canadian wares that were at times above the Canadian average. The Dions never ventured beyond the ordinary range of Canadian potting, but within the limitations of that range they were not only competent but even imaginative.

The wares today credited to the Dions include what were called in their own time 'lawn vases' or 'garden urns'. (Intended for use indoors or out, these were large, urn-shaped plant holders on detachable bases.) One such urn attributed to the Dions is in a church; others, brown-glazed over the characteristic red body, were at one time owned by members of the Dion family. The largest of these 'lawn vases' stand nearly three feet tall. While of necessity heavy in appearance, they represent skilled work.

Also accepted as of Dion make are large tobacco jars around which dance figures urged on by fiddlers. Other pieces credited to the Dions include teapots decorated with raised beavers, well-modelled jugs in a variety of designs, and ornamental figures (copied from English or American types) such as dogs and lions, the latter on rectangular bases. Old photographs taken outside the pottery show Dion workers displaying wares on planks or trays. These wares, in addition to the usual pots and dishes, include flower pots and saucers, the edges scalloped. Flower pots of this type attributed to the Dions usually have three small round holes at the top, to convert them into hanging baskets (*Plate* (40A).

Sometimes these Dion wares, whose body colour normally ranges from a dark red to a terracotta colour, are covered with a plain brown glaze, or a glaze heavily streaked with brown; sometimes the brown is flecked and mottled with other colours, such as green. About all the decorative pieces there is a sense of vitality. The figures dancing round the tobacco jars are spirited, the beavers have a primitive power, even the hanging baskets have a rough zest.

Although the Dions are not listed among the potters in such gazetteers of Canadian business as Mitchell & Co.'s 'classified directories' of 1864 and 1865, they were, nonetheless, at work at this period, even if only in a small way. In the 1861 census Jean Dion (born about 1829) is recorded as a potter working at Ancienne Lorette. Ten years later, in the census of 1871, his elder brother Antoine is given as a potter. That same year (1871) *Lovell's Canadian Dominion Directory* recorded both brothers as potters of Ancienne Lorette, 'distant from . . . Quebec 7 miles'. Until after the First World War members of the familly potted in the area, for sons of Antoine—another Antoine, Silfrid, Joseph, and Frédéric—trained by both their father and uncle, carried on the work. In the *Dominion of Canada . . . Gazetteer* for 1919, under 'Potteries', were listed both a 'Poterie Dion' and 'Dion Frères', the one in operation at Ancienne Lorette, the other at nearby Les Saules. In the 1920's, however, the effort to make Dion pottery pay was finally given up. Not even flower pots could be produced and sold in large enough quantities to be remunerative. Quebec crockery merchants, such as Renaud & Co. and Francis Thomas, had once handled Dion wares in quantity, but in the end it seemed no one really wanted those local products at any price that was realistic. The demand for hanging baskets and terrines from Lorette or Les Saules simply died away.

The Dions' best years came during the period when Dion earthenware was seen regularly in provincial fairs. *The Mercantile Agency Reference Book* for January, 1881, for example, shows that the potting business in Antoine Dion's name was rated as having an estimated capital of between $2,000 and $5,000. This rating placed the Dions with successful Canadian potters of the day. A decline in fortune obviously set in towards the last years of the century. When *The Mercantile Agency Reference Book* for March, 1899, was published, Dion

Frères, potters, had an estimated capital of under $500, and a credit rating that was understandably 'Limited'.

At one time the Dions ventured into brick-making as well as potting. On September 20, 1881, the *Montreal Gazette* reported that 'S. [Silfrid] Dion' of Ancienne Lorette had won second prize at the provincial exhibition for 'plain and moulded bricks'.

There are still those who remember the Dion pottery in its later years, with the crocks and pans set out on boards to dry in the sun. Once this was a common sight at any small Canadian pottery. Rev. Henry Scadding, though writing of an earlier day and another province, pictured the same thing when he described John Walmsley's pottery on Yonge Street, where the passer-by saw 'displayed in the open air on boards . . . numerous articles of coarse brown ware, partially glazed, pans, crocks, jars, jugs demijohns, and so forth'.[70] Scadding found such a sight 'ever pleasant to contemplate', but under changing conditions it was only when potting remained on too small a scale to pay that such a pleasant sight was possible.

In the Maritimes, provincial exhibitions provided the local potters with a chance to display their wares, just as they did in central Canada. Dominion exhibitions were also staged in such cities as Halifax (1881) and Saint John (1883), and from accounts of these industrial fairs, both provincial and Dominion, come direct reports of eye-witnesses to add a further dimension to the history of potting in Canada. The representative of the Saint John *Daily Sun*, who visited the New Brunswick provincial fair of 1880, wrote on October 5 of the products entered by the Whites of Crouchville. He not only commented on the usual wares associated with the Whites, but made mention of their less well-known attempt to compete with overseas manufacturers in certain types of ornamental earthenware:

F. & J. WHITE . . . show a large assortment of their pottery wares. From a light frame which runs along the front and sides of their section, are swung rows of hanging flower baskets in rustic, painted and other models. On shelves and stands they have a confusing array of flower pots of all sizes and styles (including some specially fine rustic ones), also a few mantle [sic] tiles and some pottery of classic mould for decorative art designs . . .

The flower pots and the 'milk pans, jugs, butter crocks, jars, etc.' (which the reporter described as set out on 'the floor of their arbor') were to be expected from the Whites, but when they undertook the making of ornamental tiles to decorate mantels and walls, they were endeavouring to enter into direct competition in the Canadian market with such great English firms as Copelands, Doultons, Mintons, and Maw & Co. All these English potteries did a big business in Canada in 'mantel tiles'.

The reporter for the *Daily Sun* noted too, the 'sample cards' of clay tobacco pipes, which the Whites had arranged on the wall of their exhibition booth in 1880, and declared that the specimens he had examined were 'well made and of smooth finish'. The reporter's opinion was obviously shared by visitors from the west, who were in Saint John with a travelling exhibit from Manitoba. The Manitoba goods (chiefly agricultural) had been shown earlier at the Dominion Exhibition held that year in Montreal. They had then been moved on to Saint

John. When the westerners in charge headed home, they took with them samples of the clay tobacco pipes from Crouchville. According to the *Daily Sun* (on October 12), the men from the west found the New Brunswick pipes 'better than are imported into Manitoba from Scotland'. It was predicted that as a result of the fair in Saint John orders would come in from western Canada for such Maritime products as canned salmon and lobster and even clay pipes.

The next year the Whites themselves took part in a Dominion exhibition, this time in Halifax. Again the *Daily Sun* sent a reporter, who, on September 24, told the readers at home that for this event Frederick J. and James A. White had erected 'a high stand' on which to show off 'tobacco pipes of all kinds', together with 'bread pans, milk pans . . . butter crocks, bean pots and a great variety of lava flower pots and saucers, pressed hanging pots . . . rustic flower stands, rustic flower pots, etc.' The display, it was felt, would be 'very attractive to lady visitors', and would give a good idea of what New Brunswick potters were capable of doing.

The 'lady visitors' at the Halifax fair had more than the Whites' display to interest them in the pottery line. Smith & Kaye, the Nova Scotia potters who had exhibited at Philadelphia in 1876, made 'an elaborate show' of their own 'pottery goods' and also put on popular demonstrations of how these wares were made.

The later years of the nineteenth century saw Canadian potting as an industry developed not only to the point where Canadians took part in great exhibitions abroad and showed the range of their products in Dominion and provincial exhibitions at home, but where the isolated worker was rapidly giving place to a body of master potters with common interests to protect. An early and bold attempt to advance the cause of potting in Canada was the formation, in 1872, of the Ontario Earthenware Manufacturers Association. The names of those who banded together in this pioneer effort to strengthen a young industry were in themselves a record of accomplishment. Simon Thomas Humberstone, the son, grandson, and great-grandson of Canadian potters, was a force in the new organization. John Brown's sons, Joseph and William, were among the founders. So, too, were the influential German potters, Jacob Ahrens and Henry Schuler.

Suitably, the Ontario men held some of their organizational meetings in Hamilton, 'the Ambitious City'. They elected William Campbell, the Hamilton pottery owner, their president, and they drafted a constitution and by-laws which they afterwards published in pamphlet form. The chief objective was price control. Attempts on the part of Canadian potters to meet the ruinous competition from abroad by equally ruinous price cutting at home had brought the Ontario manufacturers together, determined to close ranks against those who were killing their own industry. Canadian potters had been forced to try to undersell the imported wares, but the founders of the Ontario Earthenware Manufacturers Association believed that this had been carried to the point where pirates within their own business were slashing necessary profits out of existence. The result was a frail industry threatened by self-inflicted wounds. Summarized, the aims of the new association were to secure 'uniformity of price', to prevent 'injurious competition', to encourage 'good feeling' among the members, and to be ready

266

to adopt such other measures as might be 'considered essential for the protection of those in trade as Earthenware Manufacturers'.

For breaking any of the by-laws 'without satisfactory cause', a member of the Ontario Earthenware Manufacturers Association could incur the severe fine of one hundred dollars for each infraction. The machinery for imposing these fines was set up at a meeting of the association in January, 1873. It was agreed on this occasion that a member against whom complaints had been made must appear before a special session of the organization, called specifically to deal with the charges, but that the accused could be judged guilty only by a three-fourths vote of the members attending. At this time it was also decided to limit the maximum fine to four hundred dollars, or four violations of the by-laws.

At the January meeting in 1873 Simon Thomas Humberstone was present, and he made a copy of the agreement entered into that day by the representatives of thirteen Ontario potteries. It remains with his papers. In addition to Simon Thomas Humberstone himself, those signing the agreement, or affixing their mark if unable to write, were William Campbell, the president of the association, J. H. Ahrens, Joseph Bradwin, Joseph Brown, William Brown, J. H. Burns, Samuel Burns, Alexander J. Davis, Arthur Dodge, Robert Irwin, McGlade & Schuler (Peter McGlade and Henry Schuler), and William Taylor.

That such an association could be formed in the 1870's, even in Ontario where there were more potteries than in any other province, was evidence of how far Canadian potting had come from the day when a manufacturer in business on an extensive scale was one who employed someone else to hawk his wares from a pedlar's cart. Michael Whitmore, one of the more important of the pre-Victorian potters of York, advertised for a pedlar in 1830 'to hawk Brown POTTERY WARE through the country'.[71] Six months later, when Whitmore's Yonge Street Pottery was 'burnt to ashes', the loss was deplored publicly as being all the more serious for having affected one of the town's 'enterprising' businessmen.[72]

The wares on which Canadian potters built business were cheap goods, bringing in small returns unless a sufficient volume of sales could be effected. Relatively few price lists have survived, but among those that have is one from Warner & Co., Toronto stoneware manufacturers at mid-century. Dated 1856 and carrying woodcuts of the various articles made, the Warner list gives prices ranging from seventy-five cents for a dozen stoneware beer bottles to $15.00 for a dozen butter pots (six-gallon size, with covers). 'Moulded' inkstands were $1.50 a dozen, pitchers $1.25 a dozen for quart size, and small chambers $2.25 a dozen. In the 1880's Jacob Ahrens was selling pie plates at six and a quarter cents each in his Paris Pottery. His Rockingham spittoons could be had for twenty cents each and water pitchers for as little as twelve and a half cents each. In New Brunswick, at this same period, the Whites were selling half-gallon 'pancake pitchers' for seventeen cents apiece and small flower pots at twelve cents a dozen. By the end of the century Simon Thomas Humberstone was selling quart pitchers for $1.00 a dozen, small teapots for $1.32 a dozen, and hanging baskets at the rate of twenty-five for less than a cent apiece.

On such low-priced wares did a precarious industry rest. Its status was humble. The judges at the 1860 provincial exhibition in Montreal had defined it when they awarded a bronze medal to George Whitefield Farrar, of St. Johns, for his earthenware. The bronze medal, they pointed out in drawing up the prize list, was for 'excellence of manufacture in a less degree and upon articles of less importance than those obtaining the silver medal.' The gold medal was reserved for 'original inventions or for the introduction of new and important manufactures'.[73] The day came when whiteware from St. Johns won a gold medal,[74] but on the whole, Canadian ceramic products were rarely reckoned among the country's original or important manufactures; they were more commonly in the bronze medal class—'articles of less importance'.

The range of nineteenth-century Canadian potting was contained within these restrictions. With only a fleeting look at whiteware in its most practical bodies, it was limited to the 'VARIOUS DESCRIPTIONS OF Common Earthen and STONEWARE'.[75] When Canadian potters boasted, as did Walmsley & Mc-Cluskie in 1865, that 'articles of the more ornamental kinds, as well as those in common use', were being manufactured,[76] it was from the sturdy bodies belonging to that common earthenware and stoneware that the ornamental wares were made. In nineteenth-century Canadian potting, there was, as the Canadian Commission at Philadelphia admitted, virtually no place for 'the finer descriptions' of ware, and only in a small way did Canadian potters concern themselves with articles not strictly for use.

But back of the plain wares that Canadians made, sometimes skilfully, producing goods of 'excellent finish', sometimes with fumbling incompetence, lies the whole history of a stubborn effort to bring an industry into being in a new country. This persistent effort, in the face of disheartening difficulties, succeeded in lifting potting in the colonies from the farm to the factory, even if most often a small factory, working in the bleakness of imminent failure.

The range of Canadian potting appears not as something narrow and limited but as a triumphant achievement when viewed in historical perspective. What was accomplished at St. Johns and Newton Brook, at Crouchville and Brantford, at Ancienne Lorette and New Hamburg has meaning in terms beyond stone crocks and red flower pots. That meaning comes into focus in advertisements such as the two that appeared on the same mid-century day in the *New Brunswick Courier*—the one advertisement for milk pans and gallon jars to be made at the Provincial Pottery near the Valley Church (if any orders for them were left at Gillis's store in Saint John), the other for exactly the same articles announced by an importer and expected 'hourly' in a great multitude from across the sea.

CHAPTER XXII

The Staffordshire of Canada:
The Farrars

WE the undersigned, having RE-BUILT the POTTERY burned on the 14th February last . . are now ready to furnish our STONE WARE to customers as usual. E. L. FARRAR, G. W. FARRAR. *News and Frontier Advocate*, April 24, 1857.

'The Staffordshire of Canada' was the St. Johns–Iberville district of the Province of Quebec. In the nineteenth century, industrial potting was concentrated there to an unusual degree, and it was the only area in Canada where whiteware for the table was manufactured on any important scale over a period of time. The directories list more potters working in Ontario than in Quebec during the second half of the century, but it is potters of St. Johns–Iberville who have a place that is unique in Canadian ceramic history. From them came the ironstone and white granite that entered into competition with imported wares, displacing them, at least to some extent, not only on family tables but in the dining rooms of Canadian hotels and on steamboats and trains. Yet whiteware potting did not burst upon St. Johns suddenly. It was the eventual development in an area where stoneware and brown and yellow earthenware had been made for years, and where those with ambitions beyond the usual scope of Canadian potting had worked and planned for the day when whiteware would be added to the output of the district.

The valley of the Richelieu had long been associated with potting in Lower Canada. In early days, however, the centre had been St. Denis-sur-Richelieu, some miles above St. Johns. Abbé J. B. A. Allaire, writing the history of the parish of St. Denis, in 1905, stressed that 'la première industrie qui a pris une certaine extension dans la localité est celle de la poterie.' At one time—'A son âge d'or, en 1837'—almost a score of potteries were in existence. But potting, as St. Denis-sur-Richelieu knew it, was a small-scale operation. The products were the coarse earthenware milk bowls, jugs, dishes of kitchen use, and crocks of all sizes ('des terrines, des cruches, des plats et des pots de toutes dimensions'). For the most part these simple wares came only from little one-potter establishments. In Abbé Allaire's words: 'Il n'y avait toutefois le plus souvent qu'un ouvrier par établissement.' These small, one-potter establishments gave way in the face of the growth of industrial potting at nearby St. Johns. It was, said Abbé Allaire, the rise of stoneware factories ('les grandes usines de grès') at St. Johns that administered the final 'coup de grâce' to potting in St. Denis.[1]

269

At St. Johns, then, and not at St. Denis, industrial potting gained its importance in the area. Stoneware, such as was made in the American potteries to the
south, was introduced. Whiteware, in imitation of the products of Staffordshire,
eventually followed. From small beginnings factories emerged to take the place
of the one-potter effort.

In St. Johns and Iberville (on the opposite shore of the Richelieu River) the
foundations of potting on a scale large enough to be considered industrialized
were laid by the Farrar family. The Farrars, of English origin but North Americans for two centuries, were the first potters of industrial ambition in St. Johns.
Bringing with them from Vermont the traditions of New England, they worked
in Canada for not far short of a hundred years. They were never particularly
prosperous, but their influence is not to be measured by the modest ratings given
them in *Mercantile Agency Reference Books*. It was in large measure the initiative
and persistence of these Vermont Yankees that drew to the district potters who
worked and failed and tried again, and, in Victorian times, succeeded in turning
the valley of the Richelieu into the nearest approximation Canada could offer
to Staffordshire.

The Eastern Townships Gazetteer for 1875-76 gives 1841 as the date for the
beginning of the Farrar business in St. Johns. A Farrar, however, was potting
in the area even earlier. By 1840 Moses Farrar was already established there.
In that year he made the substantial contribution of twenty-five dollars towards
the erection of the St. Johns Wesleyan Methodist Chapel. Two years later, in the
enumeration of Methodists in the 'Village of St. Johns', he was listed as the head
of a household of six.[2] This early Farrar set a pattern that succeeding members
of the family were to follow: they were generous contributors to the Methodist
Church, and for years supported the work in St. Johns. In the twentieth century
the last Farrar to be a potter in the Province of Quebec used to donate specially-
made miniature jugs, flower pots, and spittoons to Methodist fund-raising
bazaars.[3]

With the Farrars life sprang into the potting business in St. Johns. They came
imbued with a family tradition of potting, for Moses Farrar, potter of St. Johns,
Canada East, was in partnership with Ebenezer Lawrence Farrar, a son of old
Isaac Brown Farrar, potter of Fairfax, Vermont. The names of the partners
appear together on stoneware crocks and on brown-glazed jugs as E. L. & M.
FARRAR/ST. JOHNS, C. E.

It is possible that Moses Farrar was not only in partnership with a son of Isaac
Brown Farrar (1771-1838)[4] but was himself a son of Isaac. C. H. Chandler, listing,
in 1914, the members of this historic New England family, made clear that not
all of Isaac's many children could be traced, and his own account fails to include
another son, George Whitefield Farrar, who, after mid-nineteenth century, had
full charge of the Canadian business. The date of Moses' birth—about 1810,
according to the 1851 census taken in Canada East—would permit him to be
a son of Isaac, and in this connection it is, perhaps, significant that Moses Farrar
named his eldest son Isaac (a boy of sixteen in 1851). The name Moses, too, was
a family name: Isaac Brown Farrar's maternal grandfather was Moses Brown
of Beverly, Massachusetts.

Few families in the potting business in nineteenth-century Canada could claim

270

deeper roots in North America than the Farrars. Jacob Farrar (c. 1620-87) had emigrated to Massachusetts as early as 1653; his wife and four children, two of whom were to be killed by Indians, followed him shortly after. Isaac Brown Farrar was Jacob's great-great-great-grandson. His father was the celebrated 'Priest' Farrar—Rev. Stephen Farrar (1738-1809) of New Ipswich, New Hampshire, who had been a classmate at Harvard of John Adams, second president of the United States. 'Pastor Patriot Counsellor' was the way Stephen Farrar was remembered even a hundred years after his death.[5]

As a young man, Isaac Brown Farrar, Stephen's son, left New Hampshire and settled in Vermont. He was there at the time of his marriage in 1795 (to a daughter of Dr. Ebenezer Lawrence, of Pepperell, Massachusetts). After a few years in Enosburg, he moved to Fairfax, where his main potting activities were to be carried on. Family records in the possession of his Canadian descendants show that he was in Fairfax in the early years of the nineteenth century, and that it was in Fairfax that at least two of his sons, Stephen Hammond and George Whitefield Farrar, were born, the one in 1805, the other in 1812.

Just when he turned to potting is not known, but that he was a potter is clear from Canadian as well as American evidence. When Isaac Brown Farrar's grandson, George H. Farrar (George Whitefield Farrar's son), died in St. Johns in 1927, the St. Johns *News* pointed out that as a potter, George H. Farrar had been following not only in the steps of his father but of his Fairfax grandfather as well.[6]

With the Farrars the history of potting in St. Johns becomes bound up with the history of potting in Vermont; it is impossible to draw any clear line of demarcation between the Farrars' American and Canadian activities in the early years. Their story in Canada at this time has to be regarded as part of the fabric of American potting history. There was a constant mingling of business interests and a going back and forth across the border. They drew other American potters to Canada. A Ballard, for example, worked for a Farrar in St. Johns. His story is told in another chapter. Warren Soule, an American potter related to the Farrars by marriage, was associated with them in the first years. Together 'Farrar & Soule' won a prize for stoneware at an industrial exhibition held in Montreal in 1850.[7]

The partnership of Farrar & Soule was still in existence a year later, when Robert W. S. MacKay published his *Canada Directory*. At this stage it was probably Moses Farrar who was in partnership with Warren Soule (Moses Farrar's wife was Caroline Soule), but Moses soon after drops out of the Canadian picture. By the mid-1850's Ebenezer Lawrence Farrar, who, like Warren Soule, for a time worked in partnershp with Moses, was doing business in St. Johns under his own name alone. An advertisement in the St. Johns *News and Frontier Advocate* indicates this:

NOTICE

I RESPECTFULLY call the attention of my numerous customers to the fact that, not withstanding the conflagration on Sunday last that consumed my Potteries, I shall be able to furnish them with my

STONE WARE

as heretofore, early in the spring.

E. L. FARRAR.

St. Johns, Feb. 18, 1857.

It would be at this period that the salt-glazed crocks and jugs marked simply E. L. FARRAR/ST. JOHNS C. E. were made (*Plate* 42A), even though Ebenezer Lawrence Farrar was not, by any means, confining his business interests to Canada. During the whole period when he must be counted a Canadian potter, Ebenezer Lawrence Farrar was also active in Vermont. American gazetteers list him as a potter of both Fairfax and Burlington, and when he died unexpectedly in Canada, in the summer of 1857, Burlington, Vermont, was given as his address. Yet at the time of his death he was the senior partner in a Farrar business in St. Johns.

The new partnership was entered into in the spring of 1857, two months after fire had destroyed the pottery that Ebenezer Lawrence Farrar had operated under his own name. This time his partner was his brother, George Whitefield Farrar (1812-81). Earlier, George Whitefield Farrar had been potting in Fairfax, as old billheads show, but now his activities were transferred permanently to Canada. His was to be an important influence on potting in St. Johns. In April, 1857, the *News and Frontier Advocate* carried the announcement of the new firm:

NOTICE

WE, the undersigned, having RE-BUILT
the POTTERY burned on the 14th
February last, have formed a Co-Partner-
ship under the firm of E.L. & G.W. FAR-
RAR, to commence from this date, and are
now ready to furnish our STONE WARE to
customers as usual.

E. L. FARRAR,
G. W. FARRAR,

St. Johns, April 13, 1857.

Ebenezer was the senior partner; George was the partner resident in St. Johns. In a very brief time, however, George was destined to have the whole Canadian undertaking on his shoulders alone. Tragedy was just ahead for Ebenezer, though no one could have foreseen it when the brothers opened their new pottery in the spring of 1857, and confidently prepared to furnish 'STONE WARE . . . as usual'.

Until the early summer of 1857 all went well. The new pottery, risen from the ashes of the old one, was an imposing establishment. John H. Walker, the Montreal engraver, was commissioned to make a woodcut view of it which appeared on billheads, and later in the year was reproduced in a full-page advertisement in the *Canada Directory for 1857-58*. As Walker engraved it, the Farrar pottery in St. Johns bore the names 'E. L. & G. W. FARRAR' in large letters high on the face of the handsome building. But before the engraving was published in the directory (delivered to subscribers at the end of November, 1857), the joint names were outdated, and it was George Whitefield Farrar who signed the text of the accompanying advertisement. Ebenezer was dead.

Late in June, 1857, Ebenezer, accompanied by his brother Stephen Hammond Farrar, who was potting in Fairfax, made a business trip to Canada. Two of the best-known crockery merchants in Canada East had agreed to act as agents for Farrar pottery made in St. Johns. One of these dealers was John C. Watson, of

272

Lemoine Street, Montreal;[8] the other was Thomas Bickell, of the Upper Town, Quebec.[9] It was to see these agents that Ebenezer Lawrence Farrar undertook the trip. On June 26 he completed his business in Quebec with Thomas Bickell. That afternoon the two brothers, Ebenezer and Stephen, started back to Montreal. Less than twenty-four hours later Thomas Bickell was called upon to identify their bodies.

Ebenezer and Stephen Farrar perished in the St. Lawrence steamboat calamity that destroyed more than two hundred lives in a matter of minutes. They had taken passage aboard the *Montreal*, leaving Quebec at four o'clock on the afternoon of June 26. The steamboat that day was crowded with Irish, Scottish, and Norwegian immigrants, and some French-Canadian *voyageurs* (going up the river to bring back a timber raft). As the *Montreal* drew away from Quebec, the passengers light-heartedly watched the progress of a rival steamboat belonging to another line. It was maintained afterwards that the two boats were not racing and, therefore, were not forcing their engines; but they were certainly moving swiftly up the river in close company. Suddenly, when the *Montreal* was opposite Cap Rouge, there was a stir among the crew. Smoke was seen, and then great lashes of fire flayed the air above the boilers. Accounts later were confused; the painful facts were not: of almost three hundred passengers aboard the *Montreal* scarcely fifty lived. The Farrars were not among them. No one knows whether they died in the panic-stricken rush that carried away deck railings and dropped a struggling, writhing mass of passengers into deep water, whether they were overcome by the enveloping clouds of smoke and flames, or whether the current swept them under as they struck out for shore. All that is known is contained in the stark brevity of a coroner's count. On July 4, 1857, the Quebec *Morning Chronicle* carried an official list of the dead. Datelined June 30, it identified bodies examined by a coroner who had worked feverishly all that last unhappy week-end in June. The names of the Farrar brothers were among the first on the list:

BODIES EXAMINED ON SATURDAY [June 27]:

1. James McLaren, of Quebec, gaoler,—Body removed by his family.
2. Ebenezer Farrar, of Burlington, identified and removed by Mr. T. Bickell, of Quebec.
3. Stephen Farrar, of Fairfax, Vermont,—brother of No. 2, also removed.

It is left to the imagination to reconstruct the feeling of horror that must have rushed over Thomas Bickell when he heard the news of the disaster on the river. Word of it ran like the fire itself around Quebec on that summer evening. All night long, crowds huddled about the Queen's Wharf, where the first bodies brought in were laid in mournful rows. Bickell must have been down there at once, walking up and down between the rows, scanning the dead faces. All that was left for him to do now for the men with whom he had been talking potting business only hours before was to arrange for coffins in which to take them away.

In St. Johns, where word from Bickell extinguished any hope there might have been, George Whitefield Farrar was left to carry on. It was necessary to let the public know that he would do just that. Three weeks after the fatal fire on the St. Lawrence he had Bickell insert a notice in the *Quebec Mercury;* it indicated briefly that there would be stoneware in the future from G. W. Farrar working alone:

STONE - WARE

G. W. FARRAR, surviving partner of the
late firm of E. L. & G. W. F A R R A R ,
Manufacturer of Stone - Ware, St. John's
C.E.

THOMAS BICKELL,

Agent, Quebec, St. John Street,

July 21, 1857.

In *The Canada Directory*, published in November that year, George Whitefield Farrar's advertisement stressed again that he would continue at the 'old stand' in St. Johns. He made clear that he was manufacturing 'first quality' stoneware, and that he would keep on hand a number of items, including ginger-beer bottles, snuff jars, fire clay and sand, and Vermont flint enamelled ware.

The reference to Vermont flint enamelled ware is of special interest in view of the Farrars' Vermont background. Christopher Webber Fenton, of Bennington, Vermont, patented a process for applying colour to earthenware in 1849. Ware glazed by this method exhibited a characteristic streaking and mottling of colours that, in powdered form, had been sprinkled over the ware which had first been burned to a biscuit state and then dipped in a transparent glaze. In the subsequent firing in the glost oven, these colours, dusted on top of the glaze, were melted into it, so that they became a part of it. The popular name for this ware was 'Flint Enamelled Ware' (powdered flint was reported to give Bennington glazes brilliance and durability). The flecks and streaks of colour commonly seen were blue, green, yellow, or orange. Frequently the effect desired was simply that of a Rockingham (brown) glaze with flecks of colour through it. In spite of the patent, others copied 'Fenton's Enamel'. Stephen Hammond Farrar, of Fairfax, was one of those said to have made a 'good quality' flint enamelled ware.[10] George Whitefield Farrar, his brother, would also have known how to make it, although his advertisement in *The Canada Directory* does not actually state that he had necessarily made everything he had on hand. It should, perhaps, be noted that in the directory itself George Whitefield Farrar is listed as both a 'potter' and 'dealer' in stone and earthenware. His usual output was concentrated on the utilitarian stoneware advertised through Thomas Bickell in the *Quebec Mercury* that same autumn:

St. John's Stone-Ware

SOLD, wholesale, at Manufacturer's
Prices, by the Subscriber, who has just
received a fresh supply, consisting of
Liquor Jars, Cream Pots, Butter Pots, &c. &c.

THOMAS BICKELL,

Agent for G. W. Farrar,

St. John Street, Upper Town,

Quebec, Oct. 29, 1857.

274

This advertisement is important because of the association of the name St. Johns Stone Ware with that of George Whitefield Farrar. Many stoneware jugs and pots, in date belonging to the middle years of the nineteenth century and later, are marked only ST. JOHNS/STONE WARE. These, it would appear from Bickell's advertisement, may be assigned to the Farrar pottery, rather than to one of the several other stoneware potteries which opened in St. Johns in emulation of the Farrars' business. John Gillespie, for example, operated such a pottery. He advertised his ware as 'Canada Stone Ware',[11] possibly because the name 'St. Johns Stone Ware' had already been appropriated by the Farrars.

Ordinary brown-glazed or Rockingham ware also came from Farrar's pottery in the days before Confederation. There is a contemporary reference to this ware in the *Montreal Gazette* on September 23, 1863. In publishing the prize list for that year's provincial exhibition, the *Gazette* announced that the Farrar entries had won first prize for both 'Stone and Rockingham Ware'.[12]

In Vermont, Ebenezer and George Farrar had both produced stoneware and perhaps the common, dark-bodied earthenware. Their brother Stephen had had the same range of production. None of them, working in the United States, had aimed as high as whiteware. But in Canada, the brother who had been left to maintain the family tradition alone began to plan for a day when tableware from fine clays that burned white in the kiln would emanate from St. Johns. That day arrived, and he had a part in bringing it about, although he never shared in the profits which finally came.

The whiteware was made at a new pottery, founded in 1873, and operated by the St. Johns Stone Chinaware Company. This new pottery was the first and almost the only successful producer of tableware in nineteenth-century Canada. The financial backing of Edward and Duncan Macdonald, private bankers, established the company on a solid basis. The Macdonalds, however, were financiers, not potters. The idea of manufacturing whiteware in St. Johns originated not with the Macdonalds, but with men who had handled clay, and of these men, George Whitefield Farrar was chief. At the time of his death, in 1881, the St. Johns *News* gave him the credit that was his due, when it said: 'Mr. Farrar . . . was undoubtedly the promoter of the St. Johns Stone Chinaware . . . factory, which is at present doing such a large and flourishing business, and as he was but a short time connected with the concern, its lack of success at the outset cannot certainly be laid to his charge.[13]

The history of the St. Johns Stone Chinaware Company is told in the next chapter. What caused its shaky start belongs in that account, but what is important to the story of the Farrars is that it was George Whitefield Farrar who had a vision of something more ambitious than anything ever before attempted in Canada. He did not give up his own stoneware and Rockingham factory—that continued all the while—but he 'promoted' the idea of whiteware for St. Johns. In Farrar's potting career his connection with the St. Johns Stone Chinaware Company was only a brief interlude; it was not for him to carry this type of earthenware into successful production. But undoubtedly, at the outset, he gave direction to a bold plan that put Canadian potting on a new level.

By the time that George Whitefield Farrar became interested in the new Stone Chinaware Company, his sons had assumed many of the burdens of his own

275

pottery. These sons, all born in Fairfax, were George H. (*Plate* 42B), Lucius E., and another Ebenezer L. ('Eben') Farrar (*Plate* 43A). The eldest, George H. (born in 1843), took charge of his father's pottery when he was still in his twenties. By 1871 the business style of the firm was in the name of George H. and Lucius E. Farrar.[14] What this second generation of Farrars potting in Canada was producing is indicated in an advertisement of 1875:

G. H. & L. E. FARRAR,
MANUFACTURERS OF
Stone, Yellow & Rockingham Ware,
AND ALL KINDS OF
FIRE CLAY LININGS FOR STOVES AND RANGES.
ALSO DEALERS IN
BEST NEW JERSEY FIRE CLAY & SAND,
ST. JOHNS, P.Q.
Orders Promptly attended to.[15]

To produce this 'Stone, Yellow & Rockingham Ware' steam power had been installed in the Farrar pottery, and forty employees were on the payroll.[16]

During all these years the Farrars had potted in St. Johns. They were shortly to move across the Richelieu River to Iberville. The reason for the move was a fire that gutted the pottery in the autumn of 1876.[17] It was ironic that the Farrars should lose their pottery that autumn, for they had escaped the devastating fire that blazed through St. Johns in June, levelling nearly the whole business district and making the town 'one picture of desolation'.[18] In June the Farrars must have congratulated themselves; less than six months later they, too, were burned out.

For a few years after the move to Iberville the business style of the firm continued as George H. & Lucius E. Farrar. It was under this style that specimens of their work were exhibited at Philadelphia in 1876, and at Paris in 1878. Later in the century the firm operated under the name of E. L. Farrar, the youngest brother. *The Eastern Townships Business & Farmers Directory for 1888-89* lists the 'earthenware factory' in E. L. Farrar's name. The *Dominion of Canada and Newfoundland Gazetteer* was still recording it that way in 1919, although 'Eben' had been drowned in the Richelieu River the summer before.

But though the pottery might be officially listed in the name of one or more members of the family, all the Farrars had a part in it. George Whitefield Farrar, for example, was not named in the directories as the owner of or even as a partner in the Farrar pottery during the last years of his life, yet he was concerned with it. His obituary, in January, 1881, makes this clear: 'At the time of his death Mr. Farrar was interested in a flourishing pottery in Iberville'. Lucius E. Farrar did eventually drop out of the business, but George H. and 'Eben' never did; they remained with it to the end of their working days, and even though the firm was long listed in 'Eben's' name alone, George H. Farrar was at all times a dominant force in it. It was he who would see the Farrar pottery through to the end.

At no time were the Farrars operating on an estimated capital of more than a few thousand dollars. In the *Mercantile Agency Reference Books* for the years after Confederation the estimated capital of their business ranged from under

$2,000 to a brief maximum of $10,000, and their credit rating from 'Fair' to 'Good' and back to 'Fair'. In this the Farrars were no different from most of the other stone and common earthenware makers. A total capital of $2,000-$5,000 was average, and this almost always implied a credit that was rated at 'Fair', the lowest category. Yet during these years the Farrars not only operated a pottery in either St. Johns or Iberville, they frequently maintained a warehouse in Montreal. A new billhead, engraved by J. H. Walker after G. H. & L. E. Farrar had taken over the business, gives the name of the pottery as the St. Johns Stone, Rockingham and Yellow Ware Factory, and adds the information that there was a warehouse at No. 26 St. Henry Street, Montreal (*Plate* 43B).

The warehouse on St. Henry Street was rented in the name of Louis Deneau,[19] who, during a period in the 1870's and 1880's, acted as the Farrars' agent in Montreal. Before Deneau brushed up the premises for the crocks and jars from the Farrar pottery, No. 26 St. Henry Street had been occupied for business by a horse dealer.[20] The connection between Louis Deneau and the Farrars resulted at one time in a firm known as Farrar & Deneau, Stoneware & Crockery. In 1876 Farrar & Deneau were operating a retail establishment in the city. [21] Later, after this partnership was terminated, Deneau used to advertise that his china, glass, and earthenware house was the 'Depot for St. Johns and Cornwall Stoneware'. An advertisement with this information appeared in *Lovell's Montreal Directory for 1883-84*.[22] By this time, of course, the Farrars were actually potting in Iberville, but their stoneware was often spoken of by the old name of St. Johns.

There is no evidence that the Farrars ever made any whiteware commercially at their own establishment. Their connection with this branch of potting lies in the fact that George Whitefield Farrar was a moving spirit behind the formation of the St. Johns Stone Chinaware Company, even though 'he was but a short time connected with the concern'. The contemporary evidence shows that what the Farrars produced commercially at their own potteries was stoneware and common earthenware.

Because it formed the chief part of their output, and because they marked much of it over the years, their stoneware is best known today. Frequently this stoneware is decorated in blue. On the early crocks and jugs made by E. L. & M. Farrar the blue decoration is often very faint and is naive in spirit. Wares belonging to the mid-1850's, and made at the pottery operated by Ebenezer Lawrence Farrar alone, may have floral decoration that is neat and tight. This is quite unlike the free sprawling blue on wares marked ST. JOHNS/STONE WARE, or G. W. FARRAR/ST. JOHNS, belonging in the main to the 1860's. End-of-the-century pieces sometimes have very simple designs—a quick clover leaf or a swirl of blue—put on by George William Farrar, 'Eben' Farrar's only son, who worked at the pottery when he was boy, and who, in later years, recounted to his children how he had put the blue on the pots when he 'was still in short pants'. (This rudimentary artistic work was a prelude to his future career, for George William Farrar left home at an early age to become a china decorator at Cassidy's crockery emporium in Montreal.)[23]

The wares produced by the Farrars in the last years of the nineteenth century and the first years of the twentieth have a variety of markings. The names G. H. & L. E. FARRAR appear on many, often with the St. Henry Street address in Montreal, or with the address, NO. 9 WILLIAM STREET/MONTREAL (another location of the warehouse). Very occasionally FARRAR & DENEAU is found impressed on stoneware. Pieces with this mark belong to the mid-1870's. Before the fire of 1876 the Farrar products were usually marked ST. JOHNS, whether or not a Montreal warehouse address was also included; IBERVILLE, P.Q. took its place after the move. From the 1880's E. L. FARRAR/IBERVILLE, P.Q. became the standard mark (*Plate* 44A); sometimes this was abbreviated to a simple E L F. Another late form of the mark occurs as E. L. FARRAR/POTTERY WORKS/IBERVILLE.

All the marks were impressed on articles of stoneware or on the lead-glazed wares which were fired at a lower temperature than the blue-decorated stoneware. The impressed marks have been noted on crocks, jars, pitchers, spittoons, bean pots, churns, cream pots, pickle jars, milk pans, jardinières, and the occasional umbrella stand. On sample wares, made in miniature, the mark was sometimes painted in black on the bottom of the piece. A sample wine jug, approximately three inches in height, in the possession of Mrs. Lottie Farrar de Bellefeuille, grand-daughter of 'Eben' Farrar, bears the black-painted identification: POTTERIES/FARRAR/IBERVILLE/1886. Samples appear to have been made of all the regular productions, for Mrs. de Bellefeuille remembers how, in the last years of the pottery, rows of samples used to be displayed in the office window in Iberville. Other members of her family possess sample churns and bean pots. Mrs. Effie Farrar Sutherland, daughter of George H. Farrar, has a brown-glazed miniature spittoon, three inches in diameter.

In addition to the stoneware, as the evidence has shown, Rockingham and yellow wares were made by the Farrars. Since others, notably in later years Elijah Bowler and Charles E. Pearson,[24] made both Rockingham and yellow wares in either St. Johns or Iberville, it is not possible to be certain who was responsible for all the wares of this type with the impressed mark ST. JOHNS POTTERY. There is, however, a strong case to be made for the Farrars, especially in view of the fact that some of these wares would seem to belong to the earlier days of George Whitefield Farrar, before either Bowler or Pearson was active. A large jug, long on loan to the Montreal Museum of Fine Arts from the collection of Paul Gouin, supports this theory. Octagonal in shape, with moulded decoration of vine leaves and grapes, and covered with a dark brown glaze over a buff body, this jug is marked ST. JOHNS POTTERY. In style and spirit it suggests the middle years of the century, when George Whitefield Farrar was winning prizes for his Rockingham ware, and when neither Elijah Bowler nor Charles E. Pearson was a master potter in the area. At this period only at the Farrar pottery could a jug requiring such proficiency have been produced.

Again, with reference to the Farrars, it is pertinent that G. H. & L. E. Farrar sometimes used the name St. Johns Pottery Works. It was under this title that their entry was catalogued at the Paris Universal Exhibition of 1878, even though their Works were then in Iberville. They also continued to use the name St. Johns Stone, Rockingham and Yellow Ware Factory after the move to Iberville, as a new billhead of this period shows. Rockingham or yellow wares marked ST. JOHNS and mid-Victorian to late Victorian in style need not, therefore, be denied a Farrar origin simply because the Works were, by that time, in Iberville.

Difficult as it is to be definite about the attribution of certain marked pieces, it is virtually impossible to assign an unmarked piece to any particular St. Johns factory, unless the history of the piece can be known beyond any doubt, and this can only rarely be the case. Two small jugs, partly brown-glazed, in the possession of George H. Farrar's daughter, may be accepted as having been made at her father's pottery, but were these jugs to be separated from their family connections, and their story lost, they would present problems in attribution that would baffle anyone aware of the pitfalls.

The interest of the Farrar history, however, reaches beyond the tentative identification of pieces which may or may not have come from their potteries. It is far more a consciousness of the stirrings of an industry that came to St. Johns with the sons and grandsons of Isaac Brown Farrar of Vermont. The lot of the Farrars in Canada was no easy one. The writer of George Whitefield Farrar's obituary pointed out that he had 'encountered many difficulties in this country'. At the beginning it was uphill work for these Americans to get started in a new environment, even though it was an environment with long pottery associations; in the end it was a losing battle against mechanization in an age that had a dwindling place for the small factory. Just as the one-potter establishments of St. Denis had been supplanted by the stoneware factories of St. Johns, so these same factories in their turn gave up an unequal struggle.

George H. Farrar, who outlived his younger brothers, was the last member of his family to be a potter in 'the Staffordshire of Canada'; of him it is still possible to gather first-hand information. His daughter and his son-in-law recall that he imported his stoneware clay from New Jersey (as his father had done); that he had a foreman named Andrew Greendale, 'on whom he could depend for almost anything'; that he fired by slabs, and that there were stokers working round the clock when the ware was in the kiln; that, however, he had those troubles with firing that plagued most Canadian potters, and that he hired a new hand who swore he knew all there was to know about firing—'but ah, it was no better'.

There are memories of how deliveries were made—in a great box sleigh in winter. It was 'a red letter day' for the Farrar children when there were wares to go to a customer in Chambly. If it was not too cold, the children were allowed to skip school and make the trip with the stoneware. Suitably mittened and wrapped, and sternly warned to keep their feet from shattering crocks and jars packed in straw, they would chant in time with the sleigh bells, as the potter's ware went racing over the snowy roads of a Canadian winter.

But there are also memories of anxieties. What the potter had to sell was a breakable product, and George H. Farrar's wife, in her house by the pottery, would listen with apprehension to catch any sound of pots banging upon pots as a shipment was loaded—'the customers won't take them if they are damaged'.

A quiet memory is that of the nightly round to see that all was locked up at the pottery. To his daughter, George H. Farrar would say, 'Come, let us go and see that all is safe at the pottery.' Together they would walk through the silent rooms, where shadows cast weird shapes upon the walls, and pots, drying in rows, suddenly swelled to mammoth size before quivering back into the darkness. An old cat, devoted to her master, always made the rounds with the potter. She would go running ahead of him, occasionally leaping upon a table or a shelf to wait silently until he had gone by, and then would slink past him again into the blackness.

As George H. Farrar approached his last years he repeatedly expressed the wish to go back to Fairfax to see the house where he was born, the son and grandson of potters. On a fine, sunny day, as he neared the age of eighty, his daughter took him. And his experience matched that of many who have made a pilgrimage to the scenes of childhood. He saw Fairfax, Vermont, again, and the house where he was born, but what had seemed of heroic size in the days of childhood turned out to be less than was remembered. Fairfax was 'just a little place'.

About two years before he died George H. Farrar sold the pottery.[25] He himself had chosen to follow his father and grandfather into the potting business, but for the next generation of Farrars, potting in St. Johns in the twentieth century had had a clouded prospect. 'Eben' Farrar's only son had found in china decorating and not in potting work that satisfied him;[26] one of George H. Farrar's two sons had died early, the other, Lawrence, was never a potter. With the death of George H. Farrar, on February 5, 1927,[27] the link between the potting traditions of New England and 'the Staffordshire of Canada' was broken. He was, as the St. Johns *News* said of him, 'the last of the Old Guard'.

CHAPTER XXIII

The St. Johns Stone Chinaware Company

... the now well-known St. John's Chinaware Factory ...
is to-day the largest of the kind in the Dominion.
Rose's *Cyclopaedia of Canadian Biography*, 1888.

The most important nineteenth-century pottery in Canada was the St. Johns Stone Chinaware Company. It was the first and only really successful producer of tableware in the country. It was, in fact, the only whiteware factory that managed to stay in existence for any length of time. Founded in 1873, the St. Johns Stone Chinaware Company lasted for a quarter of a century. At one period it employed as many as four hundred workers,[1] it had a credit rating that was 'High', and a total capital estimated at a possible $150,000.[2] To achieve this ceramic miracle in Canada the financial resources of a pair of rich brothers—merchants and private bankers—provided the essential backing. It was this strong backing, combined with the shrewd judgment of experienced business-men, that lifted a faltering and failing company to an extraordinary level of suc-cessful production for a Canadian pottery.

The story of the St. Johns Stone Chinaware Company begins with the Farrars. The evidence of George Whitefield Farrar's obituary in 1881 makes clear that he was the 'promoter' of the adventurous undertaking. This Vermont potter, born to the handling of clay, had a vision of St. Johns as a centre for the manufacture of whiteware in Canada. The result of his aspirations was the formation of a com-pany to bring a whiteware factory into being. To launch the company money had to be found. Fifty thousand dollars was the initial capital,[3] and for at least part of this large amount those who were starting something new in the Province of Quebec turned to the firm of E. and D. Macdonald.

The Macdonalds of St. Johns, Edward C. and Duncan, were remembered years afterwards by one resident of the town as 'the merchant princes of St. Johns'.[4] In *Mercantile Agency Reference Books* they were variously described as 'Speculators', 'Merchants', and 'Private Bankers'. That they put up capital to help found the St. Johns Stone Chinaware Company in 1873 is evident from the fact that even before they came to own it outright, Edward Macdonald was the president of the Company. An advertisement published in 1875, when the pottery had been in operation less than two years, furnishes proof of this:

ST JOHNS STONE CHINAWARE COMPANY,
ST. JOHNS, P.Q., MANUFACTURERS OF
White Granite, French Pearl, Plumbers' Ware, &c., &c.
ED. MACDONALD, President.
A. K. LAVICOUNT, Secretary.
WM. LIVESLEY, Manager.

Accompanying this advertisement, in the *Eastern Townships Gazetteer & Directory for the Years 1875-76*, was a picture of the plant. The title of the company, ST. JOHNS STONE CHINAWARE COMPANY, and the name DOMINION POTTERY both appeared on the face of the building. The building itself, set on the opposite side of St. George Street to the Farrars' own Stone, Rockingham and Yellow Ware Factory, was impressive in size. Impressive, too, was the fact that at this early stage '200 hands' were said to be employed in it.[5]

But even at this moment, when the St. Johns Stone Chinaware Company was employing two hundred persons and promoting its products in advertisements that pictured smoke belching from busy kilns, the Company was floundering in a morass of financial troubles. Every contemporary source speaks of the difficulties of these first years. George Whitefield Farrar's obituary referred to them while exonerating him from blame: 'He was undoubtedly the promoter of the St. Johns Chinaware . . . factory . . . and as he was but a short time connected with the concern, its lack of success at the outset cannot be laid to his charge.'[6]

When Edward C. Macdonald died in his turn, on January 25, 1889, the St. Johns *News* published a long obituary notice of him, and once again harked back to the 'series of vicissitudes' through which the Stone Chinaware Company passed during its hesitant beginning. It remained, however, for an expert on Canadian business affairs to sum up succinctly the disheartening start of whiteware potting in St. Johns. William Wickliffe Johnson, manager of the Mercantile Agency's Montreal office, said simply: 'The Company did not prove a success.'[7]

Four years after its inauguration this pioneer manufactory for the making of tableware in Canada faced complete disaster. What was being produced by it was of good enough quality to compete with certain imported wares, but its financial structure was in collapse. William Wickliffe Johnson blamed the situation on 'expensive management', and on 'a want of knowledge of the detail of the business'.[8] Whatever the reason, the future of the industry hung in the balance. It was at this point that the Macdonalds took over.

That both Edward and Duncan Macdonald were involved in the transaction would seem to be clear. Edward Macdonald's obituary stated that the Company was 'bought in' by him at this time, so that he switched from 'president' to 'proprietor'. Duncan Macdonald's notice in Rose's *Cyclopaedia of Canadian Biography*, written while Edward was still alive, was equally emphatic in asserting that it was Duncan who 'entered into the manufacture of stone chinaware'.[9] What the brothers had done was to embark on another joint enterprise, in this case one in which Edward was to have the title of 'proprietor', but in which both

282

brothers had a concern. Together they threw their money and their brains behind the task of making Macdonald's Canadian tableware pay. William Wickliffe Johnson took another look at the St. Johns Stone Chinaware Company and what he saw this time was an improvement: 'in 1877, it passed into private hands, since which time the business has been prosecuted with vigour and more satisfactory results.'[10]

A year after the Macdonalds had become the owners of the St. Johns Stone Chinaware Company a Governor-General visited the pottery. When the St. Johns *News* described the viceregal visit it echoed William Wickliffe Johnson's words: 'This industry, which has seen some trying times, is now prospering under the new management, and bids fair in a few years to become one of the largest factories on the continent.'[11]

The Earl of Dufferin arrived in St. Johns by train on an August afternoon in 1878. With his wife by his side, he was greeted by the principal residents. These included Edward Macdonald, the 'proprietor' of the St. Johns Stone Chinaware Company. Following the official presentations, the Governor-General and Lady Dufferin were driven through the streets, passing under arches from which flew banners welcoming 'Lord Dufferin, Canada's Pride' in English, French, and Irish (the last a compliment to the land of the Governor-General's ancestors). Along the route the Governor-General paused to inspect public buildings—the fire station and a church—then he was driven to the St. Johns Stone Chinaware factory at the corner of St. George and Grant Streets. Edward Macdonald was waiting to conduct him through the entire plant, explaining every 'process of crockery making' as it was being carried out at Canada's first whiteware pottery. At the end of the tour of inspection Lady Dufferin was asked to accept 'a cup and saucer and plate of china made at the factory', while the Governor-General was thanked in both English and French for his encouragement of an infant industry: 'Merci donc, mille fois merci au nom de tous les ouvriers de cette manufacture de ce que Votre Excellence a voulu venir encourager nos travaux.'

The account of this viceregal visit in the St. Johns *News* of August 23, 1878, is important, not only for the interest of the visit itself, but for the information that it contains on the state of the Company at a period when it was just beginning to emerge from its sea of troubles. With the new ownership had come a new manager. William Livesley was gone, and in his place was a man named McLaughlin, brought in by the Macdonalds. The work of the factory was now being carried on by '120 operatives' (as compared to the '200 hands' employed during the days when 'expensive management' was blamed for the Company's financial difficulties). Most significant of all was the statement that of the 120 workers 'more than half' were said to be 'English, from Staffordshire, the rest being French Canadians'.

'The mark of the Staffordshire potter is everywhere', so wrote the ceramic historians G. W. and F. A. Rhead.[12] It was even to be found in St. Johns in the Province of Quebec, though the potting industry there owed its initial impulse to Yankees from Vermont.

The St. Johns Stone Chinaware Company had been formed in the first place to produce whitewares—the same kind of white granite, ironstone, and stone chinaware Staffordshire was exporting to Canada. At the big pottery on St.

George Street the main output was of plain, sturdy, cheap table and toiletware that not only competed with the imported article in quality and price, but offered many of the same patterns. Wares which have survived in some quantity show that the St. Johns Stone Chinaware Company produced a wheat pattern in white tableware identical with that made by several Staffordshire firms. A fluted pattern turns up with the St. Johns mark, or, again, with a Staffordshire mark. A St. Johns pattern with moulded decoration of leaves and berries is indistinguishable from that made by potters working in England at the same period. The absolutely plain white ware, hard and smoothly glazed, made at St. Johns can be identified as Canadian only when marked.

Staffordshire's influence on St. Johns was first of all in the very nature of the goods produced: the white ironstone, French pearl, white granite, and stone china that were the plebian off-spring of the tough stone and ironstone chinas made famous long before by Josiah Spode and Charles James Mason. From Staffordshire came the tradition of the ware itself, from Staffordshire came many of the actual patterns and shapes into which this ware was fashioned at St. Johns, and from Staffordshire came 'more than half' the workmen who made the ware successfully in Canada.

The greatest output was undoubtedly in whiteware unrelieved by colour (*Plate* 45A), but St. Johns was also able to advertised decorated ware in every variety.[13] The evidence of what has survived shows that decoration often took the form of broad bands of enamel colour, the broad bands generally being set off by narrow lines in a contrasting tone, or in gold. In the gold, two qualities were used: a fine matt gold, and the cheap, brassy gold common to inexpensive wares of the period. The colours usually seen on St. Johns stone chinaware include a soft French pink, a lively maroon, a bright lavender, a fresh jade green, a darker green, and a biscuit colour. Sometimes these are accompanied by touches of black. Occasionally silver lustre appears on handles and rims.[14]

On some table crockery the decoration consists of small rosettes in gold sprinkled over the surface of the ware. At other times flowers, butterflies, and insects in natural colours appear on table and toilet ware in which the additional moulded decoration has been further embellished with colour. Pink and azure blue were frequently used to ornament moulded frills and ribbons.

At St. Johns large circular plaques were made to hang on the wall.[15] These are sometimes found with landscapes painted on them. Possibly some of this work was done at the factory itself, as part of the decorated ware in every variety advertised in 1879. It is obvious, however, that such plaques must also have been sold in the white to amateur artists. A fair amount of St. Johns stone china bears evidence of the craze for china painting which held Victorian women in its spell.

In addition to plaques, the ornaments produced at St. Johns included small pitchers, flower vases, and toy ware. An eyewitness describing the Stone Chinaware Company's display at the Dominion Exhibition in 1880 emphasized that the examples on view comprised 'all grades from the common delf to the exquisitely painted services and ornaments'.[16] When the Marquis of Lorne, Governor-General at that time, stopped at the Company's booth a few days later it was not ornamental ware, however, that he ordered, but practical 'sets of different kinds'.[17]

The St. Johns Stone Chinaware Company

Advertisements show that decorated ware in a choice of styles was part of the regular output at St. Johns. But decorating might also be done to special order, as advertised in 1888:

ST. JOHNS
Stone Chinaware Company
MANUFACTURERS OF
WHITE GRANITE AND C C GOODS,
COMPRISING FULL LINES OF
TABLE AND TOILET WARE,
Decorating done to order. Telephone No. 35.[18]

This special decorating was executed to the order of both individuals and companies, such as hotel and steamboat companies. A Montreal collector, for example, has a large ice-water pitcher in white stone china. It is ornamented with a broad pink band and painted in gold with the initials of the person for whom it was specially decorated. Another collector has several articles of table and toilet ware each with the name of the particular hotel for which it was originally made.

Hotel ware was an important feature of St. Johns production. From its first days the Stone Chinaware Company made a determined effort to compete with imported wares in the field of hotel, steamboat, and railway supplies. Its heavy, durable crockery was particularly suited to this market, and the Company was prepared to meet Staffordshire in furnishing such wares complete with names or crests.

Existing pieces show that St. Johns was successful in bringing in orders of this kind from widely separated parts of the country. A large milk or water pitcher has survived to show that the Lorne House, a resort hotel at Murray Bay on the lower St. Lawrence, was one that patronized the Canadian pottery. For the Lorne House the St. Johns Stone Chinaware Company made white granite wares decorated with a black-printed device incorporating the name of the hotel and the name of Chamard & Co., its owners. Earlier the St. Johns factory had secured an order from Cobourg, miles away on Lake Ontario. For Thomas Connor's Windsor Hotel in Cobourg it made a heavy ironstone decorated in sparkling green and gold; printed in a reddish brown on the face of each piece was Connor's name and the name of his establishment. A large slop jar remaining from this order (*Plate* 45B) is identical in mould with a J. & G. Meakin production of the period, another instance of a borrowing from Staffordshire by St. Johns. In the case of both the slop jar made for the Windsor Hotel in Cobourg and the pitcher turned out for the Lorne House in Murray Bay the printing of the identifying device is over the glaze.

The Windsor Hotel slop jar is of particular interest, since it can be dated within five years. White ironstone was not made at St. Johns until 1873, when the first company in Canada for its production was organized. In 1878 the Windsor Hotel in Cobourg was burned down in a spectacular fire;[19] Thomas Connor never opened it again under that name. Thus the slop jar is a product of a well-defined period. Unless it came from an order that had not yet been shipped to Ontario

285

before the fire took place, the jar would also seem to be a survivor of one of the calamities of 1878. When the Windsor Hotel was destroyed that spring it took with it three volunteer firemen, whose lives were crushed out when the front wall of the building suddenly fell upon them. The fire chief on that melancholy occasion was none other than Thomas Connor himself, whose name was printed on the wares made for the blazing hotel by potters in St. Johns.

So important was the hotel, steamboat, and railway supply business to St. Johns that the Company advertised itself as 'specialists' in this class of crockery.[20] The *Gazette* of Montreal praised its wares of this type as 'handsome' and 'extra heavy'.[21] That a company which was established only in 1873 as the pioneer producer of whiteware in Canada, and which spent its first years struggling through 'vicissitudes' and 'trying times' should have, even in those same first troubled years, challenged to any extent the experienced overseas makers of this class of industrial whiteware was in itself a triumph. It is a triumph to which the well-potted jar bearing the name of the old Windsor Hotel in Cobourg is witness.

Another type of St. Johns ware of special interest, and one which was first produced at an early date, is the tableware in the characteristic 'St. Johns blue'. An item in the *Gazette* indicates that St. Johns had this ware on the market in 1879. On September 13 that year the *Gazette* described for its readers what the Stone Chinaware Company was then showing at the provincial exhibition in Toronto. In its 'fine assortment . . . displayed with great taste' the pottery was exhibiting 'a new style' in dinner and tea ware. This 'new style' was ware in a distinctive shade of blue. The effect was obtained by colouring the body of the ware itself.

St. Johns blue varies in intensity, but it is generally a compelling colour, reminiscent of the famous Herez blue of the Persian carpet weaver. Frequently the raised decoration on the blue ware is composed of floral sprigs, standing out in white against the startling blue background (*Plate* 46A). In certain blue wares in several Montreal collections one of the white sprigs on each piece has been replaced by what may have been intended as a monogram. This raised device in white appears to combine the initial 'V' with the initial 'I' (J?). A bread tray (*Plate* 47A) has this unusual St. Johns decoration. An ambitious effort, the tray was modelled with a rolled rim and ornamental handles, and, in addition to the raised decoration in white, features sheaves of wheat and the words WASTE NOT WANT NOT on a ribbon. In execution, this competent piece from St. Johns compares not too unfavourably with similar Victorian bread trays in stone china from such important factories as those of Copeland and Davenport. It was clearly inspired by a Staffordshire model, and in the St. Johns factory it may well have been made by Staffordshire workmen employed by the Macdonalds.

As well as tea, dinner, and toilet ware, dolls' sets, in both blue and plain white, were made at St. Johns. So, too, was dessert ware, including leaf-shaped dishes and footed centrepieces. Kitchen bowls in graduated sizes were turned out in a variety of moulded patterns. Large and small strainers, milk pans, and other items connected with the dairy were part of the factory's output, in either heavy stone china or in lighter weights of 'C C and White Granite'. For the conservatory there were huge jardinières, and plant holders in regular flower-pot shape but made of whiteware (*Plate* 47B). The sickroom was supplied with stone china feeders and bed pans.[22]

On all these wares the St. Johns Stone Chinaware Company put its printed mark. This mark was generally in black, though occasionally, in the later days, it was printed in brown. Usually, though not always, the mark included the Royal Arms in some form (*Plate* 49A). Whether or not the company 'promoted' by George Whitefield Farrar for the making of whiteware adopted the name St. Johns Stone Chinaware Company at the outset, this was the name by which it was known in a very short time, and which became part of the printed mark. The place name, ST. JOHNS, was generally added underneath the Royal Arms, and might or might not be accompanied by P.Q. or QUE. The omission of P.Q. or QUE. has no significance, however, in setting a date before Confederation, as has sometimes been thought, for the simple reason that there was no whiteware factory in St. Johns until Confederation was six years old.

Proof that there was no whiteware factory in St. Johns before Confederation does not rest solely on 1873 as the date for the founding of the St. Johns Stone Chinaware Company. Other contemporary material bears out the claim that until the Stone Chinaware Company opened, whiteware was not made in St. Johns by anyone. The directories, for instance, list only stone, Rockingham, and yellow ware potters in St. Johns prior to and immediately following Confederation. The *Eastern Townships Gazetteer and General Business Directory* for 1867, the year of Confederation, makes no mention of whiteware potting in St. Johns and gives Farrar only as a 'manufacturer of stoneware'. Similarly, Lovell's *Canadian Dominion Directory for 1871* lists no makers of whiteware in St. Johns, and again names the Farrars as manufacturers of 'stone and Rockingham' ware. Finally, William Wickliffe Johnson was emphatic in stating that until the St. Johns Stone Chinaware Company was organized in 1873 no pottery in Canada had been engaged in the manufacture of white tableware.[23] It is, therefore, obvious that whether or not P.Q. or QUE. appears after ST. JOHNS on the back of a piece of whiteware, that piece was produced well after the date of Confederation.

There remains to be explained the mark IRONSTONE CHINA/ST. JOHNS, P.Q. (*Plate* 49A). This was a mark used from an early date by the St. Johns Stone Chinaware Company itself. It is found on a number of the same patterns that also appear marked in the more usual way with the name of the Stone Chinaware Company, and it is known on pieces made in St. Johns when the Company was still the only whiteware manufactory in the district. The slop jar made for the Windsor Hotel in Cobourg, which has this mark, is an example. The jar must have been ordered before the Windsor Hotel burned down in the spring of 1878, yet at that time only the Stone Chinaware Company would have been capable of producing ware of this kind and quality in St. Johns. Again contemporary sources provide the evidence. At the end of 1876, for instance, the *Gazette*, anticipating the opening of the West End Dresden Pottery, near Montreal, early in the New Year, stated that it would be only the second manufactory for whiteware in the Dominion.[24] Clearly at that time there was not in St. Johns a rival to the Stone Chinaware Company. In 1879, when the *County of Missisquoi and Town of St. Johns Directory* was published by John Lovell, there was still only one whiteware pottery listed in St. Johns, the St. Johns Stone Chinaware

Company. The slop jar made for the Windsor Hotel in Cobourg, and marked with the Royal Arms and IRONSTONE CHINA/ST. JOHNS, P.Q. must, therefore, have been a product of the company known as the St. Johns Stone Chinaware Company. It could have come from no other pottery, and it furnishes proof that the IRONSTONE CHINA mark was used by it.

According to its own advertisements, the St. Johns Stone Chinaware Company 'chiefly' manufactured white earthenware of various grades—ironstone, stone china, white granite, pearl china, and C.C. ware. Possibly experiments in porcelain were carried out, although the words 'china' and 'porcelain' when used in connection with St. Johns products are not to be taken as proof. 'China', for St. Johns, was stone china, and 'porcelain', as the Victorian potters sometimes used the term, could be just another name for the same earthenware body. (One of the Stone Chinaware Company's later rivals in St. Johns manufactured a hard earthenware which it called 'British Porcelain'.) It would be unwise now to try to define arbitrarily what was meant by 'stoneware, china, and porcelain goods of capital finish and quality' displayed by the St. Johns Stone Chinaware Company at the Dominion Exhibition of 1880.[25] It is easier by far to ascertain the names of the types of ware manufactured by nineteenth-century Canadian potters than to arrive at correct definitions of those wares, not only in terms of their own day, but in terms of their precise meaning in any particular listing. The clue, however, to the nature of these wares shown in 1880 is to be found in William Wickliffe Johnson's statement, two years later, that china (or porcelain) in the usual sense was not made commercially anywhere in Canada.[26]

While it is of interest to know the full reach of the St. Johns Stone Chinaware Company, its importance is accounted for by the great volume of heavy, white earthenware which emerged from its kilns. It was the successful production of this earthenware that in time brought the credit rating of the firm to a satisfactory level, and kept it there. It was this ware that made it possible for a Canadian pottery to enter into real, if necessarily limited competition with the English makers of earthenware for the table.

In 1874 the St. Johns Stone Chinaware Company was still too new or too uncertain to be given a rating in the *Mercantile Agency Reference Book* for the beginning of that year. The Company was listed, but following its name there was a blank. 'The absence of a Rating,' said the Agency, 'indicates those whose business and investments render it difficult to rate them satisfactorily to ourselves. We therefore prefer, in justice to these to give our detailed report on Record at our offices.' By 1881, after less than four years of Macdonald ownership, there was no doubt about the Company's standing. That year the total capital of the Company was estimated at up to $150,000. General credit was 'High'. A decade later the figures were equally gratifying. While the Company's improved status is certainly accounted for in part by the Macdonalds' own credit, there is no doubt that the volume of sales in white granite and stone china also had a significant role.

To keep up with the demand for these wares, the Macdonalds had to enlarge the pottery in St. Johns. In 1888 Rose's *Cyclopaedia of Canadian Biography* spoke of a 'recent large addition to the already extensive works', and stated that this addition 'now enables the firm to give employment to about four hundred people'. By this time Alexander Macdonald, son of Duncan, was manager. Under his vigorous drive the products of the factory were 'brought to great perfection'.[27] At exhibitions abroad, both in Great Britain and on the Continent, they won awards. The 'serious doubts'[28] that had once troubled the future of whiteware potting in St. Johns seemed safely resolved. And then fire all but wiped out the St. Johns Stone Chinaware Company.

On the evening of March 4, 1893, it happened. A despatch to the *Gazette* in Montreal called it 'a conflagration' second only to St. Johns' devastating fire of 1876, and predicted hardship and poverty for the many who were thrown out of work without a moment's warning. The fire was first noticed about supper time, but even though firemen from Iberville and a detachment from the military school arrived almost at once to help the St. Johns brigade, the flames swept out of control. All night long and on into the dawn they roared into the sky. They only died down when the entire manufacturing portion of the pottery (four large buildings surrounding a square) had been gutted. Only shortly before, 'extensive improvements' had been made to the these buildings, and 'new and improved machinery, costing about twenty-five thousand dollars' had been installed. The total loss was 'estimated at one hundred thousand dollars', and on this there was no more than 'fifty-four thousand dollars of insurance'.[29]

Calamitous as was the situation, something remained. A big wooden warehouse, on the opposite side of St. George Street, which contained 'a large quantity of ware', had been saved. And just recently the St. Johns Stone Chinaware Company had bought out one of its new rivals, 'the Dakin pottery'. At the Dakin plant it would at least be possible 'to finish' any ware that could be saved from the ruins. Even this employment, the *Gazette* pointed out, would relieve 'to some extent, the privations which must of necessity result from the consequences of such a disaster'. Then once again there were revived the old memories of the days of difficulty. Said the *Gazette*: 'It is the universal hope that the Messrs. Macdonald will, as they have already overcome so many difficulties, decide to rebuild and reap the benefits of the great experience they have sacrificed so much to acquire.'[30]

That was in 1893, twenty years after whiteware potting had first been established in St. Johns under a cloud of misfortune. For a few years the Macdonalds did carry on the business they had 'sacrificed' so much to develop. But by 1896 there were rumours that they would not do so much longer. The Montreal French-language newspaper, *La Minerve*, put the rumours into print on March 31:

Il y a déjà quelque temps que les MM. Macdonald, de Saint-Jean, sont en pourparlers avec des céramistes français pour la vente de leurs usines de céramique, à Saint-Jean. Les MM. Macdonald ont consenti à vendre le tout, y compris la clientèle, matière première, et les vaisselles en magasin, pour la somme, dit-on, de $130,000. Ils ont préféré faire un sacrifice afin de donner à la ville de Saint-Jean l'avantage d'avoir, dans un avenir rapproché, si tout s'arrange bien, la première industrie française qui se soit jamais implantée dans le pays.

Il est tout probable que M. Alex. Macdonald partira, sous peu, pour Paris.

The St. Johns Stone Chinaware Company had been born in the mind of George Whitefield Farrar, an American. It had been rescued from failure and solidly established by two brothers, grandsons of a British soldier who had died fighting against the American rebels at Bunker's Hill. They had built its success on a Staffordshire body and had employed Staffordshire workmen. Now, 'si tout s'arrange bien', the sale of its good-will, its materials on hand, and the stock in the warehouse was to be negotiated with a firm in France for a possible $130,000. Presumably this firm would introduce French ceramic methods to a pottery that already owed debts to American and British traditions.

But in spite of any plans that Alexander Macdonald may have laid on a trip to Paris to meet with French ceramists, the days of the St. Johns Stone China-ware Company were drawing to an end. When the final *Mercantile Agency Reference Book* for the nineteenth century was published in 1899, its name was gone from the list of potteries in St. Johns.[31] A new company, the Canada Stone Chinaware Company (La Compagnie de Faienceries du Canada), made a brief appearance. Then it, too, vanished from the directories.

No other pottery for the making of tableware in St. Johns was able to challenge the record of the St. Johns Stone Chinaware Company. When, in 1931, the National Development Bureau in Ottawa made a survey of the ceramic industry in Canada, it reported that there was 'no production of white table-ware of any kind' in the country.[32] The situation was exactly as it had been at the beginning of 1873.

CHAPTER XXIV

Some Other Potteries in
St. Johns and Its Vicinity

At the present time there are within the town proper and in Iberville just opposite,
eight factories for the manufacture of different kinds of stone and earthen-ware.
The Eastern Townships . . . Directory for 1888-89.

The full roll of potters in the St. Johns-Iberville area will probably never be
known. The journeyman potter one day was a master potter the next, and was
back again at the bench before a directory could record the flight of his ambition.
As in the Potteries of England, 'the Staffordshire of Canada' was a place of
tentative efforts and disappointed hopes. In any area of concentrated potting
such as this, the come and go of aspiring workmen has always defied the attempts
of historians to trace them all; for many made so little impression that no record
of any kind remained behind them save, perhaps, a few unmarked pots that now
elude or confuse attribution.

Yet there were those who were successful, for a time, in building up business
in competition with either the Farrars or the St. Johns Stone Chinaware Company. John Gillespie, maker of 'Canada Stone Ware', was one. An advertisement, published in 1858 in the St. Johns *News and Frontier Advocate*, tells what
John Gillespie was prepared to do as a potter:

CANADA STONE WARE
MANUFACTURING
ESTABLISHMENT.

———

ST. JOHNS, C.E.

———

THE Subscriber, while returning thanks to the public for the generous support extended
to the late firm, would inform them that he will continue the manufacture of STONE
WARE in all its branches, in his own name and account, and that he will keep constantly
on hand a large supply, manufactured in the most approved manner and from the best
material, which he will be happy to dispose of at prices suitable to the times.

All orders from merchants and others engaged in the sale of Stone Ware, will meet
with prompt attention.

JOHN GILLESPIE.

St. Johns, Feb. 10, 1858.[1]

The 'late firm' referred to by Gillespie may well have been the Gillespie &
Mace listed as St. Johns potters in *The Canada Directory for 1857-58.* (The

directory was published at the end of 1857.) In the earlier *Canada Directory* published in 1851 no Gillespie was listed as potting in St. Johns, but two years later the name Gillespie does occur in connection with St. Johns wares. A *Montreal Gazette* reporter noted it in describing pottery displayed at the provincial exhibition that autumn: 'We noticed some pottery by Messrs. Gillespie and Soule, of St. Johns; fire clay, chimney tops, filter bricks, tiles, drain tiles and smoking pipes, from Mr. Henderson; some bricks and tiles from St. Michel d'Yamaska.'[2]

For a brief period the young, ambitious John Gillespie (he was born only in the 1830's) managed to maintain an independent place in the potting industry of Canada. But working 'in his own name and account' proved a disheartening experience. The end of the 1850's was a period of depression in Canada, which explains his 'prices suitable to the times'. Many businesses suffered or collapsed. That the Canada Stone Ware Manufacturing Establishment did not survive the depression for long is indicated by the directories of the mid-1860's. Gillespie's name, as a master potter, is no longer to be found in them. He drops out of sight for some years, and then, in the *County of Missisquoi & Town of St. Johns Directory for 1879, 1880 and 1881*, there is again a John Gillespie, potter. If this is the same John Gillespie who earlier, in his own name, carried on the manufacture of stone ware 'in all its branches', it would appear to be John Gillespie come down in the world. There is nothing in the directory of this later date to indicate that John Gillespie, in 1879, was other than a journeyman potter.

Frequently those who engaged in potting in St. Johns and Iberville had first gained experience with either the Farrars or the St. Johns Stone Chinaware Company. Orrin L. Ballard, bearing a name almost as prominent in Vermont potting at mid-century as that of Farrar, worked at one time with E. L. Farrar. Later, for a short time, he potted in St. Johns on his own account. The *Pilot*, a Montreal newspaper, indicates this in its issue of September 30, 1858. In discussing the provincial exhibition, the *Pilot* commented: 'Mr. O. L. Ballard, formerly Farrar, St. Johns, is an extensive exhibitor of butter, cream, cake, flower, and pudding pots, water fountains, milk pails, &c. These all show a decided progress in make over former years.'

Orrin L. Ballard's 'progress in make' was sufficient to secure for him that year's first prize in both 'Stone Ware' and 'Pottery'.[3] For the best specimens exhibited in each category he received a prize of four dollars, and was given a diploma.

Both John Gillespie, advertising in the St. Johns *News* in 1858, and Orrin L. Ballard, winning prizes that same year at the provincial exhibition, marked at least some of the wares that came from their separate potteries. Their names and ST. JOHNS, C.E. impressed on blue-decorated jugs and jars identify their productions.

Ballard, like Gillespie, must have found the 1858 depression a difficult time in which to start on his own in a district where other potters were already at work. Like Gillespie he stayed in business in St. Johns only briefly. He is not listed in *Mitchell's Canada Gazetteer and Business Directory for 1864-65*. The next year, however, when Mitchell & Co. of Toronto published a new Canada directory, an O. L. Ballard re-appears as a master potter in Canada. This potter, probably the same as Orrin L. Ballard, once of St. Johns, is now listed as working in Cornwall, Canada West. Again, however, a Ballard pottery lasted only a short time. Before the 1870's the name was gone from Cornwall.

In order to trace the activities of Orrin L. Ballard in Canada, and to account for the years when he slips in and out of Canadian directories, it may be necessary to turn to Vermont sources, and to relate the O. L. Ballard of St. Johns, C.E., and the O. L. Ballard of Cornwall, C.W., to the O. L. Ballard who is recorded as potting in Burlington, Vermont.

There were several Ballards potting in Vermont in the 1850's and 1860's. Among them were two who were at one time in partnership, using the mark O. L. & A. K. BALLARD/BURLINGTON, VT. The association of Orrin L. Ballard with the Farrars in St. Johns suggests that Ballard had, as did the Farrars themselves, a Vermont background. He may have been another who had interests simultaneously in Canada and the United States (even as E. L. Farrar in the 1850's). The O. L. Ballard who departs from the Canadian directories at some time after the middle of the 1860's may, perhaps, be found again in the O. L. Ballard advertising fire brick in Burlington in 1867.[4]

In addition to their competitors in stoneware, the Farrars had rivals in the making of Rockingham and yellow ware. The most important competition in this branch of potting came in the later years of the century, when Elijah Bowler opened his St. Johns Rockingham and Yellow Ware Manufactory. Bowler's pottery came into being towards the end of the 1870's, and lasted into the 1880's. A bi-lingual advertisement, published in the *County of Missisquoi & Town of St. Johns Directory* in 1879, sets forth the different articles produced by Bowler in Rockingham and yellow ware, and reveals, too, that in St. Johns he was attempting some sort of majolica, or earthenware with coloured glazes and probably with relief decoration:

ST. JOHNS

ROCKINGHAM & YELLOW WARE

MANUFACTORY,

E. BOWLER,

PROPRIETOR,

CORNER OF

ALLEN AND ST. THOMAS STREETS,

ST. JOHNS, P.Q.

Manufacturers of

CANE, ROCKINGHAM AND MAJOLICA WARE,

Tea Pots, Milk Pans, Lip Bowls, Preserve

Jars, Round and Oval Dishes,

Spittoons, &c.

The very best Ware at the lowest price.

———

FABRICANT DE

POTTERIE, CANE, ROCKINGHAM & MAJOLICA

Théières, Plats à Lait, Bols,

Demi-Couverts, Pots à Confitures, Plats

Ronds et Ovals, Crachoirs, Etc.

Les Meilleurs Articles et les plus bas prix.

The directory that carried this advertisement described Bowler himself as 'thoroughly and practically conversant with all the details of the manufacture', and able, therefore, 'to fill orders in a manner certain to ensure thorough satisfaction'. The products of the pottery were said to be varied in design, well finished, and above all, cheap.[5]

Bowler's was another case of a St. Johns potter endeavouring to succeed in a period of business recession. At the time when he established his Rockingham & Yellow Ware Manufactory, the country was in the debilitating grip of a prolonged and severe 'period of stagnation'.[6] The effect of hard times upon Bowler's business may, perhaps, be judged from his rating in the *Mercantile Agency Reference Book* for January, 1881. In that year Bowler's total capital was reckoned at no more than a thousand dollars.

But Bowler survived the depression. He was still the proprietor of a St. Johns pottery when *The Eastern Townships Business & Farmers Directory for 1888-89* was published. He was not listed in the Mercantile Agency's *Reference Book* for January, 1892, but it may have been he who was back in the directories in 1896, this time with a partner. When John Lovell issued the 1896 *Business and Professional Directory* for Canada, he included Bowler & Knight of St. Johns. This firm, however, was not manufacturing the old Rockingham and yellow ware teapots and pudding bowls. The new trend in St. Johns potting was towards the sanitary earthenware that was to become the main ceramic output of the district in the twentieth century. Bowler & Knight were the proprietors of the Dominion Sanitary Pottery Co., manufacturers of 'closet traps, plug basins . . . and every kind of sanitary ware'.

When William Wickliffe Johnson, manager of the Mercantile Agency's Montreal office, reviewed the Canadian crockery trade in the 1880's, he noted that there was in Canada itself an increasingly important production of 'the cheaper grades of crockery, such as Rockingham, Cane, 'C C', and white granite wares, which were formerly imported altogether from Great Britain'.[7] Much of this Canadian-made earthenware of the 1880's came from the area around St. Johns. Another potter who, like Bowler, contributed to the increased production was Charles E. Pearson of Iberville. At the Dominion exhibition of 1880, in Montreal, Pearson's showing attracted particular attention. His display was visited by the Governor-General, the Marquis of Lorne. The *Herald* reporter, following the Governor-General through the buildings, wrote that Queen Victoria's son-in-law inspected 'the urns and vases of C. E. Pearson, of the Rockingham and yellow ware pottery', and noted that in this section of the exhibition he was shown 'a beautiful bisque vase, as fine as can be imported'.[8] Presumably this was the 'Bisque vase, containing various designs' which the *Star* had previously identified as 'the most ornamental feature of the display of the Rockingham and yellow ware pottery of Iberville'.[9] Not only the *Herald* and *Star*, but the *Gazette* commented upon Pearson's work: 'Charles E. Pearson of Iberville, P.Q., has a capital display of the Rockingham and yellow ware teapots, vases, dishes, all of home manufacture, and excellent goods are here to be seen.'[10]

Though 'bisque' would normally suggest an unglazed porcelain, the term, as used by the *Herald* and *Star* reporters, would probably have indicated nothing more than an unglazed body. The *Star* clearly identified this particular 'bisque' vase as the leading feature in a Rockingham and yellow ware display that could have included only earthenware.

In spite of his prominence in exhibition accounts, Charles Pearson was at this time no more prosperous than Elijah Bowler. The same *Mercantile Agency Reference Book* that gave Bowler a total capital of a thousand dollars at best, put Pearson in the same category.[11] With the exception of a mere handful of large-scale enterprises, nineteenth-century Canadian potteries were cramped and confined in their operations by inadequate financing. Pearson did not last in business for as many years as Bowler. When *The Eastern Townships . . . Directory for 1888-89* came out, Bowler was still active in St. Johns, but in the Iberville listings Charles E. Pearson was no longer among the pottery owners.

In the brown-glazed earthenware called Rockingham, and in the yellow or cane wares, Elijah Bowler and Charles E. Pearson were producing earthenware of the same type as G. H. & L. E. Farrar made, first in St. Johns and then in Iberville, at their Stone, Rockingham and Yellow Ware Factory. It would now be all but impossible to assign unmarked pieces of either Rockingham or yellow ware of this period to a particular factory, even when such pieces are believed to have a St. Johns-Iberville origin. Probably in the past, wares that actually came from both Bowler and Pearson have been considered Farrar productions, only because the Farrars have been far better known than their competitors.

During the last years of the century, ordinary earthenware and stoneware in the form of crocks and jugs and similar utilitarian articles were made at other Iberville potteries, some of which marked at least certain of their productions. Bertrand & Lavoie, listed simply as 'potters' in *The Eastern Townships Business . . . Directory for 1888-89*, sometimes used a body that is distinctly pink in colour, and reminiscent of brick clay. Adolphe Loupret, listed among the 'Stone Manufacturers' in *Lovell's Business and Professional Directory . . . of Canada for 1896-97*, produced wares that are generally of the usual buff or grey-toned stone body. Another name found on jugs is that of Calixte Goyette, listed under potters of St. Athanase (Iberville) in Polk's *Dominion of Canada . . . Directory, 1890-91*.

But important as the making of stone and common earthenware was in the St. Johns-Iberville district, the area's right to a place that was unique in nineteenth-century Canadian potting was by virtue of its whiteware. When the editor of *The Eastern Townships . . . Directory* claimed, in 1888, that St. Johns was 'the birth-place of potteries in the Dominion of Canada', he meant that it was in St. Johns that the first pottery for the making of whiteware was established. The St. Johns Stone Chinaware Company opened in 1873. In spite of all the difficulties that clouded its beginning, others saw in it an enterprise to be imitated. According to William Wickliffe Johnson, 'several' of the later potteries were started by former employees of the St. Johns Stone Chinaware Company.[12]

One firm that made a heavy stone china, indistinguishable from much produced by the St. Johns Stone Chinaware Company itself, was the British Porcelain Works. This St. Johns pottery, started in the 1880's, was owned in its early days by H. Earle, of Montreal. In 1888 it was being managed for him by Dakin & Allen in St. Johns.[13] Four years later, in the *Mercantile Agency Reference Book for January, 1892*, F. B. Dakin's name was given as the reference for the British Porcelain Works. This may, therefore, have been the 'Dakin pottery' that the

Gazette spoke of in 1893 as having been 'recently' bought out by the St. Johns Stone Chinaware Company.[14] It was, in any event, about this time that the British Porcelain Works ceased to function under that name and F. B. Dakin transferred activities to Iberville. He is listed there, in *Lovell's Business and Professional Directory . . . of Canada for 1896-97*, as F. B. Dakin & Co., 'manufacturers of vitreous sanitary ware, Rockingham, cane and white ware'.

At the British Porcelain Works, with which Frederick B. Dakin was associated in the 1880's and early 1890's, the usual strong white table and toilet goods were made (*Plate* 49B). Some of these wares were in the ubiquitous wheat pattern borrowed earlier by the St. Johns Stone Chinaware Company from Staffordshire. They were all of a stout earthenware and no more porcelain than the 'chemical porcelain' made at an earlier date by the Grainger factory in Worcester, or the 'opaque porcelain' made at countless Staffordshire potteries. The black-printed mark used on them was the Royal Arms, with BRITISH PORCELAIN WORKS above and IRONSTONE CHINA below.

Another St. Johns firm of brief existence which may have tried to manufacture whiteware in imitation of the Stone Chinaware Company, or which perhaps only dealt in it, was that of Jones & Bowers. In January, 1881, the *Mercantile Agency Reference Book*, giving Jones & Bowers a credit rating of 'Fair', listed them vaguely under 'China & Stoneware'. The partners in this firm may have been William Jones and Samuel Bowers, both of whom, in 1879, were journeymen potters in St. Johns.[15] As a firm, Jones & Bowers did not last out the decade.

Although factories grew up in St. Johns to imitate the St. Johns Stone Chinaware Company, the second whiteware factory in Canada was not in St. Johns or even Iberville, but some thirty miles away in St. Cunegonde (now part of the city of Montreal). This factory, the West End Dresden Pottery, though not in St. Johns, had nonetheless close links with the St. Johns Stone Chinaware Company. Not only was it directly inspired by the example of the St. Johns factory; it had for its manager the same William Livesley who had managed the Stone Chinaware Company in its first disturbed and doubtful days. In the *Quebec Official Gazette* (January 5, 1877) Livesley's name appears among those applying for the charter for the new firm.

The West End Dresden Pottery opened less than four years after the St. Johns Stone Chinaware Company. Its premises in St. Cunegonde were already well known, for they had earlier housed the St. Lawrence Glass Works. From St. Lawrence glass to Dresden pottery was a step which the Montreal *Gazette* anticipated in a news story on November 1, 1876:

> For some weeks past arrangements have been in progress, which are now completed, for the purpose of converting the St. Lawrence glass works into a manufactory for making both the common and fine qualities of pottery, suited to the general Canadian trade. Mr. W. Workman has not only met the wishes of the parties applying in a generous manner by making the terms easy and practicable, but has given substantial support by taking the first shares in the new company.

The Irish-born financier William Workman, once mayor of Montreal, was in a position to make things 'easy' for the new pottery. He was the director of a bank, and had been president of the St. Lawrence Glass Works.[16] The Glass Works had, in fact, been built on Workman and Delisle property; moreover, Workman had joined with Livesley and four other Montreal residents in applying for a charter for the company.

The *Gazette* story on that November day was more than a simple announcement of another new pottery; it was a summing up of the state of whiteware manufacture in Canada. To point up the Canadian situation, the *Gazette* looked first at the United States. There it found 'one whiteware factory to every million and-a-half of its population'. This was in strong contrast to Canada, where only one such factory, the St. Johns Stone Chinaware Company, was 'at present at work for the whole Dominion'. The example of this one whiteware factory in St. Johns invited St. Cunegonde to follow, not alone because there was an obvious need for more whiteware potting in Canada, but because St. Johns had demonstrated that first-class tablewares could be produced at home. In three short years this lone Canadian whiteware pottery had 'secured a character for sound ware seldom if ever, equalled in the United States'. Its products even stood up to comparison with those of 'the best makers in the mother country'. At St. Cunegonde the story could be repeated.

To strengthen the case for a second whiteware factory near Montreal the *Gazette* touched upon an argument of historic force: 'Shut out as Canada is for half the year, from the English markets, the establishment of this pottery must meet a want, and the supply of dealers at short notice cannot fail to be appreciated by all interested in the business.'

In actual fact, the land of the St. Lawrence was no longer cut off from the world for 'half the year' by the freezing of the river. Those days belonged to the earlier part of the century. Trains now connected cities like Montreal with Atlantic ports, open the year round. But old ways were slow to change. Canadian crockery dealers still got in the bulk of their supplies from England in the spring and autumn. During the winter months little new stock was imported.

To win support for Canadian-made whiteware, the *Gazette* stressed that any increase in the manufacture of these wares must ultimately benefit the china merchants. It was admitted that importers in the United States had at first greeted the whitewares made in that country with 'hostility', but 'the leading importers of Canada' were expected to take a broader view. It was believed they would see the advantages of a ready source of home supply in the winter months, and would appreciate the profit to the country of expanding industry. In so far as possible, materials obtained in Canada itself—'bone or animal charcoal, phosphate of lime, spar quartz'—were to be used at the new pottery; and 'fine ware, such as porcelain or china' might in time be attempted.

If the history of Canadian potting in general holds few instances of outstanding industrial success, the history of whiteware potting in particular has almost none. The exception is the St. Johns Stone Chinaware Company, which inspired the others. Those who tried to imitate it, however, did not have the essential backing of experienced businessmen like the Macdonalds of St. Johns. William Workman, it is true, gave practical encouragement to the West End Dresden Pottery in St. Cunegonde, but there is no evidence that he, like Edward C. Macdonald, went daily to an office in the pottery and himself directed its business affairs with shrewd and untiring zeal.[17] The life span of the West End Dresden Pottery was less than three years. It probably never, on any commercial basis, was able to produce the more expensive type of 'fine ware' that had been planned.

William Livesley had been manager of the St. Johns Stone Chinaware Company before he left it to become superintendent and general manager of the West End Dresden Pottery. It must have been with new hope and new resolve that he shook off the troubles of St. Johns and made a fresh start in St. Cunegonde. When the West End Dresden Pottery had to admit defeat, after less than three years, a way was found to give it another brief chance at success, but William Livesley's connection with the St. Cunegonde venture was over. Under a new name and new management, the West End Dresden Pottery floundered on for another four years; William Livesley returned to St. Johns. Here he made still another attempt to produce whiteware. According to the *Quebec Official Gazette* for April 11, 1885, Livesley, described as a potter and a British subject, was one of the group (which also included Charles Pearson) who made application to the provincial government for the incorporation of the British Porcelain Manufacturing Company.

The new name of the West End Dresden Pottery was the Stafford Pottery, and the man who formed the new company to run it was Mark H. Tomkins, an importing agent, dealing in china clay, Portland cement, and raw materials generally. He had an office in Montreal and a wooden warehouse in St. Cunegonde, back of the West End Dresden Pottery. The pottery was on Albert Street, and Tomkins' warehouse on Delisle, just south of Albert.[18] When he took over the West End Dresden Pottery—once a glass house and now renamed the Stafford Pottery—Mark Tomkins extended the premises west to the corner of Vinet Street, and south to Delisle, to include his warehouse. Then he listed the pottery as located at 'Albert, Vinet and Delisle'.[19]

What was made at this enlarged pottery in its last bid for life may be learned from the accounts of the 1880 Dominion exhibition. The *Gazette*, in describing the Stafford Pottery's display, spoke of Mark H. Tomkins & Co. as 'manufacturers of white earthenware, fire brick, door knobs, &c.'[20] A dark blue or 'mazarine' ware was also made, and for this and the door knobs the company won special praise from the judges at the exhibition. In addition, the Stafford Pottery of Mark Tomkins & Co. placed first, and the St. Johns Stone Chinaware Company second, in 'Potteryware'. The St. Johns firm, however, took the first prize for 'Stoneware'.[21] The 'Stoneware' was stone china.

With a flair for publicity, Tomkins arranged demonstrations of pottery making at his exhibition stand. The *Gazette* reported: 'They have employes [*sic*] at work making jugs, cover-dishes, ewers and all kinds of pressed goods, and their operations are watched with interest by numbers of spectators.'[22] A spectator who himself attracted interest was the Marquis of Lorne. The same day that he inspected Charles E. Pearson's Rockingham and yellow wares, the Governor-General stopped to watch the Stafford potters. They were making sugar bowls at the moment, and he viewed the whole process. From the *Herald's* account of the conversation between the Marquis of Lorne and Mark Tomkins comes the information that the Stafford Pottery imported all its clay from England.[23]

Over his exhibition stand in 1880 Mark Tomkins worked out a message in balls of clay: 'It is the duty of every man to endeavor that something may be added by his industry to the hereditary aggregate of knowledge and happiness.'[24] With St. Johns leading St. Cunegonde, potters of Quebec strove by their industry to add the mastery of whiteware potting to Canadian knowledge. They tackled it with something of American enterprise, British skill, and Canadian perseverance in the face of difficulties; but, in spite of it all, the frustration of failure rather than the happiness of success was the outcome at every pottery that tried to follow in the steps of the St. Johns Stone Chinaware Company. By 1883, or the early part of 1884, the Stafford Pottery was permanently out of business.

CHAPTER XXV

The Humberstones:
Canadian Potters Through the Century

Motto watch the man that grinds the glaze as a cat would a mouse.
Simon Thomas Humberstone's Notebook.

A number of families in Canada were potters through several generations. The Whites, Bristol potters transplanted to New Brunswick in the 1860's, worked near Saint John for a quarter of a century. James Foley, a grandson of Joseph White, carried the tradition into the twentieth century, but not under the White name. The Dions of Ancienne Lorette were French-Canadian potters from mid-Victorian days; the Farrars, Yankees from Vermont, potted at St. Johns from the 1840's. Only one family, however, the Humberstones of Upper Canada, achieved the truly remarkable feat of maintaining a Canadian potting tradition under the same family name through the whole of the nineteenth century. The Humberstones began potting in Canada at the end of the eighteenth century; the last of their potteries was destroyed by fire in the twentieth. In nineteenth-century Canadian ceramic history their record is without parallel.

Although the Humberstones were unique they were also typical Canadian potters. Their activities reflect the struggles and difficulties that faced all who tried to establish the potting industry on Canadian soil. Despite the fact that Simon Thomas Humberstone experimented with Egyptian black, Parian porcelain, and glorious coloured glazes, the commercial output of the Humberstones was almost entirely the common earthenware and stoneware that restricted the horizon of the typical potter of Canada.

Five generations of Humberstones potted in Ontario: Samuel Humberstone (c. 1744-1823); Thomas Humberstone (1776-1849); Thomas Humberstone, Junior (1811-95); Simon Thomas Humberstone (1846-1915); and Thomas Allan Humberstone (1887-1952).[1] Another member of the family, William Humberstone (b. 1837), eldest son of Thomas Humberstone, Junior, carried both the family name and something of the family tradition into the Northwest. He became a pioneer brickmaker in Edmonton, in days when the nearest railway was at Calgary, some two hundred miles away, and when mail arrived once a week at best.[2]

It is fitting that the Humberstones seem to have been of Staffordshire origin: 'Samuel Humberstone . . . learned his trade, the manufacture of pottery in Staf-

301

fordshire.'[3] This published statement of 1885 was based on material supplied by Thomas Humberstone, Junior, Samuel's grandson.[4] Thomas, Junior, the first of the Humberstone potters to be born in Canada, had been nearly twelve years old when Samuel died and was buried in the graveyard of the historic 'Blue Church' by the St. Lawrence, far from Staffordshire, and far from the comfortable surroundings of Philadelphia, where he had settled before the American Revolution.

When the American Revolution broke out, Samuel Humberstone, the Staffordshire potter, remained loyal. As a lieutenant in the New York Volunteers, he fought on the British side. Later, like other United Empire Loyalists, stripped of his possessions by the new republic, he fled with his family to Canada. For a few years the Humberstones found refuge in Montreal; but before the end of the eighteenth century, Samuel Humberstone had taken up his land grant in Augusta Township, Grenville County, in Upper Canada. On the south-east corner of Lot 27, Concession 1 (just at the mouth of the Mill Creek) he erected a pottery,[5] one of the first in the new province. There, under conditions of hardship and difficulty, he carried on the trade learned in Staffordshire and practised in Philadelphia, and there, in 1823, he died. The earthenware he made of local clay was the ordinary brownware, the pots and crocks needed in a pioneer community.

Samuel Humberstone's only son, Thomas, born in Philadelphia, was taught how to make pots by his father; and it is this second Humberstone who has been credited with the first pottery in York County, a pottery erected on his farm on the west side of Yonge Street, beyond Hogg's hollow (Lot 14, Concession 1).[6] The move from Grenville County to York was made by Thomas in 1798.[7] At that time, striking out for himself, he acquired two hundred acres of land which he immediately set about clearing. Like his father, Thomas had to be both farmer and potter in Canada, and wresting land from forest was for the Humberstones the first step towards both occupations.

That the younger Humberstone was able to establish himself successfully on the land is shown by an advertisement in the *Upper Canada Gazette* in 1819. On July 1, Thomas Humberstone offered for sale his holding on Yonge Street. By that time he was able to describe it as a 'valuable property', too well known to need 'encomiums'. It was only eight miles outside York, had now forty acres under cultivation, a 'never failing' well, two hundred apple trees and a large dwelling house and barn.

In yet another way Thomas Humberstone followed in his father's footsteps: he, too, enlisted as a militiaman to fight against the Americans. In the War of 1812, when the Americans seized the opportunity to push their way into Upper Canada, Thomas Humberstone rushed to join the volunteers. He fought at Detroit; at Queenston (tradition has it) he helped to carry Brock from the battlefield; he was one of those who rallied to the futile defence of York.[8] In the autumn of 1813 he was taken prisoner of war near Kingston and carried off to the United States.[9] Today his commission as a lieutenant in the East York Batallion of Incorporated Militia and his sword are preserved by his great-great-grandson. They form part of a collection of family relics that includes products of Humberstone potteries.

The Humberstones: Canadian Potters Through the Century

Samuel Humberstone had suffered by the American Revolution. The life that he had created for himself in Philadelphia, when it was British territory, was lost to him forever. Ahead lay only the troubles of a pioneer in the backwoods. His son found that the War of 1812, when Americans were again the enemy, disrupted his potting business in Canada.

Just before the outbreak of war, in June, 1812, Thomas Humberstone had secured a government contract for 'a large quantity of bricks'.[10] This was an important contract, for there were as yet very few brick buildings in York,[11] and the business of making bricks locally was wide open for exploitation by the enterprising. With a government order in his pocket for bricks to be made by him, Thomas Humberstone, in 1812, must have felt himself on the verge of expanding prosperity such as he had not yet known as a potter. In anticipation of government payment, and in order that he might 'the better be enabled to fulfill and complete' his contract, he laid out the sum of £200 currency for the purchase of a house in York, 'at the North East angle of the appropriation for a market'.[12]

And then two things happened to upset all his plans. The declaration of war with the United States and his own enlistment with the volunteers prevented his going ahead with brick-making. When he returned from fighting at Detroit and Queenston, it was to receive a further set-back. He was informed that the building he had purchased in good faith for £200 was not to be his after all. It had been discovered that this building had been erected by its original owner, Thomas Gough, 'without the sanction or authority of Government'.[13] Dr. John Strachan (who would later become the first Anglican bishop of Toronto) was keeping a school in it, and Thomas Humberstone was not to have it.

On March 11, 1813, some six weeks before military duty was to see him engaged in the defence of York itself, Thomas Humberstone directed a petition to Roger Hale Sheaffe, administrator of the government of Upper Canada. In this petition, in which he described his peacetime occupation as that of 'Potter', and in which he set forth both his father's Loyalist record with the New York Volunteers and his own recent service with 'the late General Brock to the Westward', Thomas Humberstone asked that there be granted to him the half acre of land on which stood the building he had thought he owned. His petition was read in Council on March 27, 1813, but it availed him nothing. The decision was that 'the prayer of the Petitioner cannot be complied with'.[14]

But although war had disrupted his work as a potter, and had consequently lost him both business and money, Thomas Humberstone received certain benefits for his services as a soldier. He was granted five hundred acres of land and a pension.[15] After the war he went back to potting. He made bricks and he also made 'pottery ware' described as 'useful' by Rev. Henry Scadding.[16] This useful pottery would have been the ordinary brown earthenware that his father had made. An account of the manufactures of Upper Canada, written in 1825, stated that up to that time the 'only sort of Pottery' made in the province was brownware, 'often of a very good quality'.[17]

The third Humberstone to enter the potting business in Upper Canada was Thomas Humberstone's son, Thomas, Junior. Like his father and grandfather, he, too, became a farmer and potter, and he, too, faced calamities. But the calamities that fell upon Thomas Humberstone, Junior, were of a different nature from those experienced by the earlier Humberstones. Although he certainly must have had anxious moments during the rebellion year of 1837, when he strongly supported the Tory cause, he was never driven from his country (as was his grandfather), nor taken prisoner of war by foreign invaders (as was his father). In his case, fire was the cause of his misfortunes.

According to information which he himself must have furnished for the *History of Toronto and County of York*, Thomas Humberstone, Junior, early followed 'the same trade as his father and grandfather'. The same source records that at one time he carried on a pottery at York Mills, and contemporary newspaper references and directories indicate that he also potted at Thornhill and Willowdale as well as at Newton Brook. All his potteries were on Yonge Street, and none was more than a few miles distant from 'the old homestead' where his father had erected the first pottery, and where he himself had learned his trade and worked until the beginning of the 1830's.[18]

The site which was in the end, under his son's management, to be the location of the most important of all the Humberstone potteries was in Newton Brook (on the west side of Yonge Street, just south of Steeles Avenue).[19] The first pottery that Thomas Humberstone, Junior, erected here was destroyed by fire, his house and barn going at the same time. He rebuilt the pottery, and again fire swept it away. Again he rebuilt. Then he decided to move to the opposite side of Yonge Street, but fire still pursued him. In time the new pottery, like the others, was burned to the ground. For a third time Thomas Humberstone, Junior, rebuilt a pottery and struggled back to prosperity. Since his own information indicates that there was 'no insurance whatever' on any of the potteries,[20] it is clear that Thomas Humberstone, Junior, must have faced losses almost as serious as his grandfather had suffered in a revolution, and disruptions of business perhaps even greater than invasion had brought to his father. With a streak of stubborn persistence, necessary to all those who would remain in potting in Canada, Thomas, Junior, continued as a potter until about 1870. At that time he retired to his farm, and turned over the family business to his second son, Simon Thomas.

The best known of all the Humberstone potters, Simon Thomas Humberstone not only engaged in potting for nearly fifty years; he became a well-known figure in politics as well. His father was described in his obituary as having had political affiliations that were 'rigidly Conservative'.[21] It was this allegiance that the son maintained, even as he continued the potting tradition. He was a candidate for both federal and provincial nominations for the Conservative party, and although he was unsuccessful in these bids, he was long a force in Conservative affairs in Ontario.[22] In municipal politics he served first as deputy reeve and later as reeve of York Township—'the jolly reeve' the newspapers called him, when they regaled the public with samples of his wit.[23] A political cartoon, published in the *Recorder* on September 29, 1892, shows this politician-potter as a massive figure, flying the banner of Economy (*Plate* 49c).

But while he was as ready a fighter in the political field as his grandfather had been on the battlefield, Simon Thomas Humberstone had at the same time all his father's determination to stay with potting. His was a robust and forceful

304

personality, and he brought to potting the same vitality he carried with him into the political arena. Under him 'a large pottery' was erected on the west side of Yonge Street, back where his father had been at the time of the first fire.[24] A billhead of the 1890's indicates that this was known as the Newton Brook Pottery: 'NEWTON BROOK POTTERY . . . S. T. HUMBERSTONE . . . Stone, Earthenware & Rockingham.'

Simon Thomas Humberstone's predecessors had made the ordinary brownwares and, later, the stonewares of Canadian potting. He, on the other hand, began to reach out to new achievements. The Humberstones made little use of marks, but pieces in family possession that obviously belong in shape and style to the period of Simon Thomas show the range of his vigorous experiment. In addition to the usual red flower pots—the bread-and-butter staple of the pottery —there are large flower holders on tall pedestals, ornamented with raised leaves and blossoms; there are flower vases with mottled glazes in effective greens and yellows, and in subtler shades verging on pink and on the grey-green of the sea. A small-necked pot, six and a half inches in height, is of particular interest, for on it Simon Thomas tried out a whole series of glazes, showering them on in one brilliant blaze—blues inspired by turquoise and lapis lazuli, buffs and tans and whites melting into the colour of rich Jersey cream. That he was much concerned with glaze effects and with experiments to achieve fine colours is borne out by a manuscript notebook, today in the possession of his grandson, Lewis Humberstone. There are notations in faded ink about the ingredients to be used for a white to 'rival the opal', and for a 'most beautiful and costly read [sic] inclining to purple', as well as for ordinary Rockingham glazes to give 'a fair brown'.

A buff or common red earthenware body was Simon Thomas Humberstone's usual product. His notebook, however, shows 'receipts' for Egyptian black, and for Parian. Beside the Parian formula, which calls for felspar, Simon Thomas made the notation, 'if spar can be got'. A small jug, about four inches in height, is evidence of his attempts with whiteware. The jug is unglazed and is obviously an experimental piece, but taken in conjunction with the notebook references to Parian and to an 'Ivory Boddy' [sic] to be mixed 'today', it becomes further proof that Samuel Humberstone's Staffordshire heritage came down in Canadian expression, still vigorous in the fourth generation. There is a touch of singular continuity in the fact, revealed by the notebook, that in Newton Brook, in North York, Simon Thomas Humberstone, Samuel Humberstone's great-grandson, pored over the *Pottery Gazette* from Staffordshire.

For well over forty years Simon Thomas Humberstone watched over every detail of the business he had taken over from his father. When he died suddenly of pneumonia, in 1915, his obituary was headed 'Ancestor Established First Pottery in Co. of York',[25] and the notice made clear that neither politics nor other interests of any kind had ever succeeded in separating him from 'the trade of his forefathers'. To the day of his death he had retained the 'active management' of the Newton Brook Pottery.

Papers left behind by Simon Thomas Humberstone give a good indication of the type of ware made by him for general sale. It was, of course, on the ordinary wares, and not on the more ambitious efforts, involving experiment and expense, that the prosperity of the Newton Brook Pottery had to depend. Flower pots and plant containers, such as hanging baskets, were the mainstay of the business. A typical order for them was filled on January 17, 1893, when a customer in Newmarket was supplied with 2,750 flower pots (of various sizes) and 31 baskets. The total cost to the customer was $30.11. Against this amount Simon Thomas set down the expenses to himself for delivery of the order: meals enroute for the employee making the delivery, 50 cents; tolls, 30 cents; hay for the horse, 15 cents.

Another sale, ten days later, was made to a Mrs. Oliver, of 276 Queen Street West, in Toronto.[26] Her bill came to $8.87, and for this she received sixty-three items, including 'stone pitchers', 'oval pitchers', 'nappies', 'spitts' [spittoons], gallon and half-gallon pitchers, and teapots in four sizes. The charge to her for the stoneware pitchers was at the rate of $2.25 per dozen; for the spittoons in 'No. 3' size, $0.80 per dozen; and for the largest teapots, $3.00 per dozen. The teapots were probably of the Rockingham (brown-glazed) type. In Simon Thomas Humberstone's notebook there are a number of references to 'Rock Tea Pots', as well as to glazes that give 'a nice tea Pot Brown'.

An old photograph preserved with the Humberstone papers shows a different type of product. Taken by Thomas Perkins, whose studio was on Yonge Street in the later years of the nineteenth century, the picture is of a group of ornamental vases in shapes favoured at the end of Queen Victoria's reign. The price, which was probably the price per dozen, has been written in ink across the face of each of twenty different models. These prices range from $0.60 for the smallest vase to $3.00 for the largest. It is possible that this photograph represents pieces shown by Simon Thomas Humberstone at a provincial exhibition or at a trade fair. He was a regular exhibitor at such events, and included with his papers are a number of complimentary tickets given out to those taking part in fairs and exhibitions. In showing his pottery, Simon Thomas was following the example of his father, who took part in provincial exhibitions at an early date. At the Provincial Exhibition of Agriculture, Arts and Manufactures held in Toronto in 1858, for example, Thomas Humberstone, Junior, was awarded a prize of $2.00 for a 'Flower Pot Vase'.[27]

Vases such as those in the Perkins photograph, made by Simon Thomas Humberstone, were often in a red earthenware body, and were sometimes bought by the amateur china decorator, who painted over the entire surface. At the pottery itself, Simon Thomas Humberstone's wife occasionally decorated special pieces of this kind for the family. With her, roses were a favourite form of ceramic ornamentation, and her work extended to painting imported china, later fired in her husband's kiln and kept for family use.[28]

Simon Thomas Humberstone conducted the 'active management' of his own pottery, took part in politics, and also found time to join with others in giving leadership to the potting industry in Ontario. He was one of those who founded the Ontario Earthenware Manufacturers Association, an ambitious effort to protect and advance the interests of the local potters.[29] But not even he, with his energy and influence, could offset the new difficulties which the twentieth century brought to many potters in Canada. Costly machinery and larger scales of production were needed to keep up with a new age. For the majority of those who had begun potting in the nineteenth century, the twentieth was only to compound their many serious difficulties. By the time of the First World War, when Simon Thomas Humberstone's career drew to its close, there were scarcely twenty potteries left in Canada producing earthenware or stoneware in sufficient quantities to ensure a listing in the Dominion directories.[30] The days of almost all of them were numbered.

This was the situation that faced the last of the Humberstones who was a potter. Thomas Allan Humberstone inherited the Newton Brook Pottery from his father, Simon Thomas, in the spring of 1915. The next year his brother-in-law, Clifford Alexander May, who was then a young boy, came to work for him. Clifford May remembers that there were at that time only about five or six persons employed at the pottery. The output, as he recalls it, consisted chiefly of stoneware churns and red flower pots, and he remembers going with Thomas Allan to make deliveries of the flower pots at nearby greenhouses.

Samuel Humberstone, the United Empire Loyalist, had made wares needed in a pioneer community. His son had been offered opportunities to exploit fields still new to Upper Canada. His grandson and his great-grandson had been able to keep a place in the industrial development of the Victorian age. But Thomas Allan Humberstone, Samuel's great-great-grandson had to face the realities of the twentieth century. He had been trained as a potter by his father, mastering the trade first learned by Samuel in Staffordshire in the eighteenth century, but for him, the fifth Humberstone in direct line of descent to carry on potting in Canada, the future promised no more than to the Farrars in St. Johns. Before the First World War was over, he had made the decision to close down the Newton Brook Pottery. The fires went out in the kilns, and the old building stood empty. By 1919 not even the building was left.[31] It was gutted by a fire of unknown origin, possibly started by tramps, or by children playing in the deserted rooms.

The Humberstone story is unique. It spans more than a century, and it includes men whose lives linked potting with stirring events in Canadian history: a United Empire Loyalist; a potter who fought at Queenston Heights, one of Brock's celebrated York Volunteers; another potter who watched anxiously for Toronto to be delivered from the rebel menace in 1837. But while the Humberstone story is unique, it is at the same time typical of Canadian potting. From the record of the Humberstones may be traced the whole pattern of potting in Canada, a groping, tentative struggle after goals almost always denied Canadians.

Simon Thomas Humberstone's pottery was described as 'large' in contemporary accounts,[32] but neither Simon Thomas nor any of the other Humberstones made fortunes out of potting. Nineteenth-century *Mercantile Agency Reference Books*, covering the working years of Thomas, Junior, and of Simon Thomas, show that the estimated capital of the business was only briefly as high as $10,000. In 1874 the listing under the name of Simon Thomas Humberstone actually gave the total capital of the pottery as under $2,000.[33] During the greater part of the time the rating was in the $2,500-$5,000 category.

In the plague of fires that wiped out the assets of Thomas Humberstone, Junior, there is a familiar story, repeated at many a pottery in nineteenth-century Canada. In his persistence in rebuilding, time after time, there is the essential of

Canadian potting. Only a rugged persistence carried the Canadian potter on in the face of overwhelming odds.

Like average Canadian potters of Victorian times, the Humberstones took part in provincial exhibitions, attempting there to secure notice of the locally made product, although even at these provincial exhibitions the imported wares often pressed aside the Canadian offering. Prizes were awarded to importers as well as to local manufacturers for displays of earthenware. Those giving orders for goods often went no farther than the stand of the importer, seeing in his wares what they considered a superior and sometimes cheaper product.

In nothing does the Humberstone record exemplify better the story of potting in Canada than in Simon Thomas Humberstone's efforts to produce wares to rival these products from overseas. His notebook, a document of far more than personal significance, reveals glimpses of the frustrations, difficulties, and handicaps under which the Canadian potter worked in an ill-matched attempt to share his country's crockery trade.

The notebook was not kept as a regular diary; it was written in spasmodically, as Simon Thomas was moved to set down his problems, to make notes on his experiments, or to write out a new formula for either body or glaze. One of the earliest entries is one of the most interesting, for it gives an inner view of a typical Canadian pottery in mid-Victorian times. Simon Thomas, his punctuation and spelling as individualistic as the man himself, sketched this picture in setting down the state of his own affaires on New Year's Day, 1872:

> I have orders on hand at this date to the amount of six hundred and fifteen Dollars. The clay in the celler I should suppose will last till the first of Febuary Red clay in the yard 20 till August Blue clay one Load The wood is pretty Low About 30 cord in the yard and 20 four in bush I have made arrangements for twenty more cord to be delivered ten of bass wood and ten of slabs at two Dollars per cord each kind the hay I should suppose will last till June three horses. I have three turners William Brems & Taylor. Pegler left on Christmas, John around the shop and Menge by the day Beckett Left on Christmas was getting 21 per month find himself his place is to be filled by Henry McGee on the Eight at ten Dollars found (Backed out) Jim Healy Left Christmas for Barrie 50 cents per day I have Likewise made a purchase of wood from Luvick about 150 cord at $1.75 in the bush. The burnt ware on hand stands about four kilns and the green ware is about Three kilns, Lead is low about 50 pounds Oats stand at seven Bushels.

Oats and hay for the horses who took his wares to town, and wood to fire those wares had, of necessity, as important a place in the Canadian potter's scheme of things as the clay 'in the celler', the lead for glazing, or the journeyman potter worth ten dollars a month with board thrown in.

In the notebook are illuminating sidelights on the way in which the Canadian potter, isolated from the great centres of the industry, had to be on the alert to pick up whatever he could from another man engaged in the same trade. Simon Thomas Humberstone heard that at Schuler & McGlade's pottery, in Paris, washing soda was put in the glaze for 'Fancy Rockingham', to keep it 'from peeling off'. He recorded this information in his notebook, adding that he had got it from Tom Flemming, who 'supposes it to be correct'. From the foreman of another pottery—that of James R. Burns in Toronto—he learned that the danger of the glaze crazing on Rockingham teapots was much reduced 'if the tea pots get a good hard biscuit'. Once again he made a careful note, this time with his own observation that 'it is absolutely necessary to properly dust the tea pots before Glazing and not allow them to get dusty after they are glazed as it certainly affects the lustre.'

But most interesting of all, perhaps, is the notebook account of a running battle against blistering. A blistered glaze is frequently to be found on nineteenth-century Canadian wares, and Simon Thomas Humberstone's problems must have been those of many of his fellow potters. 'For about one year,' he wrote, 'we have been troubled with blister or *blib* and as yet are unable to acct for it.' In the kiln that he had drawn that day a teapot showed 'the Old Grudge'. It was badly blistered, and the fault appeared in this case 'to be in the glazing . . . but where I cannot say'.

In considerable detail, over many months, Simon Thomas recorded his observations and experiments in a frustrating effort to conquer the blistering glaze. He drew a kiln on March 25, 1886, and commented tersely: 'Blistered all to Hell'. On another occasion he noted that his most recent labours had produced only 'a very poor miserable dirty loomy glaze . . . inclined to Blister in small spots where not well Burned'.

At one time he thought he had found the root of the trouble. He suspected that it lay in the mixing of the glaze, and not, as he had for a time believed, in the actual firing. He wrote in his notebook: 'Motto watch the man that Grinds the glaze as a cat would a Mouse you will find it will pay well to take a news paper & sit down beside the Miserable Devil let him be as trustworthy as may never trust him'.

He worked out a formula for a lead glaze which, properly mixed, was proving satisfactory. 'No Blister no nothing', he wrote beside it. But the next year Simon Thomas decided that the real fault had been all along with those who prepared the clay in the first place. Neither the firing nor the glaze itself had been responsible for his blistered pots. On June 13, 1887, he drew a kiln. In capital letters and underlined for emphasis he recorded the result:

NO BLISTER

this kiln looks all that a man could desire the clay mixers done the business, *they were the devils.*

In the main, the story of Canadian potting has to be pieced together from old directories, newspaper advertisements, exhibition accounts, and local histories. Frequently this material may be supported by marked or accepted specimens of earthenware or stoneware. Only very rarely, however, does the evidence of the struggle come to light in the words of the potter himself. The dog-eared, coverless notebook, its pages filled with the firm handwriting of Simon Thomas Humberstone, is of uncommon interest. That such a document should have survived at all is remarkable enough, but it is particularly appropriate that this unusual record should be connected with the Humberstones, whose length and constancy of effort stand unrivalled in the troubled history of Canadian potting.

CHAPTER XXVI

China Decorating in Canada

This elegant ornamental art was introduced into Canada for the first time,
by Messrs Hurd, Leigh & Co., Yonge Street, Toronto. *Journal
of the Board of Arts and Manufactures for Upper Canada.*

In china decorating as well as in potting Canadians attempted to compete with
the overseas manufacturers. Here again there was a significant link with Staffordshire. China painters from the potteries of England were brought out to the
colonies, or came out on their own initiative to seek work, and taught as well as
practised their art. As early as the 1860's Hurd, Leigh & Co., of Toronto, china,
glass, and earthenware dealers, hit upon the idea of importing wares in the white
to be decorated by English-trained workers at their own studio. The firm claimed
to be the first in Canada to introduce china decorating on this industrial level.[1]
For their enterprise, Joseph Hurd and Edmund G. Leigh won the praise of the
Board of Arts and Manufactures for Upper Canada.[2]

The Toronto firm that brought this new industry to Canada was established
in the 1850's (as Jackson & Hurd, at 72 Yonge Street); it lasted until the second
half of the 1870's.[3] In 1863, shortly after Joseph Hurd and Edmund Leigh had
taken control of the business, the decorating department was opened.[4] According
to the *Journal of the Board of Arts and Manufactures*, the first artists employed
came from England: 'Hurd, Leigh & Co. . . . sent to England for a family of
artists who had been educated at a school of design in connection with the potteries, and had long experience in working for some of the best establishments'.[5]
With these china decorators of long experience on their staff, Hurd, Leigh & Co.
began to build up new business for themselves and a new industry in the colonies.

Initial publicity centred around the advantages to Canadian buyers of tablewares made in England but decorated in Canada. The *Journal of the Board of
Arts and Manufactures* explained it to the public:

> The exceedingly beautiful wares of the English potteries are so attractive to all who have
> the least taste, that almost every family regards the possession of a set of beautiful china
> as among the first requisites of housekeeping. Unfortunately, however, the loss by break-
> age in transporting this class of goods from England to this country is so great as to raise
> the price of the articles above the convenience of many to purchase. The Messrs. Hurd,
> Leigh & Co., familiar with the pottery business in all its practical detail, resolved to
> remedy this state of things by importing their fine porcelain without the ornamental work,
> and having the artistic embellishment executed here at their own establishment.

Hurd, Leigh & Co. convinced the Board of Arts and Manufactures, who backed them publicly, that they could give the Canadian buyer better value by importing the obviously cheaper undecorated ware and having 'the artistic embellishment' put on in Canada. This, however, was only one aspect of their sales campaign. Another took the line of encouraging home manufactures. It was the theme of an advertisement prominently placed in *McEvoy & Co.'s Toronto Guide for the Provincial Fair of 1866*:

Encourage Home Manufacture

Hurd, Leigh & Co.

Gilders & Enamellers

of

China and Earthenware

Dinner Sets decorated to order

any number of pieces—upwards of

30 patterns always on hand . . .

So far from his choice being limited because of selecting from Canadian-decorated wares, the customer who bought from Hurd, Leigh & Co. would be able to choose from 'the largest number of patterns in Tea and Toilet Ware of any House in the Trade'—or so Hurd, Leigh & Co. advertised in the *Guide*. If the customer saw nothing he liked in the stock patterns 'always on hand', he could bring in his own design for decoration, and be sure that it would be executed 'at short notice'. This last was meant to point up the difference between giving an order for special china decoration to be done in Canada itself and submitting the same type of order to an English firm.

Canadian china merchants had always been ready to take orders for special decoration. Patton & Co., of Toronto, rivals of Hurd, Leigh & Co. in the crockery business, advertised regularly that they could 'furnish Dinner Services . . . with Initials or Armorial Crests'.[6] But Patton & Co., like other china merchants throughout the colonies, sent off their orders for this special decoration to the manufacturer overseas; the customer in Canada received it only after a long delay. Hurd, Leigh & Co., with china-decorating facilities 'now for the first time introduced . . . into this country',[7] promised crests, mottoes, or any other decorating work 'on the shortest notice and highest style of art'. The editors of the *Guide* added their comment that this work so quickly done at home was both 'beautiful and chaste'.

Hurd, Leigh & Co. made a success of their pioneer undertaking. A pamphlet entitled *Business Sketches of Toronto*, published about 1867,[8] only a few years after Hurd, Leigh & Co. had 'introduced' china decorating to Canada, speaks of them as having developed one of the largest trades in the province in the crockery line. Still said to be 'the only establishment in Canada' where the 'beautiful and delicate process' of china painting was attempted, Hurd, Leigh & Co. had found such a demand for their goods that the decorating department alone now kept twelve persons constantly employed.

The novelty of the industry at this time is further suggested by the attention given in the *Sketches* to the decorating side of Hurd, Leigh & Co.'s business. Gilding, as it was carried out in 'pure gold' at 72 Yonge Street, was described in detail: 'A solution of pure gold is used . . . which on being laid on the china at first has a dark hue, the other necessary colors are then put on, after which the china is placed in a furnace where it is subjected to intense heat. On being taken out the gilding is a dull yellow color, after which the articles are put in the hands of the finishers and burnished with agate or bloodstone.'

Another account of the firm in the 1860's boasted that the china decorating done in Toronto was 'equal in quality and appearance' to the best that England could offer.[9] The writer who made this claim pointed out that orders which would have gone abroad in the past were now being attended to at home, and cited the specially decorated china and earthenware in use at the Rossin House as an example. The crest on all of the ware at this Toronto hotel was the work of Hurd, Leigh & Co.

The period of Hurd, Leigh & Co.'s activity was the period when French porcelain began to crowd English products in the Canadian market. Much of their decorating work, particularly for hotels and restaurants, was carried out on French china, which they advertised along with English wares.[10] It is a piece of French porcelain that today links these Toronto importers and decorators with a famous restaurant that was one of the most fashionable eating places in Victorian Montreal. This piece, sold at auction in Montreal in 1963, a hundred years after it received its decoration in Toronto, is a large ornamental jug (*Plate* 50). Embellished with gold, and with a broad band of claret colour around the rim, the jug bears the inscription (in gilt letters): 'Toronto TO Montreal'. Worked in with the inscription are the name and device of the Terrapin Restaurant. They are done in the 'pale rose colour' that a contemporary account spoke of as typical of Hurd, Leigh & Co.'s palette.[11] The same pale rose has been used for the identification on the bottom of the piece, where HURD, LEIGH & CO., TORONTO, DECORATORS appears on a ribbon.

The Terrapin Restaurant had its beginning in Toronto. It was the successor to the St. Nicholas Saloon,[12] and it stood on land now covered by the King Edward Hotel. So successful was this restaurant that its owners, Carlisle & McConkey, were able to open branches in other parts of the country. In the last weeks of 1862 they moved into Montreal, renting premises in the Crystal Block on Notre Dame Street.[13] In Montreal the Terrapin Restaurant and Ladies' Ice Cream Saloon caught the carriage trade at once. It became the meeting place not only for those who wished to sample the 'delicacies of the season' and the stock of the 'liberally furnished bar', but for those with musical tastes. In an early Montreal advertisement, introduced by a Latin motto, 'Dum Vivimus Vivamus', Carlisle & McConkey announced 'elegant PARLOUR CONCERTS' as a regular feature of the restaurant's entertainment policy.[14] 'Soirées Musicales', with the band of the Terrapin leading in the *Victoria Rifles* quickstep or the *Corn Flower* valse, were soon events of the season.[15]

Long after the Terrapin Restaurant closed in Toronto it continued to flourish in Montreal. There, in 1873, it passed into the hands of Henry Dunne, former 'assistant to the late Mr. Carlisle'.[16] Henry Dunne kept it going for almost twenty years, and it was not until the early 1890's that the Terrapin Restaurant on Notre Dame Street went out of existence.

When the Toronto to Montreal venture had first been decided upon by the owners of the Terrapin Restaurant, there had been a flurry of excitement. Publicity in newspapers and advertising in directories in both cities called attention to the fact that this Toronto house had opened a branch in Montreal. As one of their early orders in the decorating department, Hurd, Leigh & Co. had been called upon to produce the large jug that recorded the success of this move. For years the jug, with its pale rose terrapin and its 'Toronto TO Montreal' stood in the restaurant on Notre Dame Street. It was still there when Henry Dunne took over the management and it was there when he retired. When he closed the restaurant, he took the 'Toronto TO Montreal' jug home with him. From Henry Dunne it passed to his daughter, Mrs. Charles H. Alves. It was with her possessions when she died in the 1960's. As a souvenir of the past it recalls the gaieties of Victorian Montreal, and at the same time it bears testimony to the enterprise of a Toronto importing house that brought a new industry to Canada.

Of the china merchants who followed Hurd, Leigh & Co.'s example and set up decorating departments of their own, one of the most important was the firm of W. J. Reid & Co., of London. Reid's china, glass, and earthenware business had been established in the 1840's by the Manchester-born Nathaniel Reid, father of W. J. Reid. By the 1880's this china house was doing a wholesale trade with customers 'from Halifax to British Columbia'.[17] Five travellers working throughout the country brought in the orders, and these included orders for wares whose decoration was painted on in London. In an 'immense' four-storey building on Dundas Street, known as Crystal Hall, one whole floor was given over to the china painters. A visitor to W. J. Reid & Co. called their work 'an interesting industry': 'The China decorating department is on the second flat, and here we come to an interesting industry. Artists are employed painting flowers and fancy patterns on China tea sets, dinner sets, chamber sets, lamp shades, etc., etc. The work is tastefully executed, the colors are finely blended, the whole being finished in a most artistic manner. Two kilns are used for the burning in of the patterns, so as to make them absolutely indestructible.'[18]

The wares on which the 'indestructible' patterns were painted included heavy ironstone from Staffordshire. Stone china, ironstone, and white granite were imported by Reid & Co. in such quantities that another whole floor in Crystal Hall (the third) was allotted to their display.[19] Such goods were very cheap when imported in the white; hand-painted in London they simulated the 'beautiful china' that the *Journal of the Board of Arts and Manufactures* said every housewife longed for.

An example of Canadian decoration on this type of ware is to be found in an ironstone plate from the Burslem factory of William and Edward Corn. Imported in the white, the plate was given a gold rim at Crystal Hall, and then painted with a bird in flight and a spray of clover, leaves, and berries arranged asymmetrically. On the back of the plate, in addition to the under-glaze printed mark of W. & E. Corn, is the ornate over-glaze mark (in red) of W. J. Reid & Co. This mark incorporates the information that the piece was MANUFACTURED BY CRYSTAL HALL WORKS W. J. REID & CO. LONDON CANADA. When there is no maker's mark, the words 'Manufactured by W. J. Reid & Co.' have sometimes led to the mistaken belief that Reid & Co. must have been Canadian manufacturers of ironstone. They were, however, importers and decorators, not potters.

In the 1880's, when W. J. Reid & Co. were operating an extensive china-decorating department, they were only one of the firms in London where such work was being turned out in quantity. Another firm, established about 1885, was owned by Pigot & Bryan, and known as the London Decorating Works.[20] It is not surprising to find that china decorating flourished on an important scale in London, for in London there had settled at mid-century one of the best known, most accomplished, and most influential of all the Canadian china painters (*Plate* 51A).

John Howard Griffiths (1826-98) was born in Staffordshire and worked in the Potteries as a china painter before coming to Canada. He was a younger brother of James Griffiths, a charter member of the Royal Canadian Academy, who, like John, began his career by painting china in Staffordshire. Both brothers were to be prominent in the artistic life of the colonies, but it was John who was to have wide influence through teaching, and it was he who would continue to work on china in Canada.

An undated newspaper clipping in a family scrapbook, kept by the eldest of John Griffiths' six daughters, says that he was once 'a pupil of Rippingille, of the Royal Academy' (Edward Villiers Rippingille, who exhibited at the Royal Academy in London from 1813 until 1857).[21] The clipping adds that he 'also served an apprenticeship at painting on china'. In an interview in Canada in the 1890's John Griffiths identified the pottery where this apprenticeship was served as Mintons, in Stoke-on-Trent. There he had learned to decorate china, and there he had himself invented a new way to paint upon china buttons, so as to speed up the process and put it on a more remunerative basis.[22]

Mintons was also the background for James Griffiths. Before coming to London, Canada West, James had spent a number of years as a china painter at Mintons. Their association with this important pottery was recalled in the obituaries of both brothers, in Staffordshire as well as in Canadian newspapers, after their deaths in 1897 and 1898. A third brother, Hamlet Griffiths, who remained in England, and who was the youngest of the trio, had his own connections with Mintons. After his death a Staffordshire paper recalled that he 'served his time as a hollow-ware presser at Messrs Minton's', the same factory where his elder brothers had worked as china painters.[23]

Today at Mintons there are no relevant records for the years when James and John Griffiths would have been apprentices, but there is plenty of evidence that at this factory, where the tradition of family loyalties is strong, the name Griffiths was well known in the nineteenth century.[24] The work of both brothers in Canada shows clearly that they had been trained as china painters in the Staffordshire tradition, and although James did not pursue china painting to the same extent as his brother, after he settled in London, his experience as a china painter continued to characterize his other work. The study of peonies, which he deposited as his diploma subject for the Royal Canadian Academy, and which is today at the National Gallery in Ottawa, identifies him at a glance as an artist with pottery antecedents. It is of interest that John Griffiths, the better known of the two for china painting, credited James with having had his part to play also in establishing in Canada critical standards for judging the quality of painted decoration on china. According to John Griffiths it was his brother, and not he, who first induced provincial exhibition committees to include china painting as a category in prize lists, and who was responsible for 'much of the knowledge that has circulated through the province'.[25]

In Canada neither brother was able to devote himself exclusively to art. For over twenty-five years James Griffiths was employed in the Court House at London, his painting in oils and water colours done when the day's work was over. John Griffiths, like many another Staffordshire man who came out to the colonies, combined farming with other pursuits. The land that he eventually acquired was Lot 23, Concession 1, in Westminster (then outside London). But he did not particularly care for farming, and in the end his hundred acres were primarily the concern of his only son. The son no more than the father enjoyed working on the land, but he submitted to the dictates of a Victorian parent, whose own interests were devoted with singleness of purpose to collecting paintings and china. There are family recollections of days when the farm needed some improvement or the farm house some added equipment, but John Griffiths, oblivious of these things, would arrive home with another painting or the latest example of fine porcelain to be found in London. An auction (he once bought a seventeenth-century Spanish painting for one cent at a London sale),[26] a meeting with a fellow artist (and they were all his friends, their best work upon his walls —Daniel Fowler, Harlow White, St. Thomas Smith),[27] or an account of the latest ceramic triumph from his old firm of Mintons meant more to him than the state of the crops or the percentage of butter fat in the milk.

In part, John Griffiths owed the indulgence of his tastes to the fact that, unlike many an immigrant, he had come to Canada with capital. The directories listed him in his first days in London as an 'artist',[28] but at that time he was an artist who was 'engaged in speculating and loaning money'.[29] The second half of the 1850's were, however, years of depression in Canada. John Griffiths lost heavily. He then looked around for congenial work, and for a time was employed at painting and japanning the wares of J. & O. McClary, tinsmiths and hardware merchants.[30] Later he opened a photographic studio.[31] He was deeply interested in the new art of photography and experimented with its application to porcelain, a field in which the Wedgwood firm was also experimenting at this same period in England.

But at all times John Griffiths, no matter in what other occupation he was engaged—whether in the distasteful pursuit of farming, in japanning tinware or in taking photographs—continued his enthusiasm for china painting. As one of the founders and later principal of the Western School of Art in London, he taught china painting to many. A contemporary account of the school indicates that extra afternoon classes had to be formed to accommodate those who registered for instruction in this subject.[32] In his promotion of the School of Art, John Griffiths put into practice teaching which he himself had received from Edward Villiers Rippingille. Rippingille claimed to have been the first to advocate schools of design;[33] when his old pupil became principal of the Western School of Art in Canada, he made clear that one of the chief aims of that school would be 'to build up the industries'.[34]

As a china painter and teacher of china painting John Griffiths was widely known. Newspaper references to his accomplishments were frequent. On Oc-

316

tober 22, 1889, for example, the London *Free Press* reported that 'The silver medal which was awarded to Mr. J. H. Griffiths . . . for the best collection of decorated china at the Toronto Industrial Exhibition was received by him yesterday.' This was a 'special medal', the newspaper pointed out, 'the seventh Mr. Griffiths has been awarded for his art productions'.

The prizes he took at exhibitions, both in Ontario and beyond provincial borders, established John Griffiths as one of the best-known china painters in Canada, but the most celebrated of his 'art productions' on porcelain was exhibited not at a fair but in the window of a china-decorating shop. In 1887 John Griffiths painted a porcelain tête-à-tête set that was one of Canada's official gifts to Queen Victoria on the occasion of her Golden Jubilee. Before it went off to London, England, the china painted by John Griffiths was displayed in London, Canada. The *Free Press* gave a glowing account of it:

> Messrs Pigot & Bryan, proprietors of the London Decorating Works, have on view in one of their windows, a beautiful specimen of ceramic art, which has been gotten up as a jubilee offering to the Queen, consisting of a 'tete-a-tete' set designed and executed by Mr. J. H. Griffiths, who was awarded the gold medal for china painting at the late Exhibition. The set is a masterpiece of porcelain painting. The decoration consists of a wreath of maple leaves around each piece, each leaf perfect in itself, the fibres and shades being beautifully brought out. The crown is in gold studded with jewels. Underneath this are the letters 'V.R.,' composed of small roses and leaves. The flowers, some of which are not larger than a pin's head, are marvellously executed. The handle of each piece is finished in dead gold, and they as well as the border of each are jewelled, giving the set a very rich appearance and worthy of the object for which it is intended. The tray which accompanies it is made of eight different kinds of wood grown in Canada, and is a gem in its way.[35]

To ensure that the Queen's gift was perfect, and ready in time, John Griffiths worked on two identical sets. Presumably he had no serious difficulties, nor accidents in firing, for the spare set, complete and also perfect, remained with his family. Today it is in the possession of his grand-daughter, Professor Margaret Griffiths, of McGill University.

Other family pieces, illustrating John Griffiths' work and belonging either to Professor Griffiths or to her sister, Mrs. W. H. Pike, include a self-portrait on porcelain, plaques painted with fruit and flowers in the Staffordshire manner, and plates with jewelled rims and raised gilding. Roses in their every variety were favourite subjects, and in the treatment of these flowers John Griffiths reached the peak of his skill on porcelain. He also painted figure and bird subjects, as well as arrangements of flowers other than roses. Of particular interest are samples of his work as a designer of patterns suitable for ordinary china decoration, and not intended as special show pieces. One such pattern makes use of sprays of heather in white reserves on a green ground. Not all his work was signed. The signature, when it does occur, is generally on the back of the piece, painted in red. The date is sometimes added (*Plate* 51B).

There is no evidence that John Griffiths ever intended to seek regular day-by-day employment as a china painter in Canada. Had he done so, and been dependent upon what he could earn in this way, he would have struggled for a living when he first came to the colony. His influence, had his efforts been confined to a commercial house, would probably have been slight. But the work which he did mostly on his own, 'with unabated zeal' and as part of an enthu-

317

siasm for art that 'never waned'—as his obituary put it in 1898—won wide recognition.[36] It served as an impressive example to many, set high standards, and helped to form what he himself called an understanding 'of the hall marks of a good bit of china'.[37] His teaching—and it used to be said that one could not go down the street in London, Ontario, without meeting someone who had studied china painting under John Griffiths—undoubtedly prepared many to earn a livelihood by china decorating in the later years of the century. Through John Griffiths, trained at Mintons, 'one of the chief establishments of the Potteries', Staffordshire traditions reached out in yet another way to Canada and her crockery trade.

From the beginning of the 1870's china decorating as an industry made progress. The industry tended to expand, however, in the direction of the independent decorating establishment, rather than along the lines on which Hurd, Leigh & Co. had introduced it (as an adjunct to china selling). Some china, glass, and earthenware importers, like W. J. Reid & Co., did follow Hurd, Leigh & Co.'s example, and set up their own decorating departments, but throughout the provinces there also sprang up many firms whose main business was not the selling of china, glass, and earthenware but the decorating of it to the order of both dealers and private customers. Herbert Plant established a firm of this kind in Toronto not many years after Hurd, Leigh & Co. had founded the industry. As a decorator, Herbert Plant was in business for some time, sharing the field in later days with competitors like George Prance and W. O. Littleford. In Montreal there were companies such as the Central China Decorating Company and the China & Glass Decorating Company. Similar establishments operated in other cities from Halifax to Vancouver.

With the specialized industry there opened up opportunities for the free-lance china painter and the part-time worker. If Canadian-trained, as in time a number of the china decorators were, the professional working on his own had probably taken classes at a school such as the Western School of Art in London (which owed its great debt to John Griffiths), or the School of Art and Design in Montreal (opened in connection with the Board of Arts and Manufactures for Lower Canada).[38] In Victorian times there were many outlets for the work of the china decorator maintaining his own studio. Benjamin Bloor, for example, was able to obtain commissions from Montreal plumbers. At the 1882 Dominion Exhibition in Montreal, sanitary ware decorated by Bloor and displayed 'in working order' by a plumbing firm was remarked on particularly by a *Star* reporter. Bloor's artistic work received almost as much attention in the news story as the special trap designed by the plumber to keep out sewer gas.[39]

In at least one case the decorating of imported china became a sideline at a Canadian pottery. The Montreal Pottery Company, which was established in 1893 and had its Works in Pointe St. Charles,[40] also operated a decorating business. At the pottery itself Rockingham, cane, stoneware, and terracotta were produced; but, as the *Montreal Herald* noted in 1898, 'besides manufacturing these goods, the Montreal Pottery Company also imports china and porcelain from England and France'.[41] These English and French wares were decorated in a separate department at the Works in Pointe St. Charles. The decorating side of the business advertised 'Ground Laying, Stippling, Cresting, Etc.'[42]

318

China Decorating in Canada

Side by side with the growth of china decorating as an industry went china decorating by amateurs. In Canada amateur work had become a craze by the latter part of the nineteenth century. This craze had a direct bearing on the crockery trade. Amateurs needed wares to paint, and the china, glass, and earthenware merchants were the main suppliers of these wares. Dealers in artists' materials and sometimes stationers also supplied blanks, or china 'in the white'; but their ceramic goods were generally obtained through a Canadian china, glass, and earthenware wholesaler in the first place. For the china merchant the amateur's preoccupation with china decorating meant big business, and he purposely catered to it in his advertising. Glover Harrison of Toronto, the owner of China Hall on King Street, advertised in the *Mail* on February 10, 1880, that he had just unpacked new goods which included 'two Hogsheads of French China in white, suitable for painting'.

A. T. Wiley, of Wiley's China Hall in Montreal, was an advertiser who frequently directed his sales propaganda to the china painter. One such advertisement appearing in the *Daily Witness* under the heading 'FINE ARTS IN THE HOUSEHOLD', offered 'China for Painting' along with Parian ornaments, majolica, and 'BRIC-A-BRAC in endless variety'.[43] Another of Wiley's announcements in the 1880's made a feature of 'WHITE CHINA for Oil Painting or in Water Colors'.[44]

The best china factories sold wares in the white to meet the demands of china painters, amateur and professional. John Griffiths frequently made use of Wedgwood porcelain, and his grand-daughters still have Wedgwood blanks that were with his china-painting equipment when he died. Minton and Copeland earthenware tiles were favourites with artists (*Plate* 52). A Montreal Christmas advertisement of 1881, published in the *Witness* on December 16, itemized 'Christmas paint boxes' and enamel colours for china painting, as well as Minton tiles on which to work.

Porcelain made at Limoges in France was imported in vast quantities for the use of china painters. The McCord Museum, McGill University, has coffee cups and saucers made at Limoges and decorated in Montreal at the School of Art and Design, obviously by a student not yet proficient in the technique of laying ground colours. The cups and saucers have the maker's mark, and also the mark, printed over-glaze in an oval: SCHOOL OF ART/MONTREAL/APPLIED DESIGN.

Though the craze for amateur china painting was at its height in Canada in late Victorian days, it began even before Queen Victoria came to the throne. In 1835 when a Miss Webster opened her Painting Academy in Montreal, 'in one of the new Stone Houses at the head of M'Gill Street', she put a type of china painting on a curriculum that also included japanning, wax work, and 'Transparent Painting on Glass'—this last being intended to imitate the effect of 'China Engravings'.[45] As the century progressed, announcements offering instruction in china painting increased with a rush. The ultimate seems to have been reached with an advertisement in Montreal's *Daily Witness* on December 13, 1879. The advertiser in this case confidently offered to teach 'the art of decorating china' in a single lesson.

Amateur china painting actually benefited the professional decorator, for although there might not be employment for him in a china, glass, and earthenware house or in one of the decorating establishments, or even as a free-lance worker, he could always gather a class of amateurs about him and teach. William Mill Allan (1864-1951) worked as a china painter with a Glasgow firm of crockery exporters before emigrating to British Columbia in 1890. Almost as soon as he was settled in Victoria he started a class in china painting.[46]

By the end of the century every properly educated young lady knew how to paint on china. She had studied at an art school or with a private instructor, or had at least learned the rudiments in a young ladies' seminary. Some amateurs became surprisingly good, their work ranking with that of professional china decorators. The quality and scope of this amateur china painting in Canada were strikingly demonstrated in the dinner service presented to the Countess of Aberdeen in 1898. Members of the Canadian Senate and House of Commons made this china, painted by amateurs, their farewell gift to the wife of the Governor-General, Lord Aberdeen.

With a social conscience well ahead of her time and the courage to face opposition, Lady Aberdeen all her life stirred controversy. In Canada in the 1890's her career was no different from what it had been or was to be elsewhere. But when her few years in Ottawa were over, even those who had opposed her most bitterly in some of her projects must have realized that only a gift intimately associated with Canada would be appropriate; for Ishbel, Countess of Aberdeen, was leaving behind her more real (and lasting) evidence of her interest in the welfare of Canadians than the wife of any Governor-General in the country's history. She had founded the National Council of Women of Canada, the Victorian Order of Nurses for Canada, and the May Courts of Canada. It was the women of Canada who helped to prepare her official farewell gift.

This gift was a 200-piece dinner, dessert, and coffee service of Doulton porcelain painted in Canada by 'lady artists'. Each of the many pieces was different, but each bore a Canadian scene or subject. The Women's Art Association provided the artists, selecting them after a series of competitions organized by the association's branches in Winnipeg, Hamilton, St. Thomas, Toronto, Brockville, Montreal, and Saint John. Mary E. Dignam, founder of the Women's Art Association and a stalwart supporter of Lady Aberdeen in the battle to establish the V.O.N., took charge of the project.

It was a big undertaking in china decorating that Mary Dignam supervised. There were two dozen soup plates and two dozen meat plates to be painted with Canadian historical landscape views; two dozen game plates to be painted with Canadian game birds; two dozen fish plates with Canadian fish, shells, and seaweeds; two dozen salad plates with Canadian ferns; two dozen dessert plates with Canadian fruit and fruit blossoms; two dozen cheese plates with Canadian song birds; and two dozen coffee cups and saucers with Canadian wild flowers.

The historical views ranged from the Old Magazine at Annapolis, Nova Scotia, to the Old Fort at Nanaimo, British Columbia. There were views of Quebec city, and of Brock's monument at Niagara; there was the Mohawk Church at Brantford, and the remains of the French fortifications at Louisbourg; there was the Château de Ramezay on Notre Dame Street and one of the seventeenth-century towers on Sherbrooke Street in Montreal; there was Fort Henry at Kingston, the Fish Market in Toronto, and Old Fort Garry in the Red River Territory.

The birds illustrated included the Canada goose, the bob-white, the snow bunting, and the chickadee. The fish and sea shells included the sea urchin, the scallop, the brook trout, and the lake sturgeon. On the dessert plates were such typical fruits as Niagara grapes, wild strawberries, and blueberries; and on the coffee cups and saucers flowers as characteristic of Canadian woods and fields as the dogtooth violet and the western daisy. Every piece was signed with the name of the artist, and every subject was identified.[47]

A reporter for the *Gazette* was allowed a preview of the finished work. In his dispatch to Montreal he called it 'an illustrated history of the scenery and seasons of Canada in 208 volumes', and enthusiastically predicted that it would prove 'the most valuable artistic work ever done in Canada'.[48]

The china was formally presented to Lady Aberdeen on June 13, 1898, in the Senate Chamber. An eyewitness, Lady Edgar, wife of the Speaker of the House of Commons, noted that bearded legislators wept as the once-shy Lady Aberdeen, by now an accomplished public speaker, touched on the scenes painted on china.[49] They would be, she said:

a constant living memory of the surroundings intimately connected with those various Canadian homes which have become dear to us—as we look on them . . . our thoughts will travel fondly again from east to west . . . And again we shall hear the sweet notes of the Canadian robin and blue bird heralding spring in the woods of Rideau Hall—we shall hear the whir of the wild geese crossing our lovely British Columbia lakes and mountains . . . We shall long for the exhilaration of a toboggan slide on a brilliant Canadian winter's day. We shall listen for the splash of the paddle as the canoe glides up a stately river amidst sunshine and beauty. Now we shall be speeding over the myriad hued prairies and anon we shall find ourselves in deep woods amidst the haunts of the wild flowers whose loveliness we see immortalized.[50]

To Lady Aberdeen the 'splendid gift' had a special value as the handiwork of Canadian women with whom she had shared 'common aims and common work'. As soon as she was back in Great Britain she had special cabinets built for the china painted in Canada. Today it is preserved at Haddo House in Aberdeenshire, Scotland.[51]

The remarkable extent and accomplishment of amateur china painting in Canada had been displayed in the Aberdeen service, but it remained true that this amateur work was only one aspect of an art that was also a Canadian industry, an industry that owed its establishment to Hurd, Leigh & Co. of Toronto. In its development this industry had drawn heavily upon the traditions of the English potteries. Those who had been trained in these English traditions brought to Canada their skills both as practitioners and teachers. They were men like the Minton-trained Griffiths brothers—James Griffiths, who, 'with great difficulty', persuaded provincial fair managers to recognize china painting in awarding prizes, and John Howard Griffiths, the china painter who may not have been a success at farming, but whose 'unabated zeal' for his art effectively impressed the standards of old Staffordshire upon a new country.

APPENDIX A

Concerning Marks

At almost any public library in Canada reference books on pottery and porcelain marks may be consulted. Some background notes may, however, prove helpful, since there are many popular misconceptions concerning the marking of ceramic wares. Probably the most prevalent is that if a piece of pottery or porcelain is un-marked it is necessarily old—'made before marks were used'; in short, that an unmarked piece should always be regarded as older than one bearing factory identification. This is not true. Throughout the nineteenth century there were potters who marked their wares and there were those who did not. A factory that frequently marked its products might, for one reason or another, leave some of them unmarked. In a Rockingham tea set, for example, the saucers were generally marked, the cups were not. At the Spode factory, where marking of the wares was extensively practised, some patterns were less often given the factory mark than others. The printed pattern known as 'Gothic Castle' is an example. This pattern, offering a surprising combination of the Chinese and Gothic, is very frequently found without an identifying mark of any kind. On the other hand, Spode patterns such as those adapted from Luigi Mayer's *Views in . . . Caramania* generally carry the Spode name.

Another popular misconception is that in 1891 it became 'compulsory' for English ceramic wares to be marked. Hence, all unmarked wares *ipso facto* pre-date 1891. Again this is not true. What happened in 1891 was that the effect of the McKinley Tariff Act in the United States began to be evident. At the end of September, 1890, President McKinley's highly protectionist Bill passed the Congress. This Bill, designed to encourage American industries, provided that manufactured articles of various kinds imported into the United States had to be clearly marked with the name of the country of origin. The Act came into opera-tion on October 6, 1890, and by 1891 most potters exporting to America were marking the country of origin on their wares. It was not that these potters expect-ed to sell their total output to the United States, but it was expedient to have wares ready and eligible for any order, including American. Generally speaking, the presence of the word 'England' in a ceramic mark denotes a date after

323

October 6, 1890, although occasionally the name of the country had been used earlier. An example of its use before 1890 is found in the marks of Anthony Shaw of Burslem, as given by Llewellynn Jewitt, in the 1883 revised edition of *The Ceramic Art of Great Britain*. There are other similar examples.

Where the words 'Made in England' occur (as opposed to 'England' alone), the piece so marked is of the twentieth century. This is not to say that when the word 'England' alone appears the piece is necessarily nineteenth-century, but simply that 'Made in England' belongs to the twentieth. It should be remembered, too, that American potters were under no obligation to mark their own wares with the name of the country of origin. A piece of white ironstone may be innocent of the name of any country but still be a late nineteenth- or twentieth-century product from an American potter.

A date as part of a factory mark rarely means that the piece bearing this mark was actually made at that date. It is more likely to refer to the founding of the factory in question. Thus the mark of the Worcester Royal Porcelain Company, which came into being under that name in 1862, incorporates the date '51'—a reference to 1751, the date at which Dr. Wall and his associates established their porcelain manufactory. In mid-Victorian times Coalport added '1750' to the factory mark, indicating the date claimed for the founding of that factory.

The word 'Limited' (or an abbreviation) after a firm name in a British ceramic mark belongs to the second half of the nineteenth century; it is found most often in the marks of the late Victorian period. After the Merchandise Marks Act of 1862, British ceramic marks might include the words 'Trade Mark', though their incorporation in a factory mark more usually indicates a date after August 13, 1875, when the Trade Marks Registration Act was passed.

All marks indicating the maker of a piece of pottery or porcelain—whether the name of the firm in full, the initials only, or a symbol or rebus, such as the bell which John and Matthew P. Bell, of Glasgow, used—might be impressed in the paste, printed under the glaze, or painted. In addition to the maker's mark, nineteenth-century ceramic marks often included a printed pattern name, a painted pattern number, the name of the particular body used (ironstone, ivory body, etc.), or a decorator's or artist's mark. The name of the body might be either printed or impressed; the artist's mark was sometimes incised (as on certain Doulton stonewares). Impressed or incised numbers, as distinct from painted numbers, usually had a private significance (perhaps a mould number, or a size). Some printed or impressed letters and symbols also had meaning only within the factory. Such marks are of no assistance in determining the maker of a piece of pottery or porcelain. Pattern numbers, however, in the absence of other marks, are often useful in identifying the factory. Both Spode and Davenport, for instance, produced on china an identical Imari-type pattern showing flowering plants and fencing within a formal border of red, blue, green, and gold. The pattern number, 967, identifies the Spode products.

Frequently on nineteenth-century printed wares, only a pattern name appears. Since more than one potter often made use of the same pattern name, it is not safe to jump to conclusions concerning the identification of a piece on the basis of pattern name alone. 'Friburg', for example, is a Davenport pattern name; it is also the name of a pattern registered by George Phillips, another Staffordshire potter.

Just as more than one potter might use the same pattern name, so many used a variation of the same device as part of a printed mark. Because it is possible to connect the firm of Clementson Brothers, of Hanley, with a garter device (used sometimes to mark their Canada pattern), it is not correct to assume that every piece bearing a garter device as part of a printed mark is of Clementson make. Nor does an anchor always signify Davenport, or a harp Belleek.

Canadian dealers' marks on imported wares have already been discussed (Chap. VII), but it should be remembered that china merchants in other countries also followed the practice of having their names added to the wares they sold. A name on a piece of pottery or porcelain is not always the name of the maker. As has been pointed out earlier (Chap. XIII), the presence of SHARPUS & CO. on the back of tablewares decorated with maple leaves and the Prince of Wales' Feathers has led many Canadian possessors of these 1860 souvenirs to think that Sharpus was a potter. The London firm of Sharpus & Co. was merely the retailer through whom the Canadian order was placed; the wares were made at Worcester. Rideau Hall, the viceregal residence in Ottawa, appears on earthenware marked PRIMAVESI & SONS/SWANSEA. The Primavesis were the sellers, not the makers of this brown-printed earthenware (introduced in the 1880's under the pattern name 'The World', and depicting scenes on every continent).

While marks may be extremely helpful in dating a piece of earthenware or porcelain, they may, also, at times be misleading, unless taken in historical context. Many a new collector has read in a reference book that the impressed mark SPODE was used c. 1770, and then, finding a piece of blue-printed earthenware with SPODE clearly impressed on the back, has at once assigned a 1770 date to it. But although the Spode factory did use the SPODE mark as early as the 1770's, it would be impossible for any under-glaze printed Spode ware to belong to that date, regardless of mark. No under-glaze printing was even attempted at the Spode factory, or at any other Staffordshire factory, as early as 1770. The technique was introduced later, and was only perfected over a period of time (see Chap. IX). The appearance of the mark itself and the type of ware on which it is found has always to be reconciled to any statement concerning date. In the case of the Spode factory, the word SPODE impressed was used as a mark from the 1770's until the beginning of the 1830's. Wedgwood is another factory whose marks often deceive the new collector into giving a nineteenth-century product an eighteenth-century date. The impressed mark WEDGWOOD belongs to both centuries. Experience is needed in judging the date of Wedgwood wares, apart from any marks they may have; and even then, as Sir John Wedgwood said in an interview in Montreal, in 1955, the expert may be fooled.

Some wares belonging to the nineteenth century may, however, be dated to within a few years with relative ease, through the presence of a diamond-shaped mark indicating that the design of the piece (either pattern or form) had been registered with the British Patent Office. This mark, printed under the glaze or impressed in the paste, was in use from 1842 until 1883. The letters and numbers in the corners of the diamond constituted a code, giving the year, month, and day of registration. The name of the firm applying for the registration could also be learned by reference to official documents indicated by one of the code numbers. The key to this code, in so far as the date of registration is concerned, is included here, but it should be remembered that the date represents only the earliest possible date at which a piece could have been produced under the registration. The initial registration protected the design for three years, but it could be renewed for a further period. It is not possible, therefore, to say that an example of the Clementsons' Canada pattern bearing the design registration mark for March 20, 1877, was made on that day or even in that year; it might have been produced at any time during the next few years. A manufacturer did not register all his new designs; he registered only those he considered likely to be pirated.

It is sometimes thought that the presence of the 'diamond mark' is proof that the piece in question is of British make. This is not so. Foreign manufacturers not infrequently registered designs with the Patent Office in London. In particular the French firm of Haviland & Co., which exported to Canada, registered porcelain shapes and patterns in England. Sometimes these Limoges pieces were marked with the name or initials of the firm, H. & CO., as well as with the registration mark; sometimes the 'diamond mark' alone appears impressed in the continental body. On some Japanese wares a representation of the British registration mark may be found painted in red.

The 'diamond mark', with its code letters and numbers, was discontinued in 1883. From 1884 the registration of a design was indicated by the prefix 'Rd.' followed by a number. These numbers were consecutive, and by the end of the century had passed 350,000. An article, for example, marked 'Rd. No. 352,000' would be a twentieth-century product.

THE DIAMOND-SHAPED REGISTRATION MARK

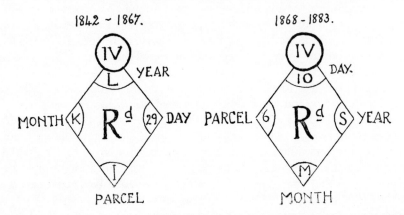

The Roman numeral (IV) in the circle at the top of the mark indicates the class of goods affected. Wood, metal, glass, and ceramic designs could all be registered, and the numeral IV was the one assigned to ceramic wares.

During the period 1842-67 the letter immediately under the circle indicated the year; the letter in the left-hand corner of the diamond indicated the month, the figure at the right the day of the month. The number at the bottom of the diamond gave the parcel number of the relevant documents filed at the Patent Office.

Appendix A

In 1868 the position of the numbers and letters changed, and a new set of code letters was used to identify the year. From that date until 1883, when the mark was discontinued, the year was indicated by the letter at the right-hand corner of the diamond; the month by the letter at the bottom, and the day of the month by the number immediately underneath the Roman numeral IV. The parcel number was then at the left-hand corner of the mark. A quick way of determining which set of code letters to consult for the year, is to remember that if a letter of the alphabet appears directly under the circle, the design was registered in the first period (1842-67); if a number is in this position, the design was registered in the second period (1868-83).

YEAR LETTERS

1842-67					1868-83			
1842	X	1855	E		1868	X	1881	E
1843	H	1856	L		1869	H	1882	L
1844	C	1857	K		1870	C	1883	K
1845	A	1858	B		1871	A		
1846	I	1859	M		1872	I		
1847	F	1860	Z		1873	F		
1848	U	1861	R		1874	U		
1849	S	1862	O		1875	S		
1850	V	1863	G		1876	V		
1851	P	1864	N		1877	P		
1852	D	1865	W		1878	D		
1853	Y	1866	Q		1879	Y		
1854	J	1867	T		1880	J		

MONTH LETTERS

1842-83

January	C	July	I
February	G	August	R
March	W	September	D
April	H	October	B
May	E	November	K
June	M	December	A

During the period in which the mark was used there were some brief changes in the code. From March 1 to March 6, 1878, for instance, the letter W was used to indicate the year, instead of D, and G then indicated the month, instead of W. For all general purposes, however, the keys as given above will serve to decipher the code.

A Check List of
Nineteenth-Century Canadian Potters

A full list of nineteenth-century Canadian potters will never be possible. Many of the pioneer potters worked only briefly and in obscurity. They were never important enough to be included in any directory, and they never advertised in any newspaper or other publication. They and their works have left no trace behind them that can now be identified. The activities of others, however, may be searched out in contemporary records. In the check list given here the names of some five hundred of these potters have been included, the proof of their work offered from contemporary sources.

The check list shows that many potters in nineteenth-century Canada combined the making of earthenware or stoneware with other business ventures. The farmer-potter was to be expected in a new land, but there was also the potter whose directory listing was under 'Furs & Pottery', or 'Pottery & Tavern', or 'boot and shoe shop, dry goods, groceries, pottery works'. There was the potter whose political affiliations assured him of additional income as village postmaster, and the potter who dealt in lumber on the side, or who was also a 'potash . . . maker'. One Lower Canada potter seems to have abandoned the handling of clay to become, for a few years, a cook in a lunatic asylum. Some ran a pottery only as an adjunct to a brickyard, or depended upon draining tiles for their main income.

The list indicates, too, how many potting traditions were mingled in the industry in Canada. The potter with the French name from Quebec is seen in company with the immigrant potter from the British Isles, the potter from the United States, and the competent band of German potters who settled in the counties of Upper Canada bordering on the Grand River. The potters of Canada came from widely differing backgrounds, but in a new land they had, nearly all, to make the same simple wares: the common red flower pots, the brownware milk pans, the jars and stoneware jugs wanted wherever the settler went. How few attempted anything more is emphasized by the scarcity of listings for manufacturers of whiteware for the table.

It may be taken that the great majority of those named in the list were the pottery owners and not journeymen (qualified employees). Though some journeymen are certainly included, the list has been drawn in large measure from the business directories of the day, and these directories tended, on the whole, to name the more important residents of an area: the proprietors of the local industries and shops, the hotel keepers, and the representatives of the professions. The journeyman potter, or the potter in business in a very small way was often overlooked. Local directories, dealing only with one county or town, were naturally more comprehensive in their listings, but even these paid more attention to the farmer with well-cleared land and the essential blacksmith than to the turner at the pottery. Census reports, however, do show that potters were far fewer than has often been assumed. From about mid-century the decennial census reports attempted to list every individual, and a study of these reports reveals surprisingly few whose activity in potting was sufficient to be recorded as the means of livelihood.

In every case the spelling of names in this list has been given as it appears in the contemporary material. It is true that there were errors in directories, newspapers, and even official documents. The handwritten list or advertisement from which the compositor set his type was at times difficult to make out, and those who compiled directory or census lists sometimes made mistakes in the first place. (An example of what appears to be an error in official records occurs in the census reports for 1851 and again for 1861, where the name of the Brantford potter, George Beech, is given as 'Beach'; when he incised his own name on the pieces he made, this English-born potter spelled it 'Beech'.) On the other hand, it is necessary to take into consideration the fact that the spelling of family names often varied considerably over the years. This is particularly true of foreign names, where the gradual anglicizing of the name changed the spelling. Some members of the family might come to spell the name one way, some another. Descendants today may spell a name very differently from the way the founder of the family in this country first wrote it, if he could write. A number of nineteenth-century potters were unable to read or write and may have had to leave any official recording of their names to others, who perhaps guessed at the spelling. As late as 1873 a master potter signing the Ontario Earthenware Manufacturers Association agreement had to sign with his mark.

To jump to hasty conclusions about a nineteenth-century spelling is sometimes to add another error. The finding of a pot with a maker's name upon it is the most satisfactory way of checking the spelling in contemporary source material, but the majority of nineteenth-century Canadian potters did not mark their work.

Because it was the custom for Canadian crockery sellers to describe themselves as 'manufacturers', where a special business arrangement existed with a potter (sometimes an overseas potter), a number of dealers have in the past been erroneously cited as Canadian potters. In the check list some of the more important of these dealers (who were never potters) have been given, in order that the errors may be rectified. Their names appear in the list within square brackets.

Confusion has also arisen because many a merchant ordered his own name and place of business impressed on crocks or jugs made for him. An example of this practice has been included. J. T. Hazen of St. Johns, Canada East, is a particularly good example of the confusion caused by this type of misinterpretation.

Since he was in business in an area where potting was extensively carried on, his name on jugs obviously of St. Johns make has meant that he has sometimes been listed among the potters of St. Johns. He was in fact a grocer, whose stoneware was made for him by a local potter. When a name on a crock or jug does not correspond to that of any known potter, it is always wise to consider the possibility of its being the name of the merchant for whom the piece was made, and not that of a hitherto undiscovered potter.

For the sake of consistency the names Quebec and Ontario have been used throughout. It should be noted, however, that prior to Confederation, Lower Canada and Upper Canada and, later, Canada East and Canada West were the terms used to designate those provinces. Marked pieces of Canadian pottery frequently have the initials c.e. or c.w. after the place name. This usually indicates a piece made at some time during the period from February 10, 1841, to July 1, 1867 (when Canada East and Canada West were the official titles of the two provinces). A few potters may have continued to use c.e. or c.w. in their marks after Confederation but most probably adopted the new names of Quebec and Ontario almost at once.

This check list does not pretend to be a complete roll of nineteenth-century Canadian potters, nor is it claimed that every contemporary reference to every potter has been included. It is, however, a list that presents contemporary material. With all its acknowledged limitations, contemporary material remains the soundest basis for historical reconstruction. On the whole it is more dependable than later recollections or hearsay evidence. The check list may be used as a starting point by those who wish to investigate further a particular potter; it may prove helpful in dating pieces. Above all it gives a detailed picture of an industry struggling into being on the humble wares of everyday use.

ABBREVIATIONS USED IN THE CHECK LIST

The use of the name of the compiler in some cases and that of the publisher in others recognizes the fact that each directory was commonly associated with a compiler's or publisher's name. Where a compiler's name appears, he was generally in effect his own publisher, the directory having been printed to his order.

BHWWD 1884-85   *The Union Publishing Co.'s . . . Business Directory for the Counties of Brant, Halton, Waterloo and Wentworth, 1884-5.* Ingersoll (Union Publishing Co., publishers) 1884.

BTD 1856   *Brown's Toronto . . . Directory, 1856.* Toronto (W. R. Brown, compiler) n.d.

CBD 1865-66   *County of Brant . . . General Business Directory for 1865-6.* Ingersoll (A. R. and John R. Sutherland, publishers) 1865.

CBD 1869-70   *County of Brant . . . Directory for 1869-70.* Toronto (James Sutherland, compiler) 1869.

CD 1851   *The Canada Directory.* Montreal (Robert W. S. MacKay, compiler) 1851.

CD 1857-58   *The Canada Directory for 1857-58.* Montreal (John Lovell, publisher) n.d.

CG 1908   *Tercentennial Edition . . . Canada's Gazetteer.* Toronto (Trade Publishing Co. Ltd., publishers) n.d.

CMD 1879-81   *County of Missisquoi and Town of St. Johns Directory for 1879, 1880 and 1881.* Montreal (John Lovell, publisher) 1879.

DCG 1865-66   *Gazetteer and Directory of the County of Grey for 1865-6.* Toronto (W. W. Smith, compiler) 1865.

DCND 1919   *Dominion of Canada and Newfoundland . . . Directory 1919*. Toronto (The Canadian Gazetteer Publishing Co., publishers) n.d.

ETD 1888-89   *The Eastern Townships . . . Directory for 1888-89*. St. Johns (E. R. Smith & Son, publishers) 1888.

FLD 1901   *Foster's London . . . Directory 1901*. n.p. (J. G. Foster & Co., publishers) n.d.

GCS 1866-67   *Gazetteer . . . of the County of Simcoe for 1866-7*. Toronto (McEvoy & Co., publishers) 1866.

GCW 1867   *Gazetteer . . . of the County of Waterloo 1867*. Toronto (Irwin & Burnham, publishers) 1867.

GGTR 1889   *Union Publishing Co.'s . . . Gazetteer . . . of the Grand Trunk Railway for 1889*. Ingersoll (Union Publishing Co., publishers) 1889.

GHB 1867   *Gazetteer . . . of the Counties of Haldimand and Brant 1867*. Toronto (Irwin & Burnham, publishers) 1867.

GSC 1851-52, etc.   *Geological Survey of Canada, Report of Progress*. Quebec, etc., various dates.

GWG 1868   *Great Western Gazetteer . . . 1868*. Toronto (M. T. Platt, compiler) 1867.

GWWD 1895   *Union Publishing Co.'s . . . Directory for the Counties of Grey, Waterloo and Wellington*. Ingersoll (Union Publishing Co., publishers) n.d. [1895].

HCB   *History of the County of Brant, Ontario*. Toronto, 1883.

HDM 1882, etc.   *Henderson's Directory of Manitoba . . .* Winnipeg (James Henderson, compiler) n.d.

HNBD 1867-68   *Hutchinson's New Brunswick Directory for 1867-68*. Montreal (James A. T. Bird, compiler) n.d.

HNSD 1864-65   *Hutchinson's Nova Scotia Directory for 1864-65*. Halifax (Thomas Hutchinson, compiler) n.d.

HTCY   *History of Toronto and the County of York*. Toronto, 1885.

ICSD 1879   *County of Simcoe . . . Directory*. Hamilton (W. H. Irwin & Co., compilers and publishers) 1879.

IETD 1875-76   *Eastern Townships . . . Directory for the years 1875-76*. Montreal (W. H. Irwin & Co., publishers) 1875.

LCDD 1871   *Lovell's Canadian Dominion Directory for 1871*. Montreal (John Lovell, publisher) n.d.

LDDC 1896-97   *Lovell's . . . Directory of . . . the Dominion of Canada for 1896-97*. Montreal (John Lovell & Son, publishers) 1896.

LOD 1882   *Lovell's Business . . . Directory of . . . Ontario for 1882*. Montreal (John Lovell & Son, publishers) 1882.

MADD 1873-74   *McAlpine's Dominion . . . Directory 1873-74*. Montreal & Halifax (David McAlpine, publisher) n.d.

MAMBD 1880-81   *McAlpine's Maritime . . . Business Directory for 1880-81*. St. John and Halifax (D. McAlpine & Co., publishers) n.d.

MANSD 1868-69, etc.   *McAlpine's Nova Scotia Directory*. Halifax (David McAlpine, publisher) n.d.

MARB 1866, etc.   These MARB references are to the *Mercantile Agency Reference Book*. Montreal, etc. (Dun, Wiman & Co., publishers) various dates.

MASJD 1874-75, etc.   *McAlpine's Saint John City Directory for 1874-75* [etc.]. St. John, etc. (McAlpine, Everett & Co., publishers) n.d.

MCD 1864-65   *Mitchell's Canada . . . Directory for 1864-65*. Toronto (J. L. Mitchell, publisher) n.d.

MCD 1865-66   *Mitchell & Co.'s Canada . . . Directory for 1865-66*. Toronto (Mitchell & Co., publishers) n.d.

MDCD 1899   *Dominion of Canada . . . Directory 1899*. Toronto (Might Directory Co., publishers) n.d.

MEOD 1869   *The Province of Ontario . . . Directory*. Toronto (H. McEvoy, compiler) 1869.

MOD 1892-93, etc.   *Province of Ontario . . . Directory*. Toronto (Might Directory Co., publishers) n.d.

MTD 1899, etc.   *The Toronto City Directory*. Toronto (J. M. Might, publisher) n.d.

MQD 1791   *Directory for the City and Suburbs of Quebec*. Quebec (Hugh MacKay, compiler) 1791.

OEMA   Ontario Earthenware Manufacturers Association.

Nineteenth-Century Canadian Potters

PCD 1890-91	*Dominion of Canada . . . Directory, 1890-91*. Toronto (R. L. Polk & Co., publishers) n.d.
POD 1884-85, etc.	*Ontario . . . Directory, 1884-85* [etc.]. Toronto (R. L. Polk & Co., publishers) n.d.
PWG 1870-71	*Counties of Perth and Waterloo Gazetteer . . . for 1870-71*. Ottawa & Toronto (James Sutherland, compiler) 1869.
QOG	*Quebec Official Gazette.*
S 1851	*Business Directory of Canada West*. Bound at the end of vol. I of W. H. Smith, *Canada: Past, Present and Future*, Toronto, 1851.
SCD 1853	*A Supplement to the Canada Directory*. Montreal (Robert W. S. MacKay, compiler) 1853.
SETG 1867	*The Eastern Townships Gazetteer*. St. Johns (Smith & Co., publishers) 1867.
SJFD 1862	*The St. John and Fredericton 1862 . . . Directory*. Saint John (Hook & Greenough, publishers) 1862.
STD 1867-68	*City of Toronto Directory for 1867-8*. Toronto (James Sutherland, compiler) 1867.
WBCD 1897-98	*The Williams' Official British Columbia Directory 1897-8*. Victoria (R. T. Williams, compiler) n.d.
WLMD 1881-82	*City of London and County of Middlesex Directory for 1881-2*. London (J. Harrison White, compiler) 1881.

ADAM, JOSEPH, St. Clements, Ont., MCD 1865-66; MEOD 1869 (listed here under Hawkesville Ont.).

AHRENS, CARL (1863-1936), b. Winfield, Ont. (s. Hermann Ahrens), d. Toronto. This Canadian artist was an accomplished potter in his younger years, having learned his craft from potters along the Grand River; 'made a success of a pottery' at Chautauqua, N.Y., in the 1890's; in 1899 took charge of the pottery at Elbert Hubbard's Roycroft community, East Aurora, N.Y.; gave up potting in 1905 to continue with painting. (Madonna Niles Ahrens, *Carl Ahrens . . .*, unpublished manuscript, pp. 5-7.)

AHRENS, HENRY, Paris, Ont., GHB 1867; MADD 1873-74; cf. AHRENS, JACOB H.

AHRENS, JACOB H., Paris, Ont., b. Germany, 1828; emigrated to Canada West in 1852; began potting in 1859, first in Waterloo and later in Brant County (HCB, p. 648); CBD 1865-66; CBD 1869-70 ('Manufacturer of Flint, Enamelled and every description of COMMON & FINE EARTHENWARE'); LCDD 1871; MARB 1872; signed OEMA agreement 1873; exhibited at Philadelphia and Paris, France (see Chap. XXI); MARB 1881; GGTR 1889 ('Ahern—*sic*— J. H. & Co.'). Examples of the work of J. H. Ahrens in the Brant Museum, Brantford, include a dog figure with the mark J. H. AHRENS impressed on the bottom; also at the museum is a price list for the 1880's (*Plate* 38).

ALLEN, H., St. Johns, Que., ETD 1888-89; cf. DAKIN & ALLEN.

ALLEN, JOHN, Beaverton, Ont., PCD 1890-91; MOD 1892-93.

ALLIN, JOHN F., Peterborough, Ont. (proprietor of the Peterborough Pottery), PCD 1890-91; MOD 1892-93; MOD 1895; MDCD 1899; CG 1908.

ANDERSON, JOHN, Orangeville, Ont., MCD 1865-66; LCDD 1871 ('boot and shoe shop, dry goods, groceries, pottery works').

ANDERSON, YORK, Davisville, Ont., LCDD 1871.

ARMSTRONG, W. J., Jarvis, Ont., PCD 1890-91. Although included with the potters in the classified index, Armstrong is listed only as a 'potash mnfr' in the Jarvis section of this directory.

BAILER, *see* BEHLER.

BAILEY, JAMES, Bowmanville, Ont., S 1851; CD 1851; about this time was briefly in partnership with JOHN BROWN (*q.v.*); CD 1857-58 ('potter and proprietor of Western hotel'); won prizes at provincial exhibitions (see the *Examiner*, Oct. 11, 1848; Oct. 8, 1851; Sept. 29, 1852; name sometimes spelled 'Baillie' in these accounts). An advt. in the *Bowmanville Messenger*, dated April 25, 1851, speaks of 'the late firm of BAILEY & BROWN', and states that Bailey, working alone, will make 'moulded ware' in toys, covered dishes, mugs, and large platters.

BAILEY & BROWN, Bowmanville, Ont., SCD 1853; *see* BAILEY, JAMES, and BROWN, JOHN.

BAKER, HENRY, Peterborough, Ont., LCDD 1871; probably the same Henry Baker listed as a potter working in the Township of Thorold, Welland Co., in *Mitchell & Co.'s . . . Gazetteer of the Counties of Lincoln and Welland for 1865*.

BALLARD, O. L., St. Johns, Que., the *Pilot*, Sept. 30, 1858, and the *Argus*, Oct. 2, 1858 (provincial exhibition accounts); mark on crock in author's collection: ORRIN L. BALLARD / ST. JOHNS C. E.; *see* Chap. XXIV.

Appendix B

BALLARD, O. L., Cornwall, Ont., MCD 1865-66; probably the same O. L. Ballard who was earlier in St. Johns, Que.; mark on blue-decorated crock in author's collection: BALLARD/CORNWALL C.W. (*Plate* 53).

BANNERMAN, ROBERT, Montreal, Que., clay pipe maker, active from the beginning of the 1860's. In LCDD 1871 Bannerman is listed as 'grocer and tobacco pipe manufacturer'; in Lovell's Montreal directory for 1888-89 Bannerman Bros. are given as 'tobacco, clay pipe and rope manufacturer' [*sic*].

BEECH, GEORGE, Brantford, Ont. In the 1851 and again in the 1861 census the name of this English-born potter is given as 'Beach', and an obvious error occurs also in the recording of his age, given, in 1851, as 31 next birthday, but as only 38 next birthday ten years later. Marked pieces indicate how he, himself, spelled his name: a picture frame in the author's collection (*Plate* 54) has the incised marking, 'Made by G. Beech / April 1862 / Brantford / Canada West'; a similar but smaller frame with the same inscription is in the McCord Museum, McGill University. Beech worked for WELDING & BELDING (CBD 1869-70). *See also* CBD 1865-66 (Beach) and GHB 1867 (Beech).

BEHLER, VALENTINE & CO., Egmondville, Ont., MADD 1873-74; presumably the same as BAILER, VALENTINE, listed in Sutherland's *County of Huron Gazetteer . . . for 1863-4;* and BOEHLER, VALENTINE, LCDD 1871; and BOHLER, VALENTINE, MCD 1864-65; MCD 1865-66; MEOD 1869.

BÉLANGER, JOSEPH, St. Denis [-sur-Richelieu], Que., CD 1857-58; MCD 1864-65; LCDD 1871.

BELL, JOHN,—, Ont., the *Globe*, Oct. 13, 1847 (provincial exhibition prize list).

BELL, WILLIAM & DAVID, Quebec, Que., primarily manufacturers of bricks, tiles, and drain pipes, but also at one time made ordinary pottery, such as brownware, yellow ware, Rockingham; also made tobacco pipes (*see* Chap. XVIII); won a prize for pottery at the provincial exhibition 1850 (*Montreal Gazette*, Oct. 24, 1850); GSC 1852-53 ('various vessels for the use of the dairy and garden, as well as water-pipes, chimney tops, and ornamental glazed bricks'); won a bronze medal for pottery at the New York fair, 1853 (*Documents Submitted by the Bureau of Agriculture to the Legislature of Canada*, Appendix II to the Journals of the Legislative Assembly, 1854-55); MADD 1873-74; exhibited drain pipes, tiles, and tobacco pipes at Philadelphia 1876; MARB 1881 ('Pipes, Pottery, &c.'); later listings mention only drain tiles, etc., e.g. *L'Indicateur de Québec*, 1888-89; the firm continued into the 20th cent.; not the makers of the tableware decorated with printed views of Quebec sometimes erroneously credited to them.

BELLEVILLE POTTERY CO., Belleville, Ont., (J. B. Ives, proprietor). In the 20th cent. this company took over the old firm of HART BROS. & LAZIER (*q.v.*); the stoneware made after the change in ownership sometimes carries the mark: BELLEVILLE POTTERY CO. / SUCCESSORS TO HART BROS. & LAZIER.

BEMISTER, W., Beaverton, Ont., MDCD 1899; cf. BEMISTER & SON.

BEMISTER & SON, Beaverton, Ont., POD 1888-89; PCD 1890-91 (J. Bemister & Son); MOD 1892-93; MOD 1895.

BEMSTEIHEL, HENRY, Milverton, Ont., PCD 1890-91; MOD 1892-93; MOD 1895; MDCD 1899; presumably the same as BEMSTEIHL, HENRY, POD 1888-89.

BENAC, DAVID, St. Johns, Que., CD 1857-58.

BENNET, JOHN, Canboro, Ont., MCD 1865-66.

BERGERON, NARCISSE, La Présentation, Que., MCD 1865-66.

BERTRAND & LAVOIE, Iberville, Que., ETD 1888-89; MARB 1890; PCD 1890-91; mark on jug in author's collection: M F G / BY / BERTRAND & LAVOIE / IBERVILLE P.Q.; *see* Chap. XXIV.

BESSE, EDOUARD, St. Denis [-sur-Richelieu], Que., CD 1851; CD 1857-58.

BESSE, JOSEPH, St. Denis [-sur-Richelieu], Que., CD 1851.

BIENSTIEL, ADAM, Bridgeport, Ont., MARB 1881; presumably the same as BIERENSHIEL, ADAM, MOD 1892-93; MOD 1895; LDDC 1896-97; MDCD 1899; and BIERENSTHIEL, ADAM, POD 1884-85; POD 1886-87; POD 1888-89; PCD 1890-91; GWWD 1896; and BIERENSTIEHL, ADAM, LCDD 1871; and BIERENSTHIL, ADAM, 1861 census (age 36 next birthday, b. Germany; from the information given here it is possible to deduce that the family emigrated to Canada about 1852); and BIERNSTHIEL, ADAM, MCD 1864-65; and BIRENSTEIL, ADAM, MEOD 1869. 'An interesting industry was started by Adam Birnstihl who operated a potting business in Lexington . . . He moved his business to Bridgeport and carried it on for many years. Many of the older folks still have specimens of his work in their homes.' (*Thirty-Eighth Annual Report of the Waterloo Historical Society*, n.p., 1950, p. 33.)

BILLS, JONATHAN, Morpeth, Ont., SCD 1853.

BITCHY, IGNATZ, Mildmay, Ont., LCDD 1871; presumably the same as BITSCHE, IGNATZ, MADD 1873-74; PCD 1890-91; MOD 1892-93; MOD 1895; MDCD 1899; and BITSCHI, IGNATZ, POD 1884-85; POD 1886-87; POD 1888-89; and BITSCHY, IGNATZ, MARB 1881.

BITSEHY, ALBERT, Wingham, Ont., PCD 1890-91.

BLACKIE, PETER, Paris, Ont., MCD 1865-66; listed as working in Lynden, Ont., LCDD 1871.

BOCHLER, JOSEPH, New Hamburg, Ont., BHWWD 1884-85; presumably the same as BOEHLER, JOSEPH, POD 1884-85; POD 1886-87; POD 1888-89; PCD 1890-91; MOD 1892-93; MOD 1895.

BOCHLER, XAVIER, New Hamburg, Ont., MADD 1873-74; presumably the same as BOEHLER, XAVIER, S 1851; CD 1857-58; MCD 1864-65; GCW 1867 ('HAS ALWAYS A LARGE STOCK OF THE BEST EARTHENWARE . . . at the lowest prices'); MEOD 1869; MARB 1881; and BOHLER, XAVIER, MCD 1865-66; LCDD 1871.

BOHLER, VALENTINE, see BEHLER, VALENTINE.

BOISSONNAULT, GEORGE & CO., Quebec, Que., MCD 1865-66 (not included in the general section devoted to potteries in this directory but given under 'Potteries' in the Quebec City section; probably only a retail outlet, since George Boissonnault is listed as a 'Grocer' in MARB 1866).

BOIVIN, JOSEPH, St. Johns, Que., CMD 1879-81.

BOIVIN, LAURENT, Les Eboulemens [Les Eboulements], Que., MCD 1864-65 (here spelled 'Boisvin'); MCD 1865-66.

BONNETERRE, ISAAC, St. Denis [-sur-Richelieu], Que., CD 1851.

BOOTH, JOHN, Thorold, Ont., LCDD 1871.

BOOTH, MATTHEW, Thorold, Ont., POD 1884-85.

BOUCK, WILLIAM, Thorold, Ont., S 1851.

BOWERS, SAMUEL, St. Johns, Que., CMD 1879-81; cf. JONES & BOWERS.

BOWLER, ELIJAH, St. Johns, Que., CMD 1879-81 ('proprietor St. Johns Rockingham and Yellow Ware Manufactory'); MARB 1881; ETD 1888-89; won prizes at provincial fairs; see Chap. XXIV.

BOWLER & KNIGHT, St. Johns, Que., LDDC 1896-97 ('Dominion Sanitary Pottery Co., Bowler & Knight props'); there is no indication that this firm produced anything other than sanitary ware; cf. BOWLER, ELIJAH.

BOYER, LOUIS, St. Johns, Que., CMD 1879-81.

BRADWIN, E. W., Mount Forest, Ont., POD 1884-85; POD 1886-87; POD 1888-89; PCD 1890-91; MOD 1892-93; MOD 1895; MDCD 1899; cf. BRADWIN, EDWARD.

BRADWIN, J. E., Wingham, Ont., POD 1886-87; POD 1888-89; cf. BRADWIN, JOSEPH.

BRADWIN, J. & E., Wingham, Ont., MEOD 1869.

BRADWIN, EDWARD, Lynden, Ont., LCDD 1871; MARB 1881 (here listed under Mount Forest, Ont.).

BRADWIN, JOSEPH, Lynden, Ont., LCDD 1871; signed OEMA agreement 1873; MADD 1873-74; MARB 1881 (listed here under Wingham, Ont.); POD 1884-85 (under Wingham).

BRANTFORD/CANADA, this mark appears on moulded wares that in appearance are late in date, and would seem to belong to the last years of W. E. Welding's pottery or to his successors.

BRANTFORD STONEWARE MANUFACTURING CO. LTD., Brantford, Ont., LDDC 1896-97 ('J. P. Hemphill, sec.-treas.'); MDCD 1899. Successors of W. E. Welding.

BRANTFORD STONEWARE WORKS, see WELDING, W. E.

BRIDDON, SAMUEL, Thorold, Ont., LCDD 1871; MADD 1873-74.

BRIÈRE, J. B., Yamachiche, Que., MCD 1865-66; GSC 1863 ('coarse earthenware is manufactured at . . . Yamachie').

BRITISH COLUMBIA POTTERY CO. LTD., Victoria B.C., advt., Victoria Daily Colonist, May 22, 1896 ('FLOWER POTS At manufacturer's prices'); LDDC 1896-97; WBCD 1897-98; MDCD 1899; DCND 1919.

BRITISH COLUMBIA POTTERY WORKS, Esquimalt, B.C., MDCD 1899.

BRITISH PORCELAIN WORKS, St. Johns, Que., ETD 1888-89 (H. Earle of Montreal, proprietor, Dakin & Allen managers); MARB 1892; mark used on white ironstone: the Royal Arms with BRITISH PORCELAIN WORKS above and IRONSTONE CHINA below; see Chap. XXIV, and Plate 49B. Included among those applying for the charter for this company, in 1885, were F. B. Dakin, William Livesley, and Charles Pearson (QOG April 11, 1885).

BRITTAIN, HENRY, Junior, Waverley, Ont., MCD 1865-66; the same as BRITTON, HENRY, Junior, CGS 1866-67; LCDD 1871; ICSD 1879; POD 1884-85; POD 1886-87; cf. BRITTAIN, HENRY, Harriston, Ont., MOD 1892-93.

BRITTAIN, HENRY, Senior, Waverley, Ont., MCD 1865-66; the same as BRITTON, HENRY, Senior, GCS 1866-67; LCDD 1871.

BRITTAIN, ROBERT J., Waverley, Ont., MOD 1895.

BRITTON, JOHN, Delaware, Ont., MCD 1864-65; MCD 1865-66.

BRITTON, WILLIAM, Waverley, Ont., GCS 1866-67.

BROWN, GEORGE A., Tara, Ont., MOD 1892-93; MOD 1895; MDCD 1899.

BROWN, JOHN, JOSEPH, and WILLIAM O., at various addresses in the Toronto area, following a brief working period in the Bowmanville district by John Brown, an English potter and modeller and the father of Joseph and William O. Brown; *see* Chap. XXI for an account of this family who emigrated to Canada in 1849; *see also* MCD 1864-65 (under Weston); MCD 1865-66 (under Carlton West); MEOD 1869 (under Weston and Don); MADD 1873-74 (under Weston). Marked pieces give the name BROWN with various combinations of initials, e.g., J. & J. BROWN, J. & W. O. BROWN (for a further reference to Joseph and William O. Brown in business together see *Nason's East and West Ridings of the County of York*, 1871). A rare mark, referring to a particular body, adds, PATENTED 1859 (*Plate* 35A).

BROWN, THOMAS, London, Ont., POD 1888-89.

BROWNCOMBE, JOHN, Welcome, Ont., LCDD 1871; the same as BROWNSCOMBE, JOHN, MEOD 1869; cf. BROWSCOMB, J.

BROWNSCOMBE, WILLIAM, Peterborough, Ont., 'Potter and Earthenware Manufacturer . . . Cream and Milk Crocks, Pans, &c., Bottles, Jars, Flower Pots, &c. always on hand and for sale low for cash' (T. & R. White's *Directory of the United Counties of Peterborough & Victoria for 1858*); MCD 1865-66; cf. BROWNSCOMBE & GOODFELLOW.

BROWNSCOMBE & GOODFELLOW, Peterborough, Ont., MARB 1881.

BROWSCOMB, J., Port Hope, Ont., *Examiner*, Oct. 11, 1848 (provincial exhibition prize list); probably should be 'Brownscombe'.

BRYCE, JAMES, Cannifton, Ont., CD 1857-58 ('manufacturer of pottery').

BULLEN, SAMUEL, Saint John, N.B., registered as a 'Potter' in 1797 (*A Register of Voters . . . of the City of Saint John*, 1785-1862).

BURNS, DENNIS, Brantford, Ont., LCDD 1871.

BURNS, JAMES H., Albion, Ont., signed OEMA agreement 1873; MARB 1881; POD 1884-85; POD 1886-87.

BURNS, JAMES R., Toronto, Ont., carried on a potting business for fifteen years in his native Ireland before emigrating to Canada in 1879; in Ontario worked first as a journeyman potter, and then purchased the TORONTO STONEWARE POTTERY (HTCY, I, 445); POD 1884-85; POD 1886-87; mark on crocks, etc.: J. R. BURNS / TORONTO.

BURNS, JOHN, Davisville, Ont., LCDD 1871; cf. BURNS, JOHN, of Yorkville.

BURNS, JOHN, Yorkville, Ont., *Globe*, Oct. 1, 1858; Sept. 15, 1859; Sept. 30, 1859 (provincial exhibition prize lists).

BURNS, MITCHELL, New Glasgow, N.S., opened a pottery or brickmaking establishment about 1850 (James Cameron, *Industrial History of the New Glasgow Area*, New Glasgow, 1960).

BURNS, SAMUEL R., various post office addresses in Ontario, PCD 1890-91 (Chester); MOD 1892-93 (Doncaster); MOD 1895 (Chester); LDDC 1896-97 (Todmorden); CG 1908 (Bolton). A Samuel Burns signed the OEMA agreement in 1873.

BURNS, THOMAS M., Charlottetown, P.E.I., MANSD 1868-69.

BURNS & CAMPBELL, Toronto, Ont., MARB 1881.

BURRITT, DAVID B. & CO., Stratford, Ont., POD 1886-87.

BURT, D., Sparta, Ont., MCD 1864-65 ('brickmaker and potter').

CADWELL, WILLIAM, New Hamburg, Ont., MDCD 1899; CG 1908; cf. CADWELL, WILLIAM of Waterloo. This family name sometimes appears as 'Kadwell'.

CADWELL, WILLIAM, Waterloo, Ont., LCDD 1871.

CALEDONIA POTTERY, St. Johns, Que., Campbell & Purvis, proprietors, LDDC 1896-97; an example of the many potteries specializing in the making of sanitary earthenware that came into being in St. Johns towards the end of the century; *see* J. D. Brosseau, *Saint-Jean-de-Québec* (St. Johns, 1937), pp. 247-53.

[CAMPBELL, J. D. & CO., Toronto, Ont., 'manufacturers of china and earthenware'. James Dykes Campbell was at one time the Canadian agent for Robert Cochran's Glasgow potteries (Verreville and Britannia); the business Campbell established in Toronto advertised as 'manufacturers' because of this Glasgow connection, but it was not a Canadian pottery. *See* annual reports of the Toronto Board of Trade, 1860, etc.]

CAMPBELL, JOHN, Montreal, Que., *Montreal Gazette*, Oct. 24, 1850 ('discretionary award' for 'flower pots' at provincial exhibition).

CAMPBELL, ROBERT, Hamilton, Ont., MARB 1881; BHWWD 1884-85 ('R. CAMPBELL, MANU-FACTURER OF Rockingham, Yellow, Terra-Cotta and Earthenware . . . Rustic Stumps and Lawn Vases in all Styles'); POD 1886-87; POD 1888-89; PCD 1890-91; MOD 1892-93; MOD 1895; LDDC 1896-97 ('Hamilton Pottery, R. Campbell'); MDCD 1899 (R. Campbell's Sons); CG 1908; DCND 1919 (R. Campbell & Sons, manufacturers of both earthenware and stoneware); *see also* subsequent directories.

CAMPBELL, WILLIAM, Hamilton, Ont., prize for 'Best pottery' at the 1866 provincial exhibition (*Journal of the Board of Arts and Manufactures for Upper Canada*, VI, 269); MEOD 1869; LCDD 1871; signed OEMA agreement 1873 as president of the association; cf. CAMPBELL, W. & R.

CAMPBELL, WILLIAM J., Brantford, Ont., 1871 census (age 30, b. Ireland); LCDD 1871.

CAMPBELL, W. & R., Hamilton, Ont., MCD 1865-66.

CAMPBELL & PURVIS, St. Johns, Que., MARB 1892; MARB 1899; *see also* CALEDONIA POTTERY.

CANADA PIPE WORKS, Montreal, Que. (W. H. Dixon & Co.), won prizes at exhibitions in the 1870's; advertised in 1876 in a pamphlet by A. Baumgarten entitled *Industrial Canada;* MARB 1881; LOD 1882; Lovell's Montreal city directory 1888-89 ('English pipe clay, D. T. and fancy pipes').

CANADA POTTERY / Stone China Ware / W. L. & Co. This mark appears on a white ironstone sugar bowl in the author's collection, in date late 19th to early 20th cent. Possibly 'W. L.' was William Livesley, an experienced whiteware potter (*see* Chap. XXIV). Cf. CANADA STONE CHINAWARE CO.

CANADA STONE CHINAWARE CO., St. Johns, Que., MDCD 1899; MARB 1899; *see* Chap. XXIII.

CAP ROUGE POTTERY CO., Cap Rouge, Que. (the name 'Cap Rouge Pottery' was used by different firms at different periods), MARB 1874; MARB 1875; exhibited at Philadelphia 1876 (*see* Chap. XXI); MARB 1881. The mark CAP ROUGE / POTTERY occurs (G. M. Fairchild, *Gleanings From Quebec*, Quebec, 1908, p. 100, describes it as appearing in relief on the bottom of a 'little yellow jug' decorated with medallions of 'a Crusader riding tilt'. Today this Cap Rouge yellow ware is sometimes called 'ochre ware' by those unfamiliar with the contemporary terms). The very high credit rating accorded the Cap Rouge Pottery Co. in the mid-1870's and early 1880's undoubtedly reflected the financial state of the company's backers (at that period John Ross & Co., prosperous Quebec grocers) and should not be taken as an indication of the volume of business in earthenware. *See also* DALKIN, J. E. & CO., and GAUVREAU, L. P. & FRÈRE.

CARLTON, WILLIAM M., Brantford, Ont., MCD 1865-66.

CARROL, S. V., Colborne [Northumberland Co.] Ont., s 1851; CD 1851 stated that Colborne had '1 pottery'.

CARTER, G. A., Ranelagh, Ont., POD 1886-87 ('flower pot mnfr.'); POD 1888-89; PCD 1890-91.

[CLEMENTSON, FRANCIS, Saint John, N.B., not a Canadian potter but an importer of china, glass, and earthenware who correctly described himself as a 'manufacturer' by virtue of his connection with the Clementson potteries in Staffordshire; *see* Chap. VI.]

CLOUTIER, ALEXIS, Quebec, Que., MQD 1791; in the Supplement to the *Quebec Gazette*, No. 1893 (following the issue for July 30, 1801), Cloutier is named as a potter working within the city.

COLE, BENJAMIN, Colborne [Northumberland Co.] Ont., LCDD 1871.

COLLINS, B. J., Orangeville, Ont., POD 1888-89; presumably the same as COLLINS, E. J., PCD 1890-91; cf. COLLINS, BERNARD.

COLLINS, BARNET, Streetsville, Ont., CD 1851 ('earthenware factory'); cf. COLLINS, BERNARD.

COLLINS, BERNARD, Orangeville, Ont., GCS 1866-67; the same as COLLINS, BARNEY, LCDD 1871?

COLLINS, DAVID, Streetsville, Ont., CD 1857-58.

COLLINS, HENRY JAMES, Orangeville, Ont., LCDD 1871.

COLLINS, WILLIAM, Streetsville, Ont., MCD 1864-65; MCD 1865-66.

COMEAU, ALARIE, St. Johns, Que., 1871 census (age 45, b. Canada); LCDD 1871; IETD 1875-76.

COMPAGNIE DE FAIENCERIES DU CANADA, *see* CANADA STONE CHINAWARE CO.

CORNELL, J. H., Toronto, Ont., BTD 1856; *see* WARNER & CO.

CORNHILL, JAMES, Chatham, Ont., LDDC 1896-97.

CORNWALL, LOUIS, Beamsville, Ont., SCD 1853.

COURTEMANCHE, FLORENT, St. Denis [-sur-Richelieu], Que., CD 1851; CD 1857-58; MCD 1864-65.

COURTEMANCHE, RÉGIS, St. Denis [-sur-Richelieu], Que., MCD 1864-65; LCDD 1871.

COURTENAY BAY POTTERY, *see* WHITE, JOSEPH & SONS.

CRANSTON, JOHN, Lynden, Ont., MARB 1881; cf. CRANSTON, JOHN & SON.

CRANSTON, JOHN & SON, Hamilton, Ont. (Wentworth Pottery), LDDC 1896-97 ('Manufacturers of White Glazed Ware, Earthenware, Egyptian Urns, and Standard Flower Pots'); MDCD 1899 ('flower pots'); CG 1908; DCND 1919 (earthenware and stoneware), and later directories.

CROWN BRICK AND POTTERY COMPANY, New Glasgow, N.S., opened in 1867 but lasted only a short time (James Cameron, *Industrial History of the New Glasgow Area*, New Glasgow, 1960); GSC 1866-69 (obtained fireclay from the Montreal & Pictou Coal Co. of Halifax).

CUDMORE, GEORGE, Don, Ont., MEOD 1869.

CULP, *see* KULP.

CURTIS, BURTON, Conestogo, Ont., originally worked the pottery that came into the possession of William Eby (*q.v.*) in the 1850's (*Kitchener-Waterloo Record*, June 21, 1967).

CURTIS, GAD, Shakespeare, Ont., MCD 1864-65; MCD 1865-66 (Gad Curtis & Son).

CURTIS, MOSES, Invermay, Ont., MARB 1881; POD 1884-85.

[CURZON, HORATIO & CO., Halifax, N.S., not Canadian potters but a firm of china, glass, and earthenware importers who advertised as 'manufacturers of china and earthenware' by virtue of English connections.]

DAFOE, R., Charlesville, Ont., s 1851; the same as DEFOE, RICHARD, Senior, CD 1851.

DAKIN, F. B., St. Johns, Que., PCD 1890-91; MARB 1892; LDDC 1896-97 ('F. B. Dakin & Co., manufacturers of vitreous sanitary ware, Rockingham, cane and white ware', Iberville); *see also* BRITISH PORCELAIN WORKS and DAKIN & REINHART; *see* Chap. XXIV.

DAKIN & ALLEN, *see* BRITISH PORCELAIN WORKS.

DAKIN & REINHART, St. Johns, Que., ETD 1888-89; *see* DAKIN, F. B.; *see* Chap. XXIV.

DALKIN, J. E. & CO., Cap Rouge, Que., LCDD 1871 ('an extensive pottery'); MADD 1873-74.

DALKIN & WILSON, *see* WILSON & DALKIN.

DANIS, ALEXIS, St. Eustache, Que., LCDD 1871; CG 1908; DCND 1919; cf. DARNS, ALEXIS.

DARNS, ALEXIS, St. Eustache, Que., MCD 1865-66; presumably the same as DAVIES, ALEXIS, MCD 1864-65; and possibly the same as DANIS, ALEXIS, LCDD 1871.

DAVEY, W. J., Owen Sound, Ont., MOD 1895; LDDC 1896-97 ('Pottery and Stoneware').

DAVIS, ALEXANDER J., Davisville, Ont., LCDD 1871; cf. DAVIS, A. J. & CO.

DAVIS, ALFRED, Davisville, Ont., LCDD 1871.

DAVIS, ALFRED, St. Johns, Que., CMD 1879-81.

DAVIS, JOHN, a John Davis of 'Yonge-Street' won prizes for pottery at the provincial exhibition held in Toronto, 1852 (*Examiner*, Sept. 29, 1852); cf. DAVIS, JOHN, of Davisville.

DAVIS, JOHN, Davisville, Ont., LCDD 1871 ('postmaster, potter'); signed OEMA agreement 1873; MADD 1873-74; won prizes at provincial exhibitions (see the *Mail*, Sept. 13, 1879); MARB 1881 (the listing here is for John Davis, Junior, 'P. O. & Pottery'). Presumably it is John Davis, Junior, who is indicated in Toronto area directories throughout the 1880's and 1890's (the listing changes to John Davis & Son and the address to North Toronto); *see also* POD 1884-85; POD 1886-87; POD 1888-89; PCD 1890-91; MOD 1892-93; CG 1908; DCND 1919, and later directories.

DAVIS, A. J. & CO., Yorkville, Ont., MARB 1866.

DAVIS POTTERY CO. LTD., Montreal, Que., MDCD 1899.

DEFOE, RICHARD, *see* DAFOE, R.

DEIFENBACHER, PHILIP, Township of Waterloo, Ont., 1861 census (age 37 next birthday, b. Germany); the same as DIEFENBACHER, PHILIP, Bridgeport, Ont., MCD 1864-65; MCD 1865-66.

DELIGNY, JACQUES, Quebec, Que. The *Quebec Gazette*, July 24, 1800, names Deligny as a 'potter' and gives his address as 'Corner of Mr. Lynd's Road'.

DESLORIER, OLIVIER, St. Johns, Que., 1871 census (age 43, b. Canada).

[DENEAU, L., Montreal, Que., not a potter but a seller of crockery who called himself a 'Manufacturer of Earthenware' by virtue of his business connections with potteries in St. Johns, Que., and Cornwall, Ont.; *see* Lovell's Montreal city directory for 1882-83; *see* Chap. XXII.]

DENIS, ALPHE, St. Eustache, Que., PCD 1890-91.

DESCHAPS, TOUSSAINT, La Présentation, Que., MCD 1864-65. [Deschamps?]

DESLAURIERS, OLIVIER, St. Johns, Que., LCDD 1871; IETD 1875-76.

DEW, JOHN, Toronto, Ont., *Examiner*, Sept. 25, 1850 (first prize for pottery, provincial exhibition).

DIEFENBACHER, *see* DEIFENBACHER.

DIEM, ALBERT, Strathroy, Ont., MADD 1873-74; presumably the same as DIM, ALBERT, LCDD 1871.

DION family, Ancienne Lorette, Que., for an account of this potting family, working in Quebec from mid-Victorian times until the 1920's, *see* Chap. XXI.

DIXON, W. H. & CO., *see* CANADA PIPE WORKS.

DODGE, ARTHUR. His name appears on the OEMA agreement, 1873.

DOIDGE, ARTHUR, Selkirk East, Man., sent 'samples of pottery' to the Dominion exhibition, Montreal, 1880 (*Gazette*, Sept. 21, 1880); MARB 1881; HDM 1882; HDM 1890; HDM 1892; MDCD 1899 (inaccurately listed here as working in British Columbia); the same as DOIDGE, A. & E., PCD 1890-91.

DOIDGE, EDWARD, Selkirk East, Man., HDM 1890; the same as DOIDGE, A. & E., PCD 1890-91.

DOMINION POTTERY. This name was used by more than one Quebec firm; MARB 1872 (Cap Rouge); MADD 1873-74 (Cap Rouge); IETD 1875-76 (St. Johns, an advt. for the St. Johns Stone Chinaware Co. has the name 'Dominion Pottery' on the building shown in the woodcut; the same woodcut but with the name 'Dominion Pottery' eliminated was later used in an advt. in ETD 1888-89); CG 1908 (Dominion Pottery Co. St. Johns, 'manufacturers of sanitary pottery').

DON BRIDGE POTTERY, Toronto, Ont., STD 1867-68 states that this pottery was established in 1852 and was taken over by EBERHARDT, NICHOLAS, (*q.v.*) in 1863.

DOLAN, THOMAS, St. Johns, Que., CMD 1879-81.

DORAN, THOMAS, St. Johns, Que., CMD 1879-81.

DRAKE, GEORGE, Beaverton, Ont., MARB 1881; POD 1884-85; POD 1886-87 ('pottery and brick mfr.'); cf. DRAKE & RAWLINGS.

DRAKE & RAWLINGS, Beaverton, Ont., MADD 1873-74.

DREYER, G., Orillia, Ont., pottery owner? Advt. in the *Gazette* (Montreal), July 12, 1873: 'POTTERY FOR SALE / TO RENT, or ON SHARES, the only / one in the District. / For particulars apply to G. Dreyer, / Orillia, Ont.'

DROLET, PIERRE, Quebec, Que., MQD 1791.

DUFOE, ERASTUS, Aultsville, Ont., CD 1857-58; this family name also appears as 'Dafoe' and 'Defoe'.

DUMAINE, HONORÉ, Cap Rouge, Que., LCDD 1871.

EARLE, H., St. Johns, Que., ETD 1888-89 ('prop. British Porcelain Works, residence Montreal'); *see* BRITISH PORCELAIN WORKS.

EBERHARDT, NICHOLAS, Toronto, Ont., took over the Don Bridge Pottery in 1863 and manufactured 'every description of stoneware' (STD 1867-68); MARB 1866; *Globe*, Sept. 26 and 27, 1866 (showing of 'admirably designed and well manufactured' pitchers, fruit jars, flower pots, etc., at the provincial exhibition); Fisher & Taylor's *Toronto Directory for 1875* ('stoneware manufacturer'); Might & Taylor's *Toronto Directory for 1877;* mark on jugs, etc.: N. EBERHARDT / TORONTO C W; presumably the same Nicheles [*sic*] Eberhardt listed under Paris, Ont., in the 1861 census (age 27 next birthday, b. France); cf. EBERHARDT & HALM.

EBERHARDT & HALM, Toronto, Ont., Irving's *Toronto Directory . . . for 1865.*

EBY, CYRUS, Markham, Ont., MCD 1865-66 (this directory also lists a Cyrus Eby under Milnesville, Ont.); LCDD 1871 (listed under Conestogo, Ont.).

EBY, WILLIAM, Conestogo, Ont., MCD 1865-66; MEOD 1869; PWG 1870-71 ('Wm. Eby's Pottery was established in 1855 . . . he manufactures brown earthen-ware'); LCDD 1871; POD 1884-85; POD 1886-87; POD 1888-89; PCD 1890-91; MOD 1892-93; MOD 1895; LDDC 1896-97; the same as ELEY, WILLIAM, MCD 1864-65 ('proprietor, Maple Hill Pottery'). William Eby, Junior carried the business into the 20th cent. *See also* CURTIS, BURTON.

ELLIOT, J., Charlesville [Aultsville], Ont., S 1851; cf. ELLIOTT, JOHN, and ELLIOTT & BROTHERS.

ELLIOTT, ADAM, Russell, Ont., MADD 1873-74; POD 1884-85; POD 1886-87; POD 1888-89; PCD 1890-91; MOD 1892-93; LDDC 1896-97; MDCD 1899.

ELLIOTT, ALEXANDER, Cannifton, Ont., POD 1884-85; MDCD 1899.

ELLIOTT, JAMES, London East, Ont., POD 1884-85.

ELLIOTT, JOHN, Aultsville, Ont., MCD 1864-65 ('brickmaker and potter'); MCD 1865-66; MEOD 1869; LCDD 1871; MARB 1872; MADD 1873-74; MARB 1881 (the listing here is for John Elliott, Junior); cf. ELLIOT, J.

ELLIOTT, WILLIAM, Aultsville, Ont., MCD 1865-66; LCDD 1871; MARB 1872; MADD 1873-74; MARB 1881; POD 1884-85; POD 1886-87; POD 1888-89; PCD 1890-91; MOD 1892-93; MOD 1895; MDCD 1899.

ELLIOTT & BROTHERS, Aultsville, Ont., CD 1857-58 ('potters and brickmakers').

ELLIS, JAMES, Dipper Harbour, N.B., advt. dated Nov. 30, 1832 (in the *New Brunswick Courier*, Feb. 2, 1833): 'EARTHENWARE MANUFACTORY / THE Subscriber . . . will be enabled / in the Spring, to supply . . . almost every article in the Earthenware / line . . . at a reduction of Ten *per cent. on former prices* . . .' Crocks, dishes, pans, jars, tiles, and chimney tops were listed among the pottery's products.

ELMSDALE POTTERY, Elmsdale, N.S., HNSD 1864-65 ('R. MALCOLM, MANUFACTURER OF STONE & BROWN EARTHEN WARE . . . Also, Manufacturer of . . . Bricks').

ELSON, J. B., London, Ont., *Examiner*, Oct. 18, 1854 (provincial exhibition prize list); cf. ELSON, JOSEPH.

ELSON, JOSEPH, Hyde Park Corner, Ont., MCD 1864-65; MCD 1865-66.

ELSON, PETER, Hyde Park Corner, Ont., MEOD 1869; LCDD 1871 ('farmer, potter'); MADD 1873-74.

EMPEY, GORDON, Charlesville, Ont., S 1851; CD 1851.

ENSMINGER, P., Markham, Ont., MCD 1864-65.

ERCHENBERGER, SAMUEL, Delaware, Ont., MARB 1881; POD 1884-85; POD 1886-87; POD 1888-89; PCD 1890-91.

FAIT, HENRY, New Aberdeen, Ont., S 1851.

FARLEY, HENRY, St. Johns, Que., CMD 1879-81.

FARLEY, JOSEPH, St. Johns, Que., CMD 1879-81.

FARRAR. For members of this potting family, working in the Province of Quebec from the 1840's, *see* Chap. XXII.

FARRAR & SOULE, St. Johns, Que. (Moses Farrar and Warren Soule), CD 1851; *see* Chap. XXII.

FERGUSON, JOHN, Enfield, N.S., LCDD 1871.

FITZMAURICE, BERNARD, Paris, Ont., 1871 census (age 18, Irish origin); presumably the same as FITZMAURICE, BERNARD, London, Ont., WLMD 1881-82; MOD 1895; LDDC 1896-97; MDCD 1899; FLD 1901; cf. FITZMAURICE & UNGER.

FITZMAURICE, HENRY J., London, Ont., WLMD 1881-82.

FITZMAURICE, JAMES, London, Ont., MARB 1881; cf. FITZMAURICE & UNGER.

FITZMAURICE, MICHAEL, Paris, Ont., 1871 census (age 20, Irish origin); presumably the same as FITZMAURICE, MICHAEL, London, Ont., WLMD 1881-82; cf. FITZMORRIS, M., Brantford, Ont., LCDD 1871.

FITZMAURICE & UNGER, London, Ont., POD 1886-87; POD 1888-89; PCD 1890-91; MOD 1892-93.

FLACK & VAN ARSDALE (or VANARSDALE) Cornwall, Ont. (David A. Flack and Isaac H. Van Arsdale), MEOD 1869; ('stone ware manufacturers'); LCDD 1871; MARB 1872; MADD 1873-74; MARB 1881; POD 1884-85; POD 1886-87; POD 1888-89; PCD 1890-91; MOD 1892-93; MOD 1895; LDDC 1896-97; MDCD 1899; CG 1908. Frequently the stoneware was marked FLACK & VAN ARSDALE / CORNWALL, O. Flack, according to J. G. Harkness, was an American who settled in Cornwall (*Stormont, Dundas and Glengarry*, n.p., 1946, p. 369). Louis Deneau was at one time the agent for Flack & Van Arsdale in Montreal (*see* Montreal city directories for the 1880's).

FLEMING, THOMAS, Paris, Ont., 1871 census (age 16, Irish origin).

FOLEY, *see* POOLE & FOLEY.

FORAND, FRANK, St. Johns, Que., CMD 1879-81.

FORAND, LOUIS, St. Johns, Que., CMD 1879-81; the same as FORANT, LOUIS, 1871 census (age 24, b. Canada).

FOSTER, LEONARD, Hamilton, Ont., POD 1888-89; GGTR 1889; MOD 1892-93; cf. FOSTER, S. P. & CO.

FOSTER, S. P. & CO., Hamilton, Ont., MOD 1895; LDDC 1896-97; MDCD 1899 ('flower pots'); DCND 1919 ('Foster Pottery Co. Ltd.'), and later directories.

FOWLER, GEORGE O., Colborne [Northumberland Co.] Ont., LCDD 1871; MADD 1873-74; the same as FOWLER, G. C., MEOD 1869?

FOWLER, H., Colborne [Northumberland Co.] Ont., MARB 1881 ('Furs & Pottery'); cf. FOWLER, WILLIAM H.

FOWLER, ORCHARD, J., Colborne [Northumberland Co.] Ont., CD 1857-58; MARB 1866. CD 1851 lists '1 pottery' for Colborne but gives no potter's name; SCD 1853 gives the Colborne potter as O. S. Fowler.

FOWLER, TIMOTHY Y., Colborne [Northumberland Co.] Ont., LCDD 1871.

FOWLER, WILLIAM H., Colborne [Northumberland Co.] Ont., POD 1884-85; POD 1886-87; POD 1888-89; PCD 1890-91; MOD 1892-93.

FOWLER BROTHERS, Colborne [Northumberland Co.] Ont., MCD 1865-66.

FRAPPIER, F. L., Montreal, Que., listed in Lovell's Montreal city directories for the early 1880's as an 'earthenware manufacturer'; took part in provincial exhibitions (e.g. *Daily Witness*, Sept. 18, 1882: 'Mr. F. L. Frappier has a considerable show of red ware, including decorated flower pots and baskets').

FRAPPIER, ISAAC, Beauharnois, Que., LCDD 1871; cf. TRAPIER, ISAAC.

FREED, JAMES, Dundas, Ont., *Examiner*, Oct. 19, 1853 (provincial exhibition prize list).

GAHEN, JAMES, Orangeville, Ont., LCDD 1871.

GARLAND, JOHN, Oakland, Ont., 1851 census (age 30 next birthday, b. England); listed as a potter working in Colborne in Fuller's *Counties of Elgin & Norfolk Directory for 1865 & 1866*.

GARRETT, JOSEPH, Peterborough, Ont., LCDD 1871.

GAUDETTE, JEAN BAPTISTE, St. Johns, Que., CD 1857-58; LCDD 1871; 1871 census (listed as 'Gaudet', age 52, b. Canada); CMD 1879-81.

GAUDETTE, JOSEPH, St. Johns, Que., CD 1857-58; MCD 1864-65 (listed under St. Alexandre, Iberville Co., Que.).

GAUVREAU, L. P. & FRÈRE, pottery at Cap Rouge, Que., sales depot in Quebec city (potters and importers of crockery); *Quebec Morning Chronicle*, May 24, 1864, and *Quebec Daily News*, May 27, 1864 ('MANUFACTURERS OF Yellow and Rockingham Ware'); MCD 1865-66 ('CAPE-ROUGE POTTERIE'); MARB 1866 ('Yellow Ware'); *see* Chap. XXI.

GENDREAU, LOUIS, St. Denis [-sur-Richelieu] Que., CD 1851.

GENDRON, LOUIS, St. Gabriel de Brandon, Que., MCD 1864-65; MCD 1865-66.

GILBERT, CALEB, Belleville, Ont., LCDD 1871.

GILBERT, EBEN, Port Ryerse, Ont., POD 1888-89; PCD 1890-91; MOD 1892-93; MOD 1895; MDCD 1899.

GILLESPIE, JOHN, St. Johns, Que., advt. in the *News and Frontier Advocate*, April 2, 1858, for Gillespie's Canada Stone Ware; 1861 census (age 29 next birthday, b. Lower Canada); a John Gillespie is also listed in CMD 1879-81 as a potter; *see also* GILLESPIE & MACE and GILLESPIE & SOULE; *see* Chap. XXIV.

GILLESPIE & MACE, St. Johns, Que., CD 1857-58; *see* Chap. XXIV. Mark on blue-decorated pot in author's collection: GILLESPIE & MACE / ST. JOHNS C.E.

GILLESPIE & SOULE, St. Johns, Que., SCD 1853; *Montreal Gazette*, Oct. 3, 1853 (provincial exhibition account); *see* Chap. XXIV.

GLASGOW POTTERY CO., Iberville, Que., five residents of Iberville applied, in 1877, for a charter for this company (QOG May 19, 1877). The company proposed making 'pottery, pottery faience and plates of superior substances'.

GLASS BROS. & CO., London, Ont., POD 1888-89; MOD 1892-93; MOD 1895; MDCD 1899 (stoneware and pottery).

GLEESON, LYMAN, Paris, Ont., S 1851 ('potter, potash and bath brick maker').

GLOVER, HENRY, St. Johns, Que., CMD 1879-81.

GOBEAU, A. M., St. Boniface, Man., HDM 1890 ('Pottery Mfr'); HDM 1892; cf. GOBEAUX, E., PCD 1890-91.

GODIN, NAPOLÉON, St. Johns, Que., CMD 1879-81.

GOOLD, FRANKLIN P., Brantford, Ont., an American (b. 1813, New Hampshire) who came to Canada as a young man and engaged in various occupations before becoming 'a manufacturer of stoneware pottery' (HCB p. 507); MCD 1865-66; MARB 1866; GHB 1867 ('BRANTFORD STONE WARE WORKS . . . established 15 years . . . employs 12 hands, and the articles, manufactured from the best New Jersey clay, are of a superior quality'); GWG 1868; mark appears on blue-decorated jugs, etc., as F.P. GOOLD or as F.P. GOOLD & CO. An interesting account of this pottery appears in the *Journal of the Board of Arts and Manufactures for Upper Canada for the Year 1865, p. 60*.

GOSSELIN, RAPHAEL, St. Johns, Que., CD 1857-58; 1861 census ('Raphael Goselin', age 31 next birthday, b. Lower Canada); CMD 1879-81 also lists an R. Gosselin as a potter; intervening directories (e.g. LCDD 1871) list Raphael Gosselin as a cook at the lunatic asylum.

GOYETTE, CALIXTE, St. Athanase [Iberville], Que., MARB 1890; PCD 1890-91.

GRAHAM, JAMES, Orangeville, Ont., GCS 1866-67.

GRAY & BETTS, Tilsonburg, Ont. (William Gray and Spence H. Betts), POD 1884-85 ('stoneware mnfrs.'); exhibited 'Rockingham and Bristol Ware' at international exhibitions (*see* Chap. XXI); later the firm was listed as GRAY & GLASS.

GRAY & GLASS, Tilsonburg, Ont., POD 1886-87.

GROH, C., Township of Waterloo, Ont., 1861 census (aged 56 next birthday, b. Germany).

GROH, T. D., Kossuth, Ont., LCDD 1871.

GUERTIN, MARCEL, St. Denis [-sur-Richelieu], Que., CD 1851; CD 1857-58.

HAIGHT, ADAM, Sparta, Ont., MCD 1864-65.

HAINES, D. J. & SON, Blyth, Ont., PCD 1890-91.

HAINES, SAMUEL, Lynden, Ont., LCDD 1871.

HAMILTON POTTERY, *see* CAMPBELL, ROBERT.

HANCOCK, RICHARD, Enfield, N.S., HNSD 1864-65.

HANDLEY BROS. / PICTON. This mark appears on earthenware, including dog figures, made in Picton, Ont. *See* D. & P. Taylor, *The Hart Pottery* (Picton, 1966), p. 9.

HANSBURGH [?], SPENCER, Brantford, Ont., 1851 census (age 21 next birthday, b. New York State).

HART BROS. & LAZIER, Belleville, Ont. According to POD 1884-85 this firm was made up of Charles A. and Elwin E. Hart and their kinsman by marriage George I. Lazier; in reality, however, it was Mrs. George I. Lazier who was the partner, as is shown by a partnership agreement registered in the County of Prince Edward Registry Office in 1880. This later development of the Hart pottery of Picton won prizes at international as well as provincial exhibitions in the 1880's (*see* Chap. XXI). Advts. indicate that their stoneware was all made 'from the best Imported Clay' (POD 1886-87) and that 'Chemical Ware' was 'a Specialty' (LDDC 1896-97). *See also* POD 1888-89 ('Stoneware, Rockingham & Yellow-ware'); MOD 1892-93; MOD 1895; MDCD 1899. The wares were frequently marked with the firm's name; decoration in blue on stoneware included birds and flowers. The firm was succeeded by the BELLEVILLE POTTERY CO. (*q.v.*). *See also* LAZIER, GEORGE I.

HART, WILLIAM & CO., Picton, Ont., s 1851; mark on blue decorated jugs, etc.: W. HART & CO./ PICTON C. W.; this firm, established at mid-century, was the forerunner of HART BROS. & LAZIER (*q.v.*).

HAYDEN, J. B., *see* WARNER & CO.

[HAYWARD, W. H. & CO., Saint John, N.B., in the 1860's this crockery importing firm was also listed under 'Potteries', *see* MANSD 1868-69 under 'Saint John and Portland . . . Potteries'; their activities were, however, primarily those of crockery sellers; in the 1870's McAlpine's Saint John city directories listed them as agents for Whites' COURTENAY BAY POTTERY. *See also* WARWICK, WILLIAM.]

[HAZEN, J. T., St. Johns, Que., not a potter but a grocer (MARB 1866; SETG 1867; cf. 'Michon & Hazen, dry goods', SCD 1853). Hazen is an example of the confusion that often arises when an article of earthenware or stoneware is marked with the name of the person who ordered it instead of the potter who made it. Sometimes the situation is clarified when the merchant is identified as such, but frequently there is nothing to indicate that the name is not that of the maker. It is especially confusing when the merchant was in business in an area where potting was extensively carried on, such as St. Johns.]

HENDERSON, Montreal clay pipe maker. Several clay pipe manufacturers by the name of Henderson, including William Henderson, James M. Henderson, and James M. Henderson, Junior, were active in Montreal. Jesse Joseph's advt. in the *Montreal Gazette*, Dec. 27, 1847, probably refers to pipes of William Henderson's make. Another Joseph advt. (*Montreal Gazette*, June 4, 1856) mentions 'Henderson's Tobacco Pipes' by name; these were the products of James M. Henderson. Henderson listings in Montreal directories begin with William Henderson in 1848 and end with James M. Henderson & Son in the later 1870's. See also *Montreal Gazette*, Oct. 3, 1853 (provincial exhibition: 'fire clay, chimney tops, filter bricks, tiles, drain tiles and smoking pipes from Mr. Henderson'); MARB 1866. W. H. DIXON (*q.v.*) was 'successor to Henderson' about 1876. Pipes may be found with HENDERSON and MONTREAL on the stem.

HENDERSON, J., Invermay, Ont., MDCD 1899.

HESS, CHRISTIAN, Zurich, Ont., 'Manufacturer of all kinds of earthenware' (*Sutherland's . . . Huron Gazetteer . . . for 1869-70*); LCDD 1871; POD 1884-85; POD 1886-87; POD 1888-89; PCD 1890-91; MOD 1892-93; MDCD 1899.

HILL, JESSE, Salem, Ont., MCD 1864-65.

HOBSON, WALTER, Quebec, Que., MDCD 1899. Hobson was probably working in the vicinity of Quebec earlier than 1899.

HOLLINGSHEAD, ROBERT, Dundas, Ont., MEOD 1869.

HOLLINGSHEAD, WILLIAM B., Dundas, Ont., MCD 1864-65; presumably the same as HOLLINSHEAD, W. V., MCD 1865-66.

HORNING & BROWNSCOMBE, Owen Sound, Ont., GWWD 1895; MDCD 1899; CG 1908.

HORNSBY, OSWALD, Halifax, N.S., LCDD 1871.

HOWISON, HENRY, Cap Rouge, Que., Marius Barbeau (*Maîtres Artisans de Chez-Nous*, Montreal, 1942, pp. 119-25) credits the Howisons (Quebec china merchants) with an early Cap Rouge pottery, and listings in Quebec City directories for the beginning of the 1860's (e. g. 1861-62) would seem to bear this out. Possibly this was the pottery that was in the hands of GAUVREAU & FRÈRE (*q.v.*) by 1864.

HUGHES, CHARLES, St. Johns, Que., CMD 1879-81.

HUGHES, JAMES, St. Johns, Que., CMD 1879-81.

HULSE, WILLIAM J., London, Ont., PCD 1890-91; *see also* HULSE & SON.

HULSE & SON, London, Ont. (Joseph and William J. Hulse), MOD 1892-93.

HUMBERSTONE, for members of this potting family, working in Ontario throughout the 19th cent., *see* Chap. XXV.

[HURD, LEIGH & CO., Toronto, Ont., sometimes described as 'manufacturers', Hurd, Leigh & Co. were not potters but crockery importers and china decorators; *see* Chap. XXVI.]

IRELAND, NICHOLAS, Brantford, Ont., 1851 census (age 30, b. United States).

IRWIN, ROBERT, Streetsville, Ont., MCD 1864-65; MCD 1865-66; MEOD 1869; LCDD 1871; signed OEMA agreement 1873.

JACKSON, SAMUEL, St. Cunegonde, Que., Lovell's Montreal city directory, 1879-80.

JACKSON, WILLIAM, Paris, Ont., 1871 census (age 38, b. Ireland).

JACOB, JOHN, Waterloo, Ont., MCD 1864-65; GCW 1867; PWG 1870-71; the same as JACOBI, JOHN, SCD 1853; MEOD 1869; and JACOBY, JOHN, MCD 1865-66. 'In the early 60's many smaller manufacturers were kept busy supplying their wares to the growing population . . . there [was] . . . a pottery managed by John Jacobi.' (*Sixteenth Annual Report of the Waterloo Historical Society*, Waterloo, 1928, p. 31.)

JACOBI, DANIEL, Waterloo, Ont., LCDD 1871; POD 1886-87; POD 1888-89; PCD 1890-91; MOD 1892-93; MOD 1895; LDDC 1896-97; MDCD 1899 ('Jacobie, D.').

JARVIS, JOHN, Tavistock, Ont., POD 1884-85.

JAUBORD [JAUBERT ?] SIMÉON, Ancienne Lorette, Que., 1851 census. The handwriting in this return is very difficult to decipher. The first letter of the surname may not be J (H ?).

JONES, WILLIAM, St. Johns, Que., IETD 1875-76; CMD 1879-81; cf. JONES & BOWERS.

JONES & BOWERS, St. Johns, Que., MARB 1881, potters? See Chap. XXIV.

JOUBERT, CHARLES, Ste. Flavie, Que., MCD 1865-66 (incorrectly listed as 'Jonbert').

JOUBERT, EDOUARD, Ste. Flavie, Que., MCD 1865-66 (incorrectly listed as 'Jonbert').

JOUBERT, ORILE [Aurèle ?], Baie-du-Febvre, Que., LCDD 1871.

JOUBERT, P. & G. (Philippe and Gédéon), St. Denis de Bouteillerie, Que., MCD 1865-66 (incorrectly listed as 'Jonbert'); LCDD 1871.

JOYCE, THOMAS, Lower Stewiacke, N.S., LDDC 1896-97 ('Pottery and Stoneware'); MDCD 1899.

KADWELL, see CADWELL.

KEINER, JOHN, Hanover, Ont., DCG 1865-66; the same as KUEHNER, JOHN?

KELLER, J. W., Victoria, B.C., WBCD 1897-98 ('plasterer and pottery works').

KELLER & BURRIS, Victoria, B.C. (J. W. Keller and S. C. Burris), PCD 1890-91.

KENNEDY, J. A., Brantford, Ont., GGTR 1889; PCD 1890-91; MOD 1892-93; cf. KENNEDY, JOHN.

KENNEDY, JOHN, Brantford, Ont., 1871 census (age 16, b. Ireland); LCDD 1871.

KERR, ROBERT, Lynden, Ont., LCDD 1871.

KEY, HENRY, St. Johns, Que., IETD 1875-76.

KNITTLE BROS., Hawkesville, Ont., POD 1888-89.

KRITZE, GOTTLEIB, Mitchell, Ont., SCD 1853.

KUEHNER, JOHN, Hanover, Ont., MCD 1864-65; MCD 1865-66; presumably the same as KUENER, JOHN, Township of Waterloo, Ont., 1861 census (aged 39 next birthday, b. Germany; from this report it may be deduced that Kuener and his family emigrated to Canada about 1852); see also, KEINER, JOHN.

KUHNER [KUENER] CONRAD, Hanover, Ont., son of John Kuener; 1861 census (b. 1851, Germany); LCDD 1871.

KULP, JOHN, Grimsby, Ont., *Lincoln County 1856-1956* (published, 1956, by the Lincoln County Council), states that among the earliest Mennonites from Pennsylvania to settle in the area were four Kulp brothers; documents in the Registry Office of the County show that John Kulp, the potter (born in Pennsylvania in 1799; died in Lincoln County in 1874), purchased land in the Township of Grimsby in 1829. He is listed as 'potter' in the 1851 census. According to information from Harold Jarvis, Grimsby, shards excavated at the site of Kulp's pottery show him to have used a variety of glazes on red-bodied earthenware. Inscription on a crock exhibited at the Royal Ontario Museum, 1966: 'John Kulp / Grimsby / August 19th / 1843'.

LABELLE, MAGLOIRE, St. Eustache, Que., MCD 1864-65; MCD 1865-66; LCDD 1871 ('Manufacturer of earthenware'); PCD 1890-91; in the 20th cent. a David Labelle carried on a potting business at St. Eustache (see CG 1908, etc.).

LAFLAMME, F. X. M., Quebec, Que., MDCD 1899.

LAMBERT, A., St. Eugene, Ont., MCD 1865-66.

LAMBERT, ANTHONY & JOSEPH, Beauharnois, Que., SCD 1853; CD 1857-58 (Joseph Lambert only); cf. LAMBERT, ANTOINE & PIERRE, GSC 1851-52 ('Common pottery is at present manufactured at Beauharnois by Messrs. Antoine and Pierre Lambert, from clay procured behind the village; the articles made are tureens, jugs, butter and cream jars, ginger beer bottles, and such like').

LAMBERT, FRANÇOIS, St. Denis [-sur-Richelieu], Que., CD 1851; CD 1857-58; MCD 1864-65.

LAMOUREUX, IGNACE, St. Johns, Que., CMD 1879-81.

LANG, JAMES, Hudson, Que., MCD 1865-66.

LAZIER, GEORGE I. (J.), Picton, Ont., LCDD 1871; MARB 1872; MADD 1873-74; MARB 1881; POD 1884-85; POD 1886-87; mark on crock in author's collection: G. I. LAZIER / PICTON C. W. (*Plate* 55). G. I. Lazier was related by marriage to the owners of the Hart pottery, and from shortly before Confederation until the end of the 1870's the pottery was listed in directories under his name. In the 1880's the firm became HART BROS. & LAZIER (*q.v.*). For a period both Lazier's name and that of Hart Bros. & Lazier appeared contemporaneously in the directory lists (e.g. POD 1886-87); they did not, however, represent two separate potteries, only two aspects of the same business which owed its origin to WILLIAM HART (*q.v.*).

LEA, W., York Township, Ont., *Globe*, Sept. 26 and 27, 1866 (provincial exhibition prize lists, etc.).

LEE, GEORGE, residence not given in the Toronto *Globe*, Nov. 4, 1846 (provincial exhibition prize list—'Best Pottery').

LEMON, JOHN, Owen Sound, Ont., POD 1884-85; POD 1886-87; POD 1888-89; PCD 1890-91; MOD 1892-93; MOD 1895; MDCD 1899; *see also* LEMON, JOHN & JAMES.

LEMON, JOHN & JAMES, Woodford, Ont., MADD 1873-74.

LESSARD, JOSEPH, St. Johns, Que., 1871 census (age 17, b. Canada).

LINES, CHARLES, Paris, Ont., 1851 census (b. England); presumably the same as LYONS, CHARLES, Lynden, Ont., MCD 1865-66; and SINES, CHARLES, MCD 1864-65.

LINES, JOHN, Lynden, Ont., LCDD 1871.

LITTLE, CYRUS, Beamsville, Ont., 1851 census (age 52 next birthday, b. United States); s 1851; CD 1851; MCD 1864-65 ('pottery and tile manufactory'); MCD 1865-66; GWG 1868; LCDD 1871; presumably the same as LITTLE & SONS, MEOD 1869.

LIVESLEY, WILLIAM, St. Johns, Que., described as an 'earthenware manufacturer' in QOG Jan. 5, 1877. *See* Chap. XXIV; *also* BRITISH PORCELAIN WORKS.

LONDON CITY POTTERY, London, Ont., PCD 1890-91.

LOUPRET, ADOLPHE, Iberville, Que., LDDC 1896-97 (manufacturer of stoneware); *see* Chap. XXIV.

LYONS, CHARLES, *see* LINES, CHARLES.

[MCCAGHEY, DOLBEC & CO., Quebec, Que., china, glass, and earthenware importers, who described themselves as 'Manufacturers of Earthenware' in LCDD 1871 by virtue of business arrangements with certain potters. As 'manufacturers' they showed flower pots, spittoons, etc. at exhibitions. *See* the Montreal *Gazette*, Sept. 14, 1870.]

MCCALL, WILLIAM, Enfield, N.S., LCDD 1871.

MCCALLUM, ROBERT, Beaverton, Ont., MOD 1895; *compare* MCCALLUM & SMITH.

MCCALLUM & SMITH, Beaverton, Ont., MDCD 1899.

MCCLOSKEY, HENRY, Hornby, Ont., POD 1886-87; presumably the same as MCCLOSKY, HENRY, MEOD 1869; LCDD 1871; POD 1884-85.

MCCLOSKEY, JAMES, Tara, Ont., MARB 1881 ('Pottery & Tavern'); presumably the same as MCCLOSKIE, JAMES, POD 1884-85 ('hotel and pottery') and MCCLOSKY, JAMES, LCDD 1871 ('pottery'); cf. MCCLUSKEY, JAMES.

MCCLOSKY, HUGH, Hornby, Ont., MCD 1865-66.

MCCLUSKEY, JAMES, Kilsyth, Ont., MCD 1865-66; the same as MCCLUSKIE, JAMES, of WALMSLEY & MCCLUSKIE (*q.v.*).

MCCONNELL, THOMAS, Aultsville, Ont., MEOD 1869.

MCCUAIG, JAMES, Belleville, Ont., LCDD 1871 ('McCuaig's Pottery . . . J. C. Lake, manager').

MACDONALD, *see* ST. JOHNS STONE CHINAWARE CO.

MCDOUGALL, JOHN, *see* MONTREAL POTTERY CO.

MCGLADE, *see* SCHULER & MCGLADE.

MCGREEVY, PATRICK, St. Johns, Que., IETD 1875-76.

MCGUIRE, JOHN, St. Johns, Que., CMD 1879-81.

MCKNIGHT, SAMUEL, Cornwall, Ont., LCDD 1871.

MAILLET, AMABLE, St. Johns, Que., CD 1857-58 ('potter and trader'); CMD 1879-81; the same as MAYÉ, AMABLE?

MAILLET, MOISE, St. Denis [-sur-Richelieu], Que., CD 1851.

MAILLET, NARCISSE, St. Johns, Que., CD 1857-58; 1871 census (age 50, b. Canada).

MAINLAND POTTERY CO., New Westminster, B.C., WBCD 1897-98.

MALCOLM, ROBERT, Junior, *see* ELMSDALE POTTERY.

MANITOBA BRICK & POTTERY CO., An Act to Incorporate the Manitoba Brick & Pottery Company (Manitoba Statutes, Cap. XLII, Vict. 34, 1871); A. G. B. Bannatyne was named as president; *see* Chap. XXI.

MARLATT, ABRAHAM, Port Ryerse, Ont., MCD 1864-65; MCD 1865-66; MEOD 1869; LCDD 1871; POD 1884-85; POD 1886-87; MOD 1892-93; MOD 1895.

MARLATT, CLAYTON, Port Ryerse, Ont., POD 1888-89; MOD 1892-93; MOD 1895.

MARLATT, J. M., Oakland, Ont., 1851 census; cf. MARLATT, JOHN.

MARLATT, JOHN, Paris, Ont., 1861 census (age 52 next birthday, b. Canada, operator of a 'Pottery Factory').

MARSHALL, SAMUEL, Blue Hill, Shelburne Co., N.S., listed as a potter in the assessment rolls, town and county, 1786-87. Information supplied by John Langdon, Toronto.

MARTIN, T., Brantford, Ont., MCD 1865-66.

MARTIN, W. D., Cataraqui, Ont., POD 1884-85; POD 1886-87; POD 1888-89; PCD 1890-91; MOD 1892-93; MOD 1895; MDCD 1899 (the listing is given here under Conestogo, Ont.).

MARTINDALE, JOHN, Niagara, Ont., advertised in the *Gleaner*, April 10, 1824: 'WANTED, ONE or two POTTERS to whom liberal wages will be given—stability and sobriety are looked for. Apply to JOHN MARTINDALE.'

MARX, JOHN, Brantford, Ont., LCDD 1871; POD 1888-89 (with this directory the listing changes to Lynden, Ont.); PCD 1890-91; MOD 1892-93; cf. MARX & HOEHN.

MARX & HOEHN, Lynden, Ont., POD 1886-87.

MATHESON & WALLACE, New Hamburg, Ont., CD 1857-58.

MAYÉ, AMABLE, St. Johns, Que., IETD 1875-76; the same as MAILLET, AMABLE?

MAYNE, CHARLES, Elmsdale, N.S., MANSD 1896 ('manf pottery').

MEDERSCHEIN, CHARLES, Quebec, Que., 1861 census; C. Medeschein [*sic*] & Co. (St. Sauveur) won prizes for stoneware and pottery at the provincial exhibition, 1870 (Montreal *Gazette*, Sept. 16, 1870).

MÉNARD, WILFRED, St. Johns, Que., CMD 1879-81.

MERKLEY, *see* MURKLEY.

METIVIER, JOSEPH, St. Ours, Que., MCD 1865-66; the same Joseph Metivier who is listed at St. Johns, Que., CMD 1879-81?

MINOR, J., Sparta, Ont., MCD 1864-65.

MITCHELL, JOHN, Brantford, Ont., MCD 1865-66.

MONGER, E., Widder Station, Ont., MADD 1873-74.

MONTIGNY, JOSEPH, Montreal, Que., MCD 1865-66.

MONTREAL POTTERY CO., Montreal, Que., Montreal city directories 1895-1905; MDCD 1899; decorators of imported ware and makers of Rockingham, cane, stoneware, etc., some of which was marked with the name of the company. The *Herald*, Nov. 26, 1898, gives 1893 as the beginning of the Montreal Pottery Co., and names John McDougall as the proprietor. *See* Chap. XXVI.

MOONEY, JAMES, Brantford, Ont., LCDD 1871; is this a connection of the James Mooney who won a prize for draining tile in 1851 (*Examiner*, Oct. 8, 1851), the James Mooney listed in Ottawa in CD 1857-58, or the James Mooney listed under Johnstown in *Fuller's Counties of Leeds . . . and Renfrew Directory . . . 1866 & 1867*?

MOONEY, JOHN, Johnstown, Ont., LCDD 1871.

MORTON & CO., Brantford, Ont., founded at the end of the 1840's by an American, Justus Morton (b. Massachusetts c. 1800); 1851 census; CD 1851 ('stoneware factory and pottery . . . the only *stoneware* factory in C.W.'); *Examiner*, Oct. 19, 1853 (provincial exhibition prize list); CD 1857-58 ('Morton & Bennett, potters'); Morton & Bennett were succeeded by James Woodyatt, who was succeeded by F. P. Goold, succeeded in his turn by Welding & Belding, and then by W. E. Welding alone. Several articles of stoneware in the Brant Museum, Brantford, have the impressed mark: MORTON & CO / BRANTFORD C W. These include a crock with the date 1851 in blue. Another marked crock has elaborate raised decoration. *See* Chap. XXI.

MURKLEY, FREDERICK, Inkerman, Ont., MCD 1865-66; this family name also appears as 'Merkley'.

MYERS, JOHN, Carron Brook, Ont., LCDD 1871 ('earthenware manufacturer').

NEEDHAM, WILLIAM, Brantford, Ont., 1871 census (age 53, b. England).

NELLES, JOHN, London, Ont., LCDD 1871.

NEW & McFARLANE, Hamilton, Ont., MDCD 1899.

NIELSON, JOHN, Fitzroy Harbor, Ont., MCD 1865-66.

ORTH, DANIEL, Campden, Ont., 1851 census; MCD 1864-65; MCD 1865-66; MEOD 1869; MARB 1892. Orth, who lived into the 20th cent., is called 'the community's first potter' in *Lincoln County 1856-1956* (published, 1956, by the Lincoln County Council). In addition to the more usual productions, he made toy articles, and some of these are preserved at the Jordan Museum, near Vineland, Ont. A large dog figure in the author's collection (*Plate* 35B) is both signed and dated: 'D. Orth 1892'.

OSWELL, HORNSBY, Enfield, N.S., HNSD 1864-65.

OTTAWA POTTERY CO. The *Gazette* (Montreal), Sept. 24, 1879, describing the Dominion exhibition in Ottawa, stated that 'The Ottawa Pottery Company has a display of flower pots, tiles, &c.'

OUELET, LOUIS, Village des Aulnaies, Que., MCD 1865-66.

OWEN, JOHN, St. Johns, Que., CMD 1879-81.

PAGE, S., Lynden, Ont., LCDD 1871.

PARKINSON, ABRAHAM, London, Ont., POD 1886-87.

[PATTON, JAMES & CO., Montreal, Que., a crockery importing firm describing itself, CD 1851, as 'manufacturers' on the strength of business arrangements with certain potters. Crocks, etc., marked PATTON & CO. / MONTREAL and PATTON & CO. / TORONTO indicate the retailer, not the potter.]

PEARSON, CHARLES E., St. Athanase [Iberville], Que., Rockingham and yellow ware potter; Montreal *Gazette*, Sept. 20, 1880, and *Herald*, Sept. 23, 1880 (provincial exhibition prize lists, etc.); MARB 1881; wares marked C. E. P. and found in the area are probably his. *See* Chap. XXIV. Pearson was later concerned with establishing the BRITISH PORCELAIN WORKS.

PEEL, JONATHAN, Brockville, Ont., *Examiner*, Oct. 10, 1849 (won first prize at provincial exhibition for best specimen of pottery).

PEGLER, JOHN, London, Ont., MOD 1892-93; *see also* STAR POTTERY.

PETERBOROUGH POTTERY, *see* ALLIN, JOHN F.

PIGGOTT, EDWARD, Toronto Junction, Ont., MTD 1899; worked for GEORGE PLANT (*q.v.*).

PLANT, GEORGE, Mount Dennis, Ont., MTD 1899 ('Pottery and Tile Mfr.'); MDCD 1899; CG 1908.

POOLE, E. R., Enfield, N.S., HNSD 1864-65.

POOLE, SAMUEL, Enfield, N.S., HNSD 1864-65.

POOLE & FOLEY, Saint John, N.B. This partnership between Samuel Poole (an English-trained potter who had worked in Nova Scotia) and James W. Foley (grandson of JOSEPH WHITE), was formed about 1880; it lasted until near the end of the century. After the dissolution of partnership Poole and Foley each operated a Saint John pottery. The Poole pottery was eventually burned out and was not rebuilt. The Foley pottery became the Foley Pottery Ltd. in 1921. As the Canuck Pottery (Quebec) Limited it was relocated in Labelle, Que., in 1964, following a fire that destroyed the Saint John plant. In the early years of the Poole & Foley partnership, the clay for the stoneware was imported from the United States, but under the management of Fenwick D. Foley (son of James W. Foley) Canadian clay from Middle Musquodoboit, N.S., was substituted for the New Jersey clay. (*Saint John Citizen*, Sept. 27, 1937, and Fenwick D. Foley.) *See* Saint John city directories; MDCD 1899; and the *New Brunswick Blue Book and Encyclopedia*, n.p., 1932, p. 17. Poole & Foley took part in exhibitions, including the Dominion exhibition of 1883: 'The Disbrowville pottery of Poole & Foley . . . [has] a splendid exhibit of brown ware, Rockingham ware and blue ware. Butter crocks of a new class are shown, which are warranted to resist acids. They also show flower pots from 2 to 18 inches in depth. Clay tobacco pipes, a superior quality, of which there is a good assortment, complete this very creditable show.' (*Daily Sun*, Oct. 3, 1883.) A Poole & Foley cash book is in the New Brunswick Museum.

PRATT, CHARLES, London, Ont., LCDD 1871; exhibited pottery at Philadelphia 1876; *see* Chap. XXI.

PRESCOTT, BARTHOLOMEW, Enfield, N.S., MANSD 1890-97; MDCD 1899; CG 1908.

PRESCOTT, CHARLES, Enfield, N.S., HNSD 1864-65; MANSD 1890-97.

PRESCOTT, HENRY, Enfield, N.S., HNSD 1864-65; LCDD 1871; MANSD 1890-97.

PRESCOTT, JAMES, Enfield, N.S., LCDD 1871; MANSD 1890-97 (both James Prescott, Senior, and James Prescott, Junior, listed); PCD 1890-91 (James Prescott & Sons); MANSD 1896; MDCD 1899; CG 1908 (James Prescott, Senior).

PRÉVOST, ARTHUR, St. Johns, Que., CMD 1879-81.

PRIOR, THOMAS, St. Johns, Que., CMD 1879-81.

PROVINCIAL POTTERY, Saint John, N.B., an advt. in the *New Brunswick Courier*, May 12, 1849, indicates that the Provincial Pottery was near the Valley Church, Portland, was run by 'Mr. Thompson', and produced milk pans, butter crocks, preserve jars, bottles, pudding pans, and garden pots. *See* Chap. XXI.

RAMSAY, WILLIAM, Thorold, Ont., S 1851, CD 1851 ('temperance hotel, pottery, corporation clerk'); CD 1857-58.

RAYWOOD, THOMAS, St. Johns, Que., CMD 1879-81.

REEVE, THOMAS, Churchill, Ont., LCDD 1871.

RICHARDSON, WILLIAM, Brantford, Ont., 1851 census (age 18 next birthday, b. Brantford).

ROBERTSON, HENRY, Saint John, N.B., HNBD 1867-68 (listed as an importer of china, glass, and earthenware and a manufacturer of common earthen and stoneware); MANSD 1868-69; in MARB 1866 and LCDD 1871 Robertson is listed only as a crockery dealer.

ROMAINE, ROBERT, Peterborough, Ont., exhibited flower pots at Philadelphia, 1876. *See* Chap. XXI.

ROSZEL, ABRAHAM, Grimsby, Ont., a potter who married a daughter of JOHN KULP. (Information obtained from a grandson of Roszel by Harold Jarvis, Grimsby.)

RUNIONS, GORDON, Cornwall, Ont., LCDD 1871.

ST. JOHNS POTTERY. This name may have been used by more than one St. Johns firm. *See* Chaps. XXII and XXIV.

ST. JOHNS STONE CHINAWARE CO., *see* Chap. XXIII.

Nineteenth-Century Canadian Potters

ST. JOHNS STONE, ROCKINGHAM AND YELLOW WARE FACTORY, *see* FARRAR.

ST. JOHNS ROCKINGHAM AND YELLOW WARE MANUFACTORY, *see* BOWLER, ELIJAH.

SASKATCHEWAN BRICK KILN & POTTERY CO., Rapid City, Sask., HDM 1890.

SAUNDERS, C., Bolton, Ont., LDDC 1896-97; MDCD 1899.

SAUNDERS, WILLIAM, Davisville, Ont., PCD 1890-91.

SCHULER, HENRY, Paris, Ont., b. *c.* 1843 in the United States; brought up in Canada; engaged in the making of earthenware in the 1860's, changing to stoneware in 1873 (HCB, p. 678); GHB 1867; 1871 census (age 28, German origin); MADD 1873-74; exhibited stoneware at Paris (France) 1878; LOD 1882; *see* Chap. XXI.

SCHULER, W. B., Brantford, Ont., Irwin's *City of Brantford . . . Directory for the Year 1880-81* (listed here under Paris); MOD 1895; LDDC 1896-97 ('Manufacturer of flower pots, hanging baskets, seed pans, lily pots, lawn vases, glazed wares . . . ').

SCHULER & McGLADE, Paris, Ont. (Henry W. Schuler and Peter McGlade), CBD 1869-70 ('PARIS POTTERY, SCHULER & McGLADE, Proprietors . . . MANUFACTURE ALL KINDS OF Flint, Enamelled & Common Earthenware . . . Having had long experience at the business, they can ensure their customers . . . as good ware as any manufactured in Canada . . . '); LCDD 1871; MARB 1872; MADD 1873-74; signed OEMA agreement 1873 (as 'McGlade & Schuler').

SCHULTZ, AUGUST, Churchill, Ont., LCDD 1871; ICSD 1879 (listed here as a householder in the Township of Innisfil); the same as SHULTZ, AUGUST, GCS 1866-67?

SCHWAB, WILLIAM, Beamsville, Ont., 1851 census (age 51 next birthday, b. Germany); MCD 1864-65; MCD 1865-66; LCDD 1871; MARB 1872; MADD 1873-74; the same as SCHWABB, WILLIAM, CD 1851; CD 1857-58; MEOD 1869. Information supplied by Harold Jarvis, Grimsby, indicates there was William Schwab, Senior, and William Schwab, Junior.

SCOTT, J. M., Belleville, Ont., MADD 1873-74.

SEIGRIST, JOHN, Shallow Lake, Ont., MOD 1895.

SHANE & TOTTON, London East, Ont. (Hiram Shane and Henry Totton), MARB 1881; the same as TOTTON, H. & CO., WLMD 1881-82 (the partners are given here as Totton and 'Shain').

SHEARSMITH, JOSEPH, Hamilton, Ont., Cooke's *City of Hamilton Directory* 1853; CD 1857-58; MCD 1865-66.

SHERRITT, WILLIAM, St. Johns, Que., CMD 1879-81.

SIBLEY, CHARLES, Toronto, Ont., BTD 1856; cf. SIBLEY, CHARLES, London, Ont., LCDD 1871.

SINCLAIR, ALEXANDER, Kilsyth, Ont., POD 1884-85; POD 1886-87; POD 1888-89; PCD 1890-91; MOD 1892-93; MOD 1895; MDCD 1899.

SINES, CHARLES, Lynden, Ont., MCD 1864-65. [Lines ?]

SKINNER, SAMUEL, Picton, Ont., Skinner's activities are bound up with the history of the Hart pottery; he was a cousin of WILLIAM HART (*q.v.*). The pottery was listed under Skinner's name in MCD 1864-65 and also in MCD 1865-66 (as 'S. Skinner & Co.'); both S. SKINNER and S. SKINNER & CO. are found on jugs, etc. made in Picton before Confederation.

SMITH, ANTHONY, Paris, Ont., GHB 1867; 1871 census (age 29, German origin); LCDD 1871; mark on unglazed red earthenware picture frame (*See* title page) in author's collection: A. Smith (incised) and ANTHONY SMITH (impressed).

SMITH, AUBREY, Enfield, N.S., LCDD 1871 ('proprietor brickyard and pottery'); *see* SMITH & KAYE.

SMITH, GEORGE, Kilsyth, Ont., MCD 1864-65.

SMITH, JOHN P., Paris, Ont., MCD 1865-66.

SMITH, OLIVER, Brantford, Ont., 1861 census (age 42 next birthday, b. United States); MCD 1865-66; GHB 1867.

SMITH, RUFUS, Brantford, Ont., 1861 census (age 22 next birthday, b. United States); MCD 1865-66.

SMITH, THOMAS, Brantford, Ont., Irwin's *City of Brantford . . . Directory for the Year 1880-81*.

SMITH & KAYE, Halifax, N.S. (Aubrey Smith and Louis Kaye); MARB 1872 ('Bricks, and Pottery'); MADD 1873-74 (Elmsdale, N.S.); exhibited earthenware, bricks and tiles at Philadelphia 1876 (*see* Chap. XXI); McAlpine's Halifax directories 1870's and 1880's; MARB 1881; *see* SMITH, AUBREY.

SOULE, WARREN, St. Johns, Que., 1851 census (age 29 next birthday, b. United States); *see* Chap. XXII.

SPENCE, WILLIAM, Ethel, Ont., LCDD 1871; MADD 1873-74; MARB 1881.

SPENCE, WILLIAM, Hollen, Ont., MCD 1865-66.

SPENCE, WILLIAM, Port Ryerse, Ont., MCD 1865-66.

SPILKER, JOHN, Owen Sound, Ont., DCG 1865-66; LCDD 1871; MADD 1873-74; MARB 1881.

347

STAFFORD POTTERY, St. Cunegonde [Montreal], Que., operated by Mark H. Tomkins & Co. from 1879 until 1883 or early 1884; successors to the WEST END DRESDEN POTTERY (*q.v.*); advertised as manufacturers of stone chinaware and white earthenware (LOD 1882); *see* Chap. XXIV. Tomkins had been one of the applicants for letters patent for the West End Dresden Pottery (QOG, Jan. 5 and April 25, 1877).

STANWORTH, LEVI, Lynden, Ont., MOD 1895.

STAR POTTERY, London, Ont. (John Pegler, proprietor), MOD 1895; LDDC 1896-97; MDCD 1899; FLD 1901; *see also* PEGLER, JOHN.

STEELE, WILLIAM, Yamaska, Que., GSC 1852-53; a Supplement to the *Montreal Gazette* (following the issue for Oct. 11, 1853) names Steele as receiving prizes for drain tiles, paving tiles, and also for pottery at the provincial exhibition; SCD 1853; CD 1857-58; *see* YAMASKA POTTERY.

STEVENSON, THOMAS, St. Johns, Que., IETD 1875-76.

STEUMPFLE, MICHAEL, Preston, Ont., MCD 1865-66; presumably the same as STEUMPLE, MICHAEL, 1861 census (age 53 next birthday, b. Germany); and STUEMPFEL, M., GWG 1868; and STUEMPLE, MICHAEL, LCDD 1871; and STUMPFLE, MICHAEL, S 1851; CD 1857-58; MEOD 1869.

STEUMPLE, HENRY, Preston, Ont., 1861 census (age 19 next birthday, b. Upper Canada); presumably the same as STUEMPFLE, HENRY, GCW 1867; POD 1884-85; POD 1886-87; and STUMPFIE, HENRY, MDCD 1899; and STUMPFLE, HENRY, BHWWD 1884-85; POD 1888-89; PCD 1890-91; MOD 1895.

STUNDEN, GEORGE, Bolton, Ont., MOD 1895.

SYLVESTRE, ISAAC, St. Johns, Que., CD 1857-58; CMD 1879-81.

TAYLOR, JAMES, Port Hope, Ont., MDCD 1899. The pottery closed in 1918 (K. M. G. Stearns, 'Port Hope Pottery', *Canadian Antiques Collector*, June, 1967).

TAYLOR, WILLIAM, Beaverton, Ont., signed OEMA agreement 1873; MADD 1873-74 (W. Taylor & Co.); POD 1884-85 (Wm. Taylor, 'pottery, lumber and coal').

TELLIER, P., St. Cuthbert, Que., MCD 1865-66.

[THOMAS, FRANCIS T., Quebec, Que., because his name appears on the back of tablewares imported by him from Scotland, and because he sometimes described himself as a 'manufacturer' on his billheads, Thomas has on occasion been listed as a Canadian potter. He was, however, an 'importer of china, glass and earthenware, coal oil lamps, &c.' (Cherrier's Quebec city directory for 1886-87); he also handled the Rockingham and brownwares of local potters and Canadian stoneware, and probably at one time had some financial interest in a local pottery; his showrooms and warehouses were at various addresses in the Upper and Lower Towns; *see* Chaps. VII and XVIII.]

THOMAS, JOHN, working near Portland [Saint John], N.B., advertised his pottery in the *Gazette and New Brunswick Advertiser*, Jan. 26, 1815.

THOMPSON, *see also* PROVINCIAL POTTERY.

THOMPSON, JOHN, Saint John, N.B., HNBD 1867-68.

THOMPSON, MATTHEW, Saint John, N.B., SJFD 1862; HNBD 1867-68 (Matthew Thompson, Senior, and Matthew Thompson, Junior); MANSD 1868-69; LCDD 1871; MADD 1873-74; MASJD 1874-75; MASJD 1879-80; MAMBD 1880-81; *Daily Sun*, Oct. 5, 1880 (provincial exhibition account—Mathew [*sic*] Thompson, 'Lower Cove Pottery.').

TOMKINS, MARK H., *see* STAFFORD POTTERY.

TORONTO POTTERY CO., Toronto, Ont., MDCD 1899 ('Jugs Butter Pots Churns Flower Pots Chicken Fonts Rock and Cane ware'); DCND 1919, and later directories. The Toronto Pottery Co. was also a distributor of clay products, glassware, etc., and at one time maintained a Montreal outlet. Stoneware made to the order of Montreal grocers often carried both the name of the Toronto Pottery Co. and the name of the Montreal merchant.

TORONTO STONEWARE POTTERY, *see* BURNS, JAMES R.

TOTTON, HENRY, *see* SHANE & TOTTON.

TOWNSLEY, GEORGE H., Toronto Junction, Ont., MDCD 1899; MTD 1899; MTD 1901.

TRAPIER, ISAAC, Beauharnois, Que., MCD 1865-66; cf. FRAPPIER, ISAAC.

VINCENT, PIERRE, Quebec, Que., MQD 1791; incorrectly given as 'Vincant'.

VOYER, ONÉSIME, Cap Rouge, Que., LCDD 1871.

WAGNER, ANSLEM, Berlin [Kitchener], Ont., S 1851; CD 1857-58; MCD 1865-66; MEOD 1869; PWG 1870-71.

WAGNER, JOSEPH, Berlin [Kitchener], Ont., GCW 1867; LCDD 1871; MADD 1873-74; MARB 1881.

WAGNER, MARTIN, Berlin [Kitchener], Ont., PWG 1870-71.

WALLACE, JOHN, Hamburg, Ont., S 1851; cf. MATHESON & WALLACE.

WALLACE, ROBERT, New Hamburg, MCD 1865-66 (this same directory lists also a Robert Wallace as a potter in Paris, Ont.).

WALLER, WILLIAM, Brantford, Ont., 1871 census (age 33, b. Ireland); LCDD 1871.

WALLY, WILLIAM, St. Johns, Que., CMD 1879-81.

WALMSLEY, JOHN, Toronto, Ont. Rev. Henry Scadding (*Toronto Of Old*, Toronto, 1878, p. 432) describes a 'rude pottery works . . . carried on by Mr. John Walmsley' where 'coarse brown ware, partially glazed, pans, crocks, jars, jugs, demijohns, and so forth' were made; *see* Chap. XXI.

WALMSLEY, WILLIAM, Kilsyth, Ont., MCD 1865-66; MEOD 1869; MARB 1872; *see also* WALMSLEY & McCLUSKIE.

WALMSLEY & McCLUSKIE, Kilsyth, Ont. (William Walmsley and James McCluskie), DCG 1865-66 ('The Earthenware manufacture of Walmsley & McCluskie has attained considerable proportions, the Pottery having now been in successful operation for several years; and many articles of the more ornamental kinds, as well as those in common use, are now produced at the works.'); later Walmsley operated alone under his own name.

WALTZ, JOHN, Heidelburg, Ont., CD 1857-58.

WARNER & CO., Toronto, Ont. (W. E. Warner, J. B. Hayden, J. H. Cornell), BTD 1856 ('MANU-FACTURERS OF STONE WARE . . . Pottery Near the Don Bridge East'); CD 1857-58. Cf. DON BRIDGE POTTERY.

WARWICK, WILLIAM, Saint John, N.B., was the brother-in-law of W. H. Hayward, with whom he established a china, glass, and earthenware importing business in 1855 (*see* Chap. V). He also established a pottery at East Saint John (*Telegraph Journal*, June 14, 1928). This pottery is said to have been the forerunner of Joseph White's Courtenay Bay Pottery (*New Brunswick Blue Book and Encyclopedia*, n.p., 1932, p. 17, and White-Foley family papers). W. Warwick & Co. are listed under 'Earthenware Manufacturers' in SJFD 1862. In 1861 'Warwick & Hayward' won a prize for 'Pottery-Ware' at the provincial exhibition (*New Brunswick Courier*, Oct. 12, 1861). *See also* WHITE, JOSEPH & SONS.

WATSON, JOHN, Montreal, Que., MDCD 1899.

WEAVER, *see* WEBER.

WEBER, JACOB, Egmondville, Ont., MARB 1881 (spelled 'Weaver' in this listing; this family name was spelled both 'Weber' and 'Weaver', but Jacob, the potter, was generally given as 'Weber'); POD 1884-85; POD 1886-87; POD 1888-89; PCD 1890-91; MOD 1892-93; MOD 1895; MDCD 1899. Newton MacTavish, writing of Egmondville as it was in the 1880's, recalls 'Weber the potter', as well as 'Sutherland the weaver, Hill the blacksmith . . . and Cresswell the artist.' (*Ars Longa*, Toronto, 1928, p. 1.)

[WEDGWOOD, JOSEPH, Montreal, Que., not a potter in Canada but an importer of china, glass, and earthenware, who styled himself a 'manufacturer' by virtue of his connection with the owners of the Wedgwood Works in Staffordshire; *see* Chap. VI.]

WELDING, WILLIAM E., Brantford, Ont., an American (b. 1819 in New York State) who settled in Canada in 1841 and eventually became a travelling salesman for Morton & Co.'s Brantford stoneware; with a partner (W. W. Belding) bought out the pottery in the late 1860's; in the 1870's W. E. Welding built a new pottery on the site of the old one, which had burned, and went into business on his own (HCB p. 543); exhibited at international events in the 1880's (*see* Chap. XXI); Toronto *Evening Telegram*, Sept. 3, 1879 (provincial exhibition); MARB 1881; BHWWD 1884-85; POD 1886-87; POD 1888-89; PCD 1890-91; MOD 1892-93; MOD 1895; *see also* WELDING & BELDING; mark used on brown pots (*Plate* 56) and on blue decorated crocks: W. E. WELDING / BRANTFORD, ONT. About 1894 Welding sold the pottery to a joint stock company, which continued operations until early in the 20th cent. Shards excavated at the site of the pottery include teapot lids with beaver finials.

WELDING & BELDING, Brantford, Ont. (William E. Welding and William W. Belding), this partnership lasted five years (HCB p. 543); MEOD 1869; CBD 1869-70 ('fire and cupola brick and stone-ware manufacturers'); LCDD 1871; MARB 1872; MADD 1873-74; mark on blue decorated jugs, etc.: WELDING & BELDING / BRANTFORD.

WELLER & FRID, Albion, Ont., PCD 1890-91; the same as WILLER & FRID, POD 1888-89.

WELLS, ROBERT, Stratford, Ont., MOD 1892-93.

WELLS, WILLIAM, Beamsville, Ont., exhibited a flower pot and saucer and red clay for pottery making at Philadelphia 1876; *see* Chap. XXI.

WENTWORTH POTTERY, *see* CRANSTON, JOHN & SON.

WEST END DRESDEN POTTERY, St. Cunegonde [Montreal], Que., letters patent applied for (QOG Jan. 5, 1877) under the name of the Montreal Porcelain Company; *see* Chap. XXIV.

WESTCOTT, ROBERT, Peterborough, Ont., LCDD 1871; MADD 1873-74; exhibited at Philadelphia 1876; *see* Chap. XXI.

WHEELER, THOMAS, Brantford, Ont., 1871 census (age 34, b. United States); the same as WHEELER, THOMAS, Belleville, Ont., LCDD 1871?

WHITE, JOSEPH & SONS, Crouchville [East Saint John], N.B., Joseph White (1799-1870), William D. White (1833-74), Frederick J. White (1838-1919), James A. White (1841-1928). This potting family from Bristol, England, settled in New Brunswick in the early 1860's and worked the Courtenay Bay Pottery for many years. For an account of their contribution to the industry in Canada *see* Chap. XXI. *See also* MARB 1866; HNBD 1867-68; LCDD 1871; MARB 1872; MADD 1873-74; MARB 1874; MARB 1881; *see also* Saint John city directories. At one time James A. White was also a dealer in china, glass, and earthenware in Saint John (MANSD 1868-69). The family potting tradition was carried into the 20th cent. by James W. Foley, a son of Joseph White's eldest daughter, Charlotte Amelia; *see* POOLE & FOLEY. The Whites do not seem to have followed the practice of marking their wares. A great-grandson of Joseph White—the Saint John potter, Fenwick D. Foley—has, however, a red flower pot, ornamented with raised decoration, which is attributed by him to the White pottery. Price lists in Mr. Foley's possession show that the Whites made a wide range of articles, including 'lava' and 'acorn-painted' flower pots, 'bariole' bakers, Rockingham pitchers with 'miser' decoration, rustic 'stumps' and hand basins 'washed' (lined) inside.

WHITE BROS., Owen Sound, Ont., PCD 1890-91 ('brick mnfrs and pottery'); MOD 1892-93.

WHITE, HANLEY & CO., Brockville, Ont., POD 1884-85.

WHITEHOUSE, MOSES, London, Ont., CD 1857-58 ('drain tiles and stoneware manufactory').

WHITMORE, MICHAEL, York [Toronto], Ont., advertised for two journeymen potters (*Canadian Freeman*, Jan. 18, 1827); advertised for a pedlar 'to hawk Brown POTTERY' made at his Yonge Street Pottery 'four miles from York' (*Colonial Advocate*, April 29, 1830); in the autumn of 1830 the Yonge Street Pottery was destroyed by fire (*Colonial Advocate*, Oct. 14, 1830); *see* Chap. XXI.

WIDEMAN, JOSEPH, Almira, Ont., MCD 1865-66; MARB 1881 (the listing here is under Markham, Ont.); POD 1884-85 (under Milnesville, Ont.); POD 1886-87 (this directory lists a Joseph Wideman at Milnesville and also a Joseph Wideman at Markham); POD 1888-89 (Markham); PCD 1890-91 (Markham); MOD 1892-93 (near Markham); MOD 1895 (Markham); MDCD 1899 (Markham).

WILLER, *see* WELLER.

WILLIAMSON, JOSEPH, Almira, Ont., MCD 1864-65.

WILSON, JOHN, Bowmanville, Ont., S 1851; CD 1851; SCD 1853 (here entered under the category of 'Removed, Discontinued or Altered' since 1851).

WILSON & DALKIN, Cap Rouge, Que., MADD 1873-74 (here the name is given as 'Wilson & Dakin'); MARB 1874. G. M. Fairchild (*From My Quebec Scrapbook*, Quebec, 1907, p. 74) says 'Messrs. Dalkin & Wilson erected a large pottery' which had 'an able American' as 'superintendent'.

WINFIELD, THOMAS, Hamilton, Ont., LCDD 1871.

WOODYATT, JAMES, Brantford, Ont., in 1857 leased the pottery of MORTON & BENNETT. According to information supplied by a member of the Woodyatt family to Donald B. Webster, Curator of Canadiana, Royal Ontario Museum, he gave up the pottery in 1859.

YAMASKA, POTTERY, St. Michel d'Yamaska, Que., 'Pottery and Brick Works', had Quebec agents to sell their tiles and brownware (*Quebec Gazette*, June 8, 1853, and *McLaughlin's Quebec Directory*, 1855); won prizes at provincial exhibitions, *see* Supplement to *Montreal Gazette*, Oct. 15, 1853; Yamaska roofing tiles and bricks also won recognition at the New York World's Fair in 1853 (*Montreal Gazette*, Jan. 27, 1854); *see* STEELE, WILLIAM.

PLATE 1. Joseph Shuter, typical of the early Montreal merchants who dominated the crockery trade of both Upper and Lower Canada. Plaster bust. [*Château de Ramezay*]

PLATE 2A. Ironstone made in Staffordshire by the Clementsons for the Methodist New Connexion Church, Toronto, and the Methodist Church of Canada.

PLATE 2B. Brown-printed platter, Lasso pattern, by J. Goodwin, the Seacombe Pottery, Liverpool. In the 1850's there were Goodwin warehouses in Quebec and Toronto.

PLATE 3A. Printed mark (late 1860's to mid-1870's) on wares made in Staffordshire for the Quebec china merchants, McCaghey, Dolbec & Co.

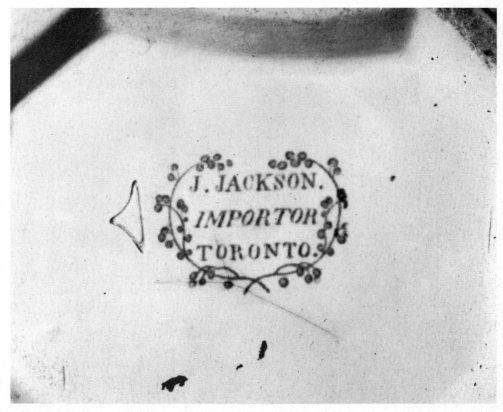

PLATE 3B. Printed mark (1850's to 1860's) on wares made for James Jackson, Toronto china merchant. IMPORTOR was later altered to IMPORTER.

PLATE 4A. Wedgwood cream-coloured ware. From early days 'Wedgwood's finest Queen's Ware' was offered to Canadians in 'setts'. This border was No. 156 in the first pattern book.

PLATE 4B. Spode tureen (*c.* 1820). Many factories followed Spode in making the fine-quality, blue-printed earthenware that was sold in Canada as 'Best Blue'.

PLATE 5. Spode coffee-pot in the body advertised in Montreal, Nov. 4, 1799, as 'Egyptian black'. Many makers produced it, continuing it throughout the nineteenth century. Ht. 9¼ in.

PLATE 6A. Pink-printed earthenware (*c.* 1830) by W. Ridgway. Ridgway himself journeyed from Staffordshire to Canada to estimate the potentials of the market.

PLATE 6B. Early Spode stone china baskets. Spode introduced stone china in 1805; soon a host of potters was shipping varieties of stone china to the colonies.

PLATE 7A. Mason's ironstone plate (*c.* 1819), from a double dinner service ordered by the Montreal merchant, Thomas Torrance, with his initials in gold.

PLATE 7B. Green-glazed basket, Copeland & Garrett. Earthenware of this green-glazed type was advertised in Saint John, April 25, 1835, and was popular throughout the century.

PLATE 8. Bread tray, opaque china, from 'the well known Firm of . . . DAVENPORT & CO.' At mid-century such Davenport earthenware was sold at Montreal shipside auctions.

PLATE 9. Mocha jug (cane body, blue decoration). Mocha was a form of the 'dipt ware' mentioned frequently in Canadian advertising from the 1840's. Ht. 8½ in.

PLATE 10A. Victorian bowl, purchased in Scotland and probably of Scottish manufacture. Earthenware bowls of this type are dubbed 'Portneuf' when found in Quebec.

PLATE 10B. Bowl of similar type, purchased from a Quebec farm house. These wares, called 'Portneuf', came from British potters and were of 'a bright, fancy character'.

PLATE 11. Doulton stoneware vase, muted colours, dated 1877, and signed by Florence E. Barlow. Purchased when new by E. B. Greenshields, Montreal. Ht. 10 in.

PLATE 12A. De Morgan dish (copper lustre) and vase (ruby lustre) purchased when new by E. B. Green-shields, Montreal. Painted marks. Ht. of vase 9½ in.

PLATE 12B. Maw and Minton tiles typical of thousands imported for house decoration. F. & J. Morgan (1880) guaranteed Maw installations despite Quebec climate.

PLATE 13A. Chinese plate. Porcelain such as this was still known as 'India china' in Canada at the beginning of the nineteenth century and offered for sale under that name.

PLATE 13B. Worcester plate, Barr, Flight & Barr (c. 1810), decorated in blue, red, pink, and gold. Throughout the century Worcester was stressed in Canadian advertising.

PLATE 14A. Worcester mug. Surprisingly extensive importations of eighteenth-century wares such as this paved the way for Worcester's nineteenth-century popularity.

PLATE 14B. Marked Rockingham cup and saucer. Rockingham was offered at Canadian trade sales such as that held by Adam Macnider in Montreal, Sept. 26, 1832.

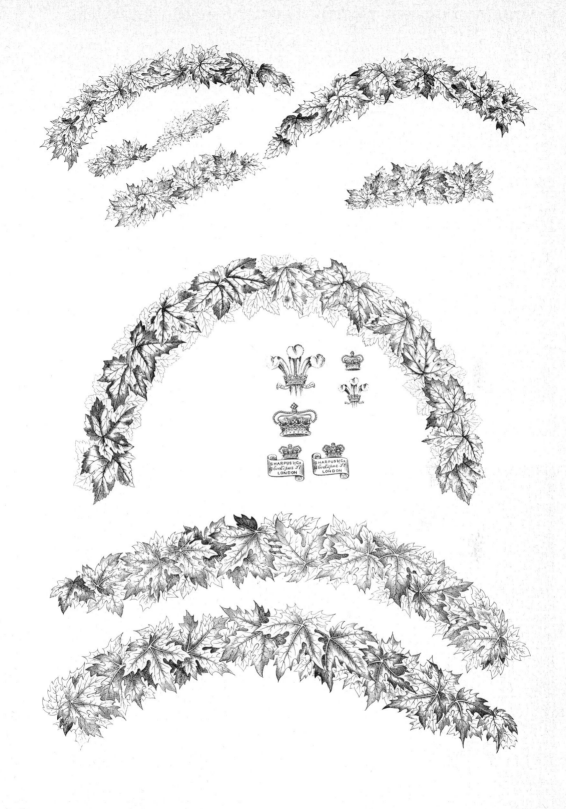

PLATE 15. Proof from an old copperplate, showing border, centre, and backstamp on Worcester porcelain made for the Prince of Wales' Canadian visit, 1860. [*Worcester Royal Porcelain Co. Ltd.*]

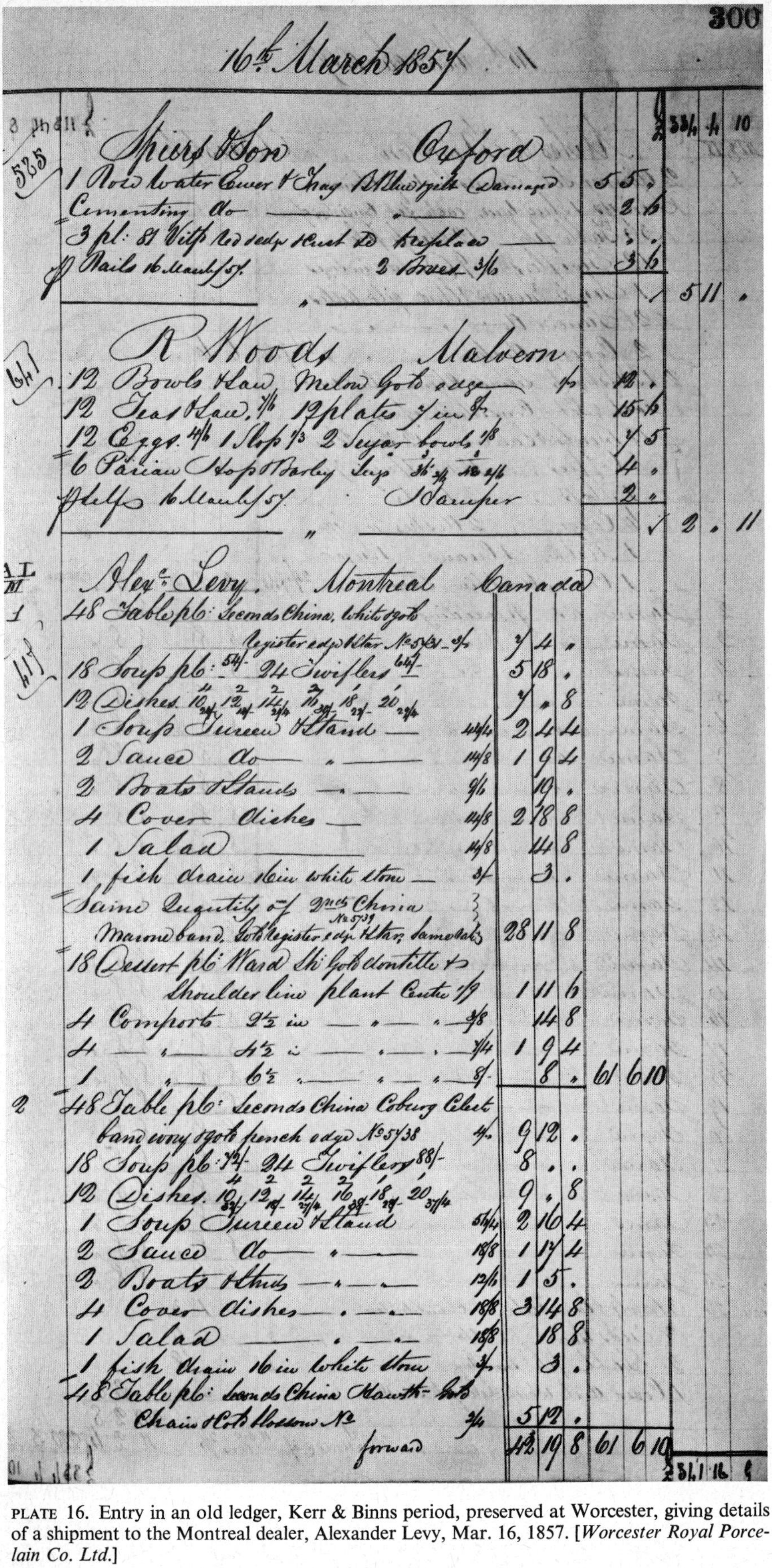

16th March 1857

PLATE 16. Entry in an old ledger, Kerr & Binns period, preserved at Worcester, giving details of a shipment to the Montreal dealer, Alexander Levy, Mar. 16, 1857. [*Worcester Royal Porcelain Co. Ltd.*]

PLATE 17A. Copeland & Garrett teaware (*c.* 1840) printed with pansies, a favourite flower of the period. The products of this factory penetrated even into the far Northwest.

PLATE 17B. Minton porcelain. By mid-century Minton such as this sepia-printed cup and saucer (shape designed 1846) was being praised by name in Canada and offered as 'celebrated' ware.

PLATE 18. Porcelain bottles (*c.* 1830). 'Rich Ornaments, English China' were the boast of Canadian dealers. Coalport and Minton are both credited with this type. Both exported to Canada.

PLATE 19A. Comport from a late Victorian Aynsley dessert service painted with Muskoka views, this one entitled 'Shooting Logs at Bala Falls'.

PLATE 19B. Belleek cup and saucer in a design registered in 1868. Canadians considered this new Irish porcelain 'Very Elegant'.

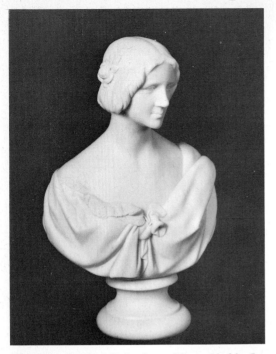

PLATE 20A. Copeland Parian bust of Jenny Lind by Joseph Durham. This was one of the Parian titles advertised in the Toronto *Globe*, Sept. 5, 1856.

PLATE 20B. J. Ridgway, Bates & Co. Parian bust of the military hero, Colin Campbell. This Staffordshire firm of the 1850's had a resident agent in Canada.

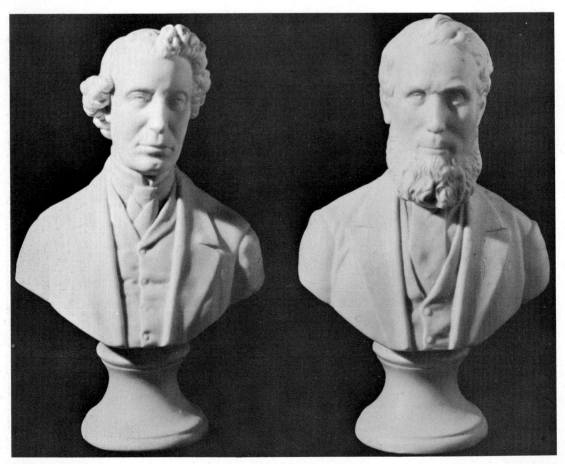

PLATE 20C. Parian busts (*c.* 1878) of Sir John A. Macdonald and Hon. Alexander Mackenzie (first and second Prime Ministers of Canada). Marked R C.

PLATE 21A. Parian bust (maker unknown) of Toronto's
Ned Hanlan, who became champion oarsman of the
world on Nov. 15, 1880.

PLATE 21B. Parian jug (maker unknown) depicting characters from Shakespeare. Ht. 6½ in. From the 1840's Canadian dealers advertised 'Parian
Jugs . . . in great variety'.

PLATE 22A. French porcelain tea set painted with moss roses in pink and brown. Both the porcelain and the decoration were very popular with Canadian housewives in Victorian days.

PLATE 22B. Galluba & Hofmann bisque figure (c. 1888). Continental bisque ornaments flooded Victorian Canada. This one is typical of many that came from Germany.

PLATE 23. Enoch Wood & Sons plate, dark blue, with a view of Montmorency Falls. Note Governor Haldimand's observation 'house' on wooden platform (upper left).

PLATE 24. Podmore, Walker & Co. ewer printed in sepia with a view of Quebec taken from Bartlett's *Canadian Scenery*. British America series. Ht. 10¾ in.

PLATE 25. Podmore, Walker & Co. gravy tureen, light blue, with a view of the Chaudière Bridge from Bartlett's *Canadian Scenery*. A figure from 'Navy Island' appears on the stand.

PLATE 26A. Bartlett's 'Chaudière Bridge (near Quebec)', as published in the early 1840's in *Canadian Scenery*.

PLATE 26B. Proof from an old copperplate showing Bartlett's 'Chaudière Bridge' as it appeared on earthenware made by F. Morley & Co. and by Ashworths, Morley's successors. [*Geo. L. Ashworth & Bros. Ltd.*]

PLATE 27. F. Morley & Co. soup plate with Bartlett's view of the Chaudière Bridge. From a service originally owned by Sir William Dawson, principal of McGill University.

PLATE 28A. Bartlett's 'Church at Point-Levi' (Lévis) as published in the early 1840's in *Canadian Scenery*.

PLATE 28B. Proof from an old copperplate showing Bartlett's 'Church at Point-Levi' as it appeared on earthenware made by F. Morley & Co. and by Ashworths, Morley's successors. [*Geo. L. Ashworth & Bros. Ltd.*]

PLATE 29. F. Morley & Co. plate printed in light blue with Bartlett's 'Church at Point-Levi'. The pattern name for this series was 'Lake'.

PLATE 30A. Unmarked plate, dark blue, with a view of Quebec. Possibly this nineteenth-century plate owes something to R. Short's view of Quebec published in London, 1761.

PLATE 30B. Tableware by E. Walley, Cobridge, printed in grey with Canadian symbols on an ironstone body whose moulded form (shape and design) was registered in 1856.

PLATE 31A. Maple pattern cream jug by T. Furnival & Sons. This brown-printed earthenware was popular in the 1880's. Ht. 4¾ in.

PLATE 31B. Teapot from the Bo'ness pottery of J. Marshall & Co., printed in black with a view from the series entitled 'Canadian Sports'. Ht. 9¼ in.

PLATE 31C. Ewer, Canadian view (Natural Steps, Montmorency River), made in Glasgow for Quebec china merchant F. T. Thomas. Hollow pieces in this series were first made in the 'Square Shape' fashionable in the 1880's.

PLATE 32A. Blue platter (Edwards) with decoration inspired by the 1840 achievement of a Canadian, Samuel Cunard, who established transatlantic mail service by steam.

PLATE 32B. Mulberry platter, pattern name 'Acadia'. Decoration and name reflect interest in Cunard's early steamships, the *Acadia* being famous for speed. Maker unknown.

PLATE 33A. E. F. Bodley & Son plate (*c.* 1880) made for the Beaver Line. Bodleys of Staffordshire produced much ironstone to the order of Canadian shipping companies.

PLATE 33B. Bodley plate (*c.* 1880) printed in brown with the traditional Willow pattern, made for use on ships of the Allan Line.

PLATE 34A. Davenport plate identified on the back as 'Montreal', and featuring the 'superb' St. Lawrence steamboat *British America* (built 1829). Printed in pink.

PLATE 34B. Sproule's 'View of Montreal From St. Helen's Island' (published in 1830) which probably furnished the Davenport artist with some of his material.

PLATE 35A. Penny bank in a body patented, 1859, by Toronto potter John Brown. Rare example of pottery under a pre-Confederation patent. Fully marked. Ht. 13½ in.

PLATE 35B. Red earthenware dog with brown, orange, and green mottled glaze. Marked and dated (1892) by Daniel Orth, Campden, Ont. Ht. 9¼ in.

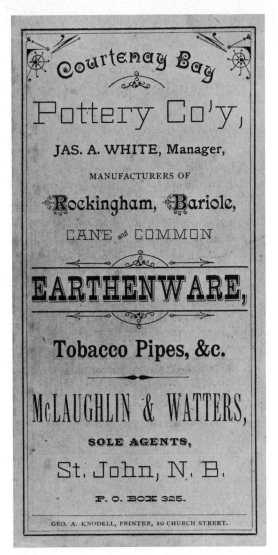

PRICE LIST.

Courtenay Bay Pottery Co.,
ST. JOHN, N. B.

Bread Pans..

				Per doz.
No. 1 Bread Pans,	....	....		$7 50
2 " "		....	....	5 00
3 " "		....	....	3 00

Milk Pans.

No. 1 Milk Pans,	....	....		$2 50
2 " "		....	....	2 00
3 " "		....	....	1 40
4 " "		....	....	1 00

Cream Crocks.

4 Gallon	....	....	....	$7 00
3 "		....	....	5 00
2 "		....	....	3 30
1½ "		....	....	2 25
1 "		....	....	1 80
½ "		....	....	1 00
¼ "		....	....	80

Butter Crocks, Covered.

6 Gallon,	....	....	....	$15 00
5 "		....	....	11 00
4 "		....	....	9 00
3 "		....	....	6 50
2 "		....	....	4 50
1½ "		....	....	3 25
1 "		....	....	2 60

Preserve Jars, Covered.

2 Gallon,	....	....	....	$4 50
1½ "		....	....	3 25
1 "		....	....	2 60
½ "		....	....	1 60
¼ "		....	....	1 20

PLATE 36. Price list, 1880's, for White's Courtenay Bay Pottery, Crouchville, N.B. The Whites were English potters who emigrated to New Brunswick in the 1860's.

PLATE 37A. James A. and Frederick J. White of the Courtenay Bay Pottery. Frederick returned to England in 1875 to manage the family pottery in Bristol.

PLATE 37B. Interior of J. H. Ahrens' pottery, Paris, Ont., painted in May, 1883, by Paul Wickson. A flash flood carried the pottery away later that summer. [*Paris Public Library*]

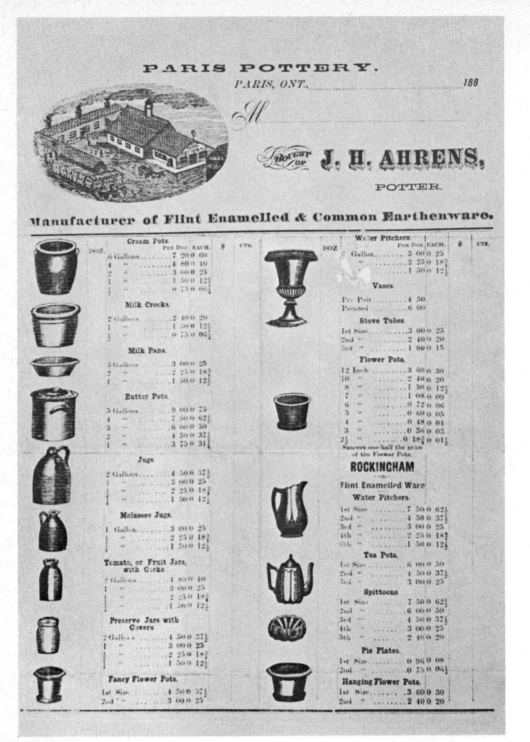

PLATE 38. Price list, 1880's, for J. H. Ahrens' pottery, Paris, Ont. Ahrens showed samples of his work at international exhibitions. [*Brant Museum, Brantford*]

PLATE 39. Yellow ware jug, early shape, crudely potted. Probably Canadian-made. Both Quebec and Ontario potters used moulded decoration of beavers and maple leaves. Ht. 9¼ in.

PLATE 40A. Red earthenware flower pot or hanging basket, glaze streaked with brown. Attributed to the Dions, Ancienne Lorette, Que. Ht. 5 in.

PLATE 40B. Red earthenware jugs, various glazes, from Brant and Waterloo counties, Ontario. The jug at the left has the initials E C on the bottom. Hts. 8 to 8¾ in.

PLATE 41. Jug (ht. 8¼ in.) and dish similar to wares found in the vicinity of Quebec city. Spittoon of a type attributed to Waterloo County, Ontario.

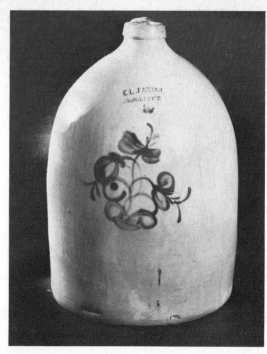

PLATE 42A. Stoneware jug marked E. L. FARRAR/ST. JOHNS C E. Contemporary price lists call these 'jugs'; today they are popularly known as 'crocks'.

PLATE 42B. George H. Farrar (d. 1927), the last member of this historic Vermont family to be a potter in the Province of Quebec. Photographed with his wife.

PLATE 43A. 'Eben' Farrar (d. 1918), younger brother of George H. Farrar. The pottery in Iberville, Que., was operated under his name for years.

PLATE 43B. Farrar's STONE, ROCKINGHAM AND YELLOW WARE FACTORY, as depicted in the 1870's by the Montreal engraver, J. H. Walker. [*McCord Museum, McGill University*].

PLATE 44A. Stoneware pot marked E. L. FARRAR/IBER-VILLE P. Q. 'Eben' Farrar's granddaughter recalls that these were the 'best sellers' in the factory's last years.

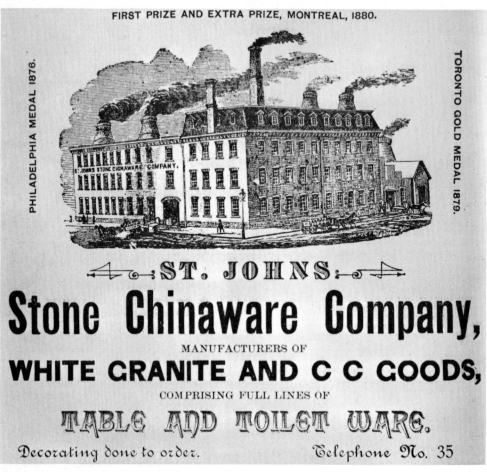

PLATE 44B. Advertisement for the St. Johns Stone Chinaware Company in *The Eastern Townships Business & Farmers Directory for 1888-89.*

PLATE 45A. Ewer and basin, the St. Johns Stone Chinaware Company. This Company (founded 1873) was Canada's most successful producer of whiteware in the nineteenth century.

PLATE 45B. Ironstone slop jar, green and gold decoration, made by the St. Johns Stone Chinaware Company for T. Connor's Windsor Hotel, Cobourg. Ht. 14¾ in.

PLATE 46A. Teapot in the blue body introduced by the St. Johns Stone Chinaware Company in the 1870's. Ht. 9 in.

PLATE 46B. Blue milk jug, moulded design, the St. Johns Stone Chinaware Company. This jug occurs in several sizes and in white as well as blue. Ht. 6¼ in.

PLATE 47A. Blue bread tray, the St. Johns Stone Chinaware Company. It is rare to find as ambitious a St. Johns piece as this intricately moulded tray. L. 13¼ in.

PLATE 47B. Flower pot or jardinière, the St. Johns Stone Chinaware Company. A variety of articles was made for the plant-loving Victorian housewife. Ht. 8¼ in.

PLATE 48A. Articles of toilet ware, the St. Johns Stone Chinaware Company. Toilet sets were frequently decorated with bands of colour (lavender, pink, green, etc.).

PLATE 48B. Jug for ice water, the St. Johns Stone Chinaware Company. This type of jug was a good selling line with North American potteries. Ht. 9½ in.

PLATE 49A. Two of the marks found on wares made by the St. Johns Stone Chinaware Company. The form of the Royal Arms varied.

PLATE 49B. Ironstone jug made at the British Porcelain Works, St. Johns. This firm (founded in the 1880's) was a rival of the St. Johns Stone Chinaware Company. Ht. 7¾ in.

PLATE 49C. Simon Thomas Humberstone, fourth generation Ontario potter who was also active in politics. Political cartoon published in the *Recorder*, Sept. 29, 1892.

PLATE 50. Terrapin Restaurant jug, (c. 1863) decorated by Hurd, Leigh & Co., Toronto, who claimed to have introduced professional china decorating to Canada. Ht. 9½ in.

PLATE 51A. John Howard Griffiths (d. 1898), the Minton-
trained china painter of London, Ont., whose work was
presented to Queen Victoria.

PLATE 51B. Wedgwood porcelain plate painted with roses
by J. H. Griffiths. One of the last pieces painted by him,
it is signed and dated in the year of his death.

PLATE 52. Hand-painted Copeland tile (12 x 11 in.). Canadian dealers frequently advertised both Copeland and Minton tiles 'in the white', offering them to amateur china painters.

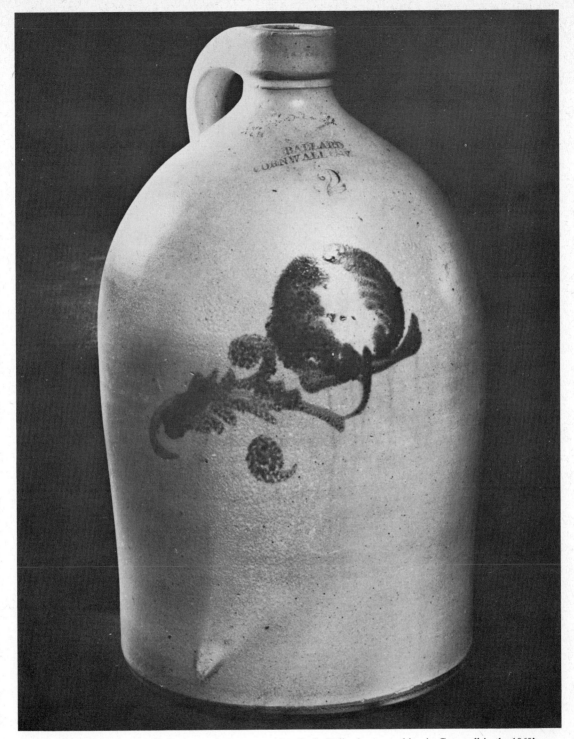

PLATE 53. Stoneware jug marked BALLARD/CORNWALL C W. O. L. Ballard was working in Cornwall in the 1860's.

PLATE 54. Picture frame, reddish-brown glaze, incised on the back: 'Made by G. Beech/April 1862/Brantford/Canada West'. 8¾ x 7¼ in.

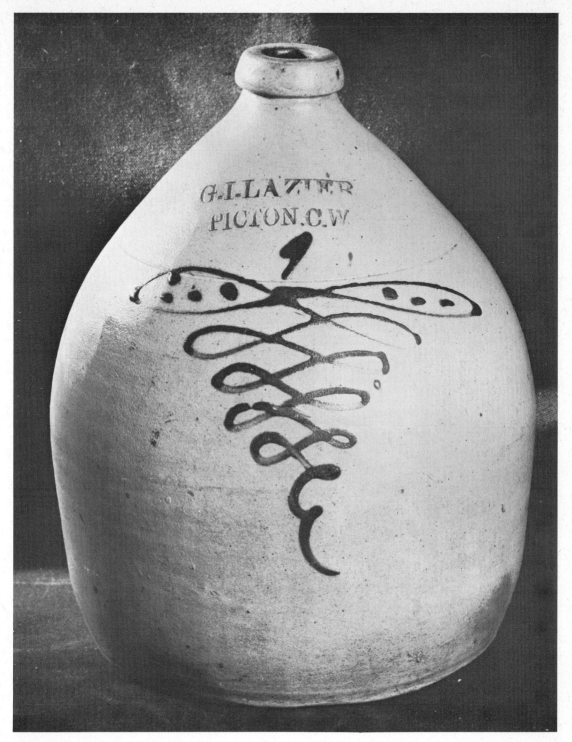

PLATE 55. Jug marked G. I. LAZIER/PICTON. C. W. Lazier was related by marriage to the Harts, potters of Picton and Belleville. As Hart Bros. & Lazier, they exhibited their work in Europe and England.

PLATE 56. Brown, covered pot, W. E. WELDING/BRANTFORD, ONT. Such utilitarian ware was a staple of this confident Ontario potter who complained that others were reluctant to compete against him.

Notes on I: OVER THE ATLANTIC BY SAIL

1. The *Scotsman* was a regular trader to Quebec and Montreal in the 1830's, the *Coeur-de-Lion* in the 1840's (*cf.* the *Montreal Gazette*, Sept. 15, 1835, Aug. 6, 1842).
2. Indicated by advertisements in the *Montreal Gazette*, Sept. 23 – Oct. 4, 1844.
3. *Ibid.*, Oct. 9, 1844.
4. *Ibid.*
5. *Ibid.*, Jan. 14, 1857.
6. *Novascotian*, Jan. 27, 1845. Bernard O'Neil, whose name is spelled in a variety of ways in contemporary newspapers and directories, was in the china business in Halifax for over thirty years.
7. *Times and Daily Commercial Advertiser* (Montreal), April 16, 1845.
8. *Montreal Gazette*, April 15, 1846.
9. *Ibid.*, Feb. 24, 1847.
10. *New Brunswick Courier*, Mar. 27, 1847.
11. Anon., *A Cheering Voice From Upper Canada* (London, 1834), p. 12.
12. Capt. W. Moorsom, *Letters From Nova Scotia* (London, 1830), p. 47.
13. *Montreal Gazette*, May 27, 1854.
14. Journal of a voyage over the Atlantic to Quebec in 1854, kept by George Roberts; printed in E. A. Collard, 'All Our Yesterdays', *Gazette*, June 3, 1960.
15. *Montreal Gazette*, Jan. 14, 1843.
16. *British American Journal*, April 15, 1834.
17. *Literary Transcript & General Intelligencer* (Quebec), June 1, 1839.
18. *Montreal Gazette*, June 5, 1824. At this period the *Gazette* was published twice a week during the season when the port was open, once a week during the winter.
19. J. Arnold Fleming, *Scottish Pottery* (Glasgow, 1923), p. 109.
20. Henry Fry, *The History of North Atlantic Steam Navigation* (London, 1896), p. 140.
21. *Montreal Gazette*, June 17, 1854.
22. Fleming, p. 211.
23. *Montreal Gazette*, Oct. 25, 1842.
24. William T. Baird, *Seventy Years of New Brunswick Life* (Saint John, 1890), p. 131.
25. *Royal Gazette and Nova Scotia Advertiser*, Oct. 7, 1800.
26. *Royal Gazette and New Brunswick Advertiser*, April 10, 1809.

Notes on II: FROM MONTREAL TO UPPER CANADA

1. John J. Bigsby, *The Shoe and Canoe* (London, 1850), I, 108.
2. The figure for 1851 was 1,447 tons of earthenware and glassware from the opening of navigation to Aug. 31. *Montreal Gazette*, Sept. 28, 1852.
3. Isaac Weld, *Travels Through . . . the Provinces of . . . Canada*, 4th ed. (London, 1800), p. 341.
4. Anon., *A Cheering Voice From Upper Canada* (London, 1834), p. 11.
5. Martin Doyle [W. Hickey], *Hints on Emigration to Upper Canada Especially Addressed to the Lower Classes . . .* (Dublin, 1831), p. 85. The word 'delf' is here used in the sense of any common crockery.
6. Bigsby, I, 108.
7. Rev. William Haw, *Fifteen Years in Canada* (Edinburgh, 1850), pp. 115-16.
8. Catherine Parr Traill, *The Backwoods of Canada*, new ed. (London, 1846), p. 108.
9. See, for example, the appeal to the crockery buyers of Upper Canada made by Goodwin Brothers, of Quebec, in *The Canada Directory*, 1851.
10. Quoted in the *Montreal Gazette*, May 17, 1841.
11. Bigsby, I, 108; Sir Charles Dilke, *Greater Britain* (London, 1868), I, 69.
12. *Gleaner*, May 17, 1823 (advertisement dated April 30).
13. Some transportation of goods from Montreal to Upper Canada did take place by sleigh, but, for bulky wares like crated crockery, this winter trade was too small to have any real bearing on the general picture.
14. *Gleaner*, Dec. 20, 1823.
15. *Montreal Gazette*, Oct. 31, 1842; also in the Hamilton *Gazette* and Toronto *Patriot*.
16. *A Cheering Voice*, p. 11.
17. *British American Journal*, Sept. 30, 1834.
18. Rev. Henry Scadding, *Toronto Of Old* (Toronto, 1878), p. 469.
19. *York Gazette*, Oct. 3, 1810.

20. *Examiner*, Jan. 1, 1840 (advertisement dated July 30, 1839).
21. *Niagara Chronicle*, July 17, 1851.
22. *A Cheering Voice*, p. 12.
23. Advertisement by Larocque, Bernard & Co., St. Paul Street. *Montreal Gazette*, Oct. 26, 1833.
24. Rev. William Bell, *Hints to Emigrants in a Series of Letters from Upper Canada* (Edinburgh, 1824), p. 56.
25. *Kingston Chronicle*, Jan. 1, 1819.
26. *Upper Canada Gazette*, Oct. 22, 1821.
27. *Gleaner*, Dec. 20, 1823.
28. *Ibid.*, Jan. 10, 1824.
29. Thomas Storrow Brown, 'Montreal in 1818', *The New Dominion Monthly*, Mar., 1870.
30. Bell, pp. 52 and 56.
31. Edward Allen Talbot, *Five Years' Residence in the Canadas* (London, 1824), I, 84-86.
32. *Brockville Gazette*, Aug. 9, 1832 (the advertisement is dated May 23).
33. A long advertisement in the *Brockville Gazette*, May 1, 1829, outlined the services they offered.
34. *Bytown Gazette*, Nov. 10, 1836.
35. For the Ottawa & Rideau Forwarding Co.'s rates see the *Montreal Gazette*, April 11, 1837.
36. See Hamilton's advertisement in the *Examiner*, Oct. 27, 1841.
37. Ross, Matthie & Co. had established their forwarding line that year and had put on an advertising campaign for Toronto business. See the *Examiner*, Oct. 27, 1841.
38. For a forwarder's advertisement offering services by both bateaux and Durham boats, see the announcement by John McPherson & Co., of Prescott, in the Niagara *Gleaner*, April 5, 1823.
39. See their advertisement in the *Montreal Gazette*, May 2, 1839; also James Croil, *Steam Navigation* (Toronto, 1898), p. 319.
40. *Montreal Gazette*, May 7, 1835.
41. D'Arcy Boulton, *Sketch of His Majesty's Province of Upper Canada* (London, 1805), p. 45.
42. *Montreal Gazette*, April 15, 1837.
43. *Ibid.*, April 4, 1837.
44. *Ibid.*, April 15, 1837.
45. According to the merchants' reckoning, the old tariff for taking 1 hhd of earthenware up the river was 12/4, and for 1 crate, 6/–; under the new tariff the charges could be as high as 3 guineas and £1. 17*s.* 8*d. Montreal Gazette*, April 15, 1837.
46. *Ibid.*
47. *Ibid.*, Aug. 12, 1845.
48. See James Patton's advertisement in the *Montreal Gazette*, Oct. 7, 1854.
49. *Ibid.*, April 18, 1855.
50. *Ibid.*, May 17, 1841.
51. Erastus Wiman, *Annual Report of the Board of Trade with a Review of the Commerce of Toronto for 1860* (Toronto, n.d.), p. 25.
52. Erastus Wiman, *Annual Report of the Board of Trade with a Review of the Commerce of Toronto for 1862* (Toronto, 1863), p. 26.
53. *Kingston Chronicle*, Jan. 7, 1820.
54. Erastus Wiman, *Annual Report of the Board of Trade . . . for 1860*, p. 25.

Notes on III: BY RED RIVER CART AND YORK BOAT

1. *Nor'-Wester*, Dec. 28, 1859.
2. For an account of such an attack see the *Nor'-Wester*, Sept. 24, 1862.
3. Anon., *Chronicles By the Way* (Montreal, 1879), p. 27.
4. Rev. George Bryce, *Manitoba: Its Infancy, Growth, and Present Condition* (London, 1882), p. 338.
5. *What to Bring and How to Come to Battleford* [1882]; quoted in E. H. Oliver, 'The Beginnings of White Settlement in Northern Saskatchewan', *Transactions of the Royal Society of Canada*, Section II (1925), 92.
6. Information supplied by Miss Alice Johnson, Archivist, Hudson's Bay Company.
7. H.B.C. Arch. A. 25/7, fo. 58d.

8. Donald Ross to James Hargrave, quoted in M. A. MacLeod, ed., *The Letters of Letitia Hargrave* (Toronto, 1947), p. lvi.
9. H.B.C. Arch. B. 235/d/122, fos. 6d., 9d., 10d.-11.
10. James Hargrave to Tom Potts, quoted in MacLeod, p. cvi.
11. Joseph James Hargrave, *Red River* (Montreal, 1871), p. 164.
12. Letitia Hargrave to Dugald Mactavish, quoted in MacLeod, p. 78.
13. Hargrave, p. 164.
14. *Montreal Gazette*, April 15, 1837.
15. *Montreal Herald*, Aug. 7, 1819.
16. *Gazette* (Montreal), Oct. 4, 1879.
17. Hargrave, p. 163.
18. *Ibid.*
19. James Hargrave to Donald Ross, quoted in MacLeod, p. lxxxii.
20. MacLeod, p. cvii.
21. *The City of Winnipeg . . . Metropolis of the Northwest* (Winnipeg, 1886), p. 17.
22. *Winnipeg . . . and Her Industries* (Chicago and Winnipeg, 1882), p. 26.
23. Rev. George Bryce, *A History of Manitoba, Its Resources and People* (Toronto, 1906), p. 453.
24. *Nor'-Wester*, June 11, 1862.
25. Charles Annandale, ed., *The New Popular Encyclopedia* (London, etc., 1902), XII, 264.
26. *Nor'-Wester*, Aug. 30, 1860; they were still advertising eight years later (*Nor'-Wester*, Dec. 12, 1868).
27. Hargrave, p. 144.
28. Charles Mair, writing from Red River, Nov. 3 and 27, 1868, quoted in Hargrave, pp. 451-52. For an advertisement for crockery offered by Mair see the *Manitoba News-Letter*, Dec. 14, 1870.
29. *Nor'-Wester*, July 28, 1860.
30. Given as *Anson Northrup* in some contemporary sources, but consistently spelled *Anson Northup* in the *Nor'-Wester* and by such authorities on the Northwest as Alexander Begg. She was named after the American who built her.
31. For example, Letitia Hargrave, in a letter written from York Factory, Sept. 5, 1845, reveals that the Company refused that year to carry goods for Andrew McDermot and James Sinclair, 'so none of them will have very well stocked shops'. MacLeod, p. 208.
32. *Nor'-Wester*, Sept. 28, 1860.
33. Myles Pennington, *Railways and Other Ways* (Toronto, 1894), pp. 142-46.
34. Henry Fry, *The History of North Atlantic Steam Navigation* (London, 1896), p. 144.
35. Hargrave, p. 34.
36. *Ibid.*, p. 61.
37. Pennington, p. 142.
38. Mary FitzGibbon, *A Trip to Manitoba* (London, 1880), pp. 44-45.
39. Mrs. Cecil Hall, *A Lady's Life on a Farm in Manitoba* (London, 1884), pp. 29-30.
40. For example, see Francis Clementson's advertisement in *Hutchinson's Saint John Directory, 1863-64.*
41. Published in the *Nor'-Wester*, June 11, 1863, under the heading: 'THE YORK ROUTE CLOSED TO PRIVATE TRADERS'.
42. Kew visited the Red River Territory in 1865. At that time he set up a commission office that eventually became the firm of Kew, Stobart & Co.
43. Hargrave, p. 292.
44. *Ibid.*, p. 301.
45. *Nor'-Wester*, June 11, 1862.
46. *Manitoba Gazette*, Aug. 5, 1874.
47. *The City of Winnipeg . . . Metropolis of the Northwest* (Winnipeg, 1886), pp. 158-59.
48. *Gazette*, April 8, 1878.
49. So styled by the *Daily Witness;* he was appointed to the Senate in 1904. H. J. Morgan, *The Canadian Men and Women of the Time* (Toronto, 1912), p. 306.
50. R. C. Russell, *The Carlton Trail* (Saskatoon, 1955), pp. 85-86.
51. Anon., *Chronicles by the Way* (Montreal, 1879), p. 64.
52. Information supplied by Dr. Russell's widow, and by George Shepherd of the Western Development Museum, Saskatoon.
53. C. P. Mulvaney, *The History of the North-West Rebellion* (Toronto, 1886), p. 338.
54. *McPhillips' . . . Business Directory of the District of Saskatchewan . . . 1888* (Qu'Appelle, N.W.T., 1888), p. 45.

Notes on III: By Red River Cart and York Boat

55. [G. H. Ham], *The New West* . . . (Winnipeg, 1888), p. 129.
56. *Ibid.*
57. C. P. T., 'Description of Fort Walsh', *The Canadian North West*, August, 1880.
58. *Ibid.*
59. E. H. Abbott to George Shepherd, Jan. 16, 1965.
60. *Globe* (Toronto), Dec. 27, 1868.

Notes on IV: AROUND THE HORN AND ON BY MULE

1. Matthew Macfie, *Vancouver Island and British Columbia* (London, 1865), p. 90.
2. *British Columbian*, Dec. 10, 1864, Dec. 8, 1866.
3. *Ibid.*, Mar. 20, 1869.
4. H.B.C. Arch. A. 67/27, fo. 401.
5. Reminiscences of Mrs. Arthur Fellows, quoted in N. de B. Lugrin, *The Pioneer Women of Vancouver Island* (Victoria, 1928), p. 177.
6. See p. 32.
7. Reminiscences of Mrs. J. D. Pemberton, quoted in Lugrin, p. 285.
8. *Emigrant Soldiers' Gazette*, Feb. 5, 1859.
9. Reminiscences of Mrs. Robert Burns McMicking, quoted in Lugrin, p. 245.
10. The usual route for passengers by that time was by steamship to Halifax or Quebec and by railway to the west coast, but sailing ships were still carrying both passengers and goods around the Horn. See Molyneux St. John, ed., *The Province of British Columbia . . . Information for Intending Settlers* (n.p., n.d.), p. 55.
11. After the union an *ad valorem* duty of 12½% was imposed on both earthenware and porcelain. *British Columbian*, Mar. 13, 1867.
12. Macfie, p. 116.
13. Quoted in Macfie, p. 92.
14. *Ibid.*, pp. 112-13.
15. R. Byron Johnson, *Very Far West Indeed* (London, 1872), p. 53.
16. Armstrong's advertisement appeared in the first issue of the *British Columbian*, Feb. 13, 1861.
17. *Guide to the Province of British Columbia for 1877-78* (Victoria, 1877), p. 407.
18. J. B. Kerr, *Biographical Dictionary of Well-Known British Columbians* (Vancouver, 1890), pp. 250-51.
19. *British Columbian*, Nov. 29, 1865.
20. F. W. Howay, *British Columbia, the Making of a Province* (Toronto, 1928), p. 140.
21. His advertisement was still running in the *British Columbian* on Nov. 29, 1865; it was dated April 17.
22. H. H. Bancroft, *History of British Columbia* (San Francisco, 1890), p. 59.
23. A. G. Doughty and Gustave Lanctot, eds., *Cheadle's Journal* (Ottawa, 1913), p. 225.
24. *Ibid.*, p. 226.
25. Quoted in Macfie, p. 229.
26. Johnson, p. 49.
27. J. A. Lees and W. J. Clutterbuck, *B.C. 1887 A Ramble in British Columbia* (London, 1888), p. 234.
28. The Potteries Committee of Inquiry, which sat in England in 1893, found that 'potters suffer an excessive mortality in following their occupation'. See the Duchess of Sutherland, 'On the Dangerous Processes in the Potting Industry', in Harold Owen, *The Staffordshire Potter* (London, 1901), p. 281.
29. Mark S. Wade, *The Thompson Country* (Kamloops, 1907), p. 110.
30. R. C. Mayne, *Four Years in British Columbia and Vancouver Island* (London, 1862), p. 92.
31. [G. H. Ham], *The New West* (Winnipeg, 1888), p. 170.
32. *British Columbian*, Feb. 24, 1864.
33. *Industries of Canada* (Toronto, 1887), p. 47.
34. *Ibid.*
35. *The City of Winnipeg . . . Metropolis of the Northwest*, (Winnipeg, 1886) p. 103.
36. *Ibid.*
37. Macfie, p. 107.

38. *British Columbian*, Mar. 20, 1869.
39. *The British Columbia Directory for the Years 1882-83*, p. 129.
40. See p. 159.
41. Reminiscences of Mrs. Robert Burns McMicking, quoted in Lugrin, p. 245.
42. Johnson, p. 49.
43. *Ibid.*
44. *Ibid.*
45. *Ibid.*

Notes on V: ANYBODY'S BUSINESS

1. Thomas Doige, *An Alphabetical List of the Merchants, Traders and Housekeepers Residing in Montreal* (Montreal, 1819).
2. See advertisements: *Montreal Herald*, June 13, 1818; *Canadian Courant*, Oct. 2, 1821; *Spectateur Canadien*, Dec. 8, 1821.
3. *Montreal Gazette*, Oct. 13, 1832.
4. *Colonial Advocate*, Mar. 10, 1831 (the advertisement is dated Dec. 10, 1830).
5. *New Brunswick Courier*, June 16, 1838.
6. *Ibid.*, May 29, 1852.
7. Even after Francis Clementson was dead, the business that continued under his name was still advertising cigars in a china shop. See *McAlpine's Saint John . . . Directory for 1879-80*, p. 63.
8. *McAlpine's Nova Scotia Directory for 1890-97*, p. 750.
9. *Henderson's Directory of Manitoba . . . for . . . 1882*, p. 80.
10. W. H. Hayward began in partnership with a brother-in-law, William Warwick. Later they separated. In 1928 the two families joined again in china-selling, but by 1955 only the Haywards were still in the business, although the name 'Hayward & Warwick' continues. Information supplied by W. H. Hayward, Senior, grandson of the founder.
11. *McAlpine's Saint John . . . Directory for 1879-80*, p. 128.
12. Erastus Wiman, *Annual Report of the Board of Trade with a Review of the Commerce of Toronto for 1860* (Toronto, n.d.), p. 25.
13. *Canadian Courant*, May 29, 1819.
14. *Ibid.*, Sept. 18, 1819.
15. John M'Gregor, *British America*, quoted in [Catherine Parr Traill], *The Backwoods of Canada*, 4th ed. (London, 1839), p. 35n.
16. *Montreal Gazette*, Sept. 1, 1806.
17. Rev. J. D. Borthwick, *History of Montreal Including the Streets* (Montreal, 1897), p. 117.
18. When A. B. Buxton (proprietor of Liverpool House) died, a two-day auction disposed of his stock. The *New Brunswick Courier*, April 24, 1844, urged retail dealers and housewives both to attend.
19. *Winnipeg . . . and Her Industries* (Chicago and Winnipeg, 1882), pp. 8 and 23.
20. *Novascotian*, Aug. 6, 1860.
21. Anonymous reminiscences of the Prince of Wales' visit to Saint John, *Daily Sun*, Feb. 1, 1901.
22. *Ibid.*
23. *Montreal Gazette*, Sept. 24, 1860.
24. *Ibid.*, Oct. 13, 1860.
25. *Ibid.*, June 23, 1791.
26. *Ibid.*, May 27, 1805. The sale took place the year after McTavish's death, and was held on behalf of his widow.
27. Rev. William Haw, *Fifteen Years in Canada* (Edinburgh, 1850), p. 116.
28. *Times* (Halifax), Nov. 4, 1834.
29. *Montreal Gazette*, April 17, 1846.
30. Sir James E. Alexander, *L'Acadie* (London, 1849), I, 275-76.
31. *Montreal Gazette*, Nov. 4, 1805.
32. *Ibid.*, May 17, 1865.
33. For example, dinner and breakfast sets of 'Liverpool Ware' used at the Hotel, No. 22, Hollis Street, Halifax, were sold in 1827. *Novascotian*, Nov. 15, 1827.

34. William Ridgway (1788-1864), son of Job Ridgway and brother of John, operated a number of potteries, but as 'Ridgway, Son & Co.' he was in business for only a decade; that decade ended in 1848, the year before the first Donegana's Hotel was burned. It is through William Ridgway that Ridgway Potteries Ltd., suppliers of the Canadian market in the twentieth century, trace their connection with this famous potting family.
35. John Palmer, *Journal of Travels in . . . Lower Canada* (London, 1818), p. 212.
36. A. Baumgarten, *Industrial Canada* (Montreal, 1876), p. 26.
37. Henry Taylor, *The Present Condition of United Canada* (Toronto, 1850), p. 84.
38. *Quebec Mercury*, July 19, 1819.
39. *Novascotian*, Feb. 17, 1845.
40. Baumgarten, pp. 26, 30.
41. *British Standard*, June 19, 1861.
42. *Daily Witness*, Aug. 25, 1880. Wiley's China Hall had opened two days before.
43. *Novascotian*, Oct. 31, 1859.
44. *Yarmouth Herald*, Dec. 14, 1854.
45. See advertisements in the *Prince Edward Island Register*, Jan. 8, 1820, and the *Canadian Intelligencer*, Sept. 17, 1828.
46. *Daily Witness*, Sept. 11, 1880.
47. *Montreal Gazette*, Dec. 6, 1854.
48. Both pounds and dollars were in use at this time in Canadian currency; it was not unusual to find both quoted in one advertisement.
49. *Montreal Gazette*, Jan. 24, Jan. 29, 1833.
50. *Ibid.*, Sept. 5, 1836, Mar. 22, 1850.
51. *Ibid.* Jan 10, 1833.
52. *Halifax Gazette*, Aug. 22, 1752.
53. *Montreal Transcript*, Mar. 18, 1854.
54. *Montreal Gazette*, May 21, 1866.

Notes on VI: A WEDGWOOD IN MONTREAL AND OTHER UNEXPECTED LINKS

1. Thomas Storrow Brown, 'Montreal in 1818', *The New Dominion Monthly*, March, 1870.
2. Llewellynn Jewitt, *The Wedgwoods . . .* (London, 1865), p. 99.
3. Information supplied by W. A. Billington, Curator of the Wedgwood Museum.
4. Eliza Meteyard, *The Life of Josiah Wedgwood* (London, 1865-1866), II, 49.
5. The *Canadian Courant* was still running this advertisement on Feb. 1, 1817.
6. Information supplied by W. A. Billington.
7. *Montreal Herald*, Nov. 2, 1816.
8. Wedgwood Archives, Keele University.
9. *Montreal Herald*, Nov. 2, 1816.
10. *Ibid.*, June 21, 1817.
11. *Ibid.*, June 6, 1818.
12. *Ibid.*, June 27, 1818.
13. Joseph Wedgwood to Josiah Wedgwood, Nov. 18, 1817. Wedgwood Archives.
14. Meteyard, II, 49.
15. The St. Paul Street premises were offered for rent by the owners or agents as early as Feb. 7, 1818 (*Montreal Herald*, Mar. 7, 1818), but it was not until a year later that Joseph Wedgwood himself put his store up for rent (*Montreal Herald*, April 17, 1819). Presumably he had made arrangements to struggle on a little longer.
16. Josiah Wedgwood to Messrs. Irvine, Leslie & Co., June 25, 1819. Wedgwood Archives.
17. *Montreal Herald*, Sept. 4, 1819.
18. For example, in the *Mercantile Agency Reference Book* for 1866 Francis Clementson, John Watson & Co. (Montreal), and Patton & Co. (Toronto) all had the same 'pecuniary strength'; Clementson's credit rating was 'High', the others merely 'Good'.
19. *Centennial of Canadian Methodism* (Toronto, 1891), p. 98.
20. *Ibid.*
21. Llewellynn Jewitt, *The Ceramic Art of Great Britain* (London, 1878), II, 332.
22. Alexander Sutherland, *Methodism in Canada* (London, 1903), p. 327.
23. *Yarmouth Herald*, Aug. 16, 1855.
24. He was born in 1818; the business in Saint John was established in 1847.

Notes on VI: A Wedgwood in Montreal and Other Unexpected Links

25. Memorandum by Mrs. B. A. MacDonald (great-grand-daughter of Thomas Stubbs) in the files of the New Brunswick Museum.
26. *The Dominion Illustrated*, Saint John, N.B., Special Number, Feb. 14, 1891.
27. *New Brunswick Courier*, Oct. 29, 1853.
28. *The Dominion Illustrated*, Special Number.
29. *New Brunswick Courier*, Nov. 3, 1855.
30. *Hutchinson's Saint John Directory, 1863-64.*
31. See pp. 69, 172.
32. *New Brunswick Courier*, Dec. 1, 1855.
33. Miss Ella Gale gave this cup and saucer to the museum in 1953.
34. George Stewart, *The Story of the Great Fire in St. John* (Toronto, [1877]), pp. 186, 249.
35. *The Dominion Illustrated*, Special Number.
36. Information supplied by Rev. Robert A. Kirtley, Minister of Bethesda Methodist Church, Hanley.
37. One of these announcements is preserved in an old scrapbook in the New Brunswick Museum.
38. In Lot 1889 Linden Avenue. Records of the Fernhill Cemetery Company.
39. *The Dominion Illustrated*, Special Number.
40. *Lovell's Montreal Directory for 1888-89.*
41. *The Canada Directory* (Montreal, 1851).
42. Joseph Mayer, *On the Art of Pottery With a History of Its Progress in Liverpool* (Liverpool, 1873), p. 89.
43. *Ibid.*, p. 90.
44. *Ibid.*, p. 90n.
45. The Toronto warehouse was gone by the 1860's.
46. J. Arnold Fleming, *Scottish Pottery* (Glasgow, 1923), p. 97.
47. Quoted in Fleming, p. 98.
48. Fleming, p. 99.
49. *Gazette* (Montreal), Mar. 25, 1896.
50. *Montreal Gazette*, Feb. 11, 1845.
51. *Ibid.*, Aug. 12, 1846.
52. *Montreal Transcript*, July 27, 1847.
53. *Montreal Gazette*, Aug. 6, 1841.
54. *Ibid.*, May 1, 1845.
55. *Ibid.*, Sept. 5, 1850.
56. *Ibid.*, May 8, 1842.
57. Robert Anderson was one of the original shareholders of the Montreal Ocean Steamship Co. (the early name of the Allan Line).
58. His obituary gives the date as 1859 (*Gazette*, Mar. 25, 1896), but it was actually in 1854 that Thomson & Minchin began styling themselves 'Successors to Robert Anderson' (*Pilot*, Mar. 21, 1854).
59. *Gazette*, Mar. 25, 1896.
60. *Ibid.*

Notes on VII: CANADIAN CHINA DEALERS' MARKS ON IMPORTED WARES

1. Joseph Shuter's dates are taken from family records in the possession of J. G. R. Shuter, his great-grandson.
2. Shuter Street, running north from Sherbrooke Street near the Royal Victoria College, passed through what had been Joseph Shuter's estate. In 1964 the name was changed to Aylmer.
3. Rev. Robert Campbell, *A History of the Scotch Presbyterian Church St. Gabriel Street, Montreal* (Montreal, 1887), p. 233.
4. *Montreal Herald*, Jan. 11, 1817.
5. Thomas Doige, *An Alphabetical List of the Merchants, Traders and Housekeepers Residing in Montreal* (Montreal, 1819), p. 169. Wilkins, later the Hon. R. C. Wilkins, was resident in Upper Canada.
6. *Montreal Gazette*, April 28, 1836.
7. *Canadian Courant*, Aug. 16, 1823; *Montreal Gazette*, June 14, 1830, July 4, 1833.
8. *Montreal Gazette*, April 30, 1836.
9. *Canadian Courant*, Aug. 16, 1823, June 5, 1824.

Notes on VII: Canadian China Dealers' Marks on Imported Wares

10. *Montreal Gazette*, May 10, 1836.
11. *Montreal Gazette*, June 3, 1834.
12. J. G. R. Shuter.
13. For Enoch Wood's Montreal connections see Chap. XVI.
14. Montreal city directories 1848-50.
15. Montreal city directories 1857-60.
16. So listed in *MacKay's Montreal Directory . . . 1861-62*.
17. So styled in an advertisement in *The Eastern Townships Gazetteer* (St. Johns, 1867).
18. *Montreal Gazette*, May 5, 1824.
19. *Montreal Herald*, Nov. 26, 1898.
20. Information supplied by A. T. Brodeur, President of Cassidy's Ltd.
21. One of those who purchased a Brownfield dinner service at Staffordshire Hall was Benjamin Martin, a cheese manufacturer from Dunham, Que. His service, with the Boxer Brothers' mark, has come down to grandchildren.
22. *Quebec Mercury*, Dec. 28, 1839.
23. *Literary Transcript*, June 1, 1839.
24. Quebec city directories.
25. *La Revue Canadienne*, April 17, 1846.
26. *La Minerve*, June 25, 1870.
27. *Montreal Gazette*, April 15, 1867.
28. The Quebec directories do not list Thomas as a crockery dealer until that year.
29. *L'Indicateur de Québec & Lévis 1897-98*.
30. *Lovell's . . . Business Directory for the Province of Quebec, 1910-11*.
31. See Chap. XVIII.
32. J. Ross Robertson, *Landmarks of Toronto* (Toronto, 1898), III, 62.
33. *Industries of Canada—Historical and Commercial Sketches of Toronto* (Toronto, 1886), p. 111.
34. Glover Harrison began his china business in 1864. Before he opened at 71 King Street East he was very briefly at Number 49, the number that was to be his again in later years. Marks giving his address as 49 King Street East almost always refer to the years after 1880.
35. Toronto city directories 1890-1901.
36. *Globe*, Dec. 13, 1866; *Mail*, Sept. 10, 1879.
37. In 1881, when he had been in business more than fifteen years, Harrison's estimated capital was only $5,000-$10,000.
38. *Industries of Canada*, p. 111.
39. C. C. Taylor, *The Queen's Jubilee and Toronto 'Called Back'* (Toronto, 1887), p. 313.

Notes on VIII: THE WEDGWOOD TRADITION IN CANADA

1. *Montreal Herald*, Special Edition, April 21, 1865.
2. *Daily Witness*, Oct. 5, 1881.
3. *Royal Gazette and Nova Scotia Advertiser*, Mar. 20, 1798.
4. *Quebec Gazette*, Aug. 5, 1802.
5. *Montreal Gazette*, Sept. 26, 1803.
6. *Royal Gazette and New Brunswick Advertiser*, May 27, 1811.
7. *Montreal Herald*, May 10, 1817; *Montreal Gazette*, Aug. 31, 1850.
8. *Gazette*, Dec. 16, 1899.
9. Wedgwood bone china belongs to two periods: 1812-22, and from 1878 on.
10. *Montreal Gazette*, May 5, 1808.
11. Josiah Wedgwood, Experiment Book, 1759, quoted in Wolf Mankowitz, *Wedgwood* (New York, 1953), p. 27.
12. Faujas de St. Fond, quoted in E. A. Sandeman, *Notes on the Manufacture of Earthenware* (London, 1921), p. 6.
13. *The Staffordshire Pottery Directory . . . and an Account of the Manufacture of Earthenware* (Hanley, 1802), p. 40.
14. An advertisement in the *Royal Gazette and New Brunswick Advertiser*, Mar. 9, 1790, offered both delft and stoneware (salt-glazed ware); another on Nov. 11, 1800, offered stoneware.
15. Josiah Wedgwood quoted in Mankowitz, p. 128.
16. *Royal Gazette and New Brunswick Advertiser*, Mar. 9, 1790.

Notes on VIII: The Wedgwood Tradition in Canada

17. *The Staffordshire Pottery Directory*, 1802, pp. 42-43.
18. *Montreal Gazette*, July 29, 1790.
19. *Quebec Gazette*, Aug. 5, 1802.
20. *Montreal Gazette*, Oct. 22, 1804.
21. John Ashton Shuttleworth to Wedgwood & Byerley, Greek Street, Soho, London, Sept. 14, 1791; now in the Wedgwood Archives, Keele University.
22. *Ibid.*
23. Eliza Meteyard, *A Group of Englishmen* (London, 1871), pp. x-xiii.
24. The letter, from an agent of the Lieutenant-Governor's in England to the Wedgwood firm, points out that, as the wares have not yet been delivered to him, they will be too late for the autumn convoy: 'the ships are all gone'. Wedgwood Archives.
25. The order is dated Nov. 30, 1815. Wedgwood Archives.
26. *Gazette* (Montreal), May 4, 1965.
27. Josiah Wedgwood, quoted in Llewellynn Jewitt, *The Wedgwoods* (London, 1865), p. 187.
28. William Pitt, *A Topographical History of Staffordshire* (Newcastle-under-Lyme, 1817), p. 349.
29. William Evans, *Art and History of the Potting Business* (Shelton, [1846]), p. 19.
30. Wedgwood & Bentley Catalogue, 1773, quoted in Jewitt, p. 214.
31. *Nova Scotia Gazette*, Aug. 29, 1786.
32. *Ibid.*, Feb. 8, 1780.
33. *Montreal Gazette*, Dec. 18, 1815.
34. *Literary Transcript*, Nov. 15, 1838.
35. *New Brunswick Courier*, July 12, 1845.
36. *Mail*, Nov. 28, 1879.
37. *Daily Witness*, Dec. 20, 1879.
38. The jugs were in 'Florence' and 'Dutch' shapes, and the orders for them, in the Wedgwood Archives, are dated Feb. 6, 1850, and Dec. 23, 1851. See also the *Great Exhibition of the Works of Industry of All Nations, 1851. Official Descriptive . . . Catalogue* (London, 1851), II, 718.
39. Josiah Wedgwood, quoted in Jewitt, p. 341.
40. *Daily Witness*, Dec. 14, 1885.
41. Advertisements for these wares in Canada may be found in Montreal's *Gazette*, Dec. 23, 1870, and *Daily Witness*, Dec. 20, 1879.
42. *Quebec Mercury*, Jan. 7, 1811.
43. *Daily Witness*, Oct. 20, 1882.
44. Jewitt, p. 391.
45. *Montreal Gazette*, Sept. 20, 1832.

Notes on IX: PRINTED WARES: FROM WILLOW TO FLOWING BLUE

1. *Gazette*, Oct. 13, 1868.
2. William Evans, *Art and History of the Potting Business* . . . (Shelton, [1846]), pp. 37-39.
3. *Montreal Gazette*, June 11, 1825.
4. *Prince Edward Island Register*, Dec. 4, 1827.
5. *Canadian Courant*, Aug. 16, 1823.
6. *Montreal Gazette*, July 8, 1830.
7. *Ibid.*, May 31, 1832.
8. Catalogue of the Gerrard Sale, Montreal, Sept. 22-23, 1828.
9. *Canadian Courant*, Sept. 4, 1819. The Duke of Richmond was buried in the Cathedral of the Holy Trinity, Quebec.
10. *Montreal Gazette*, April 10, 1824.
11. Simeon Shaw, *History of the Staffordshire Potteries* (Hanley, 1829), p. 235.
12. *Missiskoui Post*, Aug. 5, 1835.
13. *Bytown Gazette*, Nov. 10, 1836.
14. E. Morton Nance, *The Pottery & Porcelain of Swansea & Nantgarw* (London, 1942), p. 175.
15. *Montreal Gazette*, July 5, 1844.
16. *Globe*, Jan. 9, 1847; *Examiner*, Jan. 13, 1847.
17. *Times and Daily Commercial Advertiser*, Oct. 8, 1845.
18. Information supplied by the late Dr. John F. McIntosh, of Westfield Beach, N.B., and Westmount, Que.

19. See p. 85.
20. Charles Dickens, *A Plated Article* (Stoke-on-Trent, n.d.), p. 18, reprinted from *Household Words*, 1852.
21. Henry Wadsworth Longfellow, 'Keramos', *Harper's Magazine*, December, 1877.
22. Llewellynn Jewitt, *The Ceramic Art of Great Britain* (London, 1878), I, 168.
23. *Montreal Gazette*, Jan. 10, 1833.
24. *Yarmouth Herald*, May 7, 1841.
25. *Novascotian or Colonial Herald*, May 3, 1838.
26. *Montreal Gazette*, Sept. 18, 1855.
27. *Niagara Chronicle*, Dec. 26, 1850.
28. W. C. Prime, *Pottery and Porcelain of All Times and Nations* (New York, 1879), p. 409.
29. *Spring and Summer Catalogue. The Robert Simpson Company Limited* (Toronto, 1904), p. 156.

Notes on X: STONE, IRONSTONE, AND GRANITE

1. Simeon Shaw, *History of the Staffordshire Potteries* (Hanley, 1829), p. 229.
2. William Evans, *Art and History of the Potting Business* . . . (Shelton, [1846]), p. 7.
3. *Montreal Gazette*, April 16, 1829.
4. *Ibid.*, Aug. 15, 1839.
5. *Yarmouth Herald*, Oct. 25, 1833.
6. *Montreal Gazette*, April 5, 1855.
7. James Croil, *Steam Navigation* (Toronto and Montreal, 1898), p. 309.
8. Thomas Storrow Brown, 'Montreal in 1818', *The New Dominion Monthly*, Mar., 1870.
9. Rev. Robert Campbell, *A History of the Scotch Presbyterian Church St. Gabriel Street, Montreal* (Montreal, 1887), p. 314.
10. This is the date given in a family tree prepared by Dr. David J. G. Wishart, only son of Thomas Torrance's youngest daughter.
11. *Montreal Gazette*, April 12, 1827.
12. Cyrus Thomas, *Contributions to the History of the Eastern Townships* (Montreal, 1866), pp. 267-70.
13. This ironstone china was first seen by the author in the 1930's; its present owner is unknown.
14. Reginald G. Haggar, *The Masons of Lane Delph* (n.p., 1952), p. 45.
15. A plate from this service is in the author's collection.
16. Not, of course, to be confused with the 'white stone' that in eighteenth-century advertisements had indicated salt-glazed wares.
17. *Montreal Transcript*, Aug. 22, 1843.
18. *Great Exhibition of the Works of Industry of All Nation, 1851. Official . . . Catalogue* (London, 1851), II, 727.
19. Llewellynn Jewitt, *The Ceramic Art of Great Britain* (London, 1878), I, 255.
20. See Chap. XIX.
21. A piece so marked is in the author's collection.
22. J. T. S. Lidstone, *The Thirteenth Londoniad . . . Giving a Full Description of the Principal Establishments in the Potteries* (the Potteries, 1866), p. 54.
23. J. Arnold Fleming, *Scottish Pottery* (Glasgow, 1923), p. 111.
24. In the 1860's James Dykes Campbell and then James Fleming represented the Britannia Pottery in Canada.
25. *Montreal Gazette*, July 4, 1833.
26. *Novascotian*, Feb. 23, 1846.
27. *Niagara Chronicle*, July 17, 1851.
28. *Nor'-Wester and Pioneer*, Oct. 26, 1869.
29. *Yarmouth Herald*, Aug. 16, 1855.
30. *Montreal Gazette*, July 17, 1861.
31. Catherine Parr Traill, *Pearls and Pebbles* (Toronto, etc., 1895), pp. 169-70.
32. Catherine Parr Traill, *The Canadian Settler's Guide*, 5th ed. (Toronto, 1855), pp. 30-35.
33. H. H. Langton, ed., *A Gentlewoman in Upper Canada: the Journals of Anne Langton* (Toronto, 1950), p. 126. Cf. ' . . . broken crockery—an irreparable misfortune in the back woods!' Basil Hall, *Travels in North America . . . 1827 and 1828* (Edinburgh, 1829), I, 243.

34. *Nor'-Wester*, July 28, 1860.
35. Mrs. Mabel Perkins to George Shepherd, Jan. 23, 1965.
36. H. S. ('Corky') Jones to George Shepherd, Jan. 11, 1965.
37. Sarah Thompson to Rebecca Robson, Nov. 26, 1857 (unpublished letters in the author's possession).
38. Sarah Thompson to Rebecca Robson, May 6, 1859 (unpublished letters in the author's possession).
39. The St. Antoine Suburbs were west of the city as it then was, and included part of the present St. Antoine Street.
40. *Montreal Gazette*, Dec. 21, 1849.
41. *Daily Witness*, Oct. 10, 1882.
42. Charles Wyllys Elliott, *Pottery and Porcelain* (New York, 1878), p. 340.
43. William C. Prime, *Pottery and Porcelain of All Times and Nations* (New York, 1879), p. 409.
44. *Women of Canada, Their Life and Work* (Compiled by the National Council of Women of Canada) (n.p., 1900), p. 412.

Notes on XI: FOR THE KITCHEN AND THE COUNTRY: BROWNWARE TO 'PORTNEUF'

1. Llewellynn Jewitt, *The Ceramic Art of Great Britain* (London, 1878), I, 131.
2. *New Brunswick Courier*, July 9, 1836.
3. *Montreal Gazette*, June 13, 1841.
4. See Chap. XXI. W. J. Pountney, *Old Bristol Potteries* (Bristol, 1920), p. 249, gives the date as about 1835; some other writers have put it slightly later.
5. *Quebec Gazette*, May 16, 1765.
6. *Royal Gazette*, May 27, 1811.
7. *British Colonist and St. Francis Gazette*, Dec. 23, 1824.
8. *Montreal Gazette*, Nov. 5, 1831. Advertisement by McKinnon & Boyd of Bytown.
9. *Yarmouth Herald*, Jan. 31, 1856.
10. *Montreal Gazette*, Oct. 3, 1853.
11. *Quebec Gazette*, June 8, 1853. Abraham Joseph was one of the principal commission agents of Quebec at this time; in securing his services the Yamaska Pottery was making a determined effort to sell its products.
12. *McLaughlin's Quebec Directory* . . . [1855].
13. *Evening Leader*, Dec. 4, 1871.
14. For example, Warner & Co., stoneware manufacturers, were offering water filters in 1856. *Brown's Toronto . . . Directory, 1856*.
15. *Missiskoui Standard*, June 7, 1836.
16. *British Colonist and St. Francis Gazette*, June 18, 1829.
17. See p. 38.
18. 'Yellow Ironstone Pie Dishes'. *Montreal Gazette*, Dec. 19, 1845.
19. Llewellynn Jewitt, 'Rockingham China', *The Art Journal*, New Series (London, 1865), IV, 348.
20. *Montreal Gazette*, July 8, 1846.
21. See Chap. VIII.
22. *Eastern Townships Gazetteer & Directory* . . . *1875-76* (Montreal, 1875), p. 275.
23. L. P. Gauvreau & Frère's advertisement in the *Quebec Daily News*, May 27, 1864.
24. William Evans, *Art and History of the Potting Business* . . . (Shelton, 1846), p. 28.
25. *Ibid.*
26. J. Arnold Fleming, *Scottish Pottery* (Glasgow, 1923), pp. 65 and 195.
27. Llewellynn Jewitt, *The Ceramic Art of Great Britain*, revised ed. (London, [1883]), p. 564.
28. 'Called sponged ware here, and "spatterware" in America.' John Bedford, *Talking About Teapots* (London, 1964), p. 140. See also Alice Winchester, *How to Know American Antiques* (New York, n.d.), p. 74.
29. *Niagara Chronicle*, July 17, 1851.
30. *Montreal Gazette*, July 1, 1851.
31. *Montreal Commercial Advertiser*, Oct. 4, 1862.
32. A group of British ceramic experts consulted were unanimous in this opinion. A. R. Mountford, Director of the City Museum and Art Gallery, Stoke-on-Trent, pointed out that the decoration on the peacock bowl (*Plate* 10B) was not a transfer print.

33. *Montreal Gazette*, May 2, 1873.
34. See p. 223.
35. Author's collection. It would be possible to hazard a guess concerning this mark, for certain letters can be made out, but a guess sometimes proves misleading.

Notes on XII: EARTHENWARE FOR DECORATION: ON TABLE, MANTEL, AND WALL

1. Catherine Parr Traill, *The Canadian Settler's Guide*, 5th ed. (Toronto, 1855), pp. 30-35.
2. *Novascotian*, April 17, 1843.
3. *Montreal Gazette*, Dec. 19, 1845, and *Montreal Transcript*, Aug. 15, 1846.
4. *La Revue Canadienne*, Aug. 14, 1846.
5. *Montreal Herald*, July 5, 1817.
6. *Montreal Gazette*, Dec. 6, 1848.
7. *Kingston Chronicle*, May 14, 1831.
8. *Montreal Gazette*, April 27, 1857.
9. *Morning Courier*, Aug. 14, 1835.
10. G. M. Fairchild, *Gleanings From Quebec* (Quebec, 1908), p. 99.
11. *Montreal Gazette*, July 17, 1861.
12. *Great Exhibition of the Works of Industry of All Nations, 1851. Official . . . Catalogue* (London, 1851), II, 710.
13. James Dafforne, 'Porcelain and Pottery', *The Illustrated Catalogue of the Universal Exhibition, Published with the Art Journal* (London, 1868), p. 298.
14. *Daily Witness*, Sept. 29, 1880, and Nov. 15, 1882.
15. *The City of Winnipeg . . . Metropolis of the Northwest* (Winnipeg, 1886), p. 103.
16. *Daily Witness*, Sept. 17, 1880.
17. Dafforne, p. 293.
18. *McAlpine's Dominion Business . . . Directory 1873-74* (Montreal and Halifax, n.d.), p. 72.
19. J. T. S. Lidstone, *The Thirteenth Londoniad . . .* (the Potteries, 1866), pp. 35-36.
20. *Montreal Gazette*, Dec. 26, 1862.
21. *Daily Witness*, Dec. 1, 1885.
22. *New Brunswick Courier*, Dec. 4, 1858.
23. *Daily Witness*, Nov. 30, 1882.
24. A. T. Wiley's advertisement in F. W. Terrill, *A Chronology of Montreal* (Montreal, 1893), p. 349.
25. *The City of Winnipeg . . .* , p. 103.
26. L. M. Solon, *The Art of the Old English Potter*, 2nd ed. (London, 1885), p. 48. (Solon's name appears variously on his publications. Sometimes it is given as 'Marc Louis' and at other times as 'Louis Marc'.)
27. J. S. Ingram, *The Centennial Exposition* (Philadelphia, n.d.), p. 405.
28. *Ibid.*, pp. 405-6.
29. *Ibid.*, p. 406.
30. *Ibid.*, p. 408.
31. *Ibid.*, p. 407.
32. Taken from his tombstone.
33. A. M. W. Stirling, *William De Morgan and His Wife* (New York, 1922), p. 204.
34. *Daily Witness*, Dec. 16, 1881.
35. *Ibid.*, Dec. 10, 1883.
36. *The City of Winnipeg . . .* , p. 158.
37. Information supplied by J. E. Hartill, a great-great-great-grandson of Thomas Minton, and Managing Director of Mintons Ltd. The story is also told in J. A. Langford, *et al*, *Staffordshire and Warwickshire, Past and Present* (London, n.d. [c. 1875]), I, lxiv.
38. *New Era*, Sept. 19, 1857.
39. When the house was demolished a Victoria resident salvaged fragments of this set of tiles. One of these fragments, now in the author's possession, bears the Minton mark.
40. For example, at the Dominion Exhibition of 1880 the Montreal furniture makers, Owen McGarvey & Son, exhibited a cabinet into which Minton tiles had been set.
41. The fireplace and mantel are now owned by John R. Minty, Westmount.
42. Lidstone, p. 8.
43. *Cherrier's Quebec Directory for . . . 1880*.
44. Charles L. Eastlake, *Hints on Household Taste*, 3rd ed. (London, 1872), pp. 50-51.
45. *Ibid.*, p. 53.

Notes on XIII: BRITISH PORCELAIN IN THE CANADIAN MARKET

1. *Montreal Gazette*, Sept. 24, 1824.
2. John Howison, *Sketches of Upper Canada*, 2nd ed. (Edinburgh, 1822), p. 58.
3. 'From Quebec to Niagara in 1794. Diary of Bishop Jacob Mountain', *Rapport de l'Archiviste de la Province de Québec pour 1959-60* (Quebec, 1960), p. 141.
4. Statistics given in The Toronto Board of Trade annual reports for the 1850's and 1860's show that, on an average, there was still nearly fifteen times as much earthenware as porcelain imported.
5. *Montreal Gazette*, Dec. 4, 1824.
6. Marjorie Wilkins Campbell, *McGillivray Lord of the Northwest* (Toronto, 1962), p. 142.
7. *Montreal Gazette*, Aug. 6, 1798.
8. *Montreal Herald*, Jan. 14, 1815.
9. *Canadian Courant*, Jan. 14, 1824.
10. *Montreal Gazette*, June 11, 1825.
11. See also *Royal Gazette*, Nov. 11, 1800.
12. *Quebec Gazette*, June 26, 1777.
13. *Novascotian*, Jan. 1, 1788.
14. *Canadian Courant*, Feb. 1, 1817.
15. *Prince Edward Island Register*, Sept. 19, 1826.
16. *New Brunswick Courier*, Nov. 23, 1839.
17. *Examiner*, June 23, 1841.
18. *Montreal Gazette*, Sept. 20, 1832.
19. *Ibid.*, Jan. 10, 1833.
20. John Haslem, *The Old Derby China Factory* (London, 1876), p. 166.
21. *Montreal Gazette*, Dec. 23, 1863.
22. *Ibid.*, Oct. 27, 1865.
23. Ledger entry for Mar. 16, 1857. Archives of the Worcester Royal Porcelain Co. Ltd.
24. See Chap. V.
25. [Henry J. Morgan], *The Tour of H.R.H. the Prince of Wales . . .* (Montreal, 1860), pp. 124-127. Sir Fenwick Williams acted as host at the luncheon, since he was occupying Dorval Island for the summer, but Sir George Simpson provided for the entertainment.
26. *Niagara Argus*, Oct. 29, 1845.
27. *Daily Witness*, Sept. 14, 1883.
28. *Royal Commission for the Chicago Exhibition, 1893, Official Catalogue of the British Section*, London, 1893.
29. *Montreal Gazette*, May 4, 1829.
30. See Chaps. III and IV.
31. H.B.C. Arch. B. 235/d/122, fos. 6d., 9d., 10d.-11.
32. *Art Union*, November, 1846.
33. *McAlpine's Dominion . . . Directory 1873-74;* see also Polk's *Ontario Gazetteer . . . 1884-5.*
34. *Daily Witness*, Dec. 19, 1885.
35. *Ibid.*
36. Anonymous reminiscences of the Prince of Wales' visit to Saint John, *Daily Sun*, Feb. 1, 1901.
37. Information supplied by J. E. Hartill, Managing Director of Mintons Ltd.
38. The firm is now John Aynsley & Sons Ltd.
39. J. T. S. Lidstone, *The Thirteenth Londoniad . . .* (the Potteries, 1866), p. 46.
40. In 1963 in the possession of a Toronto antique dealer.
41. The Coalport factory was moved to Staffordshire in the twentieth century.
42. *The Industries of Canada* (Toronto, 1887), p. 47.
43. *Daily Witness*, Dec. 19, 1885.
44. *Evening Leader*, Sept. 6, 1871.
45. *Daily Witness*, Dec. 20, 1881.
46. See Chap. XIV.
47. Jennie J. Young, *The Ceramic Art* (London, 1879), p. 388.
48. *Gazette*, Dec. 19, 1870.
49. *Evening Leader*, Oct. 7, 1871.
50. *Mail*, Sept. 10, 1879.
51. Llewellynn Jewitt, *The Ceramic Art of Great Britain* (London, 1878), II, 489.
52. Charles L. Eastlake, *Hints on Household Taste*, 3rd ed. (London, 1872), p. 227.
53. *Ibid.*, p. 226.

Notes on XIII: British Porcelain in the Canadian Market

54. *Daily Witness*, Dec. 23, 1880.
55. Young, p. 388.
56. Letter by Brigadier James Price in *Country Life*, Mar. 27, 1958.
57. C. C. Taylor, *The Queen's Jubilee and Toronto 'Called back'* . . . (Toronto, 1887), p. 313.
58. *Ibid.*
59. *Montreal Gazette*, May 24, 1823.
60. *New Brunswick Courier*, Oct. 5, 1833.
61. *Novascotian*, Aug. 3, 1836.

Notes on XIV: PARIAN WARE

1. *Montreal Gazette*, April 27, 1864.
2. *Ibid.*, April 13, 1866.
3. *Ibid.*, Sept. 22, 1865.
4. *Ibid.*, May 15, 1866.
5. [S. C. Hall], 'Illustrated Tour in the Manufacturing Districts . . . ', *Art Union*, November, 1846.
6. 'Exposition of British Industrial Art at Manchester', *Art Union*, January, 1846.
7. *Great Exhibition of the Works of Industry of All Nations, 1851. Official . . .Catalogue* (London, 1851), II, 711-12.
8. Charles Dickens, 'A Plated Article', *Household Words*, 1852, republished by W. T. Copeland & Sons (Stoke-on-Trent, n.d.), p. 14.
9. *Montreal Gazette*, Sept. 22, 1865, and Sept. 28, 1865.
10. *Great Exhibition . . . Official . . . Catalogue*, II, 711.
11. *Examiner*, Dec. 14, 1853.
12. *The Illustrated Exhibitor* (London, [1851]), p. 37.
13. *The Crystal Palace and Its Contents* (London, 1852), p. 229.
14. *Times* (London), May 28, 1845, quoted in the *Montreal Gazette*, July 15, 1850.
15. *Montreal Gazette*, Oct. 10 and Dec. 24, 1853.
16. Information supplied by Arnold Mountford, Director of the City Museum and Art Gallery, Stoke-on-Trent.
17. *Montreal Gazette*, April 26, 1866.
18. *Montreal Herald* (weekly edition), Oct. 10, 1878.
19. *Montreal Star*, Nov. 15, 1880.
20. Quoted in the *Montreal Gazette*, July 14, 1879.
21. *Gazette* (Montreal), Oct. 9, 1876.
22. *Ibid.*, Dec. 23, 1864.
23. *The British Columbia Directory for the Years 1882-83.*
24. *Hutchinson's Saint John Directory, 1863-64.*
25. *Montreal Gazette*, May 10, 1866.
26. *Ibid.*, Dec. 20, 1860.
27. Advertisements for the Art Union of London, *Montreal Gazette* (weekly edition), Feb. 21, 1852; *Montreal Gazette* (daily), Feb. 4, 1856.
28. *Montreal Gazette* (weekly edition), Feb. 21, 1852.
29. *Novascotian*, Jan. 17, 1848.
30. *Montreal Gazette* (weekly edition), Feb. 21, 1852.
31. [S. C. Hall], 'Fine Art in Porcelain Statuary', *Art Journal*, August, 1849.
32. Llewellynn Jewitt, *The Ceramic Art of Great Britain*, revised ed. (London, [1883]), p. 423.
33. For example, busts of musicians and classical figures were marked in this way; so, too, was a bust of Princess Mary (the future Queen Mary).
34. *The Illustrated Exhibitor* (London, [1851]), p. 116.

Notes on XV: PORCELAINS OTHER THAN BRITISH

1. *Montreal Gazette*, July 30, 1829.
2. *New Brunswick Courier*, Oct. 12, 1833.
3. *Ibid.*, Nov. 23, 1839.
4. For example, L. Cauffman's advertisement for china plates, cups and saucers 'just received from Paris' in *Poulson's American Daily Advertiser*, Jan. 20, 1817.
5. *Brown's Toronto General Directory, 1856.*

6. *Globe*, Sept. 5, 1856.
7. See Chap. X.
8. *Montreal Gazette*, Dec. 23, 1863.
9. *Daily Witness*, Dec. 23, 1880.
10. Jennie J. Young, *The Ceramic Art* (London, 1879), p. 323.
11. *Daily Witness*, Dec. 19, 1885.
12. *Montreal Herald*, June 15, 1881.
13. See for example, *Daily Witness*, July 12, 1881.
14. *Gazette*, Dec. 16, 1899.
15. *Daily Witness*, Nov. 23, 1885.
16. The Quebec Suburbs of Montreal were in the eastern part of the city, on the road leading to Quebec.
17. *Daily Witness*, Dec. 21, 1880.
18. *Montreal Gazette*, Dec. 8 1856.
19. *Ibid.*, December 16, 1899.
20. *Daily Witness*, Sept. 15, 1883.
21. *Industries of Canada . . .* (Toronto, 1887), p. 48.
22. *Montreal Gazette*, Dec. 15, 1856.
23. *The British Columbia Directory for the Years 1882-83.*
24. *Daily Witness*, Nov. 24, 1885.
25. In New York directories, 1847-1855, he is listed as 'Cartlidge'.
26. See Chap. XIV.
27. *Centennial of Canadian Methodism* (Toronto, 1891), p. 97.
28. John Spargo, *Early American Pottery and China* (New York, 1926), p. 279.
29. *Gazette*, Dec. 18, 1880; see also *Daily Witness*, Dec. 20, 1880. Compare Francis Clementson & Co.'s advertisement in the Saint John *Daily Sun*, Dec. 23, 1880.
30. *British Columbian*, Mar. 20, 1869.
31. *Royal Gazette*, June 28, 1837.
32. *Daily Witness*, Dec. 10, 1883.
33. *Ibid.*, Nov. 27, 1882.
34. *Ibid.*, Dec. 20, 1883.
35. *Ibid.*, Dec. 20, 1883; Nov. 26, 1885.
36. *Royal Gazette*, Nov. 11, 1800.
37. *The City of Winnipeg . . . Metropolis of the Northwest . . .* (Winnipeg, 1886), p. 103.

Notes on XVI: ENOCH WOOD: HIS CANADIAN VIEWS AND MONTREAL AGENT

1. Simeon Shaw, *History of the Staffordshire Potteries* (Hanley, 1829), p. 30.
2. John Ward, *The Borough of Stoke-upon-Trent* (London, 1843), p. 264.
3. Dr. Benjamin Silliman, *A Tour to Quebec in the Autumn of 1819* (London, 1822), p. 86.
4. Ellouise Baker Larsen, *American Historical Views on Staffordshire China*, revised ed. (Garden City, N.Y., 1950), p. 31.
5. Ross Robertson, ed., *The Diary of Mrs. John Graves Simcoe* (Toronto, 1911), p. 74.
6. *Ibid.*, p. 75.
7. Isaac Weld, *Travels Through the . . . Provinces of Upper and Lower Canada*, 4th ed. (London, 1800), p. 254.
8. [John Cosens Ogden], *A Tour Through Upper and Lower Canada* (Litchfield, 1799), pp. 31-33.
9. Anthony Trollope, *North America* (London, 1866), p. 62.
10. Alice Morse Earle, *China Collecting in America* (London, 1892), pp. 369-71.
11. Larsen, p. 21. For Larsen's list of Wood's Canadian titles, see p. 31.
12. Alexander Marjoribanks, *Travels in South and North America* (London, 1853), p. 269. See also James Stuart, *Three Years in North America* (Edinburgh, 1833), I, 140.
13. Chisholm's *All Round Route and Panoramic Guide to the St. Lawrence River* (Montreal, 1871), p. 32.
14. Ward, p. 264.

Notes on XVI: Enoch Wood: His Canadian Views and Montreal Agent

15. Rev. Robert Campbell, *A History of the Scotch Presbyterian Church St. Gabriel Street, Montreal* (Montreal, 1887), p. 428.
16. J. T. S. Lidstone, *The Thirteenth Londoniad* . . . (The Potteries, 1866), p. 57.

Notes on XVII: BARTLETT FOR THE TABLE

1. The remaining pieces of this service were inherited by Sir William Dawson's daughter, the wife of Professor Bernard J. Harrington, of McGill. From Mrs. Harrington they passed to her daughter, Miss Clare Harrington, who remembers as a small child seeing them set out on a large dresser in her grandmother's kitchen. Through the kindness of Miss Harrington a plate from this service is in the author's collection.
2. Sir William Dawson, *Fifty Years of Work in Canada* (London and Edinburgh, 1901), p. 15.
3. Ellouise Baker Larsen, *American Historical Views on Staffordshire China*, revised ed. (New York, 1950), pp. 193-94, considers the engraving entitled 'Outlet of Lake Memphremagog' the source of one of the ceramic views.
4. *Novascotian*, April 17, 1843.
5. Information supplied by A. R. Mountford, Director, City Museum and Art Gallery, Stoke-on-Trent.
6. John Ward, *The Borough of Stoke-upon-Trent* . . . (London, 1843), p. 100.
7. Information supplied by J. S. Goddard, Chairman of George L. Ashworth & Brothers Limited, and grandson of John Shaw Goddard.
8. See p. 196.
9. Larsen, pp. 195, 203, says the source of this Morley (and Podmore, Walker & Co.) view was 'probably' a Currier & Ives lithograph, which would necessarily push the date of the earthenware to the end of the 1850's at the earliest. It is, however, clearly an adaptation of Bartlett's 'Indian Scene', as published in *Canadian Scenery*, and, therefore, available to the potters from the early 1840's.
10. Through the kindness of Miss Harrington a plate from this service is also in the author's collection. Its decoration is a combination of transfer printing and bright enamel colours.
11. Information supplied by J. S. Goddard.

Notes on XVIII: OTHER CANADIAN VIEWS AND EMBLEMS

1. Bernard Rackham, *Catalogue of the English Porcelain . . . Collected by Charles Schreiber . . . and the Lady Charlotte Elizabeth Schreiber* (London, 1928), I, 131. For the dates of Houston's engravings of Wolfe portraits see J. Clarence Webster, *Wolfe and the Artists* (Toronto, 1930), pp. 26-34, where 1766 and 1767 are held to be the earliest possible dates.
2. Rackham, p. 173. This mug was earlier catalogued as of Liverpool manufacture; later it was attributed to Longton Hall. The three portraits of Wolfe attributed to Gainsborough were all painted after Wolfe's death. See Webster, p. 34.
3. A. Doughty and G. W. Parmelee, *The Siege of Quebec and the Battle of the Plains of Abraham* (Quebec, 1901), III, 221-22.
4. This painting is now in the National Gallery of Canada. *The National Gallery . . . Catalogue of Paintings* (Ottawa, 1948), p. 124.
5. C. Reginald Grundy, 'British Military and Naval Prints', *Connoisseur*, Oct., 1914. The engraving was first published in 1776.
6. Joseph R. and Frank Kidson, *Historical Notices of the Leeds Old Pottery* (Leeds, 1893), p. 72.
7. William Turner, *Transfer Printing* (London, 1907), pp. 70, 134.
8. Ellouise Baker Larsen, *American Historical Views on Staffordshire China*, revised ed. (New York, 1950), p. 210.
9. Arthur Hayden, *Chats on English Earthenware* (London, 1909), p. 341.
10. C. P. Lucas, *The Canadian War of 1812* (Oxford, 1906), pp. 148-49.
11. Later the British authorities permitted Capt. Lawrence's body to be removed to the United States.

Notes on XVIII: Other Canadian Views and Emblems

12. Larsen, p. 155, gives this woodcut as the source, but a comparison of the ship on earthenware with a copy of the woodcut in the New Brunswick Museum shows so little resemblance that some other source must be looked for if the identification of the *Shannon* is to be proved in this way.
13. E. A. Barber, *Anglo-American Pottery* (Indianapolis, 1899), p. 39.
14. Note accompanying his gift of several pieces of this ware to the Château de Ramezay, Montreal.
15. For Howisons as china merchants see *McLaughlin's Quebec Directory*, 1855, and *Lovell's Montreal Directory*, 1874-75.
16. Llewellynn Jewitt, *The Ceramic Art of Great Britain*, revised ed. (London [1883]), p. 476.
17. *Daily Witness*, July 4, 1885.
18. Information supplied by J. Bailey, Managing Director, Furnivals (1913) Limited.
19. See p. 184.
20. J. Arnold Fleming, *Scottish Pottery* (Glasgow, 1923), p. 189.
21. The same pattern name was used by other potters, so that the pattern name alone is not sufficient for identification of a piece.
22. See p. 9.
23. See p. 96.
24. Marius Barbeau, *Maîtres Artisans de Chez-Nous* (Montreal, 1942), pp. 127, 179.
25. *L'Indicateur de Québec*, 1888-89.
26. *Geological Survey of Canada Report of Progress For the Year 1852-3* (Quebec, 1854), p. 54.
27. *L'Indicateur de Québec*, 1888-89.
28. J. M. LeMoine, *Picturesque Quebec* (Montreal, 1882), p. 94.
29. Fleming, p. 115.
30. *Royal Gazette and Nova Scotia Advertiser*, May 15, 1798.
31. *Montreal Gazette*, Dec. 28, 1844.
32. *Ibid.*, May 7, 1853.
33. *Ibid.*, May 2, 1873.
34. For example, *Lovell's Canada Directory for 1857-58.*
35. *Montreal Gazette*, Oct. 20, 1866.
36. *Daily Witness*, Sept. 12, 1885.

Notes on XIX: NAUTICAL CROCKERY

1. James Croil, *Steam Navigation* (Toronto and Montreal, 1898), p. 74.
2. This is the date given in W. P. Jervis, *The Encyclopedia of Ceramics* (New York, 1902), p. 179; others cite 1841 and 1843. Llewellynn Jewitt gives 1842 as the date when James Edwards purchased the Dale Hall Pottery for himself. Llewellynn Jewitt, *The Ceramic Art of Great Britain*, revised ed. (London [1883]), p. 456.
3. Jewitt, p. 456.
4. Commander C. R. Vernon Gibbs, R.N., *Passenger Liners of the Western Ocean* (London, 1952), p. 60.
5. *Pilot*, Sept. 24, 1857.
6. *Nor'-Wester*, July 28, 1860.
7. Pilot, July 29, 1861.
8. F. Lawrence Babcock, *Spanning the Atlantic* (New York, 1931), p. 67.
9. The date at which the name of the company became officially the Cunard Steamship Co. Ltd. is given as 1878 in Frank C. Bowen, *A Century of Atlantic Travel* (Boston, 1930), p. 13.
10. J. T. S. Lidstone, *The Thirteenth Londoniad* . . . (The Potteries, 1866), p. 52.
11. Croil, p. 231.
12. *Ibid.*, p. 233.
13. Jewitt, p. 471.
14. *Montreal Gazette*, Jan. 2, 1854.
15. On Nov. 28, 1870, the *Gazette* carried an advertisement for the Montreal Ocean Steamship Co.; the next day a new advertisement was headed 'Allan Line'.
16. The plate in the author's collection is marked only OPAQUE PORCELAIN.
17. See p. 311.
18. *Gazette*, May 21, 1869.

Notes on XX: DAVENPORT AND CANADA

1. James Strachan, *A Visit to . . . Upper Canada in 1819* (Aberdeen, 1820), p. 25.
2. [Catherine Parr Traill], *The Backwoods of Canada*, 4th ed. (London, 1839), p. 27.
3. *Ibid.*, p. 28.
4. In an advertisement in the *Montreal Gazette*, Aug. 29, 1833, Sproule offered his services in all three capacities.
5. Ellouise Baker Larsen, *American Historical Views on Staffordshire China*, revised ed. (New York, 1950), p. 173.
6. *Montreal Gazette*, Nov. 23, 1829. On the plates the name appears incorrectly as W. L. Leney.
7. Fred. A. McCord, *Hand-Book of Canadian Dates* (Montreal, 1888), p. 60. Elsewhere the date is given as 1826.
8. Newton Bosworth, *Hochelaga Depicta* (Montreal, 1839), pp. 177-78. See also James Croil, *Steam Navigation* (Toronto, 1898), p. 311. The *British America* was 170 feet long, with a 30 foot beam. She had engines of about 150 horsepower.
9. *Montreal Transcript*, June 21, 1838.
10. *Ibid.*, July 7, 1838.
11. *Montreal Gazette*, May 19, 1838.
12. J. T. S. Lidstone, *The Thirteenth Londoniad . . .* (The Potteries, 1866), p. 108.
13. *Montreal Gazette*, Oct. 15, 1851.
14. John Ward, *The Borough of Stoke-upon-Trent* (London, 1843), p. 157.
15. John M. Clarke, *Sketches of Gaspé* (Albany, 1908), p. 68.
16. W. P. Jervis, *The Encyclopedia of Ceramics* (New York, 1902), p. 138.
17. For example, see advertisements for china and glass in the *Montreal Gazette*, May 28, 1831; *ibid.*, June 14, 1854; *Novascotian*, Jan. 27, 1845.

Notes on XXI: THE RANGE OF CANADIAN POTTING

1. William Wickliffe Johnson, *Sketches of the Late Depression* (Montreal, 1882), p. 177.
2. See p. 305.
3. See p. 275.
4. See p. 296.
5. The evidence of the *Mercantile Agency Reference Books* is very clear on this. Only a handful of Canadian potteries operated on large capital, and in some cases the rating given these fortunate few certainly reflected the rating of the backers rather than the actual volume of business.
6. Mark Tomkins imported all the clay for his whiteware from England (see p. 298). In 1863 a report prepared for the Geological Survey of Canada stated that 'No clays fit for the finer kinds of pottery have as yet been found in the country'. According to a government report of the present century (1931) stoneware clays are only sparingly distributed in Canada.
7. Before Confederation these tariffs varied in the different colonies according to the amount of potting being carried on. At the end of the century there was a 35 per cent tariff on ironstone, white granite, C. C., brownware, stoneware, and Rockingham—all wares made in Canada at that time.
8. John Lambert, *Travels Through Canada . . . in the Years 1806, 1807 & 1808* (London, 1814), I, 104-5.
9. *A Register of Voters . . . [1785-1862]*, Saint John, n.d.
10. *Gazette and New Brunswick Advertiser*, Jan. 26, 1815.
11. M. Smith, *Geographical View of . . . Upper Canada* (New York, 1813), p. 67.
12. A. Backwoodsman [William Dunlop, M.D.], *Statistical Sketches of Upper Canada for the Use of Emigrants* (London, 1832), p. 7.
13. James B. Brown, *Views of Canada and the Colonists*, 2nd ed. (Edinburgh, 1851), pp. 357-65.
14. Alexander Begg, *Emigrant's Guide to Manitoba*, contained at the end of '*Dot It Down*' (Toronto, 1871), p. 378.
15. Manitoba Statutes, Cap. XLII, Vict. 34, 1871.
16. H. Y. Hind, *et al.*, *Eighty Years Progress of British North America* (Toronto, 1863), p. 695. Although the pottery was not mentioned by name it was probably the Elmsdale Pottery of R. Malcolm.

17. This letter, dated Sept. 29, 1825, was published in the *Colonial Advocate*, April 12, 1827. The writer is not to be confused with Peter Russell (1733-1808), who was administrator of Upper Canada in the 1790's.
18. Petition for a Patent, dated Toronto, Dec. 8, 1858.
19. *Commemorative Biographical Record of the County of York, Ontario* (Toronto, 1907), pp. 442-43.
20. *Examiner*, Sept. 25, 1850.
21. *Commemorative Biographical Record of the County of York*, p. 443.
22. *History of Toronto and the County of York* (Toronto, 1885), II, 214.
23. *Examiner*, Sept. 29, 1852.
24. Crown Law Department of Upper Canada, Letters Patent granted to John Worthington and John Brown, Feb. 9, 1859. Pre-Confederation Patent No. 917, now in the Patent and Copyright Office, Ottawa.
25. In Sir John A. Macdonald's handwriting on the folder containing the relevant documents. His signature follows the note.
26. Specifications and Descriptions, Pre-Confederation Patent No. 917.
27. *Ibid.*
28. *Ibid.* 'The increased demand for sewerage pipe especially, would in a very few years become a heavy item in the Provincial imports unless checked.'
29. Petition for a Patent dated Toronto, Dec. 8, 1858.
30. He so describes himself in his application for a patent.
31. Just as G. H. and L. E. Farrar of St. Johns were part of a potting business listed in their names in the 1870's, but in which their father, G. W. Farrar, was also actively concerned.
32. *Commemorative Biographical Record of the County of York*, p. 443.
33. Information supplied by Mr. Fenwick D. Foley, great-grandson of Joseph White.
34. *New Brunswick Blue Book and Encyclopedia* (n.p., 1932), p. 17.
35. W. J. Pountney, *Old Bristol Potteries* (Bristol, 1920), pp. 268-69 and p. 322. The City Art Gallery, Bristol, has a collection of wares (spirit kegs, etc.) attributed to the pottery of Joseph & James White.
36. Pountney, p. 269.
37. Family records supplied by Fenwick D. Foley. Pountney seems to have been unaware of the Canadian chapter in the White potting history, although he mentions that 'Mr. F. J. White and his son left Bristol in 1893 and established a business at . . . Denver, Colorado.' This was a small business for the making of fine stoneware, but a depression set in just about the time F. J. White arrived in Denver, and for some years the family experienced financial difficulties.
38. The Whites averaged an estimated capital of $2,000-$5,000, and a credit rating of 'Fair'.
39. *Daily Sun*, Mar. 7, 1885.
40. A link with Joseph White, however, continued. His grandson, James W. Foley, formed a partnership with Samuel Poole and together they founded a business that has twentieth-century expression in the Canuck Pottery (Quebec) Ltd. at Labelle, Que.
41. *Montreal Gazette*, Aug. 7, 1847.
42. *New Brunswick Courier*, Mar. 27, 1847.
43. See the advertisement in *Mitchell & Co.'s Canada . . . Directory for 1865-66*, Toronto, n.d.
44. *The Canada Directory*, Montreal, 1851. Morton was an American.
45. *Montreal Gazette*, Dec. 19, 1853.
46. *Report of the Canadian Commission at . . . Philadelphia, 1876* (Ottawa, 1877), p. 33.
47. *Ibid.*, p. 22.
48. *Ibid.*, Appendix No. 3, 'International Awards', p. 2; *Gazette* Sept. 30, 1876.
49. *Gazette*, Nov. 1, 1876.
50. *Report of the Canadian Commission at . . . Philadelphia, 1876*, Appendix No. 2, 'Catalogue of Canadian Exhibitors', p. 10.
51. *Report . . . on the . . . Manufactures, &c., of Ontario . . . at . . . Philadelphia, 1876* (Toronto, 1877), p. 32.
52. *Ibid.*, p. 210.
53. *Canadian Illustrated News*, Dec. 1, 1877.
54. *Paris Universal Exhibition . . . Official Catalogue of the Canadian Section* (London, 1878), p. 126. 'Rockingham' and 'Flint Enamelled Ware' were not actually synonymous, but terms were sometimes used loosely. See p. 274 for Flint Enamelled Ware.
55. *History of the County of Brant, Ontario* (Toronto, 1883), p. 648.
56. *Ibid.*, p. 678.

Notes on XXI: The Range of Canadian Potting

57. *Paris . . . Catalogue of the Canadian Section*, p. 127.
58. *Ibid.*
59. *Paris Universal Exhibition . . . Report for the Canadian Commission* (Ottawa, 1881), p. 38.
60. The certificate is today in the possession of G. H. Farrar's daughter, Mrs. Effie Farrar Sutherland.
61. G. M. Rose, ed., *A Cyclopaedia of Canadian Biography* (Toronto, 1888), p. 630.
62. *Antwerp Universal Exhibition, 1885, Official Catalogue of the Canadian Section* (London, 1885), p. 20.
63. *Ibid.*, p. 21. *The Mercantile Agency Reference Book* for January, 1881, estimates Welding's capital as $10,000-$20,000. He was a manufacturer of fire and cupola bricks as well as of pottery.
64. *Antwerp . . . Catalogue of the Canadian Section*, p. 20.
65. *Evening Telegram*, Sept. 3, 1879.
66. *Gazette*, Sept. 19, 1873.
67. *Ibid.*, Sept. 20, 1877. In these provincial exhibition accounts 'pottery' always meant 'earthenware'; 'stoneware' was a separate category; fire bricks, drain tiles and building bricks were listed by name, and had nothing to do with 'pottery'.
68. *Daily Witness*, Sept. 20, 1881.
69. *Ibid.*, Sept. 24, 1881.
70. Rev. Henry Scadding, *Toronto Of Old* (Toronto, 1878), p. 432.
71. *Colonial Advocate*, April 29, 1830.
72. *Ibid,*, Oct. 14, 1830.
73. *Montreal Gazette*, Oct. 5, 1860.
74. 'Toronto Gold Medal 1879' was featured by the St. Johns Stone Chinaware Company in advertising.
75. Henry Robertson's advertisement in *Hutchinson's New Brunswick Directory for 1867-68* (Montreal, n.d.), p. 777.
76. *Gazetteer and Directory of the County of Grey for 1865-66* (Toronto, 1865), p. 143.

Notes on XXII: THE STAFFORDSHIRE OF CANADA: THE FARRARS

1. Abbé J. B. A. Allaire, *Histoire de la Paroisse de Saint-Denis-sur-Richelieu* (St. Hyacinthe, 1905), p. 345. Joseph Bouchette (*The British Dominions in North America*) gave the number of potteries in St. Denis as twelve in 1831.
2. Records of St. Johns United Church (formerly St. Johns Methodist Church).
3. George H. Farrar, for over sixty years a member of St. Johns Methodist Church. Mrs. Effie Farrar Sutherland, his only daughter, remembers well her father's regularly donating such articles to the bazaars.
4. Farrar birth and death dates given in this chapter have been taken from four sources: family records, Canadian census records, church records, and Chandler's *History of New Ipswich*. There are discrepancies, but none of more than a year or two.
5. 'The children of his people' erected a tablet to him in 1909, placing it in the building that had succeeded the church in which he preached in New Ipswich. 'Patriot', on the tablet, refers to the Farrars' support of the American Revolution.
6. Undated clipping in the possession of Mrs. Effie Farrar Sutherland.
7. *Montreal Gazette*, Oct. 24, 1850.
8. *The Canada Directory for 1857-58.*
9. *Quebec Mercury*, July 23, 1857.
10. John Spargo, *Early American Pottery and China*, reprinted ed. (New York, 1948), p. 316.
11. See p. 291.
12. Through what is obviously a typographical error the name of G. W. Farrar appears as G. G. Farrar.
13. Undated clipping in the possession of Mrs. Effie Farrar Sutherland. G. W. Farrar died on Jan. 28, 1881. In some of these published accounts Farrar's middle name is given the phonetic spelling 'Whitfield', but an old record in Mrs. Sutherland's possession gives the correct spelling.
14. *Lovell's Canadian Dominion Directory for 1871.*
15. *Eastern Townships Gazetteer & Directory . . . 1875-76.*
16. *Ibid.*, p. 172.
17. Information supplied by Mrs. Effie Farrar Sutherland. G. W. Farrar's obituary also mentions the burning of the pottery in the autumn of 1876.

18. *News and Frontier Advocate*, emergency ed., June 22, 1876.
19. *Lovell's Montreal Directory for 1874-75*.
20. *Lovell's Montreal Directory for 1873-74*.
21. *Lovell's Montreal Directory for 1876-77*.
22. The Cornwall stoneware would have been from the pottery of Flack & Van Arsdale.
23. Information supplied by Mrs. Lottie Farrar de Bellefeuille, daughter of George William Farrar.
24. See pp. 293-95.
25. Within a few years there was another fire, 'and that was the end'. Mrs. Lottie Farrar de Bellefeuille.
26. When the demand for hand-painted china died out, George William Farrar turned to embroidery designs. For many years his embroidery patterns were carried by the Montreal *Star*.
27. The burial entry for George H. Farrar is in the register of the Anglican church in Iberville, for George H. Farrar was buried from the church to which his wife belonged.

Notes on XXIII: THE ST. JOHNS STONE CHINAWARE COMPANY

1. G. M. Rose, ed., *A Cyclopaedia of Canadian Biography* (Toronto, 1888), II, 630.
2. *The Mercantile Agency Reference Book*, Montreal, etc., January, 1881.
3. William Wickliffe Johnson, *Sketches of the Late Depression* (Montreal, 1882), p. 178.
4. W. M. Ryder, *Memoirs* (St. Johns, 1900), p. 68.
5. *Eastern Townships Gazetteer & Directory . . . 1875-76* (Montreal, 1875), p. 172.
6. Undated newspaper clipping [January, 1881] in the possession of G. W. Farrar's granddaughter, Mrs. Effie Farrar Sutherland.
7. Johnson, p. 178.
8. *Ibid.*
9. Rose, II, 630.
10. Johnson, p. 178.
11. *News*, Aug. 23, 1878.
12. G. W. and F. A. Rhead, *Staffordshire Pots and Potters* (London, 1906), p. 337.
13. *County of Missisquoi and Town of St. Johns Directory for 1879, 1880 and 1881* (Montreal, 1879), p. 13.
14. Articles from a toilet set in the author's collection are decorated with bands of maroon set off by green and biscuit colour and further embellished with silver lustre.
15. The McCord Museum, McGill University, has such a plaque.
16. *Gazette*, Sept. 17, 1880.
17. *Montreal Herald*, Sept. 23, 1880.
18. *The Eastern Townships Business & Farmers Directory for 1888-89* (St. Johns, 1888), p. 102.
19. On April 25. Henry J. Morgan, ed., *The Dominion Annual Register and Review . . . 1878* (Montreal, 1879), p. 231.
20. *Lovell's Business . . . Directory for . . . Canada for 1896-97* (Montreal, 1896), p. 1070.
21. *Gazette*, Sept. 13, 1879.
22. Marked examples of every type of St. Johns ware mentioned in this chapter are either in the author's collection or have been seen by the author.
23. Johnson, p. 178.
24. *Gazette*, Nov. 1, 1876.
25. *Ibid.*, Sept. 17, 1880.
26. Johnson, p. 177.
27. Rose, II, 630.
28. Johnson, p. 177.
29. *Gazette*, Mar. 6, 1893.
30. *Ibid.*
31. Nor was there any mention of the St. Johns Stone Chinaware Company in the *Dominion of Canada . . . Directory 1899*. The first provincial business directories of the new century did not list it. The name of the Company did, however, appear in *Wright's Classified Business Directory . . . of . . . Canada and Newfoundland*, dated 1900, but this directory contained much information that was outdated.
32. *The Ceramic Industry of Canada (with special reference to the manufacture of white ware)* (Ottawa, 1931), p. 4.

Notes on XXIV: SOME OTHER POTTERIES IN ST. JOHNS AND ITS VICINITY

1. *News and Frontier Advocate*, April 30, 1858.
2. *Montreal Gazette*, Oct. 3, 1853.
3. *Argus*, Oct. 2, 1858.
4. *Burlington Free Press*, May 25, 1867.
5. *County of Missisquoi & Town of St. Johns Directory for 1879, 1880 and 1881* (Montreal, 1879), p. 153.
6. William Wickliffe Johnson (Montreal, 1882), p. 7.
7. *Ibid.*, p. 176.
8. *Montreal Herald*, Sept. 23, 1880.
9. *Montreal Star*, Sept. 15, 1880.
10. *Gazette*, Sept. 18, 1880.
11. *Mercantile Agency Reference Book* for January, 1881.
12. Johnson, p. 178.
13. *The Eastern Townships Business & Farmers Directory for 1888-89* (St. Johns, 1888).
14. *Gazette*, Mar. 6, 1893.
15. *County of Missisquoi . . . Directory for 1879, 1880 and 1881.*
16. William Workman was a director of the City Bank; his name appears as president of the St. Lawrence Glass Works in early advertisements for that company.
17. E. C. Macdonald's obituary in the *News* described him as being in his office early and late, called him one of the most astute businessmen in the community, and declared that it was with reluctance that he took even a day's recreation.
18. *Hopkins' Atlas of the City and Island of Montreal* ([Montreal], 1879), p. 77.
19. *Lovell's Montreal Directory for 1881-82;* today this site is occupied by a brick building housing General Steel Wares Ltd.
20. *Gazette*, Sept. 18, 1880.
21. *Ibid.*, Sept. 21, 1880.
22. *Ibid.*, Sept. 18, 1880.
23. *Montreal Herald*, Sept. 23, 1880.
24. *Montreal Star*, Sept. 15, 1880; *Daily Witness*, Sept. 18, 1880.

Notes on XXV: THE HUMBERSTONES: CANADIAN POTTERS THROUGH THE CENTURY

1. These dates have been supplied from family records by Lewis Humberstone, great-great-great-grandson of Samuel Humberstone.
2. *Henderson's Manitoba, Northwest Territories and British Columbia . . . Directory for 1890* (Winnipeg, 1890), p. 546. Later William Humberstone went into other business in the west.
3. *History of Toronto and County of York* (Toronto, 1885), II, 191.
4. Simon Thomas Humberstone himself probably wrote the account of the family that appeared in the *History of Toronto*, drawing on material given him by his father, Thomas Humberstone, Junior, who was then still living. (Lewis Humberstone to author, April 24, 1964.)
5. *History of Toronto* II, 191; and Lewis Humberstone to author, Jan. 18, 1964.
6. Rev. Henry Scadding, *Toronto Of Old* (Toronto, 1878), p. 445; *History of Toronto*, II, 191-92; obituary of Simon Thomas Humberstone (undated clipping in family scrapbook now in the possession of Lewis Humberstone).
7. *History of Toronto*, II, 191.
8. *Ibid.*, p. 192; also family papers.
9. Scadding, p. 445; *History of Toronto*, p. 192.
10. Public Archives of Canada, U.C. Land Petitions 'H', Bundle 10. No. 65 (RG1, L3, vol. 227).
11. The first brick buildings in York were of imported bricks.
12. PAC, U.C. Land Petitions 'H', Bundle 10. No. 65 (RG1, L3, vol. 227).
13. *Ibid.*
14. Memo entered on Thomas Humberstone's petition. PAC.
15. *History of Toronto*, II, 192.
16. Scadding, p. 445.
17. *Colonial Advocate*, April 12, 1827 (the account was written two years earlier).
18. *History of Toronto*, II, 192; Lewis Humberstone to author, Oct. 12, 1966.

Notes on XXV: The Humberstones: Canadian Potters through the Century

19. Lewis Humberstone to author, Jan. 7, 1966.
20. *History of Toronto*, II, 192.
21. Undated clipping in family scrapbook [December, 1895].
22. Simon Thomas Humberstone's obituary. Undated clipping in family scrapbook [March, 1915].
23. Undated clipping in family scrapbook.
24. *History of Toronto*, II, 192.
25. Undated clipping in family scrapbook [March, 1915].
26. Might's *Toronto City Directory for 1893* gives J. K. Oliver, 276 Queen Street West, as a fruit dealer.
27. *Globe*, Oct. 1, 1858.
28. Pieces in family possession.
29. See p. 266.
30. Fewer than twenty (excluding manufacturers of tiles, drain pipes and sanitary ware) are listed in the *Dominion of Canada and Newfoundland Gazetteer . . . 1919*, Toronto, 1919.
31. According to the recollections of Thomas Allan Humberstone's widow, the pottery burned in the autumn of 1918.
32. *History of Toronto*, II, 192.
33. *Mercantile Agency Reference Book*, for July, 1874.

Notes on XXVI: CHINA DECORATING IN CANADA

1. *Mitchell's Canada Gazetteer and Business Directory for 1864-65* (Toronto, 1864), p. 816. The name 'Canada' then applied only to what are now the provinces of Ontario and Quebec.
2. *Journal of the Board of Arts and Manufactures for Upper Canada*, quoted in James Sutherland, compiler, *City of Toronto Directory for 1867-8* (Toronto, 1867), p. 336.
3. Sutherland, p. 335, gives 1857 as the date for the founding of the firm. In the early 1870's Hurd, Leigh & Co. are still listed as importers and decorators, but by 1875 the firm is gone.
4. Sutherland, p. 335.
5. Quoted in Sutherland, p. 336.
6. *Brown's Toronto General Directory, 1856* (Toronto, 1856).
7. *Annual Review of the Commerce of Toronto for 1867* (Toronto, 1868), p. 58.
8. There is no date of publication given, but internal evidence suggests 1867, or a little later; Hurd, Leigh & Co. are said to have been 'over ten years in business' (the firm was established in 1857).
9. Sutherland, p. 335.
10. *C. E. Anderson & Co.'s Toronto City Directory for 1868-9* (Toronto, 1868).
11. Sutherland, p. 335.
12. *Grand Trunk Railway Gazetteer . . . and Business Directory, 1862-63* (Toronto, 1862).
13. *Montreal Gazette*, Jan. 2, 1863.
14. *Ibid.*
15. *Ibid.*, July 31, 1863.
16. *Ibid.*, Nov. 1, 1873.
17. *Industries of Canada* (Toronto, 1887), p. 47; *History of the County of Middlesex, Canada* (Toronto and London, 1889), p. 1075.
18. *Industries of Canada*, p. 47.
19. *Ibid.*
20. Newspaper clipping in family scrapbook kept by John Griffiths' eldest daughter, Eliza Griffiths, and now owned by his grand-daughter, Mrs. W. H. Pike. Over the clipping has been written 'From Free Press 1887'.
21. *Victoria and Albert Museum Catalogue of Water Colour Paintings*, revised ed. (London, 1927), p. 448.
22. Undated clipping, E.G. scrapbook. From internal evidence the interview was after August, 1897, and before October, 1898.
23. Undated clippings, E.G. scrapbook.
24. J. E. Hartill, Managing Director, Mintons Ltd., to author, April 16, 1964.
25. Interview with John Griffiths. See note 22 above.
26. *Ibid.*

27. John Griffiths' collection of contemporary Canadian art was described as 'magnificent' by the reporter who interviewed him in the 1890's. Some of the paintings now hang in the National Gallery of Canada.
28. *The Canada Directory for 1857-58* (Montreal, 1857), p. 272.
29. *The History of the County of Middlesex*, quoted in John Griffiths' obituary. Undated clipping [October, 1898], E.G. scrapbook.
30. *Ibid.*
31. *Mitchell & Co.'s Canada Classified Directory for 1865-66* (Toronto [1865]), p. 88.
32. Undated clipping, E.G. scrapbook.
33. *Victoria and Albert Museum Catalogue of Water Colour Paintings*, p. 448.
34. Undated clipping, E.G. scrapbook.
35. Undated clipping in *Ibid.*
36. Undated clipping [October, 1898] in *Ibid.*
37. Interview with John Griffiths. See note 22 above.
38. *Gazette*, April 2, 1870.
39. *Montreal Star*, Sept. 16, 1882.
40. *Montreal Herald*, Nov. 26, 1898.
41. *Ibid.*
42. *Dominion of Canada . . . Business Directory 1899* (Toronto, n.d.), p. 611.
43. *Daily Witness*, Sept. 17, 1880.
44. *Ibid.*, Sept. 29, 1880.
45. *Montreal Gazette*, June 20, 1835.
46. *Colonist*, Aug. 18, 1951.
47. Marjorie Lady Pentland, to author, Oct. 8, 1962. Lady Pentland, daughter of Lady Aberdeen, supplied a complete list of all the pieces presented to her mother on June 13, 1898.
48. *Gazette*, June 14, 1898.
49. Lord and Lady Aberdeen, '*We Twa*' (London, 1926), II, 140.
50. *Gazette*, June 14, 1898.
51. The present owner is Major the Earl of Haddo, D.L., C.B.E.

Index

431

Index

431

432

Chambly, 117
Charles, Joseph, 78
Charlottetown, 116, 168
Château de Ramezay Museum, 71, 93
'Chaudière Bridge', 213-15
Cheadle, Dr. Walter Butler, 57-58, 172
Chemical porcelain, 130, 296
'*Chesapeake* and *Shannon*', 221-22
Cheverton, Benjamin, 181
Chimney ornaments, 149-51, 155; *see also*
   Figures
China & Glass Decorating Co., 318
China decorating, 277, 280, 284-85, 306,
   311-21
Chinese wares, 52, 59, 126, 130, 164-66, 175,
   197
Chinic, Martin, 106
Chippawa, 22
Chippewas, 43-44
Christie, Alexander, 19, 119, 145
Chrystler's Farm, 13
'Church at Point-Levi', 215
'City' views, 221
Clarke, Rev. Adam, 151
Clarkson, Thomas, 27
Clementson, Brothers, 81, 83-84, 96, 133
Clementson, Francis, 64, 69, 80-84, 87-88,
   93, 131-32, 138, 172, 186
Clementson, Joseph, 80-82, 131-32
Clerke, Francis, 118
Clerke, Thomas, 5, 64
Cleverdon, John, 73
'Clytie', 182
Coalbrookdale, *see* Coalport
Coalport, 58, 173, 187
Cochran, Alexander, 226-28
Cochran, Robert, 9, 86-87, 226
Coldwell, William, 40, 43
Colonial and Indian Exhibition, 262
Columbia, 231-33
Cooke, Robert, 184
Cooper, Samuel, 64, 82
Copeland & Garrett, 32, 47, 52-53, 59, 119,
   171, 177-78, 186-87, 286
Copeland wares, 33, 36, 58, 98, 143, 154,
   157-58, 170-71, 173, 175, 178-82, 185, 187,
   191-92, 265, 319
Copeland, William, 171
Copeland, William Taylor, 32-33, 47, 53,
   110, 170, 177, 180
Cork & Edge, 151
Corn, W. & E., 314
Cornwall stoneware, 277, 293
Coteau du Lac, 23-24
Courtenay Bay Pottery, *see* White, Joseph

Cowan, George, 109
Creamware, xii, 71, 79, 103-11, 113, 137,
   243-44, 294; *see also* Queensware
Crouchville, xiii, 253-56, 268
Cumberworth, Carlos, 180
Cunard, Sir Samuel, 231-36; *see also* 'Boston
   Mails'
Cuvillier & Co., 119, 139

Dakin & Allen, 295
Dakin, Frederick B., 295-96
Dakin Pottery, 289, 295
'Dancing Girl', 180
Danish earthenware, 158
Dannecker, Johann Heinrich von, 180
Darling, Adam, 110, 135, 173, 184, 192-93
Davenport, Henry, 244
Davenport, John, 243
Davenport, wares, xiii, 91-92, 119, 173,
   243-45, 286; Davenport's 'Montreal',
   239-243
Davenport, William, 244
Davies, J. P. & Co., 59, 197
Davis, Alexander J., 267
Davis, Hon. T. O., 46-48, 63
Dawson, Sir William, 129, 210-11, 215-16
Deblois & Mitchell, 66, 70, 243
Delft, 71, 105-6, 113, 158, 229
'Delights of Matrimony', 196
Demi-porcelain, 130
De Morgan, Evelyn, 158
De Morgan, William, 157-58, 171
Deneau, Louis, 277-78
Derby, 58, 67, 98, 168, 173, 175, 178
Derbyshire, 137
Devany, Lawrence, 66, 71, 143, 185
Dickens, Charles, 121, 150, 179, 182, 234
Dickson, Campbell, & Co., 58
Dignam, Mary E., 320
Dion family, potters, 263-65, 301
Dipped ware, 143-45
Dodge, Arthur, 267
Dominion Pottery, 282
Donegana's Hotel, 71, 131
Dougall, John, 20-21
Douglass, John, 94-95
Doulton, Henry, 155
Doulton, wares, 10, 154-58, 171, 173, 193,
   265, 320
Dowling, John, 22
Drean, Henry, 19
Dresden, 70, 193-94
Duck Lake, 47-48

436